WORLD HISTORY

To Jeffrey Davis
for support and encouragement

WORLD HISTORY
A Chronological Dictionary
of Dates

Rodney Castleden

Shooting Star Press Inc
230 Fifth Avenue, New York, New York 10001

This edition printed for
Shooting Star Press Inc.
230 Fifth Avenue - Suite 1212
New York, NY 10001

Shooting Star Press books are available at special
discounts for bulk purchases for sales promotions,
premiums, fund-raising, or educational use.
Special editions or book excerpts can also be
created to specification. For details contact:
Special Sales Director, Shooting Star Press Inc.,
230 Fifth Avenue, Suite 1212, New York,
NY 10001

ISBN   1 56924 213 5

Printed and bound in Great Britain

PREFACE

The aim of this reference book is to provide as continuous and detailed a narrative of the story of the human race as we can fit into a small book. The human race has existed for 2 million years, and we get occasional glimpses of earlier hominid ancestors as far back as 3 and 4 millions years ago. However, the early evidence is very patchy and cannot yet be assembled into a continuous scenario with any reliability. This argues for a relatively late start. It is also clear that the *modern* human race – the one to which we all belong – came into being very suddenly 40,000 years ago. It was then that rapid cultural advances started to happen: people started making new kinds of tools and adopting new styles of living that included trade, ceremonial burials and more ambitious and prolific artwork. By 35,000 BC we even see hints at territorial conquest. We see all the signs and characteristics of the human race that *we* belong to – uniquely restless, enquiring, resourceful, inventive and adventurous.

This book is very much an outline of human history and prehistory: it has not been possible to include everything that has happened. For instance, it would have cluttered the text too much to put in the births and deaths of all prominent people, so I have included a sample, mainly to give an idea of time scale and period flavour. It is difficult to strike the right balance between covering the multitude of events happening all over the world at any moment, which might be complete but confusing, and giving a continuous narrative. I have tried to resolve the problem by following, for the later periods especially, a limited number of themes and narrative threads. Whether this succeeds is for the reader to judge, but I hope that what emerges is a vivid and kaleidoscopic picture of the human story as an extraordinary web of interactions among individuals, groups and nations, and between people and their environment – sometimes with all-too-predictable sometimes with quite unpredictable outcomes. I hope it will help the reader towards an awareness of his or her own place in the human story, and towards a perception of the present that we currently share not as a climax but as a passing note in an endlessly complicated symphony.

The pre-classical period, that is, from 38,000 BC to around 750 BC, can be dated thanks to refinements in the radiocarbon

Preface

dating method. With corrected or 'calibrated' dates adjusted using calibration tables devised during the last five years it is possible to achieve an accuracy of within 100 years for dates as old as 2,000 BC. The reader should bear in mind that the older the date is, the wider the margin of error. From around 3,000 BC in Egypt and the Middle East and 750 BC in Europe greater accuracy is possible because dated documents exist. Even so, there are inconsistencies among the source documents and sometimes dates given in chronicles for the period AD 400–1000 contradict one another. Sometimes they conflict with radiocarbon dates – a useful check on the reliability of ancient historians! I have tried to resolve these inconsistencies to the best of my ability, always opting for the dates favoured by recent scholarship.

Rodney Castleden

KEY TO ICONS

✐ Architecture: the year given is the year of design, unless otherwise stated

✐ Art: the year given is the year of public exhibition

▢ Literature: the year given is the year when published, unless otherwise stated

♯ Music: the year given is the year of first performance, unless otherwise stated

BC

38,000 *Homo sapiens* emerges in Africa and the Middle East as a new human species with less physical power but a larger brain capacity than Neanderthal man. *Homo sapiens* advances rapidly at the expense of rivals. People colonize Australia and North America, probably for the first time.

37,000 In Eurasia a warm interlude or interstadial (the Hengelo) begins.

36,000 People living on Mount Carmel (in the Skhul Cave) are of transitional type, not pure Neanderthal, implying that 'modern' man may be a mutant type, a rapidly evolving form.

35,000 The Hengelo interstadial ends. During the much colder period that follows in Eurasia, *Homo sapiens* becomes the dominant species on Earth. These 'Advanced Hunters' dispossess the Neanderthalers of their hunting grounds. Descendants of the Neanderthalers are, nevertheless, to survive in refuges in outlying regions, such as Java and parts of Africa.

34,000 The Aurignacian culture appears.

32,000 Advanced Hunters reach Syria. At Lake Mungo (Australia), colonists feed on fish and shellfish from a series of lakes; they cook on hearths and in a clay oven.

30,000 The Dyuktai culture appears in Siberia, producing stone tools similar to those of later North American peoples, suggesting that the peoples of the two areas are linked. The Denekamp interstadial, another warm phase, starts now. The milder climate may haved encouraged people to colonize Siberia, later enticing them out onto the land bridge connecting Siberia with Alaska. Advanced Hunters reach Italy, Spain, Portugal, North Africa. At Cueva Morin (Spain) two graves are covered with mounds; the body in one has had its head and feet cut off. An offering of cooked meat and ochre is deposited in a pit.

 La Ferrassie cave art (France): animals and female genitals carved or painted on flat limestone plaques

28,500 New Guinea is peopled by colonists arriving from Asia or Australia.

27,000 The Aurignacian culture dies out in France to be replaced by the Gravettian culture. People (*Homo*

sapiens) colonize Japan at about this time, although they may have arrived via land bridges or ice sheets as long as 5,000 years ago. The Denekamp interstadial ends and the climate cools dramatically, especially in mid-high latitudes. Trading in flints begins in Central Europe.

25,000 Advanced Hunters in the Dordogne valley develop baited toggles that become wedged in a fish's mouth when the fishing-line is pulled taut. The first people are arriving in North America by way of Siberia and the Bering Strait land bridge. A woman dies at Lake Mungo (Australia): her skull is identical to that of a modern aborigine. Hers is the earliest cremation known.

23,000 The dynamic Gravettian culture centres on Central and Eastern Europe. The Gravettians are great mammoth hunters, spreading to the west and south to become well established in Greece and Italy, then penetrating to southern France, Spain, Portugal and Britain. The Gravettian thrust to the east reaches the Urals. The Gravettians produce the first portable art in the world. At Předmost (Czech Republic) mammoth bones are collected and carved with geometric patterns; 20 people are buried in a pit 40 metres/131 feet long, covered with flat stones and mammoth shoulder blades. It will never be known what events led up to the mass burial.

20,000 The Solutrean culture appears, producing fine laurel-leaf stone points for spears (France only). In the rest of Europe, the Gravettian culture continues. The production of female figurines implies a fertility cult. People living in the Franchthi Cave (Greece) hunt wild ass and gather plants. By this time the southern parts of Australia are colonized, and there is a settlement at Tiapacoya in Mexico.

    🐚 Ivory figure of Arctic hunter (Buret', Siberia)
    Kapova Cave paintings of mammoth, horse, rhinoceros (Urals)
    Ivory figurine of bird (Mal'ta, Baikal region)
    Baked clay figurines (Pavlov, Czech Republic)
    Venus of Willendorf (Austria)
    Ivory horse, rhinoceros, mammoth (Vogelherd, Germany)
    Paintings of horses; negative silhouettes of hands (Pech-Merle, France)

Sculpture of woman holding bison horn (France)
Koonalda Cave paintings (S. Australia)

18,000 Advanced Hunters are in Africa from about this time. The first microliths appear in Africa. These, the first arrowheads, seem to show that the bow and arrow were invented in Africa. The sea level is at its lowest level for the last 100,000 years, marking the maximum extent of the huge ice sheets covering Canada and Northern Europe: the sea is 130 metres /426 feet below its present level, leaving large areas of continental shelf exposed as dry land.

16,500 The Solutrean culture in France ends, and the Magdalenian culture begins. On Mount Carmel (Israel) people tend flocks of gazelles.

16,000 🖌 Mammoth bone houses (Mezhirich, Ukraine)
Skin and bone tents (Pushkari, Russia)
Stone and mud beehive huts (Israel, Syria, Iran, Iraq)

14,000 People settle at Meadowscroft, Pennsylvania (U.S.). The sea begins to rise as the ice sheets shrink.
🎨 Lascaux Cave paintings (France)
Mas d'Azil spear-thrower (France)
Venus of Lespugue (France)

13,500 A sea level rise of about 40 metres/131 feet floods large areas of lowland; the result of the melting of the North American ice sheet.

13,000 Stone grinders are used in the Near East for milling wild cereals. They are used in Australia, too, showing an interest in exploiting grass seeds. People are now living in the Yukon valley having crossed the Bering Straits land bridge.

12,000 The dog is domesticated from the Asian wolf (Iraq) and used for tracking game. Near Petra, flocks of goats are domesticated. The Bering Straits land bridge is flooded by the rising sea.
🎨 Altamira Cave paintings (Spain)
Rock engravings (Grotto d'Addaura, Spain)
Stag plaque (Lortet, Spain)
Font de Gaume cave paintings (France)

11,000 As major climatic changes are under way, vast areas of wild grasses appear in the 'Fertile Crescent'. Hunters kill mastodon at Taima (Colombia). The mammoth becomes extinct in the Ukraine.

10,500 People settle in southern South America. People living in Patagonian caves hunt guanaco and a species of horse that will later become extinct.

10,400 The short Bølling interstadial begins.

10,000 The Bølling interstadial ends. The Older Dryas phase, a period of intense cold begins when glaciers re-form in Britain. Goats are domesticated in Mesopotamia by the hunter-gatherer community which earlier domesticated the dog. A key mesolithic culture, the Natufian culture, emerges in the Near East. The Natufians (Late Hunters) live where the ancestors of wheat and barley grow wild and they use reaping knives, querns, pestles and mortars to harvest and process wild grain. The population grows as food supplies improve; there are Natufian villages of up to 50 houses (round huts) with large cemeteries. The Natufians still have no pottery, weaving, domesticated plants or animals and rely on hunted gazelles for much of their food. They bury their dead ceremoniously with ornaments, beads and headdresses. Egyptians are dying by acts of violence: half the people in Jebel Sahaba cemetery have been murdered.

  Drawings of crow, horse's head, women engraved on slate (Gönnersdorf, Germany)
  Bone spear-thrower in the form of a horse (France)
  Batons of command (Europe)
  Drawing of mammoth on slate (Gönnersdorf, Germany): our last sight of the mammoth before it becomes extinct

9,800 The Allerød interstadial begins.

9,500 At Kow Swamp (Australia) at least 40 people with narrow heads, prominent brow ridges and back-sloping foreheads are living. They seem to be a remarkable survival of *Homo erectus* living in the same region as well-established *Homo sapiens*, and must have lived separately from the rest of the aboriginal Australians.

9,000 The Allerød interstadial ends in rapid cooling. In the short Upper Dryas cold phase that follows, glaciers and ice caps grow again in Canada and Northern Eurasia. People reach the southernmost tip of South America. An early shrine, built at Jericho, consists of a clay platform with sockets for totem poles; there may have been a substantial Natufian village beside or round this shrine. The neolithic begins in Egypt and Mesopotamia. Mesolithic hunters in India build round huts with stone foundations. At Kostienki (Ukraine) people live in an oval longhouse 35 metres/115 feet long with nine hearths along its axis, sleeping hollows in the floor and six female figurines made of limestone. Fork-shaped wooden arrows are made at Ahrensburg (Germany). At Tlokowo (Poland) 112 wooden statues are thrown or placed in a lake by stone age hunters.

    ✎ Tlokowo statues (Poland): first wooden ritual statues in Europe

8,400 A winter camp at Los Mallaetes Cave (Spain) is a base for hunting goats, ibex and rabbits.

8,300 The Upper Dryas cold phase ends, and with it the Ice Age. This is the most important single environmental change in human history or prehistory. The ice melts back rapidly in high latitudes and other places warm up and experience major ecological changes. Open tundra areas in central North America and Central and Northern Europe are invaded by birch and pine trees; low-lying areas are flooded by the rising seas. The Magdalenian culture comes to an end (Europe). Some people follow the reindeer north to occupy new hunting grounds in Denmark and North Germany. In the Mediterranean lands of southern Europe the climatic changes are less critical, allowing Gravettian and other Advanced Hunting traditions to evolve gradually. As the North American ice sheet fragments, Clovis culture sites are colonized in Beringia (the still-dry Bering Straits land bridge) and Central U.S. The giant Irish deer becomes extinct (U.K.); musk ox, giant deer, lion and hyena become extinct (Ukraine). At Arene Candide (Italy) people hunt red deer, boar, bear and also collect shellfish. They bury their dead with ceremony, decorating them with necklaces of animal teeth: even the children are buried with ochre-painted pebbles and capes made of squirrel tails.

8,000 Woolly rhinoceros becomes extinct (Europe). Reindeer dies out in Denmark. Mesolithic people (Late Hunters) occupy the whole western Mediterranean region now.

Hunting magic suggests that their religion focused on animals. A continuing rise in sea level separates New Guinea from Australia. By now, large stone tools have almost disappeared in favour of small (Microliths). The larger points were used as spearheads and were appropriate to open-terrain hunting (tundra or grassland), whereas the smaller points are used as arrowheads, appropriate to hunting in woodland; the change in technology results in part from changes in climate and vegetation. In the Near East, permanent settlement in mudbrick villages becomes normal. Jericho, perhaps the first attempt in human history at a walled town, is built. Its wall is 4 metres/13 feet high with a stone-built lookout tower 10 metres/33 feet in diameter. The houses are also circular. Emmer wheat is domesticated for the first time in the Jordan valley. Barley is domesticated in the Fertile Crescent.

    The Tower at Jericho (Israel) (which still stands over 8 metres/26 feet high)

    Engravings of zebra and other animals (Wonderwerk Cave, S. Africa)

7,500   Sea level is 30 metres/98 feet below its present altitude and rising rapidly. People living on a brushwood platform beside a lake at Star Carr in the Vale of Pickering (U.K.) hunt deer with dogs; they also perform hunting rituals wearing antlered headdresses.

7,300   The Fall of Jericho. The walled town is abandoned or destroyed.

7,250   The domesticated dog appears in Denmark. People again inhabit the Franchthi Cave (Greece); they fish in the sea and collect obsidian for tool-making from the island of Melos.

7,200   Sheep are domesticated in Greece. A dug-out canoe is lost at Pesse (Netherlands).

7,100   At Çayönü Tepesu (Turkey) copper is hammered and shaped for the first time.

7,000   Barley is grown in Greece. Emmer (domesticated) wheat is grown in Turkey and Iran. A pre-pottery settlement is founded at Çatal Hüyük (Turkey), but is then deserted. Rainfall is significantly higher in Egypt from this time until 6,000 BC, making the wide floodplain and delta of the Nile moist, fertile and attractive to human settlement. Jericho is rebuilt and re-inhabited after a gap of 300 years. It is rebuilt with square houses and finely finished plaster floors covered with round rush mats. The people of Jericho tend goats and grow pulses and vetches. Obsidian is imported by the people living at Knossos (Crete).

     Plaster-modelled portrait faces built onto skulls, one with a painted moustache: the first recorded moustache (Jericho, Israel)

6,800 The Kurdistan village of Jarmo is founded: 30 dwellings house 200 people.

6,500 A herd of bison is stampeded by hunters into a hidden gully at Olsen-Chubbock, Colorado (U.S.), killing 200 beasts. The hunters use stone knives to dispatch and butcher the bison. The land bridge joining Britain to Europe is flooded: Britain becomes an island.

6,400 The wheel is invented at about this time by Sumerians in the Tigris-Euphrates basin; this will facilitate all kinds of construction work and transport and may be seen as one of the key inventions of the interglacial, along with the domestication of plants and animals.

6,250 The settlement of Çatal Hüyük (Turkey) develops into a town. At Çayönü (Iraq) the pig is domesticated for the first time.

6,200 The aurochs, ancestor of domestic cattle, is domesticated at about this time (Yugoslavia).

6,000 The first true pottery appears, at Jericho: this key invention opens the way to easier and more efficient food preparation. Settled farming communities emerge in Greece. In Switzerland dogs and plough oxen are domesticated. The Swiss lake-dwellers collect wild flax or cultivate it to make fibrous ropes, nets, etc. make bread out of cereal grains and keep dried apples and peas in their houses built on stilts.

5,508 The Year of Creation as adopted in Constantinople (7th century AD) and used for 1,000 years by the Eastern Orthodox Church.

5,500 Copper is smelted for the first time from malachite (copper carbonate) by workers in Iran. This is the first metal to be produced that can be drawn, moulded and shaped, although it is too soft to hold a cutting edge.

5,490   The Year of Creation as calculated by early Christians in Syria.

5,300   At the Téviec and Hoëdic cemeteries in Brittany (France), people are buried with antlers in substantial stone-built graves, the forerunners of megalithic tombs.

5,150   At Culver Well, Portland (U.K.) people live on winkles, limpets and plant roots.

5,000   The dingo, the only animal to be domesticated by aborigines, arrives, possibly by boat, from South-East Asia. Farming villages are widespread in Eurasia. The domestication of plants and animals is just beginning in the New World. The sea has risen to about 10 metres/33 feet below its present level. Large areas of useful lowland have been lost in the Nile Delta and the Persian Gulf. Savage warfare breaks out between communities in the Tigris and Euphrates valleys in a struggle for water and land; at other times they collaborate to build irrigation channels. The lands bordering the Nile begin to dry out. In response to this climatic change, the Egyptians build systems of irrigation channels. These two irrigation-based cultures (Mesopotamia and Egypt) are evolving towards civilization. In the Americas, maize and beans are cultivated. Farming begins in Malta. In Denmark the death rate among women is 40 per cent higher than among men, presumably because of the perils of child-bearing.

     ✑ Dissignac passage graves, Saint-Nazaire (France)

4,850   Farming begins in Jersey and Guernsey (U.K.).

4,800   The first small-scale attempts at farming in Britain in forest clearings.

4,700   ✑ Kercado chamber tomb: the first megalithic monument in France

     ✐ Decorated wooden paddle, Tybrind Vig (Denmark)

4,650   ✑ Earliest tomb chamber at Barnenez (Tomb C) (France)

4,500   ✑ Anta de Poço da Gateira passage grave, Evora (Spain)

4,450   ✑ Stone alignments of St-Just, Brittany (France)

4,400   Mt. Mazama in Oregon (U.S.) explodes in a massive eruption. The uppermost 2,500 metres/8,200 feet of the 4,250-metres/3,940 feet high volcano are blown off

leaving a huge crater. After the eruption, water draining
down into the crater forms a lake 9.5 km/6 miles across –
Crater Lake.

    ☞ Tomb A at Barnenez, Brittany (France)

4,250 The main period of passage grave construction begins in
Brittany.

4,200 Agriculture begins in Denmark.

4,000 ☞ Le Petit Chasseur chamber tombs (Switzerland)

3,880 The Grand Menhir Brisé and other standing stones are
raised in Brittany. The Grand Menhir weighs 348 tonnes
and takes an estimated 3,800 people to raise it. The
standing stones are later taken down and broken.

    ☞ The Grand Menhir Brisé (France)

3,855 Dolerite is made into axes at Le Pinacle, Jersey (U.K.).
The axe-makers build fires where they cook beef, mutton
and pork; they eat bread from stone platters.

3,800 The sea reaches 8 metres/26 feet below its present level.

3,500 ☞ Tumulus St. Michel burial mound, Morbihan
(France)

    Cueva del Romeral passage grave, Malaga (Spain)

    Mgarr and Ggantija Temples (Malta)

3,400 ☞ Mnajdra and Hagar Qim Temples (Malta)

3,300 The 30-year-old 'Iceman' dies of hypothermia sheltering
from a snowstorm beside the Similaun Glacier in the
Alps. He carries a copper axe, a quiver with 14 arrows, a
flint dagger and a framed backpack. He will be found on
11 Sep, AD 1991.

    ☞ Tarxien Temples and Hypogeum (rock-cut temple)
(Malta)

    North and South Stone Circles, Avebury (U.K.)

3,250 Building work on passage graves in Brittany stops.

    ☞ La Hougue Bie passage grave (Jersey, U.K.)

    Gavrinis passage grave (France)

    ✍ Men, Boats and Animals wall painting, Hierakono-
polis (Egypt)

3,200 The northern and southern kingdoms of Egypt are
united under Menes, the first king of the First Dynasty. Menes is the earliest human being in prehistory
whose name we know. Wheeled carts are in use in the
Near East. There is a large-scale volcanic eruption at an
unidentified location.

       ℮ Tustrup ritual centre, Jutland (Denmark)
          Mastaba (royal tomb) at Saqqara (Egypt)
       ⛢ Statue-menhirs at Le Petit Chasseur (Switzerland)

3,125   The entrance to the Gavrinis passage grave is deliberately sealed after a series of fire rituals.

3,100   The great henge consisting of a circular bank and ditch is laid out at Avebury. Stonehenge is laid out as a much more modest earth circle with two portal stones to mark the midsummer sunrise. Los Millares in Spain is created as a fortified settlement and regional seat of power for the next 500 years.
       ℮ Avebury henge (U.K.)
          Stonehenge earth circle (U.K.)
          Los Millares (Spain)
       ⛢ Naqada Vase (Egypt)
          Palette of King Narmer (carved slate) (Egypt)

3,000   Cotton is woven in the Indus valley. Clay tokens are made at Susa (Iran).
       ℮ Grønhøj passage grave, Jutland (Denmark)
       □ *Gilgamesh* (written in Sumerian cuneiform, first known written myth)

2,900   The Sahara Desert in Northern Africa has its beginnings as over-grazing and over-cultivation lead to soil exhaustion. Dolphins are hunted in the Black Sea, although in many parts of the world there is a taboo against molesting them. Potatoes are cultivated in the Andes. The Third Dynasty in Egypt is founded by King Zoser, who rules with help from Imhotep, counsellor, physician and architect. The pyramid of Zoser at Saqqara is built by Imhotep. This Step pyramid is the world's first large stone structure, a tomb that replicates earlier, lower brickwork buildings called mastabas.
       ℮ Anghelu Ruju rock-cut tombs (Sardinia)
          Everstorfer Forst burial chambers, Mecklenburg (Germany)
          Step pyramid, Saqqara (Egypt)

2,870   King Zoser dies.

2,800   The yin and yang philosophy of nature is originated in China by the Emperor Fu Hsi; health and peace require equilibrium among the five elements, wood, fire, earth, metal, water. The sickle is invented in the Tigris and

Euphrates valleys: a curved wooden haft is fitted with flint teeth. It becomes the dominant tool for harvesting grain.

2,780 The henge bank at Avebury is raised in height.

2,750 According to Herodotus, the port of Tyre is founded at this time; Tyre's rise to power begins. Silbury Hill is built close to Avebury for some unknown ceremonial purpose.

    ⚏ Havelte West megalithic tomb, Drenthe (Netherlands)

       Silbury Hill (U.K.)

2,700 The new principles of Chinese herbal medicine and acupuncture develop partly from the yin and yang principles.

2,680 Snefru, first king of Egypt's Fourth Dynasty, dies, succeeded by his son Khufu (or Cheops).

2,675 The Great Pyramid of Khufu at Giza, 'Cheops is one belonging to the horizon', rises to a height of 147 metres/480 feet and consists of limestone blocks weighing 5 tonnes. It takes 20 years to complete.

    ⚏ Hemon, Khufu's Vizier: The Great Pyramid

2,657 Khufu dies, succeeded by his son Khafre (or Chephren), third ruler of the Fourth Dynasty.

2,650 🗿 Diorite statue of Khafre, Giza (Egypt)

2,640 ⚏ The Second Pyramid at Giza, 'Great is Khafre': orders of Khafre

    🗿 Orders of Khafre: The Great Sphinx (image of the god Harmachis carved out of rock), Giza (Egypt)

2,630 Khafre, third king of Egypt's Fourth Dynasty, dies, succeeded by Menkaure (or Mycerinus).

2,610 The Third (and smallest) pyramid is built at Giza on the orders of King Menkaure.

    ⚏ The Third Pyramid at Giza, 'Menkaure is divine'

2,600 Menkaure dies.

    ⚏ Roknia megalithic cemetery (Algeria)

    🗿 Goat Caught in Thicket (gold offering stand), Ur (Iraq)

       Prince Rahotep and his wife Nofret (painted statue) (Egypt)

2,595 📖 *Nei Ching* (earliest medical text): Huang Ti (China)

2,590 ⚏ Ramshog chamber tomb, Skane (Sweden)

2,550   The people living near Stonehenge and, presumably, its builders build an impressive earthen bank and ditch round their township at Durrington Walls.
      ◢ Durrington Walls superhenge (U.K.)

2,500   The Iron Age begins in the Middle East. The smelting temperature of 1,500°C/2,764°F is much higher than that needed to smelt copper, and the new metal will not come into common use for 1,000 years. The Sumerians develop a cuneiform script alphabet of around 600 signs from the thousands of pictograms used for the Gilgamesh myth.
      ◢ Ziggurat of Ur-Nammu, Ur (Iraq)
        The Great Sarsen Circle at Avebury (U.K.)
      ◒ Diadem of Queen Shub-Ad, Ur (Iraq)
        Ti Watching a Hippopotamus Hunt (painted relief), Saqqara (Egypt)

2,475   Maize is domesticated in Central America. Potatoes and sweet potatoes are cultivated in South America. Olive trees are cultivated in Crete, which grows rich from its exports of olive oil and timber.

2,350   The Akkadian Empire is founded by Sargon I of Sumer; the Akkadians will rule Mesopotamia for 200 years. Sumer's city-state civilization reaches its peak and the empire incorporates the advances the Sumerians have made, giving them wider currency.
      ◢ Pyramid of Teti, Saqqara (Egypt)

2,300   Rice from the Indus valley is introduced into northern China, where civilization has reached similar levels to those at Harappa and Mohenjo-Daro in the Indus valley.

2,250   By this time all the stone-built graves in Brittany have been abandoned and sealed up.

2,205   The Xia Dynasty that will rule much of China for 700 years is founded. The Chinese domesticate sheep, goats, pigs, oxen and dogs, and mill grain for the first time.

2,200   ◢ Giovinazzo chamber tomb, Bari (Italy)
      ◒ Victory stele of Naram-Sin

2,150   A consignment of bluestones is taken from the Preseli Hills in Wales to be made into a double stone circle within the earth circle at Stonehenge. The route follows well-established trade routes.

2,100   ◢ The Carnac alignments (France)

Sarsen Circle and Trilithons at Stonehenge (U.K.)
Temple of Enlil and ziggurat at Nippur (Iraq)
West Kennet post circles, near Avebury (U.K.)

2,000 Byblos (Lebanon) becomes a major port exporting
Lebanese timber to Egypt. Phylakopi on Melos
(Greece has become a centre for exporting the obsidian
found on the island. Phoenician and Cretan ships use
square sails on one, two and even three masts. Amen-
hemhet I becomes King of Egypt, founding the Twelfth
Dynasty. Decimal counting appears in Babylonia, which
replaces Sumer as the dominant power in the Middle
East. Farmers in the Near East raise both beef and dairy
cattle. In Egypt, attempts to domesticate oryx, antelope
and gazelle are abandoned in favour of hunting, fishing,
fowling and gathering to supplement flood plain agriculture. Water melon is cultivated in Africa, tea and
bananas in India, apples in the Indus valley, figs in
Arabia. Agriculture develops in Central America.

 Diadem of princess Enannatumma, High Priestess
of Ur (Iraq)

1,970 Amenemhet I dies, succeeded by his son (co-regent since
1,980 BC) Sesostris.

1,955 Hammurabi becomes King of Babylon.

1,950 Hammurabi conquers the whole of Mesopotamia and
imposes a definitive code of laws.

1,935 Sesostris I of Egypt dies, succeeded by his son Amenemhet II. The new king increases trade with Punt.

1,920 Feeding the Oryxes (wall painting), Tomb of
Khnum-hotep, Beni Hasan (Egypt)

1,913 Hammurabi dies.

1,903 Amenemhet II of Egypt dies, succeeded by his son
Sesostris II.

1,900 Copper is mined on Parys Mountain, Anglesey (U.K.)

1,887 Sesostris II of Egypt dies, succeeded by his son Sesostris
III, who rules over 1600 km/1000 miles of the Nile
valley.

1,860 Mount St. Helens erupts (U.S.).

1,850 A canal is dug through the Nile's first cataract at about
this time.

1,849 Sesostris III of Egypt dies, succeeded by his son Amenemhet III.

1,840 Large volcanic eruption in the Massif Central (France).

1,830 Amenemhet III develops mines in the Sinai peninsula at about this time to keep Egypt prosperous, as well as setting up a vast irrigation system.

1,800 Copper is mined on Plynlimon in Wales (U.K.). Taboos against eating pork appear amongst certain groups in the Near East, possibly because they are sheep-rearing people and the pig is seen as the livestock of their farming enemies. A regular ferry service in 15-metre/49-foot wooden boats runs across the Humber Estuary, close to the site of the later Humber Bridge.

   ✍ Monte d'Accoddi (a stone-built ceremonial 'high place') (Sardinia)

   🐾 Ferriby boats and winch (U.K.)

   📖 *Emmerkar and the Lord of Aratta* (epic poem on clay tablets) (Sumeria)

1,792 The death of Amenemhet IV (acceded 1,801) brings the Twelfth Dynasty to an end.

1,777 ✍ Pyramid of Khendjer at Saqqara, one of the last pyramids to be built (Egypt)

1,750 The great cities of Harappa and Mohenjo-Daro in the Indus valley collapse. Several centuries of crude irrigation have made the soil saline; crop yields have fallen to a point where the cities can no longer be supported.

1,700 Babylonians use windmills to pump water for irrigation. Copper mining begins at Great Ormes Head, Wales (U.K.). Smallpox breaks out in China. Abraham, a prince of Ur, moves to Canaan and founds a religion that will attract many followers in the Middle East: Judaism replaces human sacrifice with animal sacrifice. Knossos on Crete is destroyed, perhaps by an earthquake.

   📖 Law code of Hammurabi (clay tablet)

      The Ebers Papyrus shows that Egyptians suffer from tooth decay and eye problems

1,680 Hyksos tribesmen from Palestine and Syria invade Egypt. Wearing sandals, they are able to outfight the Egyptians on hot sand.

1,650 The Jewish religion is developed by Abraham's grandson Jacob. Vesuvius erupts on a huge scale (the 'Avellino' eruption).

      🏛 Temple of Baal-Berith (Canaanite)

1,628   There is a very large volcanic eruption, possibly the eruption of Thera that destroys the bronze age city of Akrotiri on Santorini (Greece). The Chinese Bamboo Annals report 'yellow fog, a dim sun, then three suns, frost in July, famine and the withering of all five cereals', possibly the effect of fall-out from the volcanic eruption. The Shang Dynasty begins in China, precipitated by the omens.

1,600   Knossos on Crete is rebuilt within a century of its destruction. A dazzling and original civilization flourishes at Knossos and the other palace-temple centres on Crete.

      🏺 Crystal bowl in the form of a duck, found in Grave Omikron, Mycenae (Greece)
          Snake Goddess figurines, Knossos (Greece)

1,575   🏺 Gold portrait masks from graves at Mycenae (at about this time)

1,568   The New Kingdom is inaugurated at Thebes by the Eighteenth Dynasty King Ahmose I, who begins to drive out the Hyksos invaders and reunite Upper and Lower Egypt.

1,550   The mainland Greek city of Mycenae is becoming a major centre of power.

      🏺 Lion's Head Rhyton, Mycenae (Greece)

1,540   King Ahmose invades Nubia and fights the Libyans and Syrians to secure Egypt's borders.

1,545   Ahmose I of Egypt dies, succeeded by his son Amenhotep I.

1,540   Amenhotep I invades Nubia and fights the Libyans and Syrians to secure Egypt's borders.

1,525   Amenhotep I dies; his successor, not of royal blood, is Thutmose I.

1,520   A colossal volcanic eruption destroys all life on the island of Thera, including the bronze age city of Akrotiri (traditional date: the event may have happened in *1,628* instead).

1,515   🏛 Temple of Osiris at Abydos (restored)
         Hypostyle Halls at Karnak, and two pylons and two obelisks.

      📖 Rock inscriptions near the Nile's third cataract

record Thutmose's achievements.

1,512 Thutmose I of Egypt is deposed and succeeded by his illegitimate son Thutmose II, who reigns with his half-sister and wife Hatshepsut.

1,504 Thutmose II dies young. Hatshepsut rules as Regent for her infant nephew Thutmose III.

1,503 Hatshepsut assumes title 'queen'.

1,500 Nomads from the steppes of central Asia push into the Indian subcontinent, bringing flocks of sheep and herds of cattle. Horse-drawn vehicles are devised by the Chinese, who also use the wheel for making pottery, and make silk. Geometry helps the Egyptians re-survey field boundaries obliterated by the annual flooding of the Nile. Water buffalo are domesticated by the Chinese.
  Harvester Vase, Agia Triadha (Crete)
  Map of Nippur (clay tablet) (Iraq)

1,485 Two obelisks at Karnak: Hatshepsut
  Temple on the Nile near Thebes (walls decorated with pictures of an expedition to the land of Punt): Hatshepsut
  The Blind Harpist (bas-relief at Karnak)

1,483 Thutmose III comes of age; in his reign Egypt will reach its zenith, its control extending from the Nile's fourth cataract as far east as the Euphrates. The title 'pharaoh' comes into use at this time. Thutmose III builds walls round Hatshepsut's obelisks at Karnak and tries to efface all evidence of her existence.

1,470 Hove Barrow, Sussex (royal burial) (U.K.)
  Earls Barton Barrow, Northants (royal burial) (U.K.)

1,450 Thutmose III dies after a triumphant reign of 33 years. He is succeeded as pharaoh by his son Amenhotep II.
  Vapheio gold cups (Greece)

1,424 Amenhotep II of Egypt dies, succeeded by his son Thutmose IV. The new pharaoh marries a Mitannian princess, forms alliances with Babylonia and the Mitanni, leads military expeditions to Nubia and Phoenicia, and completes the last obelisk of Thutmose II, his grandfather.

1,417 Thutmose IV dies, succeeded by his son Amenhotep III.

1,400 The Iron Age begins in Anatolia, as a larger-scale way of smelting iron is found. The Talayotic culture begins in

Majorca. The last megalithic tomb is built, at St. Georges de Levezac (France).

    ✍ St. Georges de Levezac chamber tomb (France)

    🗺 Three Deities (ivory figurine), Mycenae (Greece)

1,380 Babylonia recognizes Egyptian supremacy in the Near and Middle East. The Egyptians complete a canal connecting the Nile with the Red Sea; it will be used for 700 years.

    ✍ Orders of Amenhotep III: Thebes (monumental city of temples, pylons, colossi)

    Orders of Amenhotep III: Hypostyle Halls at Karnak

    Orders of Amenhotep III: Temple of Amun at Luxor

1,379 Amenhotep III dies, succeeded by Amenhotep IV (Ikhnaton), his son.

1,374 Ikhnaton introduces monotheism in Egypt; his cult centres on the worship of the sun god or solar disc, Aten. Possibly under the influence of his wife Nefertiti, he opposes the priests of Amun. The Hittites under their King Suppiluliumas take advantage of Egypt's military weakness to build an empire extending south from their heartland in central Anatolia to the borders of Lebanon.

1,360 🗺 The Daughters of Ikhnaton (wall painting) (Egypt)

    Bust of Queen Nefertiti (Egypt)

1,358 Ikhnaton dies, succeeded by his nine-year-old son-in-law Tutankhamun. The new pharaoh has accepted the new faith of his wife and her father.

1,357 Tutankhamun returns to the religion of the priests of Amun and moves Egypt's capital back to Thebes from the new city of Akhetaton.

1,350 According to the inhabitants of Mycenae, Perseus founded the city and is reputed to have ruled here at this time. The Egyptian throne is seized by Harmhab, an army officer. Tutankhamun is probably murdered or killed in battle during this coup. Harmhab reorganizes Egypt's administration and founds the Nineteenth Dynasty. Impregnable walls are built round the hill of Mycenae turning it into a citadel.

1,349 The Pharaoh Tutankhamun is buried at Thebes with a vast treasure.

  ✉ Tutankhamun's gold mask and vulture collar
   Tutankhamun the Harpooner (gilded wooden statue)
   Tutankhamun's Golden Shrine

1,327 Harmhab of Egypt dies, succeeded by the elderly Ramesses I.
   ✍ Orders of Ramesses I: Hypostyle Hall at Karnak

1,325 Ramesses I dies, succeeded by his son Seti I.
   ✉ Workmen Carrying a Beam (limestone relief), Tomb of Horemheb at Saqqara (Egypt)

1,304 Seti I of Egypt dies after making peace with the Hittites in Syria. He is succeeded by his son Ramesses II.
   ✍ Seti I and Ramesses I: Colonnaded Hypostyle Hall, Karnak Sanctuary at Abydos: Seti I

1,300 In Mesopotamia an alphabetic script is developed that is a refinement of the cuneiform alphabet invented in *2,500 BC*.

1,280 ✍ The Citadel at Tiryns (Greece)

1,275 Captive Israelites leave Egypt to begin a migration that will eventually lead them to Canaan; their leader Moses lives at about this time.

1,272 Ramesses II of Egypt marries a Hittite princess and arranges a permanent peace with the Hittites.

1,260 ✍ Tomb of Orestes at Mycenae (Greece)

1,250 King Atreus rules at Mycenae, extending the walls of the citadel.

1,240 ✍ Seti's Temple at Abydos (completed)
   Temples at Karnak and Luxor
   Orders of Ramesses II: Mortuary Temple at Thebes with colossal statues of Ramesses II
   Temple of Abu Simbel in Nubia
   Atreus or Agamemnon? Lion Gate at Mycenae
   'Treasury' (Tomb) of Atreus at Mycenae (Greece)

1,237 Ramesses II of Egypt dies after ruling for 67 years; his son Merneptah succeeds.

1,230 ✍ Tomb of Clytemnestra, Mycenae (Greece)

1,221 Egypt is invaded by Libyans; they are defeated by Merneptah's army.

1,215 Merneptah dies.

1,200 The remaining Jews in Lower Egypt are expelled. Philistines settle in Canaan.
   ✉ Figure-of-eight Shield Fresco, Mycenae (Greece)

1,198   The Twentieth Dynasty establishes itself in Egypt as its second king, Ramesses III accedes to the throne. He rallies the Egyptians against a confederation of Philistines, Sardinians, Greek Danaoi and other 'Sea Peoples'.

1,193   Priam's city of Troy falls to Greek armies under Agamemnon after a long siege (the Trojan War).

1,190   At Mycenae, the east wing of the royal palace is destroyed by fire, then rebuilt, possibly associated with a palace revolution. In Homer, Agamemnon is murdered on his return from Troy and eight years later, Orestes kills Clytemnestra and Aegisthos. There is a naval battle between the Sea Peoples and Egyptian forces of Ramesses III.

1,170   The first recorded strike by working people occurs at the Thebes' necropolis; when the wages are delayed, builders refuse to work.

1,160   Ramesses V of Egypt dies of smallpox.
               Viaduct at Mycenae (Greece).

1,159   Eruption of Mount Hekla in Iceland.

1,146   Nebuchadnezzar I accedes as King of Babylon.

1,141   The Israelites join battle with the Philistines and lose 7,000 men. The Israelites' sacred Ark of the Covenant is taken to Ashdod by the Philistines. The outbreak of plague that follows is taken by the Israelites to indicate divine wrath on their behalf.

1,125   Battle of Megiddo.

1,122   The Chinese Zhou Dynasty is founded by Wu Wang, who overthrows the Emperor Zhou Hsin.

1,120   Mycenae and Tiryns are destroyed, possibly by Dorian invaders, bringing the Mycenean civilization to an end.

1,116   Tiglath-Pileser I begins a reign that will bring his Middle Assyrian Empire to its peak.

1,100   Assyrian forces under Tiglath-Pileser reach the Mediterranean after subjugating the Hittites.

1,050   The Fall of Shiloh.

1,025   The prophet Samuel annoints Saul as King of Hebron.

1,012   The Battle of Mount Gilboa ends in defeat and death for Saul and his eldest son Jonathan at the hands of the Philistines. David succeeds as King of Hebron.

1,005   Jerusalem falls to David King of Hebron, who is anointed King of Judea by Samuel.

1,000   The Iron Age spreads across central Europe, and iron tools and weapons become more common.

       ◻ *Rig Veda*, Hindu hymns (at about this time)

990   At about this time Absalom, King David's third son, kills Amnon in revenge for the rape of his sister Tamar; David banishes Absalom from Judea.

978   Absalom regains David's favour but then leads a rebellion. David's nephew Joab suppresses the rebellion and kills Absalom.

961   King David of Judea dies, succeeded by his son Solomon, who makes alliances with Egypt's ruling priests and with Hiram King of Tyre. Solomon executes Joab for having killed Absalom.

950   ✍ The Great Temple of Jerusalem: orders of Solomon
       Royal palace and city wall at Jerusalem: orders of Solomon

936   King Hiram of Phoenicia dies.

935   The throne of Egypt is usurped by the Libyan Shishak, who founds the Twenty-second Dynasty.

922   King Solomon of Judea dies, succeeded by his son Rehoboam. Ten northern tribes secede when Rehoboam refuses their demands to be released from taxation; they establish the separate kingdom of Israel and Jeroboam emerges as its king.

920   Palestine is invaded by Shishak, the Egyptian pharaoh, who plunders Jerusalem.

915   Rehoboam of Judah dies, succeeded by Abijah.

913   Abijah dies, succeeded by Asa.

901   Jeroboam I King of Israel dies, succeeded by Nadab.

900   Nadab King of Israel dies, succeeded by Baasha. The first towns in Italy are founded by Etruscans emigrating from Lydia during a famine.

885   Lycurgus is said to have founded the laws and institutions of Sparta at this time.

884   Assurnasirapli II becomes King of Assyria.

880   Assurnasirapli II defeats Babylonia and revives the empire.

878   Assurnasirapli II annexes Phoenicia as he acquires the entire eastern Mediterranean coast.

877   Baasha King of Israel dies, succeeded by Elah.

876   Elah is succeeded by Zimri (for seven days) and then by

Omri as King of Israel.

873 King Asa of Judah dies. Omri sets his capital on the Hill of Samaria.

870 🏛 Palace at Nimrud: Assurnasirapli II
🗿 Human-headed winged lions (sculpture), Nimrud

869 Omri dies: Ahab becomes King of Israel.

860 🗿 Ivory sphinx, King Ahab's palace

859 Assurnasirapli II dies, succeeded by his son Shalmaneser.

853 The Battle of Qarqar between Israel and Syria is indecisive.

850 The *Iliad* and the *Odyssey* are inscribed at about this time according to Herodotus (but they may have been written down 50 years ago): they represent an accumulation of myth, folktale and history acquired by oral tradition over a period of many centuries. Ahab King of Israel dies.
🗿 Stele of Mesha, King of Moab (Israel)
Bronze reliefs, Balawat gates
📖 Homer: *Iliad* and *Odyssey*
The Fan-Li manuscript (fish cultivation): Fan-Li

849 Ahaziah King of Israel dies, succeeded by Jehoram.

842 Jehoram King of Israel is killed and succeeded by Jehu. Jehu extends his purge of Israel to Judah, murdering King Ahaziah and his brothers: Jezebel is killed by being thrown from a window. Jehu has Ahab's 70 sons beheaded, removing all claims to the throne.

841 🗿 Black Obelisk of Shalmaneser III, public square at Nimrud (Jehu is shown kneeling before the Assyrian king)

815 Jehu King of Israel dies, succeeded by Joahaz.

814 Carthage is founded in North Africa by Phoenician colonists.

812 Shamshiadad V of Assyria, son of Shalmaneser, dies, succeeded by his brother Adadnirari V. The king's mother Sammuramat (or Semiramis) holds the real power.

802 Joahaz King of Israel dies, succeeded by Jehoash.

800 Rice becomes a major part of people's diet in China.
📖 The *Vedas* (religious epics) written at about this time

786 Jehoash King of Israel dies, succeeded by Jeroboam II.

783 Amaziah King of Judah dies, succeeded by Uzziah.

776 The first recorded Olympic games are held at the confluence of the Alpheus and Cladeus rivers at Olympia, although many of the buildings within the enclosure are already hundreds of years old. Only pure Greeks without criminal records may compete. The competition is limited to a footrace of 182 metres/200 yards.

772 ⚜ Temple of Artemis at Ephesus (Turkey)

771 The Zhou capital of China at Hao is destroyed by invaders from the north.

770 The Zhou capital is moved to Luoyang on the Yellow River.

753 According to later legend, Rome is founded by Romulus and Remus.

750 The prophet Amos lives at about this time.

746 Jeroboam II King of Israel dies, succeeded by Zechariah.

745 Tiglath-pileser III of Assyria accedes to the throne

742 Jotham becomes King of Judah. The prophet Isaiah is born.

737 Menachem King of Israel dies, succeeded by Pekahiah.

736 Pekahiah dies, succeeded by Pekah.

735 Jotham King of Judah dies, succeeded by Jehoahaz. Judah is invaded by allied Syrians and Israelite forces.

732 King Pekah of Israel dies, succeeded by Hoshea. The Siege of Damascus: Syria falls.

730 ✑ Ivory figurine of a youth, Athens

724 At the 14th Olympiad a second footrace is added (804 metres/880 yards).

722 The Hill of Samaria, Israel's capital and citadel since *879 BC*, falls to Assyrian forces after a siege lasting three years. King Shalmaneser V of Assyria dies, succeeded by his son Sargon II. Sargon claims the victory over the Israelites and takes 27,000 prisoners.

721 The 27,000 Israelites are taken off by the Assyrians, never to be seen again – the 'lost tribes of Israel'.

720 At the 15th Olympiad a long-distance race, 12 circuits of the stadium, is added to the games.
     ⚜ Sargon II: Citadel at Dur Sharrukin (Khorsabad)

716 Archilochus, the first known lyric poet, is born on Paros (Greece).

712 The siege of Ashdod.

710   Ethiopian invaders conquer Egypt

709   🝔 Stele of Sargon II at Cition

708   The pentathlon (long jump, javelin, 182-metre/200-yard sprint, discus, wrestling) is added to the Olympic games.

705   King Sargon II dies, succeeded by Sennacherib.

701   King Luli of Tyre and Sidon escapes from Tyre with his fleet. Assyrian forces invade Palestine. Phoenician colonists plant olive trees in Spain. China's minister of agriculture teaches the peasants crop rotation and how to dig drainage ditches; he also rents out farm equipment and stores grain surpluses to provide free food in time of famine.

700   Sennacherib besieges Hezekiah in Jerusalem and then inexplicably withdraws, fulfilling Isaiah's prophecy that Zion 'could not fall'. Aqueducts are built to carry water to the cities of the Near East.

       📖 Hesiod: *Theogony* (at about this time)

698   The Greeks begin to colonize the Mediterranean, motivated mainly by a need to find new food sources as Greece's indigenous population expands.

       📖 Sennacherib's Clay Prism (boasting how he shut up Hezekiah 'like a caged bird'

696   The 23rd Olympiad is held at Olympia; boxing is added to the games, which are increasingly a preparation for war.

693   The Assyrian King Sennacherib destroys Babylon.

690   Under Sennacherib, Nineveh has become a city of matchless splendour, where art and literature flourish.

687   Hezekiah dies and Manasseh becomes King of Judah. Isaiah disappears from public life.

       📖 Isaiah: *Book of Isaiah*

682   At Greece's 25th Olympiad the first equestrian event is held, a four-horse chariot race.

681   Sennacherib dies, succeeded by Esarhaddon.

672   Stele of Esarhaddon at Zinjirli (Syria)

671   The Assyrians invade Egypt.

668   Esarhaddon dies, succeeded by Ashurbanipal.

660   🝔 Wooden statuette of Hera, Samos (Greece)

658   Byzantium is founded by Greek colonists from Megara

650   The hillsides of Greece are bare of trees, which have been cut down to provide wood for houses, ships and charcoal

for metal-working; this leads in many areas to soil erosion and reduced food production. The 33rd Olympiad includes a no-holds-barred contest of boxing and wrestling.

🦉 Owl perfume vase (Greece)

642 Manasseh King of Judah dies, succeeded by Amon.

640 Amon King of Judah dies, succeeded by Josiah.

636 Solon, the Athenian statesman, is born.

632 Cylon, a handsome Olympic victor, seizes the Acropolis in a bid for power but is murdered by the Archon Megacles.

630 Ivory relief of Perseus beheading Medusa, Samos (Greece)

626 The prophet Jeremiah is born. King Ashurbanipal of Assyria dies and the Assyrian empire begins to decline. Ashurbanipal is succeeded by Nabopolassar.

625 Metal coins first appear in Greece. Stamped with the image of an ear of wheat, the coins are a reminder that until now grain has served as the medium of exchange; coins are lighter, easier to transport, and do not go mouldy.

624 Periander, tyrant of Corinth, invites the aristocracy to a party and has his soldiers strip the women of their gold jewellery; the gold will be used to finance his government.

621 The Athenian lawgiver Draco issues a code of laws that makes almost every offence punishable by death. The Law of Moses devised by the Israelite leader imposes dietary restrictions, allowing meat only from sheep, cattle and goats, and forbidding meat from camels, hares, rock badgers and pigs. Also 'unclean' is anything 'that dies of itself'.

620 Alcaeus, the first lyric poet of whom we know, is born on Lesbos.

614 Assur falls to the Medes.

612 Nineveh falls to the Medes and the Chaldeans. The fall of the Assyrian capital will soon be followed by the collapse of the Assyrian Empire. The poetess Sappho is born on the island of Lesbos.

610 The Egyptian Pharaoh Psammetichus I dies, succeeded by Necho II.

609 A new canal connecting the Nile with the Red Sea is begun by the Egyptian Pharaoh Necho. The canal is destined not to be completed: more than 120,000 men die in the attempt. Josiah King of Judah dies at Megiddo, succeeded by Jehoahaz II and, shortly afterwards, by Jehoiakim.

605 Nabopolassar King of Assyria dies. Necho's army is defeated at the Battle of Carchemish by the Chaldean son of Nabopolassar, who begins a dazzling 43-year-long reign at Babylon as Nebuchadnezzar II.

604 The Chinese philosopher Lao-tse is born.

600 Cyrus the Great is born. Marseilles is founded by Greek colonists, who establish the colony of Lacydon. At about this time, Africa is circumnavigated by the Egyptians, anticlockwise, taking three years.

    ✏ Orders of Pisistratus: Old Temple of Athena, Acropolis, Athens

    Orders of Periander: Stone Slipway connecting Saronic and Corinthian Gulfs

597 Jerusalem falls to Nebuchadnezzar II's army, who carry the Jews off into exile, the 'Babylonian captivity' that will last until *538 BC*. The prophet Jeremiah dies.

589 The walled city of Lachish in Judah falls to Nebuchadnezzar.

588 Nebuchadnezzar besieges Jerusalem.

    ☐ The Lachish letters

586 Periander tyrant of Corinth dies, succeeded by his nephew Psammetichus. Nebuchadnezzar's army destroys the Great Temple of Jerusalem.

582 The first Pythian games are held.

575 ✏ Orders of Nebuchadnezzar: Ishtar Gate and Hanging Gardens, Babylon

573 The Phoenician city of Tyre falls to Nebuchadnezzar's army after a siege of 13 years.

570 The poet Anacreon is born.

    ✉ The Calf-bearer (the earliest Attic statue from the Acropolis)

565 Athenian forces from Megara conquer Salamis under the command of their general Pisistratus. Taoism is founded by the Chinese philosopher Lao-tse; this liberal religion teaches that form and ceremony are useless, advocating righteousness instead.

    📖 Lao-tse: *Tao Te Ching*

563 Siddhartha Gautama, the Enlightened One or Buddha, is born.

562 Nebuchadnezzar II King of Babylon dies, succeeded by his son Evil-Merodach.

561 The Athenian general Pisistratus makes himself tyrant but is quickly driven out by Lycurgus, who leads the city's nobility, and Megacles the Alcmaeonid, who mobilizes the middle class.

560 Babylon's Evil-Merodach is deposed and killed by conspirators. He has released Jehoiakim, the King of Judah who had been imprisoned in Babylon for 36 years.

559 Solon dies. Athens restores Pisistratus, who has won the support of Megacles. At about this time, Croesus King of Lydia adopts metal coinage to replace commodities as a medium of exchange.

556 Pisistratus is again expelled from Athens after breaking with Megacles. He goes off to amass a fortune mining in Thrace. Babylon's last king, Nabonidus, accedes to the throne.

551 Confucius or Kung Fu-tse, the Chinese philosopher, is born.

550 Cambyses I, King of Anshan, dies and is succeeded by his son Cyrus, who is 50 and creates a Persian empire by uniting Medes, Persians and other tribes. Miltiades the victor of Marathon is born at about this time.

549 Armenia becomes a Persian satrapy after 63 years under the kings of Media.

546 Croesus King of Lydia is surprised at Sardis by Persians under the command of Cyrus the Great. Cyrus conquers Lydia but spares Croesus.

540 Athens restores Pisistratus to power. He exiles his opponents, confiscates their lands and uses them to benefit the poor, making the sharecroppers landowners. Pisistratus introduces the cult of Dionysus in an attempt to break down the power of the Athenian nobility by way of its hereditary priesthood.

539 Cyrus the Great of Persia defeats the Babylonian King Nabonidus. Cyrus enters the city of Babylon (*20 Oct*) amid popular rejoicing.

538 Prince Belshazzar, the son of King Nabonidus, tries to expel Cyrus's army but fails. Cyrus destroys the city of Babylon and allows the captive Jews to return to Jerusalem after 49 years in exile.

📖 Cyrus the Great: The Cyrus Cylinder (confirms Cyrus's policy of letting the captives return home)

533 Siddhartha Gautama (Buddha) renounces luxury and tries asceticism.

529 Cyrus the Great of Persia is killed in battle against tribesmen east of the Caspian Sea. He is 71 years old and is succeeded by his son Cambyses II.

✍ Tomb of Cyrus at Pasargadae (Iran)

528 Buddhism has its beginnings in India; Siddhartha Gautama finds enlightenment at the age of 35 after a severe penance at Buddh Gaya, near Benares. Siddhartha found the ascetic life futile and now travels up and down the Ganges founding monastic orders of a new religion.

527 Pisistratus tyrant of Athens dies, succeeded by his sons Hippias and Hipparchus.

525 Cambyses II of Persia defeats Psamtak III of Egypt at Pelusium, adding the Nile delta to his empire. He loses 50,000 men in a sandstorm. Aeschylus, Athenian dramatist and founder of Greek tragedy, is born at Eleusis.

522 Cambyses II of Persia learns that a usurper has seized his throne, Gaumata, a priest from Media; Cambyses dies on his way home.

521 Persia's 'false' king Gaumata is killed in battle by Darius Hystaspis, the son-in-law of the late Cyrus. The Persian nobility make Darius king.

520 A Carthaginian fleet of 60 ships under the command of Hanno lands 30,000 settlers at the mouth of the Rio de Oro in West Africa: the colony will survive for 50 years. The Persian Emperor Darius orders a canal dug to connect the Nile with the Red Sea, a project begun a century ago by the Pharaoh Necho.

✍ Orders of Darius: Nile-Red Sea Canal

🏺 Sarcophagus with married couple reclining, Cerveteri (Italy)

📖 Orders of Darius: Inscriptions in Persian, Elamitic and Babylonian on a cliff near Behistun, Iran (listing Darius's achievements)

518   The Greek poet Pindar is born in Boeotia.

516   ✎ The Great Temple of Jerusalem rebuilt

514   Harmodius and Aristogeiton conspire to assassinate the Athenian tyrants. The plot is bungled: Hipparchus is killed but Hippias escapes. Harmodius and Aristogeiton are executed.

512   ✎ Bridge of boats across the Bosporus: Mandrocles the Samian (for Darius to cross into Europe)

510   ✎ Theatre at Delphi

509   The Tarquin (Etruscan) King of Rome is overthrown and Rome becomes a republic. Tarquinius Superbus is driven out by a people's army.

500   The Greek philosopher Anaxagoras is born.

499   Battle at Lake Regillus: the Romans win a decisive victory over the Etruscans.

496   The Greek tragedian Sophocles is born.

495   Confucius resigns as prime minister of Lu when his ruler gives himself up to pleasure. For the next 12 years Confucius wanders from state to state teaching moral precepts and a utilitarian philosophy: 'What you do not like done to yourself, do not do to others'.

494   Battle of Sepeia near Tiryns, between Argos and Sparta; Cleomenes of Sparta is victorious. Argive generals are murdered as they dine, laming Argos for 20 years. Battle of Lade: Persians blockade Miletus, defeat the Greek fleet and take Miletus. Persian soldiers burn the Temple of Apollo at Didyma. The mainland Greeks are profoundly demoralized by the Persian domination of Caria.

492   Thrace and Macedonia are conquered by Mardonius, Darius's son-in-law. The Persians take the Cyclades and land in Attica.

490   The Battle of Marathon (*15 Sep*) gives Athens her first great victory, but also begins a long period of conflict with Persia.

     ✎ Mound of Marathon

     🎨 Relief of Darius and Xerxes Giving Audience, Treasury at Persepolis

489   The Athenians wage an unsuccessful campaign against Paros. The veteran Athenian general Miltiades is imprisoned; he dies of gangrene in prison. Cleomenes of Sparta becomes violently insane, hitting out at everyone in sight; his family keep him under restraint and he commits suicide.

488   ✍ The Audience Hall, Persepolis (begun)

486   Darius dies, succeeded as King of Persia by his son Xerxes

    ✍ Tomb of Darius I, Persepolis

485   Herodotus, Greek historian and geographer, is born

    ✍ Second Temple of Athena, Acropolis, Athens (pre-Periclean)

    ✍ The Ephebe of Critios, Acropolis, Athens: Critios (earliest marble classical statue)

484   The Greek dramatist Euripides is born.

483   ✍ Canal of Athos

    📖 Confucius: *Analects* (at about this time)

481   Pythius, the richest man in the Persian empire, entertains Xerxes and the whole Persian army at Celaenae in Cappadocia. When Pythius asks Xerxes to release his eldest son from military service, Xerxes has the young man cut in half.

480   Two bridges across the Hellespont are destroyed in a storm. Xerxes has the engineers beheaded and the Hellespont given 300 lashes of the whip in punishment. New bridges are made out of 670 triremes. It takes his armies two days to cross. *19 Aug*: Battle of Thermopylae, ending in victory for the Persians under Xerxes. The Persian armies, totalling 200,000, overwhelm and destroy a force of 300 Spartans and 700 Thespians under the command of Leonidas; the heroic stand of this small force enables the main Greek force to escape. Once the Persians break through the Pass at Thermopylae, they sack Athens, whose citizens flee to Salamis and the Peloponnese. The Second Temple of Athena is destroyed in the sack of Athens. *23 Sep*: Battle of Salamis: the Greeks are victorious. The Athenian general Themistocles lures the Persians into the Bay of Salamis, where over 1,000 Persian vessels are rammed and sunk by fewer than 400 Greek ships. Xerxes withdraws to Anatolia, but leaves a rearguard army under Mardonius. *2 Oct*: total eclipse of the sun at 2 pm. The omen prevents the Greeks from following and routing the retreating Persian army.

    ✄ Tomb of the Lionesses, Tarquinia (Italy)

479   *27 Aug*: Battle of Plataea. The Persian commander Mardonius is defeated by the Greeks under the command of Pausanias. The rout ends the Persian invasions of Greece. Buddha dies, aged 84, after feasting on pork.

475   Iron comes into common use in China nearly 1,000 years after its use became common in the Near East.

474   The Greek poet Pindar moves to Thebes; Pindar composes lyric odes to celebrate triumphs in the Olympiads.

472   📖 Aeschylus: *The Persians*

471   Themistocles is ostracized on a groundless charge of collaborating with the Persians.

470   Alfalfa is grown by the Greeks, who have been introduced to the plant by their enemies, the Persians. Naxos rebels against the League and is bullied into submission.

469   Cimon, Miltiades' son, takes a fleet east and defeats the Persians at the Battle of the Eurymedon River; this action reopens the old trade route from Greece to Egypt.

468   Cimon and his fellow commanders act as judges at the Greater Dionysia, an unprecedented privilege. They choose Sophocles, who is only 28, in preference to the older Aeschylus (57), whom they see as a dangerous radical. This is the first known instance of a literary prize awarded for political correctness.

467   📖 Aeschylus: *Seven Against Thebes*

466   Benghazi is founded on the North African coast by the citizens of Cyrenaica.

    ✄ Temple of Zeus at Olympia

465   Xerxes King of Persia dies, succeeded by Artaxerxes I.

460   Egypt is taken over by Persia. Themistocles commits suicide rather than submit to an order from the Great King Pericles to take arms against his own countrymen. Thucydides is born near Athens at about this time.

    ✄ Temple of Hera at Paestum (Italy)

    🗿 Statue of Poseidon (bronze) (Greece)

458   Ezra guides a caravan of exiles from Babylon back to Judah. The Roman general Lucius Cincinnatus is summoned from his small farm by the Senate to defend Rome against the approaching Aequians. Cincinnatus gathers troops, attacks and defeats the Aequians, then resigns his dictatorship and returns to his farm.

☐ Aeschylus: *The Oresteia* (with which Aeschylus wins his last prize)

457 Pericles makes Athens pre-eminent in architecture and the arts while at the same time preparing for war with Sparta. Athens has about 100,000 slaves (30 per cent of the population): 20,000 work in the silver mines at Laurion, producing Athens' wealth.

456 Aeschylus dies, aged 69, having written 90 plays of which only seven will survive.

454 The philosopher Socrates is born.

450 Celts cross the Channel and colonize the British Isles. Alcibiades and the dramatist Aristophanes are born.

✍ Temple of Theseus, Athens (completed)

449 Pericles proposes an inter-state Panhellenic Congress, to be held at Athens, to discuss the restoration of shrines destroyed by the Persians, the establishment of sacrifices vowed to the gods in *480*, and the policing of the seas. Sparta vetoes his proposal. Pericles earmarks 5,000 talents from the allied funds for the restoration of Athens' temples.

448 The rebuilding of the Acropolis at Athens begins under the direction of architects Ictinus and Callicrates.

✍ Ictinus and Callicrates: The Acropolis, Athens

447 At the Battle of Coronea, Athens loses Boeotia.

446 The Spartans invade Athens: Pericles bribes them to turn back when they reach Eleusis.

☐ Sophocles: *Ajax*

445 Peace treaty between Athens and Sparta. Nehemiah arrives in Judah and becomes its governor.

✍ Temple of Poseidon at Cape Sounion (completed)

444 Thucydides criticizes Pericles' extravagant building programme, denouncing the design for the new 12-metre/40-foot high ivory and gold statue of Athena in the Parthenon as vulgar.

✦ Pheidias: Statue of Athena Parthenos, Parthenon, Athens (design)

442 ☐ Sophocles: *Antigone*

441 The Athenian prize for drama is won by Euripides; he made his first attempt to win the prize 14 years ago, but his plays have been regarded, until now, as too sensational.

440 The Greek philosopher Heracleitus at Ephesus teaches that all is mutable. Principles are constantly changed through an incontrovertible law of nature: worlds are alternately created and destroyed. The Samians revolt against Athens and are crushed, but at a cost of 1,200 talents.

 Parthenon frieze sculptures (the 'Elgin' Marbles), Athens

438 The poet Pindar dies.

 The Parthenon, Athens (completed): Ictinus and Callicrates

437 Pheidias the sculptor cannot account for all the gold used in making the Athena statue and leaves Athens in disgrace after completing his masterpiece.

 Pheidias: Statue of Athena Parthenos, Parthenon (completed)

435 A gold and ivory statue of Zeus is completed at Elis by the Athenian sculptor Pheidias. The sculpture will be called one of the seven wonders of the ancient world.

 Pheidias: Statue of Zeus, Elis

434 Xenophon is born.

433 Pericles forms an alliance with Corcyra (Corfu), the bitter enemy of Corinth, and renews alliances with the Rhegium and Leontini in the west in an attempt to cut off Sparta's food supply. Corinth appeals to Sparta to take arms against Athens; the appeal is supported by Megara (ruined by Pericles' economic sanctions) and Aegina (heavily taxed by Pericles).

432 A decree against atheism is issued in Athens, aimed at the free-thinking philosopher Anaxaporas: he leaves Athens. The Peloponnesian Wars begin in Greece following a revolt by Potidaea in Chalcidice against Athens. Pericles blockades Potidaea. Sparta seizes the opportunity to declare war on Athens; Corfu declares war on Corinth. Socrates, aged 22, saves the life of Alcibiades, the 18-year-old nephew of Pericles, at Potidaea.

431 Archidamus II King of Sparta gains support by calling for the liberation of the Hellenes from the yoke of Athenian tyranny. Pericles improves Athens' defences, planning to lay waste the Megarid while the Spartans are preoccupied with agricultural work. The Greek physician Empedocles puts forward the idea that the body has four 'humours' (blood, bile, black bile and phlegm): this concept will dominate medicine for centuries to come.

📖 Euripides: *Medea*

430 *Aug*: Athens sends a peace mission to Sparta, with no success. The Athenians take Potidaea in the winter after a siege; by this time the port of Athens, Piraeus, is gripped by plague. One quarter of the population of Piraeus die. The plague – possibly a severe form of scarlet fever – does not affect the Peloponnese, although the Spartans kill every visitor to avoid contagion. Rome also falls victim to the plague.

429 The Athenian admiral Phormio wins victories at Chalcis and Naupactus at the entrance to the Corinthian Gulf. In Athens, thousands die of the plague. *Sep*: Pericles himself dies of the plague, which wipes out up to two-thirds of the population of Athens. Many Athenians lose their fear of the gods and their respect for the law. Hippocrates the physician is spared by the plague. He is the first to say that diseases are neither spontaneous nor supernatural in origin. Plato is born at about this time.

428 The revolt of Mitylene, the chief city of Lesbos.

📖 Euripides: *Hippolytus*

427 Archidamus II King of Sparta dies after reigning for 49 years. *Jul*: Mitylene surrenders to Athenian forces; the Athenians punish the citizens severely. *Aug*: Plataea surrenders when starvation threatens. The Athenians slaughter the Plataeans and destroy their city.

426 Corfu's democratic faction massacres Spartan supporters and secures Corfu for Athens. The Athenian general Demosthenes and the demagogue Cleon vigorously revive Athens' military forces. Demosthenes proposes an offensive strategy designed to make Sicily, Boeotia and the Peloponnese spheres of Athenian influence. *Jun*: Demosthenes travels to Acarnania and raises a large army with the intention of invading Boeotia by way of Phocis. His army is surprised and attacked in the forest and Demosthenes barely escapes. He reaches the Athenian base at Naupactus and secures it just in time to keep a large Spartan army under Eyrylochus from taking it.

Demosthenes shatters the prestige of Sparta and returns to Athens in triumph.

425 An Athenian fleet called up by Demosthenes traps the Spartan navy in Navarino Bay. A Spartan force landing on the island of Sphacteria is cut off from rescue; negotiations between Athens and Sparta reach stalemate. Cleon overwhelms the 292 Spartans stranded on Sphacteria and takes them back to Athens where they are held hostage. Sparta sues for peace but Cleon refuses. The historian and geographer Herodotus dies at about this time.

   📖 Euripides: *Hecuba*
      Aristophanes: *The Acharnians*

424 A congress at Gela in Sicily hears Hermocrates of Syracuse argue in favour of excluding foreign powers. An Athenian naval force is sent home by the Sicilians. Pagondas of Thebes crushes an Athenian army at Delium using cavalry. The Spartan general Brasidas marches through Boeotia and Thessaly to Chalcidice, where he offers protection to cities rebelling against Athens. The city of Amphipolis surrenders before it is reached by a naval force from the north under Thucydides. The vengeful Cleon exiles Thucydides for 20 years.

   📖 Sophocles: *Oedipus Rex*
      Aristophanes: *The Knights*

423 *Apr*: the Truce of Laches is designed by Athens to stop Brasidas getting any further. Brasidas ignores the truce, takes Scione and Mende, and moves towards Athens with the intention of freeing the hostages. Athens sends troops to retake Mende.

   📖 Sophocles: *Women of Trachi*
      Aristophanes: *The Clouds*

422 Cleon of Athens and Brasidas of Sparta meet in battle outside the city of Amphipolis; both are killed.

   📖 Aristophanes: *The Wasps*

421 *11 Apr*: the Peace of Nicias brings a temporary end to the Peloponnesian war. The Peace is negotiated by King Pleistoanax of Sparta and Nicias, an Athenian mineowner. Alcibiades organizes an anti-Spartan alliance between Athens and the democracies of Argos, Mantinea and Elis.

✍ Erechtheum, Acropolis, Athens

📖 Aristophanes: *The Peace*

420 Corinth and Boeotia do not support the Peace of Nicias.
Athens has released the Spartan hostages, but kept Pylos
and Nisaea because Sparta is holding onto Amphipolis.
A Quadruple Alliance (Athens, Argos, Mantinea, Elis)
organized by Alcibiades confronts an alliance between
Sparta and Boeotia.

📖 Euripides: *The Suppliant Women*

419 King Agis of Sparta gathers an army at Philus and
marches on Argos at night. The attack fails because of
weakness in the Boeotian troops, but Agis is able to force
a treaty with Argos.

📖 Euripides: *Andromache*
Sophocles: *Electra*

418 *Aug*: the Battle of Mantinea is the major land battle of the
War, giving Sparta victory over Argos, which has broken
the treaty with Sparta at Alcibiades' insistence. Alcibiades is unpopular in Athens, and he is not re-elected
general; Sparta is able to break up the Quadruple
Alliance helped, albeit unwittingly, by Alcibiades' enemies in Athens. Alcibiades presses the Athenians to
conquer Syracuse, Sicily and Carthage and so gain extra
troops to enable them to end the war against Sparta. This
extraordinary plan wins the support of the Athenians.

416 Athenians massacre the inhabitants of Melos.

415 Athenians prepare a fleet to send to Sicily. *6/7 Jun*: on the
eve of departure, they are (deliberately) given a bad omen
– the Herm busts in the streets of Athens are myster-
iously mutilated during the night. Alcibiades is accused
of the crime and also of profaning the Eleusinian mysteries. He asks for an immediate inquiry, but is ordered
to set sail. He escapes to Sparta on the return voyage,
learning that he has been sentenced to death while in
Siciliy. He openly joins the Spartans and persuades them
to assist Syracuse. *Nov*: an Athenian landing in Syracuse
Great Harbour leads to little of practical value.

📖 Euripides: *The Trojan Women*
Xenophon: *The Polity of Athens* (anonymously)

414 The Athenian commander Lamachus is killed by Syracusans. Sparta's fleet under Gylippus arrives to rein-

force the Syracusans. Athens responds by sending a second fleet under Demosthenes.

📖 Aristophanes: *The Birds* (satirizing the Sicilian expedition)

413 *Jul*: Demosthenes arrives at Syracuse but is defeated in a night attack. He urges Nicias to leave. Nicias delays because soothsayers advise waiting until after the lunar eclipse of *27 Aug*. The Athenian fleet is by then trapped in the harbour and destroyed in the Battle of Syracuse in September. Nicias and Demosthenes take to the hills with an army, but they are caught by the Syracusans and executed. The survivors of the massacre are worked to death in the quarries at Syracuse. Archelaus I becomes King of Macedonia; he lures Euripides to his court.

📖 Euripides: *Electra*

412 Spartans begin to distrust Alcibiades, who has antagonized King Agis; he withdraws to the court of Tissaphernes the Persian satrap, advising Tissaphernes to withdraw his support from Sparta and at the same time conspiring with the oligarchic party in Athens. Sparta's allies break away from her one by one.

📖 Euripides: *Helen*
   Eupolis: *The Demes*

411 *Jul*: the democracy of Athens is overthrown by Antiphon, Peisander and Phrynichus, who open secret negotiations with Sparta. They are overthrown by the moderate Theramenes. The Athenian navy decides to recall Alcibiades from Sardis and his election is ratified by the Athenians at Theramenes' persuasion *Sep*: the Spartan fleet is defeated by the Athenians in the Hellespont.

📖 Euripides: *Iphigenia in Tauris*
   Aristophanes: *Lysistrata; The Women at the Thesmophoria*

410 Alcibiades defeats the Spartan navy and its Persian supporting army at Cyzicus in the Sea of Marmara. Sparta begins negotiations but Cleophon, the new Athenian demagogue, lets the opportunity go. Democracy is reestablished in Athens.

409 Alcibiades recaptures Byzantium, clears the Bosporus, securing Athens' supply route for grain from the Black

Sea region.

📖 Sophocles: *Philoctetes*

408   *16 Jun*: Alcibiades enters Athens in triumph and is
appointed general with unlimited powers. He leaves
for Samos to rejoin the fleet. Lysander, the Spartan
admiral, assembles a huge fleet at Ephesus with help
from the Persian satrap Cyrus.

📖 Euripides: *Orestes*

407   Lysander refuses to be lured out of Ephesus to join battle
with Alcibiades, who has to sail north to collect fresh
supplies, leaving behind a squadron under his friend
Antiochus. Antiochus disobeys orders, goading Lysander, who responds to the challenge by emerging from
Ephesus to rout the Athenians at Notium. The defeat
gives Alcibiades' enemies in Athens the excuse they want
to strip Alcibiades of his command.

406   Disgraced, Alcibiades flees to the Hellespont and is
replaced by a committee of generals, one of whom is
trapped in Mitylene by Callicratidas, the Spartan admiral who replaces Lysander. Athens raises a fleet and
sends it under Conon to relieve the siege of Mitylene.
Conon is defeated but returns to gain victory in the Battle
of Arginusae. Cleophon rejects Sparta's renewed peace
offer; Sparta yields to pressure from Cyrus for Lysander
to take a fleet to the Hellespont. Euripides dies, aged 77.

📖 Euripides: *The Bacchantes*; *Iphigenia in Aulis* (unfinished)

405   The Athenian fleet follows Lysander to the Hellespont.
Sep: the Athenian fleet is destroyed while it is drawn up
on the beach at Aegospotami. Conon escapes from the
carnage with just 10 triremes. Lysander blockades Piraeus; Pausanius King of Sparta lays siege to Athens. The
tragedian Sophocles dies, aged 91: only seven of his 120
plays will survive.

✍ The Erechtheum, Acropolis, Athens (completed)

📖 Aristophanes: *The Frogs*

404   Cleophon is tried and executed as Athens is starved
into submission. *25 Apr*: the Athenians surrender and
the First Peloponnesian War comes to an end. Xenophon writes, 'This day was the beginning of freedom
for Greece'. Theramenes secures terms that save the

city from destruction but her defensive wall is torn
down to the music of flutes. The oligarchy of the
'Thirty Tyrants' takes power under Critias, who has
Theramenes forced to drink hemlock for alleged
treason. Alcibiades is murdered in Phrygia at Lysander the Spartan's request.

403 Battle of Munychia: victory for the Athenian Thrasybulus over the Spartans. Thrasybulus restores democratic institutions in Athens and grants an amnesty to all
except oligarchic extremists.

401 Cyrus the Younger of Persia leads a revolt against his
brother Artaxerxes II but is defeated and killed at the
Battle of Cunaxa. Greek commanders in the rebel army
are executed, but the 33-year-old Xenophon takes command of 10,000 soldiers and leads them to safety on the
Black Sea coast. The Greek historian Thucydides dies,
aged 60.

   📖 Thucydides: *The Peloponnesian War*
      Sophocles: *Oedipus at Colonus* (presented posthu-
      mously at Athens)

399 The Greek philosopher Socrates is condemned for
corrupting the young. He drinks hemlock and dies at
the age of 70. Archelaus I King of Macedonia dies.

396 The Etruscan city of Veil falls to a Roman army after a
10-year siege. The Romans progressively erode the
Etruscan civilization in Italy.

393 Amyntas III becomes King of Macedonia.
   🏛 The Long Walls of Athens (rebuilt)
   📖 Aristophanes: *The Ecclesiazusae*

388 📖 Aristophanes: *Plutus* (last work)

387 Fire destroys the Etruscan walls of Rome.

386 A law is passed in Athens that one play by the 'Old
Masters' – Aeschylus, Sophocles and Euripides – must
be revived each year; the Athenians have become inti-
midated by their own past. Plato's Academy is founded.
The dramatist Aristophanes dies.

384 Aristotle and Demosthenes are born.

380 📖 Plato: *Republic*
      Isocrates: *Panegyricus*

371 *Jun*: a treaty between Athens, Thebes and Sparta is
drafted, but Thebes insists on signing for all Boeotian

cities and negotiations collapse. Cleombrotus King of Sparta invades Boeotia. *Jul*: Battle of Leuctra; Thebes is victorious over Sparta. None of the city-states is able to gain the ascendancy and skirmishes continue.

370 Amyntas III King of Macedonia dies. His two sons Perdiccas and Philip will rule Macedonia.

362 Battle of Mantinea; Thebes is victorious but because its leader Epaminondas is killed in the battle it is unable to capitalize on the victory. The Greek city-states once again relapse into chaos.

359 King Perdiccas of Macedonia dies in battle against the Illyrians, succeeded by his brother Philip II; Greek affairs abruptly resume shape and pattern.

356 The Temple of Artemis at Ephesus is burned down by Herostratus, who destroys one of the seven wonders of the ancient world in a perverted though successful bid for immortality. Alexander the Great is born, the son of Philip of Macedonia.

354 A tomb enclosed by Ionic columns is built at Halicarnassus in Caria for King Mausolus; it will become one of the seven wonders of the ancient world. Xenophon dies.

 ✍ Mausoleum, Halicarnassus

351 ✎ Statue of Mausolus, Halicarnassus

350 References to wheat appear in Greek writings for the first time.

 ✍ Polykleitos: Theatre at Epidauros

349 Philip of Macedonia sets out to conquer the Chalcidic Peninsula. As the fate of its capital, Olynthus, hangs in the balance, Demosthenes urges the Athenians to go to the aid of the Olynthians, but nothing is done.

348 Olynthus falls to Philip.

347 Plato dies.

346 The Athenians try unsuccessfully to negotiate a peace treaty with Philip, who offers only an endorsement of the *status quo*, including all his territorial gains to date: the Peace of Philocrates.

344 Aristotle travels from Athens to Lesbos to study natural history. Aristotle is a follower of Plato and his father is physician to the king of Macedonia.

 📖 Demosthenes: *Second Philippic* (warns that Philip will not rest until Athens falls)

343   The dramatist Menander is born.

342   Aristotle returns to Macedon, at the invitation of King Philip, to teach; his pupils include Philip's son Alexander.

341   Epicurus the philosopher is born in Samos.

340   Philip of Macedon fails in a siege of Byzantium; the sentries may have seen Philip advancing by the light of the crescent moon and adopt the crescent symbol of their goddess Hecate as the emblem of Byzantium

338   Philip of Macedon defeats Theban and Athenian armies in the final struggle for Greek independence. *2 Aug*: Battle of Chaeronea in western Boeotia. Philip's 18-year-old son Alexander commands the left wing of his army. Philip suspects Alexander and Olympias, Alexander's mother, of plotting against him. He divorces Olympias and removes Alexander from public life.

336   Philip of Macedon is assassinated at Aeges during the wedding feast of Olympias' brother Alexander of Epirus. Philip had recently consulted the Delphic Oracle to find out whether he would conquer the Great King; the Oracle replied ambiguously, 'The bull is garlanded. All is done. The sacrifice is ready'. It is assumed that Alexander and Olympias did, as Philip suspected, conspire to have him killed. Alexander succeeds to the Macedon throne.

335   Aristotle returns to Athens from Macedon and opens a lyceum containing a museum of natural history and a library. Aristotle advises abortion for parents with too many children: 'The neglect of an effective birth control policy is a never-failing source of poverty, which in turn is the parent of revolt and crime.' Alexander destroys Thebes.

334   Alexander invades Asia. He is victorious in the Battle of the Granicus, defeating a Persian army that includes 10,000 Greek mercenaries.

     ✍ Monument of Lysicrates, Athens

333   *Oct*: Battle of Issus; Alexander defeats the Persian army but the Emperor Darius III escapes.

332   Alexander takes over Egypt and founds the city that will later be called Alexandria.

331   *1 Oct*: Battle of Arbela in Mesopotamia. Alexander wins another major victory, losing only 500 men against

Persian losses estimated at 90,000. Alexander now controls the Persian Empire. Wheat is grown extensively in south-east England and threshed in the shelter of great barns, according to a report by a traveller from the Greek colony of Massilia (Marseilles).

330 Darius III the Persian king is murdered by his satrap Bessus. Alexander destroys the great city of Persepolis, the Persian capital. The atomic theory proposed by the Greek philosopher Democritus says that matter is composed of tiny atomic particles, and that everything happens through cause and of necessity.

329 Alexander conquers Samarkand in central Asia.

327 Alexander invades northern India and plans to take the Ganges valley; he is persuaded to abandon his plans by his exhausted army. Alexander appoints Nearchus as admiral. Nearchus has Indian shipwrights build 800 ships, then uses Indian pilots to take Alexander's forces by sea to the Persian Gulf and Babylonia.

325   📖 Timotheus of Miletus: *The Persae* (earliest surviving Greek papyrus)

324   📖 Menander: *A New Comedy*

323 Alexander the Great dies in Babylon aged 32, possibly of malaria, possibly of pneumonia following a lung wound, possibly of poison; he has begun to show signs of mental disturbance. Aristotle is accused of impiety in the reaction following Alexander's death, and doubtless reflecting on Socrates' fate, he withdraws to Calcis in Euboea. Alexander's generals Antigonus, Antipater, Seleucus, Ptolemy, Eumenes and Lysimachus struggle for control of the Macedonian Empire. Ptolemy becomes Governor of Egypt.

  ✍ Ptolemy I: Museum and Library at Alexandria

322 The philosopher Aristotle dies at Calcis, aged 62. Demosthenes the orator dies, taking poison to avoid being captured and executed.

321 Battle of the Caudine Forks: Samnites trap and defeat a Roman army in a pass near Beneventum.

319 Alexander's general Antipater falls ill and names the elderly Regent Polysperchon as his successor; the nomination is challenged by Antipater's son Cassander, who is 31.

317   Ardvates, the Persian satrap of Armenia, liberates his country from Seleucid control.

316   Polysperchon, Regent of Macedonia, is overthrown by Cassander, who seizes Olympias, Alexander's mother, and has her put to death; he marries Thessaloniki, the half-sister of Alexander, and rules jointly with her. Eumenes and Antigonus, rivals for control of Macedonia, join battle in Media using cavalry and elephants. Antigonus captures Eumenes' baggage and camp followers, giving them back in exchange for Eumenes himself who, a week later, is murdered by his guard.

315   Cassander founds the Macedonian port of Thessalonica.

314   Antigonus promises freedom to any Greek city who will support him against Cassander. The Aetolians form an alliance with Antigonus: Cassander marches against them with his allies Ptolemy, Seleucus and Lysimachus.

312   Battle of Gaza: Ptolemy and Seleucus defeat the one-eyed Antigonus, who is captured but released. Rome receives its first pure drinking water supply as engineers complete an underground aqueduct into the city.
    ✒ Appius Claudius Caecus: Appian Way (begun)

310   Cassander has Roxana, Alexander's widow, executed along with her young son Alexander IV.

308   Ptolemy is defeated in a naval battle off Cyprus by Demetrius Poliorcetes, son of Antigonus.

307   Demetrius Poliorcetes lays siege to Rhodes, employing 30,000 men to build siege towers, including the siege tower called Helepolis, which requires 3,400 men to move it, and a ram 55 metres/180 feet long. The siege fails.

305   The Seleucid Empire of Babylonia is established by Seleucus, who is now 53. He adopts the name Nicator and extends his territory as far as the Indus. In Egypt, governor Ptolemy makes himself King Ptolemy I Soter (Saviour). The poet Callimachus is born in Libya.

301   Battle of Ipsus in Phrygia. This ends Antigonus' campaign; he is killed at the age of 81 by the armies of Lysimachus and Seleucus. Nomadic tribes begin to occupy northern China. The Athenian philosopher Epicurus recommends luxury and indulgence, but also prudence, honour and justice. The Chinese build a

drainage system to reduce river flooding in Szechwan's Red Basin.

📖 Theophrastus: *On Stones*

300 Carthage in North Africa begins to gain economic ascendancy in the Mediterranean by trading in slaves and the products of the African interior, including ivory and lion and leopard skins.

🛥 The Hjortspring boat (Denmark)

📖 Euclid: *Elements*

297 Cassander King of Macedonia dies aged 53. Demetrius Poliocertes returns to Greece with the intention of gaining control of Macedonia and Asia.

🏛 Sostratus of Cnidus: Pharos of Alexandria

295 Athens falls to Demetrius after a long siege; Lachares tyrant of Athens is killed. The Battle of Sentium near Anconum; Roman legions defeat Samnites and Gauls and force peace on the Etruscans.

292 🛥 Chares of Lindos: Colossus of Rhodes (bronze statue of Helios)

289 The Chinese philosopher Mencius (Meng Zu) dies, aged about 83 after a lifelong attempt to unify China.

288 Demetrius is driven out of Macedonia by Lysimachus, helped by Pyrrhus King of Epirus; Seleucus, Ptolemy and Lysimachus form an alliance to block Demetrius' plans to conquer Asia.

287 Archimedes is born at Syracuse.

285 Ptolemy Soter King of Egypt abdicates, aged 82, after reigning for 38 years. He is succeeded by his son Ptolemy II Philadelphus, initially with the daughter of Lysimachus as his wife. Demetrius Poliocertes is deserted by his army and he surrenders to Seleucus, who imprisons him for life.

🏛 Pharos of Alexandria (completed at a cost of 800 talents, this lighthouse will aid navigation for 1,600 years)

284 Ardvates, satrap of Armenia, dies after reigning for 33 years.

283 Demetrius Poliocertes dies in prison.

282 Ptolemy III is born.

281 Seleucus Nicator defeats and kills Lysimachus at the Battle of Corupedium. Seleucus makes himself King of Syria.

280   Seleucus tries to take Macedonia, but falls into a trap set by Ptolemy Ceraunus, who murders him and takes Macedonia for himself. Seleucus is succeeded by Antiochus I Soter. Pyrrhus King of Epirus defeats a Roman army at Asculum and says, 'Another such victory and we are ruined'. The Achaean League is formed by 12 towns in the northern Peloponnese.

      ✆ Chares of Lindos: Colossus of Rhodes (made from spoils left by Demetrius Poliocertes when he raised his siege in *305 BC*, and one of the seven wonders of the ancient world) (completed)

279   Celtic tribesmen invading Macedonia kill Ptolemy Ceraunus, but fierce tribesmen from the mountains force them to move east.

276   First Syrian War begins.

275   The Museum and Library of Alexandria maintain and support scholars from all countries, encouraging learning and research in all disciplines.

274   In China the Emperor Qin Shihuang is born, the illegitimate son of a merchant and a prostitute.

272   Ptolemy of Egypt annexes Miletus, Phoenicia and western Cilicia after defeating his half-brother Magas and Antiochus I Soter; the First Syrian War ends. Rome's war with Pyrrhus of Epirus ends after 10 years when Tarentum surrenders to the Romans.

270   Rome recaptures Rhegium from the Mamertine tribe and defeats the Brutians, Lucanians, Calabrians and Samnites. Rome's supremacy in the peninsula of Italy is established. The Athenian philosopher Epicurus dies.

268   The Roman silver denarius coin is minted for the first time.

267   Antigonus II, King of Macedonia, suppresses a rebellion by an Athenian-led coalition of Achaeans, Arcadians and Spartans which has tried to eject the Macedonian garrisons.

265   The Greek mathematician Archimedes devises the Archimedean screw for raising irrigation water.

264   A Punic War between Rome and Carthage begins

262   Macedonian forces under Antigonus II lay siege to Athens, which surrenders.

260   Battle of Mylae off the north coast of Sicily: the Romans' first naval victory over Carthage. Gaius Nepos commands quinqueremes modelled on a Carthaginian vessel found beached on the Italian coast. The third emperor of India's Mauyra dynasty, Asoka, adopts Buddhism.

254 The Roman playwright Plautus is born.

249 The last Zhou emperor of China is deposed.

247 Hannibal is born.

246 The Qin dynasty is founded by Emperor Qin Shihuang. Ptolemy II of Egypt dies, aged 63, succeeded by his son Ptolemy III, who invades Syria seeking revenge, for the murder of his sister Berenice.

245 Babylon and Susa fall to the armies of Ptolemy III.

244 Ptolemy IV is born.

243 Ptolemy III is recalled from his Syrian campaign by a rebellion in Egypt. Corinth joins the Achaean League.

240 The Roman poet Callimachus dies.

237 Hamilcar Barca, 33, leads a Carthaginian army in an invasion of Spain.

234 The Roman Censor Marcus Porcius Cato is born.

228 Hamilcar Barca is killed in battle. His command in Spain passes to his son-in-law Hasdrubal.

224 An earthquake destroys the Colossus of Rhodes.

223 Mesopotamia's King Seleucus III Soter is murdered and succeeded by his brother, Antiochus III.

222 Mediolanum (Milan) is taken by Roman legions after being occupied by Ligurians, then Etruscans, then Celts.

221 Hasdrubal, the Carthaginian general, is assassinated. His command passes to Hannibal, the 26-year-old son of Hamilcar Barca, and his brother Hasdrubal. Ptolemy III of Egypt dies, aged 61, succeeded by his son Ptolemy IV and his sister-wife Arsinoe III. The Qin Emperor Shihuang unites China after conquering six warring states.

220 ✍ The Flaminian Way, between Rome and Rimini (completed)

219 The Fourth Syrian War: Antiochus III King of Syria takes the province of Coelo-Syria from Egypt.

218 The Second Punic War starts. Hannibal's Carthaginian army attacks Rome's Spanish allies. He besieges and takes the town of Sagunto, then crosses the Alps to defeat a Roman army at the Ticino, and at the Trebbia River.

217   *24 Jun*: Battle of Lake Trasimene in Umbria: Hannibal defeats and almost annihilates an army led by Gaius Flaminius. The lake is red with the blood of 16,000 Romans. Egyptian soldiers under Ptolemy IV Philopater defeat the Seleucid army at Raphia.

216   *2 Aug*: Battle of Cannae: Hannibal's Carthaginian army defeats an army of 70,000 Roman soldiers, of which 50,000 are slaughtered. Hannibal lacks the siege equipment needed to take Rome itself, and instead destroys the Romans' crops. Rome is deserted by her allies.

215   📖 Titus Plautus: *The Menaechmi* (at about this time)

214   ✐ The Great Wall of China (begun as an earthwork)
         📖 Titus Plautus: *The Merchant*

213   📖 Titus Plautus: *The Comedy of Asses*

212   The Qin Emperor Shihuang burns writings and has some scholars buried alive.

211   Antiochus III removes Armenia's King Xerxes and divides the country into two satrapies.

210   The Qin Emperor Shihuang dies, aged 49, after uniting China, starting the building of the Great Wall and the new capital of Xian. Buried near his tomb are 8,000 life-size terracotta soldiers and horses.
         🐚 Orders of the Qin Emperor: Terracotta Army, Xianyang (China)

207   Battle of Metaurus in Umbria; a Carthaginian army under Hannibal's brother Hasdrubal is defeated by a Roman army under Claudius Nero and Livius Salinator. Hasdrubal is killed in battle. Three years of famine begin in China.

205   The Roman historian Polybius is born in Arcadia.

204   Roman forces commanded by Scipio besiege Carthage. The Carthaginians sacrifice 100 boys in an attempt to make the god Moloch raise the siege.

203   The Han dynasty is founded as the last Qin Emperor dies; the dynastic change may have been brought about by the famine, seen as an omen. *19 Oct*: Battle of Sama; Scipio defeats a combined army of Carthaginians and Numidians under Hannibal and forces Carthage to surrender, ending the Second Punic War. In Egypt, Ptolemy IV is succeeded by Ptolemy V.
         📖 Titus Plautus: *The Casket* (at about this time)

201 Carthage gives all her Mediterranean possessions to Rome, agrees to pay an indemnity of 200 talents a year for 50 years, and destroys all but 10 of her warships. Battle of Chios: Philip V of Macedon is defeated by Attalus of Pergamum.

200 Battle of Panium: Antiochus III gains a decisive victory over Egypt's Ptolemy V Epiphanes in the Fifth Syrian War.

⚞ Great Serpent Mound, Ohio (at about this time)

▢ Titus Plautus: *Stichus*

197 Battle of Cynoscephalae in Thessaly: Romans under Flaminius defeat Macedonians under Philip V. Philip surrenders Greece, reduces his army to 5,000 men and his navy to five ships.

196 ▢ Titus Plautus: *The Haunted House*

195 ▢ Titus Plautus: *The Persian*

194 ▢ Titus Plautus: *The Pot of Gold*; *The Rope*

193 ▢ Titus Plautus: *The Weevil*

192 Antiochus III invades Greece with a Syrian army at the invitation of the Aetolians.

191 At Thermopylae a Roman army routs the army of Antiochus III, repeating the strategy used by Xerxes in *480 BC*. Cisalpine Gaul becomes a Roman province.

▢ Titus Plautus: *Pseudolus*

190 Battle of Magenta, near Smyrna: Roman victory over Antiochus III. The Syrian king is forced to surrender all his European and Asiatic possessions as far east as the Taurus mountains and to surrender Hannibal. Hannibal nevertheless escapes.

189 ▢ Titus Plautus: *The Two Bacchaides* ('He whom the gods love dies young')

188 ▢ Titus Plautus: *The Captives*

186 ▢ Titus Plautus: *Amphitryon*

185 ▢ Titus Plautus: *Casina*

184 The playwright Plautus dies, aged 70.

183 Hannibal poisons himself at the court of Prusia I King of Bithynia, whom he knows is about to betray him to the Romans. Parma and Pisa become Roman colonies.

181 Ptolemy V of Egypt dies, succeeded by Ptolemy VI.

179 ⚞ Pons Aemilius, Rome (the world's first stone bridge is completed across the River Tiber)

172   The Macedonian King Perseus defeats a Roman army: the battle is the start of a new war between Rome and Macedonia.

170   Paved streets are laid out in Rome. They are passable in all weathers, but add considerably to the traffic noise.

168   Battle of Pydna: a Roman victory over Perseus King of Macedonia. Lucius Aemilius Paulus, the Roman general, returns to Rome with King Perseus in his triumphal procession. Captured Macedonians are sold into slavery in Rome, females fetching 50 times the price of males. Antiochus IV Epiphanes King of Syria outlaws Judaism, destroys the Great Temple of Jerusalem and tries to convert the people of Judea to idolatry. The huge amounts of loot brought home by Paulus from Macedonia enable Rome to release Roman citizens from direct taxation.

167   Mattathias of Modin, a Jewish priest defies Antiochus' ban on Judaism. Mattathias escapes into mountains outside Lydda with his sons and begins a revolt.

166   📖 Terence (Publius Terentius Afer): *The Women of Andros*

       🎵 Flaccus (Terence's fellow-slave): *Flute Music for The Women of Andros*

165   Mattathias dies: his sons continue the revolt. Judas Maccabaeus and his brothers retake Jerusalem from the Syrians. They cleanse the Great Temple, destroy the idols and restore Judaism. Jews later commemorate the event in the annual feast Hanukkah.

       📖 Terence: *The Mother-in-law*

163   Antiochus IV of Syria dies, succeeded by his son of 10, who reigns briefly as Antiochus V under the regency of Lysias.

       📖 Terence: *The Self-Avenger*

162   Antiochus V, the 11-year-old King of Syria, is killed by his cousin Demetrius I Soter.

161   📖 Terence: *The Eunuch; Phormio*

160   The new governor of Judaea is killed in battle by the Maccabees. At the Battle of Elasa, shortly after, Judas Maccabaeus is killed. His brother Jonathan succeeds as leader and will make Judea an almost independent state by the time of his death.

📖 Terence: *Brothers*

159 Terence, the Carthaginian playwright who started life as a slave, dies, aged about 31.

157 Cato helps arbitrate a truce between Carthage and Numidia.

153 January 1 becomes the first day in the civil year in Rome, changing the shape of the calendar. A rebellion in Spain has obliged Roman consuls to take office earlier than the traditional date of 15 March.

150 The Roman censor Marcus Porcius Cato urges that, 'Carthage must be destroyed'. Carthage has attacked Numidia, whose 88-year-old King Masinna is an ally of Rome. In Syria, a usurper, Alexander Balas, claims to be Antiochus IV's son; he defeats Demetrius I Soter (also a usurper) in battle and kills him. The Romans support Alexander and he accedes to the Syrian throne.

⚖ Stoa of Attalos, Athens

149 The Romans invade North Africa and besiege Carthage. The Carthaginians offer to surrender, but refuse to leave the city. Cato the Elder dies, aged 85.

146 Carthage falls to Scipio Emilianus. Roman deserters set fire to the Temple of Aesculapius, choosing death by fire instead of execution. Hasdrubal surrenders his garrison; his wife throws herself and her children into the flames of the burning temple. Carthage becomes the Roman province of Africa; the Third Punic War comes to an end. Ptolemy VI of Egypt dies, succeeded by Ptolemy VII. 50,000 Carthaginian men, women and children are sold into slavery.

145 Alexander Balas of Syria dies in battle near Antioch. His son by Cleopatra Thea succeeds to the throne as Antiochus VI.

144 ⚖ Aqua Marcia Aqueduct, Rome

143 The usurper Tryphon of Syria traps Jonathan Maccabaeus and kills him at Bethshean. Jonathan's brother Simon succeeds to the leadership of the rebels.

142 Antiochus VI, the boy-king of Syria, dies and is succeeded by Demetrius II Nicator, son of Demetrius I Soter. Judea wins its independence from Syria under Simon Maccabaeus, who sends an embassy to Rome and begins minting coins.

141 The Jews under Simon Maccabaeus liberate Jerusalem while Demetrius II Nicator is preoccupied with the conquest of Babylonia.

140 Wu Di begins a 53-year reign as Emperor of China (Han dynasty).

135 Rome's first Slave War starts. Slaves on Sicilian estates revolt under the leadership of Eunus, a Syrian who styles himself King Antiochus; they hold the towns of Henna and Tauromenium against Roman armies.

134 Simon Maccabaeus, ruler of Judea, is treacherously murdered with 300 followers by his son-in-law the governor of Jericho. Simon is succeeded by his son, John Hyrcanus.

133 Tiberius Gracchus is elected Roman tribune. He proposes limiting land holdings (of public land) to 126 hectares/312 acres per person, but there is resistance to this reform from large landowners in Etruria and Campania; Gracchus is murdered. The great estates continue to grow at the expense of small peasant holdings.

132 The Slave War ends as Roman troops capture Eunus and execute him and his supporters; of 70,000 slaves taking part in the revolt, 20,000 are crucified.

129 Scipio Emilianus is found dead after voicing approval of reforms to land holding that would favour Italian peasants. He has probably been murdered.

123 Gaius Gracchus is elected Roman tribune on a platform similar to that of his dead brother. Gaius puts through a more extreme programme, including a law that protects the poor against famine. State control of the grain supply follows; this will enable unscrupulous demagogues to win popular support by giving out free grain.

120 ✍ Temple of Concord, Rome (first large-scale use of concrete)

117 ✍ Temple of Castor, Rome

116 Ptolemy VII of Egypt dies.

110 Romans cultivate oysters; the first Western attempt to domesticate marine wildlife. Cultured oyster beds are established at Baia near the site of Naples; the local oysterman Sergius Orata becomes rich selling oysters to wealthy Romans.

105 Roman armies are defeated at Arausio on the River Rhone by the Cimbri.

104 John Hyrcanus the Judean leader dies after a 30-year reign, succeeded by his son Aristobulos I, who completes the conquest of Galilee.

103 Aristobulos I dies, aged 38, succeeded by his brother Alexander Jannaeus. A second Slave War erupts in Sicily, under the leadership of Tryphon and Athenion; slaves provide much of the power for Roman agriculture.

102 Battle of Aix-en-Provence: Roman troops under Gaius Marius defeat Teutons and Sciri. The people of Provence salute his triumph. Julius Caesar is born.

101 Battle of Campi Raudii near Vercellae: Roman troops under Gaius Marius and Quintus Lutatius Catulus defeat the Cimbri. Marius is treated as a national hero. Chinese ships reach the east coast of India for the first time, using a magnetic compass to aid their navigation.

100 Plebeian tribunes Saturnius and Glaucia advocate cheaper corn for the poor. Aristocrats in the Roman Senate outlaw the popular leaders; Saturnius and Glaucia are murdered with the connivance of the general Gaius Marius.

99 The second Slave War ends when a Roman army under Marcus Aquillius defeats an army of slaves.

96 Antiochus VIII King of Syria is murdered by his favourite Heracleon after dividing his kingdom with his half-brother Antiochus IX.

95 Antiochus IX is defeated in battle and killed by his half-brother's son, who now succeeds as Seleucus VI.

94 Artanes King of Armenia Minor is deposed by Tigranes II.

93 Tigranes II forms an alliance with Mithridates King of Parthia by marrying his daughter Cleopatra. He invades Cappadocia in the name of Mithridates, but Roman forces under Lucius Cornelius Sulla force Tigranes to retreat.

92 Mithridates II of Parthia forms an alliance with Rome and makes preparations to invade Mesopotamia.

91 Italian rebels set up a 'Republic of Italia', with a capital at Corfinium, and declare war on Rome.

88 Mithridates the Great King of Parthia dies after conquering Mesopotamia. Tigranes II of Armenia invades Parthia to recover the 70 valleys that were paid for his ransom in *95 BC*; he succeeds in reducing the size of Parthia and extending the borders of his own country. Mithridates VI King of Pontus begins the first of his three wars on Rome. Civil war breaks out in Rome as the legions suppress the Republic of Italia rebellion and fresh legions are raised to fight Mithridates of Pontus.

87 The Roman general Sulla marches on Rome, where he kills the demagogue Publius Sulpicius Ruffus and other rebels before leaving for Asia. A new demagogue appears – Lucius Cornelius Cinna.

86 Athens falls to Sulla's forces, which defeat the armies of Mithridates and his allies.

84 Gaius Valerius Catullus is born. Sulla compels Mithridates to make peace, evacuate the territories he has conquered, surrender 80 warships and pay 3,000 talents. Sulla sails for Brundisium. Antiochus XII King of Syria is killed on a military expedition against the Nabataeans.

83 Mark Antony is born.

82 *Nov:* Sulla defeats Samnites in the Battle of the Colline Gate, then appoints himself dictator and moves to punish cities that have failed to support Rome.

81 Sujin, the Japanese Emperor, begins a major shipbuilding enterprise in an effort to provide more seafood for his people.

80 Sulla, the Roman dictator, stops the distribution of free grain.

79 Sulla voluntarily retires from public life after making substantial reforms in the Roman legal system.

78 Sulla dies, aged 60. The Democratic Marcus Aemilius Lepidus begins to undo his work. Thwarted, Lepidus raises a rebel army in Etruria, but Quintus Lutatius Catulus defeats him in battle outside Rome.

77 Lepidus' army is routed by forces under Gnaeus Pompeius, aged 29, who forces Lepidus to flee to Spain where he dies.

75 The Greek physician Asclepiades of Bithynia insists that disease is a result of an inharmonious motion of the particles that make up all the tissues of the body. Many are helped by his recommendations relating to bathing, dieting and exercise, including Mark Antony.

73 A third Slave War breaks out, under the leadership of Spartacus, a slave from Thrace who has become a gladiator. Spartacus takes Mount Vesuvius with the help of his fellow gladiators. Herod the Great is born.

72 Spartacus' slave army is defeated by Roman legions.

71 Mithridates VI King of Pontus is expelled from his country by Roman legions under Lucullus; he takes refuge at the court of Tigranes II King of Armenia. Crassus defeats Spartacus. Pompey returns from Spain and destroys what is left of the slave army.

70 Pompey and Crassus break with the Roman nobility, using their troops to gain consulship. The poet Virgil is born (*15 Oct*). Tigranes II of Armenia completes his conquests; his empire now stretches from the Ararat valley to the city of Tyre on the Mediterranean. Tigranes calls himself 'king of kings' and begins work on a new capital to be called Tigranocerta. Phraates III begins to restore order in Parthia. Pompey and Crassus resume the distribution of free grain in Rome.

⚜ The Snettisham Treasure (gold torcs) (U.K.)

69 Roman forces under Lucius Licinius Lucullus defeat Tigranes II King of Armenia after his seizure of Syria. Lucullus presses into the mountain country of Armenia and Parthia. Cherries from Pontus are sent to Rome by Lucullus, introducing a new fruit tree to Europe.

68 As some of his troops mutiny, Lucullus is forced to retreat south. The King of Pontus begins a campaign to retrieve his kingdom. Crete falls to Roman legions. Cleopatra is born.

67 Pirates interfering with Rome's grain imports from Egypt are defeated by Quintus Caecilius Metellus. Antiochus XIII is treacherously murdered by the Arabian Prince of Emesa.

66 Tigranes II, King of Armenia falls into Pompey's hands; Pompey fines him 6,000 talents and releases him on condition that he now rules as Rome's vassal. Mithridates flees to the Crimea. Lucullus returns to Rome and begins entertaining on an extravagant scale.

65 Pompey reorganizes Roman territories in Asia and Syria, leaving Cappadocia, Galatia, Judea, Lycia and Eastern Pontus as client kingdoms. Pompey introduces apricots, peaches, plums and quinces to Rome from the East.

64 Pompey takes Jerusalem after a siege as he moves to subdue Judea. Lucius Catiline, 44, rallies the discontented debtors and ruined aristocrats of Rome in a conspiracy. The poet Horace is born.

63 Pompey conquers Palestine and makes it part of the Roman province of Syria. The authorities in Rome arrest Catiline and his fellow conspirators; Cicero, the Roman consul, makes speeches against Catiline in the Senate and the conspirators are executed. Mithridates discovers that a rebellion in Pontus is led by his son, and commits suicide in the Crimea. A shorthand system is invented by Marcus Tiro, who was once Cicero's slave.

62 The city of Florence is founded. Augustus is born.

60 A ruling triumvirate is created by Gaius Julius Caesar, who is now 42 and returns from his governorship of Spain. He forms an alliance with Pompey and Crassus.

59 Rome's triumvirate distributes Campanian estates among Pompey's war veterans. The triumvirate is strengthened by Pompey's marriage to Caesar's daughter Julia.

58 Julius Caesar invades Gaul with the intention of enriching himself and creating an army that will rival Pompey's. He defeats the Helvetii at Bibracte (Autun) and the German Ariovistus near Vesontio (Besançon).

57 Caesar's troops defeat the Belgae in north-west Gaul. In Rome the demagogue Appius Claudius Pulcher becomes praetor. The Senate gives Pompey the power to control Rome's grain supply as a grain shortage threatens.

  📖 Titus Lucretius Caro: *De Rerum Natura*

56 Caesar defeats the Veneti in Brittany, the Aquitani in south-west Gaul, and then meets Crassus and Pompey at Luca; they plan how to overcome mounting opposition to their triumvirate in Rome.

  📖 Gaius Valerius Catullus: *Ave atque Vale*

55 Pompey and Crassus are made Roman consuls. The Senate extends Caesar's command in Gaul for another five years; Crassus is given command over Syria, and

Pompey over the Hispanic Provinces. Crassus leaves for the East; Pompey stays in Rome.

   📖 Cicero: *On the Orator*

54 Julius Caesar's expedition to Britain. The reconnaissance opens southern England to Roman influence. Pompey's wife Julia dies, and the triumvirate begins to disintegrate. Appius Claudius Pulcher becomes consul. Crassus loots the Temple at Jerusalem.

52 Vercingetorix, the chief of the Averni tribe and leader of the Gauls, surrenders to Julius Caesar after a siege.

51 Caesar's conquest of Gaul is complete.

   📖 Julius Caesar: *On the Gallic War*.

50 🐚 Scenes of a Dionysiac Mystery Cult (wall-painting), the Villa of the Mysteries, Pompeii (Italy)

49 Julius Caesar leads his legions across the River Rubicon into Italy to begin a civil war.

48 Caesar defeats Pompey at Pharsalus in Thessaly (*29 Jun*) and becomes absolute ruler of Rome. Pompey escapes to Egypt, but he is killed at Pelusium. Caesar arrives in Alexandria, hears that Pompey has been murdered, then remains in Egypt where he fights a war on behalf of the dethroned Queen Cleopatra. Her brother Ptolemy XII Philopater is killed and a brother succeeds him as ruler.

47 Caesar moves onto Asia Minor where he defeats Pharnaces III King of Pontus near Zela (*2 Aug*). He announces his victory in the dispatch, 'Veni, vidi, vici.'

46 Julius Caesar returns to Italy, suppresses a rebellion in Campania, crosses to Africa and annihilates a 14-legion republican army under Scipio at Thapsus (*6 Apr*). Most of the republican leaders are killed. Cato commits suicide. Caesar returns in triumph to Rome with Cleopatra as his mistress (*Jul*) and is made dictator for 10 years. He sails for Spain, where resistance is led by the sons of Pompey. Caesar returns to Rome with prisoners who include Vercingetorix, who is executed.

45 Julius Caesar defeats Pompey's sons at Munda. *Sep*: Caesar returns to Rome and adopts his great-nephew Octavian as his son. Caesar introduces a new (Julian) calendar of 365¼ days; the first day of the year is to be 1 January. He has commissioned the Greek mathematician and astronomer Sosigenes of Alexandria to devise the new calendar.

44 Julius Caesar is made dictator of Rome for life. Mount Etna erupts. *15 Mar*: Julius Caesar is assassinated in the Senate by conspirators including Decimus and Marcus Brutus (former governors of Gaul) and Gaius Cassius Longinus. Cleopatra returns to Egypt with her son Caesarion; she murders her brother Ptolemy XIII Philopater. Mark Antony, 39, persuades the Romans to expel Caesar's assassins.

43 Mark Antony marches north to remove Decimus Brutus from Mutina (Modena), but he is defeated and forced to move west by Octavian, who is now 19. Octavian compels the Senate to elect him consul *Nov*: Octavian joins Mark Antony and Marcus Lepidus to form a second triumvirate. The Roman poet Ovid is born. *7 Dec*: agents of Mark Antony murder Cicero with Octavian's connivance.

42 Julius Caesar is deified by the triumvirate, who erect a temple to him in the Forum. Tiberius is born. Cassius is defeated by Mark Antony and Octavian at the Battle of Philippi and kills himself after hearing a rumour that Marcus Brutus has also been defeated. Brutus has in reality defeated Octavian, but he is defeated three weeks later; he, too, commits suicide.

41 Cleopatra meets Mark Antony at Tarsus. Like Caesar eight years ago, Mark Antony succumbs to Cleopatra's attractions; he follows her to Egypt.

📖 Virgil: *Eclogues*

40 Antony's wife Fulvia and his brother Lucius Antoninus make war against Antony, but are defeated at Perusia. Fulvia dies, leaving Antony free to remarry. He marries Octavian's sister Octavia. Octavian takes Gaul from Lepidus.

✐ Tower of the Winds, Athens

39 The triumvirate of Rome signs the Pact of Mycaenum, which recognizes the pirate Sextus Pompey as ruler of Sicily, Corsica, Sardinia and the Peloponnese. Pompey can interfere with Rome's grain imports, which puts him in a position to dictate terms. Octavian divorces his second wife and marries Livia.

38 Octavian conquers Spain and begins to dominate the triumvirate. Mark Antony returns to Egypt.

    🖎 Agesander, Polydorus and Athenodorus: The Laocoön (sculpture)

37 Herod the Great becomes King of Judea, two years after his confirmation as ruler by Antony, Octavian and the Roman Senate.

36 Octavian's general Marcus Vipsanius Agrippa clears the Mediterranean for Roman trade by defeating Sextus Pompey, who flees to Miletus where he dies. Lepidus' troops desert to Octavian, who imprisons Lepidus at Circeii. Antony is defeated by a Parthian army and he retreats to Armenia. He marries Cleopatra, despite his existing marriage to Octavia.

32 Octavian raises fears in Rome that Cleopatra will try to dominate the Roman Empire. He publishes what he says is Antony's will, in which the East is bequeathed to Cleopatra. Antony divorces Octavia.

31 *2 Sep*: Battle of Actium: Octavian is victorious at sea, becoming master of the Roman world. Cleopatra escapes to Egypt, followed by Antony, whose army surrenders to Octavian.

30 Antony commits suicide after hearing that Cleopatra has killed herself. In fact, she still lives. *29 Aug*: Cleopatra commits suicide after failing to seduce Octavian when he arrived at Alexandria. Cleopatra's son Caesarion is murdered; Egypt becomes a Roman province. The sundial is invented by the Chinese.

    🏛 Arch of Tiberius, Orange (France)

    📖 Virgil: *Georgics*

29 Greek sailors employed by Octavian re-open the ancient trade routes between Egypt and India. Peace returns to the Roman world.

27 *23 Jan*: The Roman Empire is founded by Octavian, who receives the name Augustus Caesar from the Senate. Octavian makes himself emperor, adopting the title Imperator Caesar Octavianus, soon changing this to Augustus Caesar.

    🏛 Temple of Vesta, Tivoli (Italy)

      Arch of Augustus, Rimini (Italy)

25 📖 Marcus Vitruvius Pollio: *De Architectura*

24   Augustus acts to reduce the high price of spices in Rome. He appoints the prefect of Egypt, Aeilius Gallus, to lead a campaign to bring the south Arabian spice kingdom into the Roman Empire.

23   The Roman conquest of Minorca brings the long-lived megalithic culture of the Mediterranean finally to an end.

21   Regensburg is founded on the River Danube.

20   🏛 Herod the Great: Great Temple of Jerusalem (rebuilding begins)

19   Virgil journeys to Athens to spend three years in the East, meets the Emperor Augustus who persuades him to return to Italy. *21 Sep*: Virgil dies at Brundisium, aged 50.

    🏛 Pont du Gard, near Nimes (France)

    📖 Virgil: *The Aeneid*

18   📖 Ovid (Publius Ovidius Naso): *Amores*

17   📖 Horace (Quintus Horatius Flaccus): *Carmen Saeculare*

16   Tiberius' son Drusus is born.

    🏛 Maison Carrée, Nimes (France)

15   The frontier of the Roman Empire is extended to the upper Danube.

    🏛 Augustus: Temple of Dendur, Lower Nubia (Egypt)

    📖 Ovid: *Heroides*

14   Augsburg is founded as Augusta Vindelicorum

13   🏛 Theatre of Marcellus and Shrine of Peace, Rome

12   The Jewish theologian Philo is born.

10   🏛 Temple of Vesta, Forum Boarium, Rome

9   The Emperor Claudius is born.

7   Jesus is born at about this time, probably at Nazareth. The year of Jesus' birth is determined by later astronomers on the basis of a conjunction of Saturn and Jupiter within the constellation Pisces, which gives the appearance of a huge new star; it also fulfils a prophecy made by Jewish astrologers at Sippar who predicted the arrival of a Messiah at a time when the two planets would meet.

5   Alternative date for Jesus' birth; Chinese and Korean annals refer to a nova that blazes in the sky for 70 days this spring. The population of the world approaches 250 million.

4 Herod the Great King of Judea dies, aged 69. He is succeeded by his son Archelaus.

AD The year of Jesus' birth as calculated by Dionysius Exiguus in *AD 525*: it is the year AUC 753 in the Roman calendar.

1 Addedomarus, King of the Trinovantes in southern England, dies and is probably buried in the Lexden Tumulus at Colchester; he is succeeded by Dubnovellaunus. Rice imported from China is cultivated for the first time in Japan.

    🏛 Lexden Tumulus, Colchester (U.K.)
        Broch of Mousa, Shetland (U.K.)
    🗺 Desborough Mirror (U.K.)
    📖 Ovid: *The Art of Love*
        Lucius Junius Moderatus Columella: *On Rural Matters* (urging crop rotation as a means of improving yields)

3 The Emperor Galba is born.

5 Lombard tribes on the lower Elbe are defeated by Roman legions.

6 The Chinese require candidates for political office to take civil service examinations.

    🏛 Temple of Castor and Pollux, Forum Romanum, Rome

7 📖 Ovid: *Metamorphoses*

8 Augustus exiles Ovid to Tomis, a Roman outpost on the Black Sea, for his immoral poetry. Ovid destroys his masterpiece when he hears that he has been banished, but copies made by his friends and admirers survive.

9 Battle of the Teutoburg Forest: Germanic tribes under the leadership of Arminius annihilate three entire legions under Publius Quinctilius Varus. Varus throws himself on his sword as 20,000 Roman soldiers are massacred. Varus' head is sent to Augustus. The independence of the German territories is assured. The Hsin Emperor Wong Mong frees China's slaves. Tasciovanus, King of the Catuvellauni in southern England, is succeeded by his son Cunobelinus (Cymbeline), who recaptures Camulodunum.

10 Cunobelinus reigns over much of southern England from his headquarters at Camulodunum as a tributary ally of the Roman Empress.

12   The Chinese repeal land reforms made by Wong Mong, in response to protests. Caligula is born.

14   The Emperor Augustus dies at Nola, aged 76 (*19 Aug*); he is succeeded by Tiberius Claudius Nero, who is 55 and the son of Augustus' widow Livia by her first marriage.

16   Tiberius' son Drusus defeats Arminius, breaks up his Germanic federation and recovers the eagles of the legions lost in the Battle of the Teutoburg Forest. The Romans consider the defeat of Varus honourably avenged.

17   The Emperor Tiberius sends his nephew Germanicus to Armenia to supervise the installation of a new king.
     ✐ Sardis synagogue (Turkey)

19   Germanicus is poisoned in Syria. Piso, the Syrian legate, is charged with the murder and commits suicide.

20   🛡 Battersea Shield (bronze) (U.K.)

23   Drusus, Tiberius' son, is poisoned by Lucius Aelius Sejanus, prefect of the guard, who plans to take the imperial throne for himself and increasingly dominates Tiberius. China's enlightened Emperor Wong Mong is killed in a revolt. Pliny the Elder is born.

25   The eastern Han dynasty is founded by Kwang Wudi. Sejanus persuades Tiberius to retire from the hostile atmosphere in Rome and settle on Capri.

26   Pontius Pilate becomes procurator of Judea.

30   📖 Aulus Cornelius Celsus: *On Medical Matters* (*De Res Medicos*)

31   Sejanus is executed on Tiberius' orders; Tiberius has realized the extent of Sejanus' plotting.

33   At about this time Jesus of Nazareth leaves Galilee for Jerusalem to observe the passover. The Roman procurator Pontius Pilate has Jesus crucified for sedition, probably on *3 Apr*. The Emperor Otto is born.

34   Paul is converted to Christianity after a visionary experience.

36   The Emperor Nerva is born.

37   Paul makes his first visit to Jerusalem. The Emperor Tiberius dies, aged 78, suffocated on his sickbed at Caligula's orders. He is succeeded by his nephew Gaius Caesar, nicknamed Caligula. The historian Josephus is born in Jerusalem.

38 The Emperor Nero is born. The tetrarch Agrippa visits Alexandria with spearmen ostentatiously dressed in silver and gold armour; Flaccus, Roman governor of Egypt, is affronted and deprives Egyptian Jews of their civic rights and herds them into a small area of the city. This is the first ghetto in history.

40 Cunobelinus, King of much of southern England, dies and is succeeded by his sons Togodumnus and Caractacus. The Greek merchant Hippalus sails from Berenice on the Red Sea coast of Egypt to Madras and back. Hippalus has discovered that the winds reverse during the year, the south-west monsoon winds favouring voyages from Egypt to India, the north-east trades favouring the return trip. The poet Martial is born. The Emperor Caligula is murdered by a tribune of the guard (*24 Jan*) and succeeded by Tiberius Claudius Drusus Nero Germanicus (Claudius). The Emperor Titus is born. Agrippa I becomes King of Judea, appointed by Caligula, temporarily breaking the rule of the Roman procurators. Claudius leads an expedition to conquer Britain. Londinium (London) is founded by the Romans.

44 The apostle James, who has preached the divinity of Jesus, becomes the first Christian apostle to be martyred, executed on orders from Herod Agrippa. King Herod Agrippa dies, aged 54, and Judea once more becomes a procuratorial province of Rome. Agrippa's 17-year-old son, also called Herod Agrippa, is studying at the court of Claudius in Rome.

48 Roman legions invade Wales. Herod Agrippa II becomes King of Judea.

49 Claudius expels Jewish Christians from Rome.

50 Paul arrives in Corinth. Cologne is founded as Colonia Agrippina on the site of Oppidum Ubiorum, the chief town of the Ubii tribe. Claudius fortifies the town at the request of his bride Agrippina, who was born there.

    ☞ Theatre, Orange (France)

    Acqua Claudia, aqueduct from the Campagna to Rome.

52 The Emperor Domitian is born.

53 The Emperor Trajan is born.

54 *(13 Oct)* Claudius dies, aged 63, after eating poisonous mushrooms given him by a physician in the pay of the Empress Agrippina, who hopes to rule Rome through her son Nero, who is 16.

55 ☐ Pedianos Dioscorides: *De Materia Medica*
Paul: *Letter to the Corinthians*

57 Authorities at Caesarea arrest Paul and hold him for trial.
☐ Paul: *Letter to the Romans*

59 The Emperor Nero has his mother put to death at the instigation of his adviser Lucius Annaeus Seneca. Paul is taken under arrest to Rome, but shipwrecked on Malta on the way.
☐ Paul: *Letter to the Philippians*

60 Festus succeeds Felix as procurator of Judea. Paul arrives in Rome.

61 London is sacked by the Trinovantes and Iceni of East Anglia; the Iceni are led by their queen Boudicca. Roman troops crush the revolt. Boudicca commits suicide. To protect London from further attacks, Roman engineers surround it with a stone wall.
✍ City Wall, London (U.K.)

62 Roman authorities allow the apostle Paul to stay in Rome, but under house arrest.

63 A fire beginning in some wooden booths in the Circus Maximus destroys over half the city of Rome *(18 Jul)*. Nero begins rebuilding to a master plan that gives the city wide, straight streets and broad squares. Persecution of Christians begins in Rome. Paul is probably executed at about this time.
✍ Third Temple of Jerusalem (completed)

65 A conspiracy to kill Nero comes to light; suspects are executed or forced to take their own lives.
☐ *Gospel according to Saint Mark*

66 Nero's favourite Gaius Petronius is accused of treason; he is arrested at Cumae and ordered to commit suicide.
☐ Petronius: *Satyricon*

67 A Roman army under Titus Flavius Vespasianus, now 58, enters Galilee to suppress a revolt by the Jews. The Jewish general Joseph ben Matthias holds the fortress Jotapata against a siege, but surrenders after 47 days to Vespasian and gets a sympathetic hearing from the Roman general.

68 Nero is sentenced to death by the Roman Senate under pressure from the praetorian guard, which recognizes the legate Servius Sulpicius Galba as Emperor. *9 Jun*: The Emperor Nero commits suicide aged 30.

📖 Flavius Josephus: *History of the Jewish People*

69 Legions on the Rhine refuse to recognize Galba as Emperor and salute instead the legate Aulus Vitellius, who is 54. *15 Jan*: Galba is murdered by Marcus Salvius Otho, friend of Nero, and the Senate recognizes Otho as Emperor. *19 Apr*: Vitellius defeats Otho in the Battle of Bedriacum near Cremona; Otho commits suicide. Vitellius now faces a challenge from Vespasian. *1 Jul*: the prefect of Egypt proclaims Vespasian Emperor. *Oct*: the Senate recognizes Vespasian as Emperor. *20 Dec*: the Emperor Vitellius dies in a street battle, leaving Vespasian unopposed.

70 Vespasian returns from Jerusalem, where he has bottled up the Zealot leader John of Giscala; Vespasian leaves his son Titus to continue the siege. *7 Sep*: Jerusalem falls. The Roman troops sack the city and destroy most of the Third Temple; only the 'Wailing Wall' is left standing. The Romans abolish the Jewish high priesthood and the Sanhedrin. Panic hits Rome as adverse winds delay grain imports from North Africa.

🎨 The Ixion Room, House of the Vettii, Pompeii (Italy)

71 🏛 Orders of Vespasian: Arch of Titus (celebrating Titus' sacking of Jerusalem); Public Lavatory, Rome

77 Gnaeus Julius Agricola arrives in Britain to complete the conquest begun by Claudius.

79 *23 Jun*: Vespasian dies, succeeded by his son Titus, who is 38. Chester is founded by Roman troops in England. *24 Aug*: Mount Vesuvius erupts; ash and mud bury the cities of Pompeii and Herculaneum. Pliny the Elder takes refuge with a friend at Stabiae, eventually dying of suffocation, along with thousands of others, from poisonous fumes.

80 Anthrax epidemic sweeps through the Roman Empire, killing thousands of people and animals. Anthrax and an extended drought in eastern Asia cause tribes in the interior to begin to move westwards; some 30,000

people and 40,000 horses are on the move, forming a cultural group that will become known eventually as the Huns. In Rome, three months of celebrations mark the opening of the Colosseum; 500 wild animals and many gladiators are killed as part of the entertainment.

    ⚔ Orders of Titus: The Colosseum, Rome

    📖 Martial: *Book of Spectacles*

81 *13 Sep*: Titus dies, succeeded by his brother Titus Flavius Domitianus (Domitian), who is 29.

83 Agricola's forces in northern Britain defeat the Caledonians.

84 The Emperor Domitian recalls Agricola to help repel 'barbarian' invaders along the Rhine and Danube valleys.

86 The Emperor Antoninus is born.

90 📖 A Greek sea-captain: *The Periplus of the Erythraean Sea (Sailing Round the Indian Ocean)*

95 A severe form of malaria appears in the rural areas round Rome, taking the fertile Campagna out of food production.

96 *18 Sep*: the Emperor Domitian is stabbed to death; the Empress has conspired with courtiers to bring about Domitian's death. He is succeeded by Marcus Cocceius Nerva, who is 60.

97 The Emperor Nerva recalls the general Marcus Ulpius Trajanus (Trajan) from the Rhine and formally adopts him in the Temple of Jupiter on the Capitol.

98 *25 Jan*: the Emperor Nerva dies suddenly, aged 63, succeeded by his adopted son Trajan.

100 The Romans temporarily lose control of Scotland: for a time the northern frontier is marked by the Tyne valley.

105 Paper-making is perfected by Chinese eunuch Tsai Lun, who is praised by the Emperor for his method of making paper from bark, hemp and rags.

106 Dacia (Romania) becomes a Roman province; Trajan has defeated Decebalus King of Dacia in battle.

    ⚔ Bridge over the Tagus, Alcantara (Spain)

110 📖 Suetonius: *Of Illustrious Men*

114 Trajan annexes Armenia to the Roman Empire.

    ⚔ Trajan's Column and Basilica of Trajan, Rome

115 The Romans occupy Mesopotamia.

    📖 Tacitus: *Annales*

116 Trajan annexes Assyria and marches to the Persian Gulf to conquer Parthia.

117 *8 Aug*: Trajan dies in Cilicia; aged 63; his kinsman Publius Aelius Hadrianus succeeds by adoption. Jews massacre Greeks and Romans at the news of Trajan's death. The historian Cornelius Tacitus dies, aged 60.
 📖 Tacitus: *Historia*

118 Rome's population now exceeds 1 million.
 ✍ Orders of Trajan: Roman Forum

120 ✍ Orders of Hadrian: The Pantheon, Rome

121 📖 Suetonius: *The Lives of the Caesars*

122 ✍ Hadrian's Wall (U.K.)

123 The Emperor Hadrian meets the King of Parthia and averts a war.

125 Plutarch, the Delphic priest and biographer, dies. Plague and famine sweep North africa
 📖 Juvenal: *Satires*

128 Roman agriculture declines as cheap imports from North Africa depress wheat prices, making it less profitable to farm. Galen, the Greek physician, is born.

130 ✍ Orders of Hadrian: Temple of Olympian Zeus, Athens (completed); Temple of Hadrian, Ephesus

132 The Jewish population of Jerusalem is indignant at the building of a shrine to Jupiter on the site of their Temple; a two-year insurrection begins.

135 Roman troops under Julius Severus retake Jerusalem. The leader of the insurrection, Simon Bar-Kokhba, is killed near Caesarea and the Jewish War of Freedom is over. Hadrian orders the site flattened and a new city, Aelia Capitolina, built on it; Judea is renamed Syria Palestine. A diaspora begins, as Jews are barred from Jerusalem and survivors of the massacre are spread across the empire.

136 ✍ Orders of Hadrian: Hadrian's Villa at Tivoli (Italy)

138 *10 Jul*: Hadrian dies at Baiae, aged 62. He is succeeded by his recently adopted son Antoninus, who goes directly to the Senate to confer divine honours on Hadrian; he is consequently called Antoninus Pius.

139 ✍ Orders of Antoninus: Tomb of Hadrian

140 ✍ Orders of Antoninus: Antonine Wall (barrier against Picts and Caledonians) (U.K.)

146 The Emperor Septimius Severus is born.

155 Polycarp dies, a Christian martyr, in Smyrna.

161 *7 Mar*: the Emperor Antoninus Pius dies at Lorium in Etruria, aged 73. He is succeeded by his adopted son Marcus Annius Verus, who is 40 and will be known as Marcus Aurelius.

162 The Emperor Commodus is born.

166 In Italy, land is taken from peasant farmers to give to returning soldiers, which has adverse effects on agriculture.

167 Marcus Aurelius repels the first full-scale attack on Rome by 'barbarian' invaders.

168 Marcus Aurelius and his co-emperor Lucius Verus conquer the Marcomanni, a tribe living to the north of the Danube but which has been occupying north-western Italy for several years.

169 Lucius Verus dies, aged 39, leaving Marcus Aurelius to rule alone. The Marcomanni break the peace concluded last year; a Roman army annihilates them.

174 Marcus Aurelius defeats the Quadi tribe.

175 Legions in Asia revolt under Avidus Cassius' leadership. The officers who encourage him to proclaim himself Emperor shortly afterwards assassinate him and send his head to Marcus Aurelius.

    📖 Tatian: *Harmony of the Gospels*

176 Marcus Aurelius returns to Rome after his successful campaign north of the Alps; he and his son Commodus are given a triumph.

177 Systematic persecution of Christians begins again in Rome. Many take refuge in the catacombs and worship in secret; the fish becomes a secret symbol of Christianity

180 *17 Mar* Marcus Aurelius dies, aged 58, succeeded by his son Commodus.

    🏛 Triumphal Column to Marcus Aurelius, Rome

    📖 Galen: *Methodus Medendo*

    Marcus Aurelius: *Reflections*

183 Commodus escapes an assassination attempt and puts many distinguished Roman citizens to death on suspicion of complicity.

189 Plague kills as many as 2,000 people a day in Rome. Sick and dying farmers are unable to tend or harvest their crops. Food shortages lead to riots. The Roman mob blames the grain shortage on the prefect Cleander, who is sacrificed to the mob.

192 *31 Dec*: Commodus is murdered. His mistress Marcia and his chamberlain Eclectus have found their names on an execution list and hire a wrestler to strangle the Emperor.

193 Publius Pertinax, aged 67, is chosen against his will by the Senate to succeed as Emperor. His strict rule quickly stirs opposition. *28 Mar*: Pertinax is murdered by the praetorian guard. The empire is auctioned and goes to the wealthy senator Didius Julianus. Legates in Pannonia, Britain and Syria oppose the appointment. Septimius Severus, the Pannonian legate, offers his troops huge bonuses if they will accompany him at once to Rome. *1 Jun*: Septimius Severus enters Rome in full battle array and has Didius Julianus put to death.

196 The Emperor Septimius Severus sacks Byzantium.

197 *19 Feb*: Septimius Albinus, the British legate, is defeated and killed by Septimius Severus at Lugdunum (Lyons).

200 The Japanese Empress Jingu sends a fleet to invade Korea. At the sight of the huge ships, the Koreans surrender at once and offer tribute. Westward-drifting Huns invade Afghanistan.

201 The medical writer Galen dies.

204 There is a trade recession at Leptis Magna in North Africa. The Emperor is a native of Leptis, so he helps the city by buying up the province's olive oil for free distribution in Rome.

  ☞ Arch of Septimius Severus, Rome

205 Plotinus, the last great classical philosopher, is born.

211 *4 Feb*: The Emperor Septimius Severus dies at Eboracum (York), aged 64. He is succeeded by his son Augustus, who is known as Caracalla.

212 The Edict of Caracalla: Roman citizenship is extended to all free inhabitants of the empire.

213 ☞ Baths of Caracalla, Rome

216 The Persian sage Mani is born.

217 *8 Apr*: the Emperor Caracalla is murdered by his own officers. He is succeeded by the Mauretanian Macrinus, who is 53.

218   *8 Jun*: Macrinus is killed in battle near Antioch. He is succeeded by the Syrian Varius Avitus Bassianus, a 14-year-old who claims to be the son of Caracalla and who calls himself Heliogabalus (the name of the Syrian sun god).

222   *11 Mar*: the Emperor Heliogabalus is murdered by the praetorian guard and is succeeded by his cousin and adopted son, the 14-year-old Bassianus who takes the name Severus Alexander.

226   In Persia the Sassanian dynasty is founded by the rebel prince Ardashir who has gained control of the region round Persepolis. Ardashir defeats Artabanus at Hormuz; Artabanus is killed.

234   Bread rather than grain is issued to the poor of Rome by decree of Severus Alexander.

235   Severus Alexander buys peace from the Alemanni tribe when it invades Gaul. *18 Mar*: Severus Alexander is murdered by his own troops on the Rhine; they proclaim the Thracian Maximinius Emperor, he is 62.

238   The Roman provinces in Africa disagree with Maximinius' appointment, electing their proconsul Gordianus Emperor. Gordianus is 80 and a descendant of Trajan; he yields to pressure to accept the appointment. The Senate recognizes him, but supporters of Maximinius besiege Gordianus at Carthage for a month. Gordianus' son is killed and Gordianus commits suicide when he hears the news. Gordianus' grandson is proclaimed Emperor Gordianus III. *Jun*: the praetorian guard murder Maximinius and name Gordianus III sole Emperor.

242   ✍ Palace of Shapur I, Ctesiphon (Iran)

244   The Roman Emperor Gordianus III drives the Persians back across the Euphrates, defeating them in the Battle of Resaena. Gordianus III is murdered during an army mutiny instigated by the Arabian Marcus Philippus, who is proclaimed Emperor. Philippus makes peace with the Persians.

245   The Emperor Diocletian is born.

248   The Emperor Phillipus holds games to celebrate the millennium of the founding of Rome in *753 BC*.

249   The Roman commander Decius puts down an army revolt in Pannonia. Loyal troops proclaim Decius Emperor. Phillipus advances to Verona to oppose the usurper, but he is killed by Decius' troops.

250 Gunpowder is invented at about this time by Chinese chemists, who mix saltpetre and sulphur. The Roman Emperor Decius begins another large-scale persecution of Christians in an attempt to restore and reinforce the institutions of ancient Rome. The Emperor Constantius is born.

251 The Emperor Decius and his son die in battle against the Goths in the swamps of the Dobrudja. Decius' successor, the general Gallus, makes peace with the Goths, bribing them not to return.

253 Soldiers campaigning along the Danube elect Aemilianus governor of Pannonia as their Emperor. Aemilianus defeats and kills Gallus but dies himself soon afterwards. A supporter of Gallus, Valerianus, who is 60, succeeds as Emperor.

254 Origen, the Christian scholar and teacher, dies.

255 The plague which appeared two years ago spreads through Egypt and and right across Europe.

   ☐ Cyprian, Bishop of Carthage: *De Mortalitate*

256 The plague causes great loss of life in Alexandria; thousands embrace Christianity.

258 Cyprian Bishop of Carthage is beheaded.

260 The Emperor Valerian is defeated by Shapur I King of Persia at Edessa, treacherously seized during a parley and flayed alive. His son Gallienus, now 42, succeeds as Emperor. The Roman Empire comes under attack from Berbers, Franks, Vandals, Palmyrans and Goths – as well as the plague. The value of the Roman denarius falls, paralyzing trade.

267 Prince Odenaethus of Palmyra is assassinated, apparently on Gallienus' orders; Odenaethus' wife, Septimia Zenobia, takes power in Palmyra and lays plans to extend her kingdom from the Black Sea to the Nile.

268 Gallienus is murdered by his own troops at Mediolanum (Milan) during a siege of the pretender Aureolus. Aureolus is killed by another pretender, Aurelianus, who becomes Emperor.

269 The Roman Emperor Claudius II holds off the Goths as they invade the Balkans. Zenobia Queen of Palmyra conquers Egypt, giving her control of Rome's grain supply.

270 The Emperor Claudius II dies of plague, succeeded by his brother Quintillus. Quintillus is deserted by his troops and commits suicide; he is succeeded by his brother's associate Aurelianus. Plotinus, the philosopher, dies. The silver content of the Roman denarius has fallen to 0.02 per cent.

271 The Alemanni are ejected from Italy by Aurelianus' troops. Aurelianus abandons trans-Danubian Dacia, settling its Roman inhabitants in a new Dacia (part of Moesia); he also begins work on new fortifications for the city of Rome.

272 Aurelianus besieges Palmyra, captures Zenobia and her young son Vaballathus on the banks of the River Euphrates, and forces the Queen of Palmyra to walk in gold chains in front of the Emperor's chariot in a triumphal procession; Zenobia's life is spared. Three Christians are beheaded on the road to the Temple of Mercury that stands on a hill in Lutetia (Paris); the hill will later be named Montmartre and the Sacré Coeur will be built on the site of the temple.

273 Aurelianus sacks Palmyra in response to a revolt.

274 Aurelianus puts down a rebellion at Chalons and returns to Rome in triumph. A huge oar-powered ship, 30 metres/ 100 feet long, is built on the orders of the Japanese Emperor Ojin; the Japanese will not use sails for 700 years.

275 Roman forces pull back from Transylvania and the Black Forest; the Danube and Rhine form the Empire's borders. The situation has become so dangerous that Aurelianus switches his attention to improving Rome's fortifications. Aurelianus is killed by his own officers and succeeded by Tacitus, an elderly senator who is appointed against his will.

    ✍ Porta Nigra, Trier (Germany)

276 The Emperor Tacitus is killed by his own troops after defeating the Goths in Asia Minor. He is succeeded by his brother Florianus, who is also killed and succeeded by Probus. The Persian philosopher Manes, aged 60 is executed for heresy. Manes claimed divine revelations and that he was the final prophet of God; his teachings combine Zoroastrian dualism with the Christian belief in salvation. The Zoroastrian priests brought about his downfall but his disciples will gain widespread support for 'Manichaeism'.

282 The Emperor Probus tries to clear the Egyptian canals after driving the Franks and Alemanni out of Gaul. Probus is killed by his own troops and succeeded by Aurelius Carus.

283 The Emperor Aurelius Carus dies, succeeded by his son Numerianus.

284 Numerianus is assassinated, succeeded by his Illyrian general Diocletian. Diocletian rules the East from Nicomedia in Bithynia, while his associate Herculius controls the West from Milan.

288 The Emperor Constantine is born.

290 ⚼ Amphitheatre, Verona (Italy)

300 The London Basilica, by far the largest building in Britain, is demolished.

⚼ Palace of Diocletian, Split (Yugoslavia)

301 The Emperor Diocletian at Nicomedia limits prices in an abortive effort to alleviate the economic distress caused by the collapse of Roman currency. The King of Armenia makes Christianity an official state religion; he is the first head of state to do this.

302 ⚼ Baths of Diocletian, Rome

303 *24 Feb*: general persecution of Christians begins in the Roman Empire under Diocletian's orders. His intention is to strengthen the ailing Empire by reviving the old religion.

305 *1 May*: the Emperor Diocletian abdicates at the age of 60 and retires to Salona, succeeded by Galerius co-ruling with Flavius Valerius Constantius.

306 The Roman co-emperor Constantius dies, aged 56, outside Eboracum (York) during a campaign against the Picts and Scots. The troops recognize his son Constantinus as Emperor, but Galerius raises Severus as his co-emperor instead.

307 *11 Nov*: Severus dies; Galerius replaces him with Licinius. Constantinus proclaims himself Emperor, but has effective rule only in Britain and Gaul.

308 The Roman despot Maxentius, recognized by the praetorians, banishes his father to Gaul.

309 The Persian Shah Shapur II is born. Anthrax spreads across the Roman Empire, sharply reducing the population.

311 The Roman Emperor Galerius dies after Maxentius drives him out of Italy (*May*). The Emperor Constantine begins his march on Rome. Hun invaders from the north sack the Chinese city of Luoyang, killing 30,000 people.

312 *28 Oct*: Battle of the Milvian Bridge, 6km/4 miles outside Rome: Constantine defeats the despot Maxentius and kills him, becoming absolute ruler of the Western Empire. Constantine claims to see a vision in the sky, of a luminous cross; it carries the words, 'In hoc signo vinces' (By this sign you will conquer).

    ✍ Orders of Constantine: Arch of Constantine, Rome

313 Constantine and Licinius accept Christianity and return property recently confiscated from Christians.

314 *8 Oct*: Battle of Cibalae: Constantine defeats his co-emperor, who loses most of the Balkans.

317 China is divided by the founding of Northern and Southern dynasties.

320 Rulers of the Gupta dynasty begin the unification of northern India after 500 years of disunity.

321 Constantine forbids work on the Sabbath. He also orders convicts to grind flour for Rome in an effort to hold down rising food prices.

322 The Emperor Valentinian is born.

323 *3 Jul*: Battle of Adrianople: Constantine's son Crispus defeats Licinius' navy. Licinius has angered Constantine with his anti-Christian policy. *18 Sep*: Licinius is again defeated, at the Battle of Chrysopolis in Anatolia.

324 Constantine has Licinius executed and reunifies the Empire, ruling alone from the Euphrates to the Clyde. Christianity is declared the official religion of the Roman Empire.

325 The Council of Nicaea summoned by Constantine is the first great council of the Christian church. It supports the doctrine that Christ and God are of the same substance.

328 The Holy Sepulchre, the tomb where Jesus was buried, is discovered in Jerusalem.

330 *11 May*: Constantinople is dedicated as the new capital of the Roman Empire. Constantine has had his city built on the site of ancient Byzantium.

331 The Emperor Julian is born.

333 The Romans begin withdrawing troops from Britain.

335 *17 Sep*: the Church of the Holy Sepulchre in Jerusalem is consecrated; it is built round the remains of Jesus' tomb and the rocky knoll, Golgotha, where he was crucified.

    ✍ Church of the Holy Sepulchre, Jerusalem

336 The priest Arius is tortured to death for promoting the view, contradicting the Nicaean Council, that Christ and God are of different substances.

337 *22 May*: the Emperor Constantine dies, aged 49. He is succeeded by his wife Fausta's three sons.

340 One of the co-emperors, Constantine II, is killed in battle at Aquilea in northern Italy. Coptic Christianity is introduced into Ethiopia.

346 The Emperor Theodosius is born.

350 The Emperor Constans is murdered by his general Magnetius during a coup; Magnetius becomes Emperor of the West.

    ✍ Sta. Costanza Church, Rome

351 Constantius II defeats Magnetius at Mursa and pursues him into Gaul.

353 *Aug*: Magnetius is defeated and commits suicide. Constantius II rules alone and unopposed.

354 St. John Chrysostom and St. Augustine are born.

355 Alemanni tribesmen cross the Rhine into eastern Gaul.

356 *19 Feb*: Constantius II orders the closure of all pagan temples in the Roman Empire.

357 *28 Apr*: Constantius II sets foot in Rome for the first time.

    25 Aug: Constantius' cousin Julian defeats the Alemanni at Strasbourg, pushing them back across the Rhine.

358 The Emporor Gratian is born.

359 ✑ Sarcophagus of Junius Bassus, Rome

360 The Huns invade Europe. The Picts and Scots cross Hadrian's Wall and attack Roman troops in England. The Mildenhall Treasure is buried in England, probably by the family of the Roman general Lupicinus following his arrest.

🖎 Basilica on the site of Hagia Sophia, Constantinople

361 *3 Nov:* the Emperor Constantius II dies near Tarsus in Cilicia, aged 44. He was on his way to meet his cousin Julian, whom Constantinople acknowledges as the new Emperor. A licensing system for practising physicians is introduced in Constantinople.

363 The Emperor Julian is the last champion of polytheism, which he tries to re-establish. *26 Jun:* Julian is mortally wounded in a battle against the Persians, succeeded by Jovian, captain of the imperial bodyguard.

364 Jovian signs a treaty with Shapur II Shah of Persia, ceding Armenia to Persia. He is found dead at Dadastana on the way back to Constantinople. He is succeeded by the general Valentinian, who appoints his brother Valens co-emperor in the East.

370 At Capernaum in Syria Palestine, the synagogue is rebuilt on a grander scale to compete with the 'house-church' that has been built nearby on the ruins of the house of St. Peter.

🖎 Synagogue at Capernaum

371 The new Persian Empire reaches its peak under Shah Shapur II as Rome and Persia renew hostilities.

372 The Huns make inroads into the West. They defeat the Alans and the Heruls, destroy Hermanric's Ostrogothic Empire and massacre the Visigoths. Buddhism reaches Korea from China.

375 *17 Nov:* the Emperor Valentinian dies, aged 53 on the Danube. He is succeeded as emperor in name only by his four-year-old son, Valentinian II, but Gratianus, the boy's 17-year-old half-brother, is *de facto* emperor.

376 The Romans attempt to force Visigoths, who have settled in Moesia, on the 'Roman' side of the Danube, to move back across the river.

378 *9 Aug:* Battle of Adrianople: mounted Visigoths defeat the Roman army, killing the Emperor Valens. The power of cavalry in warfare is demonstrated for the first time. Gratian summons his general Theodosius to replace Valens as Emperor in the East.

379 *19 Jan:* Theodosius assumes power in the East. He comes to terms with the Visigoths, settling them as allies in the Balkans. In Persia, Shah Shapur II dies, aged 70; he has humiliated the Romans, conquered Armenia, rebuilt the city of Susa and founded Nishapur. Athanasianism becomes the dominant view in the Church and Christianity the dominant religion in the Empire.

383 Gratian is deserted by his legions at Lutetia (Paris) and handed over to one of the generals who has mutinied against him. *25 Aug*: Gratian is assassinated, succeeded by Magnus Maximus, leader of the mutiny against Gratian. Magnus Maximus is recognized by Gratian's younger brother Valentinian II and his co-emperor Theodosius, and rules in Britain, Gaul and Spain.

388 Magnus Maximus enters Italy but is defeated by Theodosius at Aquileia and subsequently murdered; Valentinian II, who is now 17, continues as co-emperor.

390 A rebellion in Macedonia leads to fierce reprisals from Theodosius, who has 3,000 massacred at Thessalonica. Ambrose Bishop of Milan presses Theodosius to do public penance on *25 Dec*.

391 Fire destroys the Library at Alexandria, Theodosius has ordained that non-Christian works should be destroyed.

392 *15 May*: the co-emperor Valentinian II is assassinated at Vienne in Gaul. The Frankish general Arbogast, who is behind the murder, sets up Eugenius as Emperor. Theodosius is shocked and angered at the murder of his 21-year-old co-emperor and marches against him.

394 *6 Sep*: Eugenius dies in battle against the forces of Theodosius. Arbogast escapes into the mountains but kills himself two days later.

395 *17 Jan*: the Emperor Theodosius dies at Milan, aged 49. The Empire splits into two. Theodosius' son Arcadius rules the Eastern Empire from Constantinople, while Honorius rules from Milan; Honorius is only 10, and the real power is in the hands of his master of troops, a Vandal called Stilicho. The split in the Empire is intended to be temporary, but proves permanent.

396 Augustine becomes Bishop of Hippo.

397 Stilicho ejects Alaric and the Visigoths from Greece.

399 [] St. Augustine: *Confessions*

400 The Emperor Leo I is born.

401 Visigoths penetrate northern Italy.

402 *6 Apr*: Battle of Pollentia: Roman forces under Stilicho

defeat and halt the Visigoths.

405 The Emperor Honorius closes the Colosseum; it is an austerity measure, but also a sign that the Roman 'civilization' is closing down.

406 Non-Roman forces led into Itlay by Radagaisus are defeated at Florence (*23 Aug*) by Stilicho's troops. Large numbers of Vandals are led across the Rhine into Gaul by their King, Gunderic. Butter, introduced by the invading Vandals, Alans and Sciri, begins to replace olive oil.

407 Romans withdraw from Britain as they are needed to defend Rome.
The British Isles return to native rule after 360 years of Roman rule.

408 The Visigoths under Alaric lay siege to Rome. *22 Aug*: Stilicho, master of the Roman troops, is murdered on Honorius' orders. Arcadius, Emperor of the Eastern Empire, dies, aged 31, succeeded by his seven-year-old son Theodosius II; the boy's sister Pulcheria holds the real power. Alaric the Visigoth King exacts tribute from Rome.

409 Alaric invades Italy again. The Vandals cross the Pyrenees into Spain.

410 The Huns introduce trousers, which replace togas, and stirrups for horse-riding. *14 Aug*: Alaric's siege of Rome succeeds; the Visigoths sack Rome. Alaric dies shortly afterwards.

411 The self-appointed Emperor Constantine, who has gained control of Britain, Gaul and Spain, is defeated near Arles and captured; he is executed at Ravenna. The British ascetic Pelagius visits Hippo and pays a call on Augustine, whose views he disagrees with, but Augustine will not meet him.

412 A Visigoth army moves into Gaul under Ataulf, Alaric's brother.

414 *1 Jan* Ataulf King of the Visigoths marries Galla Placidia, the sister of the Roman Emperor Honorius, at Narbonne. Theodosius II the Byzantine Emperor hands over power to his sister Pulcheria, who is 15.

415 Visigoths invade Spain and conquer territory newly taken by the Vandals. *Mar*: in Alexandria, the new

Christian Bishop Cyril incites a mob to pull the Neo-platonist philosopher Hypatia from her chariot, strip her and scrape her to death with oyster shells.

417 Galla Placidia remarries the Roman general Constantius.

421 The Emperor Honorius makes Constantius, his brother-in-law, co-emperor. Constantius III dies in September. The Eastern Emperor, Theodosius II, sends an army to fight the Persians.

422 Theodosius II makes peace with Varahran King of Persia, and agrees an annual tribute to the Huns to keep them at bay. The Colosseum is damaged during an earthquake.

426 The Emperor Zeno is born.
   📖 St. Augustine: *The City of God*

427 Changsu King of Korea moves his capital to Pyongyang.

429 80,000 Vandals invade North Africa. Gaiseric King of the Vandals leads his troops across the Straits of Gibraltar.

430 The Vandals progress along the North African coast, besieging Hippo *28 Aug*: Bishop Augustine dies during the siege of Hippo, aged 76. Patrick is sent from Britain as a missionary to Ireland. Anastasius I, the Eastern Emperor, is born.

431 Nestorius, patriarch of Constantinople, is deposed by the Council of Ephesus for preaching the heresy that in Jesus there were two persons, one human, one divine. Nestorius is banished to the desert of Libya, but his ideas are disseminated by followers. The cult of the Virgin begins to spread westwards from Byzantium after the Council of Ephesus issues a decree recognizing Mary as Mother of God.

433 Attila becomes leader of the Huns.

439 Childeric I, the Frankish King, is born. *29 Oct*: the Vandals take Carthage. Genseric King of the Vandals makes Carthage his capital, seeing the strategic value of controlling North African grain production and exports.
   📖 *Codex Theodosianus* (summary of Roman law)

441 Saxon settlers establish a colony in Essex, England.

443 The Alemanni settle in Alsace, eastern France.

444 The Chinese invent the wheelbarrow.

446 The Britons make a last appeal to Rome to defend them against invasion, Honorius tells them to defend themselves. Buddhists in China are persecuted by the Wei Chinese. Monks and nuns are murdered and temples destroyed. The Confucianism of the Han Chinese gains ascendancy over Buddhism.

449 England is settled piecemeal by Angles and Saxons.

450 The Polynesian chief Hawaii-Loa discovers the Hawaiian Islands at about this time; he has sailed across more than 3,000 km/2,000 miles of open ocean from the island of Raiatea, near Tahiti. Metal horseshoes come into common use in Europe and the Near East. The Graveney Boat, a Saxon sailing vessel, founders at Southampton in England. The people living at the religious cult centre of Gudme in Denmark become very rich, presumably making money out of visiting pilgrims.

451 Battle of Chalons: the Huns are defeated by a Roman force under Flavius Aetius; the Romans are helped by the Visigoths.

452 Karu the Japanese Crown Prince is killed by his brother Anko. Anko becomes Emperor on the death of his father Ingyo. The Huns are reduced in numbers by plague and food shortages.

453 Attila the leader of the Huns dies. Huns remaining in Italy are driven out by the Romans.

455 The Vandals sack Rome. The city of Chichen Itza is founded by the Mayan people on the Yucatan Peninsula, Central America; it consists of 15.5 square km/6 square miles of temples, pyramids, plazas and dwellings. The Mayan civilization is based on maize cultivation. Orae Favianae (Vienna) is ravaged by a scarlet fever epidemic. In Italy, city dwellers desert the towns for the countryside where they will be less obvious targets for barbarian attack; barter replaces organized trade based on currency, as the Roman civilization disintegrates.

456 The Japanese Emperor Anko is murdered by the 10-year-old son of his uncle Okusaka, whom Anko himself killed. The boy, Mayuwa, is killed along with other princes by Anko's brother Yuryaku, who succeeds as Emperor.

466 The Huns invade Dacia. Leo I, Emperor of the Eastern Empire, beats them off with the aid of generals Anagastus and Anthemius. The Frankish King Clovis I is born.

467 Leo I has Anthemius elected Emperor of the West; together they assemble a fleet of over 1,000 ships to attack the Vandal empire in North Africa.

468 The forces of Genseric the Vandal King surprise the Imperial Fleet commanded by Leo I's brother-in-law Basiliscus. Half the vessels of the Imperial Fleet are destroyed. Leo I successfully fends off another Hun invasion of Dacia.

471 Basiliscus murders Aspar the Goth, on the grounds that Aspar was responsible for the failure of the 468 expedition, although Basiliscus himself was to blame. The Goths in reprisal attack the approaches to Constantinople, but the attack is called off as Zeno, Leo's son-in-law, has Ardaburius the leader of the Goths murdered.

472 The Emperor Anthemius is killed by the barbarian general Ricimer, who appoints instead Olybrius. *19 Aug*: Ricimer dies, whereupon Gundobad the Burgundian takes control of the army of the Western Empire. *2 Nov*: the Emperor Olybrius dies, leaving the Western Empire without an emperor.

473 Gundobad names Glycerinus Emperor. Julius Nepos marches on Rome at Leo I's instigation, removes Glycerinus and makes himself Emperor of the West on *24 Jun*.

474 Leo I of the Eastern Empire dies, aged 74, succeeded by Zeno.

475 Roman commander Orestes expels the Emperor Julius Nepos and names his own son, Romulus Augustus, Emperor of the Western Empire.

476 *28 Aug*: the Western Empire founded by Augustus is formally ended at Ravenna; for some time the Empire has been protected and managed by the Germanic tribes. The last Emperor, Augustulus (Romulus Augustus), is formally deposed by the Saxon leader Odovacar; the 'barbarian' king treats the boy kindly, sending him to live at Naples on a large annual pension. The Eastern Emperor Zeno is compelled to abdicate by Basiliscus, who takes the throne.

477 Zeno retakes the Eastern throne from Basiliscus.

480 The Visigoths have built an empire that extends from

Gibraltar to the Loire valley and from the Bay of Biscay to the Rhine valley; their capital is at Toulouse. St. Benedict is born.

481 Childeric I, King of the Franks dies, aged 44, succeeded by his son Clovis I.

482 The Eastern Emperor Zeno tries unsuccessfully to resolve the differences between the eastern and western churches.

📖 Emperor Zeno: *Henoticon*

488 An army of Ostrogoths under Theodoric invades Italy at Zeno's instigation.

490 Ostrogoths under Theodoric besiege Ravenna.

491 Zeno dies, aged 65, succeeded by a palace official, Anastasius I, who marries Zeno's widow Ariadne.

493 The Saxon (Herulian) leader Odovacar surrenders Ravenna to Theodoric after a long siege. Theodoric invites Odovacar to dinner and has him murdered, then unifies Italy as an Ostrogoth kingdom.

495 The Chinese Weis dynasty establishes Luoyang as its capital.

496 Clovis leads the Franks to victory over the Alemanni near Strasbourg. Clovis becomes a Christian convert; he is baptized by his friend Remy Bishop of Reims.

500 Bavaria is invaded by the Marcomanni from Bohemia. The Mayan culture evolves in Central America. Incense is introduced in Christian church services to cover up the smell of unwashed worshippers. Dionysius Exiguus, the man who will fix Jesus' birthday as *25 Dec*, is born.

📖 *The Susruta* (classic of Indian medicine, written at about this time)

502 Gundobad King of Burgundy issues a legal code making Romans and Burgundians subject to the same laws. The Persians sack the city of Amida in Mesopotamia in a struggle against the forces of the Eastern Empire. In China, Xiao Yan marches on Nanjing and compels the Qi rulers, to whom he is related, to abdicate; Xiao Yan becomes Emperor, founding the Liang dynasty.

505 An earthquake in Italy causes further damage to the Colosseum in Rome.

507 Clovis and his Frankish army defeat the Visigoths in the Battle of Campus Vogladensis. Clovis and Gundobad, his ally, kill Alaric II King of the Visigoths and Clovis annexes the Visigoth kingdom of Toulouse. The Visigoths keep control of Spain.

508 The Franks are driven out of Provence by the Ostrogoths under Theodoric; the Ostrogoths also recover Septimania (later called Languedoc) from the Visigoths. The infant Visigoth King Amalaric is Theodoric's grandson and Theodoric steps in to act as his regent. Clovis establishes his capital at Lutetia (Paris), close to his newly conquered lands.

510 Anicius Boethius, the Roman philosopher, is appointed consul by his friend Theodoric, who rules his Ostrogoth kingdom from his base at Ravenna.

511 *11 Nov*: Clovis King of the Franks dies, aged 45. The Frankish kingdom is divided into four by his sons Theodoric, Childebert, Lothair and Chlodomer, who rule from their four respective capitals: Metz, Paris, Soissons and Orleans.

513 Eruption of Mount Vesuvius.

516 Gundobad King of Burgundy dies, succeeded by his son Sigismund, who converts his people from Arianism to Christianity.

517 Buddhism is introduced to central China by the convert Emperor Wu.

518 Anastasius I, the Byzantine Emperor, dies on *9 Jul*, aged 88. He is succeeded by his Illyrian bodyguard, Justinus I.

519 Reconciliation between the eastern and western churches.

520 ⬚ Priscian: *Institutionis Grammaticae* (codifies Latin grammar)

521 St. Columba is born at Gartan in County Donegal Eire.

522 Ancius Boethius is arrested on a charge of conspiring against Theodoric, and imprisoned at Pavia. Boethius insists that the letters alleged to have been written by him to the Emperor Justinus are forgeries.

524 Boethius is executed. Sigismund King of Burgundy is killed by Chlodomer and succeeded by Godomar. War breaks out again between Rome and Persia.

⬚ Boethius: *The Consolation of Philosophy*

525 Ethiopians invade and conquer the Yemen. The Egyptian Cosmas Indicopleustes explores the Nile valley.

📖 Cosmas Indicopleustes: *Topographia Christiana* (at about this time)

Dionysius Exiguus: *Easter Tables* (gives Jesus' birth date incorrectly as 25 December, 753 years after the foundation of Rome, ie the year AD 1. The error is perpetuated in all subsequent Christian calendars)

526 Theodoric the Great, King of the Ostrogoths, dies on *30 Aug*, aged 72, succeeded by his grandson, the 10-year-old Athalaric; Athalric's mother Amalasuntha acts as regent. An earthquake at Antioch kills over 200,000 people.

✍ Theodoric the Great's Tomb at Ravenna (Italy)

527 Justinus I, Emperor of the east, adopts his nephew Justinian as co-emperor on *1 Apr. 1 Aug*: Justinus I, aged 77, dies of an infected wound; succeeded by Justinian.

528 Battle of Daras: Justinian's commander Belisarius, who is only 23, leads imperial forces to victory over the Persians.

529 Benedict of Nursia founds the Benedictine order of monks. Plato's academy in Athens is closed down by Justinian because 'unChristian' activities are suspected. Many scholars emigrate to Syria and Persia.

📖 Justinian: *Codex Vitus* (code of civil law)

530 Battle of Callinicum: Belisarius is defeated by the Persians.

531 Justinian's laws prohibit Jews from testifying against Christians.

532 *Jan*: The Nika insurrection destroys a large area of Constantinople. Justinian panics, but his influential wife Theodora persuades him not to flee. Belisarius' troops massacre 30,000 of the rebels. Justinian signs a permanent peace with Chosroe King of Persia, freeing his troops for campaigns in the West. The Franks invade Burgundy.

533 Belisarius leads his army into North Africa, defeating the Vandals and reclaiming the province for the Emperor Justinian.

534 Malta becomes a Byzantine province. The Visigoths who control Spain make Toledo their capital.

535 Belisarius invades Sicily, then moves north with the intention of taking over the Ostrogoth kingdom of Italy.
    ✍ Christian Basilica, Leptis Magna in North Africa

536 Haze covers the Mediterranean region for the entire year, at the end of which there is a very severe winter; it is likely that volcanic dust from an eruption in Indonesia is responsible. *9 Dec*: the fall of Rome, as Belisarius' troops regain Italy from the Ostrogoths.

537 The Ostrogoth leader Witiges besieges Rome in an attempt to recover the city, but the siege fails.
    ✍ Anthemius of Tralles and Isidore of Miletus: Church of St. Sophia, Constantinople (dedicated *27 Dec*)

538 Buddhism arrives at the court of the Japanese Emperor Senka, by way of Korea.

539 Belisarius' army takes Ravenna and captures the Ostrogoth leader Witiges. Belisarius is recalled to Constantinople and the Ostrogoths begin to reclaim Italy. Under a new leader, Totila, Milan is besieged and its 300,000 inhabitants are massacred. Senka Emperor of Japan dies, aged 72, succeeded by his half-brother Kinmei, who is 30.

540 The Persians invade Syria and take Antioch. Byzantine rule in Italy is brought to an end by Totila the Ostrogoth. The Roman statesman Cassiodorus retires from public life, retreating to the monastery of Vivarium that he had founded; he devotes his time to copying and translating Greek works. Pope Gregory I is born.

541 Justinian devises plans to conquer Gaul and Britain, but is forced to cancel them when he contracts plague. Hildebad King of the Ostrogoths dies, succeeded by his nephew Totila. The Great Plague of Justinian spreads throughout Europe, bringing agriculture to a halt and causing widespread food shortages.

542 📖 Gildas: *De Excidio et Conquestu Britanniae* (history of Britain)

543 Belisarius completes the reconquest of North Africa.

546 Rome falls to the Ostrogoths under Totila after several years of Byzantine rule. So many have fled that Rome's population is down to 500. Cassiodorus founds another monastery, at Beneventum.

547 The Great Plague of Justinian reaches Britain, where Ida accedes to the throne of Bernicia.

    🖎 Church of St. Vitale at Ravenna (octagonal) Italy

548 Theodora Empress of Byzantium dies, aged 40, Justinian is left to rule alone.

549 The Persians take Petra. The last games are held in Rome; the ritualized cruelty of the games is finally made impossible by people the Romans call barbarians.

    🖎 Church of St. Apollinare at Classe near Ravenna (Italy) (completed)

550 Toltecs overrun the Yucatan Peninsula in Central America; they conquer the Teotihuacan civilization. St. David converts the Welsh to Christianity.

    🖎 Orders of Justinian: Nea Church and Hospice, Jerusalem

    🖾 The Last Supper mosaic, Church of St. Apollinare near Ravenna (Italy)

    📖 Procopius: *De Bellis* (Persian, Vandal and Gothic wars)

    Grammaticus: *Hero and Leander* (poem)

551 A Byzantine fleet defeats an Ostrogoth fleet.

552 Battle of Tagina: Byzantine army under Narses, replacing Belisarius, defeats the Ostrogoth army and kills Totila King of the Ostrogoths. Justinian initiates the European silk industry; he has sent Christian missionaries to China to smuggle silkworms out. Buddhist images and sutras reach Japan. The leader of the Soga clan urges the acceptance of these gifts and the Emperor permits the building of a temple to house and worship the Buddhist images. An epidemic sweeps the countryside, and the images are thrown into the Naniwa canal.

553 Narses annexes Rome and Naples for Byzantium.

    📖 Procopius: *Anecdota* (ossip about Justinian, Belisarius and the Empress Theodora)

554 Narses becomes prefect of Italy, completing his conquest of Italy for the Emperor Justinian. Justinian's Pragmatic Sanction orders that lands taken from the Ostrogoths should be restored to their original owners; this proves to be impracticable.

558 Clotaire I King of Soissons reunifies the Frankish kingdom on the death of Childebert King of Paris. Plague continues to kill many.

559 An army of Slavs and Huns reaches the gates of Constantinople; Belisarius comes out of retirement to drive them off.

560 Eormenric King of Kent dies, succeeded by his son Ethelbert I.

    📖 Cassiodorus: *Institutiones* (music theory)

561 Clotaire (or Lothar) I, King of the Franks, dies. His sons divide the Frankish kingdom again; Sigibert rules Austrasia, Guntram rules Burgundy, Chilperic rules Soissons and Charibert rules Paris.

563 St. Columba, the Irish missionary, founds the monastery of Iona.

565 Justinian the Byzantine Emperor dies, aged 83, succeeded by his nephew Justin II. In the north of Italy the Lombards drive the Byzantines south but let them keep Ravenna.

568 Alboin the Lombard ruler founds a kingdom in northern and central Italy.

569 The prophet Mohammed is born.

571 Kinmei the Emperor of Japan dies, aged 62, succeeded by his son Bintas.

572 Alboin King of the Lombards takes Pavia, giving him almost all of Italy. A new war breaks out between Persia and Byzantium.

573 Sigibert, King of Austrasia, encouraged by his wife Brunhilda, declares war on his brother Chilperic King of Soissons. Chilperic has murdered his wife Galswintha, Brunhilda's sister, in order to marry his mistress Fredegund. King Sigibert appeals to the Germans to the east of the Rhine for help, and they 'oblige' with atrocities round Paris and Chartres.

575 Sigibert pursues his brother Chilperic to Tournai. As Sigibert is raised in triumph on a shield, he is assassinated on orders from Fredegund. Sigibert is succeeded by his son Childebert II, with Brunhilda as regent.

577 Battle of Dyrham, at which Cuthwine and Ceawlin fight against the Britons, killing three of their kings, Coinmail, Condidan and Farinmail.

578 Justin II the Byzantine Emperor dies insane, succeeded by his general Tiberius as Tiberius II Constantius.

579 Theodric King of Bernicia dies, succeeded by Friduuald.

Chosroes I King of Persia dies after reigning for 48 years over a kingdom that stretches from the Oxus to the Red Sea.

580   The Lombards successfully drive the last of the Ostrogoths in Italy north of the Alps.

581   Yang Jian, chief minister of the northern Zhou, founds the Chinese Sui dynasty by killing his ruler, the last of the Zhou emperors and declaring himself the Emperor Wendi.

582   Byzantine Emperor Tiberius II Constantius dies, succeeded by his son-in-law Flavius Tiberius Mauricios. Penda, King of Mercia in Britain is born, the son of King Pybba. Cassiodorus dies, aged 92.

     ☐ Cassiodorus: *The Ostrographia* (an account of Ostrogoth rule)

584   Chilperic of Neustria dies, succeeded by his son Clotaire II.

585   Friduuald King of Bernicia dies, succeeded by Hussa. Leovigild King of the Visigoths puts down an insurrection led by his son Hermenegild. Leovigild imprisons and kills his son, then conquers the entire Iberian Peninsula. Bintas, Emperor of Japan, dies, aged 47, and is succeeded by his brother Yomei, who is 45. The King of Paikche (part of Korea) sends another image of Buddha to Japan; another temple is built; the Soga chief converts three girls and makes them nuns. Another epidemic follows and Moriyc Mononobe burns the temple down.

586   Leovigild King of the Visigoths dies, succeeded by Recared. Moriyo Mononobe and Okoshi Mononobe denounce Buddhism as a foreign religion conflicting with native Shintoism, but Yomei the new Emperor supports Buddhism. Shinto religion adopts many Buddhist images to give a Buddhist counterpart to every Shinto deity.

587   The Japanese Emperor Yomei dies, aged 47, succeeded by Sushun, nephew of Iname Soga. Agents of Iname Soga murder Moriyo Mononobe. The Visigoths are converted to Christianity under Recared. The first Japanese Buddhist monastery is founded.

588   The Persian Emperor Hormizd is deposed and murdered

after several defeats by the Byzantines. He is succeeded by his son Chosroes II. The Lombards are converted to Roman Catholicism under their new King Authari.

589 The Sui Emperor Wendi reunifies the Chinese Empire when he defeats Chen forces at Jian-kang (later Nanjing), bringing the Chen dynasty to an end. The Persian army deposes Chosroes II, who leaves for Constanantinople.

590 Pope Gregory I claims papal absolutism in an attempt to unite Italian opposition to rule by the Lombards. Authari King of the Lombards dies, succeeded by Agilulf. Plague strikes Rome but subsides when Pope Gregory sees a vision of the Destroying Angel sheathing its sword on Hadrian's mausoleum, which is renamed the Castel Sant' Angelo. Gregory I reforms courts, repairs Rome's aqueducts, reintroduces the grain dole for the poor.

591 Battle at Adam's Grave near Alton Priors in England. Ceawlin is deposed and succeeded by Ceol as King of Wessex ('Old King Cole'). Hussa King of Bernicia dies and is succeeded by Ethefrith. The Byzantine Emperor Maurice restores Chosroes II to the throne of Persia in return for territorial concessions. Lombard forces under Agilulf advance in northern Italy

593 Ceawlin, deposed King of Wessex, dies. Aethelfrith son of Aethelric succeeds to the kingdom of Northumbria.

596 Pope Gregory instructs Augustine to go to Britain.

597 Augustine lands in Kent with a mission to convert Ethelbert King of Kent and High King of southern England to Christianity. Augustine becomes Archbishop of Canterbury. *8 Jun*: St. Columba dies on Iona. Ceol King of Wessex dies and is succeeded by Ceolwulf.

600 The Mayan civilization in Central America approaches its peak, with a wealthy monarchy, temples, sophisticated architecture and sculpture.

611 Ceolwulf King of Wessex dies and is succeeded by Cynegils.

614 ☐ Clotaire II King of the Franks: *Edictum Chlotacharii* (defining rights of kings, nobles and Church)

615 The Persians sack Jerusalem and take the 'True Cross', on which Jesus is believed to have been crucified, as part of the booty.

616 The Persians invade Egypt. Aethelfrith King of Northumbria dies and is succeeded by Edwin. Ethelbert King of Kent dies and is succeeded by his son Eadbald. Redwald King of East Anglia takes an army into Mercia and defeats the Northumbrians on their own frontier.

618 In China the Tang dynasty is founded; an official of the Sui regime has the Emperor Yangdi murdered and installs himself as the Emperor Kao Zu.

619 In Canterbury, Archbishop Laurentius dies and is buried beside Augustine; he is succeeded by Mellitus as Archbishop of Canterbury. Jerusalem is sacked by the Persians.

620 Chosroes II takes Rhodes and restores the Persian Empire as it was under Darius I.

622 City authorities in Mecca oppose Mohammed's teachings; the prophet flees on *16 Jul* to Medina. The Byzantine Emperor Heraclius lands at Issus and defeats the Persian army in the Battle of Issus.

624 Mohammed's followers surprise a Meccan caravan returning from Syria, defeating more than 1,000 Meccans.

625 King Redwald of East Anglia and overlord (*bretwalda*) of England dies and is buried at the royal burial ground at Sutton Hoo; the famous ship burial uncovered in *1938–9* is thought to be his. Persian forces attack Constantinople, but Heraclius fends off the attack.

626 In Japan Umako Soga dies. The city of Edinburgh is founded by King Edwin of Northumbria.

627 Edwin King of Northumbria is baptized at Easter by Paulinus. Chinese Emperor Kao Zu abdicates and is succeeded by his son Tai Zong. Opponents of Mohammed move on to Medina and massacre 700 Jews. The Byzantine Emperor Heraclius invades Assyria. *12 Dec*: Battle of Nineveh gives the Byzantines a decisive victory over Mesopotamia. At the same time then successfully beat off an attack on Constantinople by the Avars.

628 Chosroes II King of Persia is imprisoned after a military mutiny following the Battle of Nineveh. *3 Apr*: Chosroes is murdered by his son, who succeeds him as Kavadh II and makes peace with Heraclius. Prisoners are exchanged and the 'True Cross' is returned to Jerusalem. Mecca falls to Mohammed, who writes to the world's rulers explaining the Muslim faith. The Japanese Empress Suiko dies, aged 74 and is succeeded by the Emperor Jomei.

629 Clotaire II King of the Franks dies and is succeeded by his son Dagobert, who is advised by Arnulf Bishop of Metz and Pepin the Elder. The Emperor Heraclius restores Jerusalem to Byzantine suzerainty. Mohammed returns to Mecca in triumph with the *Koran* in which the principles of Islam are laid down.
   ☐ The *Koran*

630 The Tang court in China receives its first Japanese embassy.

632 Allied forces of Penda of Mercia and Cadwallon of North Wales defeat the Northumbrian army at the Battle of Hatfield. Edwin King of Northumbria is killed in the battle with his son Osfrith; Osric, son of Aelfric, succeeds Edwin. Penda becomes King of Mercia. *7 Jun*: Mohammed dies aged 63. The prophet's followers choose Abu Bekr to succeed him as ruler of Islam, giving him the title Caliph; Medina is his seat of power.

633 Muslim forces attack Persia. Christian churches at Alexandria, Jerusalem and Antioch are turned into mosques. Osric of Northumbria dies and is succeeded by Oswald.

634 The Caliph Abu Bekr dies on *22 Aug*, aged 61 and is succeeded by Mohammed's adviser Omar.

635 Muslims under Khalid ibn-al-Walid take Damascus, which becomes the seat of the Caliphate. Gaza is also taken by the Muslims. In India, the Chalukyas fend off an invasion attempt by Harsha. The port of Basra is founded at the head of the Persian Gulf at the confluence of the Tigris and Euphrates.

636 Bishop Aidan chooses the island of Lindisfarne as his base, within sight of King Oswald's Bamburgh Castle. *15 Aug*: Battle of Yarmuk, east of the Sea of Galilee: Islamic forces defeat a Byzantine army and gain Syria.

637 Persian forces are defeated by the Arabs at Tunis and Ualula. The Muslims compel their new subjects to learn Arabic, building an empire united by language.

638 Jerusalem falls to Islamic forces under Caliph Omar. A second Arab army penetrates Mesopotamia; a third penetrates Persia, and the Persians appeal for aid from China.

639 Dagobert I, King of the Franks, dies on *9 Jan.* He is succeeded by his six-year-old son Clovis II of Neustria and Burgundy. Arab armies invade Armenia and Egypt.

640 Byzantine forces are defeated at Heliopolis by an Arab army; the Islamic conquest of Egypt progresses. The Chinese Emperor Tai Zong sends a mission to India to study techniques of sugar refining in the Bihar region; sugar cultivation and manufacture will soon be developed in China.

641 King Oswald of Northumbria, 6th overlord of the Southern English, is canonized after his death in battle against Penda at Maserfield (Oswestry?); Oswald is succeeded by Oswy. The Japanese Emperor Jomei dies, aged 48, succeeded by his widow the Empress Kogyoku.

642 Battle of Niharvand: the Arabs finally defeat the Persians. The Persian King Yezdigird III appeals to China for help, to no avail; his lands are incorporated into the Caliphate. Alexandria falls to the Arabs; Cyrus the city patriarch makes the condition that the Muslims guarantee free exercise of religion

         ✍ Amr Mosque, Cairo

         City of Palenque (Central America)

644 Famine in Japan kills thousands. *Jun: coup d'état* in Japan. Iruka, grandson of Umako Soga is killed by Nakano-oeno-oji and Nakatami Kumatari. The Empress Kogyoku is removed and Kotoku the grandson of the Emperor Bintas is made Emperor. Nakano-oeno-oji becomes Prime Minister and Crown Prince. The Taika period begins, as the Japanese adopt the Chinese practice of naming periods. Alexandria rebels against Arab rule as a Byzantine fleet comes into view; the Byzantines recapture the city, but Egypt's Arab governor Abdalla ibn Sa'd manages to get it back again. He then works to build an Arab fleet.

646 In Japan a Great Reform decree establishes centralized government (Chinese-style) with the Emperor ruling from a palace in a fixed capital.

648 Arab invaders take Cyprus.

651 Persian ex-King Yezdigird III is murdered in a miller's hut near Merv. Bishop Aidan dies in the parish church at Bamburgh. At the same moment Cuthbert, a shepherd in the Lammermuir Hills, sees a vision of a host of angels, which he later connects with Aidan's death and interprets as a call to serve God.

653 Recessuinth, King of the Visigoths draws up a legal code that establishes equality between Goths and Romans.

⌷ Recessuinth: *Liber ludicorium*

654 Arabs plunder Rhodes. Kotoku, Emperor of Japan, dies, aged 58; the deposed Empress Kogyoku is restored under the name Saimei. Anna King of East Anglia dies and is succeeded by Aethelhere. Battle of Winwaed: King Penda of Mercia and 30 other kings and princes are killed, including King Aethelhere of East Anglia, who is succeeded by Ethelwold. Oswiu, King of Bernicia rules Mercia.

655 A Byzantine fleet under the personal command of Emperor Constans II is defeated by an Arab fleet off the coast of Lycia.

656 Caliph Othman, aged 80 is assassinated at Medina. He is succeeded by Mohammed's nephew Ali ibn Abi Talib, but there is disagreement over the succession. *9 Dec*: Battle of the Camel: the new Caliph defeats the opposition.

661 Wulfhere, son of King Penda of Mercia, attacks the Isle of Wight and gives it to Ethelwold King of Sussex. The Caliph Ali is assassinated and succeeded by Muawiya, who moves his seat of government to Damascus, founding the Omayyad Caliphate. Supporters of Caliph Ali are later called Shiites. The Empress Saimei of Japan dies, aged 67, and is succeeded by Tenji, son of the Emperor Jomei.

663 The Synod of Whitby in England; Roman Christianity prevails over Celtic Christianity. Constans II moves the Byzantine court from Constantinople to Italy as he tries to re-establish Rome as the seat of Empire. He meets resistance from the Lombards and no later Byzantine emperor will visit Rome.

664 Arab forces invade Afghanistan, Kabul falls to the Arabs.

668   The Byzantine Emperor Constans II dies in his bath at Syracuse on *15 Jul*; his death at 37 during an insurrection is probably the result of foul play. The Byzantine court returns to Constantinople. Arabs invade and devastate Anatolia on an annual basis. Constans is succeeded by his three sons, Tiberius, Heraclius and Pogonatus.

669   St. Wilfrid, the great art patron, is installed as Bishop of Northumbria; he chooses York as the centre of his diocese. Constantinople is under siege from Arab forces. Theodore of Tarsus becomes Archbishop of Canterbury.

670   *15 Feb*: The death of King Oswiu ends the Northumbrian supremacy in England: he is succeeded by Egfrith.

671   Tenji, the Emperor of Japan, dies, aged 45, and is succeeded by his son Kobun; Tenji's brother Ooama objects that Kobun's mother was a commoner and that the emperor must be entirely of royal blood.

672   Cenwalh King of Wessex dies and is succeeded by his Queen, Seaxburg, for a year. St. Chad, Bishop of Lindisfarne, dies. The Japanese Emperor Kobun is deposed by his uncle Ooama and commits suicide. Ooama makes himself Emperor under the name Tenmu.

673   Aescwine succeeds to the throne of Wessex. St. Etheldreda, daughter of Anna, King of East Anglia, founds the monastery at Ely. The Venerable Bede is born; he will later write *Ecclesiastical History of the English Nation*.

674   Wulfhere, King of Mercia, dies and is succeeded by Ethelred son of Penda. Building work begins on Hexham Abbey under Wilfrid's direction, using stone from the Roman camp at Corbridge; most Roman architecture in Britain is to suffer this fate.

   ✍ Hexham Abbey Crypt (U.K.)

675   Childeric of the Franks is murdered while hunting; the assassination leads to civil war in the Frankish kingdom.

677   The Byzantines destroy an Arab fleet at Syllaeum, temporarily ending the Arab threat to Europe.

678   A comet appears in August, shining like a sunbeam for three months. Bishop Wilfrid is expelled from his bishopric by King Egfrith; he sets out for Rome by way of the Netherlands. The Arabs lift their blockade of Constantinople and establish a 30-year peace. Caliph Muawiya dies at Damascus and is succeeded by his son Yazid, but Kufans in Iraq invite al-Husain, son of Caliph Ali, to accept the Caliphate.

680 The Bulgarians defeat a Byzantine army. Pogonatus now rules alone in Constantinople as Constantine IV. *10 Oct*: Battle of Kerbela: Caliph Yazid defeats al-Husain, who is deserted by the Kufans and killed. Wilfrid tells Pope Agatho in Rome of the founding of the monastery at Peterborough; the Pope sends a deed for the monastery back to King Ethelred. Wilfrid returns to England with vestments and ornaments for his new church at Hexham. Hilda abbess of Whitby dies.

  🕮 Wilfrid's Chair in Hexham Abbey

681 Khan Asparukh leads migrant Bulgar tribes across the Danube, subdues the Slavs who live there and founds the kingdom of Bulgaria.

682 Muslim forces overrun the North African coast, occupying Tripoli, Tangiers and Carthage; the last Byzantine bases in North Africa have fallen to Islam.

685 Centwine, King of Wessex, is deposed and succeeded by Ceadwalla. At York, Theodorus Archbishop of Canterbury consecrates Cuthbert as Bishop of Hexham, at the command of Egfrith. *6 Feb*: Hlothere, King of Kent dies and is succeeded by his son Eadric. *20 May*: King Egfrith is killed in the Battle of Nectansmere and succeeded by his brother Aldfrith; Northumbrian domination of England is ended. Constantine IV dies and Justinian II succeeds him at the age of 16.

686 Eadric, King of Kent, dies and is succeeded by his son Oswini. Tenmu, Emperor of Japan, dies and is succeeded by his widow Jito.

  ✍ Orders of Tenmu: Yakushi Temple at Nara (completed)

687 Caedwalla King of Wessex attacks Kent, where his brother Mul is burned to death. *20 Mar*: St. Cuthbert dies on Farne Island. Venice elects its first Doge and begins its rise to power. Pepin gains a victory at Testry, uniting the Frankish kingdom.

688 Caedwalla abdicates and goes to Rome; Ine becomes King of Wessex and draws up the earliest code of British laws to survive. In Rome, Caedwalla is baptized Peter by Pope Sergius; seven nights later he dies in his baptismal vestments and is buried in St. Peter's. Charles Martel is born, the son of Pepin II.

689 Justinian II defeats the Slavs in Thrace, deporting many of them to Anatolia.

690 Wihtred, son of Egbert I, becomes King of Kent. Archbishop Theodorus, the last Roman archbishop, dies and is buried at Canterbury.

691 ✍ Orders of Caliph Abd al-Malik: Dome of the Rock, Jerusalem (completed)

692 Brihtwold Abbot of Reculver becomes the first English Archbishop of Canterbury on *1 Jul*. Battle of Sebastopol in Cilicia: the Arabs defeat Justinian II.

694 The people of Kent confer with Ine King of Wessex, offering to pay compensation for killing Mul.

695 The Emperor Justinian II is deposed by his army officers, who cut off his nose and send him into exile in the Crimea. One of the officers, Leontius, becomes Emperor.

697 In England, the Mercians kill Osryth, Ethelred's Queen and the daughter of Oswiu King of Northumbria. The Arabs destroy Carthage. Empress Jito of Japan abdicates, aged 32; she is succeeded by Momu, the 14-year-old grandson of Tenmu.

698 Byzantine Emperor Leontius is deposed and succeeded by the fleet commander, who reigns as Tiberius III Apsimar. Willibrord Bishop of Utrecht discovers the island of Heligoland.

　　🕮 Bewcastle Cross, Cumbria (U.K.)
　　　The Lindisfarne Gospels (U.K.)

700 🕮 Echternach Gospels (Luxembourg)
　　📖 *Beowulf* (Old English epic poem) (at about this time) (U.K.)
　　　Dandin: *The Adventures of the Ten Princes* (India)

701 Japanese Emperor becomes sole landowner in Japan. Arab mariners sail for the first time to the Spice Islands.

702 Justinian II Rhinometus once again becomes Byzantine Emperor.

　　✍ Umayyad Mosque at Damascus
　　　Orders of Duke Hetan II: Round Church at Marienberg (Germany)

707 Momu Emperor of Japan, dies aged 24, and is succeeded by his aunt Gemmei.

708 Drinking tea becomes popular among the Chinese, partly because a boiled drink is far safer than water that has not been boiled.

709 Ceolred becomes King of Mercia; Cenred and Offa journey to Rome, Cenred remaining in Rome until his death. Bishop Wilfrid dies at Oundle and is buried at Ripon.

   ✍ Oratory at Mont Saint-Michel

710 Nara (Heijo) becomes the fixed capital of Japan.

   ✍ Orders of Empress Gemmei: Palace at Nara, Japan.

711 Arabs and Berbers (Moors) from North Africa invade Spain under Tariq ibn Ziyad, defeating the Visigoths under King Roderick. Battle of Wadi Bekka: Roderick is killed. Tariq takes Cordova and the Visigoth capital, Toledo. Justinian II opposes rebel troops under the leadership of a soldier called Bardanes. The troops defeat Justinian in Anatolia and put him to death in December; Bardanes is declared Emperor with the name Philippicus.

712 The Moors take Seville. Samarkand falls to an Arab army under the 17-year-old Abu Qasim al-Thagafi. The Muslim general Mohammed ibn-Kasim makes the first Arab conquests in the subcontinent of India, taking Sind.

   📖 Yasumaro Ono: *Kojiki* (first history of Japan)

713 Xuanzong becomes Emperor of China. The Byzantine Emperor Philippicus is deposed and succeeded by Anastasius II. Aldwulf King of East Anglia dies and is succeeded by Alfwold.

715 Gemmei Empress of Japan abdicates, aged 54 and is succeeded by her daughter Gensho. Pepin the Short is born, the son of Charles Martel.

   🏛 Landscape Mosaic, Great Mosque at Damascus

716 The Emperor Anastasius is deposed in an army insurrection. He is succeeded by a tax official, Theodosius. The Moors take Lisbon. The Chinese landscape painter Li Su Xun dies, aged 65. Osred King of Northumbria is killed; he is succeeded by Cenred. Ceolred King of Mercia dies and is succeeded by Ethelbald. Ethelred ex-King of Mercia also dies.

717 An Arab army lays siege to Constantinople; Theodosius is deposed and succeeded by Leo III. A new Arab Caliph takes office, Omar II; he grants tax exemptions to true believers.

    🐛 Buddha with the Gods of the Sun and the Moon (bronze), Nara, Japan

718 Cenred King of Northumbria dies and is succeeded by Osric son of King Aldfrith.

720 The Moors cross the Pyrenees and take Narbonne. A Muslim force invades Sardinia.

    📖 Yasumaro Ono: *Nihonshoki* (Japanese chronology)

722 Queen Ethelburg destroys Taunton, which the King of Wessex built.

724 Japanese Empress Gensho abdicates and is succeeded by her nephew Shomu. Shomu orders that the houses of the Japanese nobility must be roofed with green tiles as in China.

725 Wihtred King of Kent dies after a reign lasting 34 years; he is succeeded by his son Ethelbert II. Parsees following the teachings of Zoroaster move to India and are welcomed by the local ruler, a Hindu.

726 Ine King of Wessex dies in Rome and is succeeded by Ethelheard. The Greeks rebel against the rule of Leo III, who forbids the worship of icons in an attempt to stamp out superstition. Pope Gregory II attacks Leo III's policy. A Greek fleet sets sail for Constantinople with a rival emperor but it is destroyed by the Byzantine fleet with an incendiary mixture known as 'Greek fire'. There is a volcanic eruption on Santorini.

729 Two comets appear. Osric King of Northumbria dies and is succeeded by Ceolwulf.

730 Pope Gregory II excommunicates Emperor Leo III.

731 The Mayan Empire in Central America enters its period of ascendancy. Tatwine becomes Archbishop of Canterbury.

    📖 Venerable Bede: *Ecclesiastical History of the English People*

732 *11 Oct*: Battle of Tours: a huge Moorisl. army invading southern France under Abd ar-Rahman is defeated by the Frankish leader Charles Martel, who is now 44. Abd ar-Rahman is killed. The Moor advance into Europe is brought to a halt in this decisive battle. Bubonic plague strikes Constantinople. Pope Gregory II orders Wynfrith Boniface, Archbishop of Hesse, to forbid Christian converts to eat horsemeat; this is to differentiate them from the pagan Vandals, who regularly eat horsemeat as part of their religious rites.

735 Death of the Venerable Bede, the English scholar. Charles Martel conquers Burgundy.

737 Theodoric IV King of the Franks dies: a six-year interregnum follows. Christians from the south invade Egypt to protect the patriarch of Alexandria.

739 Charles Martel is asked by Pope Gregory III to help in fighting the Lombards and Arabs. Boniface founds bishoprics at Passau, Ratisbon and Salzburg.

741 The city of York is burned down. The Byzantine Emperor Leo III dies, aged 61 and is succeeded by his son Constantine V. Charles Martel dies, aged 53 on *22 Oct* after dividing his territory between his sons Carloman (Austrasia, Alemannia, Thuringia) and Pepin (Neustria, Burgundy, Provence).

742 The Byzantine Emperor Constantine V makes a renewed attack on the worship of images.

743 Childeric III succeeds to the Frankish throne left vacant in 737. Ethelbald King of Mercia and Cuthred King of Wessex lead armies against the Welsh.

✎ Palace at Mshatta, Jordan

744 There are many shooting stars. Swabia becomes part of Childeric III's Frankish Empire. Lombard rule ends as King Liutprand dies, aged 54.

745 Constantine V invades Syria in the continuing war against Islam. Wynfrith Boniface, Archbishop of Mainz, is given pepper, still a very rare and costly spice, by the Roman Gemmulus.

746 Constantine V retakes Cyprus from the Arabs, who lose a large fleet. Constantinople is struck severely by plague. Pepin's brother Carloman abdicates unexpectedly, retires to a monastery near Rome, leaving Pepin to rule the entire Frankish realm.

747 The Emperor Charlemagne is born, the eldest son of Pepin III (the Short).

748 Cynric Atheling of Wessex is killed. Eadbriht King of Kent dies and is succeeded by Ethelbriht.

    🔗 Todai Temple at Nara (completed) (Japan)

749 Alfwold King of East Anglia dies; his kingdom is divided among his heirs Hun, Beonna and Alberht. Battle of the Zab: the Caliph Marwin is defeated. Aistulf becomes King of the Lombards. Shomu, Emperor of Japan, abdicates, aged 48, and is succeeded by his daughter Koken.

    🐉 The Neighing Stallion (fire-clay sculpture) (China)

750 The Abbasid Caliphate is founded by Abu-Abbas al-Sarah, who has most of the Umayyads massacred. Plague follows famine in Spain.

    🐉 Crucifixion (bronze book cover) (Ireland)

751 Charles Martel's son Pepin the Short is crowned at Soissons by the Archbishop of Mainz (Boniface), becoming Pepin III in a new coronation ceremony that gives the monarch great prestige. The first paper-making factory in the Muslim world is established at Samarkand: Chinese prisoners have revealed how paper is made.

752 🐉 Rushanabutsu (17 metres/55 feet high statue of the Buddha), Nara (Japan)

754 Pepin II is crowned again at St. Denis by Pope Stephen II; the new Frankish dynasty is proclaimed to be holy (the Pope has appealed to Pepin for help against the Lombards).

756 The Donation of Pepin establishes the papal states and launches the papacy as a temporal power. Pepin III takes lands that legally belong to the Eastern Empire and gives them to the Pope, in effect recognizing papal claims to be heirs to the Empire in Italy. Abd-al-Rahman I is proclaimed Emir of Cordova on *15 May;* he makes the city the capital of Moorish Spain. He is the only Umayyad prince to have escaped the massacre of 750. Xuanzong, the Emperor of China, abdicates following the death of his favourite concubine Yang Guifei. The Emperor's bodyguards demanded her death and the Emperor permitted her to be strangled by his chief eunuch. The Mongol adventurer An Lushan seizes the capital and proclaims himself Emperor. Cuthred King of Wessex dies and is succeeded by Sigeberht. Ethelbald King of Mercia and overlord of the Southern English is killed at Seckington and buried at Repton.

757 Offa seizes the kingdom of Mercia, uniting most of England under his rule; Offa becomes overlord of the Southern English, assuming the title 'rex totius Anglorum patriae'. Sigeberht King of Wessex is deposed and killed and is succeeded by Cynewulf. An Lushan is assassinated at Luoyang, ending an insurrection that has caused the death of millions of people. The Arab writer Ibn al-Mukaffa is tortured at Basra on orders from Caliph al-Mansu; his limbs are cut off and he is thrown, still alive, into a furnace.

758 Edbriht King of Northumbria becomes a monk and is succeeded by his son Osulf, who is killed by his own household. Kohen, Empress of Japan, abdicates and is succeeded by her cousin Junin.

759 Frankish forces retake Narbonne from the Moors.

    📖 *Manyoshu* (anthology of Japanese poetry)

760 Cuthbert Archbishop of Canterbury dies.

761 The Japanese Empress Mother Koken is cured of illness by the priest Dokyo, who becomes Koken's court favourite; the Emperor Junin's jealousy is aroused. Moll Ethelwold becomes King of Northumbria.

762 Caliph al-Mansur moves the Arab seat of power to Baghdad, where he builds a new capital. Ethelbert King of Kent dies and is succeeded by his son Eardwulf.

764 Nakamaro Fujiwara leads a revolt against the Japanese Empress Mother Koken. The revolt is suppressed, Junin is forced into exile and Koken reascends the throne with the name Shotoku: Dokyo is her prime minister. Ceolwulf King of Northumbria dies.

765 Following Ceolwulf's death, Alhred becomes King of Northumbria. For the first time a three-field crop rotation system is mentioned in Europe. Baghdad nears completion, ringed by three lines of brick walls.

768 *24 Sep*: Pepin the Short dies, aged 54, and is succeeded by his son Charles, who will later be known as Charles the Great or Charlemagne. Pepin's son Carloman becomes King of Austrasia.

    ✐ Orders of the Fujiwara family: Kasuga Shrine at Nara, Japan

770 The Japanese Empress Shotoku dies, aged 52, succeeded by Konin, grandson of Tenji.

771 *4 Dec*: Carloman King of Austrasia dies; Charlemagne becomes King of all the Franks and marries Hildegarde of Swabia.

772 Charlemagne wages war on the Saxons.

773 Charlemagne subdues the Lombards and is crowned King of Lombardy.

774 The Northumbrians drive their King, Alhred, out of York; instead they take Ethelred I, the son of Moll, as their leader. Charlemagne visits Rome, where he confirms the Donation of Pepin but also makes it clear that he is sovereign even in the papal lands.

775 The Byzantine Emperor Constantine V dies, aged 56, and is succeeded by his son Leo IV. Caliph al-Mansur dies, aged 63, and is succeeded by his son al-Mahdi. The people of Tibet conclude a boundary agreement with the Chinese.

776 Mercian and Kentish armies meet in battle at Otford in Kent.

777 Charlemagne invades Moorish Spain, but is stopped at Saragossa.

778 Charlemagne's rearguard is attacked and annihilated on *15 Aug* at Roncesvalles in the Pyrenees; Charlemagne's paladin Roland is killed in action. Byzantine forces defeat the Arabs at Germanikeia and drive them out of Anatolia.

📖 *Chanson de Roland* (French epic poem)

779 Cynewulf King of Wessex and Offa King of Mercia meet in battle near Benson in Oxfordshire; Offa is victorious.

🖋 Orders of Offa: Offa's Dyke (earthwork to keep Welsh out of England)

780 The Byzantine Emperor Leo IV dies, aged 30, and is succeeded by his 10-year-old son Constantine VI (mother Irene as Regent). Irene restores image worship in the Byzantine Empire. Charlemagne encourages the use of the three-field crop rotation.

781 Konin Emperor of Japan dies, aged 73, and is succeeded by his son Kanmu. Nestorians in China build Christian monasteries.

782 Arab armies advance to the Bosporus. Charlemagne takes Saxon hostages at Verdun and makes Saxony a Frankish province, imposing Christianity on the Saxons.

783 Widukind leads a Saxon rebellion against Charlemagne and massacres a Frankish army. Charlemagne kills his Saxon prisoners and reinvades Saxony. Cyneheard kills Cynewulf King of Wessex and is himself killed; Brihtric becomes King of Wessex.

785 Charlemgne once again subdues the Saxons. Their leader Widukind is reconciled and baptized. Caliph al-Mahdi dies and is succeeded by his son al-Hadi. The Japanese strongman Tanetsugu Jujiwara marries his granddaughter to the grandson of Emperor Kanmu, anticipating that the 11-year-old Heizei will accede to the throne.

786 Caliph al-Hadi dies and is succeeded by his brother, Harun al-Rashid, who will make Baghdad the dazzling centre of Arab culture and greatly extend the power of the eastern Caliphate.

787 The Council of Nicaea sanctions the worship of icons in the Christian Church. The first Viking raids on Britain.

789 A dispute arises between Offa and Charlemagne; as a result Frankish ports are closed to English merchants.

790 A Byzantine army mutiny against the Empress Mother Irene places the 19-year-old Constantine VI in command of the Empire. The Utrecht Ship is built. Irish monks reach Iceland in skin-frame vessels.

792 Constantine VI recalls his mother and makes her co-ruler. Offa has Ethelbert King of East Anglia beheaded; later Offa is stricken with remorse, which leads him to order a tomb for Ethelbert housed in a great church, which eventually becomes a cathedral.

793 Vikings raid and destroy the church at Lindisfarne; they also ransack Egfrith's monastery at Jarrow. Many are later drowned when their ships break up in bad weather, some survivors swim ashore only to be slaughtered on the beach at Tynemouth by Northumbrians. A paper mill is established at the new city of Baghdad as the Arabs spread the Chinese technique of paper-making.

794 In Japan the seat of government is transferred to Heian (later called Kyoto). The first Viking raids on Scotland.

795 The first Viking invasion of Ireland. Charlemagne forbids the export of food from his Empire in an attempt to avoid food shortages.

796 Offa king of Mercia dies on *26 Jul* after reigning for 40 years. His death marks the end of Mercian dominance in England and the beginning of the rise of Wessex. Offa's son and successor Egfrith dies and is succeeded by Cenwulf. Osbald accedes to the Northumbrian throne but is deposed after only 27 days, succeeded by Eadwulf.

797 The Byzantine Emperor Constantine VI is seized and blinded by orders of his mother Irene; she now becomes the first Byzantine Express.

798 Cenwulf King of Mercia ravages Kent, stamping out the attempted Kentish coup against him. The Kentish King Eadbert is taken to Mercia, where his eyes are put out and his hands cut off; the Kentish dynasty is ended, and Cenwulf governs Kent through his brother Cuthred.

799 ✍ Abbey Church of St. Riquier (France)

800 Charlemagne is crowned head of the western Roman Empire on Christmas Day, but Irene, Empress of the eastern Roman Empire refuses to recognize him. Viking raids on the monastic community on Iona are reported: 68 monks are killed at Martyrs' Bay. In Central America, town-based royal dynasties come to an end in what is clearly a major social and political change, but the Mayan way of life continues in the rural areas.
📖 ▯ *Book of Kells*

802 Brihtric King of Wessex dies and is succeeded by Egbert. The Byzantine Empress Irene is deposed and exiled to Lesbos where she is supposed to support herself by spinning; her minister of finance succeeds her as Nicephorus I.

805 The Japanese Buddhist priest Saicho has spent the last three years visiting Chinese Buddhist temples, and returns with tea. Ex-Empress Irene dies on Lesbos.

806 Eardwulf King of Northumbria is deposed and exiled, succeeded by Elfwald. Kanmu Emperor of Japan dies, aged 69, and is succeeded by his son Heizei, a manic-depressive. Famine hits Japan.

807 Cuthred King of Kent dies. Arabs pillage Rhodes.
▯ *Book of Armagh* (Ireland)

808 Elfwald King of Northumbria dies and is succeeded by Eanred son of King Eardwulf. Fez is founded as a tent colony in Morocco: it will become the cultural centre of North Africa.

809 The great Caliph Harun al-Rashid dies on *24 Mar*, aged 46, at Tus in Persia, during an expedition to suppress a rebellion. His son al-Amin succeeds him, but another son, Mamun, is recognized in Persia: Mamun begins a revolt against al-Amin. The Japanese Emperor Heizei abdicates and is succeeded by his brother Saga.

    ✏ Abbey Church of St. Vicenzo (101 metres/330 feet long)

810 Reservoirs at Kairouan (Tunisia)

811 The Byzantine Emperor Nicephorus invades Bulgaria. The Bulgarians under King Krum surprise the Byzantine army and kill the Emperor. Nicephorus' son Staurakios succeeds; he is succeeded in turn by his brother-in-law, Michael I Rhangabe. In Java a magnificent temple called Borobudur is built by the Buddhist Sailendra rulers. On the shores of Lake Titicaca (Peru) the Tiahuanaco civilization reaches its peak. Its influence stretching all the way to the Pacific coast, the civilization is overextending itself; wars with the neighbouring Huari are weakening it.

    ✏ Borobudur Temple (Java)

812 The Byzantine Emperor Michael sends an embassy to Charlemagne's court, formally recognizing him as Emperor of the West. Charlemagne in return recognizes Venice and Dalmatia as Byzantine possessions.

813 The Byzantine army led by general Leo deposes Michael I and replaces him with Leo V. Caliph al-Amin surrenders Baghdad after Tahir, his brother's general has offered peace terms, but al-Amin is treacherously murdered on *25 Sep*. He is succeeded by his brother al-Mamun.

814 *28 Jan*: Charlemagne dies of pleurisy, aged 71. He is succeeded as Holy Roman Emperor by his son Louis I. The noble Minamoto family has its beginnings in Japan when 32 of the Emperor's children are made commoners or Buddhist priests as an economy measure. Omurtag, Khan of the Bulgars, makes a 30-year treaty with the Byzantines, gaining new territories in the Balkans.

    📖 Han Yu: *Memorial on the Bone-Relic of the Buddha* (an attack on the Emperor of China's worship of a holy relic)

817 The Holy Roman Emperor Louis the Pious partitions the Empire. His son Lothair is given most of Burgundy and Francia, his son Louis the German receives Bavaria, and his son Pepin receives Aquitaine; the whole nominally retains its unity under a single Emperor, Lothair. Ziyadat Allah becomes third Aghlabid King of Ifriqiyah (Tunisia). The Aghlabids have broken away from the Abbasid empire to form a separate Muslim kingdom. Bernard, King of of Italy and one of Charlemagne's grandsons, rebels against Louis' proposed division of the Empire because he has been excluded from it. He is captured, taken to Gaul and blinded on Louis' orders; he dies three days later.

820 The Byzantine Emperor Leo V is murdered in the mosque of Santa Sophia by supporters of his general Michael, who has been sentenced to death for conspiring against Leo. Leo is succeeded by Michael as Michael II Psellus (the Stammerer).

821 A treaty between China and Tibet agreeing the independence of Tibet is ratified at Chang'an.

822 Louis does public penance for causing the death of Bernard.

824 The Chinese writer who dared to criticize the Emperor, Han Yu, dies, aged 56.

825 The children of the late Emperor Kenmu are made commoners to reduce the imperial budget; they are given the family name Taira. Egbert King of Wessex decisively defeats Beornred King of Mercia at the Battle of Ellandun (near Swindon).

 Animal Head on Prow, Oseberg Ship (Norway)

 Dicuil: *De Mensura Orbis*

826 Crete is conquered by Muslim pirates who will use the island as a base. Harald Klak is baptized at Louis' palace at Ingelheim. He aspires to the throne of Denmark and gains Frankish backing, taking with him to Denmark a Frankish monk called Askar, who begins the slow job of converting the Danes to Christianity.

827 Arabs sent from Tunisia by Ziyadat Allah invade Sicily.

828 Idris II King of Morocco dies; Morocco is divided between his two sons.

829 The Byzantine Emperor Michael II dies and is suc-

ceeded by the religious fanatic Theophilus. Louis offends his three remaining sons by changing his inheritance settlement to provide for Charles, his son by his second marriage (to Judith of Bavaria).

📖 *Annales Regni Francorum* (French history)

831 The Sicilian city of Palermo falls to the Tunisian Arabs. Anskar is appointed Bishop of Hamburg by the Pope, with the responsibility of converting Scandinavia.

832 The Byzantine Emperor Theophilus issues an edict against idolatry.

833 Caliph al-Mamun dies and is succeeded by his brother al-Mu'tasim, who chooses Samarra as his capital. Junna, the Emperor of Japan, abdicates, aged 47, in favour of his nephew Ninmio. Louis the Pious is deserted by his army and imprisoned by his eldest son, Lothair, who acts as sole ruler.

834 Louis is rescued by loyalists and reinstated at Metz; Lothair returns to his sub-kingdom in Italy. Caliph al-Mamun founds a 'House of Wisdom' in Baghdad, where ancient Greek scholarly texts are translated into Arabic.

835 Dougan, the first King of the Saifawa dynasty of Kanem-Bornu (Chad, Niger and Nigeria), dies at Njimi, his capital city.

837 Naples fends off an Arab attack.

838 The Persian religious revolutionary Babk is executed on 4 *Jan* at Samarra on the orders of Caliph al-Mu'tasim.

839 King Egbert dies, leaving a strengthened and enlarged kingdom of Wessex, which is the core of what will later be England. He is succeeded by his son Ethelwulf.

840 The Holy Roman Emperor Louis the Pious dies on 20 *Jun*, aged 62, at Ingelheim after suppressing a revolt by his son Louis the German. His son Lothair, now 45, succeeds him as Emperor and attempts to take back all the lands of Charlemagne. Louis' son Charles, now 17, succeeds as King of France and joins forces with his half-brother Louis the German in blocking Lothair's plan. The English under ealdorman (duke) Wulfheard repel a Viking attack on Southampton.

📖 Einhard: *Vita Caroli* (Life of Charlemagne)

841 Battle of Fontenoy: Lothair is defeated by Charles the

Bald and Louis the German, but remains Emperor until his death.

842 The Byzantine Emperor Theophilus dies and is succeeded by his three-year-old son Michael III; his mother Theodora serves as Regent and neglects his education. Caliph al-Mu'tasim dies at Samarra.

    ✍ Orders of Caliph al-Mu'tasim: Mosque at Samarra (with spiral minaret)

843 The Treaty of Verdun, concluded between Louis the Pious' sons, gives Lothair the title Emperor, Italy, the valleys of the Rhône, Sâone and Meuse and the capital cities of Rome and Aix-la-Chapelle. Charles receives the remainder of Gaul, and Louis the German receives lands to the east. The treaty breaks the unity of the Empire. Lothair is to have no power over his brothers' dominions.

844 Lothair has his son Louis crowned King of Italy in Rome by Pope Leo IV.

845 The Taoist Chinese Emperor Wuzong suppresses Buddhism; he seizes the wealth amassed in Buddhist monasteries and temples. Hamburg is raided by Vikings, who destroy Anskar's church; Anskar is forced to flee, but he sets up a new missionary base at Bremen.

847 Pope Leo IV repairs and enlarges the walls of Rome, which were badly damaged in Arab raids last year. The Arab mathematician who invented square roots, Mohammed al-Khwarizmi, dies in Baghdad.

    ✍ Orders of Pope Leo IV: Leonine Wall, Rome

849 King Alfred is born at Wantage, the fifth son of Ethelwulf King of Wessex. Wystan, heir to the Mercian throne, is murdered by his godfather.

850 The Norseman Rurik makes himself ruler of Kiev. The Japanese Emperor Ninmio dies, aged 40, and is succeeded by his son Montoku. The Sican culture evolves in northern Peru. In India, the Chola people are gaining power under the leadership of their King, Vijayalaya. Arab scientists invent the astrolabe, an aid to navigation. Salerno University is founded. The Yiddish language has its beginnings: Jews settling in Germany develop their own language which includes elements of Hebrew and German.

851 Vikings sack Canterbury Cathedral, but they are defeated by Ethelwulf King of Wessex and Kent. In Rome the Colosseum and Leonine Wall are damaged by a severe earthquake.

852 Malamir Czar of Bulgaria dies. The Umayyad Emir of Cordova Abd ar-Rahman II dies and is succeeded by Mohammed I. Coal is mentioned for the first time in English chronicles as a supplement to firewood.

853 Charles the Bald, King of the West Franks is at war with Louis the German, his half-brother. The first major Japanese painter whose name we know, Kudawara Kuwanari, dies.

855 The Holy Roman Emperor Lothair dies on *29 Sep*, aged 60, and is succeeded by his son Louis II, who is 33. He continues as King of Italy: his brother Lothair II is given part of Austrasia, renamed Lotharingia (now Lorraine); a third son, Charles, is given Provence and southern Burgundy. Ethelwulf King of Wessex takes his son Alfred on a pilgrimage to Rome; Alfred is six.

856 Ethelbald leads a rebellion against his father Ethelwulf. An earthquake at Corinth kills 45,000 people.

858 Ethelwulf is made to share his throne with his son Ethelbald; Ethelwulf dies, and Ethelbald becomes sole King of Wessex. Algeciras is attacked by Vikings, but the Arabs drive them off. The Emperor of Japan, Montoku, dies aged 31; he is succeeded by his eight-year-old son Seiwa.

860 Ethelbald King of Wessex dies and is succeeded by his brother Ethelbert. The simplified phonetic alphabet Hiragana becomes popular among Japanese women. Vikings land on Iceland for the first time. Constantinople is besieged by the Rus (Russians).

861 Vikings sack Cologne, Aix-la-Chapelle, Worms, Toulouse and Paris.

862 The Scandinavian chief Rurik founds the city of Novgorod, makes himself Grand Prince and establishes what will become the Russian royal family. The Magyars, a nomadic people from the Ukraine, move west and attack the kingdom of Louis the German.

863 The Cyrillic alphabet is invented by the Macedonian missionary Cyril and his brother Methodius.

864 Boris I Czar of Bulgaria becomes a Christian.

865 Russian Norsemen sack Constantinople. Ethelbert King of Wessex dies and is succeeded by his brother Ethelred I, the fourth son of King Ethelwulf.

866 *Apr*: the Byzantine Caesar Bardas is murdered with the consent of his nephew, Emperor Michael III. Michael's Armenian chamberlain, Basil, carries out the murder. Michael rewards him by making him co-emperor. The Fujiwaras have become the most powerful family in Japan, as Yoshifusa is appointed Regent for the boy-Emperor Seiwa. The Fujiwaras have won their position through politics and carefully planned marriages rather than by the use of violence.

867 The Macedonian dynasty is founded by the co-emperor. *Sep*: he has his co-emperor Michael III murdered and becomes Basil I. The patriarch of Constantinople, Photius, who was excommunicated by Pope Nicholas I, begins a schism with the Roman Church by issuing an encyclical against the Pope; the Pope is anathematized by the Council of Constantinople. *13 Nov*: Pope Nicholas dies.

868 Al-Jahiz, author of the *Book of Misers*, dies.
   ☐ *The Diamond Sutra*, found at Kansu, China (world's first printed book)

869 Caliph al-Mu'tazz is murdered by his troops and succeeded by al-Muqtadi. Arab invaders take possession of Malta. Cyril, the monk who with his brother composed a Slavonic alphabet known as Glagolitic, dies in Rome, aged 42; his lettering is being simplified into 'Cyrillic'.

870 Caliph al-Muqtadi abdicates under pressure from the Turks, who choose al-Mu'tamid; he moves his court to Baghdad. Lothair II dies. Lorraine is partitioned under the Treaty of Mersen, which has been forced on Charles the Bald King of Lorraine by the Holy Roman Emperor Louis II, who now gains territory west of the Rhine. King Edward the Elder of England is born.
   ✑ *The Lindau Gospels*

871 Ethelred King of Wessex is defeated by a Danish army at Reading on *4 Jan*, but is victorious at Ashdown on *8 Jan*. Saxon forces are defeated at Basing on *22 Jan* and victorious at Merton on *2 Mar*. Ethelred dies of his battle wounds in April and is succeeded by his brother Alfred.

874 The Danes move north into Mercia, where after little resistance King Burgred abdicates; the Danes set up a puppet king. Vikings begin to colonize Iceland.

875 The Holy Roman Emperor Louis II dies on *12 Aug* in Brescia, aged 50. He has named Carloman as his successor, but Charles the Bald persuades Carloman to go home, moves swiftly to Rome ahead of Louis the German, and is crowned Emperor by Pope John VIII. Xizong becomes Chinese Emperor (Tang dynasty).

876 *8 Sep*: Louis the German dies at Frankfurt, aged 72, on the point of going to war with Charles the Bald; he is succeeded by his son Carloman. Seiwa, Emperor of Japan, abdicates, aged 26, and is succeeded by his ill-equipped eight-year-old son Yozei.

877 The Danes seize Exeter while their leaders are deceitfully negotiating with Alfred. The Danish fleet is dispersed by a storm. *5 Oct*: Charles the Bald dies, aged 54, while crossing the Alps. He is succeeded as King of France by his son Louis le Begue (the Stammerer) as Louis II. Ahmad ibn Tulun, Governor of Egypt, fends off an attempt by the Abbasid Caliph to remove him from office, making Egypt independent for the first time since Cleopatra's reign. Ibn Tulun is the son of a Turkish slave who made a career in the Caliph's army and became Governor of Egypt in *868*: Tulun took over from him, establishing Fustat (Cairo) as the capital.

ℝ Orders of Ahmad ibn Tulun: Cairo Mosque.

878 King Alfred is surprised by a Danish attack at Chippenham, where he has been celebrating Christmas. Many of his men are killed but he escapes to Athelney in disguise, and he is joined by troops from all over Wessex in *May*. Battle of Edington: Alfred's English army defeats the Danes under Guthrum. Egbert II King of Northumbria north of the Tyne dies; he is the last recorded king of Northumbria.

879 Treaty of Wedmore, between Alfred and Guthrum; Guthrum is baptized and Alfred cedes England north of Watling Street to the Danes. *10 Apr*: Louis II dies at Compiègne, aged 32, and is succeeded by his young sons who reign jointly as Louis III and Carloman. They are crowned in September at Ferrière and divide the kingdom between them.

880 The Songhay Empire (West Africa) reaches its peak; its economy and military action depend to a large extent on the deployment of slaves.

881 The throne of the Holy Roman Empire, which has been vacant since *877*, is filled. *Feb*: Pope John VIII crowns Charles III King of Swabia in a ceremony in Rome.

882 *5 Aug*: Louis III King of France dies at St. Denis, aged 19; his brother rules alone. Under Oleg, Kiev becomes the capital of the Rus (Russians), replacing Novgorod.

883 Al-Muwaffiq, brother of the Caliph, suppresses the Zenj rebellion that has ravaged Chaldea since *869*.

884 The Japanese Emperor Yozei has devoted himself to his horses and is forced to abdicate, aged 16; he is succeeded by a 54-year-old great-uncle, Koko. *12 Dec*: Carloman King of France dies while hunting and is succeeded by the Holy Roman Emperor Charles III (the Fat).

885 Alfred King of Wessex retakes London from the Danes. In southern India, Aparajita King of the Pallavas is killed leading his army into battle on his war-elephant. His death brings to an end a period of great cultural achievement; the power of the Pallavas has been eroded by that of the Cholas under their King Aditya.

886 Norsemen lay siege to Paris. *Oct* Charles III arrives with a large army, but agrees to pay the invaders a large ransom to withdraw. *29 Aug*: the Byzantine Emperor Basil I dies and is succeeded by Leo VI.

887 *Nov*: the Holy Roman Emperor Charles the Fat is deposed by an assembly at Tribur; there is to be no emperor for four years. The Carolingian Empire finally falls apart. The Japanese Emperor Koko abdicates and is succeeded by his son Uda.

888 Odo Count of Paris is elected King of the West Franks to fill the gap left by Charles III's departure. He is opposed by the 10-year-old Charles the Simple, son of Louis the Stammerer; he rules from Laon as the last Carolingian King but has no real power.

890 Alfred King of Wessex develops the power of the king's courts and founds a regular army and navy. The Songhay kingdom (modern Mali and Niger) annexes Gao on the right bank of the Niger.

891   Guido of Spoleto, King of Italy, is crowned Holy Roman Emperor by Pope Stephen V. Arnulf King of the Germans defeats the Vikings in a battle on the River Dyle, driving them out of his kingdom.

892   England is invaded by a Viking fleet of 330 ships; the Vikings have brought with them their wives and children in a clear attempt to settle in England. Caliph al-Mu' tamid dies and is succeeded by his nephew al-Mu'tadid; the capital is moved back to Baghdad.

893   The Danish invasion force is defeated by Alfred's son Edward at Farnham; the Danes take refuge on Thorney Island.

   📖 Asser: *The Life of Alfred the Great*

894   The Holy Roman Emperor Guido of Spoleto dies and is succeeded by his co-emperor Lambert. Svatopluk King of Moravia dies after uniting Moravia, Slovakia and Bohemia ('Great Moravia'). The Danish invasion force in England withdraws to Essex. Symeon, the new Czar of Bulgaria, invades Thrace. The Byzantines appeal to the Magyars for help. The Magyars have been expelled from southern Russia and led by Arpad into Hungary.

896   *Feb*: the German King Arnulf is crowned Holy Roman Emperor by Pope Formosus; he sets off to establish his authority in Spoleto but is seized by paralysis on the way. Pope Formosus dies. Alfred King of Wessex and his son Edward end the Danish threat to England.

897   The Japanese Emperor Uda abdicates, aged 30, and is succeeded by his 12-year-old son Daigo. Nine months after Pope Formosus' death his body is exhumed, dressed in full papal vestments, propped up on a throne and formally put on trial for perjury. The corpse is found guilty, has its three blessing fingers cut off and is thrown into the Tiber.

898   *1 Jan*: Odo King of the West Franks dies; his rival Charles III in Laon gains sole control in France after a five-year civil war.

899   *26 Oct*: Alfred the Great of Wessex dies and is succeeded by his son Edward the Elder, who is now 29. *Dec*: Holy Roman Emperor Arnulf dies, aged 49, and is succeeded

as German King by his son Louis III, the last of the German Carolingian kings.

900 The Czechs gain the ascendancy over all Bohemian tribes. The Norseman Gunbjorn is blown off course while sailing from Norway to Iceland and discovers Greenland. Rhazes first distinguishes between measles and smallpox; he is chief physician in a Baghdad hospital. England receives her first shipment of East Indian spices. Harald Fairhair wins the Battle of Hafrsfjord and becomes the first King of Norway, uniting several separate princedoms. The city of Monte Alban in Mexico is abandoned after being sacked by the Mixtec people. Monte Alban has been the capital of the Zapotec people for 500 years and the centre of the rich Zapotec culture; the fall of their capital marks the end of the Zapotecs' culture. In Java the Hindu Matarama dynasty replaces the Buddhist Sailendo dynasty and orders the building of over 100 magnificent stone temples. The Toutse state (Botswana) is founded on the western edge of the Kalahari Desert. In Central Asia, Ismail ibn Ahmed, the Samanid ruler of Transoxiana, establishes his capital at Bokhara; his wealth depends on Bokhara's key position on trade routes between East and West.

 ₫ Chandi Lara Longgrang Temple at Prambanam (Java)

   Samanid Mausoleum at Bokhara

 □ *The Paris Psalter*

901 The 21-year-old Boso, son of the late King of Provence, is chosen King of the Lombards at Pavia; he is crowned by Pope Benedict in Rome in *Feb* as the Holy Roman Emperor Louis III. Edward the Elder, King of Wessex, takes the title 'King of the Angles and Saxons'. Abu 'Abd Allah stirs the Berbers up against the Aghlabid emir of Ifriqiyah (Tunisia).

902 The Tunisian conquest of Sicily is completed as the town of Taormina is taken from the Byzantines.

904 *31 Jul*: the Saracen corsair Leo of Tripoli storms Thessalonica; he plunders the town and abducts 20,000 people as slaves.

905 The Holy Roman Emperor Louis III is surprised and blinded by insurgents after having subdued the Lombards; he is sent back to Arles. The Christian reconquest of Spain begins, under the leadership of King Alfonso III of León and the Asturias: the province of Navarre is made a kingdom.

📖 *Kokin Wakashu* (anthology of Japanese poetry)

906 In South-East Asia, Annam gains its independence from China. Aditya, the Chola King, dies at the end of a 35-year-reign during which he has enlarged his empire across south-east India.

907 The Tang dynasty in China ends as Khitan Mongols under the leadership of Ye-lu A-pao-chi gradually conquer the territory. The Magyar chief of Hungary, Arpad, dies; the Magyars destroy the Moravian Empire and make forays into German and Italian territories. Oleg Prince of Kiev lays siege to Constantinople and so gains major trading rights. In India, the Rastrakuta people occupy most of the Deccan Plateau after repulsing the Chalukyas.

910 Edward the Elder, King of the Angles and Saxons, gains victories over the Danes and takes London and Oxford when his brother-in-law Ethelred King of Mercia dies. The Byzantine Emperor Leo VI is forced to pay tribute to the Magyars. The kingdom of Asturias is renamed León with Alfonso III as its King. William Duke of Aquitaine founds the Benedictine Abbey of Cluny.

✐ William Duke of Aquitaine: Cluny Abbey (France)

911 The Treaty of St. Clair-sur-Epte sets up the Dukedom of Normandy; Rollo the Viking (Hrolf the Ganger) becomes the first Duke of Orleans as Viking domination of the Franks increases. The last of the Aghlabid rulers of Ifriqiyah is driven out of Kairouan during a popular rising. He is succeeded by Ubayd Allah known as the Mahdi. Oleg Prince of Kiev and leader of the Rus gains a commercial treaty with the Byzantines in return for peace: the power of the Rus steadily increases. Louis the Child King of Germany dies, aged 18. *Nov:* the son of Conrad Count of Lahngau is chosen to succeed him. Lorraine switches allegiance to France.

912 Duke Rollo is baptized, taking the name Robert. The Byzantine Emperor Leo VI dies and is succeeded by his brother Alexander II.

913 The Byzantine Emperor Alexander II dies and is succeeded by his eight-year-old nephew Constantine VII Porphyrogenitus; the Regency is composed of Constantine's mother Zoe, the patriarch Nikolas and John Eladas. Bulgarian forces under the leadership of Czar Symeon threaten Constantinople when their annual tribute is not paid. Czar Symeon calls himself Emperor of the Romans.

914 Adrianople falls to the Bulgarians, but the Byzantine army soon retakes it. Ordono II becomes King of Asturias (now León).

915 Famine strikes Spain and Portugal. The Lombard King Berengar is crowned Holy Roman Emperor.

916 Ubayd Allah, the first Fatimid Caliph, makes Mahdia the capital of Ifriqiyah.

917 Czar Symeon's Bulgarian forces overrun Thrace in violation of the *913* agreement with Constantinople but in retaliation for the Byzantines' refusal to pay the agreed annual tribute.

918 *23 Sep* Conrad I King of the Germans dies; a decision about the succession is left until next year.

919 The Iberian Peninsula is again struck by famine. The south is ruled by Caliph Abd ar Rahman III, the north by Christian princes who are establishing the states of León, Castile and Navarre. *May*: at Fritzlar German nobles, previously advised by the late King Conrad, elect the Duke of Saxony King; he is known as Henry the Fowler.

922 Charles III (the Simple) King of France is deposed by his barons and replaced with King Odo's brother Robert. *29 Jun*: Robert is crowned at Reims, while Charles the Simple gathers an army to try to retake the throne. Al-Hallaj, the 64-year-old mystic, is sentenced to death for heresy. *27 March*: he is flogged, mutilated and beheaded in Baghdad. He advocated reforming the Caliphate.

923 *15 June*: Battle of Soissons: the usurper Robert is killed, but Charles the Simple's army is defeated and the barons elect Rudolf Duke of Burgundy to succeed Robert; Charles is imprisoned.

924 Magyars cross the Alps and ravage Provence. Bulgarians under Czar Symeon attack Constantinople without success. *17 Jul*: Edward the Elder, King of the Angles and Saxons in England, dies and is succeeded by his son Athelstan, who will extend the territory he has inherited.

925 Henry the Fowler King of the Germans annexes Lotharingia (Lorraine). Arabs from the Persian Gulf colonize Zanzibar.

926 Bulgarians under Czar Symeon attack Croat forces who have allied themselves with the Byzantines; Symeon is defeated. Manchuria and North Korea are annexed to the Mongol Khitan Empire.

927 Famine devastates the Byzantine Empire. *27 May*: Czar Symeon dies of a heart attack and is succeeded as Bulgarian Czar by his son Peter. *Oct*: Czar Peter signs a peace treaty with the Byzantines.

928 Louis III (the Blind) King of France dies at Arles, aged 48; he has been blind for 23 of the 27 years of his reign.

929 Wenceslas, the Christian King of Bohemia, is murdered in Prague by his non-Christian brother Boleslav. The Emir of Cordova Abd ar-Rahman III proclaims himself Caliph, establishing Spain as a major Muslim power.

930 The Japanese Emperor Daigo dies, aged 45, and is succeeded by his seven-year-old son Suzaku: ex-Emperor Uda retains power. The Carmathians, a group of Muslim extremists, sack Mecca and steal the Ka'aba, the sacred Black Stone; their motives are not known, but the success of the attack shows the growing impotence of the Abbasid caliphs.

932 In China printing is used for the first time to reproduce Confucian classics.

933 *15 Mar*: Battle of Merseburg: Henry the Fowler defeats Magyar raiders.

936 Rudolf Duke of Burgundy dies and is succeeded by Charles III's son as King of France – Louis IV d'Outremer, who is now 15. The Abbasid Caliph in Mesopotamia relinquishes power to a soldier-adventurer, Ra'iq. *2 Jul*: Henry the Fowler the German King dies at Memleben, aged 60, and is succeeded by his 23-year-old son Otto I. Tartars attack and capture Beijing.

939 Battle of Andernach: Otto I defeats Eberhard of Franconia and other rebel dukes, confirming Saxon power over all of Germany after a long period of internal rivalries since the break-up of the Frankish Empire. Vietnam gains its independence from China. In Spain, Caliph Abd ar-Rahman III builds a new city as an alternative capital to Cordova, Madmat az Zahra. The Taira and Minamoto families challenge the Japanese imperial court at Kyoto, causing anarchy in the provinces.

940 Athelstan King of England dies and is succeeded by his son Edmund. Irish-Norse Vikings under the leadership of Olaf conquer the kingdom of York, forcing the Anglo-Saxon King Edmund to cede territory. The Bogomils, followers of a Bulgarian peasant sect, are denounced by the Orthodox Church as heretics; it is as much a working-class political movement as a religious sect.

941 Igor Prince of Kiev crosses the Black Sea and plunders Bithynia and reaches Constantinople while the Byzantine fleet is in the Aegean Sea. The Byzantine fleet returns in time to drive the Rus off; the Rus fleet is almost completely destroyed by 'Greek fire'.

942 Odo Abbot of Cluny dies, aged 63, after making Cluny one of the most famous and influential monasteries in Europe.

943 Byzantine troops penetrate deep into Arab territory in order to recover the Mandylion, a unique icon which is possibly even a relic of Jesus.

944 Danish settlers help Edmund recover the lands he ceded to Olaf in *940*.

945 Igor Prince of Kiev dies in battle with Drevlianian tribesmen and is succeeded by his widow Olga, the first Slav ruler to become a Christian. Indonesians, using Madagascar as a base, invade the Sofala coast of Mozambique. In Japan, Kyoto is invaded by thousands of farmers demonstrating against the requisition of their crops. *Dec*: Shiite forces under Imad ibn Buwayhid take Baghdad; the Caliph is kept as a figurehead while Buwayhid tries to restore order.

946 *Jan*: the Abbasid Caliph al-Mustaqfi is deposed and blinded. He is succeeded by the three Buwayhid brothers, Imad, Runk and Mu'izz. Edmund I King of England dies and is succeeded by his brother Edred. Suzaku Emperor of Japan dies, aged 23, and is succeeded by his two-year-old brother Murakami.

947 Mongol Khitans found the Liao dynasty and settle the Beijing region.

950 Cordova has become Europe's intellectual centre, a city of half a million people with hospitals, medical schools and libraries. Mixcoatl, the ruler of the Toltec Empire (Mexico), is assassinated at Tula, his capital city. His people, shocked by the murder, deify him as a hunting-god. The Toltec civilization succeeds the Teotihuacan civilization which the Toltecs destroyed 300 years ago. The new ruler, Topiltzin, is a philosopher and reformer opposed to the Toltec custom of human sacrifice. In Central India, the kingdom of Chandela reaches its peak. The great Muslim philosopher al-Farabi dies, aged 80.

954 Louis IV King of France dies, aged 33, and is succeeded by his son Lothair, who is now 13; he will rule under the regency of Hugh Count of Paris. Eric Bloodaxe is murdered at York, and York is taken from the Vikings; King Edred now rules all England.

955 King Edred of England dies and is succeeded by his nephew Edwig. *10 Aug*: Battle of Lechfeld: Otto the Great of Saxony defeats the Magyars, driving them decisively to the east, ending the Magyar invasion.

956 *17 Jun*: Hugh the Great of Burgundy dies and is succeeded by his son Hugh Capet.

959 The Kilwa sultanate is founded (now the coast of Tanzania) by Ali ben al-Husain ben Ali. Following the death of Edwig, his younger brother Edgar becomes King of England. The Byzantine Emperor Constantine VII dies after reigning for 47 years. He is succeeded by his son Romanus II. King Edgar of England recalls the monk Dunstan from exile in Flanders and makes him Bishop of Worcester.

960 The Northern Song dynasty is established at Kaifeng in China by Zhao Kuangyin, who begins to reunify China. The first ruler of Poland emerges in the person of Mieszko, who has carved out a territory between the Warthe and Oder Rivers.

961 Crete is taken back from Arab pirates by a huge Byzantine fleet commanded by Nicephorus Phocas; he storms Candia and expels Muslims. Edgar King of England makes Dunstan Archbishop of Canterbury.

962 *2 Feb*: Otto I King of Saxony is crowned Holy Roman
Emperor by Pope John XII, bringing to an end a period
of chaos in Rome. Otto revives the Western Empire,
which creates friction with Constantinople, the centre of
the Eastern Empire.

963 The Byzantine Emperor Romanus II dies, aged 25,
probably poisoned by his wife Theophano, and is succeeded by his son Basil II. The general Nicephorus
Phocas, who is now 41, reigns as co-emperor. Edgar
becomes King of England. Edward the Confessor the son
of Ethelred Evil-Council (the Unready) is born.

964 Otto starves Rome into surrender, forcing the reinstate-
ment of his candidate, Leo VIII, as Pope.

965 Byzantine forces retake Cyprus from the Arabs. Al-
Mutanabbi, the great Arab poet, is killed by bandits
near Baghdad, aged 45.

967 The Japanese Emperor Murakami dies, aged 41, and is
succeeded by his insane son of 17, Reizei.

968 Dinh Bo Linh takes the title of Emperor of Dai Vet
(North Vietnam), founding the Dinh dynasty.

969 The Byzantine co-emperor Nicephorus is murdered in
his palace in a personal intrigue by his wife's lover, the
Armenian general John Tzimiskes, who now reigns as
co-emperor instead. Prince Sviatoslav of Kiev invades
Bulgaria and captures the Czar. Byzantine forces take
Antioch after a long siege, bringing 300 years of Arab
rule to an end. Reizei, the insane Japanese Emperor, is
deposed by the Fujiwara family and replaced by his 10-
year-old brother Enyu. Cairo is founded by the Fati-
mids, Muslims who have conquered much of Egypt.
     ✉ Al Azhar, the Mosque-University at Cairo

970 The Vizier Abud al-Daula founds a great hospital at
Baghdad.

971 Prince Sviatoslav of Kiev is driven out by Czar John of
Bulgaria, who annexes much of the country and restores
trading links with the Rus.

972 Maiolus Abbot of Cluny is captured on the Great St.
Bernard Pass by Arab marauders. His monks raise the
ransom for his release and put pressure on Otto the Great
to clear the European mainland of Arab interference and
make travel on the highways safe once more.

✍ The Daigo Pagoda, Kyoto, Japan (5 storeys high; completed)

973 *7 May*: Otto I Holy Roman Emperor dies, aged 60, and is succeeded by his 18-year-old son Otto II. The Fatimid rulers in Egypt set up the Sanhaja Berber family of the Zirids as Rulers in Ifriqiyah. *11 May*: King Edgar of England's coronation in Bath. Afterwards Edgar sails with his fleet to Chester where he has eight British sub-kings symbolically row him along the River Dee as a gesture of fealty.

975 King Edgar of England dies, aged 31, and is succeeded by his 12-year-old son Edward. Arabs introduce modern arithmetical notation into Europe, making calculation much easier. The northern Chinese Song kingdom defeats the southern Tang kingdom, bringing to an end the era of the Five Dynasties and Ten Kingdoms.
🐍 The Gero Crucifix, Cologne (first crucifixion image to show Jesus suffering)

976 The Byzantine co-emperor John Tzimisces dies, aged 51, on returning from a campaign against the Saracens (Arabs). Basil II, now 20, reigns alone. Samuel sets himself up as Czar of Bulgaria. Austria has its beginnings as a margraviate granted by Otto II to the Franconian Count Leopold. Caliph Hakam II of Cordova dies, aged 63. He has made the University of Cordova the most important academic institution in the world. He is succeeded by his son Hisham.

978 *18 Mar*: Edward (King Edward the Martyr) is murdered at the gates of Corfe Castle in Dorset, aged 15. He is killed by his stepmother Elfthryth, who wants her 10-year-old son to be king; he succeeds as Ethelred Evil-Council. Aix-la-Chapelle is plundered by Holy Roman Emperor Otto II, at war with Lothair King of France. Cordova's regent al-Mansur seizes power from the boy-Caliph Hisham II.

979 The Le dynasty takes power in Dai Vet (Vietnam). A Vietnamese envoy is arrested in the kingdom of Champa, so the Vietnamese send a punitive expedition to destroy the Cham capital.

980 Vladimir Prince of Novgorod calls in Viking warriors to take Kiev for him; Vladimir makes himself Grand Duke of Kiev. English ports (Southampton and Chester) come under attack from Danish raiders. The kingdom of Axum (Ethiopia) manages with help from Alexandria to repulse an invasion attempt by the Queen of Damot, but Axum's control over the Red Sea trade route is at an end.

981 Otto II marches into Apulia to fight the Arabs who have invaded Italy. The Byzantines ally themselves with the Arabs in southern Italy against Otto II, who is seen as an expansionist. Seven hundred Norse Icelanders sail for Greenland in 25 ships to start a colony. The expedition is led by Eric the Red, an exiled murderer; only 14 of the 25 ships reach Greenland.

982 The Byzantine Emperor Basil II sends troops to support the Arabs in southern Italy against Otto II. *Jul*: Otto suffers total defeat at Cortone and escapes incognito on a Greek ship to Rossano. Viking raiders continue to attack the south coast of England. Eric the Red makes landfall in Greenland and decides to settle there.

983 Otto II organizes a new campaign against the Saracens, but then hears of a general Slavic rising east of the Elbe and dies suddenly in his palace in Rome on *8 Dec*, aged only 28. He is succeeded by his three-year-old son Otto III, with the child's mother Theophano as Regent.

984 Otto III King of the Germans is seized by the deposed Duke of Bavaria, the 33-year-old Henry the Quarrelsome, who was dethroned by Otto II in *976*. Henry claims the Regency, but is forced to hand the boy over when Theophano arrives with the boy's grandmother Adelheid. Enyu, Emperor of Japan, abdicates in favour of his 16-year-old son Kazan.

985 The Danish King Harald II (Harald Bluetooth) dies after reigning for 35 years and is succeeded by his son Sweyn (Sweyn Forkbeard). The Chola people gain power over the Deccan Plateau in India, and also over the seas round India. Printers in Chengdu, Szechwan, China, succeed in producing the world's first printed book; the *Tripitaka* (the Buddhist scriptures) is printed from 130,000 wooden blocks. The achievement is a landmark in the storage and dispersal of ideas and information.

986 *2 Mar*: Lothair King of the Franks dies, aged 44, and is succeeded by his son Louis V. India is invaded by Subuktigan, the Muslim Sultan of Ghazni. Kazan the Emperor of Japan is tricked into abdicating, aged 18; he becomes a Buddhist priest and is succeeded by his brother Ichijo. Eric the Red establishes a regular colony in Greenland, where he first made landfall four years ago. Czar Samuel, reviving Bulgarian power from his base in Macedonia, defeats Basil II's counter-offensive and begins to rebuild his Empire. Bjarni Herjolfsson discovers the mainland of North America. Sailing from Iceland to Greenland, he is blown to the south of Cape Farewell and sees the coast of Labrador, describing it as 'well-forested with low hills'.

 🗏 Albucasis Abul Kasim: *al-Tasrif* (manual of surgery)

987 *May*: Louis V dies, allegedly poisoned by his mother, at the age of 20. His death ends the Carolingian dynasty; the Capetian dynasty is founded by the 49-year-old Hugh Capet after the Archbishop of Reims declares that the Frankish monarchy is not hereditary but elective and engineers Hugh's election. Anatolia is taken over by the Barons Bardas Phocas and Bardas Skleros, who threaten the power of Emperor Basil II. Grand Duke Vladimir of Kiev sends out envoys to scrutinize the religions of his neighbours. They report that the Muslim Bulgarians are miserable, that the Germans' temples have 'no beauty', and that the ritual of the Orthodox Church in Constantinople is awesome: 'We no longer knew whether we were in heaven or on earth, and we know not how to tell it'.

988 Constantinople is under threat from Bardas Phocas and Bardas Skleros. Grand Duke Vladimir of Kiev is baptized at Kherson in the Crimea, taking the Christian name Basil in the Emperor's honour; he marries the Emperor's sister Anna and begins the mass conversion of Russians to Eastern Orthodoxy. Sabuktigin of Ghazni occupies Kabul and establishes Ghaznivid power there.

989 The Byzantine Emperor Basil II drafts in 6,000 Russian troops to defeat Bardas Phocas at Abydos in Anatolia on 13 *Apr*, bringing the Anatolian threat to Constantinople to an end. Bardas Skleros concedes in the face of superior forces.

990 Forces from Ghana take the Berber town of Awdaghost, which controls the Saharan trade routes, as the kingdom of Ghana makes new gains. The King of Ghana has become the most powerful ruler in non-Islamic Africa, ruling a territory that stretches from the Senegal River to the Niger, south of the Sahara.

991 Battle of Maldon: Norsemen under Olaf overcome an heroic English attempt to stop them invading, and penetrate deep into the interior of England.

992 The first recorded ruler of Poland, Mieszko I of the house of Piast, dies after a reign of over 30 years and is succeeded by Boleslav the Brave. The 25-year-old Boleslav begins an invasion of Pomerania to give Poland access to the Baltic Sea. The Sailendras of Sumatra attack the rival kingdom of Mataram in Java and kill the King of Mataram.

993 Olaf Skutkonung, son of Eric the Conqueror, becomes the first Christian King of Sweden. Khitan Mongols annexe Korea to their expanding Mongol Empire.

994 Boleslav King of Poland conquers eastern Pomerania. The Tomaras found the city of Delhi in India. The Norse King Olaf and the Danish King Sweyn fail in their attempt to capture London but cause much damage throughout southern England. The English pay them to go away but the attacks continue.

995 Basil II incorporates Syria into the Byzantine Empire as his troops take Aleppo and Homs. At about this time Leif Ericsson, the son of Eric the Red, buys Bjarni Herjofsson's ship in Greenland and sets sail for the west, lands on the Labrador coast Bjarni discovered in *986*, and overwinters there.

996 *May*: Otto the Great's grandson is crowned Otto III in Rome. The 16-year-old dreams of reconstructing the Roman Empire and is regarded by his teachers as 'the wonder of the world'. He has already invaded the Italian peninsula and replaced the Pope with his cousin Bruno (Pope Gregory V). Byzantine troops under Basil II recover Greece from the Bulgarians. Samuel King of the Bulgarians is defeated on the Sperchelos River: his supporters are bribed to defect. *14 Oct*: Hugh Capet dies in Paris, aged 58, and is succeeded by his son Robert II.

The (Christian) Duke Geza of the Magyars dies and is succeeded by his son Stephen I. The Copts flee from Muslim Egypt to Ethiopia, fearing persecution. Leif's brother Thorvald sails from Greenland to Vinland (Labrador), intending to set up a colony. He is involved in a skirmish with the natives and is killed by an arrow; his crew spends the winter in North America before returning to Greenland.

997   Samuel Czar of Bulgaria makes attacks on Byzantine Greece; he is defeated and seriously wounded. The war of attrition between Samuel and Basil II continues.

998   Mahmud becomes King of the Ghaznavid people in Afghanistan.

999   In Syria, Basil II defeats an Arab counter-offensive against Antioch and Aleppo. Boleslav King of Poland exploits the chaos in Bohemia by attacking Silesia, Cracow and Moravia. Christians throughout Europe throng the churches, often surrendering jewels and even waggon-loads of belongings in the hope of being in a state of grace on Judgement Day. Many are astonished that the world does not end on 31 December. In fact the millennium ends at the close of the year 1000, not 999.

1000 Olaf I Tryggvesson is killed in a battle with the Kings of Sweden and Denmark; Norway is left without a king and the Danes take over the country. Boleslav King of Poland unites Bohemia and Moravia. Ceylon (Sri Lanka) is invaded by the Cholas under their King Rajaraja the Great. Seljuk Turks occupy Transoxiana, the territory east of the Oxus River. Basil II, the Byzantine Emperor, attempts to conquer Bulgaria again. In North America, the Southern Cult evolves in the lower Mississippi valley. Mexican-influenced, the people make objects of carved shell, metal and pottery showing a preoccupation with death; they focus on such sites as Emerald and Grand Village. The Iroquois people in north-east North America live in villages and cultivate beans and maize. Ethiopia is almost overrun by non-Christian, non-Islamic people from the south. The Polynesians have reached New Zealand in the last stage of the greatest migration and navigational feat in human history. Their ancestors began this migration in about *1500 BC* from the east Indies, reaching Easter Island and Hawaii by about *AD 400*; they are now the most widely dispersed racial group on earth. Churches are built, especially in France and Germany, to express gratitude for the postponement of the Day of Judgement; Duke Stephen I founds the monastery of Gran. The Indian mathematician Sridhara recognizes the importance of the zero. *25 Dec*: Duke Stephen, who has been in power since *997*, is crowned first King of Hungary with regalia sent by Pope Sylvester II.

     Bridge of the Ten Thousand Ages, Foochow (China) (completed)

     Fan K'Uan: Travellers on a Mountain Path

1001 The Mayan civilization in Central America is in retreat; over-use of the land, soil erosion and malnutrition take their toll as the population levels drop.

1002 *23 Jan*: the Holy Roman Emperor Otto III dies of malaria at Paterno, aged 22, while on campaign against the Romans. He is succeeded as King of the Franks and Bavarians by his cousin Duke Henry of Bavaria, who is now 28. The Vizier al-Mansur, chief minister of Caliph Hisham II of Cordova, dies, aged 63; the Caliphate begins to decline without his guidance. The Byzantine armies of Basil II overrun Macedonia, defeating the Bulgarians at Vidin. Ethelred II of England orders a massacre of Danish settlers.

1003 The Danish King Sweyn (Forkbeard) ravages the English coast and exacts tribute in recompense for the massacre last year. Thorfinn Karlsefni leaves Greenland with three ships for a three-year exploration of North America. His attempts at colonization are unsuccessful. *May 12*: Pope Sylvester II, the first French pope, dies.

1004 Zhenzong, the Song Emperor of China, concludes a peace treaty with the Liao empire of the Khitan Mongol nomads, which costs the Chinese 100,000 ounces of silver and 200,000 bolts of silk a year, an extortionate tribute many Song officials find humiliating and offensive. The Lombard King Ardoin is defeated by Henry King of Bavaria, who has himself crowned King of Lombardy at Pavia on *14 May*. Ardoin nevertheless carries on fighting and much of Pavia is destroyed by burning and many of its citizens killed.

1005 Kenneth III King of Scotland dies and is succeeded by Malcolm II.

1006 Muslims settle in northern India. Mount Metrop in Java erupts; the Hindu King Dharmawangs is killed in the eruption and the Temple of Borbudar, the largest temple in South-East Asia, is badly damaged.

1007 Ethelred II King of England pays the Danes for two years free of attacks.

1008 Mahmud of Ghazni defeats Hindu forces at Peshawar as he expands his empire. The Persian writer Al-Hamadhani dies at Harat; he invented the literary form called the *Maqamah*, a cameo short story in rhyming prose.

1009 Egypt's Fatimid Caliph al-Hakim destroys the Church of the Holy Sepulchre in Jerusalem. There are demands across Christian Europe for a crusade to recover the Holy Land from Muslim control.

1010   ✐ Orders of King Rajaraja of Chola: Brihadisvara Temple at Thanjavur, Southern India (61 metres/200 feet high)

   ⬚ Mansur Abu'l-Quasim Firdwasi: *The Book of the Kings* (epic poem)

1011 Ichijo Emperor of Japan dies, aged 31, and is succeeded by his cousin Sanjo.

1012 Ethelred II pays the Danes another huge sum to stop them attacking England. 'Heretics' – Christians professing unorthodox beliefs – are for the first time persecuted in Germany.

1013 The Danes once more attack and conquer England; Ethelred II takes refuge in Normandy. Cordova's Caliph Hisham II dies and is succeeded by Sulaiman al-Mustain.

1014 Henry of Bavaria the German King recognizes Benedict VIII as Pope and is crowned by him as Holy Roman Emperor Henry II on *14 Feb*. *Feb*: the Danish King Sweyn Forkbeard dies suddenly at Gainsborough and is succeeded by his son Canute. Canute, who is 20, returns to the safety of Denmark as Ethelred comes back from Normandy to reclaim his throne. *23 April*: Battle of Clontarf: fighting rages all day between two Irish factions. The victorious Munster army is led by Brian Boru, the 87-year-old High King of Ireland; the other, led by Mael Morda King of Leinster, is aided by the Vikings. Morda himself breaks through Brian Boru's bodyguard and stabs Boru to death. Morda is later tortured to death by the High King's army. Basil II, the Byzantine Emperor, annexes part of Bulgaria and orders that the Bulgarian army is to be blinded.

1015 Olaf II of Norway re-establishes Norwegian independence. Canute returns to England and is recognized as King in Wessex.

📖 Shikibu Murasaki: *The Tale of Genji*
Sei Shonagon: The Pillow-Book of Sei Shonagon

1016 Sanjo, the blind Emperor of Japan, abdicates, aged 40, and is succeeded by Ichijo's eight year-old son Goichijo. *30 Nov*: Ethelred II King of England dies, aged 48, and is succeeded by his son Edmund Ironside, who is chosen King by the people of London; Canute is chosen to succeed by the witan at Southampton. Battle of Ashingdon in Essex: Canute routs Edmund's army but permits him to reign in the south until his death. Edmund dies later in the year, aged 26; Canute rules all England.

1017 Canute divides England into four earldoms for ease of administration.

1018 Battle of Cannae: the Lombards and Normans are defeated by a Byzantine army. The Bulgarians submit to Constantinople, which regains Macedonia. The Polish-German War is ended by the Treaty of Bautzen.

1019 Jaroslav the Wise, Prince of Kiev, begins a long reign during which he will codify Russian law.

1020 Olaf II King of Norway is recognized as King by people living in the Orkneys, Shetlands and Faeroes.

🏛 Bemberg Cathedral

1021 The Byzantine Emperor Basil II sends an army to invade Armenia. An epidemic of St. Vitus' dance sweeps across Europe.

1022 In southern Italy a Byzantine army is defeated by forces of Holy Roman Emperor Henry II. Harold II King of England, son of Earl Godwin, is born. The Synod of Pavia decrees that the higher clergy must be celibate.

🏛 Orders of Michinaga Fujiwara: Hojo Temple

1024 *13 Jul*: the Holy Roman Emperor Henry II dies, aged 51, and is succeeded as German King and Roman Emperor by his son Conrad II. Olaf King of Sweden dies: 110 years of religious wars between Swedes and Goths follow.

1025 Boleslav the Brave makes himself King of Poland, gaining independence from the Holy Roman Empire, but dying within a few months. He leaves a Poland that has become a powerful nation stretching from the Danube to the Baltic Sea. Boleslav's son Mieszko II succeeds him. *15 Dec:* the Byzantine Emperor Basil II dies, aged 69, after reigning for 49 years and is succeeded by his brother, Constantine VIII.

1026 Canute defeats Norwegian and Swedish attempts to take Denmark from him and begins a pilgrimage to Rome. Do-re-mi is introduced into music by Benedictine monk Guido d'Arezzo.

1027 Duke Richard the Good of Normandy dies and is succeeded by his son Robert I (le Diable). William the Conqueror is born, the son of Robert of Normandy. Conrad II is crowned Emperor in the presence of Canute King of England and Denmark and King Rudolf of Burgundy. The Archbishops of Milan and Ravenna cannot agree which of them is to lead the new Emperor to the altar: they exchange insults and punches at the church door. Japan's prime minister Michinaga Fujiwara dies, aged 62. The Mayas of Central America suffer an epidemic that hastens the decline of their civilization.

1028 Canute conquers Norway, which he now rules along with Denmark and England. The Byzantine Emperor Constantine VIII dies, aged 68 and is succeeded by his daughter Zoë; she marries and her new husband becomes co-emperor Romanus III. Sancho III of Navarre conquers Castile; he has also conquered León and proclaims himself King of Spain.

   📖 *Eiga* (Japanese history)

1030 Hakon, the Governor of Norway appointed by Canute, dies: ex-King Olaf of Norway sees this as an opportunity to regain his throne. Olaf is defeated and killed by Canute's much larger army at the Battle of Stikelstad. The Byzantine Emperor Romanus III invades Syria and is defeated in a battle with Muslim emirs. The Ghaznavid ruler of Afghanistan Mahmud dies and is succeeded by his son Masud, who promptly blinds his brother Mohammed. Masud's empire stretches from the Ganges valley to Persia.

≠ Speyer Cathedral (Germany)

📖 Avicenna (Abu Sina): *Canon of Medicine* (major influence on medical thinking)

1031 *10 Jul*: Robert the Pious King of France dies, aged 61, and is succeeded by his 23-year-old son Henri I. The Caliph of Cordova Hisham III is deposed, ending, the Umayyad Caliphate.

1032 *2 Feb*: Rudolph III King of Burgundy dies. He has no heir, so the Holy Roman Emperor Conrad II claims Burgundy and unites it with the Empire. Robert II Duke of Normandy helps Henry of France defeat his mother Constance and bring to an end the civil war in France.

1033 Mieszko II King of Poland is defeated by German and Russian armies. Many in France believe that this year, the millennium of Jesus' death, will bring with it the end of the world; many go on pilgrimages. Castile regains her independence from Navarre.

1034 The Byzantine Express Zoë poisons her husband, Romanus III, and marries the weak Michael IV. Mieszko II King of Poland dies; his death begins a six-year civil war. Bretislav the Restorer ravages Silesia. Malcolm II King of Scotland dies and is succeeded by his grandson Duncan.

1035 Sancho III of Navarre dies, aged 65, having ruled Navarre for 35 years and Castile for eight. The kingdom is divided among his sons and he is succeeded in Castile by his second son, Ferdinand I. *12 Nov*: King Canute dies at Shaftesbury in England, aged 39; his sons are unable to hold England and the Norwegians are able to break away from Denmark: Canute's empire disintegrates. Rajaraja the Great dies after reigning for 50 years and engineering the supremacy of the Cholas in southern India.

1036 Goichijo Emperor of Japan dies, aged 28 and is succeeded by his brother Gosuzaku. Guido d'Arezzo pioneers modern musical notation.

1037   Ferdinand I King of Castile conquers the kingdom of León and makes himself King of León. *Jun 13*: Avicenna (Abu Sina), the great Persian medical scholar and philosopher, dies at Isfahan.

1038   Stephen I King of Hungary dies, aged 61, after reigning for 40 years and is succeeded by his nephew Peter Orseolo.

1039   *4 Jun*: The Holy Roman Emperor Conrad II dies; at Utrecht, aged 49 he is succeeded as German King by his son Henry. An English army is defeated by the Welsh Prince Gruffydd of Gwynedd and Powys.

1040   *17 Mar*: King Harold I of England dies and is succeeded by Harthacnut (or Cnut II), the son of Cnut by Emma. *Jun*: Harthacnut arrives in England with a large fleet and is crowned King. *14 Aug*: Macbeth murders Duncan King of Scotland; Macbeth himself becomes King. The Turks defeat the Ghaznavid ruler Masud; he returns to Ghazni where he is murdered and succeeded by his blind brother Mohammed. Guido d'Arezzo, the music teacher who devised the modern system of musical notation, dies.

1041   Peter Orseolo King of Hungary is driven out by Samuel Aba, a usurper. Henry King of the Germans defeats Bretislav King of Bohemia and forces him to pay homage. Eardwulf of Northumbria is murdered and succeeded by the Danish Siward the Strong. The Byzantine Emperor Michael IV dies and is succeeded by his nephew Michael V. Movable clay type for printing is used at about this time by the Chinese printer Pi Sheng.

1042   Harthacnut King of England dies, aged 23, and is succeeded by the son of Ethelred Evil-Council, the 42-year-old Edward the Confessor. The Byzantine Emperor Michael V imprisons the Express Zoë, but the aristocracy rises against him, locks him up in a monastery and releases Zoë. She marries Constantine IX, whom she takes as co-emperor. The Seljuk Turks rebel against the Byzantines. The Almoravids, Saharans Muslims, invade Morocco in what they see as a 'holy war'.

1043   King Edward the Confessor is crowned at Easter. He has been aided by the rich and powerful Earl Godwin, whose daughter Edith he will shortly marry. Henry III King of the Germans moves to stop Samuel Aba of Hungary, who has invaded eastern Bavaria. In Apulia, power passes to the Norman brothers William and Drogo de Hauteville.

1044   Peter Orseolo of Hungary is restored by Henry III of Germany; Henry gains control over Hungary by winning a great victory at the Battle of Menfo in July. Burma has its beginnings in the kingdom of Pagan; the Burmese and the Mons end their rivalry for control of the territory and, instead, agree to join forces. Koreans complete a great defensive wall across the Korean peninsula to keep out Mongol raiders. Pope Benedict IX is deposed in favour of Sylvester III.

1045   Gosuzaku Emperor of Japan dies, aged 36, and is succeeded by his 16-year-old son Goreizei. Benedict retakes the papal throne by force, then abdicates, selling the papacy to Gregory VI.

⬚ Abu Raiham Mohammed: *Tarikh-ul-Hind* (human geography of India)

1046   The German King forces Gregory VI to abdicate on the grounds of his simony (buying his office) and ratifies the depositions of Sylvester III and Benedict IX. He installs, instead, the Bishop of Bemberg as Clement II. In return, the German King is crowned Holy Roman Emperor Henry III on Christmas Day in Rome by his appointee, Pope Clement II.

1047   Magnus I King of Norway and Denmark dies; he is succeeded in Norway by Harald Haardrade (Harald III) and in Denmark by Sweyn Estrithson (Sweyn II). The Holy Roman Emperor Henry III restores the Duchies of Swabia, Bavaria and Carinthia. Peter Orseolo of Hungary is deposed by his cousin András, who reigns as András I.

1048   The Afghan scholar Abu Raiham Mohammed al-Biruni dies.

1050   The Byzantine Empress Zoë dies, aged 70; her older sister Theodora shares the throne with Constantine IX. Harald III founds the city of Oslo. Anawrahta becomes King of Burma, which makes huge cultural and economic advances under his leadership.

✍ Temple of the Warriors, Chichen Itza, Yucatan
   Temple at Pagan and Shwezigon Pagoda (Burma)

📖 Abu L'Al al-Ma'arri: *Luzumiyyat* (13,000 verse poem, written at about this time)

1052 The Pisans take Sardinia from the Arabs. The Seljuks seize Isfahan.

1053 *23 Jun*: Robert Guiscard the Norseman defeats the papal army raised by Leo IX at Civitate; Pope Leo is captured. Robert takes Benevento from the Byzantines and founds the Norman Empire in southern Italy.

✍ Pisa Cathedral (Italy)

1054 King Macbeth of Scotland is defeated at Dunsinane near Perth by Malcolm, son of Duncan, whom Macbeth murdered. Malcolm is aided by the Danish Siward Earl of Northumberland. Henri I King of France invades Normandy and is defeated at Mortemer. Jaroslav Prince of Kiev dies at Vyshgorod after successfully extending his control as far as the Baltic Sea. The Eastern (Orthodox) and Western (Roman) Churches break apart as Pope Leo IX (the 'antipope' Bruno) excommunicates Michael Cerularius Patriarch of Constantinople and his followers. Leo's war against the Normans in southern Italy ends in defeat and he is captured; he dies on *19 Apr*, aged 51. *5 Jul*: a star in Taurus explodes in a supernova visible by daylight for 23 days and at night for another year and a half; the luminous gas cloud created by this colossal explosion will later be called the Crab Nebula.

1055 Siward the Strong, Earl of Northumberland, dies after helping Malcolm Canmore to the Scottish throne. He is succeeded by Tostig, a son of Earl Godwin of Wessex. The Byzantine Emperor Constantine IX dies, aged 55, leaving his sister-in-law Theodora to rule alone. Turks led by Toghril-Beg enter Baghdad to liberate the Abbasid Caliphate from the Shiites. Toghril-Beg re-establishes Sunni power and makes himself the Caliph's temporal master. Awdaghost (in Mauretania) is captured by Islamic (Almoravid) invaders from the north.

1056 *5 Oct*: the Holy Roman Emperor Henry III dies, aged 38, at Pfalz Bodfeld and is succeeded as German King by his five-year-old son Henry IV, his mother Agnes of Poitou acting as Regent. The blind poet Abu L'Ala al-Ma'arri dies, aged 77, at El-Marra in Syria. The Byzantine Empress Theodora dies, aged 76, ending the Macedonian dynasty; she is succeeded by Michael VI.

1057 The Comnenus dynasty is founded by Isaac I Comnenus, an army officer who is proclaimed Emperor by the rebels who overthrow Michael VI. *15 Aug*: King Macbeth of Scotland is killed by Malcolm Canmore and is succeeded by his stepson Lulach at Lumphanan.

1058 King Lulach of Scotland is killed by Malcolm Canmore, who succeeds as Malcolm III. William of Normandy defeats Godfrey of Anjou at the Battle of Varaville. Grand Duke Casimir I of Poland dies, aged 43, and is succeeded by his son Boleslav II (the Bold).

1059 The Byzantine Emperor Isaac I Comnenus abdicates in favour of an administrator, who reigns as Constantine X. The Treaty of Melfi cements relations between the Papacy and Robert Guiscard, who swears fealty to the Church; he is in return recognized as Duke of Apulia and Sicily, even though Sicily is occupied by Saracens. Nicholas II, the new Pope, restricts the right to participate in future Papal elections to cardinals only.

1060 András I of Hungary is deposed by his brother, who succeeds as Belá I. West Africa is conquered from Ghana by Arabs supported by Berbers greedy for the salt mines of Ankar. *4 Aug*: Henri I King of France dies, aged 52, and is succeeded by his eight-year-old son, Philip I.
🕮 Christ as Ruler of the World (mosaic), Daphni (Greece)

1061 Malcolm III of Scotland invades Northumberland. King Spytihnev of Bohemia dies and is succeeded by Vratislav II. After the Almoravids' successful conquest of the Zanata in Morocco, Yusuf ben Tashfin succeeds to the Moroccan throne.

1062 Anno II Archbishop of Cologne seizes the 11-year-old Henry IV, King of the Germans. In this, the *coup d'état* of Kaiserswerth, Henry is forced to give up power to Anno and Adalbert Archbishop of Bremen. Marrakesh is founded as a tent settlement by Abu Bakr, who then invades Spain.

1064 *9 Jun*: Ferdinand I of Castile takes Coimbra from Portuguese defenders. Solomon, the new King of Hungary, takes Belgrade from the Byzantines. The Turks conquer Armenia. 'Granaries' set up by Ying Zong, the

Chinese Emperor, take surplus grain after harvests and release stocks in times of shortage.

1065 The University of Parma is founded. Ferdinand I of Castile dies after beginning the reconquest of Spain from the Moors; he is succeeded by his son Sancho II. Vikings build a longship at Dublin; it will later be taken across the North Sea and deliberately sunk in a Danish sea inlet.

  ! Westminster Abbey (consecrated) (U.K.)

1066 A comet appears in the skies: it will later be identified as 'Halley's Comet'. *5 Jan*: Edward the Confessor, King of England, dies and is succeeded by his brother-in-law Harold Godwinson Earl of Wessex (Harold II). Harald Haardraade (King Harald III of Norway) is invited by Tostig Earl of Northumberland to come to England and take the throne from Harold; he arrives with a large fleet. *25 Sep*: Harald Haardraade is killed at the Battle of Stamford Bridge, in which Harold II of England successfully defends his throne against the Norwegian invasion and Tostig's treachery. *28 Sep*: Duke William of Normandy arrives at Pevensey Bay (southern England) with a Norman invasion fleet. Harold rides south with his army to meet William. *14 Oct*: Battle of Hastings: the Normans are victorious and Harold is killed. *25 Dec*: William Duke of Normandy is crowned King William I of England in Westminster Abbey.

1067 The Chinese poet Wang An-shih campaigns to reduce corruption in the government administration and the army. The Byzantine Emperor Constantine X Dukas dies, aged 60. His widow succeeds him, marrying a general who co-rules as Romanus IV Diogenes. Boleslav II King of Poland takes Kiev. A Chinese edict maintains a state monopoly of gunpowder. The first leper hospital in the world is founded by the Castilian soldier Ruy Diaz de Bivar, better known as El Cid. Malcolm III King of Scotland marries Margaret, the sister of the Saxon Edgar the Atheling. Margaret takes the Black Rood to Scotland, beginning Scotland's gradual change from the Celtic-Columban rites to Roman Catholic ritual.

1068 Shen Tsung becomes Emperor of China. Goreizei, Emperor of Japan, dies, aged 39, and is succeeded by his brother Gosanjo.

1069 William I of England suppresses a Saxon rebellion in the north; the Normans establish their feudal superiority in a 'harrying of the north', devastating the region between York and Durham. Wang An-shih, now Chinese Prime Minister, reforms his government by raising salaries to make it possible for government officials to afford to be honest.

1070 The Order of the Knights of St. John is founded at Jerusalem by merchants from Amalfi to look after the Hospital of St. John. A Danish fleet that arrived in English waters last year is bribed to go away; the dispersal of the Danes leads to the collapse of Hereward the Wake's Saxon rebellion (in the Fens) against the régime of William the Conqueror.

     ☞ Baptistry, Florence (Italy)

1071 *16 Apr*: Byzantine rule in Italy ends: Bari falls to Robert Guiscard after a long siege. *26 Aug*: Battle of Manzikert: ends Byzantine power in Asia Minor. The Emperor Romanus falls into enemy hands, is released, but is blinded when he tries to regain his throne; he dies shortly after this. Officials at Constantinople select Constantine X's son to succeed, as Michael VII.

     ☞ Cathedral of San Marco, Venice (completed) (Italy)

1072 Sancho of Castile is murdered at the siege of Zamora while fighting against Sancho IV of Navarre. He is succeeded by his brother Alfonso VI, who continues the reconquest of Castile with help from El Cid. Gosanjo Emperor of Japan abdicates because of illness and is succeeded by his 19-year-old son Shirakawa. 10 *Jan*: Palermo falls to Robert Guiscard and his brother Roger.

     ☞ Parma Cathedral (completed) (Italy)

1073 Robert Guiscard's Norman forces take Amalfi from Gisulf of Salerno, angering the new Pope, Gregory VII. Ex-Emperor Gosanjo of Japan dies, aged 39.

1074 The Peace of Gerstungen ends the conflict between Henry IV and the Saxons. Solomon King of Hungary is defeated by his cousin who succeeds as Géza I. Pope Gregory VII excommunicates Robert Guiscard and all married priests.

1075 The Seljuk Turk Malik Shah subdues Syria and Palestine. In New Mexico an earthquake destroys trails up to the top of the Enchanted Mesa; the tribes-people living there are stranded and starve to death. The survivors found a new settlement, Acoma, the Sky City, 5 km/3 miles away; it will become the oldest continuously inhabited town in North America. The Synod of Rome passes decrees against simony (buying and selling church offices). A revolt against Hildebrand's confirmation as Pope gathers, led by German bishops. Pope Gregory VII declares that the Bishop of Rome is absolute sovereign of the Church.

Bayeux Tapestry (depicting the events surrounding the Battle of Hastings)

1076 Kumbi, the capital of Ghana, is plundered by Almoravids, the Muslims who are gradually overrunning West Africa; overgrazing hastens the fall of the Ghana Empire. Henry IV calls the Synod of Worms under pressure from his German bishops; they withdraw their allegiance to Pope Gregory VII and declare him deposed. As a result, Henry IV demands Gregory's abdication. In retaliation, Gregory assembles a Lenten Synod in Rome, suspends and excommunicates rebellious priests and deposes and excommunicates Henry. Political chaos follows. *Oct*: the Diet of Tribor orders Henry to humble himself and stand trial before *27 Feb* next year.

1077 Géza I King of Hungary dies and is succeeded by Belá I's son, Ladislas I. Ladislas supports the Pope and restores order and prosperity in Hungary. The Polish nobility rebel while King Boleslav II is in Russia reinstating one of his relatives on the throne of Kiev; Bishop Stanislas takes the side of the rebels against Boleslav's autocratic rule. *21 Jan*: Henry IV does penance at Canossa and wins absolution. The King presents himself as a penitent after a mid-winter crossing of the Alps with his wife Bertha to avoid a public trial at home. Hildebrand accepts Henry's promises and oaths of contrition. The German nobles elect Rudolf of Swabia as anti-king in Henry's place, with approval from papal legates. The Almoravids (Muslims from the northern Sahara) seize the Ghana Empire, still the richest kingdom in West Africa. This makes the Almoravids wealthier than the sultans they vowed to overthrow 20 years ago A second Almoravid army crosses into Spain.

    ⊞ St. Albans Cathedral (begun) (U.K.)

    Lewes Priory, first Cluniac monastery in England

1078 William I of England is defeated by Philip I of France, who is supporting Robert Curthose, William's son, against Norman-English pressure. The Byzantine Emperor Michael VII abdicates and is succeeded by a soldier chosen by the army, Nicephorus III.

    ⊞ Old Sarum Cathedral (U.K.)

1079 Stanislas Bishop of Cracow excommunicates Boleslav II King of Poland and denounces his excesses. Stanislas joins the conspiracy against the King, who has him assassinated on *9 May* while he is saying Mass in his cathedral. Pope Gregory VII excommunicates Boleslav and Polish rebels have the excuse they need to drive him out of Poland; Boleslav leaves for Hungary and is succeeded by his brother Ladislas I Hermann. Peter Abelard is born near Nantes.

    ⊞ Winchester Cathedral (rebuilding begun) (U.K.)
    Hereford Cathedral (begun) (U.K.)

1080 Rudolf of Swabia is defeated and killed, ending the civil war in the German states. Henry IV, having regained his position, is once again deposed and excommunicated by Pope Gregory, but this time the Pope is deposed by a synod which attempts to install a new Pope.

    ⊞ York Minster (present structure begun) (U.K.)

1081 The Byzantine Emperor Nicephorus III abdicates under duress; a general succeeds as Alexius I Comnenus. Ex-King Boleslav II of Poland dies in exile in Hungary. The German King Henry IV invades Italy; he places Matilda Marchioness of Tuscany under the imperial ban for supporting Gregory VII. Henry accepts the Lombard crown at Pavia and sets up a council to recognize the Archbishop of Ravenna as Pope Clement III.

1082 The German King Henry IV besieges Rome and finally gains entry. He tries but fails to gain a reconciliation with Pope Gregory VII. The Romans agree to call a synod to rule on the dispute between Henry and Gregory. Robert Guiscard defeats the Byzantine forces of Alexius I Comnenus and takes Durazzo.

    ⊞ Rochester Cathedral (completed) U.K.

1083 A synod meets in Rome to resolve the quarrel between

Pope Gregory and the German King Henry IV. The Japanese strongman Yoshiiye Minamoto sets off to suppress a rebellion from the Kiyowara family in North Japan.

🪶 Ely Cathedral (present structure begun) U.K.

📖 Sima Guand: *Comprehensive Mirror for Aid in Government* (chronology of China's history commissioned by the Emperor Ying Zong)

1084 The Synod of Rome declares Pope Gregory deposed and recognizes the anti-pope Clement III. *31 Mar*: Clement crowns Henry. The newly recognized Emperor attacks fortresses still in Gregory's control but withdraws across the Alps as Robert Guiscard's Norman forces advance from southern Italy. The Normans sack Rome. Pope Gregory is unable to remain in Rome; he leaves for Salerno.

📖 Peter Crassus: *Defensio Henrici IV*

1085 *25 May*: Alfonso VI King of Castile takes Toledo; the centre of Arab science and learning falls into Christian hands. Alfonso adopts the title 'Emperor of Toledo'; strategically, the loss of Toledo is disastrous to the Muslims, significantly weakening their power base in Spain. Pope Gregory VII dies on *25 May* (the same day as the fall of Toledo) at Salerno; Henry IV extends the 'Peace of God' over the Holy Roman Empire. *15 Jul*: Robert Guiscard the Norman dies of fever, aged 60, after regaining Corfu; the Duke is succeeded by his brother Roger, who has conquered Sicily.

🎨 The Carrizo Christ (ivory crucifix), León (Spain)

1086 The magnetic compass is pioneered by Shen Kua, the Chinese waterworks director; he sees the needle as pointing south. The Oath of Salisbury makes English vassals directly responsible to the crown, prohibiting them from private wars. The Japanese Emperor Shirakawa abdicates, aged 33, and is succeeded by his seven-year-old son Horikawa. This begins a long sequence of voluntary abdications after which the ex-emperor retains effective power. *23 Oct*: the Almoravid army in Spain defeats Alfonso VI of Castile's army at Zallaka. The Berber leader of the Almoravids, Yusuf ibn Tashfin, sends cartloads of heads of Christians to the chief cities

of Spain and the Maghrib as propaganda for his victory.
📖 *The Great Survey* or '*The Domesday Book*' (an inventory of England's agricultural resources and land ownership)

1087 William I invades the Vexin in France in retaliation for raids on his territory. He burns the town of Mantes, but when he rides out to see the destruction, his horse stumbles on the cinders and William sustains severe internal injuries. He is carried to Rouen, where he dies on *9 Sep*, aged 60. He is succeeded by his third son, William Rufus in England and his eldest son, Robert Curthose, in Normandy. Genoa and Pisa take control of the western Mediterranean from the Arabs. The Byzantine Emperor Alexius I Comnenus is defeated at the Battle of Drystra by Bogomils (heretic peasants) in Thrace and Bulgaria.

1088 In England there is a rebellion in support of Robert Curthose.
⟡ Otranto cathedral (completed) Italy

1089 *28 May*: Lanfranc Archbishop of Canterbury dies; the Archbishopric remains empty for four years. *Jun*: Antioch falls to the Crusaders.
⟡ Worcester Cathedral (begun) U.K.

1090 William II of England wages war on his brother Robert in Normandy.

1091 Malcolm III of Scotland invades England but is horrified at the size of the English army that confronts him, readily agreeing to offer William II homage and acknowledge him as overlord. In the Treaty of Caen, William and Robert agree terms; whichever of them lives the longer will inherit the domains of the other. Duke Roger Guiscard completes his conquest of Sicily and goes on to take Malta.
⟡ Chichester Cathedral (U.K.)

1092 Vratislav II King of Bohemia dies and is succeeded by Bretislav II. The Near Eastern Muslim sect known as the assassins murder the Seljuk Vizier Nizam al-Mulk
⟡ Tewkesbury Abbey (U.K.)

1093 *13 Nov*: Malcolm III and his eldest son Edward are trapped and killed at a place that will be called Malcolm's Cross; his death brings the Scottish invasion of England to an end. Malcolm's widow, Queen Margaret, dies four days later; the new King of Scotland is Donald Bane, Malcolm's brother.

  ✍ Durham Cathedral (U.K.)

1094   *15 Jun*: El Cid takes Valencia after a nine-month siege. He violates all the conditions of surrender by ordering the Cadi ibn Djahhaff burned alive and massacring many of the citizens. El Cid now in effect rules a kingdom that includes most of Murcia and Valencia. The anti-pope Clement III is deposed and Pope Urban II is installed in his place. King Donald Bane of Scotland is deposed in *May* and succeeded by Duncan II, Malcolm's younger son. 12 *Nov*: Duncan II dies and is succeeded by the reinstated Donald Bane.

  ✍ St. Mark's Basilica, Venice (completed)

1095   Ladislas I King of Hungary conquers Dalmatia and Croatia, introducing Catholicism and persecuting non-Christians. He dies suddenly on *29 Jul*, aged 55, as he is about to join the crusade, and is succeeded by his nephew Coloman. The Byzantine Emperor Alexius requests aid against the Seljuk Turks. Pope Urban proclaims the crusade on *27 Nov* at the Synod of Clermont, and excommunicates Philip I of France for adultery. William II of England calls a council at Rockingham to settle a dispute with Anselm Archbishop of Canterbury; to William's consternation, Anselm appeals to Rome, arguing that he cannot be tried by a secular court.

1096   Alexius Comnenus provides food and escort for the Crusaders, exacting an oath of fealty from the leaders in an attempt to protect his rights over any 'lost provinces' of the Greek Empire. More than 30,000 men join the First Crusade, converging on Constantinople. The world's first university is founded at Salerno in Italy. Shirakawa the Japanese Emperor is so distraught at the death of his daughter Teishi that he shaves his head and becomes a Buddhist priest, but he retains his control over secular affairs.

  ✍ Canterbury Cathedral Crypt (U.K.)

1097   Umme, the first King of Kanem-Bornu (Niger and Nigeria), dies after being converted to Islam. King Donald Bane of Scotland is deposed for a second time;

with William II's intervention, he is succeeded by Edgar, a son of Malcolm III. Archbishop Anselm sails from Dover to confer with the Pope, leaving the Canterbury estates in the King's hands. *30 Jun*: Battle of Nicaea: a combined force of Crusaders and Byzantine Greeks take the Seljuk Turks' capital. Walter the Penniless, a French knight, is killed after leading a great crowd of people through Europe in what is called the Peasants' Crusade. The First Crusade has been inspired as much by population pressure as by religious zeal or a desire for plunder.

  🏛 Westminster Hall, London (U.K.)

1098 After a nine-month siege by Bohemund of Otranto, Antioch falls to the Crusaders; so many of Bohemund's men have died that it has not been possible to bury all the corpses. Magnus III King of Norway takes the Orkneys, Hebrides and Isle of Man. Philip I King of France makes his son Louis responsible for resisting attacks instigated by William II of England and William III of Normandy. The Cistercian order of monks is founded at the monastery of Citeaux by Robert de Molesmes and Stephen Harding.

1099 El Cid is defeated by the Almoravids at Cuenca and dies, aged 59; his widow continues to hold Valencia against the Moors. *15 Jul*: Jerusalem falls to the Crusaders. The Crusaders brutally kill 40,000 people (Jews and Muslims) and set fire to mosques and synagogues as the First Crusade comes to an end. A kingdom of Jerusalem is founded under the Norman knight Godfrey de Bouillon: he is elected King and assumes the title Defender of the Holy Sepulchre. Disease and starvation have reduced the number of Crusaders from 300,000 to 60,000; most of the survivors head for home.

1100 *18 Jul*: Godfrey de Bouillon King of Jerusalem dies, aged 39, and is succeeded by his brother Henry Count of Flanders, helped by Tancred Prince of Galilee. *2 Aug*: William II of England is killed, aged 44, by an arrow while hunting in the New Forest. Sir Walter Tyrel, who fired the arrow, flees the country to avoid trial. Also in the hunting party is William's brother, who succeeds him as Henry I and takes possession immediately of the Treasury at Winchester. There is suspicion that William's death may not have been an accident.

1101 Robert Curthose. Duke of Normandy returns from the Crusade and invades England, trying to take the throne from his younger brother Henry, who has assumed the throne in defiance of an agreement made between Robert and William II. Robert is bought off in the Treaty of Alton and he renounces his claim to the English throne. *22 Jun*: Duke Roger I Guiscard of Sicily dies, aged 70, at Mileto in Calabria; he is succeeded by his son, Roger II. The Song Emperor of China Hui Zong ascends the throne, He founds the Imperial Academy of Painting, Hui Zong himself is an accomplished painter.

    ✍ Baptistry, Florence (Italy)

1102 Ladislas I King of Poland abdicates in an effort to secure peace His 16-year-old son Boleslav III (Wrymouth) gains the throne after a violent power struggle with his brother. Coloman I King of Hungary completes his conquest of Dalmatia. Alfonso VI lifts the Almoravids siege of Valencia, which began last year; he empties and burns the city.

1103 Magnus III King of Norway leads an army to invade Ireland but is killed in battle.

1104 Baldwin I King of Jerusalem takes Acre; Raymond of Toulouse takes the port of Byblos. Bohemund of Otranto appears at Epirus with an enormous army raised in Italy to challenge the supremacy of the Byzantine Emperor Alexius Comnenus. Mount Hekla in Iceland erupts violently, devastating farms within a 70-km/45-mile radius; this is the first of 14 eruptions of Hekla in the next 850 years.

1105 The Holy Roman Emperor Henry IV is captured by his 24-year-old son, also called Henry, who declares that he owes his excommunicated father no allegiance. A diet at Mainz forces the Emperor to abdicate, but the conditions of the abdication are broken and the ex-Emperor is imprisoned at Ingelheim.

1106 Henry IV escapes from Ingelheim to Cologne and begins to gather an army to oppose his treacherous son, but he dies on *7 Aug*, aged 54, at Liège. Pope Paschal II refuses to allow Henry a Christian burial because he was excommunicated. He is succeeded by his son as Henry V.

28 Sep: Battle of Tinchebrai: Duke Robert Curthose of Normandy is defeated by Henry I of England. Henry takes Robert home in chains and puts him in the Tower of London; he will remain a prisoner until his death in *1134*.

    ✍ Tiverton Castle (U.K.)

1107 King Edgar of Scotland dies and is succeeded by his brother Alexander I. Horikawa Emperor of Japan dies, aged 28, and is succeeded by his four-year-old son Toba; Toba's grandfather Shirakawa is still the real power in Japan.

    🐍 Renier of Huy: Bronze Font in St Bartélemy church, Liège (Belgium)

1108 Philip I of France dies, aged 56, and is succeeded by his son Louis VI. The Byzantine Emperor Alexius defeats Bohemund of Otranto at Durazzo. In Japan, the Taira and Minamoto clans join forces to punish the warrior monks of the Enryakujj Temple on Mount Hiei near Kyoto.

1109 Boleslav III King of Poland defeats the Pomeranians at the Battle of Naklo and the Germans under Henry V at the Battle of Hundsfeld. King Louis VI of France goes to war against England. Crusaders take Tripoli and Beirut. Alfonso VI King of Castile dies and is succeeded by his daughter Urraca. Anselm Archbishop of Canterbury dies and the Archbishopric is left vacant for five years.

1110 Bretislav II Duke of Bohemia dies and is succeeded by Ladislas I. Henry V invades Italy and concludes an agreement with Pope Paschal II at Sutri. The Pope promises to crown him Emperor and restore his lands to him, including those given by earlier kings to the German church. A miracle play is performed at Dunstable, the earliest known.

    ✍ Tournai Cathedral nave (France)

1111 *12 Feb*: Henry V arrives at St. Peter's, Rome for his coronation. When Pope Paschal reads the treaty terms ordering the clergy to restore the fiefs of the crown to Henry, there is uproar. The Pope is unable to crown Henry, so Henry leaves Rome taking the Pope with him as hostage; the Pope crowns him under duress.

1112 The Portuguese monarchy is founded on the death of

Henry of Burgundy, Count of Portugal. Henry's three-year-old son succeeds him as Afonso Henriques, with his mother Teresa as Regent, and begins a long reign. The Holy Roman Emperor Henry V is excommunicated by the Synod of Vienna.

    ✍ Exeter Cathedral (U.K.)

1113 Pisa conquers the Balearic Islands. Vladimir Monomakh, great-grandson of Vladimir the Great, becomes Grand Duke of Kiev at the age of 60; in addition to campaigning against the Cumans on the steppes, Vladimir writes works describing the conditions of everyday Russian life. The Knights of the Hospital of St. John resolve to fight for the defence of the Holy Land.

    ✍ Hexham Abbey (U.K.)
       Church of St. Nicholas, Novgorod (early example of onion-dome style) (Russia)

    ✧ The Gloucester Candlestick

1114 Toledo withstands an attack by the Almoravids. Coloman King of Hungary dies after conquering Croatia.

1115 A young Burgundian nobleman, Bernard, founds a monastery at Clairvaux. The Jurchan nomads from Manchuria overthrow the Khitan Mongol Liao, who were their overlords, and found the Jin dynasty. Akuta, the Jurchan chieftain, becomes the first emperor of the new Jin state.

    ✧ Christ Pantocrator Mosaic, Daphni (France)

1116 Coloman I King of Hungary dies, aged 44, and is succeeded by Stephen II

1117 Magnus Earl of Orkney (St. Magnus) is murdered on the island of Egilsay in Orkney.

1118 The Byzantine Emperor Alexius I Comnenus dies, aged 70, after ordering the Bogomil leader Basilius burned to death. He is succeeded by his son, John II Comnenus. Toba, the 15-year old Emperor of Japan, takes as his wife Shoshi, the beautiful 17-year-old mistress of his grandfather, ex-Emperor Sirakawa. Shoshi is pregnant with Shirakawa's son Sutoku. Alfonso of Aragon retakes Saragossa from the Almoravid King Ali ibn-Yusuf on *18 Dec* and makes the town his capital. *21 Dec*: Thomas Becket, later Archibishop of Canterbury (St. Thomas), is born in London, the son of a merchant.

1119 Charles le Bon becomes Count of Flanders; he is a son of Canute IV, King of Denmark. Henry I of England defeats the Normans in a skirmish at Bremule and continues to keep his brother Robert in captivity. Pope Gelisarius II, Pope since last year, dies at Cluny. He came to France to escape the acrimonious conflict between the Holy Roman Emperor and the Papacy; he is succeeded by Pope Callixtus II.

1120 Henry I of England makes peace with Louis VI of France, when his only legitimate son, the heir to the English throne, is drowned in the sinking of the *White Ship* off Harfleur in the English Channel. Measurement of latitude and longitude is pioneered by the Anglo-Saxon scientist Welcher of Malvern; in 1092 he observed the solar eclipse and used this observation to calculate the time difference between England and Italy.
         Notre Dame la Grande, Poitiers (France)
         St. Albans Psalter

1121 The Byzantine Emperor John II Comnenus takes southwest Anatolia back from the Turks. The Concordat of Worms condemns Peter Abelard the French theologian for his teachings concerning the nature of the Trinity. Fulbert has Abelard castrated for secretly marrying Fulbert's niece Héloïse. Abelard withdraws to a monastery, where he is joined by Héloïse, a former student: he later founds the Priory of the Paraclete and installs Héloïse as prioress.

1122 The Emperor John II Comnenus and his Byzantine troops wipe out the Patzinak Turks in the Balkans. The Holy Roman Emperor Henry V renounces the right of investiture with ring and crozier at the Pope's persuasion; the Concordat of Worms held in *Sep* also recognizes freedom of election of the clergy. This ends the 50-year dispute between Holy Roman Empire and the Papacy.

1123 The Byzantine Emperor John II defeats Serbian forces in the Balkans. Frederick Barbarossa is born, the son of Duke Frederick of Swabia. The First Lateran Council forbids priests to marry. Shirakawa, ex-Emperor of Japan, imposes a Buddhist-inspired law forbidding the killing of any living thing. The Persian poet and mathematician Omar Khayyam dies is Eastern Persia.

📖 Omar Khayyam: *The Rubaiyat*

1124 Stephen II of Hungary is defeated in battle by the forces of the Byzantine Emperor John II, who supports a claim to the Hungarian throne by Belá, blinded on orders from King Coloman. *27 Apr*: Alexander I King of Scotland dies, aged 46, and is succeeded by his brother David.

✏️ Rochester Cathedral (completed) U.K.

1125 Venetian forces pillage Rhodes, occupy Chios and attack Lesbos and Samos. *23 May*: the Holy Roman Emperor Henry V dies, aged 44, at Utrecht. *30 Aug*: Lothair is chosen King at Mainz with papal support. *13 Sep*: Lothair is crowned at Aix-la-Chapelle. The Almohades conquer Morocco.

🎨 Adoration of the Magi (carved whalebone) (Spain)

📖 William of Malmesbury: *History of the Kings of England* (U.K.)

1126 Lothair III makes his son-in-law Henry the Proud Duke of Bavaria. The Peace of 1126 ends the war between the Byzantine Emperor and the Venetians and Hungarians. The Jin capture Kaifeng, the Song capital, and seize two Song Emperors, Huizong and his son Qinzong. The Song were tricked into paying the Jin protection money, but the Jin came back again and took everything.

✏️ Cathedral of St. James the Great, Compostela (major pilgrimage centre) (Spain)

1127 Roger II of Sicily claims possessions on the Italian mainland, including the overlordship of Capua. The people of Apulia resist attempts to unify them with Sicily and win support from Pope Honorius II, who excommunicates Roger and claims feudal overlordship to Norman possessions in southern Italy. Charles the Good, Count of Flanders, is murdered; Louis VI of France attempts to install Robert Curthose of Normandy as ruler of Flanders, but the Flemish towns themselves (Bruges, Ypres and Ghent) insist on their own candidate, Thierry of Alsace.

1128 Pope Honorius' coalition against Roger of Sicily fails and he invests him as Duke of Apulia at Benevento. Afonso Henriques assumes power in Portugal at the age of 19, rescinding his mother's agreement to accept Castilian overlordship; Afonso defeats Alfonso VII of Castile at the Battle of São Mamede and exiles his mother Teresa.

⌁ David I of Scotland: Holyrood Abbey, Edinburgh (U.K.)

1129 *Sep*: Duke Roger II of Sicily gains recognition as Duke of Apulia at Melfi from the barons who resisted his appointment. Queen Urraca of Castile dies and is succeeded by her son Alfonso VII. Shirakawa, ex-Emperor of Japanese dies, aged 76, on *7 Jul*; his grandson Toba becomes the power behind the Emperor Sutuku.

1130 *13 Feb*: Pope Honorius II dies. Innocent II is elected but an anti-pope, Anacletus II, is also elected and Innocent flees to France. Duke Roger of Sicily supports the anti-pope and is crowned at Palermo by Pope Anacletus, initiating a long war with Bernard of Clairvaux, Innocent's champion. Bernard calls Roger a 'half-heathen king'.

⌘ Last Judgment (sculpture), Autun Cathedral (France)

1132 The Almohad Abd al-Mu'min is recognized as Caliph.

1133 Lothair II, the German King, arrives in Rome with Pope Innocent II to find St. Peter's in the anti-pope's hands; he is crowned by Innocent at the Church of the Lateran, instead, on *4 Jun*.

⌁ Durham Cathedral (completed) (U.K.)

1134 The German House of Brandenburg has its beginnings when the Holy Roman Emperor Lothair II makes Albrecht the Bear head of the Nordmark. Gijimasu, the third ruler of the Hausa city of Kano (northern Nigeria), dies, aged 39, after designing the city's mud-brick defensive walls.

1135 The Holy Roman Emperor Lothair II receives homage from King Eric II of Denmark; the Byzantine Emperor John II implores him to help get rid of Roger II of Sicily. *1 Dec*: Henry I of England dies, aged 67, and is succeeded by his nephew Stephen of Blois, who presses his claim to the throne even though Henry has a daughter, Matilda, the widow of the late Holy Roman Emperor Henry V. Her succession was accepted by the English barons in *1126*. A struggle for the English throne begins.

⌘ Last Judgment (carved typanum), Conques (France)
📖 The Bury *Bible*

1136 In response to last year's appeal from the Byzantine Emperor, the Emperor Lothair II invades southern Italy and takes Apulia from Roger II King of Sicily.

    ⚥ Orders of the Abbé Suger: Church of St. Denis (France)

    📖 Peter Abelard: *Historia Calamitatus Mearum*

1137 *1 Aug*: Louis VI King of France dies, aged 56, and is succeeded by his 16-year-old son, Louis VII. Gruffydd ap Cynan, Prince of North Wales, dies, aged 56; his sons Owen and Cadwallader work to revive Welsh power. Antioch is forced to pay homage to the Byzantine Emperor John II. *4 Dec*: the Holy Roman Emperor Lothair II dies, aged 67, in the Austrian Tyrol while retreating from Italy after a conflict over who should control Apulia.

1138 The House of Hohenstaufen in Swabia begins its century-long domination of the German states when Conrad is chosen German King for the second time on *7 Mar* at Koblenz. Conrad is crowned on *13 Mar* at Aix-la-Chapelle. Bavaria's Henry the Proud refuses to offer allegiance to Conrad and consequently loses Bavaria to Leopold IV, Margrave of Austria. A struggle between 'Ghibellines' (the Hohenstaufens) and 'Guelphs' (Henry's family) ensues. Boleslav III of Poland dies, aged 62; his realm is divided into four principalities. The Battle of the Standard: King David of Scotland is defeated when he invades England in support of the Empress Matilda against King Stephen.

    📖 Geoffrey of Monmouth: *History of the Kings of Britain*

1139 The civil war in England gets under way as the Empress Matilda lands at Arundel in Sussex with an army to support her claim to the throne. The Portuguese gain their independence from the Moors and begin to establish their identity as a sovereign nation. *25 Jul*: Afonso Henriques leads, his Portuguese army to victory over the Moors at the Battle of Ourique. The Igbo people of the lower Niger (West Africa) are making fine bronze castings, the first of several West African cultures to do so. The Igbo are politically disunited, but they have spiritual unity under their religious leader, the Eze Nri. A Lateran

Council settles the Anacletus schism which arose when rival factions of cardinals elected two popes in *1130*.

1140 Sobeslav I of Bohemia dies and is succeeded by Ladislas II. The fortress of Weinsberg is taken from the Welf family ('Guelph') by Conrad III. He lets the women of the town leave, taking as much as they can carry on their backs; each woman comes out carrying on her back a husband, father or son, who escape to safety. *3 Jun*: Peter Abelard is condemned for heresy by the Council of Sens, which is orchestrated by Bernard of Clairvaux (St. Bernard); Abelard sets off for Rome to present his defence.

☐ *Gospel Book of Abbot Wedricus*
Gratian: *Decretum*

1141 *Feb*: King Stephen of England is taken by surprise and captured as he besieges Lincoln Castle. Matilda reigns for six months, then Stephen's supporters buy his release in exchange for the Earl of Gloucester, Matilda's half-brother. Belá II, the blind King of Hungary, dies after taking terrible revenge on his enemies; he is succeeded by Géza II.

1142 Conrad III, the German King, makes peace with the Duke of Saxony, the 13-year-old Henry the Lion, son of Henry the Proud. Henry is confirmed as Duke of Saxony, while the Duchy of Bavaria, taken from his father, is conferred on Conrad's stepbrother Henry Jasomirgott, the Margrave of Austria. The Empress Matilda is driven out of Oxford after Stephen besieges the city; a five-year anarchy begins. Peter Abelard dies, aged 63, on his way to Rome to exonerate himself. His body is given to Héloïse, his wife, for burial.

1143 The Treaty of Zamora obtains Castile's recognition of Portugal's independence. Afonso Henriques is proclaimed King of Portugal and begins a 42-year long reign. The Byzantine Emperor John II dies, aged 55, and is succeeded by his 23-year-old son, Manuel I. Geoffrey of Anjou becomes Duke of Normandy on the news that his father Foulkes le Jeune, King of Jerusalem (*1131–1142*), died last year, aged 51. The Romans assert their political independence of the Pope. In Jerusalem, Foulkes' widow, Queen Melisande, rules alone.

1144 *25 Dec*: Zangi Sultan of Mosul takes Edessa after conquering Muslim northern Syria; this prompts calls for another crusade.

1145 Pope Eugene III is forced out of Rome by Arnold of Brescia, who is a student of Peter Abelard and a great fighter of corruption among the clergy; Arnold was condemned along with Abelard in 1140, and now he turns Rome into a republic modelled on ancient Rome. Almohad forces under Abd al-Mu'min defeat an Almoravid army at Tlemcen. The Almoravid ruler Tasfin ben Ali dies and the Almohads gain support among Berber groups as the Almoravid rulers lose their hold over Spain. Bernard of Clairvaux, now 54, preaches a Second Crusade.

    ✍ Bridge at Ratisbon (over the River Danube)

1146 *14 Sep*: Zangi Sultan of Mosul is murdered. His son, the Sultan Nur ad-Din, consolidates Zangi's conquest of Edessa.

1147 Marrakesh falls to Almohad forces, ending almost a century of Almoravid rule in North Africa and Spain. The Second Crusade begins; 500,000 men assemble under the leadership of Louis VII and Conrad III, but there is no overall command. Many men are lost to starvation, disease and fighting. The diversion of the Second Crusade enables King Roger II of Sicily to seize the Greek islands and pillage Corinth, Thebes and Athens. War begins between Sicily and the Byzantine Empire.

1148 The Byzantine Emperor Manuel I buys Venetian aid to resist Roger II. Returning Crusaders bring back sugar from the Middle East.

1149 The Venetian mercenaries retake Corfu for the Byzantines. *Jun*: Nur ad-Din kills Raymond of Poitiers, the Prince of Antioch, for urging the launching of the Second Crusade to halt Nur ad-Din's progress in the Near East.

    📖 Avenzoar (Abu Mervan ibn Zuh): *Theisir* (medical work, advocates bloodletting as a therapy)

1150 King Sverker of Sweden is deposed and succeeded by Eric IX. Albrecht the Bear inherits Brandenburg. The University of Paris is founded.

   ✐ Angkor Wat (very large funeral temple of the Khmer
King Suryavarman II, centrepiece of his capital)
Orders of Tsaraki dan Gijimasu: City Walls, Kano
(completed)
Wooden dome of the Ulu Mosque, Erzurum
📖 *The Black Book of Carmarthen*
Peter the Lombard: *Sentences*

1151 A Chinese army retakes Beijing from the Tartars. Ghazni
is burned by the princes of Ghur. *7 Sep*: Geoffrey of
Anjou dies, aged 38, and is succeeded by his son Henry,
who is now 18. The first plague and fire insurance policy
is issued in Iceland.

1152 *15 Feb*: the Holy Roman Emperor Conrad III dies at
Bemberg, aged 58, and is succeeded by his nephew
Frederick III, Duke of Swabia; he is of both 'Guelph'
and 'Ghibelline' blood, so it is hoped that he will end the
destructive rivalry that has divided the German states. *9
Mar*: Frederick is crowned at Aix-la-Chapelle. Louis
VII's marriage to Eleanor of Aquitaine is annulled; she
has produced no male heir. She marries Henry Plantagenet, the 19-year-old Count of Anjou and Duke of
Normandy who gains more than half of France by the
marriage. *Mar 31*: Baldwin III, now King of Jerusalem,
lays siege to the citadel of Jerusalem, exiles his mother
and co-ruler, Melisande, to Nablus. Alauddin of Ghur
sacks Ghazni in Afghanistan, driving out the last Ghaznavid ruler and bringing the short-lived Ghaznavid
Empire to an end.

1153 *24 May*: King David I of Scotland dies at Carlisle, aged
69, and is succeeded by his grandson, Malcolm IV, who
is only 12. Baldwin III King of Jerusalem takes Ascalon,
the last remaining Fatimid possession in the Holy Land.
20 Aug: Bernard (St. Bernard) dies at Clairvaux, aged 63:
he was Abbot of Clairvaux since *1115*. King Stephen of
England's son Eustace dies, leading Stephen to recognize
Matilda's son Henry Plantagenet as heir to the English
throne; Henry accordingly does homage to Stephen at
Winchester.

1154 *26 Feb*: King Roger II of Sicily dies in Palermo, aged 60,
and is succeeded by his son William (the Bad). Damascus
surrenders to the Sultan Nu ad-Din of Aleppo. *25 Oct*:

King Stephen of England dies, aged 54, at Dover; he is succeeded by his adopted son Henry Plantagenet, who is crowned at the age of 21. *14 Dec*: Adrian IV (Nicholas Breakspear) is elected the first and only English Pope. Mount Hekla erupts in Iceland.

1155 Arnold of Brescia is placed under an interdict by Pope Adrian IV and forced to leave Rome. He is betrayed by Frederick III (Barbarossa) and hanged in Rome. Pope Adrian gives Ireland to Henry II of England. The Carmelite order of monks is founded by Berthold, a knight from Calabria, on Mount Carmel in the kingdom of Jerusalem.

    📖 *Winchester Psalter* (Psalter of Henry of Blois)
    John of Salisbury: *Entheticus*

1156 Frederick Barbarossa makes Austria a Duchy, giving it special status; he also makes Bohemia an hereditary kingdom. King William of Sicily destroys the Byzantine fleet at Brindisi on *28 May* and recovers Bari from Greeks who have been encouraged to revolt by the Pope. *18 Jun*: William and the Pope come to terms at Benevento and William is confirmed as King. Frederick Barbarossa adds Upper Burgundy to his domain by marriage. The ex-Emperor of Japan, Toba, dies aged 53, during a struggle over the succession. His son Sutoku enlists the help of Tameyoshi Minamoto and Tadamasa Taira; they oppose Sutoku's half-brother Goshirakawa, who is supported by Yoshitomo Minamoto and Kiyomori Taira. Tameyoshi Minamoto is killed by his own son and by Kiyomori Taira. Sutoku fails in his attempt to rule and is exiled. Goshirakawa remains as Emperor.

1157 Frederick Barbarossa invades Poland and forces Duke Boleslav IV to submit. Later, the Diet of Besancon permits Duke Boleslav to call himself 'king'. King Eric IX invades Finland and forces the Finns to become Christians. In Rome, Frederick Barbarossa's army is wiped out by plague. King Alfonso VII of Castile dies, aged 32, in the Sierra Moreno on his way home to Toledo after a campaign against the Almohades, whose power increases. Alfonso's son succeeds him as Sanchez III.

1158 Goshirakawa Emperor of Japan abdicates and is succeeded by his 15-year-old son Nijo, but retains power; he gives Kiyomori Taira a higher status than Yoshitomo Minamoto, and Minamoto is dissatisfied. King Sanchez III dies and is succeeded by his infant son Alfonso VIII. *Jun*: Frederick Barbarossa leaves on a second expedition to Italy, beginning a long struggle with the Pope.

1159 Henry II's Chancellor Thomas Becket, now 41, leads an invasion army into Toulouse to assert the territorial rights of Eleanor of Aquitaine, Henry's wife; Louis VII drives the English army out. Noboyori Fujiwara and Yoshitomo Minamoto depose and imprison the Japanese Emperor Nijo and his father Goshirakawa. The palace revolution is staged while Kiyomori Taira is away from Kyoto visiting the Kumano Shrine. Nijo escapes from the palace disguised as a lady-in-waiting. Kiyomori returns when he hears what has happened, kills Fujiwara and Minamoto and reinstates Nijo. The Arabs retake the lands in Tunisia conquered by King Roger of Sicily.

📖 John of Salisbury: *Policratus* (first medieval political philosophy)

1160 Henry II of England comes to terms with Louis VII of France, but the peace is fragile. Arabs expel the Normans from North Africa. Kiyomori Taira is raised to the nobility by ex-Emperor Goshirakawa. *3 Feb*: the Emperor Frederick Barbarossa commits atrocities at the Italian city of Crema in an attempt to suppress rebellion. Angered by seeing the Cremans dismembering their prisoners on the city walls, he orders his own prisoners, children included, to be tied onto siege engines and hurled at the walls. Once inside the city, Barbarossa destroys it.

📖 Jean Bodel: *Jeu de St. Nicholas*

1162 Barbarossa destroys Milan, dispersing its citizens among four villages. Theobald Archbishop of Canterbury dies. Henry II appoints his chancellor Thomas Becket Archbishop, in spite of Becket's warning that he should not do this; Becket now sees his role as championing the rights of the Church.

1163 Henry II returns from France and begins to quarrel with Becket, who protects clerical privileges at the Council of Woodstock.

☕ Orders of Pantaleo: Tree of Life Mosaic, Otranto Cathedral (Italy)

1164 *13 Jan*: Council of Clarendon: Henry II obtains ratification for a code based on the practice of Henry I, the 'Constitutions of Clarendon'. Thomas Becket, supported by his bishops, rejects the Constitutions because they limit the power and freedom of the Church. The rift between King and Archbishop widens. *6 Oct*: Council of Northampton; this develops into a trial at which Becket is guilty of feudal disobedience. In fear of his life, Becket rides away to Grantham in the middle of the night. *2 Nov*: Becket leaves England in secret and goes into voluntary exile. He persuades Pope Alexander III to condemn the Constitutions. Héloïse dies and is buried beside Peter Abelard. Bones alleged to be those of the three kings who visited the infant Jesus are brought to Cologne Cathedral for veneration.

1165 The Byzantine Emperor Manuel I forms an alliance with Venice against Frederick Barbarossa, who takes an oath in *May* to support the anti-pope Paschal III against Pope Alexander III. *9 Dec*: Malcolm IV King of Scotland dies, aged 24, and is succeeded by his brother William the Lion. Nijo Emperor of Japan abdicates and is succeeded by his infant son Rokujo.

1166 *7 May*: King William I of Sicily dies and is succeeded by his 13-year-old son William II.

☕ Orders of Saladin: Cairo Citadel

☕ Lion Monument (bronze), Brunswick

♫ A monk at Ely: *The Song of Canute*

1167 Frederick Barbarossa enters Rome by force on his fourth Italian expedition. He has the anti-pope Paschal III enthroned, but a sudden outbreak of plague destroys his army and he returns to Germany. Copenhagen is founded by Axel Archbishop of Lund, a soldier who has delivered Denmark from Wendish pirates. Oxford University has its beginnings.

1168 The Japanese Emperor Rokujo is deposed and succeeded by his uncle, the seven-year-old Takakura.

1169 The dispossessed King of Leinster seeks help in recovering his crown. Strongbow, the Earl of Pembroke, invades Ireland with a band of Norman adventurers; this is the beginning of Norman-English rule in Ireland. Saladin becomes Vizier of the Fatimid Caliph of Cairo; as Vizier, Saladin holds more real power than the Caliph, who is mainly a ceremonial figure.

1170   *14 Jun*: Henry II has his son, the young Prince Henry, crowned by Roger Archbishop of York on *14 Jun*. He uses the style 'King of the English' and is even referred to by some chroniclers as 'Henry III'. Thomas Becket is furious that his rights have been violated in this way and persuades Pope Alexander III to suspend Roger of York.
13 Nov: Albrecht the Bear of Brandenburg dies, aged 70.
2 Dec: Thomas Becket returns from exile to Canterbury.
29 Dec: Thomas Becket is murdered in Canterbury Cathedral by four of Henry II's knights, on Henry's orders

🖙 West Front Sculptures, Chartres Cathedral (France)
📖 Chrétien de Troyes: *Le Chevalier à la Charette*

1171   Henry II lands at Waterford to claim Ireland as his own, after Strongbow has installed himself as King of Leinster and roused Henry's suspicions. Benedict, the custodian of Thomas Becket's shrine in the crypt at Canterbury, records 14 miraculous cures among the pilgrims who come to the shrine; a major cult begins. Saladin abolishes the Caliphate, becoming effective sovereign of Egypt.

1172   Henry II of England receives homage at Caskel Rock in Tipperary from Irish princes; Henry is in Ireland partly to escape the criticism of Pope Alexander III for his part in Becket's murder. Henry's wife raises Aquitaine against him and he is forced to make a reconciliation with the Pope. Pierre Valdes, a Lyons moneylender, founds the Waldensian movement, an ascetic Christian sect.

📖 Wace: *Roman de Rou* (chronicle of the Dukes of Normandy)

1173   Henry II of England and Ireland has his wife Eleanor of Aquitaine held prisoner; his sons Henry, Richard and Geoffrey mount a rebellion against him. Thomas Becket is canonized, a further embarrassment to Henry II. Stephen III of Hungary dies and is succeeded by Belá III. Saladin seizes Aden.

1174   Frederick Barbarossa buys Sardinia, Corsica, Spoleto and Tuscany from Henry the Lion's uncle, Welf VI. Nur ad-Din Sultan of Aleppo dies and is succeeded by an 11-year-old boy; the fight for the Regency destabilizes the Muslim world. Amaury King of Jerusalem dies and is succeeded by a 13-year-old leper, Baldwin IV; here, too, a struggle for the Regency follows. Henry II does public penance at Canterbury for Becket's murder.

   ⚜ Bonnano Pisano: Leaning Tower of Pisa (bell tower) (Italy)

   ▯ William FitzStephen: *Life of St. Thomas Becket*

1175 India is invaded by Persians led by the Sultan Mu'izz-ad-din. In Lyons, the ascetic group called the Waldensians cause the Church authorities anxiety. In Central America, the Toltec Empire collapses as neighbouring states, especially Cholula, gradually take over the rich Toltec cotton lands. Saladin gradually welds Egypt and Syria into a single pan-Arab power, with serious implications for the Holy Land in the middle; Saladin plans to take the Holy Land for himself.

   ✎ Virgin and Child (silver-gilt on wood), León (Spain)

1176 *29 May*: Battle of Legnano: the Lombard League defeats Frederick Barbarossa, who is severely wounded. Saladin mounts a campaign to drive the Christians from the Kingdom of Jerusalem. The Welsh found an annual Eisteddfod festival of music, poetry and drama at Cardigan Castle.

1177 Frederick Barbarossa and Pope Alexander III sign the Treaty of Venice, settling a six-year peace between the Lombard League and the Holy Roman Emperor. Henry II of England and Louis VII of France sign the Treaty of Ivry, mediated by Pope Alexander. Saladin is defeated by Baldwin IV of Jerusalem at Ramleh. The Khmer capital Angkor Wat falls to Champa invaders.

1178 *30 Jul*: Frederick Barbarossa is crowned King of Burgundy at Arles.

1179 The Pope forbids the Waldensians to preach without the permission of the bishops.

1180 *18 Sep*: Louis VII dies, aged 59, after reigning for 43 years; he is succeeded by his 15-year-old son Philip II Augustus. *24 Sep*: the Byzantine Emperor Manuel I Comnenus dies, aged 60, after reigning for 37 years.

He is succeeded by his 12-year-old son with his mother Maria as Regent. A rising against Japan's ruling Taira family begins as Kiyomori Taira alienates the imperial family. One revolt is led by an imperial prince, another by Yorimasa Minamoto who is killed by the Taira. A general rising on *17 Aug* is led by Yoritomo Minamoto and his father-in-law Tokimasa Hojo. Takakura, the Emperor, abdicates and is succeeded by his two-year-old son Antoku. The Minamoto army wins a series of victories.

1181 Nicholas of Verdun: Shrine of the Magi (gold and enamel), Cologne Cathedral Germany

1182 Andronicus Comnenus leads a revolt against the Empress Maria of Antioch. This prompts a massacre of Italians. The Emperor Alexius, now 14 years old, is forced to sign a death warrant for his mother's execution. A Constantinople mob proclaim Andronicus Emperor; he co-rules with Alexius as Andronicus I Comnenus. Waldemar the Great King of Denmark dies, aged 51, and is succeeded by his 19-year-old son Canute VI.

1183 The 15-year-old Byzantine Emperor Alexius II Comnenus is strangled by agents of his uncle and Co-emperor, who now assumes sole power. The Peace of Constance ends the conflict between Lombards, Pope and Barbarossa. Saladin conquers Syria, takes Aleppo and becomes Sultan. The Taira clan is driven out of Kyoto by Minamoto warriors led by Yoshinaka. The Minamotos install Gotoba, the three-year-old half-brother of the Emperor Antoku as the new Emperor.

 Saigyo-hosi: *Senzaishu*

1184 The Great Diet of Mainz, a huge medieval pageant organized by Frederick Barbarossa; his two sons are knighted. Cyprus wins her freedom from the Byzantines. The Georgians make the 25-year-old Tamara their Queen; she raises Georgia's prestige and political power to a peak. In Japan, Yoshinkaka, the Minamoto general, is killed by the Taira at the Battle of Ichinotani. Peter Valdes (Waldo) is excommunicated by Pope Lucius III.

 Modena Cathedral (completed) (Italy)

1185 The Japanese Emperor becomes a puppet as the Shoguns (generals) assume power. *24 Apr:* the Minamoto clan defeats the Taira at the Battle of Danoura. The Emperor Antoku is drowned and the imperial sword is lost. The five-year-old Gotoba reigns without real power as Japan enters a long period of civil wars among the feudal lords. A Norman army attacks the Byzantine Empire, taking Durazzo, storming Thessalonica and routing the Greeks. Isaac Angelus, representing the Greek aristocracy, deposes the Byzantine Emperor Andronicus I, who is executed. Isaac becomes Emperor as Isaac II Angelus. A large-scale Bulgarian rebellion begins under the boyars Peter and John Arsen, who win support from the Cumans against extortionate Byzantine revenue agents. Many Greeks in the Balkans will be annihilated in the revolt and much of the region is devastated. Saladin seizes Mosul and begins his conquest of Mesopotamia. Afonso Henriques King of Portugal dies, aged 76, and is succeeded by his son Sancho I. The three largest cities in the world are Kyoto, Cordova and Constantinople.

✍ Orders of Sultan Ali bin Hasan: Mosque at Kilwa (East Africa)

1186   The Kamakura period begins in Japan under the Minamoto clan leader Yoritomo. Frederick Barbarossa stages another spectacle, this time a triple coronation in Milan: he has himself crowned King of Burgundy, his son Henry crowned 'Caesar' and Henry's bride Constance crowned Queen of the Germans. Barbarossa prepares for a Third Crusade as fears for the Holy Land mount.

1187   Provoked by an attack on one of his caravans, Saladin cuts down a group of Templars and Hospitallers at Tiberias in *May*, and defeats a Christian army at the Battle of Hittin on *July. Sep* Saladin besieges Jerusalem, and takes the city on *2 Oct.* The Punjab is conquered by Mohammed of Ghor, who rules at Ghazni

✍ Verona Cathedral (completed) (Italy)

1188   Prince Richard of England pays homage to Philip II of France for the English possessions in France. This homage is offered in Henry II's presence at the Conference of Bonmolins. In the struggle that follows Henry II is overpowered. He escapes but is forced, after a chase to Angers, to concede all Richard's demands, including naming Richard as his successor. Philip III imposes a Saladin tithe to raise money for the Third Crusade, the first tax ever levied in France. The Sultan of Kilwa, Ali bin Hasan, dies after creating a powerful city-state on the Indian Ocean coast of Africa.

   ✍ Pont Saint Benezet, Avignon (the 'Pont d'Avignon' of the French folk song)

1189   *6 Jul*: Henry II dies at Chinon, aged 54, and is succeeded by his son Richard. Richard and Philip II exchange pledges of mutual good faith as they prepare for the Third Crusade. King William II makes peace with the Byzantine Emperor Isaac II Angelus and dies in November, aged 36, as he prepares to join the Crusade. The Japanese Shogun Yoshitsume is attacked and defeated by his brother Yoritomo; Yoshitsume and his family commit suicide. *3 Sep*: Jews are massacred in England at Richard I's coronation. The first paper mill in Christian Europe is established at Herault in France, 38 years after the opening of a mill in Muslim Spain; parchment is still virtually the only writing material in Europe.

   ✍ Monreale Cathedral (Sicily)

1190   *10 Jun*: the Holy Roman Emperor Frederick Barbarossa drowns, aged 67, while crossing or, perhaps, bathing in the River Calycadnus in Cilicia; it is not clear how the accident happened. Barbarossa is succeeded by his son Henry VI. Undeterred by Barbarossa's fate, Philip II prepares to join the Third Crusade. About 500 Jews taking refuge in York Castle are massacred by young men about to leave on the Crusade; attacks on Jews are widespread in England in the run-up to the Crusade.

   ✍ Lincoln Cathedral Choir

   ▯ Maimonides (Moshe ben Maimon): *Guide for the Perplexed* (advice from a rabbi about tactical conversion)

1191   Richard I of England embarks on the Third Crusade but spends a winter quarrelling with Philip II in Sicily. *Mar*: leaves Messina and conquers Cyprus. *Jun*: he joins the siege of Acre and plays a major part in reducing Acre. Philip II falls ill and returns to Paris after concluding an alliance with the new Holy Roman Emperor Henry VI against Richard I, with whom he has quarrelled. Richard meanwhile gains a victory over Saladin at Arsuf and leads the Crusaders to within a few miles of Jerusalem. The Order of Teutonic Knights is founded at Acre. Zen Buddhism is introduced to Japan by Aeisai, a priest returning from China.

1192 Yoritomo Minamoto is appointed Shogun by Emperor Tsuchi; he continues his attempt to crush the Fujiwara clan in northern Japan. The Crusaders follow unreliable and dishonest guides into the desert; famine, disease and desertion reduce their numbers from 100,000 to only 5,000. Richard I makes a truce with Saladin; under it the Christians are allowed to keep the ports they have taken and have unrestricted access to the Holy Sepulchre in Jerusalem. *9 Oct*: Richard I leaves for England in disguise. *20 Dec*: Richard I is captured in Vienna by Leopold of Austria who imprisons him in Durenstein Castle.

1193 Hubert Walter becomes Archbishop of Canterbury. Richard I is handed over to the Holy Roman Emperor Henry VI, who resents the help Richard I and his family have given to that of his rival, Henry the Lion. The Emperor demands from the English a ransom of 130,000 marks for the return of the King. The Aztecs of Central America invade Chichemec territory and conquer the Chichemec people. Indigo dye is imported from India to Britain for dyeing textiles. Saladin, the Sultan of Egypt, dies at Damascus on *4 Mar*, aged 52, and his Empire is divided among his quarrelling relatives. Saladin has briefly united the Muslim world.

1194 Norsemen discover Spitzbergen. In China, the Yellow River makes a spectacular change of course, flowing southwards from the Shandong massif; the river will retain this new course until *1853*. Richard I returns to England following the payment of the first part of the ransom; the Emperor will never be paid in full. Richard remains in England before returning to mainland Europe, leaving the administration in Hubert Walter's hands. Walter has organized the collection of the ransom and suppressed a plot to overthrow Richard by his brother Prince John. Richard's army defeats Philip II's army at Freteval, regaining his French possessions through the Truce of Verneuil. Norman rule in

Italy ends after almost a century as Holy Roman Emperor Henry VI reduces Sicily with help from Genoa and Pisa, ending the reign of King Tancred. Henry is crowned King of Sicily and plans a huge Empire with its base in Italy.

    ✍ Chartres Cathedral France

    ☐ *The Elder Edda* (Scandinavian mythology)

1195 Isaac II Angelus, the Byzantine Emperor, is deposed by his brother Alexius while out hunting; Alexius III Angelus is proclaimed Emperor by his troops. He captures Isaac, has his eyes put out and imprisons him despite Isaac's rescuing him from captivity in Antioch.

1196 Belá III of Hungary dies and is succeeded by his son Emeric. The Holy Roman Emperor Henry VI persuades the diet at Wurzburg to recognize his two-year-old son as King of the Romans.

1197 Henry VI goes to Italy to persuade Pope Celestine III to crown his son Frederick King of the Romans, but the Pope refuses. Henry prepares to set off on a crusade against the Byzantine usurper Alexius III Angelus, but he falls ill while hunting at Messina and dies on *28 Sep*, aged 32. Civil war breaks out in Germany. Henry VI's (Ghibelline) brother Philip of Swabia is supported by Philip II of France. The Guelph Otto of Brunswick is supported by Richard I of England. The Bulgarian revolutionary Peter Arsen is assassinated by rival boyars. His brother Kaloyan Joannitsa becomes Czar of the Bulgarians. Duke Ottakar I of Bohemia, deposed in *1193*, is restored. In India, the great monastery of Nalanda, a centre of Buddhist studies, is destroyed by the Arabs.

    ✍ Orders of Richard I: Château Gaillard (completed)

1198 The new Pope, Innocent III, excommunicates Philip II of France for repudiating his marriage to Ingeborg, the sister of King Canute VI of Denmark. Public opinion forces Philip to effect a reconciliation with the Pope. Ibn Rushd, the great Muslim scientist and philosopher, dies in Marrakesh, aged 78.

1199 The Declaration of Speyer confirms the right of German princes to elect the German king. Yoritomo Minamoto, Shogun of Japan, dies, aged 52; a council of 13 assumes power under Yoritomo's widow Masako and her father Tokimasa Hojo. Richard I of England becomes enmeshed in a dispute with the Vicomte de Limoges, ravages Limousin (central France) and besieges the castle of Chalus. While directing an assault on the castle Richard is shot in the shoulder by a crossbow bolt. *6 Apr:* Richard I dies, aged 32. He is succeeded by his brother John.

🕮 Tomb of Henry II and Eleanor of Aquitaine, Fontevrault (France)

1200 The Peace of Le Goulet ends the conflict between France and England. The Mayan culture of Central America finally dies out. The Mayas' crop yields have dropped spectacularly because of a failure to follow the land and because steep slopes have been unwisely cultivated, leading to rapid soil erosion; the Maya people have not managed their land properly. The city of Cuzco is founded in Peru by the Inca leader Manco Capac. The state of Chimu has grown into an Empire with its capital, Chan Chan near Trujillo, founded according to legend some 300 years ago by Tacayhamo who arrived from the Pacific on a balsa vessel.

🕮 Hell Scroll (Chinese)

📖 Hartmann von Aue: *Der Arme Heinrich* (German epic poem)

1201 The St. Gotthard Pass opens, a route through the Swiss Alps connecting the cantons of Uri and Ticino.

1202 Philip II of France confiscates Anjou, Aquitaine and Poitou from King John of England. John's troops, nevertheless, defeat French forces at Mirabeau. King John's young nephew, Prince Arthur vanishes under mysterious circumstances at Rouen, probably murdered by order of King John to remove a claimant to the English throne. Pope Innocent III offers the command of a Fourth Crusade to Boniface III Count of Montferrat. The Doge of Venice Enrico Dandolo, who is 94, has dissociated himself from earlier crusades because Venice does a great deal of trade with the Arabs, but this time he agrees to provide ships in exchange for half of all the booty and an undertaking from the Crusaders that they first sack Zara on the Dalmatian coast for him. *Nov:* the

Crusaders sack Zara; in consequence, the Pope excommunicates the Fourth Crusade. Court jesters make their first appearance in the royal courts of Europe.

📖 Leonardo Fibonacci: *Liber Abaci* (mathematics, introducing Arabic numerals from North Africa and the zero from India)

1203 *Jul*: crusaders reach Constantinople; the usurper Alexius III takes flight and dies in exile. The Crusaders release the blind Emperor Isaac II Angelus from a dungeon and restore him to the throne, but he has lost his mind and his son Alexius has to rule as Regent. Mohammed of Ghor conquers Upper India. The Almohads begin their conquest of the Balearic Islands. The Bretons rebel against King John of England.

🏛 Temple of Nataraja, Chidambaram (completed) (southern India)

📖 Wolfram von Eschenbach: *Parzival* (German epic romance of the Holy Grail)

1204 The blind Byzantine Emperor Isaac II Angelus is deposed again. General Mourzouphles usurps the throne, has Isaac's son put to death and is proclaimed Emperor as Alexius V Ducas. He tries to defend Constantinople against the Crusaders. *12 Apr*: Constantinople falls to the Crusaders; Alexius is driven out of the city and later arrested in Morea and executed. Pope Innocent III sends Peter of Castelnau and the Abbot of Citeaux to eradicate the Cathar 'heresy' in Languedoc. The whole of Normandy, apart from the Channel Islands, is now in French hands. A new Latin Empire is established at Constantinople with the count of Flanders, Baldwin IX as the first (elected) Emperor, Baldwin I. A Venetian, Thomas Morotinople, becomes Patriarch of Constaninople; the Doge of Venice Enrico Dandolo receives 'a quarter and a half' of the eastern Empire, which expands Venice's sphere of influence. The Empire of Trebizond is founded by Byzantine leaders under Alexius Comnenus at Trebizond in northern Turkey. David Comnenus bases himself at Sinope, Theodore Lascaris in Bithynia, Theodore Mancaphas at Philadelphia, Manuel Maurozomes in the Meander valley, and Leo Gabalas in Rhodes. An independent Greek Empire is founded by Michael Angelos Comnenus, based at Epirus. Thessalonica is sacked by Count Boniface III, leader of the Fourth Crusade; Boniface rules Greece and Macedonia as King of Thessalonica. Emeric I of Hungary dies and is succeeded by his infant son, Ladislas III. Bubonic plague decimates the Crusaders and brings the Fourth Crusade to an end.

1205 Enrico Dandolo the Doge of Venice dies, aged 97. The brother of Emeric I of Hungary dethrones his infant nephew Ladislas III and reigns as András II. King Philip Augustus of France takes Anjou from the English. The Duchy of Athens is founded by the Crusader Othon de la Roche.

1206 Mohammed of Ghor is assassinated after a reign that has established Muslim power in India. His Viceroy Kuthuddin-Aibak, a former slave, takes over Delhi as the first independent Muslim ruler of northern India. Theodore Lascaris, son-in-law of the former Emperor Alexius III, is crowned Emperor at Nicaea. The Uigurs who live on the borders of China are overrun by Mongol forces led by their chief, the 44-year-old Temujin, who is proclaimed Genghis Khan at Karakoram.

1208 *21 Jun*: Philip of Swabia, the German, King, is murdered at Bamberg by Otto of Wittelsbach, Count Palatine of Bavaria, to whom Philip has refused the hand of his daughter Beatrix; Otto is 26 and Beatrix is 10. Otto is chosen to succeed Philip on *11 Nov* at Frankfurt and betrothed to Beatrix. Genghis Khan conquers Turkestan. A vassal of Raymond IV of Toulouse kills Peter of Castelnau on *15 Jan*; Pope Innocent III excommunicates Raymond, who is held responsible for the murder. King John of England objects to the Pope's candidate for Archbishop of Canterbury, so Innocent places England under an interdict on *24 Mar*. Pope Innocent preaches an Albigensian Crusade against the heretic Cathars of Albi and a Waldensian Crusade against the followers of Peter Valdes (or Waldo)

1209 After a siege by the Crusader Simon de Montfort, Earl of Leicester, Carcassonne surrenders. De Montfort captures the Albigensian 'heretics'. Otto of Wittelsbach invades Italy, meets Pope Innocent III at Viterbo and is crowned Emperor on *4 Oct*, as Otto IV. Otto's coronation is followed by fighting between German and Roman soldiers. As a result the Pope asks Otto to leave Roman territory, but Otto refuses to go until he receives compensation for the losses suffered by his troops; then he breaks his treaty with the Pope by taking property Innocent has annexed to the church. *Nov*: Pope Innocent III excommunicates King John of England for continuing to oppose the election of Stephen Langton as Archbishop of Canterbury.

1210 *18 Nov*: Pope Innocent III excommunicates the Holy Roman Emperor Otto IV; Otto, nevertheless, completes his conquest of southern Italy. The Pope approves the foundation of a new religious order, the Friars Minor; there are 12 friars, who have come to Rome in order to gain official approval and recognition with their leader, Francesco Bernardone (Francis of Assisi), who is now 27.
⬜ Gottfried von Strassburg: *Tristan und Isolde* (unfinished German epic poem)

1211 *Mar*: Sancho I King of Portugal dies, aged 57, and is succeeded by his son Afonso II. Genghis Khan invades China. Otto IV is deposed by the German princes.

1212 The German princes elect Frederick, the 17-year-old grandson of Frederick Barbarossa, to succeed as Holy Roman Emperor. Otto returns from Italy to deal with his enemies; Frederick arrives in Germany from Sicily and is crowned at Mainz on *9 Dec*. Earlier, on *16 Jul*, Alfonso VIII of Castile succeeds in breaking the power of the Almohades (Moors); the Battle of Las Navas de Tolosa is a crushing defeat for the Moors and drives them out of Iberia. The Venetians conquer Crete. A Children's Crusade sets out for the Holy Land led by a 12-year-old boy, Stephen of Cloyes, who rides in a decorated cart surrounded by a retinue of young noblemen. Slave dealers kidnap many of the young people before they have even left Marseilles. The Order of the Poor Clares is founded by Clara of Assisi, who is 18, with the help of Francis of Assisi.

1213 *12 Sept*: Battle of Muret: victory for the Crusaders under Simon de Montfort, who has used the Crusade as a pretext for invading Iberia. Pedro II of Aragon is killed resisting de Montfort; Pedro's five-year-old son Jaime I is put into the care of the Knights Templar at the Pope's insistence. Stephen Langton, Archbishop of Canterbury, arrives in England after spending several years out of the country. He absolves King John, who submits to the Pope's will.

1214 *17 Jul*: Battle of Bouvines: the French victory establishes France as a military power, puts Flanders under French control and gains the imperial crown for Frederick II. An anti-Capetian alliance is formed by King John of England, Otto IV, the Counts of Flanders and Boulogne and many other feudal lords from Belgium and Lorraine; the alliance is defeated in the battle by professional cavalrymen fighting for Philip II Augustus. William the Lion King of Scotland dies, aged 71, after reigning for 49 years and is succeeded by his son Alexander II. Genghis Khan and his Mongol horsemen (cavalry again) successfully capture Beijing; the Chinese Emperor has already fled the city.

1215 *Jun*: The Magna Carta limiting the power of the English monarchy is sealed at Runnymede. *Jul*: the German nobles crown the Hohenstaufen King Frederick II at Aix-la-Chapelle. The deposed Emperor, Otto IV, will die in three years' time, leaving Frederick's position undisputed. The Fourth Lateran Council forbids trial by ordeal. The Dominican order of monks is founded by the Spanish priest Dominic, Canon of Osma Cathedral.

1216 *Jan*: French mercenaries land in England to help King John in his struggle against his own barons. *May*: Louis Coeur de Lion, the French Dauphin, lands in England. Barons who last year supported King John now defect to Louis, as do many of John's French mercenaries. Louis is unable to take Windsor or Dover. Eric X Cnutsson, King of Norway, dies. Genghis Khan turns to the west and invades the Near East with 60,000 horsemen, destroying ancient centres of civilization and spoiling irrigation works. *Oct*: King John overcomes the rebellion in the north of England but becomes ill with dysentery. He reaches Newark Castle. *19 Oct*: King John dies at Newark, aged 38, and is succeeded by his nine-year-old son Henry III with William Marshal Earl of Pembroke as Regent. Gaucelm Faydit, the French troubadour who accompanied Richard I of England to the Holy Land, dies, aged about 70.

1217 After being defeated at Lincoln and Sandwich the French troops in England return to France. Afonso o Gordo, King of Portugal, defeats a Moorish army at Alcacer do Sal. Salamanca University is founded by King Alfonso VIII of León; Cambridge University is founded in England. The bakers of Vienna pay homage to Duke Leopold VI as he prepares to leave on a crusade against the Moors: they offer him rolls in the shape of crescents.

1218 *19 May*: the deposed Emperor Otto IV dies, aged 36. Genghis Khan conquers Persia. Pope Innocent III preaches a Fifth Crusade as the Sultan Malik-al-Adil is succeeded by Malik-al-Kamil. Denmark adopts the Danneborg as its flag (the oldest surviving national flag).

1219 *Jan*: the Minamoto clan's control of the Japanese shogunate comes to an end with the assassination of Shogun Sanetomo as he is returning from the shrine at Kamakura. His uncle Yoshitoke Hojo, who has encouraged the assassins, installs Yoritsume Fujiwara as Shogun; the Hojo family will retain real power for the next century.
 ✍ Qutb-ud-Din: Minaret in Delhi (tallest building in Asia completed)

1220 The German King Frederick promises the new Pope Honorius III that he will undertake responsibility for a new crusade, *22 Nov*: the Pope crowns Frederick Holy Roman Emperor. The Dresden Boys' Choir is founded at the Kreuz-Kirche.
 ✍ St. Peter's Cathedral, Geneva (completed) (Switzerland)
 Rock-cut churches, Labilela (Ethiopia)
 Salisbury Cathedral (U.K.)
 🕲 Death of the Virgin (sculpture), Strasbourg Cathedral (France)
 Habbakuk (stained-glass window), Bourges Cathedral (France)

1221 In Japan, the Hojo family exiles the four ex-Emperors to various small islands and installs the four-year-old son of the exiled Juntoka as Emperor. *Jun*: the Hojos depose him, replacing him with the nine-year-old Gohorikawa. Genghis Khan sacks Samarkand on his march west. *6 Aug*: Dominic, the founder of the Dominican religious order, dies at Bologna, aged 51.

1222 The Mongols reach Europe for the first time as Genghis invades Russia. The Council of Oxford establishes *23 Apr* as St. George's Day. The University of Padua has its beginnings.

    ✑ Effigy of Bishop Evrard (bronze), Amiens Cathedral (France)

1223 Battle of the Kalka River: the Mongols under Subutai defeat a Russian army. They do not capitalize on their victory but, instead, retreat into Asia. *Mar*: Afonso II of Portugal dies, aged 36, and is succeeded by his son Sancho II. *14 Jun*: Philip II Augustus King of France dies, aged 57, and is succeeded by his son Louis VIII.

1224 The French take English possessions between the valleys of the Loire and the Garonne. Francis of Assisi has a vision of an angel. The Jodo Shin (True Pure Land) sect is founded by the Japanese theologian Shinran Shonin; this will become the most popular religious sect in Japan, rivalled only by Zen.

    📖 Yaqut ibn 'Abdullah: *Geographical Dictionary*

1225 The manufacture of cotton begins in Spain.

    ✍ Reims Cathedral (France)
    📖 Guillaume de Lorris: *Roman de la Rose*
    🎵 *Carmina Burana* (German drinking songs)
        Sumer is icumen in (round song)

1226 The Teutonic Knights are commissioned to conquer and convert Prussia. *3 Oct*: Francis of Assisi (St. Francis) dies, aged 44. *8 Nov*: King Louis VIII of France dies at Montpensier, aged 39 and is succeeded by his son, the 12-year-old Louis IX.

    📖 Walther von der Vogelwiede: *Kreuzlied*

1227 Genghis Khan dies, aged 65; his Empire is divided among his three sons. A Bavarian knight tours Europe wearing a long blonde wig and a woman's dress; he is Ulrich von Lichtenstein and he claims to be jousting on behalf of his own and all other ladies. Ulrich succeeds in popularizing the sport of jousting, in which role-playing of this kind is common. Henry III declares himself of age, begins personal rule, but continues to be strongly influenced by Hubert de Burgh. *8 Sep*: Frederick II sets sail from Brindisi on a new crusade to the Holy Land, but his army is struck by fever. *11 Sep*: Frederick lands at Otranto out of consideration for his troops, but is suspected of temporizing by Pope Gregory IX. *29 Sep*: Pope Gregory excommunicates Frederick. Frederick spends the rest of the year quarrelling with the Pope. Toshiro, the Japanese potter, returns to Japan after spending four years in China learning porcelain manufacturing techniques; he pioneers manufacturing porcelain in Japan.

    ✍ Beauvais Cathedral (France)
      Toledo Cathedral (Spain)

1228 An army is sent by Pope Gregory IX to invade the lands of Frederick II, whom he now calls a 'non-Christian' King. The Sixth Crusade embarks for the Holy Land under Frederick's leadership. Francis of Assisi is canonized just two years after his death.

    🐛 📖 Yogacara calligraphers: *Doctrine of Stages* (Japan)

1229 *18 Feb*: Frederick II signs a treaty with the Egyptian Sultan Malik-al-Kamil, Saladin's nephew, who is ready to surrender Bethlehem, Nazareth, Jerusalem and an access corridor from the port of Acre for the use of Christian pilgrims. *18 Mar*: Frederick enters Jerusalem and crowns himself King in the Church of the Holy Sepulchre, basing his right to the title on his marriage to Isabella, daughter of the late King John of Jerusalem. *Jun*: Frederick II returns to Italy and easily defeats his enemies there. Aragon conquers the Balearic Islands. At Toulouse the Inquisition forbids laymen to read the *Bible*. The town of Turku is founded by the Finns, who build a cathedral there and declare the new town their capital.

    📖 Thomas of Celano: *First Legend* (sketch of St. Francis)

1230 Ottakar I of Bohemia dies and is succeeded by his son Wenceslas I. *Jul*: the Treaty of San Germano ends the conflict between Pope Gregory IX and Frederick II. *24 Sep*: Alfonso IX of León dies without an heir; León accepts Ferdinand of Castile as its sovereign, uniting the two kingdoms. Berlin is founded on the site of a former Slavic settlement. Crusaders returning from the Holy Land to England bring leprosy with them. Adam de la Halle, the French composer, is born at Arras in northern France.

Orders of Louis IX: Monument to King Dagobert

Bartolomew Anglicus: *On the Properties of Things* (popular encyclopaedia)

1231 The Japanese Shogun forbids his people to sell their children into slavery. Antony of Padua dies, aged 36. Frederick II founds a medical school at Salerno; the curriculum includes three years of logic, five of medicine, one of practice, with a diploma to be awarded at the end of nine years. The school is directed by Nicolaus Praepositus.

1232 The Nasrides dynasty comes to power in Granada with the accession of Mohammed I: he focusses Muslim resistance to the Christian reconquest of Spain. Ezzelino IV comes to power in Verona. Antony of Padua is canonized by Pope Gregory IX.

1233 Henry III of England faces insurrection by his barons, led by the Earl of Pembroke. Mongol forces under the leadership of Subutai capture a Chinese ammunition factory at Bian Qin. Pope Gregory entrusts the work of the Inquisition to the Dominicans.

1234 France annexes Navarre. Pope Gregory IX canonizes Dominic, the founder of the Dominican order.

1235 The Mongols annexe the Qin empire. In West Africa, Malinke warriors led by Sundiata Keita defeat Sosso warriors at Kirina and win their freedom from the Sosso King Samanguru Kante. Sundiata Keita begins to expand his Mali kingdom, annexing parts of Ghana. Hungary's András II dies and is succeeded by his son Belá IV. Surgeons in Salerno dissect human bodies for the first time since the Ptolemaic enlightenment of Alexandria in the 3rd century BC. Frederick II commissions Michael Scot to translate Aristotle from Greek into Latin.

1236 Khwaja Muinuddin Chishti, the founder of the Chishti Sufi order, dies at Ajmir in Rajasthan, aged 97. The Sultan of Delhi, Altamsh, dies; he has enlarged and strengthened the Muslim Empire of northern India, escaped destruction by the Mongol hordes of Genghis Khan and conquered Bengal and Sind. He is succeeded by his daughter Raziya, the first woman to rule in the subcontinent of India. Theodoric of Lucca pioneers anaesthesia; he advocates the application of sponges soaked in a narcotic to patients' noses before operations.

1237 The Mongols use gunpowder and possibly firearms to conquer much of eastern Europe. They devastate Poland, led by general Subutai, who is now 65, and the Khan Ogadai. The Mongols introduce spectacles into Europe. Moscow falls to the Mongols.

1238 The Holy Roman Emperor Frederick II fails in an attempt to take Brescia from the Lombard League. Pope Gregory IX is alarmed at the projected marriage between Frederick's illegitimate son Enzio and the heiress to Sardinia, Adelasia, and makes an alliance with the Lombard League. *28 Sep*: Valencia surrenders to Jaime I King of Aragon. Alexander, now 18, is elevated to the rank of Prince by the city of Novgorod.
    ✍ Orders of Louis IX: Foulque Castle

1239 *20 Mar*: Pope Gregory IX excommunicates Frederick II again, calling him rake, heretic and anti-Christ.

1240 Raziya Sultana of Delhi is assassinated. Alexander Prince of Novgorod wins the name Nevsky on *15 Jul* when he defeats a Swedish army under Birger Jarl on the banks of the Neva River. Mongols of the Golden Horde conquer Kiev. Sundiata Keita and his Mali army take over what remains of the Ghana Empire. Richard of Cornwall and Simon de Montfort lead a new crusade to the Holy Land.

1241 The Battle of Liegnitz in Silesia: victory for the Mongols of the Golden Horde, who destroy an élite force of Teutonic knights, cutting an ear from each corpse and counting the ears later like so many rats' tails. This is the climax of the 18-year Mongol invasion of eastern Europe; there is widespread fear in Europe that the Mongols will not stop until they reach the Atlantic. *22 Aug*: Pope Gregory IX dies, aged 94, as the Holy Roman Emperor Frederick II advances against him. Ships of the new Hanseatic League (Baltic trading community) use new navigational aids, such as the rudder. *Dec*: the Mongol

Khan Ogadai dies in Mongolia; when news of his death
reaches the Golden Horde in Europe they begin to
retreat.

1242   The Holy Roman Emperor Frederick II visits his German realms, which have been threatened by Mongol
invasion. The Mongol Horde withdraws across the
Carpathians and regroups at Sarai on the lower Volga
under the command of Batu, the grandson of Genghis
Khan. *5 Apr*: Battle of Lake Peipus in Livonia: Alexander Nevsky defeats the Teutonic Knights.

1243   A five-year truce is agreed between England and France.
Innocent IV is elected Pope. Famine strikes the German
towns infested by black rats that have come westwards
out of Asia with the Mongols. *26 Jun*: the Seljuk Turkish
army is wiped out in Asia Minor by the Mongols.

1244   The Muslim mercenaries of Pasha Kwarazmi of Egypt
recapture Jerusalem, prompting a call for a Seventh
Crusade. Ceuta, Tlemcen, Mekner and Seville recognize the suzerainty over Tunis of Yahya, the Hafsid
monarch. Rome University is founded.

1245   *27 Jul*: Frederick II is deposed by a council at Lyons
after they find him guilty of sacrilege and suspected
heresy. Fighting breaks out in the German states as
the Pope orders the German nobility to elect a new
King. Sancho II King of Portugal is deposed by Pope
Innocent IV, who offers the throne to Sancho's brother
Afonso III. Louis IX prepares to head a Seventh
Crusade, against his mother's advice.

    📐 Westminster Abbey (rebuilding) (U.K.)

1246   *22 May*: the German electors choose Henry Raspe
Landgrave of Thuringia as their King. *5 Aug*: Henry
Raspe defeats Frederick's 18-year-old son Conrad at the
Battle of Nidda. Conrad enlists the aid of his father-in-
law Otto II, Duke of Bavaria, to drive Henry out of
Thuringia. The last Austrian Babenberg Duke, Freder-
ick II, dies; the deposed German King Frederick II
seizes the vacant Dukedom of Austria.

    📕 Wernher der Gertenaere: *Meier Helmbrecht* (earliest
German peasant romance poem)

1247   Lombard Guelphs take Parma while its imperial garrison
is off guard. Frederick II lays siege to Parma with a large

army. Two Franciscans begin an inquisition in the French diocese of Vienne, prompted by stories that Jews are ritually murdering Christian children; the Pope disowns them. Belá IV of Hungary founds the city of Buda to replace the city of Pest destroyed by the Mongols. Belá populates the new city with German colonists. Siena University is founded. *22 Jul*: John of Plato Carpini, a plump elderly Italian monk, arrives as a Papal Envoy with two other monks at the court of the great Khan Guyuk at Karakorum just in time to witness Guyuk's inauguration. Guyuk is keen to get in touch with the great priest who rules the west and sends John back in *Nov* with a letter to the Pope.

1248 *Feb*: the Lombards besieged at Parma break out while Frederick is off hunting; they ransack the wooden town Frederick has built and named Vittoria in accordance with a prediction by his astrologers. The Genoese take Rhodes. *Aug*: Louis IX of France embarks as leader of the Seventh Crusade, setting sail for Egypt; he is accompanied by his three brothers and the chronicler Jean de Joinville. *23 Nov*: after a two-year siege, Seville surrenders to a Christian army led by Ferdinand III of Castile; Seville's Muslim inhabitants flee to Granada. The Spanish poet Gonzalo de Berco dies, aged 68.

1249 Alexander II of Scotland dies at Kerrera, aged 51, on his way to subdue the Western Isles; he is succeeded by his eight-year-old son Alexander III. Bolognese troops capture and imprison Enzio King of Sardinia, the 24-year-old illegitimate son of the Holy Roman Emperor Frederick II. The Hague becomes the seat of Dutch government; Count Willem II builds a castle there. The Seventh Crusade invades Egypt, takes Damietta, marches on Cairo, but is halted before reaching Mansura. Roger Bacon makes the first known European reference to gunpowder in a letter written at Oxford; Bacon fights to make science part of the curriculum at Oxford University.

☙ Tomb of Siegfried III Archbishop of Mainz, at Mainz

1250 *6 Apr*: Battle of Fariskur: Egyptian forces massacre the Crusaders. Louis IX falls into the hands of the new

Egyptian Caliph Turanshah. *30 Apr*: Turanshah releases Louis IX after he agrees to evacuate Damietta and pay a huge ransom. The Egyptian Caliph advances from Mansura to Fariskur; the Emirs who have raised him to the throne are increasingly troubled by his conduct, and they overthrow him. The Mamelukes rule Egypt for over 250 years. *13 Dec*: The Holy Roman Emperor Frederick II dies at Fierentino, aged 55, after reigning for 38 years. He is succeeded by his son Conrad IV, who is now 22. The Crusaders introduce the Arabic decimal system into Europe.

📖 Vincent of Beauvais: *Speculum naturale, Historiale, doctrinale* (early French encyclopaedia)

Yukinaga Shinanozenji: *Heike* (epic poem about the Taira clan)

1251 Farm workers in northern France rise in a widespread insurrection. They assemble at Arras and Paris. The riots that result meet with ruthless countermeasures.

🏛 Temple of Thirty-Three Spaces, Kyoto (rebuilt)

1252 Ferdinand III of Castile dies, aged 53, and is succeeded by his son Alfonso X. By order of the grand Khan, Alexander Nevsky becomes grand Duke of Vladimir, replacing his own elder brother, Andrew. The new Duke works to prevent any further Mongol invasion. The Ahom kingdom is founded in Assam. The Inquisition uses instruments of torture for the first time.

🏛 Church of St. Francis, Assisi (Italy)

🏛 Ono Coroemon: The Kamakura Daibutsu (12-metre/40-foot statue of the Buddhist deity Amida)

1253 Wenceslas II of Bohemia dies and is succeeded by his son Ottokar II. In Japan, a Buddhist monk called Nichiren preaches a sermon denouncing the traditional sects of Zen and Jodo and establishes a new sect of his own based on the Lotus sutra. The Sorbonne is founded as the first college of the University of Paris by Robert de Sorbon, chaplain to Louis IX.

1254 *21 May*: the German king Conrad IV dies in Italy, aged 26. The election of his two-year-old son Conradin is blocked by papal and German opponents of Conrad and his father, Frederick II. The 19-year Great Interregnum in the Holy Roman Empire begins. King Louis IX of

France returns from Egypt and the Holy Land to restore order among warring factions in France. Henry III of England accepts the Pope's offer of the throne of Sicily.

1255 Sundiata Keita King of Mali dies at Timbuktu. He has made his Empire the largest and richest in Africa south of the Sahara, with gold mines at Bure, copper mines at Takkeda and salt mines at Taghaza. The throne of Sicily is given to Henry III's 10-year-old son Edmund Earl of Lancaster.

   📖 Ulrich von Lichtenstein: *Frauendienst* (autobiographical verse novel) (Germany)

     Thomas of Celano: *Dies Irae* (hymn) (Italy)

1256 Hulegu, brother of Kublai Khan, wipes out the Persian Assassins, brings the Persian Caliphate to an end, and founds the Ilkhan dynasty that will rule Persia until *1349*. Venice and Genoa go to war. Thomas Aquinas, a 31-year-old Italian scholar, is given papal dispensation to receive his Master of Theology degree at Cologne University; normally the university requires Masters of Theology to be at least 34. The monastic order of Augustine Hermits is founded.

1257 Richard of Cornwall, the 48-year-old brother of Henry III of England, is elected King of the Romans.

1258 *17 Jan*: Hulegu Khan of Persia puts to rout the last remaining army of the eastern Abbasid Caliphate. *10 Feb*: Hulegu Khan's Mongols sack Baghdad and massacre tens of thousands of people ending the Caliphate that has ruled from Baghdad since *762*. Hulegu withdraws on hearing the news, that his brother Mangu is dead. *10 Aug*: Conradin's Regent Manfred has himself crowned King on hearing a rumour that Conradin the boy-king of Jerusalem is dead. Manfred refuses to abdicate when it turns out that the rumour is untrue, insisting that Sicily needs a strong ruler. Pope Alexander IV excommunicates him. Mongol invaders ransack Hanoi. A flagellant movement starts up in Europe as a result of widespread famine.

   ✐ La Sainte-Chapelle, Paris (completed) (France)

     Salisbury Cathedral, (completed) (U.K.)

1259 Louis IX of France gives up Limousin and Perigord to England in exchange for renunciation of English claims to Poitou, Maine and Normandy. The Song armies of China make the first known use of firearms propelling bullets; they fend off Mongol invaders with bullets shot from bamboo tubes. The Hanseatic towns (Rostock, Lubeck and Wismar) agree not to let pirates or robbers dispose of stolen goods in their cities. A large-scale unidentified volcanic eruption leaves an acidity layer in the ice at both poles.

1260 In China, the Yuan dynasty is founded by Kublai Khan, now 44 and a grandson of Genghis Khan; he has himself elected by his army at Shant-tu. Kublai Khan has sent an envoy, Hao Jing, to the court of the Song Emperor inviting the Song to acknowledge Kublai Khan as the 'Son of Heaven' in return for a measure of self-rule; the Song rightly suspect this to be a ruse and imprison Hao Jing, but it makes no difference to Kublai Khan's seizure of power in China. The Mamelukes now ruling Egypt save the country from the Mongols at Ain Jalut in Palestine, preserving one of the last refuges of Muslim culture. Hulegu Khan has taken Damascus and Aleppo, but the Mamelukes kill Hulegu's general Ket Buqa, then revive the Caliphate by inviting a descendant of the Abbasid house to Cairo and giving him the title Mustansir l'Jllah. Mansa Ule, King of Mali, whose capital is Timbuktu, sets off on a pilgrimage to Mecca. The Venetian merchants Niccolo and Mateo Polo sail from Constantinople for the Crimean port of Sudak.

    ⁐ Chartres Cathedral (consecrated) (France)
    🛇 Choir Screen, Naumburg Cathedral (Germany)
    Nicola Pisano: Marble Pulpit, Pisa Baptistry (Italy)

1261 *25 Jul*: the Latin Empire ends as Constantinople falls to Alexius Stragopulos leading a Greek army. He takes advantage of the absence of the Venetian fleet to cross the Bosporus and drive out Emperor Baldwin II. The Palaeologi family takes power as Michael VIII Palaeologus restores Byzantine control. Ottokar the Great of Bohemia annexes Styria.

    ⁐ York Minster

1262 Haakon IV of Norway unites Greenland and Iceland with Norway. Alexander Nevsky persuades the Tartars to desist in their demand for Russian military service.

Crusaders in Spain recover Cadiz from the Moors. Pope Urban IV decides to bring Hohenstaufen power in Italy to an end and offers the kingdom of Naples and Sicily to Charles d'Anjou, Louis IX's brother.

1263 A Venetian fleet off the Greek island of Spetsopoula attacks a Genoese convoy of merchantmen and fighting galleys; this leads to a partitioning of sea power in the eastern Mediterranean. Alexander III of Scotland defeats Haakon IV of Norway in a struggle to gain control of the Hebrides; *12 Oct*: the Battle of Largs leaves King Haakon in a hopeless position. Haakon heads for home but dies on the way, aged 59, after reigning for 46 years. Alexander Nevsky, Grand Duke of Vladimir, dies, aged 43.

1264 Henry III of England is at war with his own barons; he is captured in *May* by Simon de Montfort, Earl of Leicester, after being defeated at the Battle of Lewes. Two days after the battle Henry's 25-year-old son Edward also surrenders; de Montfort becomes effective governor of England. De Montfort proposes a new form of government for England, in which a Council of Nine would be appointed to advise the King on his choice of ministers.

   📖 Thomas Aquinas: *Summa Contra Gentiles*
      Roger Bacon: *De Computo Naturali*

1265 Simon de Montfort's Parliament; burgesses are called as representatives of certain boroughs for the first time. Prince Edward escapes from custody, gains support from the lords of the Welsh Marches. *4 Aug*: Battle of Evesham: defeat, death and dismemberment of Simon de Montfort. Pope Clement IV grants Charles d'Anjou all the privileges of a crusade as Charles sails for Rome, narrowly escaping capture by Manfred King of Sicily. He reaches Rome safely and is crowned King of the Two Sicilies.

1266 Dictum of Kenilworth, restoring Henry III of England's full authority. The Isle of Man and the Hebrides are ceded to the Kingdom of Scotland by Norway. *26 Feb*: Charles d'Anjou, King of the Two Sicilies, meets his rival Manfred in battle near Benevento; Manfred is killed in battle, aged 33.

    ✍ Sanjusangendon Temple, Kyoto (completed)

    📖 Roger Bacon: *Opus Maius*

1267 Henry III of England recognizes Llewellyn ap Gruffyd as Prince of Wales by the Treaty of Montgomery. *Nov*: Pope Clement IV excommunicates Conradin for claiming sovereignty over Sicily; Conradin's fleet, nevertheless, defeats Charles d'Anjou's fleet.

    ✍ Kublai Khan: the town of Khanbelig (Beijing)

1268 An earthquake in Asia Minor kills 60,000 people. *Jul*: Conradin is well received by the Romans. *Aug*: his troops are defeated at Tagliacozzo by Charles d'Anjou's army. Charles' agents capture Conradin at Astura: he is tried for treason and beheaded. The execution of the 16-year-old shocks Europe, not least because it has the tacit approval of Pope Clement IV. Henry III of England and Louis IX of France are antagonized; the Germans are estranged from the Roman Church. The Mameluke Sultan Baybars takes Jaffa and Antioch. *29 Nov*: Pope Clement IV dies at Viterbo and will not be replaced until *1276.*

    ✍ Cathedral of Notre Dame, Amiens (completed) (France)

1269 Louis IX of France orders Jews in his country to wear 'the figure of a wheel cut out of purple woollen cloth' sewn onto their clothes, front and back.

1270 Louis IX of France leads an Eighth Crusade, arrives at Carthage and dies of plague on *25 Aug* as his army is reduced by heat and disease. Louis is succeeded by his 25-year-old son Philip III. The German poet and minnesinger Tannhäuser dies, aged 65. In Ethiopia, Yekuno Amlak comes to power, founding the Solomonic dynasty with his capital at Ankober. In Majorca, Raymond Lull is intent on converting Muslims to his version of chivalrous Christianity.

    ✍ Orders of Louis IX: Walls of Carcassonne (France)

1271 Marco Polo, who is now 17, joins his father and uncle as they begin a journey to India and the Far East.

1272 Prince Richard King of the Romans dies, aged 62: he suffered paralysis late last year following the murder of his son Henry of Cornwall by the sons of the late Simon de Montfort. A silk-reeling machine is invented, spurring the use of silk textiles. Philip III's uncle, Alphonse of Poitiers, dies and Languedoc comes under French control. *16 Nov*: Henry III of England dies at Westminster and is succeeded by his eldest son Edward I, although Edward hears of this only later while in Sicily on the Crusade.

 ✎ Orders of Gilbert de Clare: Caerphilly Castle (U.K.)

1273 The Great Interregnum ends on *29 Sep* with the election of the Count of Hapsburg as German King. He vows to lead a new crusade and is thereupon recognized by Pope Gregory X as Holy Roman Emperor. *24 Oct*: Pope Gregory X, crowns the Count of Hapsburg as Emperor Rudolph I at Aix-la-Chapelle. Thomas Aquinas breaks off his work on *Summa Theologica*, which he has been writing since *1267*, with the words, 'Such things have been revealed to me that all I have written seems as straw, and I now await the end of my life'. The Persian poet and Mystic Jalal-al Din Rumi dies, aged 66; he founded the Order of the Dancing Dervishes.

 ✎ Drum Tower, Khanbelig (Beijing)

 🏛 Pietro Cavallini: Mosaics for Church of Santa Maria Maggiore, Rome

 📕 Thomas Aquinas: *Summa Theologica*

1274 *3 Jan*: Thomas Aquinas, the Christian philosopher, dies at the Papal Court in Rome, aged 48. *11 Jul*: Robert Bruce is born at Turnberry, Ayrshire in Scotland. *2 Aug*: Edward I arrives in England. *18 Aug*: Edward I is crowned at Westminster. *Oct*: Kublai Khan sends an invasion fleet to Japan. *19 Oct*: 700 vessels with 28,000 troops begin landings at Hakata Bay in Kyushu equipped with cannons and poisoned arrows. *20 Nov*: a typhoon strikes, sinking over 200 ships of the invasion fleet, drowning 13,000 men; the survivors retreat.

1275 Amsterdam is chartered by Floris IV Count of Holland. Marco Polo enters the service of Kublai Khan.

 ✎ Lichfield Cathedral (U.K.)
  Cathedral of Notre-Dame, Lausanne (completed) (Switzerland)

 📕 William of Saliceto: *Chirurgia* (account of human dissection)
  Moses de León: *Zohar*

1276   Rudolph, the German King, outlaws Ottakar the Great
of Bohemia but when Ottakar submits to Rudolph,
Rudolph allows him to keep Bohemia and Moravia.
The first war between the Welsh and the English begins
as Llewellyn ap Gruffyd refuses to pay homage to
Edward I.
🎵 Adam de la Halle: *Le Jeu de la Feuille*

1277   In England, Roger Bacon is imprisoned for heresy.
Edward I invades North Wales, forcing Llewellyn's
surrender. Bulgaria's Czar Constantine Asen is killed
by a peasant usurper. *30 Jun*: Baybars Sultan of Egypt
dies.

1278   The new German King Rudolph of Hapsburg defeats
Ottokar of Bohemia at Durnkrut on *26 Aug*; Ottokar is
killed, aged 48, and is succeeded by his seven-year-old
son as Wenceslas II. Andorra in the Pyrenees becomes an
autonomous republic. The glass mirror is invented.

1279   Afonso III King of Portugal dies, aged 69, and is
succeeded by his 18-year-old son Diniz. Kublai Khan
overcomes the last Song resistance, reunifying China
under the Yuan dynasty. In England John Pecham
becomes Archbishop of Canterbury.

1280   Marco Polo visits Hangchow and is amazed to find it an
even greater city than Venice, with a population of
900,000 and 'so many pleasures that one fancies oneself
in Paradise'. Kublai Khan summons Egyptian experts to
improve Chinese techniques of refining sugar: the Egyptians have acquired a reputation for making pure white
sugar.

1281   Kublai Khan sends a second invasion fleet to Japan, but
the Japanese are again saved by a typhoon, which
destroys most of the Mongol invasion fleet; only a fifth
of the Mongol and Korean landing-force survives. Khan
Mangu Temir, leader of the Golden Horde, dies at
Astrakhan.
📖 Jean de Meun: *Roman de la Rose* (extended version
of Guillaume Lorris's poem)

1282   The Prince of North Wales, Llewellyn ap Gruffyd, leads
a new rebellion against Edward I of England, but is killed
in a skirmish near Builth Wells. The Sicilian Vespers
rebellion starts in a church near Palermo at vespers on *31*

Mar and leads to a massacre of the French; it triggers a war that lasts for years. Sicilian nobles support the rising against French arrogance and cruelty and persuade Pedro III King of Aragon to claim the Sicilian throne. *Sep*: Pedro arrives in Sicily.

1284 Kublai Khan leads a 500,000 strong Chinese army into Vietnam. Guerillas trained by Tran Hung Dao succeed in virtually annihilating this huge invasion army. *4 Apr*: Alfonso the Wise, King of Castile, dies at Seville, aged 63, and is succeeded by his second son Sancho IV. *25 Apr*: Edward II is born at Caernarvon Castle, the third son of Edward I.

1285 *7 Jan*: Charles I, King of the Two Sicilies, dies at Foggia, aged 58, in the middle of preparations to invade Sicily again. His son Charles the Lame is a prisoner of the King of Aragon. *5 Oct*: Philip III (the Bold) of France dies of plague during his retreat from Gerona and is succeeded by his son Philip IV. The plague that kills the French King has also turned the French army back from Aragon.

   ✏ Last Judgment (carved tympanum), Bourges (France)

   🎭 Adam de la Halle, the Hunchback of Arras: *Le Jeu de Robin et de Marian* (pastoral drama)

1286 *16 Mar*: Alexander III of Scotland falls from his horse on a night ride to see his new Queen at Kinghorn. *19 Mar*: Alexander dies of his injuries, aged 43, after reigning for 35 years. He is succeeded by his infant grand-daughter Margaret, 'Maid of Norway', the daughter of Eric II of Norway. Pedro King of Aragon holds off a French invasion of Catalonia, but dies on *8 Nov*, aged 50, and is succeeded by his son Alfonso III.

1287 Kublai Khan sends an army to invade Burma.

1288 Alfonso III, the new King of Aragon, releases Charles the Lame on condition that Sicily remains in Aragon's possession and that he persuade his cousin Charles of Valois to renounce his claim on the kingdom of Aragon, which has been given to him by Pope Martin IV. The composer Adam de la Halle dies in Naples.

1289 *22 Feb*: Pope Nicholas IV takes office. Charles II (the Lame) meets him at Rieti, where the Pope absolves him of the promises he made to the King of Aragon and crowns him King of the Two Sicilies. The Pope excommunicates Alfonso III; Charles of Valois prepares to take Aragon, helped by Castile. Block printing is employed for the first time in Europe at Ravenna. *29 Apr*: Qala'un the Caliph of Egypt seizes Tripoli on the coast of Asia Minor.

1290 The University of Lisbon is founded. Magnus Ladulos King of Sweden dies, aged 50, and is succeeded by his 10-year-old son Birger III. The Ottoman Empire has its beginnings in an Islamic principality founded by Othman al-Ghazi, chief of the Seljuk Turks. The Khalji Dynasty of Delhi is founded by the Firuz Shah Jalal-uddin, who overthrows the Muslim slave dynasty. *8 Jun*: Beatrice Portinari de'Bardi, Dante's Beatrice, dies, aged 24. *10 Jul*: Cuman rebels murder Ladislas IV of Hungary. He is succeeded by an older kinsman, András III. *26 Sep*: Margaret Queen of Scotland, the 'Maid of Norway', dies at the age of seven in Orkney on her way to marry the six-year-old Edward of Caernarvon, an act which would have united the Crowns of England and Scotland: foul play is suspected. The first Scottish interregnum begins. Edward I of England begins his attempt to rule Scotland. *27 Sep*: an earthquake in Chihli, China kills 100,000 people. *1 Nov*: massacre of Jews at York Castle.

    Giovanni Cimabue: Madonna Enthroned
       William Torel: Tomb of Eleanor of Castile (bronze)
       Eleanor Crosses at Geddington, Hardingstone and
       Waltham (U.K.)

1291 *15 Jul*: Rudolph I the German King dies at Speyer, aged 73; he has been unable to procure his son Albrecht's election as his successor. *1 Aug*: Switzerland has its beginnings in the League of the Three Forest Cantons (Uri, Unterwalden and Schwyz); the league is formed for mutual defence, but independence from Austria is not claimed. Mameluke forces take the port of Acre, ending Christian rule in the East; enthusiasm for crusades is on the wane in Europe and the Knights of St. John of Jerusalem settle in Cyprus. The Venetians move their glass ovens to the island of Murano for fear of setting their city on fire.

    Pietro Cavallini: Apse Mosaics, Santa Maria in

Trastevere (Italy)

1292 *5 May*: Adolf of Nassau is elected King of the Germans.
17 Nov: The first interregnum in Scotland ends; John
Balliol, 43, succeeds to the throne, selected out of 13
competitors by Edward I of England. *30 Nov*: John
Balliol is crowned at Scone after swearing fealty to
Edward I.

1293 The Chinese send an expedition to take Java, and fail.
Florence excludes from its guilds any person not actively
practising a profession; this effectively excludes the
nobility from any share in the city government, creating
factions. *May*: an Anglo-Gascon fleet defeats a larger
Norman-French fleet off the coast of Brittany. Philip IV
of France confiscates Gascony and summons Edward I to
his court, precipitating war between England and
France. *20 May*: an earthquake at Kamakura in Japan
kills 30,000 people.

  Pietro Cavallini: Mosaics, Santa Cecilia in Trastevere, Rome

1294 Roger Bacon, the founder of experimental science, dies.
Edward I of England starts a series of expeditions against
Philip of France in an effort to retake the Gascon
fortresses. Paper money with both Chinese and Arabic
characters is printed and used at Tabriz in Azerbaijan.
Famine strikes England. *12 Feb*: Kublai Khan, the
conqueror and ruler of much of Asia, dies, aged 78,
after reigning for 35 years and establishing the Yuan
dynasty of Chinese Emperors. The death of his favourite
son Zhenjin and his wife Chabi had saddened him and
turned him into a recluse. He is buried in a secret grave in
the Kentai Mountains. The great Khan who founded
Beijing is succeeded by his grandson Timur Oljaitu.

1295 The Model Parliament sits at London, based on the
principle *Quod omnes tangit ab omnibus approbetur* (let
that which touches all be approved by all). John Balliol
King of Scotland ignores Edward I's summons to attend
him and, instead, forms an alliance with Philip IV of
France, prompting the English to invade Scotland.
Sancho King of Castile dies, aged 37, and is succeeded
by his nine-year-old son, Ferdinand IV. Marco Polo
returns to Venice after travelling from *1275* until *1292*

in Kublai Khan's service. The first spectacles are made in Italy, making life easier for scholars and copyists.

    ✍ Arnolfo di Cambio: Church of Santa Croce, Florence (Italy)

    🎨 Giovanni Cimabue: Madonna with St. Francis
        Master Honoré: David and Goliath, in Prayer Book
        of Philip the Fair

    📖 *The Harrowing of Hell* (English miracle play)

1296 Battle of Curzola: Genoese victory over a Venetian fleet. The Genoese capture 7,000 Venetians, among them Marco Polo, who commanded one of the galleys; he is thrown into prison. The Sicilians elect their governor King (Frederick II) after he refuses to give Sicily up to the Pope; Carlos II of Naples attacks, beginning a six-year war. The Marineds capture Morocco's capital from the Berber Almohades. The elderly Turkish ruler of Delhi, Jalal-ud-din, is murdered by his nephew Alaud-din, who usurps his throne. *10 Jul:* John Balliol abdicates, forfeiting the Scottish throne for contumacy. Edward I of England takes the government of Scotland into his own hands in the second Scottish interregnum; he also, in a symbolic act, takes the Stone of Destiny from the Abbey at Scone to Westminster Abbey. Balliol is imprisoned.

1297 The Confirmation of Charters reaffirms the English Magna Carta of *1215*. English barons angered by the loss of Gascony and middle class groups angered by rising taxes force Edward I to reaffirm the great charter and to agree not to levy taxes without a grant from Parliament. The giant moas become extinct in New Zealand. *22 Aug:* Edward I sails for Flanders. *11 Sep:* Battle of Stirling Bridge: Scots troops under William Wallace defeat the English. The Burmese become vassals of the Chinese Mongol.

1298 The invention of the spinning wheel revolutionizes textile production. Jacobus de Varagine, Archibishop of Genoa, dies aged 68, after completing his chronicle of Genoa up to the year *1296*. *2 Jul:* Battle of Gollheim near Worms: the German King Adolf of Nassau is deposed and killed by his own electors. His rival, Albrecht of Austria, succeeds as Albrecht I. *22 Jul:*

Battle of Falkirk: Edward I's troops defeat those of William Wallace showing the power of the English longbow for the first time.

   ✐ Arnolfo di Cambio: Palazzo Vecchio, Florence (Italy)

   📖 Jacobus de Varagine: *The Golden Legend*

1299 Pope Boniface VIII persuades Edward I of England to release John Balliol and his son Edward from captivity and allow them to settle in France.

   📖 Marco Polo: *Book of Various Experiences*

1300 The first brandy is distilled at Montpellier by Professor Arnaud de Villeneuve. The papacy reaches its zenith as Pope Boniface VIII holds a jubilee to mark the beginning of a new century (although it does not actually begin until 1301): enormous revenues are generated by the 'pilgrim industry' and used for the subjugation of Sicily. The Hanseatic League is strengthened by a network of trading agreements among towns on the Baltic Sea and German estuaries. *13 Apr*: The composer Guillaume de Machaut is born. *29 Aug*: The poet Guido Cavalcanti dies in Florence, aged 45.

1301 The death of András III of Hungary brings the Arpád dynasty to an end. A civil war begins. The Ottoman Osman defeats a Byzantine army at Baphaion.

   ✐ Coronation Chair, Westminster Abbey (U.K.)

1302 The Black Guelphs (the Neri) triumph in Florence and drive out the White Guelphs (Bianchi), Dante the poet among them. The Estates-General of France is convened for the first time; representatives of the towns meet to show support for King Philip in his struggle against the Pope. *11 July*: Battle of the Spurs at Courtrai in Flanders; Guy de Dampierre leads Flemish burghers agaisnt the French and defeats them.

   ✐ Zhao Mengfu: Water Village

   📖 John of Paris: *De Potestate Regia et Papali* (defends authority of the king)

1303 The Universities of Rome and Avignon are founded. France returns Gascony to Edward I of England. Philip the Fair of France sends Guillaume de Nogaret to capture Pope Boniface and take him back to France to face trial. *8 Sep*: Nogaret and Sciarra Colonna enter the papal apartment, find Boniface in bed, threaten to kill him, and take him prisoner, Nogaret and Colonna are forced to make their escape, but the Pope is taken to Rome and confined there by the Orsini family. *Oct*: Pope Boniface dies humiliated in the Vatican.

    ⌂ Glastonbury Abbey (largely rebuilt) (U.K.)

1304 Ilkhan Ghazan, the Mongol ruler of Persia, dies and is succeeded by his brother Uljaitu. The 18-year-old Franciscan missionary Oderico da Pordenone sets out to retrace Marco Polo's journey to China.

    ⌂ Giotto di Bondone: Arena Chapel, Padua (Italy)

1305 Raimond de Got is elected Pope, as Clement V. Wenceslas II of Poland abdicates and dies, aged 34; he is succeeded by his son Wenceslas III. *3 Aug*: the Scots patriot and army commander William Wallace is surprised in his sleep by Sir John Menteith and 60 men who take him prisoner. Wallace is given a show trial. He protests that he cannot be a traitor because he has never been a subject of the English Crown. *23 Aug*: Wallace is executed in London.

    ✍ Giotto di Bondone: The Life of Christ; Last Judgment; Pietà

    Giovanni Pisano: Madonna and Child (sculpture)

    📖 Pietro Crescenzi: *Opus Ruralium Commodorum* (book on agriculture)

1306 The murder of Wenceslas III of Bohemia at the age of 17 is followed by an interregnum. Wenceslas is succeeded in Poland by the former King of the principality of Great Poland, Ladislas IV. The Knights of St. John of Jerusalem purchase Rhodes. France arrests, robs and expels her Jews. England also expels some 100,000 Jews.

    ✍ Giotto di Bondone: The Lamentation; Christ Entering Jerusalem

1307 Philip IV of France seizes the property of the Knights Templar, who have turned their order into a state within the state. Roger di Flor, a German soldier-adventurer, leads 6,000 Catalan mercenaries in an attack on Constantinople; the attack fails and Roger is assassinated on the orders of Emperor Andronicus II and his son and co-emperor Michael IX. *7 Jul*: Edward I of England dies at Burgh-on-Sands near Carlisle during a march north into

Scotland to engage Robert Bruce. *8 Jul*: Edward I is succeeded by his son Edward II. Piers Gaveston, previously banished by Edward I, is recalled by Edward and created Earl of Cornwall.

📖 Dante Alighieri: *The Divine Comedy* (including *Inferno*, *Purgatorio* and *Paradiso*) (work begun on this poetic imaginary journey through Hell, Purgatory and Paradise in the year *1300*)

1308 The French step up their attacks on the Knights Templar. With Pope Clement V's approval, torture is used to extract incriminating confessions. *10 Jan*: the Templars are suppressed in Britain. *25 Jan*: Edward II of England marries Isabella, daughter of Philip IV of France; while Edward is in France, the Earl of Cornwall is regent. *25 Feb*: Coronation of Edward II. *Mar*: in Parliament the English earls demand that the King banish Gaveston, who leaves for the Lieutenancy of Ireland. *1 May*: Albrecht I of Austria refuses demands from his nephew John for John's hereditary domains; Albrecht is murdered at the 18-year-old John's orders and is succeeded by the Count of Luxembourg, Henry VII.

1309 Robert Bruce holds his first Parliament at St. Andrews in Scotland. *9 Mar*: the 'Babylonian Exile' of the papacy begins; Clement V moves the papal court to Avignon at the request of his friend Philip of France.

🏛 Doge's Palace, Venice (begun) Italy

1310 The English Parliament appoints Lords Ordainers (21 peers) to reform government and regulate the King's household: another attempt to limit the power of Gaveston. Venice establishes a Council of Ten to rule the city.

1311 Robert Bruce leads the Scots in raids across the border into England. The English Parliament confirms that baronial consent to any royal appointment is required.

🏛 Notre Dame Cathedral, Reims (completed) France
🎨 Giovanni Pisano: Pulpit, Pisa Cathedral (completed) (Italy)

Duccio di Buoninsegna: Christ Entering Jerusalem

1312 The Knights Templar are abolished in France. Piers Gaveston, Edward II's favourite, is kidnapped by the Earl of Warwick and murdered; Edward II is forced to stand aside and let the Lords Ordainers rule. Lyons is incorporated into France under the Treaty of Vienne. French mariners rediscover the Canary Islands. Ala-u-din's army conquers the Indian Deccan.

1313 *Apr*: John Balliol, ex-king of Scotland, dies. *24 Aug*: the Holy Roman Emperor Henry VII dies near Siena, aged 44. John, the nephew of Albrecht I of Austria, is executed for his uncle's murder.

  📖 Dante Alighieri: *De monarchia*

1314 *Mar*: Jacques de Molay, the 71-year-old Grand Master of the French Knights Templar, is taken before the Inquisition in Paris, found guilty of heresy and burned at the stake. *24 Jun*: Battle of Bannockburn: Robert Bruce's army defeats Edward II's much larger army. Edward escapes only with difficulty from the battlefield and sails to Berwick; the independence of Scotland is assured. *25 Nov*: Louis of Bavaria is crowned King of the Germans at Aix-la-Chapelle. Louis is opposed by Duke Frederick of Austria, who is chosen by a minority of the electors and begins a lengthy civil war with Louis. *29 Nov*: Philip IV of France dies, aged 69, and is succeeded by his 25-year-old son Jean of Navarre, King of Navarre since 1305; he reigns briefly as Louis X of France.

  🏛 St. Paul's Cathedral, London (completed) (U.K.)

1315 Famine affects large areas of western Europe and will continue for the next three years. The Italian surgeon Mondino de Luzzi carries out the first public scientific dissection of a human body.

  🎨 Giovanni Pisano: Madonna (marble statue) in Prato Cathedral

1316 Lithuania's Prince Witen dies and is succeeded by his brother Gedymin. The domain is controlled largely by the Teutonic Knights and the Livonian Knights of the Sword. Dominican monks are sent to Ethiopia by Pope John XXII to search for a legendary Christian King named Prester John *5 Jun*: Louis X of France dies suddenly, aged 26; his brother, who is 22, succeeds as Philip V.

1317 France adopts the Salic Law, which excludes women from succeeding to the throne.

1318 The army of the Sultan of Delhi conquers the kingdom of Maharashtra in the central Deccan. The German poet Heinrich Frauenlob von Meissen dies, aged 68; he founded a school of meistersingers at Mainz and his nickname, 'Frauenlob' (praise of women), arose because he preferred to use the word *Frau* (woman) instead of *Weib* (wife). The Scots take Berwick and threaten to conquer the whole of England.

1319   Truce between Scotland and England.

1320   The Peace of Paris ends the conflict between France and Flanders, which keeps its independence. Ladislas IV of Poland is finally crowned, 14 years after taking power. The Muslim Tughlak dynasty of western India is founded by the Turkish Shah Ghiyas-ud-din Tughlak; as Gharzi Khan he moves his capital 6 km/4 miles east of Delhi to the new city of Tughlakabad. *6 Apr*: the Declaration of Arbroath by the Scottish Parliament asserts Scottish independence from England. Hugh Despenser and his son rise in favour at Edward II's court.

    Pietro Cavallini: Frescoes for the Church of Santa Maria Donnaregina

    The 'Pearl Poet': *Sir Gawain and the Green Knight*

1321   The University of Florence is founded. *Jan*: the Despensers defend their castles. *Apr*: Civil war breaks out in England. *24 May*: the Earl of Lancaster calls an assembly of the chief barons of northern England; they promise to act together to preserve the peace and defend the realm. *19 Aug*: Parliament formally judges the Despensers and sentences them to total forfeiture and banishment. *14 Sep*: Dante Alighieri dies, aged 56, at Ravenna in the 20th year of his exile from Florence.

    Dante Alighieri: *De Vulgari Eloquentia* (unfinished study of the Italian vernacular)

1322   The great Chinese artist and calligrapher Zhao Mengfu dies, aged 68. The English-Scottish truce expires, and Scots cross the border to raid England as far south as Preston. *2 Jan*: Philip V of France dies at Longchamp, aged 28, and is succeeded by his brother Charles IV. *Feb*: Thomas Earl, of Lancaster is denounced as a rebel. *16 Mar*: Edward II defeats his opponents at Boroughbridge. *22 Mar*: Edward II orders the summary execution of the Earl of Lancaster at Pontefract. This is the first time in England that a summary sentence of death and forfeiture for high treason has ever been passed on a peer of the realm. *2 May*: Statute of York, revoking the earlier Ordinances. Edward II creates Hugh le Despenser Earl of Winchester. *28 Sep*: Battle of Muhldorf: the German King Louis IV is victorious and Frederic Duke of Austria is taken prisoner.

    ≐ Alan of Walsingham: Octagon Lantern, Ely Cathedral (U.K.)

1323 Pope John XXII canonizes Thomas Aquinas. *30 May*: the Treaty of Northampton is a recognition of Robert Bruce's title to the throne of Scotland.

1324 Godaigo Emperor of Japan tries unsuccessfully to regain power from the Regent Tatatoki Hojo. Godaigo is betrayed but denies everything.

    ≐ York Minster (completed) (U.K.)

    ☐ Marsilius of Padua and John of Jandun: *Defensor Pacis* (a treatise against the popes' temporal power)

1325 Amir Khusrau, writer, composer and poet to six sultans of Delhi, dies, aged 95; he has become known as 'the Parrot of India'. Queen Isabella, Edward II of England's wife, crosses to France on the pretext of arranging the marriage of her son, the 12-year-old Edward, to Philippa of Hainault, who is 11. Once there, she refuses to return to Edward's court unless he will get rid of the Despensers. The German King Louis of Bavaria accepts Frederick of Austria as co-regent, but joint rule proves a failure. Ghiyas-ud-din Tughlak, Sultan of Delhi is murdered and succeeded by his son, Mohammed Tughlak. In Central America, the Aztec Empire emerges as the culmination of a history that has seen the evolution of the Olmec, Teotihuacan and Toltec cultures.

1326 *6 Apr*: Brusa, the capital of Bithynia, surrenders to an Ottoman army after a siege lasting nine years. The first Ottoman Emir Osman I dies, aged 67, and is succeeded by his son Orkhan I. *25 Sep*: Queen Isabella, Roger Mortimer and Prince Edward land at Orwell in Suffolk and assume royal power. The Despensers are captured and hanged. *26 Oct*: Prince Edward, Edward II of England's son, is proclaimed Keeper of the Realm. *16*

Nov: Isabella's men capture Edward II and imprison him in Kenilworth Castle.

1327 The Treaty of Corbeil re-establishes the 'auld alliance' between France and Scotland. Much of the city of Munich is destroyed by fire. *13 Jan*: a group of bishops and magnates takes an oath at the Guildhall in London to uphold the Queen's cause. *15 Jan*: the Archbishop of Canterbury announces in Westminster Hall that the King is deposed. *16 Jan*: Edward II of England is kept as a prisoner. *20 Jan*: Edward II agrees to abdicate. *25 Jan*: Edward III, Edward II's son, becomes King of England. *Mar*: Meister Eckhart, the German Dominican mystic, dies at Avignon. *21 Sep*: ex-King Edward II of England is secretly murdered in Berkeley Castle on Roger Mortimer's orders.

1328 *17 Jan*: the German King Louis of Bavaria is crowned Holy Roman Emperor by Sciarra Colonna in Rome after forcing the surrender of Pisa. The Emperor proclaims the deposition of the Pope and launches an expedition against Robert of Naples, the Pope's ally. *24 Jan*: Edward III of England marries Philippa of Hainault. *1 Feb*: Charles IV of France dies, aged 33; his death marks the end of the direct line of succession from Charlemagne. Charles is succeeded by his cousin Philip VI (Valois dynasty)

1329 Edward III crosses the Channel to Amiens to pay homage to Philip IV of France. *7 Jun*: Robert Bruce, King of Scotland, dies of leprosy at Cardross Castle and is succeeded by his five-year-old son David II.

1330 The Hapsburgs recognize Louis IV of Bavaria as Holy Roman Emperor on the death of Frederick of Austria. William of Occam, English scholar and philosopher, appeals to scientists and other scholars to give preference to simple solutions wherever possible; his exhortation becomes known as 'Occam's Razor'. *15 Jun*: Edward of Woodstock, the Black Prince, is born. *19 Oct*: the 18-year-old Edward III enters Nottingham Castle by an underground passage and surprises and arrests Roger Mortimer. *20 Oct*: Edward III takes the reins of England's government, assuming personal rule for the first time since his accession. Edward keeps his mother

Isabella imprisoned at Castle Rising in Norfolk for the remainder of her life. *29 Nov*: Edward III has Mortimer hanged as a traitor at Tyburn.

🐎 Equestrian Statue of Can Grande della Scala, Verona (Italy)

📖 Oderic of Pordenone: *Travels in Eastern Regions*

1331 Godaigo the Emperor of Japan renews his efforts – again without success – to regain power from his Hojo Regent. The Hojo capture him and exile him to Oki Island: civil war starts in Japan. Stephen Urosh IV of Serbia overthrows his father Urosh III, who is then murdered. *24 Sep*: Edward Balliol is enthroned at Scone as King of Scotland.

1332 Christopher II of Denmark is forced to abdicate by Gerhard Count of Holstein and eight years of anarchy begin. Lucerne joins the three Swiss forest cantons (Uri, Unterwalden and Schwyz) in the Helvetic confederation. The Ethiopian monastic movement is founded by Ewostatewos. *27 Sep*: Battle of Plowce: the Teutonic Knights are defeated by a Polish army under Ladislas IV Lokietek.

1333 *Mar*: Ladislas IV of Poland dies, aged 72, and is succeeded by his 23-year-old son Casimir III. *5 Jul*: the Japanese Emperor Godaigo escapes from his exile island and wins support from Takauji Ashikaga. The Regent Takatoki Hojo is besieged at Kamakura by the general Yoshisada Nitti and commits suicide; Godaigo regains power from the Shogunate and begins rebuilding the royal palaces. *19 Jul*: Battle of Halidon Hill: the Scottish army is defeated by Edward III, demonstrating for the first time the full potential of the English longbow in battle. Edward III of England supports the cause of Edward Balliol and places him on the Scottish throne. The Black Death (bubonic plague) begins in China. Composer Guillaume de Machaut becomes Canon of Reims.

1334 Mohammed Tughlak, the Mughal Emperor, welcomes the Moorish traveller Ibn Batuta with lavish gifts in the hope that he will help him conquer the world. Casimir III, the new King of Poland, encourages Jews to move to Poland as bankers and tax collectors, granting them privileges. *4 Dec*: Pope John XXII dies, aged 85, at Avignon; he is succeeded by Jacques Fournier, who will serve as Pope Benedict XII.

🐍 Giotto di Bondone: Campanile, Florence

🐌 Taddeo Gaddi: Madonna and Child with Saints and Scenes

1335 The Byzantine Emperor Andronicus III conquers Thessaly. In the Treaty of Trentschin, Casimir III of Poland cedes his claims to Bohemia. In Japan, the Hojo clan organize troops in an attempt to depose Godaigo in *Jul*. *Aug*: the warlord Takauji Ashikaga helps Godaigo defeat the Hojo.

1336 Philip IV of France's crusading armada appears in the English Channel and there is fighting between the English and the French at sea. Alfonso IV of Aragon dies, aged 37, and is succeded by his 17-year-old son Pedro IV. A Greek force takes the island of Lesbos back from the Byzantines. *Jan*: the Japanese warlord Takauji Ashikaga deposes the Emperor Godaigo and his son Morinaga and installs a new Emperor to open the Ashikaga period, a period in which independent feudal domains under local warlords will be dominant. The Hindu kingdom of Vijayanagar is founded in southern India.

🐌 Andrea Pisano: Bronze Doors of the Baptistry, Florence (completed)

1337 Mohammed bin Tughlak, Sultan of Delhi, punishes his subjects for threatening to revolt. He empties Delhi completely, forcing citizens to move to Daulatabad, 800 km/500 miles to the south, where the Sultan-Emperor is having a new capital built. *8 Jan*: Giotto di Bondone dies in Florence, aged 69. The Hundred Years' War between England and France begins, with rumours that a French fleet has been sighted preparing to sail to Scotland. *7 Oct*: Edward III casts doubt on Philip of France's legitimacy, claiming the throne of France for himself; Edward orders Philip to stand down and makes it clear that he is not prepared to compromise. *Dec*: at the request of papal representatives, Edward III agrees to suspend hostilities against the French until next March.

1338 Pisa University is founded. A decree issued by the diet of

Frankfurt declares that the electors are able to choose an Emperor without papal intervention, effectively divorcing the Holy Roman Empire from the papacy. Edward III of England gains the support of the Holy Roman Emperor Louis IV, who recognizes Edward's title to the French as well as the English crown in the Alliance of Koblenz. *6 May*: after a French attack on Portsmouth and the Isle of Wight, Edward cancels the truce and the Hundred Years War begins in earnest.

1339 Venice conquers Treviso, gaining its first mainland possession. Edward III invades France for the first time, without success.

📖 Kitabatake Chikafusa: *Jinno-shotoki* (history of Japan)

1340 The period of anarchy in Denmark ends with the murder of Gerhard Count of Holstein; Waldemar IV, youngest son of Christopher II ascends the Danish throne. The Florentine bankers financing Edward III's war with France demand and are given as collateral the Archibishop of Canterbury; the Peruzzi banking house charges 120 per cent interest. Travellers on the trade routes to and from China return to Europe with rat-borne fleas and ticks that will spread the Black Death. *26 Jan*: At Ghent in Flanders, Edward III of England solemnly assumes the arms and title of King of France, mainly to regularize the position of the Flemish towns which have allied themselves to the English cause. *24 Jun*: Edward III's fleet defeats a superior fleet of French ships. Much of the fighting is hand-to-hand, from the castle on one ship to that on another. *Sep*: Edward agrees to a one-year truce with the French. *30 Nov*: Edward III returns to England. The poet Geoffrey Chaucer is born.

🎨 The Luttrell Psalter
  Ambrogio Lorenzetti: Good Government in the City
  📖 Pegolotti: *The Merchant's Handbook*

1341 France imposes the first salt tax to help defray the cost of the war against England. Civil war starts in the Byzantine Empire as Andronicus III dies, aged 45, on *15 Jun*; his nine-year-old son and successor is challenged by the boy's guardian John Cantacuzene, who sets himself up as Emperor in Thrace. The Greek zealots rally round

John Cantacuzene and against Anna of Savoy, who rules as Regent for her son John V.

     Penshurst Place, Kent (U.K.)

1342   The Greek zealots supporting John Cantacuzene succeed in establishing a near-independent state. Charles I of Hungary dies and is succeeded by his son Louis.

     Pietro Lorenzetti: Nativity of the Virgin

1343   The Peruzzi banking house of Florence fails as Edward III defaults: the bankers are unable to collect their debts despite the elaborate measures they have taken to protect themselves. The Black Death strikes Tartars who attack some Genoese merchants returning to Europe from China, deliberately infecting them with plague by catapulting plague-corpses over the walls of the trading post of Calla. Some of the merchants die on the way home: others carry the plague to Constantinople, Venice and Genoa.

     William of Occam: Dialogues (proposing separate functions of church and state)

1344   Alfonso XI of Castile gains the southern port of Algeciras from the Spanish Moors. The Sienese painter Simone Martini dies at the papal court. In China the Yellow River overflows its banks, flooding 17 cities and 16,000 89 sq. km/6,000 square miles of farmland. After the flood subsides the river follows a new course and the Emperor commands that it should be returned to its original channel; 150,000 people are pressed into service to undertake the engineering work. The prestige of Florentine banks declines as the Bardi banking house fails. Civil war breaks out in Florence and the commune is re-established under an oligarchy of powerful businessmen. The phrase Hanseatic League is used for the first time to describe the confederation of Baltic traders.

1345   In response to a call for help by John Cantacuzene, the Ottoman Turks make their first crossing into Europe: civil war continues within the Byzantine Empire. Jacob van Artevelde is murdered in Ghent by a mob rebelling against his dictatorship; Flanders then withdraws from the war between France and England. The Aztecs build a spectacular new city on a marshy island in the Great Lake in Mexico: the founding of the city, called Tenochtitlan, marks the end of two centuries of Aztec wanderings in the Mexican lowlands. Florence undergoes its first social revolution as the artisans (the industrial proletariat) try to overthrow the oligarchy.

    ✍ Notre Dame Cathedral, Paris (completed)
       Aztec architects: City of Tenochtitlan (Mexico)
       Ponte Vecchio, Florence (completed, replacing earlier bridge swept away in the Arno flood of *1333*)

    📖 Francesco Petrarch: *De Vita Solitaria*

1346 Stephen Dushan, King of Serbia, proclaims himself Emperor of the Serbs, Greeks, Bulgars and Albanians and prepares to seize Constantinople. A violent earthquake strikes Constantinople. Shah Mirza founds a Muslim dynasty in Kashmir. The French Estates-General refuses to go on with war levies for Philip VI. *Jul*: Edward III of England leads his army into France on a second campaign. *26 Aug*: Battle of Crécy: this establishes England as a great military power; an army of dismounted men-at-arms and archers destroy a French army of mounted men-at-arms. 1,542 French knights are killed, whereas English casualties number only 50. The blind John of Luxembourg (ruler of Bohemia) is killed at Crécy and is succeeded by his 30-year-old son Charles I. *4 Sep*: Edward III and his army begin the siege of Calais. Battle of Neville's Cross: the Scots exploit Edward's absence, invade northern England and are beaten back near Durham. King David II of Scotland is taken prisoner and held to ransom. *26 Nov*: Charles I is crowned German King at Bonn and makes plans to attack the Holy Roman Emperor Louis IV of Bavaria.

1347 An independent Indian Sultanate based on Bihar, Gulbarga and Bijapur on the Deccan is founded by Bahman Shah. Jane I, Queen of both the Sicilies and Countess of Provence, opens a brothel at Avignon in an attempt to reduce the spread of sexually transmitted diseases; 'The Queen commands that on every Saturday the Women be singly examined and if any have contracted Illness by their Whoring they shall be separated from the rest, for fear the Youth who have to do with them should catch their Distempers'. Civil war in the Byzantine Empire ends with John Cantacuzene victorious: he reigns as

John VI, nominally as co-emperor with his ward John V.
May: The plutocracy in Rome is overthrown by Cola di
Rienzi; he heads a procession to the Capitol dressed in
full armour and is given unlimited powers by the
assembled crowd. Rienzi takes the ancient Roman title
'tribune' and begins a stern regime, encouraged by the
poet Petrarch. *Jul*: Rienzi proclaims the sovereignty of
the Roman people over the Empire. *4 Aug*: Calais
surrenders to the English. Edward III celebrates the
successful ending of the siege by taking as servants six of
the city's leading citizens (the 'Burghers of Calais'),
whose lives he has spared only at his wife's persuasion. Calais becomes an English colony. Rienzi offends
Pope Clement VI by proposing to set up a new Roman
Empire based on the will of the people and the Pope
empowers a legate to depose Rienzi and bring him to
trial. *Sep*: truce declared between England and France.
11 Oct: the Holy Roman Emperor Louis IV of Bavaria
dies during a bear hunt near Munich, aged 60; Charles of
Luxembourg is left the undisputed ruler of Germany.
Nov: Rienzi is denounced by the Pope as a pagan, heretic
and criminal, but Rienzi has Louis of Hungary as an ally
and gives himself up to feasting and pageantry. *Dec*:
Rienzi senses danger, abdicates and leaves Rome.

1348 The Black Death spreads across southern Europe, reaching Florence in April, France in June and England in
July. Jews are blamed for spreading the Black Death by
deliberately poisoning wells. Jews are persecuted first at
Chillon, then at Basel and Freiburg, where they are
herded into buildings and burned alive. At Strasbourg
2,000 Jews are hanged at the Jewish burial ground. Pope
Clement VI declares the Jews innocent of blame (twice)
but the persecution continues, thousands of Jews emigrating to Poland and Russia, where they meet with
greater tolerance. The University of Prague is
founded. England has its third poor summer in a row;
harvests are poor and hunger makes the population more
vulnerable to disease.

1349 Ilkhan Nushirwan of Persia dies, ending the Mongol
dynasty. The Black Death reaches Poland; it kills over
one-third of the population of England. A Scottish army

invades England and carries plague back to Scotland. Pope Clement VI denounces the flagellants who have reappeared in force as a revolutionary movement against the Jews, the rich and the Church; many are burned alive, beheaded or hanged. The composer Guillaume de Machaut enters the service of Charles King of Navarre.

Gloucester Cathedral East Window (U.K.)

1350 The Black Death spreads through Scotland and Wales. Charles IV names Prague as the imperial capital of the Holy Roman Empire, as part of his plan to transform the city into the 'Rome of the North.' *27 Mar*. Alfonso XI of Castile dies of the plague, aged 38, while laying siege to Gibraltar, the last Spanish city remaining in Muslim hands; Alfonso is succeeded by his 16-year-old son Pedro. *Jul*: Cola di Rienzi emerges from hiding, reaching Prague, denouncing the temporal power of the Pope and demanding that Charles IV deliver Italy from its oppressor. Charles IV imprisons Rienzi at Raudnitz.

Orders of Charles IV: St. Vitus' Cathedral, Prague (rebuilt) (Czech Republic)

Aztec craftsmen: Skull Carved From Crystal (at about this time)

Album of the Conqueror (Sultan Mohammed II)

The Cloud of Unknowing

1351 The Order of the Star is founded in France. Florence goes to war with Milan as Giovanni Visconti, Archbishop of Milan, tries to gain control of Tuscany. Zurich joins the Swiss Confederation. The Black Death has combined with the Hundred Years War to produce an economic and social crisis in England; the Statute of Labourers seeks to fix workers' wages, disadvantaging the labour force.

1352 The much-travelled Arab geographer Ibn Battuta arrives in Mali. He finds West African food disgusting but otherwise likes the region: 'The negroes abhor injustice and possess no sexual jealousy'. Glarus joins the Swiss Confederation. The Black Death reaches Moscow. Cola di Rienzi is tried by three cardinals at Avignon and sentenced to death. *6 Dec*: Pope Clement VI dies and is succeeded by Pope Innocent VI, who pardons and releases Rienzi.

1353 Giovanni Visconti of Milan annexes Genoa. Bern joins the growing Swiss Confederation.

☐ Giovanni Boccaccio: *The Decameron* (completed; published in *1419*)

1354 Ottoman forces take the Gallipoli peninsula and continue into Thrace. The Battle of Sapienza: the Genoese defeat the Venetians, who lose their fleet. Giovanni Visconti of Milan dies and is succeeded by his two nephews. After an interruption due to the Black Death, England resumes its Hundred Years War with France. Cola di Rienzi is given the title Senator by Pope Innocent VI and sent to Rome with Papal Legate Cardinal Albornoz. *Aug:* Rienzi enters Rome to wild acclaim and is restored to his position as tribune. *8 Oct* rioting breaks out in Rome. Rienzi tries to speak to the crowd but to no avail; he is murdered while trying to escape, disguised as a woman.

✍ Alhambra Palace, Granada (completed) (Spain)

1355 Chiang-ning (later Nanjing) is seized by Qu Yuanzhang, a 27-year-old monk leading a rebellion against the Mongol domination of China. The Byzantine Emperor John VI Cantacuzene is expelled from Constantinople; he retires to a monastery and is succeeded by his ward John V Palaeologus. Matteo Visconti of Milan is assassinated by his brothers Galeazzo and Bernabo, who rule at Pavia and Milan. Etienne Marcel, the richest man in Paris, persuades the Estates-General of Languedoc and Langue d'Oil to force John II to consult the Estates before imposing new tax levies and to let a commission from the Estates supervise the collection of taxes; King John induces the Estates-General to adjourn. Afonso IV of Portugal has his son's mistress murdered in case her brothers should gain control of the government. Pedro claims the murdered Inês was his wife and lays siege to Oporto.

✎ Taddeo Gaddi: Madonna and Child with Angels

1356 Korea lapses into disorder. The Koryo Kings have become little more than satellites of the Mongol imperial family. They stage a successful insurrection against the Mongols, but they have come to depend on the Mongols' prestige for their authority and so are unable to suppress their vassals; those vassals are encouraged by

Japanese pirates to create chaos. *18 Sep*: Cardinal Talleyrand's mediation between Henry of Lancaster and King John of France fails. *19 Sep*: Battle of Poitiers: France's army is defeated by the English under the Black Prince, who takes the French King prisoner and returns to England with King John and a host of French aristocrats for ransom. The government of France is left to the Regency of the Dauphin, the 18-year-old Charles, who is unable to keep civil order in the aftermath of the crippling battle.

1357 The merchants of Paris rebel against the Dauphin and recall the Estates General under the leadership of Etienne Marcel; the members order reforms that include relief for the poor and more frequent meetings of the Estates. The Great Ordinance passed by the Estates provides for a committee to supervise the levying and sexpenditure of taxes. Etienne Marcel forms an alliance with Charles (the Bad) of Navarre, discrediting the Estates-General and splititng it into factions. The Dauphin opposes the alliance, leaves Paris and forms his own coalition against the Estates-General. *20 May* Afonso IV King of Portugal dies, succeeded by his son Pedro I. Queen Isabella, Edward II's widow, dies.

1358 *22 Feb*: Etienne Marcel forces his way into the Dauphin's palace in Paris; the Marshals of Normandy and Champagne are murdered in the Dauphin's presence. *May*: French peasants rise violently in response to heavy taxes imposed to raise King John's ransom and the ransoms for the other aristocrats held in England. *Jun*: the rising of the French peasants is put down mercilessly, with English help. *31 Jul*: Charles the Bad of Navarre approaches Paris and gains support from Etienne Marcel, who is assassinated.

1359 Edward III launches his final French expedition. In Flanders, revolutionaries, wearing red hats, storm Bruges, trying to overturn the patrician government. Ivan II, Prince of Muscovy, dies and is succeeded by his nine-year-old son Dmitri Donskoi.

   ✐ Giotto di Bondone and others: Campanile, Florence (completed)

1360 The Treaty of Bretigny ends the first stage of the

Hundred Years War. Edward III makes great territorial gains in France and appears content with the settlement. King John II of France is to be freed on payment of 3 million gold crowns – a huge ransom. King John returns to France leaving three sons in England as hostages: he cannot raise the ransom money and is returned to England. Orkhan the Ottoman Sultan dies, aged 71, and is succeeded by his eldest son Murad I. English labourers who ask for wages above the low levels established by the *1351* Statute are ordered to be imprisoned. The Hanseatic League grows to 52 towns.

The Gagnières-Fonthill Vase, made in China, collected by successive European aristocrats

1361 Waldemar IV King of Denmark begins a war against the Hanseatic League. The Duchy of Burgundy comes into the possession of the King of France, John II: in two years' time he will give it to his son Philip. Murad I takes Adrianople, which becomes the Ottoman capital. The Black Death strikes again in England, France and Poland, taking the lives of many children.

1362 English becomes the language of pleading and judgment in courts of law in England; French is still used for documentation. The Norse King Magnus Ericson sends an expedition to look for the colonists who failed to reach Greenland; the search party enters what may have been Hudson Bay.

Palace of the Popes, Avignon (completed) (France)

William Langland: *The Vision of William Concerning Piers the Ploughman*

1363 Waldemar IV King of Denmark forces the Hanseatic League to accept peace and a limitation of its privileges. Magnus II of Sweden abdicates under duress and is succeeded by Albert of Mecklenburg.

1364 The Universities of Cracow and Vienna are founded. *8 Apr*: King John II of France dies, aged 45, he has been a prisoner in England for most of the time since his capture at Poitiers in *1356*. His body is sent home and he is succeeded by his 27-year-old son Charles V.

1365 *12 Apr*: Treaty of Guerande: the French House of Blois cedes its rights to Brittany.

Ni Zan: Autumn Landscape

1366   Amadeus of Savoy leads a crusading war against the Ottomans, taking Gallipoli.

     🖉 Meier Abdeli: El Transito Synagogue, Toledo (Spain)

     📖 Petrarch: *Canzoniere*

1367   Pedro I King of Portugal goes to the aid of Pedro the Cruel of Castile and together with Prince Edward of England, the Black Prince, they defeat Pedro's illegitimate half-brother Enrique. Enrique is forced to retreat into France for safety. Pedro of Portugal returns home, dies and is succeeded by his 22-year-old son Fernão I. 77 German towns are brought together by the Confederation of Cologne; the Confederation prepares a navy to oppose Waldemar IV of Denmark.

1368   The Chinese Ming Emperor Qu Yuanzhang drives the Mongols out of Beijing and adopts the name Hung-wu; he begins rebuilding the Great Wall of China.

1369   The state of Koryo (Korea) submits to the Chinese Ming army after 13 years of resistance to Chinese control. Tamerlane (also known as Timur the Lame or Tamburlaine) takes control of Samarkand. The 33-year-old descendant of Genghis Khan is head of the House of Jagatai and he begins to assemble a formidable armed horde. The Emperor Qu (Hung-Wu) drives the Mongols out of Shenxi and Gansu provinces. Pedro the Cruel of Castile offends the Black Prince, who abandons his cause. Pedro is besieged at La Mancha by Count Trastamara. *23 Mar*: Pedro is tricked into leaving La Mancha and his half-brother Enrique stabs him to death. Enrique succeeds as Enrique II.

     📖 Geoffrey Chaucer: *The Boke of the Duchesse*

1370   The Hanseatic League reaches its peak when it takes military action against Waldemar IV of Denmark; the Treaty of Stralsund gives the League a Baltic trade monopoly. *5 Nov*: Casimir III King of Poland dies, aged 60, in a hunting accident; he has promised his throne to Louis of Anjou, who rules through Regents.

     🖉 Exeter Cathedral (completed) (U.K.)

1371   *26 Feb*: Enrique II of Castile takes Zamora, forcing Fernão I of Portugal to give up his claims to Castile in the Treaty of Alcoutin. *26 Sep*: Battle of Chernomen:

the army of the Ottoman Sultan Murad I defeats a combined force; the rulers of Macedonia, Bulgaria and the Byzantine Empire acknowledge his suzerainty.

1372 Charles V of France regains Poitou and Brittany from England and gains control of the Channel, defeating the English at La Rochelle. The Vatican commissions an astronomer to correct the Julian calendar (in use since *46 BC*) because each year is too long by 11 minutes; the astronomer dies before he can change the calendar.

1373 John of Gaunt Duke of Lancaster invades France, leading a large army from Calais to the borders of Burgundy. Castilian troops sent by Enrique II burn Lisbon; Enrique is at war with both Aragon and Portugal. The Holy Roman Emperor Charles IV of Luxembourg annexes Brandenburg.

1374 John of Gaunt returns from the French war, hoping to succeed his father, Edward III of England. London retains the services of the Oxford scholar John Wycliffe to negotiate with Pope Gregory XI. Enrique of Castile makes peace with Portugal and Aragon at Imazan. *Jul*: a dancing craze sweeps Aix-la-Chapelle: crowds dance to exhaustion in a phenomenon that is never explained.

1375 The Kingdom of Armenia founded in *94 BC* comes to an end with the surrender of the Armenian King Levon V to the Governor of Aleppo, who has besieged Sis, the Armenian capital, with an army of Mamelukes. The Mamelukes kill many Armenians and convert the survivors to Islam; they imprison Levon in Cairo. The Treaty of Bruges: a one-year truce in the Hundred Years War. The Holy Roman Emperor Charles IV of Luxembourg formally recognizes the Hanseatic League. Waldemar IV King of Denmark dies, aged 55, and is succeeded by his five-year-old grandson Olaf II with the boy's mother as Regent.

📖 Guillaume Tirel: *Le Viander de Taillevent* (French cookery book)

1376 John Wychliffe gains substantial influence in London. Wycliffe says all authority, both secular and ecclesiastical, derives from God and is forfeit when its possessor falls into mortal sin; he attacks the worldliness of the Church. *8 Jun*: the Black Prince, Edward Prince of

Wales, dies, aged 46, of disease contracted in Spain.

1377 Pope Gregory XI accuses John Wycliffe of heresy. Wycliffe is summoned before the Bishop of London to answer charges but general street riots end the court session. *17 Jan*: the 'Babylonian Exile' of the Papacy ends as Pope Gregory enters Rome. *21 Jun*: Edward III King of England dies, aged 64, and is succeeded by his grandson, the 10-year-old Richard II: no regent is appointed. Thomas Duke of Gloucester and John of Gaunt, Duke of Lancaster, administer the government of England. The French composer Guillaume de Machaut dies at Reims.

1378 The Great Schism that divides the Catholic Church for 39 years begins as Bartolommeo Prignani is elected Pope Urban VI and announces a reform of the College of Cardinals. 13 cardinals meet at Anagni and elect Robert of Geneva Pope Clement VII, and this anti-pope establishes himself at Avignon. The Holy Roman Emperor Charles IV divides his realm among his three sons. He dies, aged 62, in Prague on *29 Nov* and is succeeded by his son Wenceslas, who is 17.

    🏛 Canterbury Cathedral Nave (U.K.)

1379 *30 May*: Enrique II of Castile and León dies, aged 46, and is succeeded by his 21-year-old son Juan I, in spite of claims by John of Gaunt, who is a son-in-law of Pedro the Cruel.

1380 *29 Apr*: Catherine of Siena, the Christian mystic, dies, aged 33, eight days after being paralyzed from the waist down. *8 Sep*: Battle of Kulikovo: the army of Dmitri Donskoi Prince of Moscow defeats the Mongols and destroys the legend of Mongol invincibility. *16 Sep*: Charles V of France dies at Vincennes, poisoned by mushrooms. He is succeeded by his 12-year-old son Charles VI.

    🏛 Cathedral of St. Etienne, Metz (completed) France
    🐍 Apocalypse Tapestry
    📖 John Wycliffe: The *Bible* (English translation)

1381 After his successful invasion of Persia last year, Tamerlane invades Russia. At the end of the three-year War of Chioggia, Venice gains supremacy over Genoa. *May*: poll tax collectors are set upon in many towns in

England. *4 Jun*: the Peasants' Revolt begins in England as the working class rises against the *1351* Statute of Labourers and this year's poll tax. *7 Jun*: Kentish rebels choose Wat Tyler as their leader. *13 Jun*: Essex and Kentish rebels enter London and Richard II withdraws to the safety of the Tower. *14 Jun*: Simon of Sudbury, Chancellor and Archbishop of Canterbury, is beheaded by the mob. *15 Jun*: Richard II summons Wat Tyler and his Kentishmen to Smithfield, and Tyler is treacherously stabbed by William Walworth Mayor of London in the King's presence.

1382 The Archbishop of Canterbury William Courtenay purges Oxford of Lollards; Wycliffe has been discredited by the Peasants' Revolt and condemned by the Church; he withdraws to the parish of Lutterworth. Reforms granted to Tyler last year are repealed; English people lose confidence in the King. The Black Death sweeps Europe, taking a heavy toll in Ireland. Revolution in Florence: wool-combers led by Michele di Lando seize the palace. Michele is exiled, shops and factories are closed and merchants and businessmen persuade surrounding landowners to cut off the city's food supply. An oligarchy is set up in Florence. *10 Sep*: Louis the Great of Hungary dies suddenly after reigning for 40 years. He is succeeded in Hungary by his daughter Maria of Anjou and in Poland by his daughter Jadwiga.

1383 Japanese *nō* drama is pioneered by Motokiyo Zeami, a 20-year-old actor and playwright; he will write 240 *nō* plays. *22 Oct* Fernão I of Portugal dies; his widow Leonora acts as Regent for his daughter Beatrix.

1384 The Count of Flanders dies and Flanders passes into Burgundian control. Juan of Castile marries Beatrix, the Portuguese Infanta, but the people of Portugal resist his claim to the throne of Portugal; Juan besieges Lisbon. *31 Dec*: John Wycliffe has a stroke at mass in Lutterworth and dies.

📖 Geoffrey Chaucer: *House of Fame*

1385 The great Chinese artist Ni Zan dies, aged 84. Heidelberg University is founded. Ottoman forces under the Sultan Murat capture Sofia. *14 Aug*: Portuguese forces defeat a Castilian army at the Battle of Aljubarrota. The illegitimate son of Pedro, João I, takes power, supported unanimously by the cortes at Coimbra.

🐚 Tomb of Bernabo Visconti of Milan

📖 Geoffrey Chaucer: *Troilus and Criseyde*

1386 *9 May*: Treaty of Windsor: an alliance between England and Portugal, signalled by the marriage of João I of Portugal and John of Gaunt's daughter Philippa. *9 Jul*: Battle of Sempach: the Swiss defeat an Austrian army under Leopold III, who is killed, at the age of 34, in the battle; the Swiss struggle for freedom from Vienna.

🏛 Milan Cathedral (Italy)

1387 Olaf II of Denmark dies, aged 17, and is succeeded by his 34-year-old mother Margaret, who will unite Scandinavia. Tamerlane has taken control of Persia and secured the borders of his Transoxianan territory with that of the Mongol horde.

1388 Charles VI of France begins his personal reign at the age of 19, following the Duke of Anjou's death. Charles replaces Philip of Burgundy with his own brother Louis Duke of Orléans, but the appointment of this dandy is unpopular and Philip gains support from Isabelle of Bavaria, the King's wife. John Purcey completes the first translation of the entire *Bible* into English, based on work begun by Wycliffe.

1389 Margaret of Denmark names Eric of Pomerania, a seven-year-old grand-nephew, as her successor. She is offered the Swedish throne; her army defeats that of the Swedish King Albert at Falkoping and takes Albert prisoner. Shams al-Din Mohammed, the poet and Muslim mystic known as Hafiz, dies at Shiraz in southern Persia. *15 Jun*: Battle of Kossovo: victory for the army of the Ottoman Sultan Murad I, ending the 'Serb Empire', a coalition of Serbs, Albanians, Wallachians and Bosnians. *16 Sep*: Sultan Murad is assassinated by Lazar, a Serbian nobleman posing as a deserter. The 69-year-old Murad is succeeded by his eldest son, the 50-year-old Bayazid I (the Thunderbolt). Bayazid has the Serbian Prince Lazar captured and put to death.

1390 The Byzantine Emperor John V is deposed by his grandson, John VII, but John V is quickly restored to the throne by his second son, Manuel. *13 May*: King

Robert II of Scotland, dies aged 74, and is succeeded by his son John, who reigns as Robert III. *9 Oct*: Juan I of Castile dies, aged 32, and is succeeded by his 11-year-old son Enrique III.

📖 *The Forme of Cury* (illuminated English cookery book)

1391 Tamerlane defeats Toqtamish, Khan of the Golden Horde. The Byzantine Emperor John V Palaeologus dies, aged 59, and is succeeded by his son Manuel II. *June*: the persecution of Jews in Seville spreads throughout Andalusia as the Spaniards look for scapegoats for the Black Death. *5 Aug*: Castilian sailors set fire to the Jewish ghetto in Barcelona: hundreds of Jews are killed. Many Jews accept conversion to escape persecution.

🏛 The Alhambra, Granada (completed) Spain

📖 Geoffrey Chaucer: *Canterbury Tales* (at about this time)

1392 The Yi dynasty of Korea is founded by the warlord I Songgye, who murders several rivals and proclaims himself King; he makes Kyonsong (later to be called Seoul) his capital. Japan is reunified after a civil war between northern and southern dynasties. The southern Emperor abdicates believing that the throne will alternate between the two branches: the northern dynasty will in reality never give up the throne.

🂠 Jacques Gringonneur: Playing Cards

1393 Bayazid I, the Ottoman Sultan, subdues Bulgaria. Tamerlane takes Baghdad. The Holy Roman Emperor Wenceslas of Bohemia has the priest John of Nepomuk tortured and drowned in the River Moldau (at Prague) for refusing to reveal the Empress's confessions. Richard II orders a cycle of sculptures to decorate the remodelled Westminster Hall.

1394 The Holy Roman Emperor Wenceslas of Bohemia is taken prisoner by Jobst of Moravia, his cousin. Richard II of England grants the poet Geoffrey Chaucer a pension of £20 a year for life.

1395 Albert of Mecklenburg, King of Sweden, renounces his throne and retires to Mecklenburg, as Queen Margaret of Denmark continues her relentless conquest of his realm. Richard II of England goes on campaign in Ireland, forcing the Irish barons to pay him homage. Gian Galazzo Visconti, ruler of Milan, assumes the title Duke, buying it from King Wenceslas. Tamerlane and his Tartar horde destroy Astrakhan.

1396 Charles VI of France makes a truce with England that will last almost two decades. Sigismund King of Hungary leads the Crusade of Nicopolis along the Danube valley, pillaging and killing along the way; the crusade is supported by both popes. The 20,000 crusaders meet a similar number of Turks at Nicopolis. *25 Sep*: Battle of Nicopolis: Turks defeat crusaders.

    ✆ Nicholas Broker and Godfrey Prest: Richard II (gilt effigy for Westminster Abbey)

1397 Bayazid I's Ottoman army lays siege to Constantinople; Jean Boucicaut, Marshal of France, defends the city. Tartars led by Tamerlane appear, distracting Bayazid from his siege. Giovanni de Medici founds the Medici banking house. Florence resists an invasion by Visconti forces from Milan. Queen Margaret of Denmark completes the conquest of Sweden, creating her grand-nephew Eric King of a united Scandinavia (the Union of Kalmar): Margaret herself continues to rule in fact.

    ✍ Orders of Shogun Yoshimitsu: Golden Pavilion, Kyoto (completed)

1398 Richard II of England moves towards a despotic regime. *16 Sep*: Richard II orders Mowbray and Bolingbroke to fight a judicial duel at Coventry to settle the dispute between them, then he intercedes and banishes them both. *24 Sep*: Tamerlane has led his Tartar army through mountain passes into northern India, crossing the River Indus. *12 Dec*: Tamerlane's Tartar horde massacre 100,000 Hindu prisoners in Delhi. *17 Dec*: Tamerlane sacks Delhi. Zhu Yuanzhang, the Ming Emperor who reunified China, dies, aged 70.

1399 *9 Jan*: Tamerlane's Tartars storm the town of Meerut, then fight their way along the Himalayan foothills towards the Indus valley. *3 Feb*: John of Gaunt dies, aged 59, and Richard II confiscates his Lancaster estate. *19 Mar*: Tamerlane reaches the Indus. *Jul*: Bolingbroke returns to England to claim his father's estates. *19 Aug*: Bolingbroke defeats and captures Richard II. *29 Sep*:

Richard is persuaded to abdicate. *30 Sep*: The usurper Bolingbroke is chosen by the English Parliament to reign as Henry IV, founding the House of Lancaster.

1400 The Holy Roman Emperor Wenceslas of Bohemia is deposed for drunkenness and incompetence. Wenceslas refuses to accept the decision and hangs onto the imperial crown for 10 years against challenges from rivals. *10 Feb*: Richard II, ex King of England, disappears while imprisoned in Pontefract Castle, he is presumably murdered on or about this date. His corpse is shortly afterwards displayed in London to prove that he is dead. *2 Aug*: Rupert, Elector Palatine of the Rhine, is elected German King at Rense. *25 Oct*: the English poet Geoffrey Chaucer dies.

📖 Jean Froissart: *Chroniques de France, d'Angleterre, d'Ecosse et d'Espagne*

1401 Tamerlane sacks Baghdad for the second time

🏛 Henry Yevele (fabric) and Hugh Herland (roof): Westminster Hall

1402 *28 Jul*: Battle of Angora (Ankara): Tamerlane defeats the Ottoman Sultan Bayazid I, whose army is hopelessly outnumbered 800,000 to 120,000. Bayazid's men desert and he is captured. Imprisoned in Ankara, Bayazid is forced to act as a footstool for Tamerlane, while Bayazid's favourite wife, Despina is forced to be a naked waitress at Tamerlane's feast; Bayazid made the mistake of insulting Tamerlane by calling his virility into question. *3 Sep*: Gian Galazzo Visconti Duke of Milan dies of plague, aged 51, while besieging Florence. His death saves Florence. Milan sinks into anarchy as his 13-year-old son Giovanni is proclaimed Duke. Rumours circulate that Richard II of England is still alive.

🎨 Lorenzo Ghiberti: The Sacrifice of Isaac (gilt-bronze)

1403 Accession of Ming Emperor Zheng Zu to the Chinese throne. The reign starts amid great unrest; there is uneasiness that the Emperor's nephew, deposed and lost in a fire, may reappear at any time, just as in England many expect King Richard to appear, alive and well, at any moment. *Mar*: the Ottoman Sultan Bayazid I dies in captivity at Tamerlane's camp, aged

43. A long interregnum starts as his sons fight for power. The Doge of Venice imposes quarantine for the first time, as a measure against the spread of the Black Death. Japan begins trading with Ming China.

☙ Tomb of William of Wykeham (painted carving) (U.K.)

1405 Yung Lo (Zheng Zu), the Chinese Emperor, orders the first Chinese exploratory voyage. A fleet of 63 junks sails to islands in the south under the command of Zheng He (or Cheng Ho), a Muslim eunuch. French troops land in Wales to support Owen Glendower's rebellion against the English. Venetian troops defeat an army assembled by the Carrara family and seize Verona, Vicenza, Padua and other lands of the Carraras and Viscontis. The Florentines buy Pisa in order to gain access to the sea. *17 Feb*: Tamerlane, the Tartar leader, dies suddenly at Atrar, aged 68. He was planning an invasion of China, but on his death his Empire quickly disintegrates.

1406 Hanseatic fishermen catch English fishermen working off Bergen; they tie the Englishmen up and throw them overboard. King Robert III of Scotland suspects the Duke of Albany of being responsible for the mysterious death of the King's eldest son David four years ago. He sends his 11-year-old son James to France for safety, but the boy is captured by English sailors. *4 Apr*: Robert III dies, aged 65; James remains in English hands. A copy of Ptolemy's *Geography* is taken to Italy from Constantinople and it is translated into Latin by James Angelus. Its availability gives a boost to the development of geographical thought in Europe, reviving the useful idea that the world is round. The Arab historian and diplomat Abd al-Rahman ibn Mohammed dies, aged 74. *25 Dec*: Enrique III of Castile dies, aged 27, and is succeeded by his infant son Juan II.

1407 The Black Death kills thousands of people in London. Zheng He returns to China with the Prince of Palembang (Sumatra) in chains. *23 Nov*: in France the Duke of Orléans is assassinated by supporters of the Burgundian John the Fearless; civil war between the Burgundians and Armagnacs follows.

1408 Zheng He sets off on a second great sea voyage; he will return this time with the King of Ceylon and the Sinhalese royal family because the people of Ceylon dare to attack He's mission. Jan Hus, a 35-year-old Bohemian priest, is denounced by fellow clergyman for his criticism of the sale of indulgences and other clerical abuses. Hus is dismissed.

1409 Venetians recover their Dalmatian territory. The Pope orders the surrender of all books by John Wycliffe, they are burned. Jan Hus is excommunicated by his Archbishop, but he continues to preach at the Bethlehem Chapel and he defends Wycliffe. Council of Pisa: the schism between Rome and Avignon is ended with both popes deposed and a new Pope, Alexander V, elected on *26 Jun*.

    ⌂ The North Bar (brick city gate), Beverley (U.K.)
    ☺ Donatello: David (sculpture)

1410 In Peru, the Inca Empire is expanding under the leadership of Viracocha Inca; the Inca social structure is also becoming more formal and hierarchical. In West Africa, Kanajejdi the King of Kano who introduced iron helmets and quilted horse armour to his Hausa cavalry dies. *4 May*: Pope Alexander V dies at Bologna under suspicious circumstances: possibly a poisoning? He is succeeded by John XXIII. *18 May*: the Holy Roman Emperor Rupert dies, aged 58 at Landskron. He is succeeded by Sigismund of Luxembourg. *15 Jul*: Battle of Tannenberg: a Polish and Lithuanian army defeats an army of Teutonic Knights.

1411 Portugal and Castile make peace; Portugal begins its rise to power. *1 Feb*: Peace of Thorn: the Slavic advance is halted but the Poles still have no access to the Baltic; the Teutonic Knights give away little, in spite of their conspicuous defeat last year at Tannenberg. *Mar*: Jan Hus continues to preach in Prague, defending John Wycliffe's teachings. *5 Jun*: Musa, an Ottoman Prince, enlists support from Serbs to attack Suleiman at Edirne; Suleiman is killed in the fighting. The Serbs ally themselves with Musa's brother Mohammed.

    ⌂ The Guildhall, London
    ☺ Andrei Rublev: Trinity (icon)

1412 Zheng He embarks on a third great Chinese exploratory voyage; this one will take him as far as the Strait of Hormuz, the entrance to the Persian Gulf. Gian Visconti Duke of Milan is assassinated; his brother Filippo is left to rule the Duchy. *28 Oct*: Queen Margaret of Denmark dies suddenly, aged 59, on board her ship in Flensborg harbour. Eric VII of Denmark and Norway (Eric XIII of Sweden) continues to reign.

1413   The butchers of Paris led by Simon Caboche take over the city and try to make the government more efficient by passing an 'Ordonnance Cabochienne'. The Armagnacs quickly regain control of Paris and end all hope of reform. The civil war in the Ottoman Empire comes to an end when Mohammed defeats and kills Musa, his brother, outside Constantinople. The Byzantine Emperor Manuel II holds another brother, Mustafa, as Mohammed reunites his imperial territories. *20 Mar*: Henry IV of England dies and is succeeded by his 25-year-old son Henry V.

   ✑ Donatello: St. Mark (sculpture)

1414   The exiled Indonesian Prince Paramesvara founds the Palembang state, an independent kingdom on the Malacca Peninsula; Paramesvara is converted to Islam. There is a Lollard plot against Henry V of England, who has most of the conspirators hanged. Pope John XXIII summons the Council of Constance at the insistence of King Sigismund of Hungary, who wants to see the unity of the Church restored. The council also has an aim the reform of Church leadership and the removal of heresy, especially that of Jan Hus, who arrives at the council under an imperial safe conduct, regardless of the judgement that may be passed on him.

   ✑ The Wilton Diptych (U.K.)

1415   An embassy from Malindi in East Africa (coast of Kenya) is sent to China. *5 May*: the Council of Constance unanimously condemns the writings of John Wycliffe and demands that Jan Hus recant his heresy in public. Hus refuses. *6 Jul*: Jan Hus is burned at the stake. The news that the imperial safe conduct has been violated causes indignation in Bohemia and a surge of Bohemian nationalism combined with demands for religious reforms. *25 Oct*: Battle of Agincourt: an English army defeats a French army. The French suffer severe losses and Normandy lies open to reconquest by the English.

🎨 Tomb of Ralph Greene and His Wife at Lowick (the couple holding hands) (U.K.)

Pol, Hermann and Jan Limburg: *Les Très Riches Heures du Duc de Berry* (Belgium)

Donatello: St. John the Evangelist (sculpture)

📖 Baru Chandidas: *Shrikrishnakirtan*

1416 Zheng He's Chinese fleet reaches Aden. The first war between the Ottoman Empire and the Venetians is won by the Venetians under their Doge Loredano, who defeats the Ottomans at the Dardanelles and forces the Sultan into a peace settlement. Henry V of England begins a three-year Normandy campaign.

🎨 Donatello: St. George (sculpture)

1417 *11 Nov*: the Great Schism dividing the Church comes to an end. The Council of Constance has deposed Benedict III, Gregory XII and John XXIII and now elects Martin V.

1418 John the Fearless of Burgundy seizes control of the government of France in the name of the Queen, Isabel of Bavaria. Charles, the Dauphin, escapes from Paris and establishes a headquarters at Bourges, taking for himself the title Regent. *31 Dec*: Henry V of England takes Rouen after a short siege.

🏛 Orders of Sultan Firuz: Principal Mosque, Gulbarga (India)

1419 Sugar cane from Sicily is planted on Madeira after Portuguese explorers land in the Madeira Islands and decide to colonize them. *Jul*: Henry V conquers most of Normandy. *19 Jul*: Followers of the executed Jan Hus (Hussites) march on Prague Town Hall to insist on the release of imprisoned preachers. They force their way into the Town Hall and throw Catholic councillors out of the windows (*The Defenestration of Prague*). *10 Sep*: John the Fearless is murdered after a stormy meeting with the Dauphin; the Burgundians return to the English alliance.

🏛 Façade of the Doge's Palace, Venice Italy

📖 Giovanni Boccaccio: *The Decameron*

1420 Sultan Firuz Bahman, ruler of the Indian Deccan, is defeated in battle at Pangal; unaccustomed to defeat, the

Sultan is a broken man. Yung Lo, the Emperor of China, moves his capital to the former Yuan capital Dadu, changing its name to Beijing ('northern capital'): the aim is to be better positioned to defend China against the Mongols, whose strength is on the increase. Nanjing becomes China's secondary capital. *21 May:* Henry V of England signs a peace treaty with Philippe, John the Fearless's successor as Duke of Burgundy, putting France and England under a single crown. Henry agrees to marry Catherine of Valois, daughter of Charles VI of France. *20 Dec:* Henry V enters Paris in triumph.

   ✍ Filippo Brunelleschi: Dome of Florence Cathedral
   ▯ ✇ Bedford *Book of Hours*
   ✇ Jan and Hubert van Eyck: The Crucifixion; The Last Judgment

1421   Florence buys Livorno, which gives the city the port it needs. Filippo Visconti subdues Genoa as he tries to reassemble the Duchy of Milan. The Ottoman Sultan Mohammed I dies, aged 34, and is succeeded by his 18-year-old son Murad II. Yung Lo (Zheng Zu) the Emperor of China sends Zheng He on a fifth major expedition. Prince Henry the Navigator, now 27, assembles pilots, astronomers, instrument makers and cartographers at Sagres in Portugal, a new science of navigation is pioneered. Over 100,000 people die in the Netherlands as the sea spills into low-lying land, forming the Zuider Zee.

   ✍ Filippo Brunelleschi: Church of S. Lorenzo, Florence (Italy)

1422   Lisbon becomes the seat of Portugal's government. Zheng He, grand eunuch of the Three Treasures, reaches the trading city of Malindi on the east coast of Africa with his Star Raft, the huge fleet sent by the Chinese Emperor to spread news of his greatness to the West. Trading with Malindi is symbolic as well as commercial: by accepting Chinese goods the African chiefs are seen by the Chinese as paying homage to their Emperor. *31 Aug:* Henry V of England dies of dysentery at Vincennes, aged 35, and is succeeded by his 9-month-old son Henry VI; Humphrey Duke of Gloucester is to rule as Protector. *1 Oct:* Charles VI of France dies in Paris, aged 53. Since the 19-year-old Dauphin was disinherited by the 1420 Treaty of Troyes, Henry VI of England is proclaimed King of France.

1423 The Venetians buy Thessalonica from Constantinople under an agreement with the Byzantine Emperor Manuel II to stop the Turks from taking the city.

 🕮 Gentile da Fabriano: The Adoration of the Magi
 Donatello: St. Louis (sculpture)

1424 The Chinese Emperor Yung Lo dies. *4 Jan*: Count Giacomuzzo Sforza drowns in the River Pescara on a military expedition against the Spanish. *21 May*: James I of Scotland, newly freed by the English after 18 years in captivity, is crowned King of Scotland at Scone. *17 Aug*: the Duke of Bedford's army defeats a combined Scots-French army at Verneuil.

 🕮 Lorenzo Ghiberti: Bronze Doors, Baptistry of San Giovanni, Florence
 📖 Thomas à Kempis: *Imitation of Christ*

1425 The Byzantine Emperor Manuel II dies, aged 75, and is succeeded by his son John VII Palaeologus. The Canary Islands fall to Henry the Navigator (Portugal), who takes them from Castile.

 🕮 Donatello: Habbakuk (gilt-bronze)
 Tomasso Masaccio: The Holy Trinity with the Virgin (fresco)
 📖 Alain Chartier: *La Belle Dame sans Merci*

1426 The Venetians go to war with Milan. The Duke of Bedford returns to England from France, arriving in London in *Jan* to mediate in a quarrel between his brother Gloucester and the Bishop of Winchester.

 🕮 Tomasso Masaccio: Virgin Enthroned

1427 The Emperor Yeshaq of Ethiopia sends envoys to Aragon in an attempt to form an alliance against the Muslims. The Duke of Bedford resumes the war in France.

 🕮 Donatello: The Feast of Herod (relief)
 Masaccio: Expulsion from Paradise (fresco)

1428 The Tepanec Empire in the Valley of Mexico is overthrown by a triple alliance of the Aztec city of Tenochtitlan, the exiled army of Nezahualcoyotl, the leader of Texcoco and the disaffected Tepanec city of Tlacopan.

The Tepanec Emperor Maxtla turned his own people against him with his cruelty. The Florentine painter Tomasso Masaccio dies, aged only 27. The University of Florence begins teaching Greek and Latin literature. Japanese transport workers strike in protest against high food prices as famine strikes Japan; the strikers are joined by farmers who wreck warehouses, temples and private houses. Vietnam regains its independence from China. Venetian troops under Carmagnola conquer Bergamo and Brescia. The Treaty of Delft ends the conflict between Flanders and England. John Wycliffe's bones are dug up by order of the Council of Constance, burned and thrown into the River Swift.

   ☞ Filippo Brunelleschi: Church of S. Lorenzo, Florence (completed)

   ☞ Robert Campin: Merode (altarpiece)

1429 Cosimo de' Medici becomes head of the Florentine banking house, at the age of 40. Joan of Arc, a 17-year-old shepherdess from Lorraine, has seen visions. She persuades an army officer to equip her with armour and take her to the Dauphin; he provides her with a small army and she liberates Orléans in May. The Duke of Bedford sends to England for reinforcements, strengthens his grip on Paris, and assigns the Regency of France to Philippe of Burgundy in accordance with the wishes of the Parisians. Joan of Arc persuades the Dauphin that he is after all the legitimate heir of Charles VI, despite the Treaty of Troyes. He is crowned at Reims on *18 Jul* as Charles VII.

1430 The Ottoman Turks under Murad II take Thessalonica. *23 May*: Joan of Arc enters Compiège near Paris and is taken prisoner. *14 Jul*: Joan is handed over to Pierre Cauchon, Bishop of Beauvais, and then to the English who imprison her at Rouen. Charles VII makes no attempt to save her.

   ☞ Filippo Brunelleschi: Pazzi Chapel, Florence (first Renaissance building)

   ☞ Donatello: David (bronze)

      Paolo Uccello: Mosaics for Church of San Marco, Venice

1431 The Chinese admiral Zheng He leads his final great exploratory voyage, one that will visit 20 different states. Joan of Arc is handed over to Pierre Cauchon by the English, who threaten to seize her again if she is not convicted of treason. Condemned, Joan is burned at the stake in Rouen on *30 May*. *16 Dec*: Henry VI of England, 10-years-old, is crowned king of France in Paris.

1432 Carmagnola, Conte di Castelnuovo, is convicted of treason by the Council of Ten in Venice after his unsuccessful campaign against Milan. The Portuguese navigator Gonzalo Cabral discovers the Azores. The Ottoman Sultan Murad II besieges Constantinople, without success. The Doge intercedes on Carmagnola's behalf. *5 Apr*: Carmagnola is beheaded.

   Fra Filippo Lippi: Reform of the Carmelite Rule (fresco)

   Jan and Hubert van Eyck: The Adoration of the Mystic Lamb (panels)

1433 The Chinese admiral Zheng He returns to China at the end of his seventh and final expedition; Mecca and 10 other states send tribute to the Ming Emperor. In spite of the success of Zheng He's enterprise, the Chinese now turn their back on the outside world. The Portuguese navigator Gil Eannes, one of Prince Henry the Navigator's captains, reaches and rounds Cape Bojador on the West African coast for the first time; the Portuguese sailors have been frightened to travel too far along this coast for fear of being burned black like the people they can see living on its shore. Florence is defeated in a war with Lucca: Cosimo de' Medici is imprisoned as an example. The Hussite Wars in Bohemia end after 13 years; Bohemia's nationalism has been asserted and the country breaks for ever from Germany. Timbuktu falls to the Tuaregs, desert camel-riders. *31 May*: Sigismund is crowned Emperor by Pope Eugenius IV. *14 Aug*: João I King of Portugal dies, age. 76, after reigning for 48 years and is succeeded by his 40-year-old son Duarte.

   Jan van Eyck: Man in a Red Turban

   John Lydgate: *Life of St. Edmund*

1434 The capital of the Khmer is moved to Phnom Penh from Angkor. African slaves are introduced for the first time into Portugal by a caravel returning from West Africa.

Engelbrecht Engelbrechtsen leads a peasants' revolt through southern Sweden, seizing castles on his way; the revolt spreads to Norway. Prokop the Great, the radical Bohemian priest, leads his followers, the Taborites, into battle at Lipany: he is defeated. Ladislas V King of Poland dies, aged 84, and is succeeded by his 10-year-old son Ladislas VI. Florence recalls Cosimo de' Medici from exile and he rules the city (for the next 30 years).

✍ Church of St. Maclon, Rouen France
    Ca' d'Oro, Venice Italy
✐ Jan van Eyck: Giovanni Arnolfini and His Wife

1435 King Eric of Scandinavia makes peace with the Hanseatic League and restores its privileges. The diet of Sweden recognizes the claims of Englebrecht Englebrechtsen and elects him Regent for the ineffectual King Eric, who has lost Schleswig to the Duke of Holstein. Movable type is used by Dutch printers at Haarlem. Alfonso V of Aragon conquers Naples, ending the reign of Giovanna II and reuniting Naples and Sicily, making Naples the focus of an Aragonese empire in the Mediterranean. *9 Sep*: the powerful Duke of Bedford dies in France; his removal fuels impatience in England for the young King Henry VI to take power into his own hands. Charles VII of France and Philippe le Bon of Burgundy sign a treaty at Arras; Philippe breaks with the English and recognizes Charles as the true and only King of France.

✐ Roger van der Weyden: The Descent from the Cross
    Luca della Robbia: Singing Angels (marble relief)
    King René of Anjou: Death Wearing a Crown
    (painting) Pisanello: The Vision of St. Eustace
    Fra Filippo Lippi: The Adoration of the Child

1436 Charles VII of France recovers Paris from English control as the English struggle to hold the Scots at bay; a Scottish army defeats the English at Berwick, on the border. The Compact of Iglau brings the Hussite Wars to an end: all parties involved agree to accept Sigismund, the Holy Roman Emperor, as King of Bohemia. In their tentative exploration of the West African coast, the Portuguese pass the Sahara and reach the Rio de Ouro.

    ✐ Filippo Brunelleschi: Dome of Florence Cathedral, the Duomo

    🐚 Donatello: Jeremiah (sculpture)

    📖 Leon Battista Alberti: *Della Pittura* (aesthetic principles)

1437   The Portuguese are defeated at Tangier by the Moors. The Moors extract a promise from the Portuguese to return to Ceuta; Fernando, the King's brother, offers himself as a hostage but the Portuguese do not return to Ceuta and Fernando is abandoned in the dungeons at Fez. *10 Feb*: James I of Scotland is stabbed to death, aged 42, by Sir Robert Graham, whom the King had banished. Graham is tortured and executed. James is succeeded by his five-year-old son James II. *Mar*: James II of Scotland is crowned at Holyrood. *9 Dec*: the Holy Roman Emperor Sigismund dies, aged 69, and is succeeded as German King by his son-in-law Albrecht of Hapsburg.

1438   Barsbay al-Zahiri, the great Mameluke Sultan of Cairo and conqueror of Cyprus, dies. The Inca dynasty of Peru is founded by Pachacutec. Eric VII of Denmark, Norway and Sweden flees from peasant rebellions and takes refuge on the island of Gotland in the Baltic Sea; he becomes a pirate. *9 Dec*: Duarte I King of Portugal dies of plague at the age of 47, leaving his brother Fernando unransomed; Duarte is succeeded by his six-year-old son Afonso V, with his uncle Pedro as Regent.

1439   Ewuare assumes power in the kingdom of Benin in West Africa, killing the previous *Oba*, his own brother. There is heavy fighting during the coup and the capital, Urbini, is taken by storm. Ewuare is determined to turn what has been until now a limited, 'constitutional' monarchy into a despotism; he orders all his subjects to be scarred with facial markings. A nephew of the Scandinavian King Eric VII assumes the throne as Christopher III. The Ottoman Sultan Murad II takes Serbia, forcing the Serbian despot George Brankovich to take refuge in Hungary. The Council of Florence confirms the union between Rome and Constantinople; the Byzantine Emperor John VIII accepts the primacy of the Pope. *31 May*: Richard Beauchamp Earl of Warwick, the most powerful subject in England, dies at Rouen where he has resided as Lieutenant of France and Normandy. *27 Oct*: the German King Albrecht II dies, aged 42, at Langendorf; he will be succeeded next year by his posthumous son Ladislas Posthumus (born *22 Feb*, 1440).

🐚 Tomb of Richard Beauchamp, Earl of Warwick, at Warwick

Jan van Eyck: Margaret van Eyck

Luca della Robbia: Marble Reliefs for Altar of St. Peter in Florence Cathedral

🎵 Guillaume Dufay: *Nuper rosarum Flores* (for the Dedication of Florence Cathedral, *25 Mar*)

1440   Battle of Anghiari: victory for the *condottiere* Niccolo Piccinino, ruler of Bologna, over Filippo Visconti of Milan. Harfleur falls to English forces under the Duke of Somerset; a peace mission to France by Cardinal Henry Beaufort fails. Eton College in England is founded by Henry VI. *2 Feb*: The Duke of Styria and Carinthia is elected to succeed the late Albrecht II. *Mar*: Ladislas VI King of Poland accepts the Hungarian throne while the infant Ladislas Posthumus remains in the care of his uncle Frederick III. *21 Sep*: Frederick I Elector of Brandenburg dies at Kadolzburg, aged 48. *26 Oct*: Gilles de Laval, Seigneur de Rais in France, is executed at Nantes by garrotting and burning for murdering 200 children; he has also been convicted on charges of heresy, sodomy, sacrilege and violation of clerical immunity. The composer Josquin des Pres is born in Flanders.

🐚 Roger van der Weyden: Christ Appearing to His Mother

Donatello: Mary Magdalene (wooden statue)

1441   The Ethiopians send an envoy to the Church Council at Florence; an act of union is signed between the two churches of Rome and Ethiopia. The city of Cuzco in Peru is founded at about this time by the first Inca leader, the great Pachacuti. African slaves are sold in the marketplaces of Lisbon: the slave trade begins. More than 20 million slaves from Africa will be transported during the next 450 years to Europe and the New World. The painter Jan van Eyck dies at Bruges.

1442 England loses all Gascon possessions except Bordeaux and Bayonne to the French. The Portuguese Prince Fernando dies in a dungeon in Fez. *12 Jun*: Alfonso V of Aragon is crowned King of Naples. *17 Jul*: Archduke Frederick III of Austria is crowned German Emperor.

1443 The Afghan ambassador and traveller Abdur Razzaq visits the city of Vijayanagar, the great capital of the Hindu Empire of Southern India. George Castriota, Governor of Albania, declares himself a Christian and his country independent from the Turks while the Sultan Murad is preoccupied with the Serbs and Hungarians. In Japan, Motokiyo Zeami, the writer of *nō* plays, dies aged 80.

 ✍ House of Jacques Coeur, Bourges France
 🎨 Stefan Lochner: Madonna with Violets

1444 The Portuguese explorer Nino Tristram reaches the mouth of the River Senegal on the West African coast. Venetian efforts to find new spice routes are stimulated by Niccolo de' Conti, who has returned to Venice after 25 years in the Middle East, India, Java and Sumatra. Pope Eugenius IV tells de' Conti to recount his adventures to the papal secretary Poggio Bracciolini as penance for renouncing Christianity during his travels. *12 Jun*: Truce of Adrianople between Christians and Ottoman Turks; George Brankovich is restored as Serbian despot at the age of 77. The Ottoman Sultan Murad II forces the Wallachian Prince Dracul to give him as hostages his son Radu and grandson, the 13-year-old Dracula. The Hungarians are used by the Pope to break the Truce of Adrianople, resuming hostilities in *Sep. 10 Nov*: Battle of Varna: Murad II crosses the Bosporus in the face of a Venetian fleet and defeats a large army of Wallachians and Hungarians, killing Ladislas VI.

 🎨 Konrad Witz: St. Peter Altarpiece (Lake Geneva as setting)

1445 Portuguese explorer Dinis Diaz reaches and rounds Cape Verde, the westernmost point of Africa. Copenhagen becomes Denmark's capital. Charles VII forms the first permanent French army.

 🎨 Domenico Veneziano: Santa Lucia Altarpiece
   Fra Angelico: The Adoration of the Magi

Paolo Uccello: Giants
Luca della Robbia: The Resurrection (sculpture)

1446 Corinth falls to the Turks, who thwart a Greek attempt to expand from the Peloponnese into central Greece. A Korean alphabet of 28 letters is devised by committee and proclaimed 'the right language to teach the people' by Sejong, the King of Korea; his reform is rejected by the educated elite who continue to use the thousands of Chinese ideograms, and the masses are unable to use the new alphabet. *15 Apr*: the Florentine architect Filippo Brunelleschi dies, aged 69, with the dome of Florence Cathedral still incomplete.

    King's College, Cambridge (U.K.)
Orders of Cormac Mc Carthy: Blarney Castle (Ireland)

    Petrus Christus: Edward Grymestone; Carthusian Monk
Stefan Lochner: The Patron Saints

1447 Shah Rukh, son of Tamerlane, dies at Samarkand after reigning for 43 years. He is succeeded by Tamerlane's grandson Ulugh-Beg, who is more scientist and scholar than ruler and warrior. Milan establishes a republic when Filippo, the last of the Viscontis, dies; Francesco Sforza is hired as military leader. Polish aristocrats choose the Grand Duke of Lithuania to succeed Ladsilas VI. The new King, 20 years old, unites Lithuania with Poland: he is Casimir IV.

    Stefan Lochner: Presentation in the Temple

1448 The Byzantine Emperor John VIII dies, aged 57, and is succeeded by his brother Constantine XI; he is the last Byzantine emperor. Johannes Gutenberg leaves Strasbourg where he has lived for several years and returns to his native Mainz; he has invented movable print type. *19 Oct*: Battle of Kossovo: Murad II defeats a Hungarian army under Janos Hunyadi. Dracula escapes from his Ottoman captors and assumes the throne of his father, who has been murdered. Realizing that his position is unsafe, Dracula abdicates after a few months and travels to Moldavia and Transylvania. The Union of Kalmar uniting the three Scandinavian kingdoms begins to disintegrate when Christopher of Bavaria dies. The

Danes elect Christian of Oldenburg King, while the Swedish nobility elect Karl Knutsson (as Charles VIII). Charles VII renews the Hundred Years War with England, seizing Maine. Charles suppresses a rebellion of French noblemen supported by his own son, the Dauphin. Charles exiles the Dauphin, who continues to conspire against him.

🎨 Pietro di Giovanni d'Ambrogio: Adoration of the Shepherds

1449 The Turkestan Prince Ulugh-Beg is executed in Samarkand on a trumped-up charge at the instigation of his son Abd al-Latif; the Khan's favourite son Abd al-Aziz is also put to death. Ulugh-Beg's death is a great loss to science. He devised a movable observatory 40 metres/130 feet long to identify 1,018 stars; his tables are so precise that his calculations of the movements of Mars and Venus differ from modern figures by only a few seconds. The Muslims feared his learning. The chief of the Mongol federation captures Ying Zong the Chinese Emperor in battle and holds him prisoner. In Japan, the Shogun Yoshimasa assumes power, ushering in a second period of Ashikaga art rivalling Yoshimitsu's. Afonso V of Portugal is persuaded by courtiers to make war on his uncle Pedro, the Regent. The Regent, who has served his country well, is killed along with his son at the Battle of Alfarrobeira.

1450 The southern African kingdom of Great Zimbabwe is disintegrating. A victim of its own success, the capital, also called Great Zimbabwe, has outgrown the agricultural resources of the region; starved, its inhabitants have abandoned it. *25 Mar*: Francesco Sforza overthrows Milan's republic, making a triumphal entry as Duke. Sforza and his son Galazzo establish a court rivalling that of the Medicis. *15 Apr*: The French defeat the English at Formigny, completing the reconquest of Normandy. Henry VI banishes the Duke of Suffolk, who is widely hated in England for his part in the sale of Anjou and Maine to France. *1 May*: Suffolk's ship is intercepted as he sails for France and the Duke himself is captured. *2 May*: the Duke of Suffolk is beheaded at sea. *18 Jun*: John Cade leads a rebellion, demanding the restoration of power to the Duke of York. Cade's Kentish rebels defeat the King's troops at Sevenoaks. *3 Jul*: the Kentish rebels enter London. *12 Jul*: Cade is hunted down and killed at Heathfield. Pope Nicholas authorizes the Portuguese to subject and reduce to perpetual slavery Muslims and other non-Christians in Africa. At about this time, the Incas start to make cultivation terraces in the Andes.

   📐 Leon Battista Alberti: Church of San Francesco, Rimini (exterior redesigned) (Italy)
     Filarete: Porta Giova, Sforesco Castle, Milan (Italy)
     Great Wall of China (rebuilding with brick facing begun)
   🎨 Paolo Uccello: The Flood; The Drunkenness of Noah
     Fra Angelico: The Annunciation (fresco)

1451 The Ottoman Sultan Murad II dies, aged 48, at Adrianople and is succeeded by his 21-year-old son Mohammed II

   📐 Leon Battista Alberti: Rucellai Palace, Florence (completed) (Italy)
   🎨 Luca della Robbia: The Ascension (polychrome terracotta)

1452 *19 Mar*: Frederick the German King is crowned Holy Roman Emperor by Pope Nicholas. *Jun*: war between the last Greek Emperor of Constantinople, Constantine, and the new Ottoman Sultan Mohammed II begins. The Sultan's Castle of Europe (Rumili Hisar) stands opposite the Castle of Asia (Anadoli Hisar) at the narrowest part of the Bosporus: this alarms Constantine. The painter Leonardo da Vinci is born.

   🎨 Roger van der Weyden: The Braque Triptych
     Lorenzo Ghiberti: Bronze Doors, Florence Baptistry

1453 The White Sheep dynasty of Persia begins, founded by Uzun Hasan. The fall of Constantinople and the end of the Byzantine Empire that has existed since the end of the Roman Empire in *AD 476*. An enormous iron chain has kept Mohammed II's fleet out of the Golden Horn, but the Sultan has 70 small ships dragged overland to support the 250,000 troops that besiege the city on *6 Apr*.

12 Apr: the Sultan orders the city walls pounded with huge cannonballs fired from an 8-metre/26-foot long cannon with 42-inch calibre. *29 May*: the walls of Constantinople are breached, the Turks enter, there is hand-to-hand fighting and the last Byzantine Emperor, Constantine XI, is killed. The Turks make Constantinople the Ottoman capital. The Pope is left with no serious rival in Europe. Since the Muslim rulers impose high tariffs on caravan shipments, European traders need new sea routes to the Orient more urgently than before, giving a spur to exploration. Greek scholars fleeing from Constantinople are welcomed by Cosimo de' Medici in Florence. The Turks introduce coffee to Constantinople. The Hundred Years War ends with the English expelled from every part of France except Calais. Henry VI has his first episode of insanity: his cousin Richard of York stands in as Regent. *24 Dec*: John Dunstable, the English mathematician, astrologer and composer, dies in London.

1454 Henry VI of England recovers from a bout of insanity and dismisses the Duke of York as his protector. At a Feast of the Pheasant for the Duke of Burgundy, 28 musicians perform inside a huge pie; a nursery rhyme commemorates the event. *9 Apr*: the Peace of Lodi ends the conflict among Venice, Milan and Florence. *18 Apr*: the Doge of Venice, Francesco Foscari, signs a treaty with the new Sultan Mohammed II. *21 Jul*: Juan II of Castile dies and is succeeded by his son Enrique IV.

1455 The Venetian navigator Alvise da Cadamosto discovers the Cape Verde Islands off the West African coast. The French poet François Villon stabs a priest to death in a street brawl and has to flee from Paris. *18 Mar*: the painter Fra Angelico dies in Rome, aged 55. *22 May*: In England the Wars of the Roses between the houses of York and Lancaster begin with the Battle of St Albans. *1 Dec*: the artist Lorenzo Ghiberti dies in Florence, aged 77.

✎ Andrea del Castagno: David (painted leather)

□ *Gutenberg Bible* (first printed Bible, one of earliest printed books using movable metal type)

1456 The Ottoman Turks take Athens and begin ruling

Greece. *14 Jul*: the Hungarian Prince János Hunyadi destroys the Ottoman fleet. *21 Jul*: János Hunyadi defeats the Ottoman army besieging Belgrade and forces Mohammed II to withdraw to Constantinople. *11 Aug*: János Hunyadi dies of plague, aged 69. Vlad Dracula, who is now 24, reassumes the throne of Wallachia.

    ✍ Leon Battista Alberti: Church of Santa Maria Novella (new facade)

    ✑ Andrea del Castagno: Niccola da Tolentino

    📖 François Villon: *Le Petit Testament* (poetry)

1457 Charles VIII of Sweden is driven out of the country. Christian I of Denmark is crowned King of Sweden in his place; the nobles Svante Stures, Sten Stures and Sten the Younger retain the real power. The artist Donatello moves to Florence at the age of 71. Freiburg University is founded. *16 Mar*: János Hunyadi's eldest son Laszlo is arrested in Buda and beheaded. Ladislas V, King of Hungary and Bohemia leaves Buda for Prague to escape the criticism following the execution of the 23-year-old Laszlo Hunyadi. *19 Aug*: Andrea del Castagno dies of plague, aged 34 in Florence, 11 days after his wife's death. *23 Nov*: Ladislas V of Hungary and Bohemia dies suddenly, possibly of poison; he is succeeded as King of Hungary by Laszlo Hunyadi's younger brother.

    ✑ Petrus Christus: Madonna with Saints Francis and Jerome

    Paolo Uccello: The Rout of San Romano

1458 Matthias Corvinus is elected to the throne of Hungary, but the throne remains in dispute. Constantinople annexes Serbia. Alfonso V of Aragon dies, aged 73, and is succeeded by his son Juan in Aragon and his illegitimate son Ferdinand in Naples. Mahmud I begins a 53-year reign in Delhi; Mahmoud will conquer Champanir and Girnar and build a great palace at Sarkhej.

    ✍ Pitti Palace, Florence (Italy)

1459 Matthias Corvinus King of Hungary challenges the legitimacy of King George Podiebrad of Bohemia.

    ✑ Andrea Mantegna: The Crucifixion

1460 *10 Jul*: Henry VI of England is taken prisoner at the Battle of Northampton and the Yorkists win. *3 Aug*.: James II of Scotland is killed when a cannon explodes near Roxburgh Castle; he is succeeded by his son James III. *25 Oct*: The Lords' Act of Accord states that Henry VI of England should keep the crown for his lifetime, but then the Duke of York and his heirs are to have it; Henry VI, captive, agrees. *13 Nov*: Prince Henry the Navigator dies, aged 66.

✐ Leon Battista Alberti: Church of San Sebastian, Mantua (Italy)

▯ The Arsenal, Venice (Italy)

✑ Luca della Robbia: Madonna and Angels (glazed terracotta)

1461 *2 Feb*: Battle of Mortimer's Cross: the Yorkists are victorious capturing Owen Glendower, who is beheaded. *17 Feb*: Second Battle of St. Albans: Queen Margaret defeats the Earl of Warwick and has her husband, Henry VI, released by the Yorkist lords. *4 Mar*: Henry VI of England is deposed, succeeded by Edward Earl of March, the late Duke of York's son, as Edward IV. *29 Mar*: Battle of Towton confirms Edward's supremacy. *28 Jun*: coronation of Edward IV of England, founding the house of York. *24 Jul*: Charles VII of France dies, aged 58, and is succeeded by his son Louis XI. Trebizond and Kastamonu fall to Ottoman forces. Japan has a plague and famine that cause a rising against the Shogun Yoshimasa.

✑ Donatello: Judith and Holofernes

▯ François Villon: *Le Grand Testament* (*. . . ou sont les neiges d'antan?*)

1462 Basil II Grand Duke of Muscovy dies, aged 47, and is succeeded by his son Ivan III, who is, in effect, the first Russian monarch. Vlad (Dracula) of Wallachia slaughters 20,000 Turks along the Danube, many by impalement, but Vlad the Impaler is deposed and replaced by his pro-Turkish brother. The Holy Roman Emperor Frederick III is besieged by radicals in the Hofburg at Vienna; the radicals are led by Frederick's own brother, Albrecht.

1463 The Holy Roman Emperor Frederick III unites upper and lower Austria following the death of his brother Albrecht. The Venetians declare war on Constantinople following Ottoman interference with their trade in the Levant.

♫ Guillaume Dufay: *Ecce ancilla Domini*

1464 The Poste Royale is founded by Louis XI of France; it is the first national postal service. *23 Apr*: the English composer Robert Fayrfax is born. *1 May*: Edward IV of England secretly marries Elizabeth Woodville. *16 Jun*: the painter Roger van der Weyden dies in Brussels, aged 63. *1 Aug*: Cosimo de' Medici dies, aged 75, in Florence while listening to Plato's *Dialogues*; he is succeeded as head of the Medici banking house by his son Piero.

1465 The Dukes of Alençon, Berri, Bourbon, Lorraine and Burgundy join forces to defeat Louis XI at Montl'hery; they force him to sign the Treaty of Conflans restoring Normandy to the Duc de Berri and towns on the Somme to Burgundy. *Jul*: Henry VI, ex-King of England, is captured by Edward IV and kept prisoner until *1470*.

🖼 Piero della Francesca: *Duke of Urbino*

1466 Pope Paul II excommunicates George Podiebrad King of Bohemia. In Florence, Luca Pitti fails in his attempt to assassinate Piero de' Medici. He is stripped of his powers and his palace is left unfinished. The Medicis form an alliance with the Vatican to finance alum mining in the papal states; the Pope will excommunicate anyone importing alum from Turks in breach of their monopoly. *13 Dec*: Donatello dies in Florence, aged 80.

🖼 Giovanni Bellini: *Pietà*

1467 In Japan, Shogun Yoshimasa names his brother Yoshime as his successor, but is challenged by supporters of his son Yoshihisa; 10 years of civil war begin in Japan. The Japanese priest and landscape painter Sesshu goes to Beijing to study, after being taught by Shubun, a Chinese painter who bcame a naturalized Japanese, bringing Japanese and Chinese art closer together.
15 Jun: Philippe le Bon Duke of Burgundy dies, aged 71, after reigning for 48 years and making Burgundy the richest country in Europe. He is succeeded by his son Charles the Bold, who makes a triumphant entry into Liège to start a 10-year power struggle with Louis XI of France.

1468 Sonni Ali King of Songhai (West Africa) takes Timbuktu from the Tuaregs. Zara Yaqub, Solomonic Emperor of Ethiopia, dies after reigning for 34 years and bringing all the Ethiopian Highlands under his rule and creating a bulwark against Islam in Africa; he became the 'Prester John' Christians in Europe have been looking and hoping for. Prince Skanderbeg of Albania dies, aged 62. Charles the Bold, Duke of Burgundy, marries Margaret, the sister of King Edward IV of England. Norway surrenders the Orkney Islands to the kingdom of Scotland. Johannes Gutenberg, the inventor of movable printing type and thus the pioneer of modern mass production of books, dies in obscurity in Mainz. *3 Dec*: Lorenzo and Giuliano de' Medici succeed their father Piero as rulers of Florence.

    Hans Memling: Donne Triptych
        Cosme Tura: Pietà

1469   *19 Oct*: the crowns of Castile and Aragon are joined in the marriage of Prince Ferdinand of Aragon and Léon and the Infanta Isabella of Castile. *9 Dec*: the painter Fra Filippo Lippi dies at Spoleto, aged 63.

    Marsilio Ficino: *Complete Works of Plato* (translated into Latin)

1470   German printers set up the first printshop in Paris. French printer Nicolas Jensen sets up in Venice as a printer and publisher after learning the craft from Gutenberg in Mainz; he is the first to use Roman rather than Gothic lettering. In Peru, the Inca army led by Topa Inca, son of Pachacuti, overruns the kingdom of Chimor, the most developed state in South America. The Inca conquest of Chimor makes the Incas the dominant people in the continent; their base is the city of Cuzco. Henry VI regains his throne briefly in *Oct*, supported by the Earl of Warwick; Londoners deride the spectacle of Henry VI being brought out in procession in an old blue velvet gown. The Duke of Clarence defects to Edward IV, who obliges Warwick to take refuge in France. Portuguese explorers (João de Santarem and Pedro de Escolar) reach the Gold Coast in West Africa (Ghana).

    York Minster (completed) (U.K.)

    Thomas Malory: *Morte d'Arthur* (completed)

1471   The Portuguese found the port of San Jorge d'el Mina on the Gold Coast to deal with the gold trade. The Portuguese take Tangier. Sten Sture the Younger repels an invasion of Sweden by the Danes. Pope Sixtus cancels the alum deal made between the Vatican and the Medici family; Lorenzo de' Medici is appointed banker to the Vatican. Ivan III, Grand Duke of Muscovy, forces Novgorod to relinquish its ties with Lithuania and pay tribute to Moscow. *Jan*: Louis XI declares war on Charles the Bold of Burgundy. Edward IV returns to England, landing at Ravenspur (now Spurn Point). *22 Mar*: Podiebrad of Bohemia dies, aged 51, in Prague and is succeeded by the Polish Prince Ladislas, son of Casimir IV, who will rule as Ladislas II. *11 Apr*: Edward IV deposes Henry VI again. *14 Apr*: Battle of Barnet: Edward defeats and kills Warwick as he tries to escape from the battlefield. *6 May*: Battle of Tewkesbury: decisive defeat of the Lancastrians; Prince Edward, the son of Henry VI, is stabbed to death by the Dukes of Clarence and Gloucester after the battle. *21 May*: Henry VI is executed secretly in the Tower of London. *26 Jul*: Pope Paul II dies, aged 54, and is succeeded by Sixtus IV.

1472 Portuguese exploration of the Atlantic coast of Africa continues. Fernando Po discovers the Fernando Po Islands and Lopo Goncalves is the first to cross the equator. Grand Duke Ivan III of Muscovy marries Zoë, niece of Constantinople's last Greek Emperor, Constantine XI; later Russian rulers use this as the basis of a claim to be the protectors of Orthodox Christianity.

    ⬈ Leon Battista Alberti: Church of San Andrea, Mantua (completed)

    🎨 Leonardo da Vinci: The Annunciation
        Andrea del Verrocchio: Tomb of Giovanni and Piero de' Medici

    🎵 Guillaume Dufay: *Ave regina caelorum* (for the Dedication of Cambrai Cathedral on *5 Jul*)

1473 In Mexico, Ayacatl, who has ruled the Aztecs since *1468*, conquers the neighbouring city of Tlatelolco. The Japanese warlord Yamana Mochitoyo dies, aged 69, and his son-in-law Hosokawa Katsumoto also dies, aged 48, in the civil war (Onin War). Cyprus falls to the Venetians. Charles the Bold of Burgundy occupies Lorraine and Alsace.

    ✍ Orders of Pope Sixtus IV: Sistine Chapel, Vatican Palace
Ryoanji Garden, Kyoto

    🖾 Martin Schongauer: The Virgin of the Rose Garden

1474 Yoshima, the Japanese Shogun, abdicates, aged 39, in
favour of his son Yoshihasa. The Union of Constance is
created to support Louis XI of France: the Coalition
makes war on Charles the Bold Duke of Burgundy.
Christopher Columbus (Cristoforo Colombo), a 23-
year-old Genoese seaman, begins speculating about
the possibility of reaching Cathay (China) by sailing
westwards from Europe. Columbus uses map projec-
tions devised by German mathematicians and Italian
map-makers at Sagres to revive the ancient Greek idea
that the earth is spherical. *27 Nov*: the French composer
Guillaume Dufay dies at Cambrai. *13 Dec*: Isabella
succeeds to the throne of Castile and León as her
half-brother Enrique IV dies.

1475 Pope Sixtus IV appoints the Pazzi family as bankers to
the Vatican, replacing the Medicis. Castile and Portugal
fight over Enrique IV's succession, but the cortes at
Segovia recognizes Isabella's right to succeed together
with her husband Ferdinand of Aragon. Edward IV of
England invades France. *29 Aug*: Louis XI meets Edward IV and negotiates the Peace of Picquigny.
10 Dec: the painter Paolo Uccello dies in Florence, aged
78.

    ✍ Winchester Cathedral (completed) (U.K.)

    🖾 Giovanni Bellini: St. Justine
      Perugino (Pietro di Cristoforo di Vannucci): The
Adoration of the Magi
      Antonio and Piero Pollaiuolo: The Martyrdom of St.
Sebastian; Battle of Ten Naked Men

    📖 Platina (Bartolomeo Sacchi): *Concerning Honest
Pleasure and Well-being* (first printed cookery book)

1476 Charles the Bold of Burgundy conquers Lorraine and
then makes war on Swiss cantons allying themselves with
Louis XI of France; he is defeated. Vlad Tepes (Dracula), who is now 43, reassumes the throne of Wallachia.
26 Dec: Galazzo Sforza, tyrant of Milan, is assassinated
in the porch of Milan Cathedral by three young noblemen; he is succeeded by his seven-year-old son Gian

Galazzo with the boy's mother as Regent.

 ✽ Andrea del Verocchio: David (bronze)

1477 Printers all over Europe are adopting Gutenberg's movable type printing press. A game called 'hands-in-and-hands-out' (cricket) is banned in England by Edward IV because it it interferes with compulsory archery practice. Columbus visits England but is unable to get financial backing for his quest for a new route to the Indies. The civil war in Japan comes to an indecisive end. Ottoman troops reach the outskirts of Venice. Louis XI of France invades Burgundy. *5 Jan*: Battle of Nancy: Swiss pikemen defeat the Duke of Burgundy's cavalry. The 43-year-old Duke, Charles the Bold, is killed in the battle; his body is later found half-eaten by wolves. *18 Aug*: the Hapsburgs gain the Netherlands through the marriage of the son of the Holy Roman Emperor Frederick III, Maximilian, to Mary the daughter of Charles the Bold.

1478 Novgorod loses its independence after a second war with Muscovy. Isabella of Castile launches an Inquisition against converted Jews who practise their original faith in secret; her Inquisition will broaden to include all 'heretics'. Lorenzo de' Medici takes 200,000 florins from Florence's city treasury to cover a default by the Medici branch in Bruges; he is excommunicated. *26 Apr*: Lorenzo and Giuliano de' Medici are attacked in Florence Cathedral; it is a conspiracy involving Pope Sixtus IV and the Pazzi family to remove the Medicis from their position of power. The 25-year-old Giuliano is stabbed to death, but Lorenzo is able to escape into the sacristy. Later he exacts cruel revenge on the Pazzi family and their supporters, hanging them from the palace windows or throwing them into the Arno.

 ✽ Sandro Botticelli: Primavera

1479 In Milan Ludovico Sforza seizes power from his nephew Gian Galazzo. Ivan III, Grand Duke of Muscovy, annexes Novgorod and deports its rebellious aristocrats to central Russia. *20 Jan*: Juan II of Aragon dies, aged 81, and is succeeded by his 26-year-old son Ferdinand (Ferdinand II of Aragon and V of Castile and León), uniting the major crowns of Spain. *25 Jan*: Treaty of Constantinople, ending the war between Venice and the

Ottoman Empire; the Venetians have to pay a tribute of 10,000 ducats a year to trade in the Black Sea. *7 Aug*: Maximilian of Austria defeats Louis XI of France, halting his penetration of Burgundy. *4 Sep*: Ferdinand and Isabella make peace with Portugal after four years of war; the Portuguese recognize Spanish rights over the Canary Islands in exchange for a monopoly of trade along Africa's west coast.

📖 Hans Memling: Mystic Marriage of St. Catherine

1480 The last Aztec Emperor, Montezuma II, is born. Pestilence causes enormous loss of life in the Mayan Empire in Central America. Ferdinand of Aragon mediates in the quarrel between Pope Sixtus IV and Lorenzo de' Medici. Ivan III of Muscovy exploits the disunity of the Tartars and stops their advance on Moscow; he frees Russia of Tartar domination. *10 Jul*: René Count of Anjou dies without an heir, aged 71: Louis XI annexes his territory. *11 Aug*: Otranto in southern Italy falls to the Ottoman Turks, but Mohammed II fails to take Rhodes.

🏛 Hôtel de Ville, Brussels (completed)

📖 Hans Memling: The Seven Joys of Mary
Sandro Botticelli: The Birth of Venus

1481 *3 May*: the Ottoman Sultan Mohammed II dies, aged 49, and is succeeded by his 34-year-old eldest son Bayzid I. *Aug*: Afonso V of Portugal dies, aged 49, and is succeeded by his 26-year-old son João II.

📖 Michael Pacher: Coronation of the Virgin (wooden shrine)

1482 Portuguese explorers sailing along the west coast of Africa discover bananas. The Bishop of Liège is killed by Guillaume de la Marck (the Wild Boar of the Ardennes), a 36-year-old Belgian soldier in the pay of Louis XI (Louis the Spider). Venice opens a war with Ferrara. *23 Feb*: the artist Luca della Robbia dies in Florence, aged 82. *27 Mar*: Mary of Burgundy, the 27-year-old daughter of Charles the Bold, dies after a hunting accident. Her husband Maximilian claims power over the Low Countries as Regent for his infant son Philip, but Flanders and Brabant reject his claim. *25 Aug*: Queen Margaret of Anjou, the widow of the murdered

King Henry VI of England, dies. *23 Dec*: the Peace of Arras ends the conflict between the Hapsburgs and Louis XI of France, who has lived in isolation for two years at Plessis-les-Tours surrounded by astrologers. Burgundy and Picardy are to become part of France,

🎨 Pietro Perugino: The Delivery of the Keys (fresco in Sistine Chapel)

1483 Tomas de Torquemada, a 63-year-old Dominican monk, takes control of the Inquisition at the request of Ferdinand and Isabella. *9 Apr*: Edward IV of England dies unexpectedly, aged 40, and is succeeded by his 12-year-old son Edward V. *30 Apr*: Richard 40, Duke of Gloucester takes possession of Edward V at Stony Stratford as his Protector and becomes effective ruler of England from this moment. *22 Jun*: Edward IV's marriage is declared invalid and his sons illegitimate. *25 Jul*: Edward V is deposed. *26 Jun*: Richard of Gloucester accedes to the English throne as Richard III. *10 Aug*: Louis XI of France dies, aged 60, and is succeeded by his 13-year-old son Charles VIII. *24 Aug*: Richard III declares his son Edward Prince of Wales; the deposed Edward V and his younger brother (the Princes in the Tower) are murdered at about this time.

🏛 William Orchard: Divinity School, Oxford
🎨 Sandro Botticelli: The Magnificat Giovanni
  Bellini: The Virgin and Child and Six Saints
  Piero Pollaiuolo: Coronation of the Virgin

1484 In Japan, the Shogun Yoshimasa introduces the tea ceremony. The Portuguese navigator Diego Cão discovers the mouth of the River Zaire and the coast of Angola. Columbus approaches João II of Portugal with his scheme to sail westwards to the Indies; King João declines. *9 Apr*: Richard III's son and heir, Prince Edward, dies. *Aug*: Richard III of England orders the body of the murdered King Henry VI to be removed from Chertsey Abbey to St. George's Chapel, Windsor. *12 Aug*: Pope Sixtus IV dies and is succeeded by Pope Innocent VIII. *5 Dec*: Pope Innocent introduces harsh measures against witches and magicians.

🏛 Silver Pavilion, Kyoto (completed)
🎨 Hieronymus Bosch: Garden of Earthly Delights

    ⬓ John Lydgate: *The Life of Our Lady*

1485 Matthias Corvinus of Hungary expels the Holy Roman Emperor Frederick III from Vienna. The Belgian La Marck is captured and beheaded for murdering the Bishop of Liège. Bruges and Ghent surrender to Maximilian of Austria after sieges. *16 Mar*: Richard III of England's wife, Anne Neville, dies. *7 Aug*: Henry Tudor lands at Milford Haven in Wales with 1800 French soldiers. *22 Aug*: Battle of Bosworth Field: Henry Tudor, Earl of Richmond, defeats the King's army. Richard III is killed in the battle and is succeeded by Henry Tudor as Henry VII. *30 Oct*: coronation of Henry VII in Westminster Abbey. Columbus travels to France and England, hoping to interest Charles VIII or Henry VII in an expedition to Cathay, but without success. *16 Dec*: Catherine of Aragon is born, the daughter of Ferdinand and Isabella.

    ✺ Giovanni Bellini: St. Francis in Ecstasy
       Carlo Crivelli: Pietà Panchiatichi
       Leonardo da Vinci: The Virgin of the Rocks

    ⬓ Thomas Malory: *Morte d'Arthur* (published posthumously by Caxton)

1486 Matthias Vorvinus of Hungary devises a law code: for a time Hungary becomes the dominant state in central Europe. In the kingdom of Gaur in India, African slaves revolt and put their own leader on the throne. The kingdom of Benin in West Africa begins trading with Portugal. *18 Jan*: Henry VII of England marries Elizabeth, daughter of Edward IV, uniting the houses of York and Lancaster and so strengthening his own (Tudor) dynasty. *16 Feb*: Maximilian of Austria becomes King of the Romans. *9 Apr*: Maximilian is crowned King of the Germans at Aix-la-Chapelle. *1 May*: Christopher Columbus successfully persuades Ferdinand and Isabella to sponsor a westward expedition to the Indies. *16 Jul*: Henry VII announces that the Princes in the Tower were murdered at Richard III's orders; some believe that Henry VII himself may have been responsible. *19 Sep*: Henry VII of England's son Arthur is born.

    ✺ Carlo Crivelli: Annunciation

📖 Juliana Berners: *Book of St. Albans*
Jakob Sprenger and Heinrich Kramer: *Malleus Maleficarum* (alleged evidence of witchcraft)

1487 Pope Innocent VIII appoints Tomas Torquemada Grand Inquisitor. In Central America, the Great Temple of Tenochtitlan is consecrated with the sacrifice of 20,000 people; the ceremony is presided over by the Aztec ruler, Ahuitzotl, who tears out the hearts of hundreds of victims himself. The Portuguese navigator Bartholomew Diaz embarks from Lisbon; a storm drives his tiny fleet round the southernmost tip of Africa. João II of Portugal sends Pedro de Covilhão to the Near East in search of a spice route and the land of Prester John.

    ✍ Orders of Emperor Ahuitzotl: Great Temple, Tenochtitlan (restored)
Palazzo Dario, Grand Canal, Venice (completed)

1488 Work goes forward on the rebuilding in brick of the Great Wall of China, first created as an earthwork 1,700 years ago, now a 7.6-metre/25-foot high brick-faced rampart. Johann Widmann, a German mathematician, invents the regular and systematic use of the symbols + and − for plus and minus. *7 Oct*: the artist Andrea del Verrocchio dies in Venice, aged 53. *Dec*: Bartholomew Diaz returns to Lisbon and reports his discovery to João II; the King renames Diaz' Cape of Storms the Cape of Good Hope, seeing it as promising a sea route to India.

    ✍ Duke Humphrey's Library, Oxford
Frauenkirch, Munich

    🎨 Andrea del Verrocchio: Equestrian Statue of Bartolommeo Colleoni (unfinished bronze)

1489 The first European typhus epidemic breaks out in Aragon, introduced by soldiers returning from Cyprus. Venice buys Cyprus from Catherine Cornaro, ending 700 years of Frankish rule there.

1490 Henry VII of England takes control of the English wool trade away from Florentine bankers and puts it in the hands of English bankers. This loss in business exposes Florence to the opponents of big business, led by Girolamo Savonarola, Prior of San Marco. The Portuguese plant sugar cane on São Tomé and transfer slaves from Benin to work the cane fields. Portuguese explorers navigate 300km/200 miles of the River Zaire: they found a trading post at São Salvador. *4 Apr*: Matthias Corvinus dies suddenly, aged 50, and is succeeded by Ladislas II of Bohemia.

  ✍ Mausoleum of Tamerlane, Samarkand (with black onyx tomb)

    Borovitzkiye Gate, the Kremlin, Moscow

  🎨 Sandro Botticelli: The Annunciation

1491 A Portuguese embassy arrives at Banza, capital of the Kongo (Angola and Zaire), to establish friendly relations with Nazinga Nkuma, King of the Kongo. Charles VIII of France annexes Brittany; Henry VII goes to war with France, making peace with Scotland to release his troops for action. Constantinople makes peace with Egypt, which gains control of Cilicia in Anatolia. Savonarola begins denouncing corruption in Florence, especially that of Lorenzo de' Medici, in a series of sermons.

  ✍ Main Entrance of the Kremlin (Gate of Salvation), Moscow

    Orders of Mohammed Quli: Hyderabad, including Charminar Arch

  🎨 Perugino: The Nativity

    Martin Schongauer: The Last Judgment (frescoes in Breisach Cathedral)

1492 In West Africa, Sunni Ali dies under mysterious circumstance after reigning for 28 years and building a huge Songhai Empire. He has had the mullahs of Timbuktu murdered for defying his authority, so he may be the victim of a revenge killing. *2 Jan*: Granada surrenders to Isabella and Ferdinand, who take the last Muslim kingdom in Spain. *31 Mar*: Ferdinand and Isabella extend the Spanish Inquisition: it orders the 150,000 Jews in Granada to sell up and leave the country 'for the honour and glory of God'. *18 Apr*: Lorenzo de' Medici dies, aged 43. *Jun*: Casimir IV King of Poland dies, aged 65, and is succeeded by his 33-year-old son John. *3 Aug*: Christopher Columbus sets sail with the *Santa Maria*, *Niña* and *Pinta*. *6 Aug*: *Pinta* loses her rudder, so the fleet stops at Tenerife for repairs. *6 Sep*: Columbus sets sail again from Tenerife. *12 Oct*: the painter Piero della Francesca dies, aged 72, near Arezzo. Columbus sights land. *28*

Oct: Columbus lands in Cuba. *6 Dec*: Columbus lands on the island of Quisqueya which he calls Hispaniola. Luis de Torres and Rodrigo make the earliest known reference to smoking tobacco. They report seeing natives who 'drink smoke'. Rodrigo de Jerez is the first European to take up smoking. *25 Dec*: *Santa Maria* runs aground and has to be abandoned.

1493   The Songhai Empire in West Africa is taken over by the 50-year-old Askia Mohammed; he will, during his reign, come to dominate the Mandingo Empire and extend his territory beyond the River Niger. *Jan*: Columbus builds a fort on Hispaniola using material from the wrecked *Santa Maria*. *4 Jan*: Columbus sets sail for home, leaving 44 men at the new Fort La Navidad. *4 Mar*: Columbus reaches Lisbon. *15 Mar*: Columbus arives at Palos. *May*: Maximilian I, King of the Germans, takes Artois and Franche-Comte from France under the Peace of Senlis. *4 May*: Alexander VI issues a Papal Bull establishing a demarcation line between Spanish and Portuguese spheres of influence; the Spanish are to hold dominion over any lands they may discover west of the line, the Portuguese over lands discovered east of the line. *24 Sep*: Queen Isabella sends Columbus back to the Indies as Governor in a fleet of 17 ships. The second voyage is financed through the sale of assets appropriated from Jews. *3 Nov*: Columbus lands on an island he calls Dominica. *22 Nov*: Columbus sights Hispaniola, sails westward to La Navidad to find that the fort has been burned down and the men have gone.

 🐱 Carlo Crivelli: Coronation of the Virgin
  Tilman Riemenschneider: Adam and Eve (sculpture)

1494   The Flemish composer Josquin des Pres is invited to become principal singer at the royal chapel of Charles VIII of France. Treaty of Tordesillas divides the world between Portugal and Spain along the same lines as those expressed in last year's Papal Bull. Ivan III, Grand Duke of Muscovy, gains his nickname 'the Great' by driving the German merchants out of Novgorod and extending his territory east to the Ural Mountains by annexing Novgorod. *11 Jan*: the painter Ghirlandaio dies in

Florence, aged 44. *14 May*: Columbus discovers Jamaica, naming it Santiago; later in the month he lands on Guadeloupe, Montserrat, Antigua, St. Martin, Puerto Rico and the Virgin islands. He goes 33 days with virtually no sleep and loses his memory. Columbus returns to Spain with 500 Caribs. Queen Isabella suggests to Bishop Fonseca that an inquiry should be held into the legality of the abduction and imprisonment of the Caribs. Theologians differ on this legal question, so Queen Isabella orders that the Caribs should be returned to their island. *11 Aug*: the artist Hans Memling dies at Bruges, aged 64. *22 Oct*: the Duke of Milan, Gian Galazzo Sforza, dies. He has probably been poisoned by his uncle Lodovico the Moor who succeeds him as Duke; Lodovico gives his niece Bianca in marriage to Maximilian the German King in return for an imperial investiture of the Duchy of Milan.

🐚 Perugino: Pietà
 Sandro Botticelli: Calumny

1495 Leonardo da Vinci submits plans to control the River Arno, which intermittently floods Florence. Leonardo is now employed by Duke Lodovico of Milan. Naples is struck by syphilis in the first documented outbreak of the disease in history, although it may earlier have been mistaken for leprosy; the disease strikes the French army in a particularly virulent form and the French call it the Neapolitan disease (while the Italians call it the French disease). The Diet of Worms tries to modernize the Holy Roman Empire, proclaiming Perpetual Peace and setting up a Court of Appeal. The Lithuanians expel their Jews. Columbus orders every native in Hispaniola above the age of 14 is to pay tribute money to Spain every three years. *Feb*: Naples surrenders to Charles VIII of France, who is crowned King of Naples. *6 Jul*: Battle of Fornovo: Ferrandino, son of the ex-King Alfonso of Naples, retakes Naples. Pope Alexander VI organizes a Holy League to drive out the French. Charles escapes to France. The French fleet is captured by the Spanish at Rapallo; a French army surrenders at Novaro. *Oct*: João II King of Portugal dies, aged 40, and is succeeded by his brother-in-law Manoel I.

ℂ Piero di Cosimo: Vulcan and Aeolus

1496   Henry VII of England refuses to recognize the Spanish and Portuguese claims of the Treaty of Tordesillas; he grants a patent to the 46-year-old John Cabot to search for new lands and govern for England any he may find. The Spanish complete their conquest of the Canary Islands; Tenerife, the largest of the islands, falls to the Spanish, who rapidly assimilate the indigenous Guanche people. In Poland, the Statute of Piotkow restricts burghers from buying land, deprives peasants of freedom of movement and gives the gentry extensive privileges. Manoel I of Portugal orders the expulsion of Jews from his country and has many massacred; he does this to please Ferdinand and Isabella, known anti-Semites, whose daughter Isabella he plans to marry. Ferrandion, the new King of Naples, dies, aged 27, on *7 Sep* and is succeeded by his uncle Frederick.

ℂ Gentile Bellini: Procession of the True Cross in St. Mark's Square

Vittore Carpaccio: The Blood of the Redeemer

Perugino: The Crucifixion

1497   Rustum Shah of Persia dies, ending the White Sheep dynasty. Lucrezia Borgia, 17-year-old Duchess of Ferrara, persuades her father Pope Alexander VI to annul her marriage to Giovanni Sforza, Lord of Pesaro; the Pope betrothes her, instead, to Alfonso of Aragon. John I of Denmark defeats a Swedish army at Brunkeberg and revives the Scandinavian Union, beginning a reign as John II. The Portuguese explorer Vasco da Gama sets sail from Lisbon to find a sea route to India round the southern cape of Africa discovered by Diaz in *1487*. A Florentine seaman, Amerigo Vespucci claims he discovered the mainland of America in *1491*; it is believed that he is an agent of the Medici family. *22 Jun*: John Cabot reaches Labrador and goes on to explore the coastline of Nova Scotia and Newfoundland. He sees huge fishing grounds off Newfoundland. *6 Aug*: Cabot returns to Bristol. *22 Nov*: Vasco da Gama rounds the Cape of Good Hope. *25 Dec*: Da Gama sails along the south-east coast of Africa on Christmas Day, giving Natal its name. Savonarola celebrates the annual carnival in Florence with a bonfire of the vanities in the Piazza della Signoria. Carnival masks, books and pictures are burned, attracting huge crowds. Savonarola attacks the alleged crimes of Pope Alexander VI and contemptuously rejects the offer of a cardinal's hat.

    ⚏ Bell Harry (central tower) Canterbury Cathedral (U.K.)

    ⚐ Leonardo da Vinci: The Last Supper (fresco)
        Filippino Lippi: The Meeting of Joachim and Anne at the Golden Gate
        Perugino: Apollo and Marsyas
        Michelangelo Buonarroti: Bacchus (sculpture)

1498 John Cabot and his son Sebastian follow the eastern seaboard of North America from Nova Scotia southwards on a second voyage. *8 Apr*: Charles VIII of France dies, aged 27, and is succeeded by his cousin the Duc d'Orléans as Louis XII. *14 Apr*: Vasco da Gama arrives at the trading city of Malindi in East Africa after calling in at Kilwa and Mombasa. *23 Apr*: Vasco da Gama makes his landfall in India at Calicut, establishing finally that there is a sea route from Portugal to India and the Spice Islands; the discovery frees Europe from dependence on Venetian and Muslim middlemen in the spice trade. Savonarola is burned at the stake for heresy in the Piazza della Signoria on the same day. *7 Jun*: Columbus embarks on a third voyage to the New World. *22 Jul*: Columbus reaches St. Vincent. *15 Aug*: Columbus reaches Grenada and goes on to discover Trinidad, landing at what seems to be the mouth of the Orinoco on the mainland of South America. 200 Spanish colonists settle in Hispaniola. The Spanish ship 600 Caribs back to Spain to be sold into slavery.

    ⚐ Piero di Cosimo: The Discovery of Honey
        Albrecht Dürer: The Apocalypse (woodcuts)
        Gerard David: Judgment of Cambyses

1499 Venice opens a four-year war with the Ottoman Empire. The Ottoman Turks take Montenegro. The Moors in Granada stage a large-scale insurrection as Inquisitor General Francisco de Cisneros forces people to convert to Christianity. London has a Black Death epidemic. Louis XII divorces Jeanne, daughter of Louis XI, and

marries Anne of Brittany, widow of Charles VIII, in
order to keep the Duchy of Brittany under the French
crown. Vasco da Gama returns to Portugal from Mozambique with pepper, nutmeg, cloves and cinnamon
after losing one-third of his men to scurvy; his success
encourages others to attempt the voyage round Africa.
Louis XII gains support from Venice for his claim to
Milan; he invades Italy, forces Lodovico's flight from
Milan and accepts Milan's surrender on *14 Sep*. The
Swiss are supported by the French against the German
King Maximilian I and gain a series of victories. *22 Sep*:
Treaty of Basel: Maximilian grants the Swiss indepen-
dence, although formal independence will not come for
over a century.

    ⌁ Campanile in the Piazza San Marco, Venice
    ⌺ Willibald Pirkheimer: *Bellus Helveticum*
        John Skelton: *The Bowge of Court* (poetry)
        Fernando de Rojas: *La Celestina* (play)

1500   The Portuguese navigator Gaspar de Corte-Real makes
the first authenticated landfall by a European in North
America since Thorfinn Karlsefni. Spanish navigator
Vicente Pinzon reaches Cape St. Roque, the eastern
tip of Brazil. Pedro Cabral reaches India with Bartholomew Diaz and Duarte Pareira to collect spices. On the
way, Cabral has been driven off-course by contrary
winds which have taken him to Brazil; he takes possession of Brazil in the name of the King of Portugal, then
resumes his voyage to India. In Germany, the writings of
Hroswitha of Gandersheim are discovered. The works of
this canoness who lived *935–972* include six grisly Latin
plays about Christian virgin martyrs, making Hroswitha
the first post-classical playwright.

    ⌁ City of Macchu Picchu, Peru
    ⌘ Hieronymus Bosch: Christ Crowned with Thorns;
        Ship of Fools
        Albrecht Dürer: Self-portrait
        Sandro Botticelli: Mystic Nativity
        Luca Signorelli: The Damned Cast into Hell
    ⌺ Sheikh Masfarma ben Uthman: *History of Bornu*
    (Niger, Chad, Nigeria)

1501   Alwand, Shah of Persia, is defeated at the Battle of

Shurur by the young leader of the Safavids, Ismail.
Vasco da Gama gains control of the spice trade for
Lisbon, cutting off the trade route through Egypt with
caravels blockading the Red Sea. Amerigo Vespucci
makes a second voyage to the New World, this time
for Portugal; his description of the coast of Brazil
expresses the conviction that this is not part of Asia
but a new continent. Gaspar de Corte-Real makes a
second voyage to North America, abducts 57 Indians
to sell as slaves, and drowns along with the slaves chained
in the hold when his caravel sinks in a storm. Spanish
settlers at Santo Domingo bring African slaves into
Hispaniola; this is the first importation of Africans into
the New World. Ivan the Great of Muscovy invades
Lithuania. The German King Maximilian I acknowledges the French conquests in northern Italy (the Peace
of Trent). Henry VII declines the Pope's request to lead
a crusade against the Ottoman Turks, who rob Venice of
Durazzo.

    Albrecht Dürer: *Life of the Virgin*
    Michelangelo Buonarroti: *Pietà*; *Bacchus*

    Gawain Douglas: *Palace of Honour*
    John Skelton: *Speculum Principis* (moral treatise for
    Prince Henry, later Henry VIII of England)

1502 The Safavid dynasty of Persia is founded by Ismail, the
rebel leader who has himself proclaimed Shah; Ismail
executes Sunnis who will not accept the Shiite brand of
Islam. In Central America, Montezuma II ascends to the
throne of the Aztec Empire at Tenochtitlan; he is 22.
Queen Isabella of Castile expels all remaining Moors
who have not been converted to Christianity. *Mar*: A
Spanish fleet takes Taranto as Ferdinand of Aragon
supports Louis XII's claims to Naples. *11 May*: Christopher Columbus embarks on his fourth voyage to the
New World. He discovers St. Lucia, Honduras, Costa
Rica. *Sep*: Amerigo Vespucci returns to Europe after his
New World voyage; his account is the basis of the name
'America'. *Dec*: the 27-year-old Cesare Borgia, son of
Pope Alexander VI, receives French help in putting
down a revolt by his captains; Borgia eliminates all his
enemies.

    ✒ Donato Bramante: The Tempietto at St. Pietro in
    Montorio
    William Vertue: Henry VII's Chapel, Westminster
    Abbey
    🎨 Lucas Cranach: St. Jerome
    Monumenta Cartographia World Map (addition of
    the New World dramatically changes people's view
    of Europe's relationship with the rest of the world)

1503 Louis XII of France abandons his claim to Naples
following the disintegration of his alliance with Ferdinand of Aragon. The Governor of Hispaniola, Nicolas de
Ovando gets royal permission to import African slaves to
relieve a labour shortage. Another 2,000 Spanish colonists arrive in Hispaniola. *18 Aug*: Julius II becomes
Pope on the death of Alexander VI (Rodrigo Borgia).
Alexander VI's ruthless son Cesare Borgia has carved out
a small principality for himself in the Romagna. The new
Pope commissions Michelangelo to design a tomb for
him. The gradual collapse of the Mongolian Golden
Horde in the extreme east of Europe allows the grand
Duchy of Muscovy to prepare for expansion. *2 Nov*:
Columbus discovers Panama. He also observes rubber;
the heavy black bouncing ball used in games by the
natives astounds the Spaniards.
    ✒ Canterbury Cathedral (completed) (U.K.)
    🎨 Lucas Cranach: Crucifixion
    Leonardo da Vinci: Leda and the Swan; The Battle
    of Anghiari

1504 In Afghanistan, Babur, a descendant of Tamerlane from
Turkestan, seizes Kabul. In Sudan, the Muslim Funj,
possibly originating far away in Bornu (Nigeria), defeat
the Christian chiefs ruling Sennar, the land between the
Blue and White Niles. In the Bavarian War, Albrecht of
Bavaria defeats Rupert, son of the Elector Palatine; the
German knight Götz von Berlichingen loses his right
hand at the siege of Landshut and has it replaced with an
iron hand. *Sep*: the Treaty of Blois settles the conflict
between France and Maximilian I. *8 Sep*: Michelangelo's
David is put on display for the first time in the Piazza
della Signoria in Florence. *7 Nov*: Christopher Columbus returns to Spain from his final voyage too ill to pay

his respects to the dying Queen. *24 Nov*: Queen Isabella
of Castile dies, aged 53, and is succeeded by her daughter
Juana and Juana's husband Philip, although they remain
in Flanders; Ferdinand rules instead.

   ✎ Albrecht Dürer: Adam and Eve (engraving)
     Lucas Cranach: Rest on the Flight into Egypt
     Michelangelo Buonarroti: David (sculpture)
   ♫ Robert Fayrfax: Mass *O Quam Glorifica*

1505 Sri Lanka (Ceylon) is discovered by the Portuguese. The
German monk and composer Adam of Fulda dies at
Wittenberg. Ivan the Great, Duke of Muscovy, dies,
aged 65, and is succeeded by his 26-year-old son Basil
III. *Jul*: the Portuguese send Francisco de Almeida to
India as its first viceroy. *24 Jul*: the people of Kilwa on
the East African coast are punished for refusing to show
Almeida the proper respect; King Ibrahim of Kilwa fails
to welcome him when he drops anchor and Almeida's
men sack the city. *Aug*: Almeida establishes forts at
Calicut, Cananor and Cochin on the Malabar coast.

   ✎ Giorgio Giorgione: The Tempest
     Raphael: Madonna and Child Enthroned with
     Saints
     Giovanni Bellini: The Virgin and Child with Four
     Saints
     Lorenzo Lotto: Bishop Bernardo de' Rossi
     Perugino: The Combat Between Love and Chastity
     Leonardo da Vinci: Mona Lisa
     Michael Sittow: Henry VII

1506 The classical sculpture Laocoön is unearthed on the
Esquiline Hill in Rome, causing a great stir. The first
Italian national army is created by Niccolo Machiavelli,
the 37-year-old Vice Chancellor of Florence: he forms a
Florentine militia. In a Lisbon riot up to 4,000 Jews are
killed. Alexander I of Poland dies and is succeeded by his
brother Sigismund I. In Korea, rebels succeed in overthrowing their cruel ruler Yonsangun. *21 May*: Christopher Columbus dies in obscurity in Valladolid, aged
55. *29 Jul*: Martin Behaim, cartographer and maker of
the earliest known globe (*1492*), dies, aged 47, in Lisbon.
13 Sep: the painter Andrea Mantegna dies at Mantua,
aged 75. *25 Sep*: Philip I of Castile dies suddenly at

Burgos, aged only 28, and his wife loses her reason; her father Ferdinand II of Aragon acts as Regent of Castile, ruling Castile as Ferdinand V.

  🏛 Donato Bramante: St. Peter's Basilica, Rome

  🎨 Lorenzo Lotto: St. Jerome in the Wilderness
      Raphael: Madonna di Casa
      Lucas Cranach: St. Catherine

  📖 William Dunbar: *The Dance of the Seven Deadly Sins* (poetry)

1507 Korean rebels place Chungjong on the throne. *23 Feb:* the artist Gentile Bellini dies, aged 77. *12 Mar:* the Florentine adventurer Cesare Borgia is killed, aged 30, while laying siege to the castle of Viana; Borgia has been fighting in the service of his brother-in-law the King of Navarre.

  🏛 Palazzo Strozzi, Florence (completed)

  🎨 Gentile Bellini: St. Mark Preaching in Alexandria

  📖 Martin Waldseemuller: *Introduction to Cosmography*
      Alvise Cadamosto: *The First Journey by Sea to the Land of the Negroes of Lower Ethiopia*

1508 Juan Ponce de León, who accompanied Columbus on his second New World voyage, explores and colonizes Puerto Rico. The Portuguese colonize Mozambique in south-east Africa. In Ethiopia, Lebna Denguel accedes to the throne. A Portuguese fleet is taken by surprise and sunk off the west coast of India by an Egyptian and Gujarati fleet: this is a triumph for Mahmud Begara, the elderly Sultan of Gujarat. John Cabot searches for a north-west passage, hoping to find a way to Cathay round the north of North America, and reaches Hudson Bay. Pope Julius II commissions Michelangelo to paint the Sistine Chapel ceiling. Maximilian I assumes the title Roman Emperor Elect on *4 Feb;* the Pope confirms that the German King shall from now on automatically be Holy Roman Emperor

  🏛 John Wastell: Fan Vault, King's College Chapel, Cambridge

  🎨 Lucas van Leyden: The Chess Player; Self-portrait (aged 14)
      Lorenzo Lotto: Madonna and Saints

  📖 Lodovico Ariosto: *Cassaria*

1509 The Ethiopians send an Armenian called Matthew as an ambassador to Portugal. The Spanish explorer Alonso de Ojeda discovers the territory that will be known as Colombia. The Portuguese explorer Diego Correa founds the first European colony in Brazil near Porto Seguro. *2 Feb*: Battle of Diu in the Indian Ocean: Portugal's Indian viceroy Francesco de Almeida destroys a Muslim fleet, establishing dramatically that Portugal controls the spice trade. In India, Krishnadevaraya becomes King of Vijayanager and repulses an attack by the forces of Sultan Mahmud of Bidar. *22 Apr*: Henry VII of England dies, aged 52, and is succeeded by his son Henry VIII. *14 May*: a French army defeats a Venetian force at Agnadello. Pope Julius II commissions Raphael to decorate the chambers in the Vatican Palace.

    🎨 Lucas van Leyden: The Temptation of St. Anthony
    Gerard David: Madonna with Angels and Saints
    📖 Alexander Barclay: *The Ship of Fools* (poetry)

1510 Japanese pirates ravage the coastal villages of southern China; some of the pirates are, in fact, Chinese, but they have disguised themselves by cutting their pigtails off. The Portuguese explorer Afonso de Albuquerque seizes the island of Goa on India's Malabar coast; this is Western Europe's first colonial possession east of Africa. Shah Ismail of Persia defeats an Uzbek army, killing Mohammed Shaybani, and extending his kingdom from the Tigris to the Oxus. The Venetian painter Giorgione dies of plague, aged 32. Sandro Botticelli also dies, on *17 May*, aged 65.

    🎨 Vittore Carpaccio: Presentation in the Temple
    Titian (Tiziano Vecellio): The Gypsy Madonna
    Sebastiano del Piombo: Salome
    Raphael: The Triumph of Galatea
    📖 *Everyman* (English morality play)
    🎼 Josquin Des Prés: *Deploration de Jehan Okenhenheim*

1511 The Papal army takes Modena and Mirandola from the French in *Jan*; the French take Bolgna in *May*. The Pope makes an alliance with Venice to drive the French out of Italy; in *Oct* he drafts Ferdinand II of Castile and Henry VIII of England into his Holy League. In the East Indies, Portuguese forces under Albuquerque capture

Malacca, the centre of the spice trade. Spanish forces under Diego Velazquez gain control; African slaves start arriving in Cuba, where the native Carib population has decreased alarmingly on contact with the Europeans. Poland establishes serfdom.

🐛 Fra Bartolommeo: St. Sebastian; Marriage of St. Catherine

Raphael: Sistine Madonna; Julius II; The School of Athens (fresco)

Andrea del Sarto: Procession of the Magi

Quentin Massys: Deposition (triptych)

Titian: The Triumph of Christ (woodcut 2.8 metres/9 feet long)

1512 The Newfoundland fishing grounds provide cod for English, French, Portuguese and Dutch ships; they use the island as a base, drying the fish there before shipping it back to Europe. Askia Mohammed the Great, King of Songhai in Africa, conquers the Hausa states of Kano, Zaria and Katsina. Spanish colonists import African slaves into Hispaniola to replace the Indian slaves who have died in large numbers from disease. The Portuguese abandon Kilwa. Pope Julius II convenes the Lateran Council to undertake reforms in the Church of Rome. Forces of the Holy League are defeated in battle at Ravenna, but the French and their German mercenaries are driven out of Milan in *May*; the Sforzas return to power in the Duchy. The Swiss take Lugano, Locarno and Ossola as a reward for assisting in driving the French out of Milan. Navarre is annexed to Castile. Bayazid II, the Ottoman Sultan is deposed by his Janissaries on *12 Apr*, aged 65; he dies under mysterious circumstances, and is succeeded by his 47-year-old son Selim I. Selim has his younger brothers strangled in *Nov*.

🐛 Michelangelo Buonarroti: The Creation of Adam (Sistine Chapel)

1513 European geographers and cartographers agree that the new discoveries to the west of the Atlantic are two new continents and are shown as such in a new, revised edition of Ptolemy. John I of Denmark (also John II of Sweden) dies and is succeeded by his 32-year-old son

Christian II of Denmark and Norway: the Swedes reject him. Peasant rebellions spread outwards from Switzerland. Ponce de Léon discovers Florida on Easter Day and goes ashore to plant orange and lemon trees. The Spaniard Vasco de Balboa is the first to see the Pacific Ocean from the New World. A Portuguese caravel reaches Canton (then called Guangzhou). Portuguese explorers discover Mauritius and Réunion (uninhabited). *9 Sep*: Battle of Flodden Field: James IV of Scotland is defeated and killed by English troops under the Earl of Surrey; James is succeeded by his son James V with Queen Margaret as his guardian. The Scottish navy is sold to France.

   🏛 Chartres Cathedral (completed) (France)
   🦢 Albrecht Dürer: Knight, Death and Devil (engraving)
   📖 Raymond Gil Vicente: *Cassandra the Sibyl* (play)
      Niccolo Machiavelli: *Il Principe*

1514 The new Pope Leo X says, 'Not only the Christian religion but nature cries out against slavery and the slave trade'. The slave trade continues to grow. 1,500 Spanish settlers arrive in Panama. The Ottoman Sultan Selim invades Persia and imposes Sunnism on the Shiite Persians. *23 Aug*: Battle of Chaldiran: Selim's 80,000 cavalrymen rout the Persian army. Though wounded, Shah Ismail escapes from the battlefield. *15 Sep*: Selim and his army enter Tabriz and massacre many of its citizens.

   🦢 Andrea del Sarto: Birth of the Virgin
      Quentin Massys: Money Changer and his Wife

1515 Spanish conquistadors found Havana, Cuba. The Spanish explorer Juan de Solis discovers the Plate Estuary in South America. The Spanish explorer Juan de Bermudez discovers Bermuda. Following Bramante's death at the age of 70 last year, the Pope appoints Raphael chief architect of the still-unfinished St. Peter's in Rome. Louis XII of France dies, aged 52 and is succeeded by his 21-year-old son-in-law François I. *29 Sep*: After defeating the Swiss and the Venetians at the battle of Maiganano, the French conclude a peace treaty; the Swiss retain most of the Alpine passes in return for France's right to enlist Swiss mercenaries. *14 Dec*:

François I makes peace with Pope Leo X. Portuguese strategist Afonso de Albuquerque takes Hormuz at the entrance to the Persian Gulf and returns to Goa to find that he has been dismissed. *16 Dec*: Albuquerque dies in Goa, aged 62.

    Orders of Cardinal Wolsey: Hampton Court Palace (completed)

    Matthias Grünewald: Isenheim Altarpiece
    Giovanni Bellini: Portrait of Fra Teodoro
    Michelangelo Buonarroti: Moses (Sculpture)
    Albrecht Dürer: Rhinoceros

    Erasmus: *Education of a Christian Prince*
    John Skelton: *Magnificence*
    Alexander Barclay: *Eclogues* (earliest pastoral poems in English)

1516 The first sugar exported from the New World to the Old is presented to King Carlos I of Spain by Hispaniola's inspector of gold mines. The Castilian Regent Jimenez forbids the importation of slaves into colonies of Spain, but Carlos I (ruling from Flanders) continues to grant courtiers licences to import slaves into the colonies. The Concordat of Bologna between François I of France and Pope Leo X gives the French King the freedom to appoint bishops and abbots. *23 Feb*: Ferdinand V of Castile and León (II of Aragon) dies, aged 63, and is succeeded by his grandson Carlos I, a 16-year-old student in Flanders. *24 Aug*: Battle of Marjdabik north of Aleppo: the Ottoman Sultan Selim defeats the Mamelukes. Selim takes Aleppo with his cannon. *26 Sep*: Selim enters Damascus, then moves on Cairo. *29 Nov*: the artist Giovanni Bellini dies in Venice, aged 86.

    Raphael: Baldassare Castiglione
    Titian: The Tribute Money
    Michelangelo Buonarroti: Dying Slave (statue)

    Ludovico Ariosto: *Orlando Furioso*
    Gil Vicente: *The Ship of Hell*
    Thomas Moore: *Utopia*

1517 Askia Mohammed, ruler of the African Songhai kingdom, is defeated by the Hausa Confederation which gains dominance east of the River Niger. The Archduke Charles grants Florentine merchants a monopoly in the slave trade. The Spanish explorer Francisco de Cordoba notices traces of an ancient Mayan civization in the Yucatan. *22 Jan*: Selim the Ottoman Sultan, sacks Cairo and the Sharif of Mecca surrenders to the Turks; Selim gains control of the holy places of Arabia, leaving Egypt in the hands of the Mameluke beys. *26 Mar*: the Flemish composer Heinrich Isaac dies in Florence. *3 Oct*: the 34-year-old Martin Luther, an Augustinian monk, nails 95 theses to the door of Wittenberg Cathedral, challenging the excesses and abuses of the Roman Church. This begins the Reformation, a long period of religious and civil unrest throughout Europe. Fra Bartolommeo dies in Florence, aged 42.

    ✍ Seville Cathedral (completed) (Spain)
    🕾 Sebastiano del Piombo: The Raising of Lazarus
       Andrea del Sarto: Madonna of the Harpies
       Quentin Massys: Erasmus

1518   Spanish colonists in Santo Domingo import more slaves from Africa to chop cane in the colony's 28 sugar plantations. The Reformation gains support from the Swiss cleric Huldreich Zwingli, who persuades the Zurich city council to exclude from the city the Franciscan monk Bernardin Samson, who sells indulgences.

    ✍ Antwerp Cathedral Spire (Belgium)
    🕾 Titian: Bacchanal; The Assumption
       Torrigiano: Effigy of Henry VII. Westminster Abbey
    📖 Erasmus: *Colloquies*
       Gil Vicente: *The Ship of Purgatory*

1519   The Spanish conquistador Hernando Cortez, now 34, embarks from Cuba to conquer New Spain (Mexico). Vasco de Balboa is beheaded in Panama for alleged treason; in reality, it is part of a struggle for power in Central America. *12 Jan*: the Holy Roman Emperor Maximilian I dies, aged 59; Spain's Carlos I is elected Emperor as Charles V. *24 Apr*: Montezuma II, the Aztec Emperor, sends envoys to attend the first Easter Mass to be celebrated in the New World. *2 May*: Leonardo da Vinci dies, aged 67, at Amboise Castle on the River Loire. *24 Jun*: Lucrezia Borgia, Duchess of Ferrara, dies, aged 39. *20 Sep*: the Portuguese navigator Ferdinand Magellan embarks from Seville in quest of a spice route to the Orient. *Nov*: Cortez takes Montezuma II prisoner and rules the Aztec Empire through Montezuma.

✍ Pierre Lescot: Château de Chambord
St. George's Chapel, Windsor (U.K.)
🎨 Peter Vischer: Shrine of St. Sebaldus (bronze), Nuremberg
Sebastiano del Piombo: The Raising of Lazarus; Christopher Columbus
📖 Gil Vicente: *The Ship of Heaven*
John Skelton: *Colin Clout*

1520 Christian II of Denmark invades Sweden. *19 Jan*: Battle of Tiveden: Sten Sture the Younger is mortally wounded and Christian advances without further opposition on Uppsala. The Swedish senators assembled there agree to accept Christian as King on condition that he rules according to Swedish custom. *31 Mar*: Christian of Denmarks signs an agreement to this effect. Sture's widow, Christina rallies the Swedish peasants to defeat the invaders. *6 Apr*: the painter Raphael Sanzio dies, aged 36, in Rome: it is Good Friday and his birthday. In Sweden, the Battle of Uppsala gives Christian a narrow victory. *7 Jun*: Henry VIII of England and François I of France meet with 10,000 courtiers near Calais on the Field of the Cloth of Gold. Henry appears as Hercules; the banquets, tournaments and spectacles leave the French treasury crippled. *10 July*: in Mexico, Cortez is driven out of Tenochtitlan by the Aztec leader, Cuauhtemoc; Cortez is forced to retreat to Tlaxcala. *Sep*: King Christian of Denmark lays siege to Stockholm. *7 Sep*: Christina surrenders on the promise of a general amnesty. *21 Sep*: Selim the Ottoman Sultan dies, aged 53, and is succeeded by his 24-year-old son Suleiman I (the Magnificent). *4 Nov*: Christian is crowned King of Sweden; *7 Nov*: the Bishops of Skara and Stragnas are beheaded at midnight in the public square at Stockholm, apparently on the King's orders. *8 Nov*: Christian's Danes kill 80 more Swedes, in spite of the promise of an amnesty. Sten's widow Christina and other Swedish noblewomen are sent as prisoners to Denmark; Sten's body is dug up and burned. *28 Nov*: Ferdinand

Magellan negotiates the Straits of Magellan and sails into the South Sea, renaming it the Pacific Ocean.

🙠 Titian: The Madonna with Saints Aloysius and Francis; Man with Glove

Raphael: Transfiguration (unfinished)

📖 Martin Luther: *Appeal to the Christian Princes of the German Nation*

🎜 Robert Fayrfax: *Music for the Field of the Cloth of Gold*

1521   *18 Apr*: Charles V's Diet of Worms orders Martin Luther to recant. Luther refuses, saying, 'Here I stand'. The German princes support him in starting an evangelical movement. Frederick the Wise of Saxony takes Luther to Wartburg for his own protection; there he will translate the *Bible* into German in defiance of the Edict of Worms. *23 Apr*: Battle of Vilialar: the Holy Roman Emperor Charles V defeats Spanish insurgents. *24 Apr*: after discovering the Philippines (*15 Mar*), Ferdinand Magellan wades ashore on Mactan with 48 fully-armed men in an attempt to subdue the native chief Lapu Lapu. *27 Apr*: Magellan is killed in a skirmish with Mactan warriors. *Aug*: Belgrade falls to Suleiman the Ottoman Sultan after a three-week siege. *27 Aug*: the composer Josquin des Prés dies. *31 Aug*: the great city of Tenochtitlan in Central America is conquered by Cortez after a battle lasting 85 days; the Aztec Emperor Montezuma II is killed in the fighting. Cortez burns the city. *24 Oct*: the composer Robert Fayrfax dies at St. Albans. *Dec*: Manoel I of Portugal dies, aged 52, Europe's wealthiest ruler; he is succeeded by his son João III.

🖊 Château de Chenonceaux, Loire valley (completed)

🙠 Parmigianino: The Marriage of St. Catherine

📖 Henry VIII: *The Golden Book* (a refutation of Luther)

1522   Charles V, the Holy Roman Emperor, drives French troops out of Milan with help from the Pope, Mantua and Florence; Henry VIII of England joins in the war against France. The Ming Emperor Jia Qing comes to power in China, expelling the Portuguese for acts of piracy. There is a slave revolt in Hispaniola. Luther returns to Wittenberg while Charles V is distracted by the war with France; he initiates church services in German. Zwingli condemns celibacy and Lent fasting; he calls on the Bishop of Constance to let priests marry. *6 Sep*: the Magellan expedition returns to Seville under the command of Magellan's Lieutenant Juan d'Elcano after the first circumnavigation of the world.

📖 Titian: The Resurrection

🎵 Sebastian Felsztynski: Hymn Book for Sigismund I of Poland

1523 *Jan*: Christian II of Denmark is deposed by the Danish nobility for cruelty and is succeeded by the Duke of Holstein as Frederick I. *19 Jan*: Huldreich Zwingli publishes his 67 Articles in Zurich: they attack the authority of the Pope and the idea of transubstantiation. *6 Jun*: the Swedish house of Vasa is founded as Gustavus I is crowned King at the age of 27. *Jun 1*: two followers of Martin Luther are burned alive at Brussels. *14 Sept*: Pope Adrian VI dies aged 64.

📖 Hans Holbein: Erasmus

1524 Aden becomes a colony of Portugal. Vasco da Gama returns to India as Portuguese Viceroy. *20 Feb*: Spanish forces in New Spain disperse the Quiche army under Chief Tecum Uman outside the city of Xeladu. The Chief kills the horse of Pedro de Alvarado, believing that man and horse are one; Alvarado in retaliation kills the Chief with his sword, spreading panic through the native warriors. *Apr*: Giovanni da Verrazano explores the east coast of North America, discovering New York harbour and giving the name Angouleme to Manhattan Island. *23 May*: Shah Ismail of Persia dies, aged 38, and is succeeded by his eldest son, the 10-year-old Tahmasp I. *29 Oct*: French troops invade Italy and retake Milan.

📖 Correggio (Antonio Allegra): Ascension of Christ
    Andrea del Sarto: The Sculptor
    Parmigianino: Self-portrait

1525 In Peru, Huayana Capac, the 11th Inca King, dies at Quito and his Empire is divided between his sons Huascar and Atahualpa. With no written language, they rule a complex, orderly society of 12 million people; engineers build suspension bridges, paved roads and irrigation systems. *8 Apr*: the Grand Master of the

Teutonic Knights, Albert von Brandenburg assumes the title Duke of Prussia. *14 May*: the German peasant rebellion is suppressed; Philip Landgrave of Hesse disperses Thomas Müntzer's army of peasants. *27 May*: Müntzer, who claims to be God's messenger, is beheaded. *1 Nov*: Francisco Pizarro sails from Panama to explore Peru: the natives call it Twwantinsuyu, the Four Corners of the World.

🎨 Andrea del Sarto: Madonna del Sacco
    Correggio: The Assumption of the Virgin

📖 Gil Vicente: *Don Duardas*
    William Tyndale: *The New Testament* (in English)

1526 Mbemba Nzinga, the Congolese King, protests to João III of Portugal that Portuguese merchants are selling his people as slaves to Brazilian sugar planters. Francisco Pizarro explores the Gulf of Guayaquil; the natives greet him as 'Viracocha', believing him to be the fulfilment of a prohecy that the 14th-century Inca King Viracocha would one day return. *14 Jan*: François I of France signs the Treaty of Madrid: he has been held captive for over a year by the Emperor Charles V following the Battle of Pavia (*24 Feb* last year). King François gives up Burgundy, Flanders, Artois, Tournai and Italy. On release, he says the terms were extorted and the treaty is invalid; he forms an alliance with Suleiman the Magnificent against Charles V. *19 Apr*: Battle of Panipat: the Indian robber baron Zahir-ud-din Babar defeats a 100,000 man army of Ibrahim shah Lodi, Sultan of Delhi, using artillery. Babar takes Agra and founds the Moghal Empire. *29–30 Aug*: Battle of Mofacs: Louis II of Hungary is killed at the age of 20 and his army is defeated by the Turkish army of Suleiman the Magnificent. Louis II is succeeded by Ferdinand, brother of Maximilian I; the Hungarian nobility, nevertheless, elect John Zapolya (once Louis' Regent). The crown of Bohemia goes to Louis' brother-in-law Frederick, elected King at 23.

🏛 Château de Chantilly (completed) (France)

🎨 Hans Holbein: Sir Thomas More and His Family
    Lucas van Leyden: The Last Judgment
    Albrecht Dürer: The Four Apostles

> Titian: Pesaro Madonna
> Andrea del Sarto: The Last Supper (fresco)

1527 Sebastian Cabot explores the Plate Estuary in South America, sailing into the Paraguay and Parana rivers. Sir Hugh Willoughby searches for a north-east passage to Cathay. Hernando Cortez completes his conquest of New Spain. The Muslim Somali Chief Ahmed Gran leads an invasion army into Ethiopia; the Negus of Ethiopia appeals to the Portuguese for help. Henry VIII appeals to Rome for dispensation to divorce Catherine of Aragon. *16 Mar* Battle of Kanvaha: the Moghal Emperor Babar defeats Rajput forces, destroying his Hindu rivals in northern India. *30 Apr*: Treaty of Westminster, an alliance between François I of France and Henry VIII of England; François renews hostilities against Charles V. *6 May*: Rome is sacked by Spanish and German mercenaries of Holy Roman Emperor Charles V. They besiege Pope Clement VII in the Castel Sant' Angelo and take him prisoner.

> Hans Holbein: Sir Thomas More
> Parmigianino: The Vision of St. Jerome
> Lucas van Leyden: The Worship of the Golden Calf

1528 The French besiege Naples in their war with Charles V; typhus eventually ends the siege in *Aug*, with the Prince of Orange leading his cavalry out of the city and cutting down the retreating French troops. Paris becomes the capital of France. The Augsburg banker Bartholomaus Welser gains the right to conquer and colonize Brazil; Welser has made his fortune trading in spices, sugar and slaves. Hernando Cortez returns to Spain to plead his case with those who revoked his authority in *1526*. Giovanni Verrazzano is killed by natives on an expedition to Brazil. Physicians in Basel force Theophrastus Bombastus von Hohenheim (known better as Paracelsus) to leave the city because of his unorthodox medical opinions; he believes, for instance, that disease is caused by external agencies. The Reformation gains acceptance in Berne and Basel. Mombasa rebels against Portuguese rule. The artist Matthias Grünewald dies at Frankfurt. Albrecht Dürer dies at Nuremberg, aged 56.

    Hans Holbein: Nicholas Kratzer; The Artist's Family
    Correggio: Madonna of St. Jerome
    Fontainebleau Palace, near Paris (completed)
    Baldassare Castiglione: *The Courtier*

1529 Francisco Pizarro returns to Spain to claim the territory he has carved out for himself in Peru. Charles V names Pizarro Governor for life and Captain-General of 'New Castile' with vice-regal powers. South American territories of New Granada (Venezuela and Colombia) are colonized by the Welsers of Augsburg: their agents explore the Orinoco valley. In Japan, monks sweep down from the Tendai monasteries on Mount Hiei onto the city of Kyoto, where they massacre adherents of the Buddhist Nichiren sect. King Askia Mohammed, ruler of the great Songhai Empire in West Africa, is deposed, aged 86; he is succeeded by Askia Bankouri. *16 Apr*: followers of Luther protest against a ruling by the diet of Speyer forbidding the teaching of Luther's ideas in Catholic states, while Catholicism may be taught in Lutheran states. *6 May*: Battle of Ghaghra: the Moghal Emperor Babur defeats the Afghan Chiefs of Bengal and Bihar. *27 May*: Ad-Din Barbarossa completes his conquest of Algeria, bringing the Ottoman Empire to its height. *5 Aug*: Peace of Cambrai, settling the conflict between France and Charles V. François I gives up all claims to Flanders, Artois and Italy and agrees to pay a ransom of 2 million crowns. Charles V renounces all claims to Burgundy. *3 Sep*: Suleiman arrives at Buda with 250,000 troops, taking the city almost at once. John Zapolya is officially proclaimed King. The Sultan marches on Vienna. *27 Sep*: Suleiman attacks Vienna but his Turkish army is decimated by cold and hunger. *Oct*: Suleiman's Ottoman army returns to Constantinople without taking Vienna, but stealing children as slaves. *17 Oct* Henry VIII of England removes Cardinal Wolsey as Lord Chancellor, replacing him with Thomas More.

    Albrecht Altdorfer: Battle of Issus
    Martin Luther: *A Mighty Fortress Is Our God!*; *Away In A Manger*

1530 The Moghal Emperor Babar dies, aged 47, and is

succeeded by his son Muhammed Humayun. In Peru, the Inca King Huascar's half brother Atahualpa moves south from Quito and destroys the town of Tumebanba. Huascar's army withdraws, leaving suspension bridges across the River Apurimac intact. Atahualpa is able to cross the river, take Huascar prisoner and reach Cajamarca. The Knights Hospitaller (Order of St. John) settle in Malta. *23 Feb*: Carlos I of Spain is crowned Charles V of the Holy Roman Empire and King of Italy by Pope Clement VII. *29 Nov*: Cardinal Wolsey dies, aged 55.

   ✒ Correggio: Adoration of the Shepherd
      Titian: Man in a Red Cap
      Lucas Cranach: The Judgment of Paris
   📖 Girolamo Fracastoro: *Syphilis or the French Disease*
      Philipp Melancthon: *The Confession of Augsburg*
      Hans Sachs: *Das Schlaraffenland* (verse)

1531 Francisco Pizarro and his brothers Gonzalo and Hernando leave Panama for Peru with just 300 – to conquer the Inca empire. Up on the altiplano, Atahualpa has his half-brother Huascar put to death and becomes the Inca (king) himself. *26 Jan*: a major earthqauke strikes Lisbon, killing 30,000 people. *6 Feb*: the Schmalkaldic League allies most of Europe's Protestant princes against the Holy Roman Emperor Charles V, who has had his brother Ferdinand elected King of the Romans. *8 Jul*: the German sculptor Tilman Riemenschneider dies, aged 71. *11 Oct*: Battle of Kappel: the Catholic Swiss cantons attack Zurich. Zwingli is killed in the fighting.
   📖 Margaret of Navarre: *The Mirror of the Soul*

1532 The armies of Suleiman II; the Ottoman Sultan, invade Hungary. The Holy Roman Emperor Charles V establishes himself at Madrid, paying for improvements to the imperial palace with taxes on Caribbean sugar; both Spain and Portugal have grown rich on their colonial enterprises. *16 Nov*: Atahualpa visits the camp of Francisco Pizarro in the Andes. Pizarro seizes the Inca and holds him for ransom; the Inca government grinds to a halt. Pizarro unintentionally reintroduces horses to South America; within three years they are seen running wild far away on the pampas.

  ✍ St. James's Palace, London

  🎨 Lucas Cranach: Martin Luther; Philipp Melanchthon

  Correggio: Jupiter and Io

  Titian: Charles V

  📖 François Rabelais: *Pantagruel*

  Ludovico Ariosto: *Orlando Furioso* (revised)

1533 Catherine de' Medici marries Henri of Valois, Duc d'Orléans; they are both 14. Frederick I of Denmark dies, aged 62, and is succeeded as King of Denmark and Norway by his 30-year-old son Christian III. Danish Catholics oppose this, hoping to make his brother Hans King; peasants hope for the restoration of the imprisoned ex-King Christian II. Basil III Grand Duke of Muscovy dies, aged 54 and is succeeded by his three year-old son Ivan IV (the Terrible). *25 Jan*: Henry VIII of England secretly marries Anne Boleyn. *6 Jun*: Ludovico Ariosto, author of the epic poem *Orlando Furioso*, dies at Ferrara, aged 59. *22 Jun*: Suleiman the Magnificent signs a treaty with Ferdinand of Hungary, who will continue to rule part of Hungary: Suleiman's nominee John Zapolya rules the remaining part. *29 Aug*: the end of the Inca Empire. Francisco Pizarro has brought Atahualpa to trial on charges of murder, sedition and idolatry. Found guilty, Atahualpa is executed by strangling. *15 Nov*: Pizarro enters Cuzco.

  🎨 Hans Holbein: The Ambassadors

  📖 Thomas Elyot: *Pasquil the Playne*

  John Heywood: *A Merry Play Between the Pardoner and the Friar*

1534 Jacques Cartier sails for the New World on François I's orders, to find a northern route to Cathay; Cartier sails into the Gulf of St. Lawrence. Francesco Pizarro returns to Spain with the crown's (one-fifth) share of the enormous ransom the Incas paid to have Atahualpa's life spared. The Inca leader Manco Capac II leads a rising against the Spanish conquistadors. Henry VIII of England breaks with the Roman Church through the Act of Supremacy which makes him head of the English Church. The Society of Jesus (Jesuits) is founded by Ignatius Loyola. A Dutch fanatic, John of Leyden, sets up a theocratic kingdom of Zion at Munster. The former innkeeper predicts the end of the world, organizes hedonistic orgies and brings the Reformation into disrepute. Michelangelo moves from Florence to Rome after completing the Medici Tomb. *5 Mar*: the painter Correggio dies, aged 45. *Jul 3*: an Ottoman army takes Tabriz from the Persians. The 20-year-old Shah Tahmasp assumes personal power, executing his Regent. *25 Sep*: Pope Clement VII dies after eating poisonous mushrooms. *25 Sep*: The Ottoman army takes Baghdad.

  ✐ Château de Chambord, Loire valley (completed)
    Antonio Sangallo the Younger: Farnese Palace, Rome

  ✑ Michelangelo Buonarroti: Tomb of Giuliano de Medici, Florence

  📖 Francois Rabelais: *Gargantua*
    Martin Luther: *Bible* (German translation)
    Polydore Vergil: *Anglia Historia*

1535 An Act of Union joins Wales to England. Tunis falls to Charles V; the pirate leader Khair ad-Din is defeated and Tunis is sacked. The vice-royalty of New Spain is founded with Mexico City (Tenochtitlan) as its capital; Antonio de Mendoza is appointed the first viceroy. In Peru, the city of Lima is founded by Pizarro, who resumes his exploration of the former Inca Empire. Jacques Cartier returns to North America, sails up the St. Lawrence to the site of Montreal and is frozen in. Munster's Anabaptist leader John of Leyden beheads one of his four wives in the Munster marketplace, justifying his action by claiming visions from heaven. *2 June*: Munster falls to Francis of Waldeck and the leading Anabaptists are imprisoned. *Jul 6*: Sir Thomas More is beheaded at the Tower of London, aged 57. *24 Oct*: Francesco Sforza II Duke of Milan dies, aged 43, without a successor; Milan becomes a suzerainty of Charles V.

  ✑ Parmigianino: Madonna del Collo Lungo
    Hans Holbein: King Henry VIII

  📖 Miles Coverdale: *English Bible* (first complete Bible in English)

1536 Hernando Cortez discovers Lower California. Jacques

Cartier return from 'New France' with 10 Huron Indians, all of whom soon die. The Anabaptist Jacob Hutter, who teaches that only hardship and suffering can be expected, is arrested and burned at the stake on the orders of Ferdinand King of the Germans. Portugal installs the Inquisition. A third war breaks out between Charles V and François I, who claims Milan following last year's death of Sforza. *Jan*: John of Leyden and some of his followers are cruelly tortured and executed in the marketplace in Munster. *12 Jun*: Menno Simons, a Friesland cleric, leaves the Roman communion after questioning infant baptism and getting unsatisfactory answers from Luther. *19 May*: Henry VIII of England has his wife Anne Boleyn executed on a charge of adultery. *30 May*: Henry VIII marries Jane Seymour. *12 Jul*: Desiderius Erasmus dies in Freiburg, aged 69. *6 Oct*: William Tyndale is condemned for heresy at Vilvorde Castle near Brussels and strangled. In West Africa, there is growing discontent at the tyrannical rule of Askia Bankour the King of the Songhai Empire. He has exiled his deposed predecessor, the 93-year-old Askia Mohammed, to an island in the River Niger.

　📖 William Tyndale: *The Practyce of Prelates*

1537 The Inca leader Manco Capac II establishes a new Inca state at Vicabamba. Gustavus I of Sweden ends the Hanseatic League's Baltic monopoly. Menno Simons preaches the 'Mennonite' view: he advocates a faith that forbids oaths and the taking of life, rejecting terms that cannot be found in the Bible – such as Trinity. Don Pedro de Mendoza leaves Buenos Aires for Spain in *Apr*, but dies of syphilis on the way back to Europe; his colony will be taken over by the Guarani people. *2 Jun*: a Papal Bull of Paul III prohibits enslavement of New World Indians in defiance of Charles V's policy; Paul excommunicates Catholic slave traders.

　🖼 Hans Holbein: Privy Chamber Fresco of the Tudor Dynasty

1538 An Ottoman flotilla takes over Yemen and Aden. *24 Feb*: the Peace of Grosswardein ends the conflict between Hungary's two kings, Ferdinand and John. *18 Jun*: the third war between François I and Charles V ends. *Sep*: a

Holy League against the Ottoman Turks brings together Pope Paul III, Charles V and the Venetians. A Venetian fleet under Andrea Doria, Doge of Genoa, is defeated at Prevesa by an Ottoman fleet. In Peru, Pizarro orders the execution by garrotting of Diego de Almagro, his 63-year-old expedition partner and former friend following a struggle for power.

🏛 Nonesuch Palace, Surrey (U.K.)

🎨 Titian: The Venus of Urbino; The Allegory of Marriage

Hans Holbein: Christina of Denmark

1539 The Franciscan missionary Marcos de Niza explores Arizona and New Mexico. Gonzalo de Quesada founds the city of Bogota. Potatoes arrive in Spain with conquistadors returning from Quito. In Paris, Ambroise Pare pioneers the manufacture of artificial limbs. *1 Feb*: Treaty of Toledo, ending the conflict between Charles V and François I. Charles suppresses a rebellion in Ghent, where citizens have refused to pay taxes to fund the wars with France.

🏛 Romano Giulio: Palazzo Ducale, Mantua (completed)

🎨 Titian: François I

Hans Holbein: Anne of Cleves

1540 The potato is introduced into France as an ornamental plant. Pope Paul III formally recognizes the Jesuit order founded six years ago. Hernando Cortez returns to Spain. Spanish explorer Hernando de Alarcon discovers the River Colorado. Jon Greenlander lands in Greenland, to find the last Norse colonist lying dead outside his hut with a dagger in his hand. *6 Jan*: Henry VIII marries Anne of Cleves at Greenwich. The marriage has been arranged by Lord Privy Seal Thomas Cromwell. *Jul*: John Zapolya King of Hungary dies, aged 53; the Turks recognize his infant son Sigismund as his successor, John II, but Ferdinand invades east Hungary, Turks invade the central plain, and the country is divided into three instead of two. *9 Jul*: Henry declares his marriage to Anne of Cleves null and void. *28 Jul*: Cromwell is beheaded at Tower Hill. *Dec*: Lopez de Cardenas discovers the Grand Canyon of the Colorado.

 ✑ Titian: Doge Andrea Gritti
Jacopo da Bassano: Adoration of the Shepherd

1541 The Portuguese send troops to Ethiopia under Christopher da Gama to expel the Somalis under Chief Ahmed Gran, who invaded Ethiopia in *1527*. Jacques Cartier makes a third expedition to North America, setting up a temporary colony at Quebec. John Calvin sets up a theocratic government in Geneva that will make the city a focus for Protestantism throughout Europe. The Catholic missionary Francis Xavier sails from Lisbon at the request of Ignatius Loyola to begin a mission to the Orient; he first visits Mozambique, Malindi and Socotra. *12 Feb*: Pizarro's Lieutenant Pedro de Valdivia founds the city of Santiago in Chile. Hernando de Soto discovers the Mississippi. *26 Jun*: Francisco Pizarro completes his conquest of Peru and is assassinated by the friends of Diego de Almagro, the 21-year-old son of the man Pizarro had executed three years ago; Almagro is made Governor of Peru, based in Lima. *24 Sep*: the Swiss doctor and alchemist Paracelsus dies in exile in Salzburg.

 ✑ Michelangelo Buonarroti: The Last Judgment (Sistine Chapel fresco)

1542 Spanish colonists under Alvar de Vaca travel 950 km/600 miles inland from the south Brazilian coast and settle at Asuncion. *13 Feb*: Henry VIII of England has his wife Queen Katherine Howard beheaded on charges of adultery. *21 May*: Hernando de Soto dies aged 46, on the banks of the Mississippi; this body is committed to river. De Soto's men descend the Mississippi under Luis de Alvarado from the river's confluence with the Arkansas River. *21 Jul*: Pope Paul III establishes the Universal Inquisition in an attempt to halt the Reformation with repression. *24 Aug*: Gonzalo Pizarro reaches the mouth of the River Amazon after an epic journey from the river's headwaters. *25 Nov*: Battle of Solway Moss: Henry VIII of England defeats James V of Scotland. *14 Dec*: James V of Scotland dies, aged 30, and is succeeded by his baby daughter Mary Queen of Scots.

1543 The Pope issues a list that forbids Roman Catholics to read certain books. The Spanish Inquisition burns Protestants at the stake for the first time. Japan receives visitors from Europe for the first time when a Chinese ship carrying two Portuguese travellers is wrecked off Kyushu; the foreigners have muskets, which the local lord buys from them and replicates. From now on firearms will be part of Japan's military equipment. *24 May*: Nikolaus Copernicus dies, aged 70. *12 Jul*: Henry VIII marries Catherine Parr. *20 Nov*: The painter Hans Holbein dies, aged 45.

  ✎ Benvenuto Cellini: Gold Saltcellar for François I
     Titian: Ecce Homo
  □ Nikolaus Copernicus: *De Revolutionibus Orbium Coelestium* (theory that the earth rotates daily on its axis and moves, with other planets, round the sun)
     Andreas Vesalius: *De Corporis Humani Fabrica* (with anatomical drawings by Titian)

1544 King Chungjong of Korea dies after reigning for 37 years. In northern Europe there is a shortage of honey as a result of the break-up of monasteries by the Reformation. *14 Apr*: Battle of Ceresole south of Turin: a French army defeats the imperial army of Charles V. *14 Sep*: English troops join those of Charles V to menace Paris; the English take Boulogne. *18 Sep*: Treaty of Crespy-en-Valois, ending the two-year war between Charles V and François I in the Netherlands. France loses Artois and Flanders, Charles renounces his claim to Burgundy but keeps Milan.

  ✎ Lorenzo Lotto: Portrait of an Old Man
     Master John: Mary I
     Benvenuto Cellini: Nymph of Fontainebleau (sculpture)

1545 Henry VIII's flagship *Mary Rose* is warped out into the Solent, where a gust of wind capsizes it; it sinks in less than a minute as the King watches. Charles V makes a truce with Suleiman the Magnificent at Adrianople. The Moghal Emperor Humayun takes Kandahar; his rival, the Emperor Sher Shah, is killed by a cannonball while laying siege to the Rajput stronghold of Kalanjar. *20 Apr*: Jean Meynier, a Provençal baron, massacres Waldensian Protestants in order to seize their lands. At Potosi on the altiplano of New Castile, the Spanish discover a silver deposit that will yield much of the wealth to fuel commercial activity in Europe for the next century and prepare the way for the Industrial Revolution. Pope Paul III convenes the Council of Trent to reform the Church; the Tridentine Decrees will effect some genuine reforms but also polarize dogma against the teachings of the Protestants. Fishing in the Baltic deteriorates, but fishing in the North Sea improves.

✟ Michelangelo Buonarroti: The Conservators' Palace, Rome

☊ Bronzino (Agnold di Mariano): Venus, Cupid, Folly and Time

☐ Thomas Cranmer: *The King's Primer*

1546 Mayans in New Spain rise against the Spanish but are defeated. At Diu in India Portuguese troops rout the Gujarati army. *18 Feb:* Martin Luther dies where he was born, at Eisleben, aged 63. *1 Mar:* The Scottish Lutheran reformer George Wishart is burned to death on Cardinal Beaton's orders. *29 May:* Beaton is assassinated for his persecution of Protestants. *7 Jun:* Peace of Ardres, ending two years of conflict between Henry VIII and François I. Charles V meets Pope Paul III, who promises money and troops to halt the Protestant movement. *3 Aug:* the Paris printer Etienne Dolet is hanged and burned for heresy and blasphemy: he has published the works of Erasmus and other humanists.

✟ Michelangelo Buonarroti: St. Peter's Basilica, Rome

☊ Titian: Pope Paul III and His Grandsons
Lucas Cranach: Martin Luther
Gerlach Flicke: Cranmer

☐ Pietro Aretino: *Orazia*

1547 The Moghal Emperor Humayun exploits quarrels among rival successors of Sher Shah Suri to regain his territories in India and take Kabul. *16 Jan:* Ivan IV, Grand Duke of Muscovy, has himself crowned Tsar (first use of this title in Russia). *28 Jan:* Henry VIII of England dies, aged 55, and is succeeded by his 10-year-old son Edward VI. *3 Mar:* François I of France dies, aged 52, after developing a fever the night he heard of Henry VIII's death – and laughed. *24 Apr:* Battle of

Muhlberg: Charles V defeats and captures the Elector of Saxony, laying siege to Wittenberg, the Elector's capital. *31 Jul*: Scots' royalists besiege St. Andrews Castle and capture the Lutheran John Knox. He is exiled and condemned to work on a French galley.

📖 Thomas Cranmer: *Book of Homilies*

1548 Ottoman forces occupy Tabriz in Persia. In Peru the Battle of Xaquixaguane gives Pedro de la Gasca victory over Gonzalo Pizarro, son of Francesco Pizarro; he has Gonzalo Pizarro executed. *Apr 1*: Sigismund I of Poland dies, aged 81, after reigning for 42 years and is succeeded by his 28-year-old son Sigismund II.

🐚 Tintoretto (Jacopo Robusti): The Miracle of St. Mark)
Titian: Equestrian Portrait of Charles V
Paolo Veronese: Bevilacqua-Lazise Altarpiece
Tomb of Sigismund the Old, Wawel Cathedral, Cracow

📖 John Bale: *Kynge Johan* (first historical drama in English)

1549 Ivan IV, Tsar of Muscovy, summons the first Russian national assembly. The first Portuguese Governor of Brazil, Thome de Souza, founds the city of São Salvador (later Bahia). *Jan*: Lord High Admiral Thomas Seymour is sent to the Tower of London for scheming to marry Edward VI to Lady Jane Grey and marry the Princess Elizabeth, the future Elizabeth I, himself. 20 *Mar*: Seymour is executed.

✏ Piero Ligorio: Villa d'Este at Tivoli, near Rome (completed)
Pitti Palace (finally completed)

📖 Thomas Cranmer: *The Book of Common Prayer*
John Cheke: *The Hurt of Sedition*

1550 In Nigeria, the Nupe tribesmen defeat the Yoruba people of the Oyo kingdom. In Europe, prices begin to rise as coins made from Mexican and Peruvian silver and gold devalue the old currencies. *Mar*: Treaty of Boulogne: peace between France and England. England gets John Knox released from his slave galley, France regains Boulogne, English troops withdraw from Scotland. *Jun*: the Japanese feudal lord who last year welcomed

Francis Xavier to Kyushu makes it a capital offence to become a convert to Christianity.

✐ Robert Smythson: Longleat House, Wiltshire (U.K.)
Andrea Palladio: Villa Rotunda and Palazzo Chiericati, Vicenza

✍ Tintoretto: Presentation of the Virgin
Bronzino: Eleanora of Toledo and Her Son
Lorenzo Lotto: A Nobleman in His Study
Michelangelo Buonarroti: Deposition from the Cross

📖 Giovanni Straparola: *Tradeci Piacevoli Notti* (fairtale collection)
Pierre de Ronsard: *Odes*
Giorgio Vasari: *The Lives of the Most Eminent Italian Architects, Painters and Sculptors*
Al-Fasi: *History and Description of Africa*

🎵 John Marbeck: *The Booke of Common Praier Noted* (modified plain chant)

1551 Ottoman Turks take Tripoli after failing to take Malta. Henri II of France disavows the Council of Trent, renewing the war against Charles V and seizing the bishoprics of Verdun, Toul and Metz. The Italian composer Giovanni da Palestrina is appointed Director of Music at the Church of St. Giulia in Rome by Pope Julius III. The National University of Mexico is founded at Mexico City in New Spain. Francis Xavier leaves Japan in *Nov* after converting only 150 people to Christianity

📖 Erasmus Reinhold: *Prudentic Tables* (contains astronomical tables)
Konrad von Gesner: *Historia Animalium*

🎵 Louis Bourgeois: *Praise God From Whom All Blessings Flow* (hymn)

1552 *22 Jan*: the Duke of Somerset, former Lord Protector of England, is executed. *May*: Maurice of Saxony, now an ally of Henri II of France, takes Augsburg. *Jun*: Maurice of Saxony almost captures Charles V at Innsbruck. *24 Jun*: in an increasingly common incident, the Portuguese ship *São João* runs aground on the Natal coast; 100 are drowned, and of the 500 who get ashore only 25 survive the walk to the nearest Portuguese base at Sofola. *20 Aug*:

Ivan IV, Tsar of Muscovy, attacks Kazan, besieging the
fortress with 150,000 men after a faction in Kazan offers
him the Khanate. Charles V lays siege to Metz which is
defended by the Duc de Guise. Charles lifts the siege and
withdraws after losing over 12,000 men in a month to
scurvy and typhus. *2 Oct*: Ivan IV takes Kazan, using
artillery to break through the citadel walls of the Tartar
capital. The Volga becomes a Russian river and Ivan
goes on to attack Astrakhan. *3 Dec*: Francis Xavier dies
exhausted near Canton in China.
- Titian: Self-portrait
- Nostradamus (Michel de Nostradame): *Centuries*
  Pierre de Ronsard: *Amours de Cassandre*
  Etienne Jodelle: *Cleopatre Captive*
  Nicholas Udall: *Ralph Roister Doister*

1553 The camera obscura devised in *1267* by Roger Bacon is
improved by a 15-year-old Italian, Giambattista della
Porta, who adds a convex lens. English explorer Richard
Chancellor reaches Moscow by way of the White Sea and
Archangel. The composer Johann Eccard is born at
Muhlhausen in Thuringia. *6 Jul*: Edward VI of England
dies of tuberculosis, aged 15, at Greenwich and is
succeeded by his Catholic half-sister Mary. A marriage
is arranged between Mary of England and Philip, son of
Charles V of Spain: Philip is to have the title King of
England but no hand in government and no right to
succeed Mary. *9 Jul*: Maurice of Saxony is fatally
wounded at Sievershausen as his army defeats that of
Albert of Brandenburg-Kulmbach. *2 Aug*: Battle of
Marciano: a French army invading Tuscany is defeated.
- Strozzi Palace, Florence (completed)
- Pieter Brueghel: Landscape with Christ Appearing
  to the Apostles at the Sea of Tiberius
  Titian: All-Saints Altarpiece

1554 Katsina in Nigeria regains its independence from the
Songhai Empire. Mehedia on the Tunisian coast falls to
Algerians under the command of the corsair Dragut.
Henri II of France invades the Netherlands. Mary
Queen of England releases the Duke of Suffolk in a
show of clemency but hardens her position when Suf-
folk once again proclaims his daughter Lady Jane Grey

the rightful Queen. *12 Feb*: Lady Jane Grey and her husband Guildford Dudley are executed. *Mar*: Mary has her half-sister Elizabeth imprisoned in the Tower to secure her own position. *25 Jul*: Queen Mary and Philip of Spain are married.

📖 Titian: Danae; Venus and Adonis

🎵 Giovanni Palestrina: *First Book of Masses*

1555 The Moghal Emperor Humayun defeats an Afghan claimant to his throne, reoccupying Agra and Delhi. Japanese pirates besiege Nanjing. *23 Mar*: Pope Julius III dies, aged 67, succeeded by Marcellus II. *Apr*: an army led by Cosimo de' Medici Duke of Florence forces a French army to end its siege of Siena and surrender. *30 Apr*: Pope Marcellus II dies, aged 54, succeeded by Paul IV. Paul orders that Rome's Jewish quarter is to be walled, creating the Ghetto of Rome. Palestrina is appointed a member of the Pontifical Choir by the Pope without examination, which creates resentment and jealousy among other choir members. *Oct*: Queen Mary restores Roman Catholicism in England, persecuting Protestants. *16 Oct*: Hugh Latimer bishop of Worcester and Nicholas Ridley bishop of London are burned at the stake at Oxford. *25 Oct*: European peace breaks out as Charles V, now 55, hands over imperial power to his brother Ferdinand and sovereignty in the Netherlands to his son Philip in a formal ceremony in the Hall of the Golden Fleece in Brussels.

✏ Giacomo da Vignola and Michelangelo: Palazzo Farnese, Rome

📖 Tintoretto: St. George and the Dragon
   Benvenuto Cellini: Perseus (sculpture)
   Michelangelo Buonarroti: Pietà for the Duomo, Florence

📖 *Popol Vuh* (Toltec holy book translated)
   Pierre de Ronsard: *Amours de Marie*

🎵 Giovanni Palestrina: *Missa Papae Marcelli*

1556 Ivan the Terrible completes his conquest of Kazan and Astrakhan, taking the lands from the Tartars; this opens the way for Russian expansion to the east. *24 Jan*: the most severe earthquake in the recorded history of the world shakes Shanxi province in China: over 830,000 people are killed in the disaster. *27 Jan*: the Moghal

Emperor Humayun dies after falling from his library roof in Delhi; he is succeeded by his 14-year-old son Jalal-ud-Din, who returns from exile. *14 Feb*: Thomas Cranmer, Archbishop of Canterbury, is dismissed from office by papal legates at Christ Church, Oxford. *21 Mar*: Cranmer refuses to recant and is burned at the stake. *17 Sep*: the Holy Roman Emperor Charles V sails from Flushing to settle as a guest at a monastery in Estremadura, having abdicated all his responsibilities. *5 Nov*: Jalal-ud-Din, now the Moghal Emperor Akbar, defeats a Hindu army in the Battle of Panipat in the Punjab; he regains the Hindustani Empire.

✐ Philibert Delorme: Château d'Anet (completed)

▯ Robert Recorde: *Castle of Knowledge*
Georg Bauer: *De Re Metallica* (textbook on mining and metallurgy) Hans Sachs: *Der Paur im Egfeur* (play)

♫ Roland de Lassus: *Book of Motets*

1557 The Portuguese found the city of São Paulo in Brazil, and the colony of Macao off the Chinese coast near Canton. A 14-year Livonian War starts as Ivan IV's troops invade Poland and the Swedes take Estonia. Cosimo de' Medici Duke of Florence becomes ruler of the former republic of Siena. *6 Jun*: João III of Portugal dies on his 55th birthday and is succeeded by his three-year-old grandson Sebastian. *7 Jul*: Mary Tudor Queen of England declares war on France in support of her husband, Philip II of Spain. *10 Aug*: Battle of St. Quentin: Spanish forces under the Duke of Savoy defeat the French under the Constable of Montmorency. The French are driven out of Italy.

✑ Pieter Brueghel: Landscape with the Parable of the Sower
Willem Boy: Gustavus Vasa of Sweden

1558 London's population reaches 200,000. English geographer and astrologer John Dee succeeds Robert Recorde as technical adviser to the Muscovy Company. *Jan 20*: Calais falls to François Duc de Guise. *21 Sep*: Charles V dies, aged 58. *17 Nov*: Mary Tudor Queen of England dies, aged 42, and is succeeded by her half-sister Elizabeth, who is now 25.

✎ Pieter Brueghel: The Fall of Icarus

Paolo Veronese: Feast in the House of the Pharisee

⎕ John Knox: *First Blast of the Trumpet Against the Monstrous Regiment of Women*

1559 Emperor Gelawdewos, who saved the Ethiopian Empire from both Ottoman and Somali invaders, then from Galla tribesmen from the south, dies in battle defending his realm. Suleiman the Magnificent helps his son Selim defeat Selim's brother Bayezid at the Battle of Konya. Bayezid and his five sons escape to Persia; Suleiman pays to have them executed. English food prices rise to three times their 1501 levels because of debasement of the coinage to raise money for wars. *1 Jan*: Christian III, King of Denmark and Norway dies, aged 55; his cousin, who reigned as Christian II, is to die still a prisoner later in the month at the age of 79. They are succeeded by Christian II's son, Frederick II. *3 Apr*: Treaty of Cateau-Cambresis ends the war started between the late Charles V and France. *20 Jun*: Henri II of France sustains a terrible head wound jousting with Gabriel de Montgomery in a tournament to celebrate the treaty and the marriage of his daughter. *10 Jul*: Henri II of France dies, aged 40, and is succeeded by his 14-year-old son François II with the Duc de Guise and Cardinal of Lorraine as Regents. *18 Aug*: Pope Paul IV dies aged 83. The Romans demolish his statue, free the prisoners of the Inquisition and destroy the Inquisitors' records.

✎ Pieter Brueghel: Netherlandish Proverbs

Titian: The Entombment; Diana and Actaeon

⎕ Pope Paul IV: *Index of Authors and Books*

1560 The Auracanian Federation (a native alliance) destroys Spanish colonial settlements in the interior of Chile. A smallpox epidemic severely reduces the Portuguese colonies in Brazil, increasing the need to import African slaves to cut the sugar cane. *Mar*: the Conspiracy of Amboise is organized by French Huguenot Louis de Bourbon and attempts to overthrow the Catholic Guise family. The Queen Mother Catherine de' Medici intervenes to thwart the Huguenots; 1,200 are hanged at Amboise. *19 Apr*: Philip Melanchthon, Luther's associate, dies at Wittenberg. *25 Jun*: Gustavus I of Sweden abdicates, aged 64, succeeded by his son Charles IX. French troops in Scotland try to support Mary Stuart's claims to the English throne. *6 Jul*: Treaty of Edinburgh ends French interference in Scottish affairs. *5 Dec*: François II of France dies aged 16, and is succeeded by his 10-year-old brother Charles IX.

   🖋 Andrea Palladio: Villa Foscari, Vicenza (completed)
   🎨 Pieter Brueghel: Children's Games

1561 *19 Aug*: Mary Queen of Scots returns to Scotland from France and gets involved in argument with the Calvinist John Knox, who denies the authority of the Pope in Scotland. Spain withdraws troops from the Netherlands. Madrid becomes Spain's capital. Giovanni Palestrina leaves the Pontifical Choir and is appointed *Maestro di Capella* at Santa Maria Maggiore in Rome. The Edict of Orléans halts the persecution of Huguenots in France. The first Flemish Calvinist refugees arrive in England. Anthony Jenkinson of the English Muscovy Company reaches Isfahan by way of Russia and begins trade with Persia.

   🖋 Sansovino dacopo Tatti: Ca' Corner della Ca' Grande, Venice
      Basilica of St. Basil, Moscow (completed)
   📖 John Knox: *Book of Discipline*
      Francesco Guicciardini: *History of Italy*
      Thomas Norton and Thomas Sackville: *Gorboduc*

1562 The English navigator John Hawkins seizes a Portuguese ship carrying African slaves to Brazil, trades 300 slaves at Hispaniola for sugar, pearls and ginger and makes a huge profit; this marks the start of English participation in the slave trade. *1 Mar*: the Duc de Guise orders a massacre of Huguenots at Vassy, setting off a series of French civil wars; the Huguenots retaliate by murdering priests. *May*: the Dutch composer Jan Sweelinck is born at Deventer. *17 Dec*: the Flemish composer Adrian Willaert, who was Chapel Master at St. Mark's for 35 years, dies in Venice.

   🎨 Titian: Europa and the Bull
      Paolo Veronese: Marriage at Cana
      Pieter Brueghel: The Triumph of Death

1563 In Japan, rice riots at Mikawa follow the requisition of crops by the Tokugawa family and imposition of heavy taxes; Buddhist temples are burned in retaliation by the feudal lord Ieyasu. The Chinese finally overcome the Japanese pirates who have been raiding the south coast of China. Ivan the Terrible orders the drowning of Jews in the River Dvina. Queen Elizabeth of England says, 'If any African were carried away without his free consent, it would be detestable and call down the vengeance of Heaven upon the undertaking'. John Hawkins sells a cargo of over 100 African slaves in Hispaniola. *Feb*: The Duc de Guise is murdered by a Huguenot, leaving Catherine de' Medici in control of the Catholic faction. *19 Mar*: the Peace of Amboise signed by Catherine ends the conflict between Catholics and Huguenots: limited toleration is granted.

✍ Tuileries Palace, Paris

✍ Pieter Brueghel: Landscape with the Flight into Egypt; The Tower of Babel

1564 Huguenots and Catholics join forces to drive the English out of Le Havre; the Peace of Troyes ends hostilities between France and England, with England renouncing all claim to Calais in return for 222,000 crowns. Elizabeth I takes shares in Hawkins' second slave trading venture and lends him a ship, overcoming her scruples. Miguel Lopez de Legazpe leaves New Spain with four ships to colonize the Philippines. The Inquisition forces Andreas Vesalius to go on a pilgrimage to the Holy Land for dissecting human bodies. An epidemic in New Spain severely reduces the numbers of Aztecs. The sweet potato reaches England on board one of Hawkins' ships retruning from New Castile, ending England's reliance on imported potatoes for its sweet potato pies. *8 Feb*: the sculptor and painter Michelangelo Buonarroti dies in Rome aged 88. *27 May*: John Calvin dies in Geneva, aged 54; Théodore de Bèze becomes the leader of French Protestantism. *Oct*: the pioneering Flemish anatomist Andreas Vesalius is shipwrecked on an island in the Ionian Sea, dying there of hunger and exhaustion.

✍ Pieter Brueghel: The Adoration of the Kings; The Slaughter of the Innocents

1565 King Afonso II of Kongo (Angola) is assassinated as he attends Mass. The Portuguese colony of Rio de Janeiro is founded in Brazil. Miguel de Legazpe founds the colony of Cebu in the Philippines. John Hawkins introduces tobacco into England from Florida. *23 Jan*: Battle of Talikota, ending the Hindu Empire of Vijayanagar. Muslim armies from Bijapur and Golconda attack a Hindu army led by the warrior Ramaraja, who is captured and beheaded; his head mounted on a long spear frightens his army into rapid retreat. *May*: Ottoman forces besiege Malta. 700 Knights of St. John led by Grand Master Jean de la Valette, who is 71, resist the Ottomans. *Sep*: Spanish forces arrive in Malta, driving off the Ottoman Turks.

    ✐ ✍ Orders of the Duke of Orsini: Sacro Bosco at Bomarzo, Tuscany

    ✐ Paolo Veronese: The Family of Darius Before Alexander

    Pieter Brueghel: Haymaking; Peasant Wedding

    Titian: The Death of Actaeon

1566 Philip II of Spain oppresses the Moriscos (Moors who have been converted to Christianity), forbidding them to wear traditional dress or speak Arabic. A German army under Maximilian II prepares to fight the Turks under Suleiman the Magnificent at Komon in Hungary, but typhus strikes and the campaign is abandoned. *9 Mar*: David Riccio, Italian secretary to Mary Queen of Scots, is stabbed to death by the Earls of Morton and Lindsay on orders from Mary's husband Lord Darnley. *2 Apr*: Margaret of Parma, Regent for the Lowlands, receives a petition for the abolition of the Inquistion; she promises to forward it to her brother Philip of Spain but raises an army.

    ✐ Pieter Brueghel: The Wedding Dance

    ▯ William Stevenson: *Gammer Gurton's Needle*

1567 French colonists in Brazil are caught and killed by the Portuguese. In Venezuela, the city of Caracas is founded by Spanish settlers. *10 Feb*: Mary Queen of Scots' husband Lord Darnley is found murdered and the Queen is suspected of complicity. *24 Apr*: Mary Queen of Scots is 'abducted' by the Earl of Bothwell. *15 May*:

Mary marries Bothwell. *Jun*: The Scottish nobility
desert Mary, forcing her to abdicate in favour of her
one-year-old son James VI. *24 Jul*: James VI is proclaimed King of Scotland. Philip of Spain sends troops
under the Duke of Alva to the Lowlands, where they take
Antwerp; the Lowlanders prepare for a war to gain their
independence.

 Titian: The Martyrdom of St. Lawrence
 Tintoretto: Christ Before Pilate
 Pieter Brueghel: Adoration of the Kings in the Snow

1568 The unification of Japan begins. Kyoto is seized by the
Taira general Oda Nobunaga, who starts subduing
feudal lords and eroding the political power of Buddhism. Mennonites flee Spanish persecution in the
Lowlands, moving to the German states, Switzerland
and Russia. In Granada, Moriscos rebel against Philip
II's restrictions. *23 Mar*: Peace of Longjumeau signed by
Catherine de' Medici with the Huguenots ends the
religious war in France. *13 May*: Mary Queen of Scots
escapes from captivity but is imprisoned again after
fleeing to England. *4 Jun*: leaders of the Flemish opposition to the Inquisition are beheaded as traitors in
Brussels; the action causes a revolt of the Lowlands.
There is a general confiscation of the estates of those who
failed to appear before the Council of Blood, including
William of Orange, who with thousands of others has left
Holland. *30 Sep*: Eric XIV of Sweden is deposed because
he has shown signs of mental illness and he is replaced by
his 31-year-old brother John III. *Oct*: Sir John Hawkins
is ambushed by the Spanish in the West Indies; the
incident precipitates an undeclared state of war between
England and Spain.

 Titian: Jacopo della Strada
 Pieter Brueghel: The Peasant Dance; Blind Leading
 the Blind

1569 Akbar captures the fortress of Ranthambor in India,
effectively ending independent Rajput power. Ottoman
troops drag their ships overland from the Don to the
Volga but still fail in their attack on Astrakhan; the
Ottoman army retreats with heavy losses. Gerhard
Kremer (Mercator) publishes his Mercator projection

map of the world, with lines of longitude and latitude drawn as straight lines, making the job of charting a course simpler. *13 Mar*: Battle of Jarnac: Catholic forces under the Duc d'Anjou defeat Huguenot forces. Louis de Bourbon is murdered while crossing the River Charente. *1 Jul*: Union of Lublin, merging Poland with Lithuania to strengthen both states against attacks from Tartars and Muscovites. *5 Sep*: the painter Pieter Brueghel dies in Brussels, aged 44.

- Pieter Brueghel: The Storm at Sea
  Mercator (Gerhard Kremer): *Map of the World* (first comprehensive world map)

1570 Large scale traffic in African slaves begins between Sierra Leone and Brazil. The Indian tribes of north-east North America form a confederation under the name Iroquois. The Mohawk brave Hiawatha persuades the Mohawk, Onondaga, Cayuga, Seneca and Mohawk tribes to form a league with a common council to settle differences peacefully. Philip of Spain's half-brother, Don John of Austria, suppresses the Morisco rebellion in Granada; the Moriscos are dispersed throughout Castile. Nagasaki opens as Japan's major port for foreign trade as regular trading with the Portuguese begins. *8 Jan*: Ivan the Terrible enters the city of Great Novgorod to begin a reign of terror; he has batches of Novgorod citizens from all classes put to death each day. *25 Jul*: Ivan the Terrible has many of his advisers and ministers publicly executed in Moscow. *8 Aug*: Treaty of St. Germain: Charles IX ends France's third religious war. *13 Dec*: the Peace of Stettin ends the war between Sweden and Denmark, recognizing Swedish independence.

- Francesco Primaticcio and Germain Pilon: Tomb of Henri II
  Tintoretto: Moses Striking the Rock
- Palladio (Andrea di Pietro): *Four Books of Architecture*
  Abraham Ortelius: *Atlas* (the first atlas)
  Roger Ascham: *The Schoolmaster* (treatise on education)
  Bartolomeo Scappi: *Cooking Secrets of Pope Pius V*

1571 The Crimean Tartars sack Moscow. In Japan, Oda

Nobunaga destroys the Enryakuji Buddhist monastery on Mount Hiei, removing his most powerful enemies. *13 Feb*: Benvenuto Cellini dies in Florence, aged 70. *19 May*: the City of Manila in the Philippines is founded; Miguel de Legazpe moves his capital from Cebu to the new city. *7 Oct*: Battle of Lepanto near Corinth: an Ottoman fleet is defeated by the Maritime League (Venetian, Genoese, Maltese and Spanish) under Don John, who frees 12,000 Christian galley slaves and kills 25,000 Turks. Constantinople quickly recovers from this reverse because the Venetians are reluctant to follow up their victory (their merchants want peace for trade).

1572 Selim II the Ottoman Sultan rebuilds his navy to a point where Don John of Austria fears to attack it. In England, the Duke of Norfolk is beheaded for conspiring with the Spanish to free Mary Queen of Scots. The Huguenot leader Henri of Navarre arrives in Paris to marry Margaret of Valois, saving his life by pretending to be converted to Catholicism. Francis Drake sets sail from England on an expedition to capture the annual silver shipment from Peru to Spain by intercepting it in Panama: he embarks in two small ships. *May*: in Peru, the Spanish conquistadors capture Vilcabamba, the fortress of the Inca rebels led by Tupac Amaru. The last of the hereditary Sun-Kings of Peru, Tupac Amaru, is converted to Christianity and then beheaded by the Spanish. *23 Aug*: the Massacre of St. Batholomew's Day: 50,000 Huguenots are killed in France. Encouraged by Catherine de' Medici, Catholics disembowel the King's adviser Gaspard, Admiral de Coligny, throwing him from his bedroom window still living. Pope Gregory XIII congratulates Catherine. *23 Nov*: the painter Bronzino dies in Florence, aged 69.

📖 Luiz Vaz de Camoes: *Cs Lusiadas*

🎼 Thomas Tallis: *Spem in alium* (40-part motet, written at about this time)

1573 In Japan, the Shogun Yoshiake takes arms against the strongman Oda Nobunaga who defeats him; Yoshiake shaves his head and becomes a Buddhist priest. In China, Wan Li succeeds to the imperial throne at the age of 10, beginning a 47-year reign as the Emperor Shen Zong. Francis Drake captures a shipment of Spanish silver from the Potosi mines in New Castile while it is being transhipped across the Isthmus of Panama. *7 Mar*: Venice concludes a peace treaty with the Turks, breaking with the Spanish; now only Crete, Paros and the Ionian Islands remain under Venetian control. *11 May*: Poland elects its first King, choosing Henri of Valois (election paid for by Catherine de' Medici). *8 Jul*: Edict of Boulogne, ending the fourth religious civil war in France.

  ✎ Tintoretto: The Battle of Lepanto
     Paolo Veronese: Christ in the House of Levi
  📖 Torquato Tasso: *Amyntas*

1574 *30 May*: Charles IX of France dies, aged 24, and is succeeded by his brother Henri of Valois, who abandons the throne of Poland at the age of 23, returns to France as King Henri III, and is dominated by his mother Catherine de' Medici; Poland is left without a King. *Sep*: Leyden comes under siege by a Spanish army. *3 Oct*: William of Orange (William the Silent) breaks the dyke to flood the reclaimed polder and sails his ships right up to the city walls of Leyden to relieve the siege with bread and herrings. *22 Nov*: the Juan Fernandez Islands in the South Pacific Ocean are discovered by Juan Fernandez. *12 Dec*: Selim II the Ottoman Sultan falls in his bath, injures his head and dies, aged 50; he is succeeded by his 27-year-old eldest son Murad III, who has his brothers strangled in his presence.

  ✎ Giorgio Vasari: Uffizi Palaces (completed; Vasari dies *27 Jun*)
  📖 Pierre de Ronsard: *La Franciade*

1575 The town of Luanda is founded by Portuguese colonists in Angola. The painter El Greco arrives in Spain after leaving his native Crete and studying painting in Italy; he settles in Toledo. *22 Jan*: Thomas Tallis, Elizabeth I's royal organist, and William Byrd, organist and composer, are granted a 21-year licence by the Queen to print and sell music. *Feb*: Protestant rebels in the Lowlands meet the Spanish Governor-General Requesens at Breda; Maximilian II acts as an intermediary and the

Governor-General agrees to withdraw troops from the Netherlands. *Oct*: Battle of Dormans: a Protestant army is defeated by Catholic troops under the Duc de Guise. *14 Dec*: the Polish nobility elects Transylvania's Prince Stephen Bathory as the new King of Poland.

🐚 Giovanni Bologna: Mercury (bronze)
   Paolo Veronese: Moses Saved

🎵 Thomas Tallis and Willian Byrd: *Cantiones* (motets)

1576 Shah Tahmasp I of Persia is murdered, aged 53, after reigning for 43 years; he is succeeded by his son Ismail II, who kills many of his relatives. Akbar, the Moghal Emperor, conquers Bengal. The English navigator Martin Frobisher, searching for a north-west passage to Cathay, discovers Baffin Land. The Danish astronomer Tycho Brahe establishes an observatory on the island of Hven in the Sound; he rejects the Copernican system, believing that the five planets revolve round the sun which inturn revolves round a stationary earth. The first playhouse in England opens at Shoreditch under actor-manager James Burbage. *19 Jan*: the poet and dramatist Hans Sachs dies, aged 81. *6 May* the Peace of Chastenoy ends the fifth religious war in France, but so many concessions are made to the Huguenots that French Catholics form a Holy League and make an alliance with Philip II of Spain. Fearing the League's power, Henri III forbids the practice of Protestantism in France. *27 Aug*: the painter Titian dies of the plague in Venice, aged about 90. *12 Oct*: Holy Roman Emperor Maximilian II dies, aged 49, and is succeeded by his son Rudolf. *Nov*: the Spanish Fury erupts. Requesens dies, leaving Spanish garrisons in the Netherlands unpaid; the Spanish troops go on the rampage in Antwerp, killing 6,000 people and destroying 800 houses. *8 Nov*: William the Silent persuades the 17 Lowland provinces to unite: the Pacification of Ghent promises resistance until freedom and independence are restored to the Netherlands.

🏛 Orders of Oda Nobunaga: Azuchi Castle, Japan
📖 Dante Alighieri: *La Vita Nuova* (first published)
   (Jean Bodin: *Six Livres de la République*

1577 Ethiopians conquer the sultanate of Harrar. In Italy, Giovanni Palestrina is told by the Pope to restore the purity of 'Gregorian' chant in church music. In France, Catholic forces defeat Huguenots, but Henri III is unwilling to let the Holy League become too powerful and grants the Huguenots generous terms. *23 Sep*: William the Silent enters Brussels in triumph to be appointed Lieutenant to the new Governor, Archduke Mathias. *13 Dec*: Francis Drake sets sail on the *Pelican* for South America; his crew includes an apothecary and Drake's personal trumpeter.

✍ Andrea Palladio: Church of the Redeemer, Venice

1578 Drake navigates the Strait of Magellan, renames his ship *Golden Hind* and ravages the Pacific coast of South America. Elizabeth I of England grants a patent to Sir Humphrey Gilbert to take and colonize 'all remote and heathen lands not in the actual possession of any Christian prince'. Gilbert sets sail in search of a north-west passage. Ismail II, Shah of Persia, dies and is succeeded by his brother Mohammed Khudabanda. *Jan*: Philip II of Spain sends an army to the Netherlands under his cousin Alessandro Farnese to support the army of Don John. *31 Jan*: Farnese attacks and defeats a Dutch patriot army at Gemblours. *Aug*: in south-east Africa, the Portuguese sign a treaty with the Munhumutapa kingdom of the south Zambezi basin. *4 Aug*: Sebastian I of Portugal is killed and his army wiped out at Al Kasr al Kebir in north-west Africa; he has waged a crusade here in spite of warnings from Philip II of Spain and Pope Gregory XIII. Both the King of Fez and the Moorish pretender are also killed in the battle. The Portuguese people cannot believe that Sebastian is dead. A 'Sebastianist' cult develops: members believe that the King is either on a pilgrimage or waiting on an enchanted island for the right moment to return. Four people turn up pretending to be Sebastian and are executed, one of them an Italian who speaks no Portuguese! *1 Oct*: Don John of Austria dies of fever; Farnese takes command of Austrian and Spanish forces in the Low Countries. Martin Frobisher returns to England from Canada without having found a north-west passage.

✍ Nonsuch House, a new house added to the row of buildings on London Bridge has been made in the

Netherlands (first known prefabricated house)

📖 Raphael Holinshed: *Chronicles of English History to 1575*

Pierre de Ronsard: *Sonnets pour Hélène*

1579 *Jan*: The Union of Arras joins the Walloons (Catholics) of the Low Countries with those of Hainaut and Artois. The Union of Utrecht joins Dutch patriots to the union, marking the founding of the Dutch Republic; the Dutch sign a military alliance with England. In India, the Emperor Akbar invites Jesuits from the Portuguese colony of Goa to visit his court. *17 Jun*: Drake puts in for repairs at a point north of the site of San Francisco, claiming possession of the territory ('New Albion') for England.

🎨 El Greco: Trinity and Assumption.

📖 George Buchanan: *De Juri Begni apud Scotos* (justifies tyrannicide)

Theodore de Bèze: *Vindiciae contra Tyrannos* (rulers must be held accountable to their subjects)

Thomas North: *Lives of the Noble Grecians and Romans* (translation of Plutarch, influencing Elizabethan poets and playwrights)

Edmund Spenser: *The Shepheard's Calendar*

1580 *26 Mar*: Drake leaves Java, sailing westward for home. *11 Jun*: Spanish conquistador Juan de Garay, Captain-General of the La Plata territory, refounds the city of Buenos Aires. *15 Jun*: Drake rounds the Cape of Good Hope. *25 Aug*: Battle of Alcantara near Lisbon: the Spanish under the elderly Duke of Alva invade Portugal and defeat the Portuguese army. Philip II is proclaimed King of Portugal as well as Spain (Philip I of Portugal). *26 Sep*: Drake enters Plymouth Harbour after circumnavigating the world. *26 Nov*: the Treaty of Fleix ends a seventh religious civil war in France.

✐ Wollaton Hall, Nottingham (U.K.)

🎨 The Great Bed of Ware (U.K.)

📖 Michel Eyquem de Montaigne: *Essais*

John Lyly: *Euphues and His England*

Torquato Tasso: *Gerusalemme Liberato*

1581 William the Silent appoints François of Valois King of the Netherlands: François is the brother of Henri III

King of France. He tries to regain Antwerp from the Spanish. Stephen Bathory of Poland invades Muscovy, defeats Ivan the Terrible and marches on Pskov. The first English colony in North America is established at Roanoke Island, Virginia *14 Jun*: Edmund Campion, the English Jesuit, is arrested as he preaches at Lyford in Berkshire, committed to the Tower of London, examined in the Queen's presence and placed on the rack three times to try to shake his Catholic faith. *19 Aug*: the architect Andrea Palladio dies, aged 71, in Venice. *20 Nov*: Campion is found guilty of conspiring to dethrone Elizabeth I. *Dec 1*: Campion is hanged, drawn and quartered.

🎵 Baltasarini: *Ballet Comique de la Reyne*

1582 In India, the tolerant Emperor Akbar attempts a fusion of the world's great religions. In China, Matteo Ricci arrives in Macao to begin an intensive study of Chinese language and culture. In Japan, Taira strongman Oda Nobunaga joins his general Hideyoshi, who has taken much of western Honshu from the Mo'ori family. His enemy, the general Akechi Mitsuhido, sets fire to the monastery where Nobunaga stays overnight and Nobunaga dies in the flames. Hideyoshi kills Mitsuhido and then begins to eliminate the Nobunaga family in a power struggle. A delegation of Japanese Christian boys sets off for Rome; they will return in four years after visiting Pope Gregory XIII. The Universities of Wurzburg and Edinburgh have their beginnings. *10 Aug*: Ivan the Terrible makes peace with Poland and Sweden after 25 years of fighting. *4 Oct*: Teresa of Avila (St. Teresa), the ascetic Christian mystic and writer, dies at Albe de Tormes, aged 67. *5 Oct*: the new Gregorian calendar replaces the old Julian calendar. The new one, devised by Aloysius Lilius, is adopted by Catholic countries in Europe today; which becomes *15 Oct*.

📖 Richard Hakluyt: *Divers Voyages Touching the Discovery of America*

Giordano Bruno: *The Shadow of Ideas*

1583 The Burmese invade Yunnan province. Dutch troops from the seven United Provinces sympathetic to Spain occupy the mouth of the River Scheldt, blocking Antwerp (held by Protestants) from sea trade. The composer Girolamo Frescobaldi is born at Ferrara. *5 Aug*: Humphrey Gilbert takes possession of Newfoundland for England, setting up a short-lived colony; Gilbert himself is lost on the return voyage.

🐚 Giovanni da Bologna: Rape of the Sabine Women (sculpture)

📖 Andre Cesalpino: *De Plantis* (first modern classification of plants)

Fray Louis de León: *The Names of Christ*

1584 In Japan, Hideyoshi gains control over the centre of the country. Bern, Zurich and Geneva form an alliance against Savoy and the Catholic cantons. The English colony on Roanoke Island (U.S.) is named Virginia after Elizabeth I by Walter Raleigh, who has secured the renewal of the colonization patent granted to his half-brother Humphrey Gilbert. *18 Mar*: Ivan the Terrible Tsar of Muscovy dies, aged 53, and is succeeded by his 27-year-old son Fedor Ivanovich, but the new Tsar is dominated by Ivan's court favourite, Boris Godunov. *10 Jul*: William of Orange (the Silent) is murdered at Delft by the Burgundian Balthazar Gerard. Spain's Philip II has offered a large reward to anyone who would assassinate William. William is succeeded by his son Maurice of Nassau, a 17-year-old student at the University of Leyden. *8 Aug*: Hideyoshi moves into Hideyoshi Castle at Osaka. *10 Aug*: François Duc d'Alençon, Henri III of France's younger brother, dies leaving the ruling family without a successor.

🏛 Hideyoshi Castle, Osaka (Japan)

1585 Sir Francis Drake sails for the West Indies to attack the Spanish. Sir Walter Raleigh sends a new expedition to Virginia under the leadership of his cousin Sir Richard Grenville and Sir Ralph Lane. Lane discovers Chesapeake Bay and stays in America as Governor of the Virginia colony. John Davis discovers the Davis Strait on the first of three voyages in search of a north west passage to the Pacific. Jamaican ginger, the first Oriental spice to be grown successfully in the New World, arrives in Europe. Another religious civil war breaks out in France (the War of the Three Henris) as the Holy

League vows to stop Henri of Navarre from succeeding to the throne. *Aug*: Treaty of Nonsuch forms an alliance between England and the Protestant Allied Provinces; Elizabeth breaks with Spain and sends an army under the Earl of Leicester to the Low Countries. *23 Nov*: the English composer Thomas Tallis dies at Greenwich, aged 80.

    Orders of Frederick II of Denmark: Kronborg Castle, Elsinore

    Simon Stevin: *La Disme* (advocating decimal fractions)

1586   The Moghal Emperor Akbar annexes the kingdom of Kashmir. The Japanese Emperor Goyozei makes Hideyoshi his Prime Minister. *1 Jan*: Sir Francis Drake surprises the fortified city of San Domingo on Hispaniola, extorting a large ransom from the Spanish Governor. *Feb*: Drake captures Cartagena. *7 Jun*: Drake burns San Agostin in Florida. *18 Feb*: Drake sets sail for England, taking Sir Ralph Lane and other surviving settlers from the failed colony in Virginia. Potatoes taken home by Drake are planted on Raleigh's estate in Ireland. *22 Sep*: Battle of Zutphen: the Earl of Leicester's army and the Dutch army defeat Spanish forces. Leicester's nephew Sir Philip Sidney is wounded in the thigh and dies 26 days later at Arnhem. The Babbington plot to assassinate Elizabeth I is uncovered. *25 Oct*: Mary Queen of Scots is accused of complicity in the Babbington Plot. *12 Dec*: Stephen Bathory of Poland dies suddenly, aged 53, and is succeeded by the 21-year-old son of the Swedish King as Sigismund III.

    Obelisk, St. Peter's Square, Rome

    El Greco: The Burial of Count Orgaz
       Tintoretto: The Legend of St. Mark

1587   Mohammed Khudabanda, the half-blind Shah of Persia, dies and is succeeded by his 30-year-old son Abbas I. Hideyoshi invades the Japanese island of Kyushu and subdues the Shimazu clan; with this act Hideyoshi, now Kampaku (civil dictator), completes his conquest of the feudal barons of Japan. *8 Feb*: Mary Queen of Scots is executed at Fotheringhay Castle by order of Elizabeth I. *19 Apr*: the invasion fleet prepared by Philip II of Spain is burnt in Cadiz harbour by Drake, delaying the invasion of England. *25 Jul:* Hideyoshi orders Jesuits to leave Japan and bans Christianity. *18 Aug:* the first English child to be born in North America, Virginia Dare, is born on Roanoke Island. *20 Oct:* Battle of Coutras: Henri of Navarre defeats the Catholic League but with no long-term effect.

  📖 Robert Southwell: *An Epistle of Comfort to the Reverend Priests*
     Christopher Marlowe: *Tamburlaine the Great*
     Thomas Kyd: *The Spanish Tragedie*

1588 In Japan, Toyotomi Hideyoshi instigates a 'sword hunt' to disarm the Japanese peasants. *4 Apr:* Frederick II King of Denmark and Norway dies, aged 53, and is succeeded by his 10-year-old son Christian IV. *19 Apr:* the artist Paolo Veronese dies in Venice, aged 59. *12 May:* Henri of Guise enters Paris and is acclaimed King of France. A popular rising forces Henri III to take refuge at Blois. *Jul:* the Spanish Armada sails against England under the command of Alonso de Guzman, Duke of Medina-Sidonia, who is 38. *31 Jul:* the Spanish Armada is engaged by the Royal Navy under Lord High Admiral William Howard, only 34 ships against 134 invading Spanish vessels – and the English ships are significantly smaller. *8 Aug:* the English defeat the Armada, helped by severe weather conditions. *23 Dec:* Henri III has Henri of Guise and his brother Louis the Cardinal murdered.

  🎨 Nicholas Hilliard: Young Man Among Roses
  📖 Christopher Marlowe: *The Tragedy of Dr. Faustus*
  🎼 Giovanni da Palestrina: *Lamentations* (introduction points out to the Pope that poverty has obliged him to omit many pieces)

1589 The Russian Orthodox Church makes itself independent from Constantinople by establishing a separate Russian patriarchate; the move is prompted by the decline of the Ottoman Empire. An English clergyman, William Lee, invents the first knitting machine; Elizabeth I refuses a patent for his stocking frame so he sets up his frame at Rouen. Sir John Harington, banished from the royal court by Queen Elizabeth for telling bawdy stories, invents the world's first flushing toilet, the 'Ajax'. *5 Jan*: Catherine de' Medici dies at Blois, aged 69. *Jul*: The Catholic party in France is revolted at the news that Henri III has ordered the murder of Henri of Guise and his brother; the King has been obliged to flee to the Huguenot camp of Henri of Navarre at St. Cloud outside Paris. *31 Jul*: Jacques Clement, a Dominican monk, murders Henri III of France at St. Cloud; Henri of Navarre is recognized as his successor, Henri IV. *2 Sep*: Battle of Arques: Henri IV of France defeats the Duc de Mayenne, head of the Catholic League.

  ✐ Kamurzell House, Strasbourg (completed)

  📖 Christopher Marlowe: *The Famous Tragedy of the Jew of Malta*

  ♫ Thoinot Arbeau: *Orchésographie* (book of French dance tunes)

1590 Shah Abbas of Persia and the Ottoman Sultan Murad III end their 12-year war. Murad enlarges his Empire to the Caucasus and the Caspian Sea, acquiring Georgia and Azerbaijan. The Shah has his father and brothers blinded. The Moghal Emperor Akbar conquers Orissa. The Sultan of Golconda, Mohammed Quli Qutb Shah, founds the city of Hyderabad on the River Musi. Hideyoshi completes the unification of Japan. *Jan*: the Catholic party in France refuses to recognize Henri IV as King, proclaiming the elderly Cardinal de Bourbon King as Charles X. *14 Mar*: Battle of Ivry: Henri IV defeats the Catholic League under the Duc de Mayenne by besieging Paris; starvation kills 13,000. *May*: 'Charles X' of France dies.

  ✐ Dome of St. Peter's Basilica, Rome (completed)
    Palazzo Balbi, Venice (completed)

  🎨 Michelangelo Caravaggio: The Cardshop

  📖 Edmund Spenser: *The Faerie Queene Books 1–3*

1591 The Japanese Rikyu Sen commits suicide on orders from Toyotomi Hideyoshi: Sen had refined the tea ceremony. The first books to be printed using movable type are produced at Nagasaki by the Portuguese Jesuit Alessandro Valegnani. Brazil is closed to all immigration except Portuguese, but African slaves are still to be imported to work on the plantations. The English John White returns to Roanoke to find that everyone has vanished. Possibly the colonists are the victims of Indian hostility; they leave behind them a message consisting of the one word 'Croatan', which does nothing to solve the mystery. Spanish and Portuguese adventurers hired by the Moroccans cross the Sahara; they use firearms to defeat a Songhai army, take Timbuktu and destroy Gao. *15 May*: the Tsarevich, nine-year-old Demetrius, is found murdered, his throat cut. The Regent Boris Godunov is suspected of complicity.

    ✍ Antonio da Ponte: Rialto Bridge, Venice (rebuilt)

    📖 William Shakespeare: *Henry VI*

1592   Mulai Ahmed al-Mansur Sultan of Morocco sends an army of Andalusian mercenaries and adventurers to invade the Songhai Empire in the African interior, using arms supplied by Elizabeth I of England. The invasion force defeats the Songhai army at Tondibi near Gao, and again at Bamba near Timbuktu; the Moroccan force retreats when no gold is found. English explorer James Lancaster rounds the Malay peninsula. Portuguese colonists settle in Mombasa on the east coast of Africa. The Spanish navigator Juan de Fuca explores the Pacific coast of North America, and claims (mistakenly) to have found the north-west passage. Galileo Galilei, 28-year-old mathematician at the University of Pisa, moves to Padua University after contradicting the accepted belief that objects fall at speeds proportional to their weight. *Apr*: the French royalist siege of Rouen is relieved. *May*: in Japan, Toyotomi Hideyoshi invades Korea after the Koreans reject his terms for trade; Hideyoshi's general Konishi takes Pusan Castle, but a Chinese ironclad sent by admiral Yi-sun-sin almost destroys the Japanese fleet.

    ✍ Palazzo Vecchio, Florence

    🎨 Tintoretto: The Last Supper

    Gheeraerts: Elizabeth I, the Ditchley Portrait

1593   Chinese troops cross the Yalu River into Korea, forcing the Japanese out of Seoul. Hideyoshi, the Japanese leader, loses a third of his troops and retreats to the south coast as winter sets in; Korean guerrillas harry his retreat. In England, coal mining gains momentum as a result of a shortage of firewood. In Sweden, the Diet of Uppsala requires King Sigismund to maintain Lutheranism as the state religion. Spanish Franciscans arrive in Japan to start missionary work in competition with the Portuguese Jesuits. The organist at Salisbury Cathedral in England loses his job for striking the Dean of Salisbury in a fit of rage. In France, the Estates-General meets in February in Paris, calling for a Catholic king. *11 Jul*: Giuseppe Arcimboldo, painter and master of revels at Emperor Rudolf's court (a haven for all kinds of eccentrics), dies in Prague, aged 66. *Jul 25*: Henri IV of France rejects Protestantism and is accepted into the Catholic faith.

🖉 Juan Bautista de Toledo: Escorial Palace, near Madrid (completed)

📖 Christopher Marlowe: *The Massacre at Paris*; *The Troublesome Reign and Lamentable Death of Edward II*

Wiliam Shakespeare: *Venus and Adonis*; *Richard III*; *Comedy of Errors*

1594 The Moghal Emperor Akbar takes control of Makran and Baluchistan. Lisbon closes its spice market to English traders, forcing them to get their spices directly from the Far East; the creation of the Dutch East India Company follows. The sweet potato reaches China, 30 years after the Spanish introduced it into the Philippines. Sir Richard Hawkins sails round Cape Horn and plunders the Spanish port of Valparaiso; he is defeated in San Mateo Bay (Peru) and taken prisoner (kept captive for eight years). *22 Mar*: Paris surrenders to Henri IV, who is then crowned at Chartres; he continues his campaign to win over France, province by province. *31 May*: the painter Tintoretto dies in Venice, aged 75. *14 Jun*: the composer Orlando di Lassus dies.

🎨 Michelangelo Caravaggio: The Musical Party

📖 Thomas Nashe: *The Unfortunate Traveller, or the Life of Jack Wilton*

William Shakespeare: *The Rape of Lucrece*; *Titus Andronicus*

Christopher Marlowe: *Dido, Queen of Carthage* (murdered *30 May, 1593*)

♒ Giovanni Palestrina: *Seventh Book of Masses* (Palestrina's 104th Mass is published in *Jan*: he dies *2 Feb* in Rome)

1595 The Dutch East India Company sends its first ships to the Far East; the Dutch found colonies on the West African coast and in the East Indies. Sir Walter Raleigh explores the River Orinoco in South America and returns to England empty-handed. The University of San Carlos is founded at Cebu City in the Philippines. Spanish troops land in Cornwall as hostilities between Spain and England continue. *6 Jan*: the Ottoman Sultan Murad III dies, aged 49, and is succeeded by his son Mohammed III, who has his 19 brothers murdered in accordance with the 'law of fratricide'. Mohammed's mother, the Sultana Valide Baffo, is the real power behind the throne. *2 Feb*: English Jesuit Robert Southwell is executed for treason. *5 Jun*: Battle of Fontaine-Française: Henry IV succeeds in driving the Spanish out of Burgundy.

🖾 Annibale Carracci: *Venus and Adonis*

📖 William Shakespeare: *Two Gentlemen of Verona; Love's Labour's Lost* Robert Parsons: *A Conference about the next succession the Crowne of Ingland* Robert Southwell: *St. Peter's Complaint*

1596 The London theatres reopen; they have been closed for three years because of plague in the city. Blackfriar's Theatre opens in London: actor-manager James Burbage converts a house into a playhouse. Sir John Harington's flushing water closet has found few buyers in England. The tomato is introduced into England as an ornamental plant. The Dutch explorer Willem Barents discovers and lands on Newland (Spitzbergen). *Jan*: the French Catholic leader, the Duc de Mayenne, surrenders to Henri IV, ending the War of the Catholic League. France forms an alliance with England and the Netherlands against Philip II of Spain, whose forces take Calais in *Apr*. *28 Apr*: Sir Francis Drake dies of dysentery aboard his ship and is buried at sea off Panama. *1 Jul*: an English fleet captures Cadiz. *Sep*: Ottoman forces under the new Sultan Mohammed III defeat a Hungarian Army at Erlau. *Oct*: Battle of Keresztes: victory for the Ottomans, who slaughter over 30,000 Hungarians and Germans. *29 Nov:* authorities in Madrid admit that Spain's economy is ruined, in part as a result of a series of expensive wars including the disastrous attempted invasion of England.

♺ Swan Theatre, London

⚞ El Greco: *View of Toledo*

📖 Robert Southwell: *The Triumphs over Death*
Sir John Harington: *Metamorphosis of Ajax*
William Shakespeare: *A Midsummer Night's Dream*
Edmund Spenser: *The Faerie Queene, Books 4–6*
George Chapman: *The Blind Beggar of Alexandria*

1597 Mount Hekla in Iceland erupts. Paul Heuter, a German traveller who visits England, notices the blackness of Elizabeth I's teeth and attributes it to the Queen's excessive consumption of sugar. Philip II of Spain sends a second armada against England, but once again his ships are scattered by a storm. Robert Devereux, Earl of Essex, sails to the Azores to capture the Spanish treasure fleet, but fails. *5 Feb:* in Japan, Toyotomi Hideyoshi crucifies 26 Christians at Nagasaki, ordering all remaining missionaries to leave the country; when most defy this order, he takes no action for fear of driving away Portuguese traders. *20 Jun:* Willem Barents dies in the Arctic while trying to find a north-east passage.

♺ Robert Smythson: Hardwick Hall, Derbyshire (completed)

📖 William Shakespeare: *Sonnets*; *Romeo and Juliet*; *Richard II*; *King John*; *The Merchant of Venice*
Francis Bacon: *Essays*

𝄽 Jacopo Peri: *Dafne*
John Dowland: *First Booke of Songs*

1598 The Dutch Admiral Wijbrand van Warwijk discovers Mauritius. In the south-west of North America, Pueblo territory is colonized by the Spanish. The Dutch set out to trade directly with the Far East and begin taking Portuguese possessions in the east. Spain and the Netherlands offer prizes for a method of ascertaining longitude. *7 Jan:* Fedor I Tsar of Muscovy dies, aged 40, and is succeeded by his brother-in-law Boris Godunov, who has been effective ruler since 1584. *15 Apr:* Edict of

Nantes: Henri IV gives Huguenots political rights equal to those of Catholics, permitting them to exercise freedom of worship in some French towns. *2 May*: Treaty of Vervins ending the war between France and Spain. Philip II is to keep Flanders, Artois and Charolais but give up Picardy. *13 Sep*: Philip II of Spain dies in the new Escorial Palace, aged 71, after reigning for 42 years. He is succeeded by his 20-year-old son Philip III. *18 Sep*: Toyotomi Hideyoshi dictator of Japan dies, aged 62; his death leaves a power vacuum and Japan is plunged into civil war. The Japanese evacuate Korea; their campaign there has been disastrous, costing 260,000 lives on the Japanese side alone.

- Francisco Becerra: Cuzco Cathedral (completed)
- El Greco: St. Martin and the Beggar
  Michelangelo Caravaggio: The Calling of St. Matthew
- Lope de Vega: *Arcadia*; *La Dragontea* (epic poem about Drake)
  Abul Fazl: *The History of Akbar*
  Tang Xiansu: *The Peony Pavilion*
  William Shakespeare: *Henry IV*
  Ben Jonson: *Every Man in His Humour*
- John Wilbye: *Madrigals, First Book*

1599 Elizabeth I of England sends the Earl of Essex to subdue the Irish rebel, the Earl of Tyrone, but he is defeated at Arklow. Thomas Dallan, the Lancashire organ builder, sets off for Constantinople with an organ, a present from Elizabeth I to the Sultan. There are now 900,000 black slaves in the New World. In the East, the Dutch set up trading posts at Banda, Amboina and Ternate. Inspired by the success of the Dutch enterprise, the merchants in London decide to form their own East India Company. The Black Death takes a heavy toll in Essen, one of Europe's largest cities. *22 Mar*: the painter Anthony van Dyck, later court painter to Charles I, is born at Antwerp. *25 Apr*: Oliver Cromwell is born at Huntingdon in England. *28 Sep*: the Earl of Essex leaves his post as Lord Lieutenant of Ireland to vindicate himself before the Queen. He returns to England. *Nov*: Essex is arrested for disobedience and banished. The Swedish Riksdag votes to depose Sigismund III, the Polish King of Sweden; his uncle Charles is appointed Regent for Gustavus' grandson.

  ✍ Commissioned by William Shakespeare and partners: Globe Theatre, London

    Montacute House, Somerset (completed)

  📖 William Shakespeare: *Julius Caesar*

1600 China has 120 million people, France 16 million, Italy 13 million, Spain and Portugal 10 million, the German-speaking states together 20 million, England 5 million, North America 1 million. *17 Feb*: the Italian philosopher Giordano Bruno is burned at the stake in Rome, condemned for heresy because he supports the Copernican view of the solar system and has suggested that there may be other worlds than this. *15 Sep*: Battle of Sekigahara: the Japanese general Ieyasu defeats the other three regents for the six-year-old son of Hideyoshi, the dead dictator. The English explorer Will Adams reaches Kyushu and is summoned to Kyoto by Ieyasu, who retains him as an adviser: Ieyasu is impressed with Adams' knowledge, especially of navigation. Ieyasu moves his capital from Kyoto to Edo. *14 Oct*: in Madrid, the theologian Luis de Molina, a disciple of Thomas Aquinas, dies. *31 Dec*: the (English) East India Company is chartered to make annual voyages to the Indies, challenging Dutch control of the trade in spices.

  ✍ Church of St. Nicholas, Panilovo in Muscovy (completed)

  🎨 Annibale Carracci: Flight into Egypt

  📖 Thomas Dekker: *The Shoemaker's Holiday*

    William Shakespeare: *Henry V; As You Like It; Much Ado About Nothing*

    Ben Jonson: *Every Man Out of his Humour*

    Oliver de Serres: *Théâtre d'agriculture des champs*

    William Gilbert: *De Magnete*

    Sir Walter Raleigh: *The Nymph's Reply to the Shepherd*

  🎵 Jacopo Peri: *Eurydice* (first presented at the wedding of Marie de' Medici to Henri IV of France, *10 Jun*, Pitti Palace)

1601 In Japan, the Regent Ieyasu improves the transport

system by ordering the establishment of 53 stations between Edo and Osaka with inns at which travellers may stay overnight and hire fresh horses. Will Adams supervises the building of 100-ton ships for the Shogun. Anthony Sherley introduces coffee to London where it sells at £5 per ounce. In India, the Mughul Emperor Akbar absorbs the Deccan kingdoms of Berar, Ahmadnagar and Khandesh into his Empire. *Jan*: the first English spice fleet sets sail from Woolwich under the command of James Lancaster; his flagship, the *Red Dragon*, is 600 tons. Queen Elizabeth puts the Earl of Essex on trial for his failure in Ireland. *25 Feb*: Essex is beheaded, aged 34. *24 Oct*: the astronomer Tycho Brahe dies at the imperial court in Prague.

🎨 Annibale Carracci: Ceiling Fresco, Farnese Palace, Rome

📖 William Shakespeare: *Twelfth Night*; *Troilus and Cressida*
John Donne: *The Progress of the Soule*
Thomas Middleton: *Blurt, Master Constable*

1602 The English mariner Bartolomew Gosnold explores 'New England'. *20 Mar*: The United East India Company is chartered by the Dutch Staats-General: it combines various companies to eliminate competition and receives sweeping powers to wage defensive wars, make treaties and build forts in the Indies. *Jun*: James Lancaster's East India Company fleet arrives at Achin, Sumatra. The local ruler has been antagonized by the Portuguese and he is happy to deal with the English, who defeated Portugal's ally. Lancaster seizes a large Portuguese galleon and loots her cargo of plate, jewels and merchandise.

📖 William Shakespeare: *The Merry Wives of Windsor*
Ben Jonson: *Poetaster*

1603 The West African ruler Idris Aloma dies after reigning over the huge Islamic state of Bornu, building it into the greatest power between the Niger and the Nile. In Japan, Tokugawa Ieyasu founds the Tokugawa Shogunate, with his headquarters at the city of Edo. Samuel de Champlain and François du Pontgrave explore the Saguenay and St. Lawrence Rivers, and hear from the Indians of the existence of the Great Lakes and Niagara Falls. Famine in Russia kills tens of thousands of people. The English East Indian Company's first expedition returns; James Lancaster sells his cargo of pepper at a good profit and is knighted. *24 Mar*: Elizabeth I of England dies, aged 69, after reigning for 45 years. She is succeeded by James I of England (VI of Scotland), son of Mary Queen of Scots, who reigns over a United Kingdom. Sir Walter Raleigh is tried for high treason; he is suspected of complicity in the 'Main Plot' to dethrone James I and sent to prison. *25 Dec*: the Ottoman Sultan Mohammed III dies, aged 37, of plague and is succeeded by his 14-year-old son Ahmed I.

- Carlo Maderna: Castel Gandolfo (completed)
- Johnde Critz: Earl of Southampton
  Annibale Carracci: Landscape with the Flight into Egypt El Greco: St. Bernardino
- Thomas Dekker: *The Magnificent Entertainment Given to King James*
  William Shakespeare: *Hamlet; All's Well That Ends Well*

1604 Samuel de Champlain explores the Atlantic coast of North America from Maine to Cape Cod. James I makes peace with Spain and concentrates English efforts on North American colonization. *6 Mar*: after the 14-year-old Duke John, younger brother of King Sigismund, renounces his claim to the Swedish throne, his uncle takes the title instead, reigning as Charles IX. *20 Sep*: the Spanish retake Ostend from the Dutch after a three-year siege.

- Pont Neuf, Paris
- El Greco: St. Ildefonso
  Michelangelo Caravaggio: The Deposition
- Michael Drayton: *The Owl*
  William Shakespeare: *Othello; Measure For Measure*
  Thomas Dekker and Thomas Middleton: *The Honest Whore*
  James I: *Counterblaste to Tobacco* ('a custom lothsome to the eye, hatefull to the nose, harmefull to the braine, dangerous to the lungs')
- Jan Sweelinck: *Psalms of David* (First Book)

1605 In Japan the Shogun Ieyasu makes his son Hidetada Co-ruler. Will Adams has become foreign adviser to the Shogun, taking the Japanese name Anshin Miura and a Japanese wife. Adams obtains from the Shogun an invitation to found a Dutch trading post in Japan. *5 Mar*: Pope Clement VIII dies, aged 70, and is succeeded by Paul V. *13 Apr*: Tsar of Muscovy Boris Godunov dies, aged 52, and is succeeded by his son, but Fedor II is soon murdered by enemies of the Godunovs. An impostor claiming to be Demetrius, son of Fedor I, enters Moscow on *19 Jun. 17 Oct*: in India, the Moghul Emperor Akbar dies, aged 62, possibly poisoned; Akbar is succeeded by his son Jahangir.

Orders of Ram Das: Golden Temple at Amritsar

El Greco: The Crucifixion; The Resurrection; St. John the Baptist

Miguel de Cervantes: *Don Quixote de la Mancha*
Michael Drayton: *Poems Lyric and Pastoral*
William Shakespeare: *King Lear*
Ben Jonson: *Volpone*

1606 Portuguese forces in the Pacific drive off the Dutch after a siege of Malacca. A Plymouth Company ship sent out in *Aug* under Henry Challons is captured by the Spanish; a second ship sent in *Oct* under Thomas Hanham and Martin Pring reaches the coast of Maine and returns with favourable reports. The Russian pretender is driven from the throne and murdered; Basil Shuiski, the boyar who has organized the coup, makes himself Tsar Basil IV. *19 Dec*: three ships of the London Company sail for Virginia (*Godspeed*, *Sarah Constant* and *Discovery*) under Captain Christopher Newport. Dutch sailors land at Cape Keerweer in Australia, making the first landing by Europeans in Australia. The painter Annibale Carracci suffers from depression and gives up painting almost completely.

Thomas Middleton: *A Trick to Catch the Old One*
William Shakespeare: *Macbeth*; *Antony and Cleopatra*
Thomas Dekker: *The Seven Deadly Sinnes of London*

1607 French colonists abandon the settlement founded by de Champlain three years ago. The Muscovy commissions

English navigator Henry Hudson to find a northern passage to China; Hudson follows the east coast of Greenland. *14 May*: Christopher Newport of the London Company founds Jamestown, Virginia. *22 Jun*: Newport sails for England, leaving the colonists in the care of Captain John Smith. By autumn the Jamestown colonists are starving. *Dec*: Captain John Smith goes up-country to trade for corn with the Algonquin Indians. He is captured and his life is spared through the intercession of the chief's 12-year-old daughter Pocahontas.

   📐 John Thorpe: Hatfield House, Hertfordshire (U.K.)

   📖 Francis Beaumont and John Fletcher: *The Knight of the Burning Pestle*
      William Shakespeare: *Timon of Athens*
      Thomas Heywood: *A Woman Killed with Kindness*
      Cyril Tourneur: *The Revenger's Tragedy*

   🎵 Claudio Monteverdi: *Orfeo*

1608 Henry Hudson searches the Barents sea for a north-east passage on a second abortive voyage. The English East India Company ship *Hector* is the first Company ship to reach India; William Hawkins hands the new Moghul Emperor Jahangir a letter from James I asking for trade; the letter is addressed to the late Emperor Akbar, and Jahangir grants the trading concessions to John Mildenhall. Paraguay is founded in South America as a Jesuit state. A Spanish royal decree legalizes the enslavement of Chilean Indians. *Jan*: Christopher Newport arrives in Jamestown with 110 new settlers: disease and hunger have reduced the original colony to 40. *7 Jan*: the fort at Jamestown is destroyed by fire. *Jun*: Holy Roman Emperor Rudolf II is forced to cede Hungary, Austria and Moravia to his brother Matthias. Captain John Smith surveys Chesapeake Bay and the Potomac River, hoping to find a passage through to the Pacific. *10 Sep*: Smith is elected President of the Jamestown Council. *29 Sep*: Newport arrives at Jamestown with a second supply ship. *Dec*: Newport embarks for England with Smith's map of Chesapeake Bay.

   📖 William Shakespeare: *Coriolanus*
      Thomas Dekker: *Lanthorne of delight*
      Thomas Middleton: *A Mad World, My Masters*

♫ Claudio Monteverdi: *L'Arianna*

Thomas Weelkes: *Ayeres or Phantasticke Spirits*

1609 Hostilities begin between America's Five Nations Iroquois and the French; Champlain has started this by killing some Mohawks at the request of the Hurons. Henry Hudson makes a third voyage, this time employed by the United East India Company. He explores the New England coast and the Hudson River as far as Albany. The London Company ship *Sea Venture* is wrecked off Bermuda, the beauty of which so delights George Somers, one of the Captains, that he returns to England to form a company to colonize Bermuda. In Japan, Dutch merchants found a trading post at Hirado at the invitation of the Shogun, ending the Portuguese monopoly in trade with Japan. The Bank of Amsterdam is founded with silver from South American ingots. *9 Apr*: Philip III of Spain signs a truce with the Dutch, recognizing the independence of the Netherlands. *10 Jul*: Duke Maximilian of Bavaria organizes a Catholic League to oppose the Protestant Evangelical Union organized by Frederick IV the Palatine Elector. *15 Jul*: the painter Annibale Carracci dies in Rome. *12 Sep*: Hudson sails far enough up the Hudson River to be sure that it is not the hoped-for north-west passage.

◿ Palazzo Contarini degli Scrigni, Venice (completed)

Basilica, Mexico City

✐ Adam Elsheimer: Flight into Egypt

Peter Paul Rubens: Self-portrait with His Wife Isabella Brant

El Greco: Fra Paravicino

📖 Richard Hakluyt: *Virginia Richly Valued*

Johann Kepler: *Astronomia Nova*

Ben Jonson: *Masque of Queens*

William Shakespeare: *Sonnets* (completed)

♫ *Pammelia* (first published book of catches, rounds and canons)

Deuteromelia (more catches)

John Wilbye: *Madrigals* (Second Book)

1610 Ralambo, King of the Andriana, extends his realm through the interior of Madagascar; he calls his kingdom Imerina, 'as-far-as-the-eye-can-see'. The Hausa

Queen Amina dies, aged 34, after extending her kingdom south to the Niger Delta. The Jamestown colonists
in Virginia prepare to abandon the colony, setting off for
Newfoundland. They meet the *Virginia* commanded by
Lord de la Warr carrying 150 new settlers and fresh
supplies; they turn round, return to Jamestown and try
again with de la Warr as their Governor. The French
Queen Mother Marie de' Medici removes Sully from
office and replaces him with her favourites, Concino
Concini, in a powerful position: oppression of the
peasants follows. In Spain, the Duke de Lerma steps
up the expulsion of the Moriscos (converted Moors)
who have contributed so much to the country's economy
and culture. *7 Jan*: using the newly invented telescope, Galileo observes the
moons of Jupiter and proves Kepler's theories about
the elliptical shape of planetary orbits correct. *14 May*:
Henri IV of France is assassinated in Paris by a 31-year-
old fanatic, François Ravaillac. Henri is succeeded by
his nine-year-old son, Louis XIII, with the boy's
mother Marie de' Medici as Agent. *Jul*: the Grand
Duke of Muscovy Basil IV is deposed by Sigismund
III of Poland, abducted to Warsaw and his throne
offered to Sigismund's son who is proclaimed Ladislav
IV. *18 Jul*: the painter Michelangelo Caravaggio dies of
malaria at Port 'Ercole, aged 36. *Aug*: Henry Hudson
makes another attempt to find a north-west passage,
backed this time by English investors. *3 Aug*: Hudson
enters and explores Hudson Bay.

   El Greco: *Laocoön*; *The Opening of the Fifth Seal*
   Peter Paul Rubens: *Raising of the Cross*

   William Shakespeare: *Cymbeline*
   Ben Jonson: *The Alchemist*
   Lope de Vega: *Peribanez*

   Claudio Monteverdi: *Vespers*

1611 The Danes declare war on Sweden. Mutineers maroon
Henry Hudson on the shore of James Bay: he is never
heard of again. The (English) Muscovy Company sends
out its first ship fitted out especially for whaling; the
Mary Margaret kills a small whale off Spitzbergen and is
lost with all hands on her return voyage. *30 Oct*: Charles

IX of Sweden dies, aged 61, and is succeeded by his 16-year-old son Gustavus II.

✎ Peter Paul Rubens: Descent from the Cross

□ Cyril Tourneur: *The Atheist's Tragedy*
Ben Jonson: *Catiline his Conspiracy*
William Shakespeare: *The Winter's Tale*; *The Tempest*
Authorized Version of the *Bible*

1612 Africans are being exported as slaves from Angola to Brazil at a rate of 10,000 a year. The Japanese begin persecuting Christians; the Shogun Ieyasu abandons his friendly attitude towards missionaries, realizing that trade with Europe can be carried on without them. A colony is founded on Bermuda. Two (English) East India Company ships defeat four Portuguese galleons off the Indian coast; the Emperor Jahangir is impressed and grants the English trading rights at Surat. Cultivating tobacco gives the Virginia settlers an export commodity, a solid economic base for the colony that has so far been lacking; Jamestown becomes a boom town. *20 Jan*: the Holy Roman Emperor Rudolf II dies, aged 59, in Prague and is succeeded by his brother Matthias. *27 Oct*: In Moscow, Polish troops surrender to the Russians under Prince Dmitri Pojarsky.

□ John Webster: *The White Devil*
Beaumont and Fletcher: *Cupid's Revenge*; *The Coxcomb*

1613 An English trading post is established at Hirado in Japan, as Will Adams tries to establish trading links between Japan and England through Captain John Saris. The East India Company sets up its first trading post in India. Dutch merchants set up a fur trading post on Manhattan Island. *20 Jan*: the Peace of Knared ends the war between Sweden and Denmark; Sweden gives up Finland. *22 Feb*: Mikhail Romanov, who is 17, is elected Tsar by the Russian boyars, ending the 'time of troubles' that has lasted since the death of Boris Godunov. *29 Jun*: the Globe Theatre in London burns down after a performance of Shakespeare's *Henry VIII*. *22 Jul*; Mikhail is crowned Tsar in the Kremlin, founding the Romanov dynasty. *28 Oct*: the first Japanese-built Western-style ship sails from Japan at the start of a three-month voyage to Acapulco in New Spain, commanded by the Samurai Tsunenaga Hasekura.

🐍 Guido Reni: The Aurora Fresco, Raspigliosi Palace, Rome

📖 William Shakespeare: *Henry VIII*

Francis Beaumont and John Fletcher: *Knight of the Burning Pestle*

Miguel de Cervantes: *Exemplary Novels* (short stories)

1614 Armand du Plessis, Duc de Richelieu, gains election to the Estates-General and engineers the dismissal of the Estates-General, which will not convene again until *1789*. The Virginia colonists resist settlement by the French in Maine and Nova Scotia. Dutch traders found Fort Nassau (Albany) on the River Hudson. *5 Apr*: John Rolfe, a Virginia settler, marries Pocahontas, daughter of chief Wahunsonacook; Pocahontas has been converted to Christianity and changed her name to Rebecca. *7 Apr*: El Greco dies at Toledo, aged 72.

✏ Andrea Palladio: Church of San Giorgio Maggiore (completed)

Bridge of Sighs, Venice

🐚 Peter Paul Rubens: Descent from the Cross

Domenichino: The Last Communion of St. Jerome

📖 John Webster: *The Duchess of Malfi*

Tirso de Molina: *La Santa Juana*

Ben Jonson: *Bartholomew Fair*

John Napier: *Mirifici Logarithmorum Canonis Descriptio* (logarithms)

🎵 Jan Sweelinck: *Psalms of David* (Third Book)

1615 Drinking chocolate from the Spanish New World is introduced into Italy, Spain and Flanders. Rubber is also introduced into Europe from South America, but as little more than a curiosity. England turns increasingly to coal, as timber grows scarce and firewood becomes more expensive. The Dutch seize the Moluccas from the Portuguese. An English fleet defeats a Portuguese fleet off Bombay in an intensifying trade war. *4 Jun*: Ieyasu, the Japanese Shogun, takes Osaka after a six-month siege. Hideyori, whose father was the dictator Hideyoshi, commits suicide and is burned in the fire that destroys his castle. *28 Jul*: Samuel de Champlain discovers Lake Huron.

♫ Mohammed Aga: Blue Mosque, Istanbul

🎨 Domenichino: Scenes from the Life of St. Cecilia

🎼 Girolamo Frescobaldi: *Recercari et Canzoni Francese*

1616 Willem Schouten, a Dutch East India Company mariner, rounds Cape Horn for the first time, naming it after his birthplace, Hoorn. English explorer William Baffin discovers Baffin Bay while trying to find the north-west passage and sailing further north (77°45′) than anyone will venture for over 200 years. Will Adams sets sail with Japanese ships for Siam; he has built the ships to expand Japanese trade in silks and other commodities. *26 Feb*: Galileo is arrested for heresy. *6 Mar*: the playwright Francis Beaumont dies, aged 34. *23 Apr*: William Shakespeare dies at Stratford, aged 52. Miguel Cervantes dies in Madrid, aged 69. *1 Jun*: the Japanese Shogun Ieyasu dies, aged 74, and is succeeded by his son Hidetada, who is now 38.

♫ Notre Dame Cathedral, Antwerp (completed)
   Inigo Jones: The Queen's House, Greenwich

🎨 Peter Paul Rubens: The Lion Hunt
   Frans Hals: Banquet of the Officers of the Guild of Archers

📖 Beaumont and Fletcher: *The Scornful Lady*
   Ben Jonson: *Poems*

1617 /A smallpox epidemic sweeps through New England, reducing the Indian population from an estimated 10,000 to 1,000. Rebecca Rolfe (Pocahontas) dies of smallpox. In Japan, the Yoshiwara red-light district is established in Edo. A vice lord has persuaded the authorities to give him a licence to operate supervised brothels. The ashes of Shogun Ieyasu are transferred from Edo to the mausoleum of Nikko. The composer Heinrich Schütz becomes Kapellmeister of the Elector of Saxony at Dresden. *9 Mar*: Gustavus II of Sweden cuts Russia off from the Baltic. In England, James I releases Sir Walter Raleigh from prison to seek gold in the Orinoco basin. *17 Mar*: Raleigh sails from England. *24 Apr*: Concino Concini, Chief Minister of France, is arrested and executed on Louis XIII's orders; the King banishes his mother to Blois, while the Duc de Luynes gains power over the 16-year-old King. *22 Nov:* the Ottoman Sultan Ahmed I dies, aged 27, and is succeeded by his 16-year-old brother Mustafa I. *31 Dec:* Raleigh's ill-fated expedition reaches the mouth of the Orinoco.

 ✿ Royal Mosque, Isfahan (completed)

1618   Richelieu negotiates a treaty between Marie de' Medici and the Duc de Luynes so that she can return from exile: Richelieu is exiled to Avignon for conspiring with the Queen Mother. The Ottoman Sultan Mustafa I is declared unfit to rule and replaced by his brother Osman II. *23 May:* the Defenestration of Prague, starting the Thirty Years' War in Europe. Bohemian Catholics destroy a Protestant church. Protestants are incensed that seven out of the 10 new governors of Bohemia are Catholic. Two governors are thrown from a window in the Hradcany Palace, marking the start of a revolt led by the Protestant Count Heinrich von Thurn; his rebel troops march on Austria. *28 Sep:* the world's first pawnshop opens in Brussels. *29 Oct:* Sir Walter Raleigh is executed following his return from South America; several Spaniards have been killed in a skirmish while Raleigh was ill in Trinidad and the expedition was temporarily under Lawrence Keymis' control. Keymis kills himself after being reproached by Raleigh. James I has Raleigh executed to pacify the Spanish.

 ✿ Thomas Holt: Bodleian Library, Oxford
 🌿 Diego Velazquez: Old Woman Cooking
    Jusepe de Ribera: Crucifixion
 📖 Torquato Tasso: *Il rey Torrismondo*

1619   The 72-year-old Dutch statesman Jan van Oldenbarneveldt is beheaded for treason after a trial ordered by Prince Maurice of Nassau. The town of Yeniseysk is founded as the capital of a gold-mining region of the same name in the interior of Asia. Richelieu is recalled to Paris from exile in Avignon to assist Louis XIII in suppressing the rebellion of the Queen Mother, Marie de' Medici. The first black slaves to arrive in the Virginia colony are landed from a Dutch privateer; slaves begin to play a role in the North American economy. 90 young

English women arrive in Jamestown to marry settlers, who have paid for their passage. *20 Mar*: the Holy Roman Emperor Matthias dies, aged 62, in Vienna and is succeeded by the recently deposed King of Bohemia, as Ferdinand II (elected *28 Aug*). *Nov*: the Protestant army under Count von Thurn lay siege to Vienna but cold and hunger force them to withdraw. *30 Nov*: the first American Day of Thanksgiving is celebrated on board the ship *Margaret* as it reaches land at Hampton, Virginia.

   Diego Velazquez: Adoration of the Magi; Water Carrier of Seville
Domenichino: Diana at the Chase
Peter Paul Rubens: The Rape of the Daughters of Leucippus
Jerome Duquesnoy: Mannekin Pis (bronze), Brussels (replacement)

1620 The Dutch mathematician Simon Stevin dies. In London, the poet, physician and composer Thomas Campion dies. Cornelius Droebbel, a Dutch engineer, tests a prototype submarine in the Thames; under pressure the hull made of wood covered with greased leather leaks badly. *8 Nov*: Battle of the White Mountain: a Catholic army under Flemish Field Marshal Count von Tilly defeats Frederick V of Bohemia. Bohemia loses its independence, lands of the Czech nobles are confiscated by Tilly, Maximilian of Bavaria and Ferdinand II. *11 Nov*: the *Mayflower* arrives at Cape Cod (left Europe *16 Sep*) with 100 'pilgrims' who have emigrated from Scrooby in England, first to Amsterdam and then to Leyden, now to America. They choose Plymouth as the site of their settlement.

   Imperial Palace of Katsura, Kyoto (Japan)
Francis Bacon: *Novum Organum*
Thomas Dekker; *Dekker, His Dreame*

1621 Parliament impeaches Francis Bacon, the English Lord Chancellor on bribery charges; he is fined £40,000 and banished, but James I pardons him and suppresses the fine. The Dutch West Indies Company is chartered by the Netherlands as it makes further inroads into the Spanish trading empire. *15 Feb*: Michael Praetorius, the German composer of Lutheran church music, dies, aged 50. *31 Mar*: Philip III of Spain dies, aged 42, and is succeeded by his 15-year-old son Philip IV. The Spanish break their *1609* truce with the Netherlands. The Indian Tisquantum has made his way back to North America from Spain, presenting himself at the 'Pilgrim' colony at Cape Cod; he shows the colonists how to catch eels and grow maize and beans, and is still well-disposed towards the white settlers. *Jul*: Sir Edwin Sandys, on King James I's behalf, tries to dissuade American colonists from growing tobacco, but they refuse to diversify. *16 Oct*: Jan Sweelinck, the Dutch composer, dies in Amsterdam.

    🐚 Nicolas Poussin: Rape of the Sabine Women
        Anthony van Dyck: Rest on the Flight into Egypt
        Guido Reni: Hercules
        Lorenzo Bernini: Rape of Prospero

    📖 Robert Burton: *Anatomy of Melancholy*
        Thomas Dekker: *Greevous Grones for the Poore*

1622 Persian forces take Kandahar from the Moghal Emperor and drive the Portuguese from Hormuz. *22 Mar*: Indians attack and destroy several Virginia settlements, killing over 300 colonists. *Apr*: Battle of Wiesloch: Protestants under Count Peter Mansfeld defeat Count von Tilly's Catholic army. *May*: Osman II the Ottoman Sultan tries to raise an army to reform the Janissaries of Constantinople. *20 May*: the Janissaries hear of his plan, march him through the city streets, strangle him, then restore the mentally defective Mustafa I. *5 Sep*: a hurricane in the North Atlantic sinks a Spanish prize galleon, the *Atocha*, and 260 passengers and 200 million pesos are lost. *Oct*: Louis XIII of France besieges Montpellier. *18 Oct*: the Duc de Rohan makes peace when Louis agrees to reaffirm the Edict of Nantes. Louis later forbids political meetings, recalls Richelieu to the Royal Council and appoints him Cardinal.

    📐 Inigo Jones: Banqueting House, Whitehall (completed) (U.K.)

    📖 Francis Bacon: *Historia Naturalis et Experimentalis*
        Michael Drayton: *Polyolbion* (second part)

1623 Count von Tilly advances to Westphalia. The Ottoman

Sultan is forced to abdicate, and is replaced by his 14-year-old nephew Murad IV. Abbas I, Shah of Persia, takes Mosul, Baghdad and all Mesopotamia from the Ottoman Turks. In Japan, Shogun Hidetada abdicates, aged 45, in favour of his 19-year-old son Iemitsu. In the Massacre of Amboina the Dutch seize 10 English traders, torture and execute them, ending English East India Company efforts to trade. The Dutch seize the Brazilian port of Pernambuco (later called Recife). The Prince of Wales (later Charles I) travels to Spain with the Duke of Buckingham, who has persuaded him to court the sister of Philip IV. 'Mr Smith' and 'Mr Brown' (the Prince and the Duke in disguise) arrive in Madrid to find the Spanish court unenthusiastic about Prince Charles and distrustful of his promises to relax English laws against Catholics. Velazquez becomes court painter to Philip IV of Spain. Thomas Weelkes, the English madrigal composer, dies. Tulsi Das, the poet of the Rama cult, dies in Benares. The English composer William Byrd dies, aged 80.

- ✐ Inigo Jones: The Queen's Chapel, St. James's Palace, London
  Francois Mansart: Church of St. Marie de la Visitation, Paris
- ✑ Gianlorenzo Bernini: David (marble)
  Anthony van Dyck: Cardinal Bentivoglio
  Guido Reni: Baptism of Christ
  Peter Paul Rubens: Marie de' Medici Landing at Marseilles
- 📖 William Shakespeare: *Comedies, Histories and Tragedies* (First Folio)
  Philip Massinger: *The Duke of Milan*
  Pedro Calderon de la Barca: *Amor, Honor y Poder*

1624 Philip IV of Spain reduces his household staff and bans the wearing of ruffs, a symbol of sartorial extravagance that goes out of fashion all over Europe as luxury gives way to austerity, the 'spirit of the age'. Japan expels all Spanish traders. Pope Urban VIII threatens to excommunicate all snuff users. *29 Apr*: Louis XIII makes Richelieu his chief minister. *10 May*: the Dutch seize Bahia, the capital of Brazil.

    🏛 Jacques Lemercier: Louvre Palace, Paris (completed)

    🎨 Frans Hals: The Laughing Cavalier

    📖 Captain John Smith: *The General History of Virginia*
    Ben Jonson: *The Fortunate Isles*
    John Donne: *Devotions upon Emergent Occasions*

1625 A Huguenot rebellion in France is led by Henri Duc de Rohan. The first English colony on Barbados is founded under Sir William Courteen. A Black Death epidemic kills 41,000 people in London. *5 Mar*: James I of England dies, aged 58 and is succeeded by his son Charles I, now 27. *22 Apr*: Fort Amsterdam is founded on the southern tip of Manhattan Island by the Dutch West India Company. *1 May*: Charles I is married by proxy to Henrietta Maria, the 16-year-old sister of Louis XIII. *2 Jul*: Breda in the Netherlands surrenders to the Spanish after a siege lasting almost a year. *8 Sep*: Treaty of Southampton, forming an Anglo-Dutch alliance against Spain. Charles I sends an abortive expedition to Cadiz.

    🏛 Inigo Jones: Covent Garden Church, London (completed)
    Katsura Rikyu Palace, Kyoto (completed) (Japan)

    🎨 Peter Paul Rubens: Marie de' Medici
    Guido Reni: Job
    Gerrit van Honthorst: The Procuress

    📖 John Donne: *First Sermon preached to King Charles*
    James Shirley: *Love Tricks*

1626 Dutch colonists buy Manhattan Island from chiefs of the Wappinger Confederacy and found the town of Nieuw Amsterdam, led by Peter Minuit. French colonists settle Madagascar; they try to drive out the Hova people who have lived there for 600 years. *Feb*: the English lutenist and composer John Dowland dies in London. *9 Apr*: Sir Francis Bacon catches pneumonia and dies, aged 65. *27 Aug*: Battle of the Bridge of Dessau: Catholic forces defeat a Danish army.

    🎨 Rembrandt van Rijn: The Baptism of the Moor; The Clemency of Titus
    Frans Hals: Isaac Massa

Peter Paul Rubens: Assumption of the Virgin
Jose de Ribera: Drunken Silenus

1627 Reykjavik, the capital of Iceland, is attacked by pirates.
Catholic armies under Wallenstein and von Tilly conquer Holstein. Wallenstein subdues Jutland and Schleswig; Christian IV of Denmark temporarily withdraws
from the Thirty Years' War. Manchu troops invade
Korea; the Manchus make Korea a vassal state, but
the Korean court and people remain loyal to the
Ming. *Apr*: Richelieu founds the Company of the Hundred Associates, which is given control of New France
and a monopoly on the fur trade and land between
Florida north to the Arctic Circle. Richelieu besieges
the Huguenot stronghold La Rochelle. *Oct*: the Moghal
Emperor Jahangir, tyrannical ruler of Delhi, dies, aged
58, while journeying from Kashmir. He is succeeded by
his 35-year-old son Shah Jahan, who has all his male
relations murdered to secure his position.

   ✍ Jacques Lemercier: Versailles (France)
     Pao Ho Tien, Beijing (one of the Three Great Halls)
   ✇ Francisco de Zurbaran: Crucifixion
     Peter Paul Rubens: The Mystic Marriage of St.
     Catherine
     Rembrandt van Rijn: The Money-Changer
     Frans Hals: Banquet of the Civic Guard; The Jolly
     Toper
   ⬛ Francis Bacon: *New Atlantis*
     Charles Sorel: *Le Berger extravagant*
     Michael Drayton: *Nymphidia*
     Francisco de Quevedo Villegas: *Los Sueños*
   🎝 Heinrich Schutz: *Dafne*

1628 The Austrian Duke Wallenstein acquires the Duchy of
Mecklenburg and assumes the title Admiral of the Baltic.
Dutch forces occupy Java. Salem is founded on Massachusetts Bay by 50 English colonists. *23 Aug*: George
Villiers, Duke of Buckingham is murdered as he prepares
to relieve La Rochelle. *28 Oct*: La Rochelle surrenders
after a 14-month siege. The Huguenots cease to be an
armed power in France.

   ✍ Braemar Castle, Scotland
   ✇ Nicolas Poussin: The Martyrdom of St. Erasmus

Jacques Callot: The Siege of Breda
Francisco de Zurbaran: St. Serapion

☐ William Harvey: *Exercitatio Anatomica de Motu Cordis et Sanguinis in Animalibus* (pioneering work on the circulation of the blood)
Francis Fletcher: *The World Encompassed by Sir Francis Drake*
Thomas Dekker: *Britannia's Honour* (masque)
John Ford: *The Lover's Melancholy*
James Shirley: *The Witty Fair One*

1629 Portuguese colonists plant the first American crops (cassava and maize) in Africa, on the coast of Angola. The Truce of Altmark ends the conflict between Sweden and Poland. The Englishmen John Mason and Sir Ferdinando Gorges acquire grant of land in North America and establish a farming community in New Hampshire. In Japan, the Kabuki Theatre becomes all-male by order of the Shogun Iemitsu, who has decided it is immoral for women to dance in public. Pope Urban VIII appoints Giovanni Lorenzo Bernini to finish St. Peter's Basilica in Rome. The singer and composer Gregorio Allegri starts singing tenor, at 47, in the Papal Chapel in Rome. *19 Jan*: Shah Abbas of Persia dies at Kaswin, aged 72, after reigning for 42 years and is succeeded by his 13-year-old grandson Safi I. The new Shah has his grandfather's advisers and generals beheaded along with all his male relations. The Persian Governor of Kandahar defects to the Uzbeks, who take over the city and province. *Mar*: Charles I dissolves the English Parliament. *29 Mar*: the Edict of Restitution issued by the Emperor Ferdinand II restores church estates in Europe as they were in 1552 and permits freedom of worship only to adherents of the Confession of Augsburg *(1530)*. Troops of the Catholic League ruthlessly enforce the edict, showing no mercy to 'heretics'. *22 May*: Treaty of Lubeck, ending hostilities between Emperor Ferdinand II and Christian IV of Denmark, who has his lands restored to him on condition that he abandon his interference in German affairs. *28 Jun*: a French edict of grace allows freedom of worship to Huguenots but denies them the right of assembly. *Sep*:

Mexico City is severely flooded. *20 Oct*: the French theologian Cardinal Pierre de Berulle dies in Paris. *15 Nov*: Bethlen Gábor of Transylvania dies, aged 49, after his marriage to a sister-in-law of Gustavus II of Sweden; he had designs on the Polish crown.

🎨 Peter Paul Rubens: Allegory of War and Peace
  Anthony van Dyck: Rinaldo and Armida
  Diego Velazquez: The Triumph of Bacchus
📖 John Ford: *The Lovers' Melancholy*
  William Davenant: *The Tragedy of Albovine*

1630 The Ottoman Emperor Murad IV defeats a Persian army and captures Hamadan, the ancient capital of Media. He retakes conquests of the dead Persian Shah Abbas, massacres the citizens of Hamadan and wrecks the town. Portsmouth is founded in the New Hampshire colony. Bubonic plague in Venice kills 500,000, hastening the city's decline. *Apr*: England makes peace with France. *Jun*: the Puritan John Winthrop arrives at Salem on the *Arabella* and appoints himself Governor. Boston is founded as the Massachusetts Bay Colony acquires 2,000 new settlers from England. *Jul*: Gustavus II of Sweden lands on the Pomeranian coast to give aid to the oppressed Protestants and resist the cruelty of Wallenstein's army. *13 Aug*: the Emperor Ferdinand II dismisses Wallenstein. *26 Nov*: in Transylvania, Bethlen Gábor is succeeded by George Rákóczi I, who is elected Prince of Transylvania by the Diet of Segesovar

🏛 Salmon de Brosse: Palais de Luxembourg, Paris (completed)
  Glamis Castle, Tayside (rebuilding) (Scotland)
🎨 Nicolas Poussin: The Triumphs of Flora
  Francisco de Zurbaran: The Vision of the Blessed Alonso Rodriguez
📖 Pierre Corneille: *Melite, or The False Letters*
  William Davenant: *The Cruel Brother*
  John Donne: *Death's Duell*
🎵 Gregorio Allegri: *Miserere* (at about this time)

1631 The Dutch authorities in Amsterdam recall Peter Minuit from Nieuw Amsterdam for granting excessive privileges to landowners and concentrating political and economic power in the hands of a few people. A shipyard is opened at Boston as cheap American timber makes an American-built ship half the price of an English ship; the 30-ton sloop *Blessing of the Bay* is one of the first ships built in Massachusetts. *13 Jan*: Treaty of Barwalde: Richelieu pledges French support for Gustavus II of Sweden and Bernhard Duke of Weimar. *20 May*: Hessian troops unsuccessfully defend the town of Magdeburg against Tilly's army; an orgy of looting, burning and murder follows, in which most of the citizens of Magdeburg are killed – 25,000 die. *17 Sep*: Battle of Breitenfeld: the strength of Catholicism in central Europe is broken as a Saxon-Swedish army of 40,000 defeats an army of equal size under Tilly.

🐚 Nicholas Stone: Effigy of John Donne

📖 John Donne: *Death's Duel* (his last sermon)

James Shirley: *The Traitor; The Humorous Courtier; Love's Cruelty*

🎼 Domenico Mazzochi: *Lamentations of Mary Magdalene*

1632 In the Deccan of India, a million people die in a famine following two years of drought. Emperor Shah Jahan orders the destruction of Hindu temples: 76 are destroyed in Benares alone. Nova Scotia is founded as the French colony of Acadia. Sigismund III of Poland dies suddenly, aged 65, after reigning for 44 years and is succeeded by his 37-year-old son Ladislas IV; Moscow instantly declares war on Poland. *5 Apr*: Gustavus II of Sweden defeats von Tilly's Catholic army at the confluence of the Danube and the Lech; Tilly is mortally wounded. *30 Apr*: Tilly dies at Ingolstadt, aged 72. Munich surrenders to the Swedes, Wallenstein tries to stop them taking Nuremberg; both armies withdraw as scurvy and typhus strike. *16 Nov*: Battle of Lutzen: the Swedish army defeats the Catholic army, but Gustavus II is killed. He is succeeded by his six-year-old daughter Christina; meanwhile Sweden is governed by Count Axel Oxenstierna.

✏ Orders of Shah Jahan: Taj Mahal

🐚 Rembrandt van Rijn: De Tulp's Anatomy

Peter Paul Rubens: The Garden of Love

Anthony van Dyck: King Charles I and Queen

Henrietta

☐ Galileo Galilei: *Dialogo de Massimi Sistemi del Mondo* (repeats his belief in the Copernican system)
John Milton: *On His Having Arrived at the Age of Twenty-Three*
James Shirley: *Hyde Park*

1633 In Japan the persecution of Christians intensifies; Christianity is seen as the faith of potential invaders of Japan. Russian forces besiege Smolensk, but the city is saved by a Polish army under the new King Ladislas IV. *1 Mar*: the English poet George Herbert dies of tuberculosis, aged 39. *12 Apr*: Galileo goes on trial in Rome. He is threatened by the Inquisition with torture on the rack and agrees to retract his defence of the Copernican idea that the sun is at the centre of the universe rather than the earth. After his submission, Galileo is confined to his villa outside Florence. René Descartes takes warning from Galileo's trial; now living in the Netherlands, he restricts his activities.

✐ Gianlorenzo Bernini: Baldacchino, St. Peter's Basilica, Rome

✑ Jacques Callot: Les Misères de la Guerre (scenes of the German wars)

☐ George Herbert: *The Temple*
William Rowley: *A Match at Midnight*
John Ford: *Tis Pity She's a Whore*
Pierre Corneille: *The Maidservant; Place Royale*

1634 Villagers at Oberammergau in Bavaria vow to put on a regular passion play if they are spared by the Black Death. Speculation in tulip bulbs reaches absurd heights in the Netherlands. Lord Calvert arrives in America to establish the Maryland settlement for both Protestants and Catholics. Jean Nicolet explores Lake Michigan and Wisconsin in search of furs and a northwest passage; crossing the huge Lake Michigan, Nicolet believes he has reached Asia and is disappointed to find that he is mistaken. Shah Jahan drives the Uzbeks out of Kandahar. The Treaty of Polianov ends the Russian-Polish war, with Ladislas IV of Poland renouncing his claim to the throne of Russia; Michael Romanov offers Poland Smolensk in exchange for recognition of his title.

18 Aug: a French priest, Urbain Grandier, is tortured and burned alive by witch-hunters at Loudun. He has insulted Richelieu and been found guilty of bewitching nuns at an Ursuline convent; their hysterical fits have attracted sightseers from all over Europe.

    Toshogu Shrine, Nikko (mausoleum for the Shogun Ieyasu completed)
    Bateman's, Sussex (England)

    Diego Velazquez: The Surrender of Breda
    Peter Paul Rubens: The Judgment of Paris; The Garden of Love

    Jean Mairet: *Sophonisbe*
    John Milton: *Comus*

1635 The Japanese Shogun Iemitsu acts to stop feudal lords becoming too rich; he orders them to visit Edo every other year and pay all the expenses of running a second household. Murad IV leads his Ottoman army against Persia; Erivan and Tabriz surrender. The Dutch invade and occupy northern Brazil. In North America, Indians destroy Dutch settlements founded two years ago in Delaware. Lope de Vega, the prolific Spanish playwright, dies claiming to have written 1,500 plays. The Peace of Prague on *20 May* settles differences between Holy Roman Emperor Ferdinand II and the Elector of Saxony; Richelieu forms an alliance with Oxenstierna (for France and Sweden). Theophraste Renaudot opens the world's first free medical clinic, in Paris. The Académie Française is founded to cleanse the French language of 'impurities'. In the Massachusetts colony, the Boston Public Latin School opens.

    Jacob van Campen: The Mauritzhus, The Hague (completed)

    Rembrandt van Rijn: Self-portrait with Saskia
    Anthony van Dyck: Charles I in Hunting Dress
    Salvator Rosa: Prometheus
    Jusepe de Ribera: The Immaculate Conception
    Peter Paul Rubens: The Apotheosis of James I
    Diego Velazquez: Prince Balthasar Carlos on Horseback; The Surrender of Breda

    James Shirley: *The Lady of Pleasure*
    Pierre Corneille: *Medea*

Francisco de Rojas Zorilla: *The Challenge of Charles V*

1636 In Japan, the Shogun Iemitsu forbids foreign travel. In North America, Dutch colonists on Manhattan Island found the town of Haarlem. Shah Safi of Persia retakes Erivan and signs a treaty with Constantinople setting his western borders. In France, the Conde-Duque de Olivares invades Beauvais and Picardy in a wild bid to restore Spanish power there. The French force Spain into a long drawn out war of attrition.

   Isaac de Caux: Wilton House near Salisbury (U.K.)

   Anthony van Dyck: Charles I in Three Positions
   Peter Paul Rubens: Landscape with the Chateau of Steen
   Rembrandt van Rijn: The Blinding of Samson

   Tristan l'Hermite: *Marianne*
   Pierre Corneille: *L'Illusion comique*
   Thomas Dekker: *The Wonder of a Kingdome*

   Heinrich Schütz: *Musikalische Exequien* (first German requiem)

1637 The Japanese calligrapher Honami Koetsu dies at Takagamine, the craft village to which he was exiled by the Shogun Ieyasu. Japanese peasants in the Shimabara Peninsula of Kyushu rise against the Shogun Iemitsu; their feudal lord Arima has, like many of them, been converted to Christianity. The Massachusetts colonists have their first hostile encounter with the Indians. In an incident known as Hankins' Scissors, one of the colonists, an ill-tempered cobbler, stabs a Pequot brave; as a result a force of 1,000 Narragansetts and 70 Mohicans destroys the fort and town at Mystic, slaughtering 600 inhabitants. The Dutch take steps to ensure a supply of African slaves for their sugar estates in the New World; they take Elmina from the Portuguese and build forts on the Gold Coast. The Swedish Queen Christina charters the New Sweden Company to establish colonies in the New World; the Dutch colonists Peter Minuit and Samuel Blommaert have encouraged the Queen's advisers. *15 Feb*: the Holy Roman Emperor Ferdinand II dies, aged 57, in Vienna and is succeeded by his 28-year-old son Ferdinand III. *Aug*: the English playwright Ben

Jonson dies, aged 65. *Dec*: the Japanese Shogun Iemitsu lays siege to the rebels on the Shimabara Peninsula.

🎨 Anthony van Dyck: Five Children of Charles I
Nicolas Poussin: The Triumph of Neptune and Amphètre

📖 René Descartes: *Discours de la Méthode*
Song Ying-xing: *Tiangong Kaiwu* (agricultural and industrial methods)
Francisco de Rojas Zorilla: *No Jealousy Without Cause*; *The Most Proper Execution for the Most Just Vengeance*

1638 Murad IV the Ottoman Sultan retakes Baghdad from the Persians, slaughtering the city's defenders after a month-long siege. In the Indian Ocean, the Dutch settle on the island of Mauritius and begin clubbing to death the dodo, the island's idigenous flightless bird. *28 Feb*: Japanese peasants occupying Hara Castle near Nagasaki surrender for lack of food. The Shogun Iemitsu's 124,000 strong siege army kills most of the 37,000 peasants; the Shogun expels Portuguese traders from Japan, suspecting their complicity in the peasant rising, and also prohibits the building of large vessels that might carry people to foreign countries, ensuring the isolation of Japan. *14 Sep*: the English clergyman John Harvard dies, aged 31, of tuberculosis after living only a year at the Massachusetts Bay colony; he leaves his library to the seminary founded at New Towne two years ago. New Towne will be renamed Cambridge because Harvard was a Cambridge graduate; the college built there is named after Harvard.

✏️ Inigo Jones: Covent Garden (first planned piazza in London)
First brick-built house in Boston, Mass.

🎨 Nicolas Poussin: Et in Arcadia Ego
Diego Velazquez: Christ on the Cross

📖 Bishop John Wilkins: *The Discovery of a World in the Moon*

🎼 Heinrich Schütz: *Orpheus und Euridice*

1639 Japan's Shogun Iemitsu finds that some Christian missionaries remain in Japan despite his 1638 expulsion order, and orders the killing of any remaining Portu-

guese, closing the ports to nearly all foreign trade. *Jun*:
the former Ottoman Sultan Mustafa I is strangled.

  🖉 Orders of Philip IV: Parque del Retiro, Madrid

  🐍 Pietro da Cortona: Ceiling Fresco, Barberini Palace,
Rome

    Jusepe de Ribera: The Martyrdom of St. Bartholo-
mew

1640 Catalonia begins a 19-year revolt against Spain in protest
against Barcelona's taxes and general denial of Catalonian rights. Portugal exploits the Catalonian revolt to
regain its independence from Spain; João da Braganza is
elected King of Portugal, but Spain does not recognize
him or Portugal's independence. Charles I of England
appoints Thomas Wentworth Earl of Strafford as his
chief adviser; Strafford prepares to lead Irish troops
against the Scots. *20 Aug*: a Scottish army crosses the
River Tweed to begin the second Bishops' War against
England, *28 Aug*: Battle of Newburn: the Scots defeat
the English. *21 Oct*: Treaty of Ripon, ending the conflict
between Scotland and England. *5 Nov*: Charles I convenes the Long Parliament. He also has Strafford im-
peached and imprisoned. Firewood in England now costs
eight times as much as it did 100 years ago, giving a
stimulus to coal mining (other prices have increased
threefold). The painter Rubens dies on *30 May* at
Antwerp.

  🐍 Louis Le Nain: The Peasant Supper

    Nicolas Poussin: The Inspiration of the Poet

    Rembrandt van Rijn: Self-portrait

    Peter Paul Rubens: Three Graces

  📖 Cornelis Jansen: *Augustinus*

    Francisco de Rojas Zorilla: *The Two Households of
Verona*

    Pierre Corneille: *Horatio*; *Cinna, or the Clemency of
Augustus*

1641 Michael Romanov, Tsar of Russia, forbids the sale and
use of tobacco; users and sellers of tobacco are to be
flogged, yet the crown will make tobacco a state monopoly for the sake of the revenue it generates. In France,
the King's brother, Jean d'Orléans, exposes a conspiracy
against Cardinal Richelieu; Henri de Ruze, Marquis de

Cinq-Mars, has used his position as Richelieu's protégé to make a secret treaty with Spain. The Japanese remove Dutch traders at Hirado to an island in Nagasaki Harbour; as they have no missionaries they are allowed to stay on condition that once a year Dutch East India Company officers visit Edo and spit on the cross. *6 Apr*: the painter Il Domenichino dies in Naples, aged 59. In London, the Archbishop of Canterbury William Laud is sent to the Tower. *12 May*: the Earl of Strafford is executed in the Tower of London. *Jul*: the Long Parliament abolishes the Star Chamber in an effort to curb Charles I's absolutism. *9 Dec*: Sir Anthony van Dyck, court painter to Charles I, dies, aged 42, in London.

🖎 Domenichino: Scenes from the Life of St. Januarius
   David Teniers: Country fair
   Frans Hals: Regents of the Hospital of St. Elizabeth
   Nicolas Poussin: The Seven Sacraments
   Anthony van Dyck: William of Orange
   Claude Lorraine: Embarkation of St. Ursula
   Rembrandt van Rijn: Manoah

📖 James Shirley: *The Cardinal*
   Pierre Corneille: *Polyentes*

1642 Shah Safi I of Persia dies, aged 26, and is succeeded by his 10-year-old son Abbas II. Paul de Chomedey founds Montreal on an island in the St. Lawrence River. The 19-year-old mathematical prodigy Blaise Pascal invents an adding machine. In America, the first baccalaureate degrees are awarded at Harvard College. In England, civil war begins as Charles I raises his standard at Nottingham. *Aug*: the Dutch mariner Abel Tasman discovers Tasmania, naming it Van Diemen's Land. *2 Sep*: in England, an Ordinance of Parliament closes the theatres 'to appease and avert the wrath of God.' *23 Oct*: Battle of Edgehill: the first military engagement of the English Civil War has no clear outcome. *Dec*: Tasman discovers New Zealand. *4 Dec*: Cardinal Richelieu dies, aged 57.

🖎 Rembrandt van Rijn: Sortie of the Banning Cock Company
   David Teniers: The Guard Room

📖 Thomas Browne: *Religio Medici*

Richard Lovelace: *To Althea, from Prison*
Thomas Hobbes: *De Cive*

1643 The New England Federation is the first union of English colonies in America (Massachusetts, Plymouth, Connecticut, New Haven). The Dutch Governor of Nieuw Amsterdam orders a massacre of the Wappinger Indians who have sought his protection from the Mohawks. The Italian mathematician Evangelista Torricelli devises the world's first barometer: he served as an amanuensis to Galileo. *14 May*: Louis XIII of France dies, aged 43, and is succeeded by his four-year-old son Louis XIV with Giulio Mazarin as Chief Minister. *19 May*: Battle of Rocroi: the French defeat a combined Spanish, Dutch, Flemish and Italian army in a major military success. Gaspar de Guzman is driven from office and exiled from Spain.

   David Teniers: Village Fete
   Rembrandt van Rijn: Three Trees
   Adriaen van Ostade: The Slaughtered Pig
   William Dobson: Endymion Porter

   Pierre Corneille: *The Death of Pompey*; *The Liar*
   Tirso de Molina: *Sly Gomez*

   Claudio Monteverdi: *L'Incoronazione di Poppea*

1644 *Apr*: in China, the Ming dynasty comes to an end with the suicide of the Emperor Chongzhen, who hangs himself as Beijing falls to the bandit and rebel leader Li Dzucheng. Li Dzucheng proclaims himself Emperor, but the Manchu Regent Dagoba and the Ming general Wu San-kuei succeed in driving Li into the provinces, where he will later be killed. The Manchus found the Qing (or Ch'ing) dynasty. *2 Jul*: Battle of Marston Moor: Oliver Cromwell's troops win the decisive battle of the English Civil War.

   Francesco Borromini: Church of S. Carlo all Quattro Fontane

   Jusepe de Ribera: St. Paul the Hermit
   Ferdinand Bol: The Three Maries at the Tomb of Christ
   David Teniers: Kitchen of the Archduke Leopold Wilhelm
   Rembrandt van Rijn: Woman Taken in Adultery

Isaac Fuller: Altarpiece, All Souls College, Oxford

☐ John Knox: *History of the Reformation of Religion within the Realm of Scotland*

John Milton: *Areopagitica*

1645 *Jan*: the imperial army under Count Gallas is defeated by an army under Lennart Torstenson and Count Konigsmark. *Mar*: Torstenson's Swedish army defeats the imperial army again at Jankau in Bohemia and conquers Moravia. *14 Jun* Battle of Naseby: Cromwell's army defeats the main Royalist army, effectively ending the English Civil War's military phase. *12 Jul*: the Russian Tsar Michael Romanov dies, aged 49, and is succeeded by his 16-year-old son Alexis. *Aug*: Ottoman forces capture Khania in Crete after a two-month siege; this starts a long struggle with the Venetians for control over Crete. In Brazil, Portuguese colonists rise against the Dutch as Prince Maurice returns to the Netherlands.

🕭 Diego Velazquez: Philip IV on a Boar Hunt

Rembrandt van Rijn: The Rabbi

David Teniers: Tavern Scene; The Dance in Front of the Castle

Bartolome Murillo: Flight into Egypt

☐ Edmund Waller: *Poems*

John Milton: *Il Penseroso*; *L'Allegro*

1646 The Swedish Count Torstenson resigns his command owing to illness; his successor, Karl Wrangel, helps lead a Franco-Swedish army into Bavaria. *5 May*: in England the Civil War ends as Charles I surrenders himself to the Scots at Newark. *Jul*: Charles rejects Parliament's proposal to control the army for 20 years; the King hopes even now to exploit differences between his opponents.

🕭 Geraert Terborch: Count Peneranda

☐ Thomas Browne: *Pseudoxia Epidemics*

Richard Crashaw: *Steps to the Temple*; *The Delights of the Muses*

Henry Vaughan: *Poems*

1647 Black Death strikes Spain. The Society of Friends (Quakers) has its beginnings in Leicestershire, England, with the teachings of clergyman George Fox. *30 Jan*: the Scots shamefully sell Charles I to the English Parliament for £400,000; he is taken to Holmby House in

Northamptonshire as Parliament and army become openly hostile to one another. *4 Jun*: Charles is seized at Holmby House by the army and taken prisoner. *6 Aug*: Charles I is taken to Hampton Court. *1 Nov*: Charles I escapes, flees to the Isle of Wight and is detained by the Governor of Carisbrooke Castle. He signs a secret treaty with the Scots, who promise to restore him to his throne by force.

📖 Francis Beaumont and John Fletcher: *Comedies and Tragedies*

1648 In the Ukraine, a pogrom by Greek Orthodox peasants results in the deaths of thousands of Jews; the Cossack Bogdan Chmielnicki leads the massacre, which is an attempt to establish Ukrainian independence from Poland by destroying the Jews who are used as tax gatherers. In Russia, Tsar Alexis abolishes the state monopoly in tobacco and reimposes the ban on smoking. *15 Jan*: the English Parliament renounces its allegiance to Charles I when it discovers his secret treaty with Scotland. *8 Aug*: in Constantinople the Janissaries dethrone the Sultan Ibrahim when he orders the lifting of the siege of Candia (Heraklion on Crete). *18 Aug*: Ibrahim is strangled by his own executioner and replaced by his eldest son, the nine-year-old Mohammed IV.

✐ Orders of Shah Jahan: Taj Mahal, near Agra (completed)

🐚 Nicolas Poussin: Landscape with the Burial of Phocion

Geraert Terborch: The Peace of Munster

Jusepe de Ribera: The Holy Family with St. Catherine

📖 Robert Herrick: *Hesperides*

John Gauden: *Eikon Basilike*

1649 Tobacco exports bring prosperity to the Virginia colony in North America. Many Royalist refugees from England arrive in Virginia. *20–27 Jan*: the trial of Charles I of England: no defence witnesses are called. *30 Jan*: Charles I is executed outside the Banqueting House in Whitehall. *5 Feb*: Charles I's 18-year-old son is proclaimed Charles II. *16 Mar*: the English monarchy is abolished; Parlia-

ment sets up a Commonwealth run by a Council of State.
12 Sep: the storming of Drogheda by Ireton's army
marks the conclusion of the reconquest of Ireland.

🏛 Inigo Jones and John Webb: Wilton House, Wiltshire (rebuilt) (U.K.)

🎨 Rembrandt van Rijn: Christ Healing the Sick
Geraert Terborch: Philip IV of Spain
Diego Velazquez: Pope Innocent X; Juan de Pereja
Nicolas Poussin: The Vision of St. Paul
Ferdinand Bol: The Four Regents of the Leper
Hospital

📖 Richard Lovelace: *Lucasta*
John Lilburne: *England's New Chaines Discovered*
René Descartes: *The Passions of the Soul*

🎼 Francesco Cavalli: *Giasone*

1650 Abbas, Shah of Persia, retakes Kandahar. In Ireland,
Archbishop James Ussher calculates from the *Bible* that
the earth was created in October, 4004 BC. The minuet is
introduced at the French court. The first coffee house in
England opens in Oxford. *14 Jan:* in France, Cardinal
Mazarin has the Great Condé and his associates arrested.
2 Feb: the Earl of Montrose returns from the mainland of
Europe to avenge the execution of Charles I but fails to
rouse the clans. *21 May:* following his betrayal by Neil
McLeod, Montrose is sentenced to death by Parliament
and executed in Edinburgh. *24 Jun:* Charles II returns to
Britain, landing in Scotland, where he is proclaimed
King. *3 Sep:* Battle of Dunbar: Cromwell's army invades Scotland and defeats an army twice its own size. *6
Nov:* William of Orange dies of smallpox, aged 24; his
son and heir (later William III of England) is born
posthumously on *14 Nov.* *19 Dec:* Edinburgh Castle
surrenders to Cromwell's troops.

🎨 Frans Hals: Malle Babbe
Rembrandt van Rijn: Jewish merchant
Nicolas Poussin: Arcadian Shepherds; Self-portrait
Jan van Goyen: View of Dordrecht
Bartolome Murillo: The Holy Family with the Little
Bird

📖 Thomas Hobbes: *Human Nature*
Henry Vaughan: *Silex Scintillans*

Anne Bradstreet: *The Tenth Muse Lately Sprung Up*
Pierre Corneille: *Andromeda*; *Nicomedes*
🎵 John Playford: *The English Dancing Master*

1651 The Japanese Shogun Iemitsu dies, aged 47, and is succeeded by his son Ietsuna. In France, the Parlement dismisses Cardinal Mazarin and releases the Great Condé; Mazarin leaves the country. *1 Jan*: Charles II is crowned at Scone in Scotland. *Aug*: Cromwell takes Perth. *3 Sep*: Royalist forces are defeated at the Battle of Worcester. *17 Oct*: Charles II escapes to France from Sussex after travelling across country in disguise. *Dec*: Mazarin returns to France with 7,000 troops to suppress the Great Condé's rebellion.

🎨 Nicolas Poussin: The Holy Family
Rembrandt van Rijn: Girl with a Broom
David Teniers: The Marriage of the Artist
Jusepe de Ribera: The Last Supper; The Institution of the Eucharist

📖 Thomas Hobbes: *Leviathan*
William Harvey: *Exercitationes de generationis animalium*
John Milton: *The Life and Reign of King Charles*
🎵 Francesco Cavalli: *Calisto*

1652 The Japanese Shogun Ietsuna survives a second coup attempt at Edo. *7 Apr*: Battle of Bleneau: the Great Condé defeats Marshal Turenne, who has changed back to the King's side. Both armies march to Paris to negotiate. *8 Apr*: Cape Town in South Africa is founded by Jan van Riebeck, a Dutch ship's surgeon, who goes ashore with 70 men, seed, agricultural implements and building materials. The Dutch are met by a Khoisan herdsman called Harry: he speaks English. *Jul*: the Duchesse de Montpensier persuades the Parisians to open the city gates to the Fronde army and turn the Bastille's guns on Turenne's royal army. A rebel government is formed and Mazarin leaves France again. The Anglo-Dutch War begins. *2 Sep*: the painter Jusepe de Ribera dies at Naples, aged 61. *2 Oct*: the Parisian middle class quarrels with the Fronde and allows Louis XIV to enter the city.

🏛 Great White Dagoba, Beijing (completed)

      ▲ Gianlorenzo Bernini: The Ecstasy of St. Theresa
      (marble)
      Rembrandt van Rijn: Portrait of Hendrickje
      Carel Fabritius: A View of Delft
      □ Shunsai Hayashi: *O-Dai-khi-Ran*

1653 The Chinese city of Amoy falls to the pirate Zheng
Chenkong, who ravages the Chinese coast with his fleet
of 3,000 junks in a struggle against the Manchus. In
France, Mazarin returns to Paris unopposed and the
rebellion is suppressed: a period of absolutism begins.
The tontine system of life insurance is devised in Paris by
the Naples banker Lorenzo Tonti; a group of investors
contributes to a fund, the proceeds of which go to the
longest surviving shareholder. Colonists in Nieuw Amsterdam build a wall across Manhattan island to protect
them from English attacks. Oliver Cromwell is proclaimed Lord Protector of the Commonwealth of England, Scotland and Ireland on *15 Dec*.
      ▲ Jan Steen: The Village Wedding
      David Teniers: The Picture Gallery of Archduke
      Leopold Wilhelm
      Rembrandt van Rijn: Aristotle Contemplating the
      Bust of Homer
      □ Izaak Walton: *The Compleat Angler*

1654 The Ukrainian Bogdan Chmielnicki renounces claims to
Ukrainian independence, swearing allegiance to Tsar
Alexis of Russia. The Russian army seizes Smolensk,
starting a long war with Poland over the Ukraine. The
German composer Samuel Scheidt dies. The German
scientist Otto von Guericke proves the existence of atmo-
spheric pressure. *6 April*: Treaty of Westminster, ending
the Anglo-Dutch War. *6 Jun*: Queen Christina of Sweden
abdicates after selling large amounts of crown property to
support the 500 nobles she has created. She leaves dressed
in men's clothes under the name Count Dohna, settles in
Rome and is succeeded by her cousin Charles X. *3 Sep*: in
the English Parliament, the republican party headed by
Vane questions Cromwell's pre-eminence. *12 Sep*: Cromwell orders the exclusion of members of Parliament
hostile to him. *12 Oct*: Rembrandt's most promising
pupil, Carel Fabritius, is killed at the age of 32 in an

explosion at the arsenal at Delft.

🖾 Geraert Terborch: Parental Admonition
Rembrandt van Rijn: Jan Stix

1655 Charles X of Sweden takes advantage of Poland's struggle with Russia over control of the Ukraine by invading Poland: the first 'Northern war' begins. English forces under Vice Admiral Penn take Jamaica from the Spanish, opening a three-year war with Spain. Oliver Cromwell suppresses a rising against his government at Salisbury and divides England into military districts to strengthen his control.

🖾 Jacob van Campen: Town Hall, Amsterdam
🖾 Rembrandt van Rijn: Woman Bathing in a Stream; The Rabbi Jacob van Ruisdael: The Jewish Graveyard
📖 Edmund Waller: *A Panegyric to My Lord Protector*

1656 Rembrandt, now 50 and ostensibly successful, declares himself bankrupt as Dutch East India shares plunge on the Amsterdam stock exchange. Dutch scientist Christian Huygens revolutionizes clockmaking by adding the pendulum. In Poland, the Swedish army defeats the Polish army at the Battle of Warsaw; Russia, Denmark and the Holy Roman Emperor declare war on Sweden. *2 Jul*: Amsterdam rabbis excommunicate rabbinical student Baruch Spinoza for heretical views; Spinoza turns to lens-grinding to earn a living. *9 Sep*: the English capture Spanish treasure ships off Cadiz. *17 Sep*: Cromwell's Third Parliament convenes. *6 Nov*: João IV of Portugal dies, aged 53, and is succeeded by his 13-year-old son Afonso VI.

🖾 Diego Velazquez: Las Meninas; Las Hilanderas
Jan Vermeer: The Procuress
📖 Thomas Hobbes: *Liberty, Necessity and Chance*

1657 The Indian bandit Sivaji raids Moghal territory in the northern Deccan. A small force under Afzal Khan is sent to repel Sivaji, who requests peace negotiations and then murders Afzal Khan. The Ottoman Turks retake Tenedos and Lemnos. Sweden and Denmark declare war as Charles X of Sweden attempts to extend his territory on the southern side of the Baltic; the Dutch intervene to stop the Swedes gaining total control of the Baltic fishery. *18–19 Jan*: the city of Edo in Japan is largely destroyed by fire, killing over 100,000 people. *2 Apr*: the Holy Roman Emperor Ferdinand III dies, aged 48, and is succeeded by his 16-year-old son Leopold I. *Apr 20*: Admiral Blake leads an English naval force in destroying the Spanish West Indies fleet off Santa Cruz. *27 Dec*: the Flushing Remonstrance, probably the earliest declaration of religious tolerance in America.

📖 Nicolas Poussin: The Birth of Bacchus
   Salvator Rosa: L'Umana Fragilità
📖 William Allen: *Killing No Murder*

1658 The Dutch naturalist Jan Swammerdam describes red blood cells for the first time. At Newcastle in England, coal production has increased sixteenfold over the last 100 years, reflecting the shortage of timber. Fur trader Pierre Radisson explores the western end of Lake Superior. The Moghal Emperor Shah Jahan becomes ill at the age of 66; his son Aurangzeb kills one of his brothers, Dara Shikoh, preparing the way to make himself Emperor next year. Charles X of Sweden invades Denmark twice but does not succeed in attacking Copenhagen. *4 Jun*: Battle of the Dunes: English and French troops defeat a Spanish relief force, and Dunkirk surrenders to the English. *3 Sept*: Oliver Cromwell dies, aged 58, and is succeeded as Lord Protector of the Commonwealth by his son, the 31-year-old Richard Cromwell

📖 Pieter de Hooch: Courtyard of a House in Delft
📖 Thomas Browne: *Urne-Buriall*
   John Bunyan: *A Few Sighs From Hell*

1659 The Spanish Infanta Maria Theresa brings cocoa to Paris. The Paris police raid a monastery and send monks to prison for consuming meat and wine during Lent. *22 Apr*: Richard Cromwell dissolves the English Parliament at the army's request. *7 May*: a 'Rump Parliament' meets and forces Cromwell to resign as Lord Protector (on *24 May*). *7 Nov*: Treaty of the Pyrenees, ending Spain's ascendancy.

📖 Diego Velazquez: Infanta Maria Theresa
   Geraert Terborch: The Letter
   Jan Vermeer: Young Girl with Flute
📖 Molière (Jean-Baptiste Poquelin): *Le dépit concoureux; Les précieuses ridicules*

Pierre Corneille: *Oedipus*
John Dryden: *Heroic Stanzas* (on Cromwell's death)
Thomas Hobbes: *De Homine*

1660 The Dutch-Khoisan War erupts at the Cape of Good Hope; the Khoisan herdsman (Harry) who greeted the Dutch settlers eight years ago is captured and imprisoned on Robben Island. In London, Samuel Pepys notes in his diary that he has drunk 'Tee (a China drink) of which I never had drank before'. In West Africa, the Kingdoms of Segu and Kaarta on the upper Niger grow stronger, rivalling the Mandingo Empire which they will soon replace. *12 Feb*: Charles X of Sweden dies, aged 37, and is succeeded by his four-year-old son Charles XI. The Treaty of Copenhagen ends hostilities between Sweden and Denmark: the Danes give up the southern tip of the Scandinavian peninsula (Scania) to the Swedes. *3 May*: the Treaty of Oliva ends the Northern War. John II of Poland gives up his claim to the throne of Sweden and abandons his last remaining territory on the Baltic coast. *8 May*: England's Commonwealth ends as Charles II is proclaimed King. *25 May*: Charles II returns to England *29 May*: Charles II returns to London. *1 Oct*: Navigation Act passed: certain commodities (tobacco, sugar, wool, indigo, apples) from the American colonies may be exported only to Britain.

  ✍ Francesco Borromini: Church of S. Ivo della Sapienza, Rome

  🖌 Rembrandt van Rijn: St. Peter Denying Christ; Self-portrait
Jacob van Ruysdael: The Morass
Jan Vermeer: View of Delft

  📖 Robert Boyle: *New Experiments Touching the Spring of the Air*
John Dryden: *Astraea Redux*
Richard Allestree: *The Whole Duty of Man*
James Harrington: *Political Discourses*
Nicolas Boileau-Despréaux: *Satires*

1661 The architect Nicholas Hawksmoor and the novelist Daniel Defoe are born. In China, the Manchu regime dictates that everyone living within 16 km/10 miles of the coast must move inland; the intention is to stop raiding by the pirate Zheng Chenkong. Shun Chih, the Manchu Emperor, dies.

📖 Robert Boyle: *The Sceptical Chymist*
Molière: *L'Ecole des maris: Les Facheux*

1662 In North America, the Wampanoag Indian chief Massasoit dies and is succeeded by his son Metacum. In China, the Emperor Shun Chih is succeeded by his son Hsuan Yeh, who reigns as K'ang Hsi, through a period of great cultural achievements. England sells Dunkirk to France. France and the Netherlands form an alliance against England. *20 May*: Charles II marries Catherine of Braganza, which initiates a profitable alliance with Portugal

🎨 Rembrandt van Rijn: The Syndics of the Cloth Guild

📖 William Rowley: *The Birth of Merlin*
Thomas Hobbes: *Mr. Hobbes Reconsidered*
Pierre Corneille: *Sertorius*
Molière: *L'Ecole des femmes*

1663 Black Death kills 10,000 in Amsterdam. Jean Colbert works to reform France's national finances. Louis XIV renews the French right to enlist Swiss mercenary soldiers, in spite of objections from Zurich and some of the Protestant cantons. *24 Mar*: Charles II grants Carolina (from Virginia south to Florida) as a reward to eight of his courtiers: they helped him regain his throne.

🏛 Christopher Wren: Pembroke College Chapel, Cambridge

🎨 Adriaen van de Velde: Jacob and Laban
Jan Vermeer: Woman with a Water Jug; Artist and Model

📖 Samuel Butler: *Hudibras*
Pierre Corneille: *Sophonisbe*
John Dryden: *The Wild Gallant*

1664 Black Death kills 24,000 in Amsterdam; the men who load the deadcarts smoke pipes, believing mistakenly that tobacco will spare them. In Japan, merchants initiate an express mail service between Edo and Osaka. In India, the bandit Sivaji sacks the town of Surat. *27 Aug*: the painter Francisco de Zurbaran dies, aged 65, in Madrid. Nieuw Amsterdam becomes New York as English soldiers take the town from the Dutch under Charles II's orders; the town is renamed after the King's brother, the Duke of York.

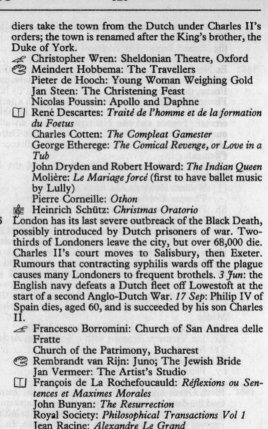

⚜ Christopher Wren: Sheldonian Theatre, Oxford

🐚 Meindert Hobbema: The Travellers

Pieter de Hooch: Young Woman Weighing Gold

Jan Steen: The Christening Feast

Nicolas Poussin: Apollo and Daphne

📖 René Descartes: *Traité de l'homme et de la formation du Foetus*

Charles Cotten: *The Compleat Gamester*

George Etherege: *The Comical Revenge, or Love in a Tub*

John Dryden and Robert Howard: *The Indian Queen*

Molière: *Le Mariage forcé* (first to have ballet music by Lully)

Pierre Corneille: *Othon*

🎵 Heinrich Schütz: *Christmas Oratorio*

1665 London has its last severe outbreak of the Black Death, possibly introduced by Dutch prisoners of war. Two-thirds of Londoners leave the city, but over 68,000 die. Charles II's court moves to Salisbury, then Exeter. Rumours that contracting syphilis wards off the plague causes many Londoners to frequent brothels. *3 Jun*: the English navy defeats a Dutch fleet off Lowestoft at the start of a second Anglo-Dutch War. *17 Sep*: Philip IV of Spain dies, aged 60, and is succeeded by his son Charles II.

⚜ Francesco Borromini: Church of San Andrea delle Fratte

Church of the Patrimony, Bucharest

🐚 Rembrandt van Rijn: Juno; The Jewish Bride

Jan Vermeer: The Artist's Studio

📖 François de La Rochefoucauld: *Réflexions ou Sentences et Maximes Morales*

John Bunyan: *The Resurrection*

Royal Society: *Philosophical Transactions Vol 1*

Jean Racine: *Alexandre Le Grand*

Molière: *L'Amour médecin*

John Dryden: *The Indian Emperor*

1666 The Cambridge mathematician Isaac Newton invents

calculus and establishes the laws of gravity. Louis XIV founds a French Academy of Sciences, emulating the Royal Society founded four years ago by Charles II in England. France and the Netherlands declare war on England. *20 Jan*: in Paris, the Queen Mother Anne of Austria dies of breast cancer, aged 64. *26 Aug*: the painter Frans Hals dies at Haarlem, aged 86. *2 Sep*: the Great Fire of London breaks out in Pudding Lane. The medieval cathedral of St. Paul's and a large area of central London are burnt. *6 Sep*: the fire burns itself out. Pratt, May and Wren are appointed to rebuild the city of London.

    Jan Vermeer: The Letter
    Gianlorenzo Bernini: Throne of St. Peter, Rome
    Edmund Waller: *Instructions to a Painter*
    Molière: *The Misanthrope*: *Le médecin malgré lui*
    John Dryden: *Annus Mirabilis*

1667 Shah Abbas II of Persia dies, aged 35, and is succeeded by his son Suleiman I. The Mogul Emperor Aurangzeb buys off the bandit Sivaji by giving him the title Rajah and letting him collect some taxes. In England, Robert Hooke demonstrates that the alteration of the blood in the lungs is the essential feature of respiration. In France, Jean Denis performs the first known blood transfusion, from a lamb into a boy. French troops invade Flanders and Hainault to start the War of Devolution. Louis XIV, now 28, takes as his mistress the Marquise de Montespan. *20 Jan*: the Treaty of Andrussovo, ending the war between Russia and Poland, ceding Kiev, Smolensk and eastern Ukraine to Russia. *21 Jul*: Treaties of Breda, ending the second Anglo-Dutch War. *18 Oct*: Brooklyn is chartered under the name Brueckelen by Mathias Nicolls, Governor of New Netherlands.

    Christopher Wren: St. Paul's Cathedral
    Gianlorenzo Bernini: St. Peter's Square, Rome
    Claude Perrault: Louvre East Front
    John Dryden: *Secret Love*; *Sir Martin Mar-All*
    Jean Racine: *Andromaque*
    John Milton: *Paradise Lost*

1668 The Black Death reaches Austria. In England, John Dryden becomes the first Poet Laureate. Sault Sainte

Marie is founded between Lake Superior and Lake Huron, the first permanent European settlement in the region. *23 Jan*: Triple Alliance, joining England, Sweden and Netherlands against France.

🏛 Christopher Wren: Emmanuel College, Cambridge

📖 Jean de La Fontaine: *Fables*
George Etherege: *She Would If She Could*
Thomas Shadwell: *The Sullen Lovers*

🎵 Dietrich Buxtehude: *Abendmusiken*

1669 The Mogul emperor Aurangzeb destroys Hindu temples and bans the practice of Hindu religion. Hindus rebel against Aurangzeb. The first Stradivarius violin is made by the 25-year-old Italian Antonio Stradivari. Famine in Bengal kills 3 million people. The Hanseatic League formed 400 years ago holds its final meeting. *27 Sep*: Ottoman Turks take Candia (Heraklion); the Venetians lose Crete. *4 Oct*: Rembrandt dies, aged 63, in Amsterdam, poor and alone.

🏛 Louis Le Vau and Jules Hardouin-Mansart: Palace of Versailles

🎨 Jan Vermeer: Girl at the Spinet

📖 Hans von Grimmelshausen: *Der Abenteuerliche Simplicissimus Teutsch das ist* (first major German novel)
Molière: *Tartuffe*
John Dryden: *Tyrannic Love*
Jean Racine: *Britannicus*
William Penn: *No Cross, No Crown*

1670 The Ukrainian Cossacks rise against the Poles; the rebellion is suppressed by General Sobieski. In India, the Mogul Emperor Aurangzeb is once again under attack from Sivaji, who has established his own Maratha state in the Deccan. Sivaji agains attacks the Gujarati port of Surat; Aurangzeb lets him levy taxes in Khandesh. Gabriel Mouton, a French clergyman, proposes a uniform decimal system of measurements to replace leagues, acres, pounds and other non-standard units commonly in use in France. Minute hands appear on watches for the first time. *6 Feb*: Frederick III of Denmark dies in Copenhagen, aged 60, and is succeeded by his son Christian V. Louis XIV of France makes a defensive alliance with Bavaria and England. *May*:

Charles II's sister Henrietta, Duchesse d'Orléans, obtains English ministerial signatures to the Treaty of Dover and then returns to France. *30 Jun*: Henrietta dies, aged 26, at St. Cloud, allegedly of poison.

  🏛 Jules Hardouin-Mansart: Les Invalides, Paris
      André Lenotre: Champs-Elysées, Paris
  🎨 Bartolome Murillo: Girl and her Duenna
      Jan Vermeer: The Pearl Necklace
      Jacob van Ruysdael: View of Haarlem
  📖 Blaise Pascal: *Pensées*
      Jean Racine: *Bérénice*
      Molière: *Le Bourgeois Gentilhomme*
      Pierre Corneille: *Tite et Bérénice*
  🎼 Jean Lully: *Music for Le Bourgeois Gentilhomme*

1671 The Welsh buccaneer Henry Morgan captures Panama City. Morgan stands trial, having violated the Anglo-Spanish Treaty, but is forgiven by Charles II and knighted. The Turks declare war on Poland. Tsar Alexis of Russia suppresses a peasants revolt led by the Don Cossacks; their leader Stenka Razin is executed. Madame de Sévigné disapproves of the condom as a means of contraception, describing it to her daughter the Comtesse de Grignan as 'an armour against enjoyment and a spider's web against danger'.

  🏛 William Bruce: Palace of Holyroodhouse, Edinburgh
  📖 John Milton: *Paradise Regained*; *Samson Agonistes*
      Thomas Shadwell: *The Humourists*
      Aphra Behn: *The Forc'd Marriage*
      William Wycherley: *Love in a Wood*
      Pierre Corneille: *Psyche*

1672 Russian serfs rebel. An Ottoman army invades Poland as a four-year war over control of the Ukraine begins. In England, the Royal Company is formed to exploit the slave trade; customs duties are imposed on goods carried from one American colony to another. The New York to Boston Post Road is built to speed up coach travel. The Black Death flares up in Europe, killing 60,000 people in Lyons and hundreds of thousands in Naples. A French army crosses the Rhine, invading the Dutch Republic; Louis XIV intends to punish the Dutch for sheltering his critics. The English support the French under secret provisions in the Treaty of Dover. *28 May*: Battle of Southwold Bay: the English defeat a Dutch fleet, after which the Dutch turn for help to the Prince of Orange. *8 Jul*: the Dutch Staats-General revive the office of Stadtholder, making William III of Orange, now 21 years old, Stadtholder for life. A crowd at The Hague murders the grand pensionary Jan De Witt and his brother Cornelius; William of Orange rewards the murderers. *6 Nov*: Heinrich Schütz, the first German composer to become well known internationally, dies, aged 87.

✍ Christopher Wren: Church of St. Stephen, Walbrook, London

🖼 Bartolome Murillo: Virgin and Child

📖 Thomas Shadwell: *The Miser*
George Villiers: *The Rehearsal*
Jean Racine: *Bajazet*
Molière: *Les femmes savantes*
John Dryden: *Marriage à la Mode*
William Wycherley: *The Gentleman Dancing Master*
Pierre Corneille: *Pulcheria*

1673 At Edo in Japan, the Kabuki actor Sannjuro Ichikawa, who is 13, invents the Aragato style which features the superman war-god; other Kabuki actors will develop this style. English surgeons fit the first metal dental fillings. In North America, the Jesuit missionary-explorer Jacques Marquette and trader Louis Joliet explore the area between the Mississippi headstreams and the Great Lakes; Joliet sees, the possibilities of of a navigable waterway from the Great Lakes to the Atlantic. The Dutch retake New York. William of Orange saves Amsterdam and the province of Holland from the French by opening the sluice gates and flooding the country. *14 Feb*: Molière dies a week after suffering a haemorrhage on stage while acting the part of the hypochondriac in his own play; he is 51. *15 Mar*: the painter Salvator Rosa dies in Rome, aged 57.

🖼 Bartolome Murillo: Madonna and Child
Edward Pierce: Sir Christopher Wren (bust)

📖 Jean Racine: *Mithridate*
Molière: *Le Malade imaginaire*

John Dryden: *Amboyna*
Jean Lully: *Cadmus et Hermoine* (Lully's first opera)

1674 Severe famine in Japan. French troops devastate the Palatinate; the Holy Roman Empire, Spain and Netherlands join in a coalition to halt the French. The Poles elect General Sobieski King as John III. *9 Feb*: Treaty of Westminster, ending the Anglo-Dutch War; New York and Delaware are returned to England. The English are now free to expand their trade networks and become prosperous while the rest of Europe becomes embroiled in debilitating wars. *6 Jun*: the bandit Sivaji has himself crowned at Raigarh in the Deccan, founding a Maratha dynasty; the military struggle with the Mogul Emperor Aurangzeb continues.

📖 William Wycherley: *The Country Wife*
Nicolas Boileau-Despréaux: *L'Art poétique*
Jean Racine: *Iphigénie*
Pierre Corneille: *Surena*
🎼 Jean Lully: *Alceste*

1675 Black Death kills 11,000 in Malta. In New England, Chief Metacum rebels against an order requiring his people to pay an annual tribute of £100; Metacum leads the Narragansett and Wampanoag Indians in attacks on over 50 colonial settlements, killing 600 people. In England there is a move to close the coffee houses, which have become gathering places for men who then neglect their families to discuss politics. *5 Jan*: Marshal Turenne defeats the Dutch at Turkheim and recovers Alsace. *27 Jul*: Marshal Turenne is killed, aged 63, by the opening shots fired in the Battle of Sassbach in Baden. The French retreat across the Rhine. *15 Dec*: the painter Jan Vermeer dies, aged 43, at Delft.

✎ Christopher Wren: Royal Observatory, Greenwich; St. Paul's Cathedral, London (work begins)
🎨 Geraert Terborch: The Music Lesson; The Concert
Caius Cibber: Raving Madness; Melancholy Madness
📖 John Dryden: *The Mistaken Husband*; *Aurengzebe*
John Bunyan: *Instruction for the Ignorant*
Thomas Shadwell: *The Libertine*
🎼 Mathew Locke: *Psyche*

Jean Lully: *Thésée*

1676 The University of San Carlos of Guatemala is founded at Guatemala City. In England, the Greenwich Observatory is established with a view to fixing a standard time and helping navigators fix their longitude. Dutch slavers buy 15,000 black slaves per year in Angola at 30 florins each, selling them in America at 300–500 florins each. *8 Feb*: Tsar Alexis of Russia dies, aged 47, and is succeeded by his 15-year-old son Fedor II. *18 Feb*: Isaac Newton writes, 'If I have seen further, it is by standing on the shoulders of giants'. Newton's Other Law is based on an aphorism of Robert Burton (*1621*), who in turn borrowed the idea from Bernard of Chartres. *Aug*: Chief Metacum is killed in battle and beheaded by colonial militiamen; his wife and children are sold into slavery. *16 Oct*: Treaty of Zuravno, ending the war between John III of Poland and the Ottoman Empire, which acquires Podolia and the Polish Ukraine and thus has a common frontier with Russia.

    ✐ Christopher Wren: Trinity College Library, Cambridge

    📖 George Etherege: *The Man of Mode or Sir Fopling Flutter*

    William Wycherley: *The Plain Dealer*

1677 Spermatozoa are discovered in human semen by Anton van Leeuwenhoek at Delft. England and France sign an agreement allowing English ships to carry Dutch cargoes. The French defeat the Dutch at Cassel. A Dutch-Danish fleet defeats a Swedish fleet at Oland. In Carolina, Culpeper's Rebellion is a protest against the enforcement of English trade laws. *1 Jan*: the first performances of Racine's *Phèdre* and Pradon's rival play of the same name. Racine is mortified at this carefully managed attempt to undermine his success. *2 Jan*: although only 38, Racine announces his retirement from writing plays. *30 Oct*: French troops in West Africa take Dutch ports on the Senegal and capture Goree near Cape Verde. *4 Nov*: William of Orange, now 27, marries 15-year-old Mary, niece of Charles II of England.

    ✐ Christopher Wren: Church of St. Martin, Ludgate, London

🐌 Pieter de Hooch: Musical Party in a Courtyard
📖 Jean Racine: *Phèdre*
John Dryden: *All for Love, or The World Well Lost*
Aphra Behn: *The Debauchee*
Andrew Marvell: *Account of the Growth of Popery*
🎵 Jean Lully: *Atys*; *Isis*

1678 French missionary Louis Hennepin discovers Niagara Falls. England is shaken by reports of a 'Popish Plot', in reality a hoax perpetrated by Titus Oates; Oates 'uncovers' a Roman Catholic plot to massacre Protestants, destroy London and assassinate Charles II. *2 Jan*: the Hamburg Staatsoper opens. *10 Aug*: Treaty of Nijmegen; Holland has returned to it the territories lost to France and Spain. *16 Aug*: the English poet Andrew Marvell dies, aged 57, after taking an overdose of opiate for the ague.

🐌 Godfrey Kneller: Charles II
📖 Thomas Durfey: *Trick for Trick*
Aphra Behn: *Sir Patient Fancy*
John Bunyan: *The Pilgrim's Progress, Part 1*
🎵 Jean Lully: *Psyche*
Johan Theile: *Adam and Eve*

1679 The composer Henry Purcell is appointed organist at Westminster Abbey, succeeding John Blow. The French explorer Daniel Greysolon reaches Lake Superior, claiming the region for Louis XIV. *29 Jun*: the Peace of St. Germain-en-Laye is forced on the Elector of Brandenburg by Louis XIV; the Elector gains nothing and has to surrender to Sweden most of Brandenburg's conquests in Pomerania. The Black Death kills over 75,000 people in Vienna.

✎ Skokloster Castle (Sweden)
Vincenzo Viviani: River Arno flood control works
📖 John Dryden: *Troilus and Cressida*
Aphra Behn: *The Feign'd Curtizans*
Thomas Durfey: *Squire Oldsapp*
🎵 Jean Lully: *Bellérophon*
Alessandro Scarlatti: *Gli Quivoco nell'amore*

1680 The Maratha leader Sijavi dies; his death is followed by fighting between Aurangzeb and the Marathas' allies, the Rajputs. The Japanese Shogun Ietsuna dies, aged 39, and is succeeded by his 34-year-old brother Sunayoshi. Europe enters a long period of economic problems accompanied by large-scale price fluctuations, peasants' revolts, famines and epidemics. *24 Jul*: the artist Ferdinand Bol dies in Amsterdam, aged 64. *25 Sep*: the English satirist Samuel Butler dies. *28 Nov*: the Italian architect Gianlorenzo Bernini dies, aged 81, in Rome.

    ✐ Jules Hardouin-Mansart: Church of Les Invalides, Paris

       Christopher Wren: Church of St. Mary-le-Bow; Church of St. Clement Danes (both in London)

    📖 John Dryden: *The Spanish Friar*

       John Bunyan: *The Life and Death of Mr. Badman*

    🎜 Henry Purcell: *Dido and Aeneas*

1681 The Chinese novelist and playwright Li Yu dies; he edited an encyclopaedia of Chinese painting and ran a theatre company. The Qing (or Manchu) Emperor Kangxi suppresses the Rebellion of Three Feudatories in the south of the country. The leader of the rebellion, the former Ming General Wu San-kuei, is killed and Qing rule is extended over the whole of China. Russia takes Tartar territory on the Volga, forcing its people to accept Christianity. France annexes Strasbourg. In England, the first bank cheques are given. In Prague, 83,000 people die of the Black Death. In North America, Pennsylvania is founded in a grant of land by Charles II to the nonconformist William Penn. The King's generosity is motivated in part by a need to discharge a £515,000 debt to Penn's father and in part by a desire to rid England of nonconformists. Penn calls the new land 'Sylvania'; Charles II adds the prefix 'Penn'. *8 Dec*: the painter Geraert Terborch dies, aged 64, at Deventer.

    ✐ Christopher Wren: Tom Tower, Christ Church, Oxford

       Baldassare Longhena: Church of the Salute, Venice (completed)

       Pierre de Riquet: Languedoc Canal, (France)

    📖 John Dryden: *Absalom and Achitophel*

       Thomas Durfey: *Sir Barnaby Whig*

       Andrew Marvell: *Miscellaneous Poems*

       Jean Mabillon: *De re diplomatica*

🎼 Jean Lully: *Le Triomphe de l'Amour*

1682 Versailles becomes the seat of French government as Louis XIV's court moves into the new château. Denis Papin, a French physicist, invents the pressure cooker. William Penn founds the city of Philadelphia. *14 Mar:* the painter Jacob van Ruysdael dies in Amsterdam, aged 53. *3 Apr:* the artist Bartolome Murillo dies at Seville, aged 64. *9 Apr:* the explorer de La Salle reaches the mouth of the Mississippi, naming the region Louisiana and claiming it for Louis XIV. *27 Apr:* Tsar Fedor III of Russia dies, aged 21, and is succeeded by his nine-year-old half-brother Peter in preference to his older but mentally defective brother, the 15-year-old Ivan. Ivan's sister Sophia orders musketeers to invade the Kremlin and kill Peter's supporters; Ivan is proclaimed Tsar with Peter as associate: Sophia as Regent holds the real power. *21 Nov:* the painter Claude Lorrain dies aged 82 in Rome.

🏛 Christopher Wren: Royal Hospital, Chelsea (U.K.)

📖 Pierre Bayle: *Thoughts on the Comet of 1680*
Saikaku Ihara: *The Life of an Amorous Man*
John Dryden: *The Medall; a Satyre against Sedition* (an attack on the Earl of Shaftesbury which forces the Earl to flee to Holland)
Thomas Otway: *Venice Preserved*
John Bunyan: *The Holy War*

🎼 Heinrich Biber: *Salzburg Mass*

1683 In Japan, the Mitsui bank opens in Edo, founded by the merchant Mitsui Takatoshi; it will grow into a major international trading company. The Chinese conquer Taiwan. Afonso VI of Portugal dies, aged 40, and is succeeded by his 35-year-old brother Pedro II. Spain declares war on France; Emperor Leopold joins Carlos (Charles) II of Spain and the Dutch-Swedish alliance against Louis XIV. Jean Colbert dies, aged 64, leaving the French navy without a champion at court: the navy soon begins to decline. In England, some defeated Whigs conspire to kill Charles II; the Rye House Plot is uncovered in *Jun.* Lord William Russell, the Earl of Essex and Algernon Sidney are arrested. *21 Jul:* Russell is executed after conviction on perjured testimony. *30*

Jul: Essex is found with his throat cut, apparently having committed suicide. *7 Dec*: Sidney is beheaded.

   ✎ Thomas Holme: Philadelphia (grid plan borrowed from Spanish towns)

     Christopher Wren: Piccadilly Circus and St. James's Palace, London

     Charlottenborg Palace, Copenhagen (completed)

   🎨 Godfrey Kneller: Sir Charles Cotterell

   📖 John Bunyan: *Greatness of the Soul*

     Bernard de Fontenelle: *Dialogues des Morts*

     William Petty: *The Growth of the City of London*

     William Penn: *General Description of Pennsylvania*

1684 In Japan, the Chief Minister Hotta Masatoshi is assassinated, aged 50, leaving the Shogun Sunayoshi with no adequate advisers. This will lead him to issue impractical edicts and create new hardships for the Japanese people. The Japanese poet Saikaku composes 23,500 verses in 24 hours at the Sumiyoshi Shrine at Osaka; the scribes are unable to keep pace with his dictation and can only count the verses. The English East India Company gains permission from Chinese authorities to build a trading station at Canton. Tea sells in Europe for less than a shilling per pound, but an import dury of five shillings makes tea too expensive for most English people to afford; the English drink more smuggled tea than legally imported tea. England has its coldest winter in living memory; the Thames and the sea as far as 3 km/2 miles out from the land freeze over.

   ✎ Jules Hardouin-Mansart: Hall of Mirrors, Versailles (completed)

   📖 John Bunyan: *The Pilgrim's Progress, Part 2*

     Thomas Burnet: *Theory of Earth*

     Thomas Otway: *The Atheist*

1685 King Wegbaja of Dahomey in West Africa dies and is succeeded by his son Akaba. In Paris, a Code Noir is issued to try to establish humane treatment of slaves on plantations in French colonies but the planters take little notice of it. French entrepreneurs found the Guinea Company to take part in the slave trade in West Africa. In England, Titus Oates is found guilty of perjury and sentenced to the pillory and life imprisonment (though he will be released in *1689* and rewarded). *6 Feb*: Charles II of England dies, aged 54 and is succeeded by his Catholic brother James, who is 51. The Duke of Monmouth claims a superior right to the throne; supported by troops, he lands at Lyme Regis in Dorset. *30 Jun*: the Earl of Argyll, Monmouth's principal supporter, is executed. *6 Jul*: Battle of Sedgemoor: Monmouth's army is easily routed and Monmouth himself is captured and beheaded. *10 Oct*: in France, the Edict of Nantes is revoked; the practice of any religion except Catholicism is banned and Huguenots are forbidden to emigrate. 50,000 Huguenots nevertheless, do emigrate from France, settling in many other countries in Europe, as well as South Africa and North America. This severely damages France's economy.

🏛 William Talman and Thomas Archer: Chatsworth House, Derbyshire

🎨 Godfrey Kneller: Philip Earl of Leicester

📖 Edmund Waller: *Of Divine Love*
    Aphra Behn: *The Unfortunate Lady*
    Thomas Durfey: *Advice to the Ladies of London*

🎼 Jean Lully: *Idylle sur la paix* (words by Racine); *Le Temple de la paix*

1686   The Institut de Saint-Louis is founded by Mme. de Maintenon for the education of daughters of impoverished nobility; the school will be known for its cookery lessons and the blue ribbon (cordon bleu) the girls wear on graduation. The English East India Company starts using force; Job Charnock moves his trading station from the besieged town of Hooghly to a defensible site nearer the mouth of the Ganges. France annexes Madagascar. *8 Jul*: Austrian troops liberate Buda from Ottoman Turks, but the pashas have left it in a poor state. Moscow declares war on Constantinople. *9 Jul*: The League of Augsburg (Holy Roman Emperor Leopold I, Carlos II of Spain, Charles XI of Sweden, Electors of Saxony, Bavaria and the Palatinate) is formed to oppose France.

🎨 Grinling Gibbons: James II (statue)

📖 Bernard de Fontenelle: *Entretiens sur la pluralité des mondes*
    Saikaku Ihara: *Five Women Who Chose Love*; *A*

>   Woman Who Devoted Her Entire Life to Love-
>   making
>   Monzaemon Chikamatsu: *Successful Kagekiyo*
>   ⚜ Jean Lully: *Armide*; *Acis et Galatée*

1687   *28 Jan*: The Japanese Shogun Sunayoshi issues a law
forbidding the killing of animals. *19 Mar*: on the Gulf of
Mexico coast of North America, the La Salle expedition
is down to 20 men; they kill their leader, La Salle, leaving
his body to the buzzards. *22 Mar*: the French composer
and director of the Paris Opera, Jean Lully, dies, aged 54,
of blood poisoning after injuring himself in the foot while
conducting with a long staff. Louis XIV has at times
appeared on stage in Lully's operatic spectacles to dance
as Apollo or Jupiter. *14 Apr*: James II of England grants
freedom of worship in England, Scotland and Wales. *12
Aug*: Second Battle of Mohacs: Charles of Lorraine
defeats the Ottoman Turks. The Venetian general Francesco Morosini reconquers the Greek Peloponnese from
the Turks and captures Athens. Morosini shells Athens,
scoring a direct hit on the Parthenon which is being used
as a munitions store by the Turks and explodes causing
enormous damage to the ancient temple. *14 Sep*: Erlau in
Hungary surrenders to an Austrian army. *8 Nov*: the
Ottoman Sultan Mohammed IV is deposed at the age of
48 by his Janissaries and imprisoned. He is succeeded by
his 47-year-old brother Suleiman II.

>   ✏ Christopher Wren: Kensington Palace, London
>   🐚 Godfrey Kneller: The Chinese Convent
>   📖 Isaac Newton: *Philosophia Naturalis Principia
>   Mathematica*
>   Aphra Behn: *The Emperor of the Moon*
>   François de la Mothe-Fénelon: *Traité de l'éducation
>   des filles*
>   John Dryden: *The Hind and the Panther*
>   Matthew Prior: *The Country Mouse and the City
>   Mouse*
>   ⚜ Heinrich Biber: *Chi la dura, la vince*

1688   A French army invades the Palatinate, devastating the
countryside on orders from de Louvois, French minister
of war. Lloyds of London has its beginnings in a marine
insurance society formed in Edward Lloyd's coffee house

in London. *10 Jun*: a son is born to James II's wife, Queen Mary, implying a likely Catholic succession. *30 Jun*: Whig leaders invite the King's son-in-law William of Orange to rule the United Kingdom. *20 Aug*: Ottoman forces surrender Belgrade to an Austrian army after a three-week bombardment. *5 Nov*: William of Orange lands in England and moves towards London. *23 Dec*: James II leaves London as William arrives, and emigrates to France.

    ⍓ Ponte de tre Archi, Venice
    ☐ Jean de La Bruyere: *Les Caractères de Théophraste*
    Bernard de Fontenelle: *Digression sur les anciens et les modernes*
    Aphra Behn: *Oroonoko*
    Thomas Shadwell: *The Squire of Alsatia*

1689 The War of the League of Augsburg involves the Dutch in a series of land wars diverting resources from their naval strength – and facilitating the rise of British sea power. In Russia, the Regent and Tsarina Sophia is deposed when it is revealed that she is involved in a conspiracy to abduct her half-brother Peter. The Treaty of Nerchinsk ends the conflict between Russia and China; the Russians agree to withdraw pioneer settlers from the Amur basin. Bostonians are dismayed at the news of James II's flight from England, restoring charter government after imprisoning Sir Edmund Andros; New Yorkers proclaim William and Mary rightful monarchs of the United Kingdom and its colonies. Indians destroy the French colony at the mouth of the Mississippi founded by de La Salle. The 17-year-old Tsar Peter is crowned in *Sep* and his marriage to the beautiful but stupid Eudoxia Lopukhina collapses; Peter leaves administration to others, occupying himself with sailing and shipbuilding.

    ✎ Meindert Hobbema: The Avenue at Middelharnis
    ☐ John Selden: *Table-Talk*
    Jean Racine: *Esther*
    Thomas Shadwell: *Bury Fair*
    John Dryden: *Don Sebastian, King of Portugal*
    Aphra Behn: *The Lucky Mistake*
    John Locke: *On Civil Government*

♭ Henry Purcell: *Dido and Aeneas*

1690 Job Charnock, East India Company official, founds the city of Calcutta on the bank of the Hooghly River, a branch of the Ganges, The Battle of Fluerus: Duc de Luxembourg, for Louis XIV, defeats the Prince of Waldeck. Spain and Savoy join the League of Augsburg against France. The Ottoman army drives the Austrians out of Bulgaria, Transylvania and Serbia, and retake Belgrade. *25 Apr*: the painter David Teniers dies in Brussels, aged 79. *30 Jun*: Battle of Beachy Head: the French defeat an English fleet under Admiral Herbert, Lord Torrington (who will be acquitted of charges that he held back in battle). *1 Jul*: Battle of the Boyne: William III's army defeats the Catholic pretender James II and his French army; the ex-King returns to exile in France.

✎ William Talman: Uppark House, Sussex
⛇ Meindert Hobbema: The Mill
📗 John Locke: *An Essay Concerning Human Understanding*
 Thomas Shadwell: *The Amorous Bigot*
 John Dryden: *Amphitryon*
♭ Henry Purcell and Thomas Durfey: *The Yorkshire Feast Song*

1691 In Japan, prospectors discover a copper and silver deposit that will make the Sumitomo family of Osaka one of the most powerful in Japan. *May*: the Ottoman Sultan Suleiman III dies, aged 50, after reigning for 35 years; he is succeeded by his 49-year-old brother Ahmed II. *12 Jul*: Battle of Aughrim: William and Mary's General Ginkel (Dutch-born) defeats an Irish army under the Earl of Lucan. *19 Aug*: Battle of Szcelankemen: Louis of Baden defeats the Ottoman Turks. During the battle the Grand Vizier Zade Mustapha Kuprili, the real power behind the last Sultan, is killed. The Turks are expelled from Hungary. *3 Oct*: Limerick surrenders to Ginkel after a siege. The Treaty of Limerick which follows grants free transport to France for all Irish soldiers who wish to go. *Nov*: the painter Jacobsz Cuyp dies at Dordrecht, aged 71.

📗 Jean Racine: *Athalie*

Thomas Southerne: *Sir Anthony Love*

♯ Henry Purcell: *King Arthur* (words by Dryden)

1692 Gottfried von Leibniz invents a calculating machine that multiplies as well as adds and subtracts. There is a violent earthquake in Jamaica; two-thirds of the pirate stronghold of Port Royal falls into the sea. William and Mary take the proprietorship of Pennsylvania away from William Penn, instead commissioning the Governor of New York, Benjamin Fletcher. The English-American clergyman Samuel Parris brings accusations of witchcraft against women in Salem in Massachusetts; 19 alleged witches will be hanged during the next two years, many on evidence supplied by 12-year-old Anne Putnam. *13 Feb*: Massacre of Glencoe, leading to years of feuding in the Scottish Highlands. Ian MacDonald, leader of the MacDonald clan, has sworn allegiance to William III but the Earl of Stair has suppressed news of the oath, conspiring with the Campbells, the MacDonalds' traditional enemies. The Campbells kill every member of the MacDonald clan under the age of 70. *29 May*: Battle of La Hogue: the French lose 15 ships and Louis XIV is persuaded that great fleets are a waste of money, leaving England and the Dutch to fight for control of the high seas. *24 Jul*: Battle of Steenkirken: the French under the Duc de Luxembourg defeat an English army.

📖 William Congreve: *Incognita*
Nehemiah Grew: *Anatomy of Plants*
Roger L'Estrange: *Aesop's Fables* (translated)

♯ John Reading: *Adeste Fidelis*
Henry Purcell: *The Fairy Queen*; *Incidental Music to Henry II*; *Ode for St. Cecilia's Day*

1693 French composer François Couperin is appointed Royal Organist at the age of 25. In England, William III initiates the national debt (never to be repaid) by borrowing £1 million at an interest rate of 10 per cent. *26–27 May*: Battle of Cape St. Vincent: the French defeat an Anglo-Dutch fleet off Portugal. *30 Jun*: Battle of Lagos: another French naval victory off the Portuguese coast. *29 Jul*: Battle of Neerwinden: a French land victory over the English.

⚘ Church of the Intercession of the Holy Virgin, Fili, near Moscow

📖 John Locke: *Ideas on Education*

William Penn: *Essay on the Present and Future Peace of Europe* (proposing federation)

Cotton Mather: *The Wonders of the Invisible World* (analysis of the Salem witch-hunt)

William Congreve: *The Old Bachelor*: *The Double Dealer*

1694 Suleiman, Shah of Persia, dies and is succeeded by his 19-year-old son Husein. In Japan, the Ukiyo-ye painter Morinobu Hishikawa dies, aged 76; he has pioneered the creation of prints depicting people's everyday lives. The Royal Navy bombards Dieppe, Dunkirk and Le Havre. France suffers severe food shortages as the French government's economic policy obstructs the flow of food into famine areas. *27 Jul*: the Bank of England is chartered; a company of merchants led by William Paterson receives the charter in return for lending the English government over £1 million.

⚘ Johann von Erlach: Frain Castle, Moravia

📖 Godfrey Kneller: Hampton Court Beauties

🎵 Henry Purcell: *Come, ye sons of art, away*

1695 Ahmed II the Ottoman Sultan dies of dropsy and is succeeded by his 32-year-old nephew Mustapha II. The Russian army under Tsar Peter the Great besieges Azov on the River Don, but the siege fails and the Turks inflict heavy casualties on the Russians. *4 Jan*: Marshal Luxembourg dies, aged 66, and is succeeded in the command of French troops in the Low Countries by the Duc de Villeroi, a less capable man. The War of the League of Augsburg continues. *Sep*: William III of England recaptures Namur. *21 Nov*: the English composer Henry Purcell dies, aged 36.

⚘ Stone guild halls, Brussels (to replace the timber halls destroyed in *Aug* by Villeroi's bombardment)

📖 Nicolaas Heinsius: *Den Vermakelyken*

William Congreve: *Love for Love*

🎵 Henry Purcell: *Indian Queen*

1696 The Polynesian pomelo tree is introduced into Barbados by Captain Shaddock; a sweeter mutation of the 'shaddock' will eventually be known as grapefruit. It is predicted that England's population will be 22 million in 3500 'in case the world should last so long'. The Assassination Plot to murder William III of England is discovered; Sir George Barclay and Sir John Fenwick are among the conspirators. Barclay is hanged; Fenwick will hang early next year. *10 Apr*: England's Navigation Act forbids the English colonies in America to export direct to Ireland or Scotland. *17 Jun*: John III of Poland dies, aged 72.

📖 Colley Cibber: *Love's Last Shift, or The Fool in Fashion*

Jean-François Regnard: *Le Joueur*

John Aubrey: *Miscellanies*

🎵 Nahum Tate and Nicholas Brady: *While Shepherds Watched Their Flocks By Night*

1697 Gold is found in Portuguese Brazil, attracting thousands of prospectors from the coast into the Minas Gerais area; many emigrate from Portugal. The Chinese conquer western Mongolia. The Russian Tsar Peter the Great tours Holland, France and England incognito: he is the first Russian ruler to travel abroad and he decides to westernize Russia. *5 Apr*: Charles XI of Sweden dies, aged 40, and is succeeded by his 14-year-old son Charles XII. *Sep*: the Poles elect Frederick Augustus I, the 27-year-old Elector of Saxony, as their new King to rule as Augustus II. *11 Sep*: Battle of Zenta: Eugene of Savoy defeats the Ottoman Turks. Eugene's troops kill 20,000 Turks, while another 10,000 Turks drown in the river; his army captures all the Ottoman artillery, thousands of camels and 10 of the Sultan's wives. *30 Sep*: Treaty of Ryswick ending the War of the League of Augsburg. France recognizes William III as King of England, Wales and Scotland, with Anne as heiress-presumptive.

✎ J. B. Fischer von Erlach: Palace of Prince Eugene, Vienna

📖 William Dampier: *Voyage Round the World*

Daniel Defoe: *An Essay upon Projects*

Charles Perrault: *Mother Goose Tales*

William Congreve: *The Mourning Bride*

John Vanbrugh: *The Provok'd Wife; The Relapse*

♯ John Blow: *I Was Glad*

Jeremiah Clarke: *Alexander's Feast*; *The World in the Moon*

1698   In West Africa, the rich Dahomey kingdom is invaded by Oyo horsemen, who will control the state for 30 years: Dahomey's wealth has been generated by supplying slaves to traders. Arabs succeed in driving the Portuguese from the east coast of Africa. The English authorities recognize the slave trade, opening it up to British merchants; the beginning of the 'Slave Triangle', a three-sided trade route round the North Atlantic. The London Stock Exchange is founded. The English engineer Thomas Savery invents the steam engine to pump water out of coal mines; it is not very effective. Captain Kidd begins his career as a pirate. Whitehall Palace in London burns down. The Russian Tsar Peter the Great returns home taking with him sunflowers that will be a major source of oil seed in Russia and eastern Europe. At the French abbey d'Hautvilliers, Champagne is invented by Dom Pierre Perignon, who uses a new strain of grape and corked bottles made of strong English glass. Most of the inhabitants of New York remain on Long Island and Manhattan Island as hostile Iroquois Indians block expansion to the west and north.

✐ Jules Hardouin-Mansart: Place Vendôme and Statue of Louis XIV, Paris

📖 Edward Ward: *The London Spy*

Rev. Jeremy Collier: *A short view of the Immorality and Profaneness of the English Stage*

1699   William Dampier explores the west coast of Australia. The Virginia colony moves its capital, after a fire last year at Jamestown, to Middle Plantation (later Williamsburg). Yellow fever kills over 300 at Charleston and Philadelphia. *26 Jan*: Treaty of Karlowitz; the Turks are forced to give up Hungary to Austria, which also gets Croatia and Transylvania, while Poland regains the Turkish part of the Ukraine, and Venice receives most of Dalmatia.

✐ Drottningholm Palace, Stockholm (completed)

📖 Colley Cibber: *Xerxes*; *Tragical History of King Richard III*

George Farquhar: *The Constant Couple, or A Trip to Jubilee*

John Toland: *Amyntor, or a defence of Milton's life*

1700 The German Protestant states adopt the Gregorian calendar devised in *1582* by order of the Diet of Regensburg; Britain and the North American colonies continue with the Julian calendar. *23 Jun*: Constantinople and Moscow sign a truce; the Russians keep Azov but give up their Black Sea fleet. The Great Northern War begins as Poland, Denmark and Russia join in opposing Swedish supremacy in the Baltic Sea; the Danes invade Schleswig, the Saxons invade Livonia and the Swedes surprise the Danes by invading Zeeland. *18 Aug*: the 18-year-old Charles XII of Sweden forces Denmark to sign the Treaty of Travendal which removes Denmark from the anti-Swedish alliance. *1 Nov*: Carlos II of Spain dies, aged 39. He is succeeded by the grandson of Louis XIV of France as Philip V.

    John Vanbrugh: Castle Howard, North Yorkshire

    Samuel Sewall: *The Selling of Joseph* (condemns slave trade)

    William Dougall: *Annie Laurie*

    William Congreve: *The Way of the World*

    Nicholas Rowe: *The Ambitious Stepmother*

1701 In West Africa, the Battle of Feyiase results in a victory for the Ashanti tribesmen over their masters, the Denkyira. The Ashanti leader, Osei Tutu, begins to build a powerful empire based on trade in gold and slaves. The English farmer Jethro Tull invents the seed-planting drill; this will increase food production by reducing seed wastage. *18 Jan*: Frederick I, the first King of Prussia, crowns himself at Konigsberg. The Holy Roman Emperor Leopold I gives the Elector of Brandenburg the right to the title in exchange for a promise of military aid. *10 Jun*: Charles XII relieves the siege of Riga by driving off a Saxon force; the Swedes go on to invade Poland. *24 Jul*: Antoine Cadillac founds the French colonial settlement of Fort Pont-chartrain (later Detroit) to control the route connecting Lakes Huron and Erie. *7 Sep*: War of the Spanish Succession begins; the Holy Roman Emperor Leopold I moves to seize

Spain's Dutch and Italian possessions. England, Holland and Savoy join the Grand Alliance.

📖 Arai Hakuseki: *Hankampu* (history of Japan's feudal lords)

George Farquhar: *Sir Harry Wildair*

Nicholas Rowe: *Tamerlane*

1702 Dutch jurist Cornelius van Bynkershoek rules that a nation's territory extends 3 miles (4.8 km) offshore. *8 Mar*: William III of England dies, aged 51, after a fall from his horse. He is succeeded by his sister-in-law Anne *11 Mar*: *The Daily Courant* begins publication, London's first daily newspaper. *14 May*: the War of the Spanish Succession widens as the Grand Alliance declares war on France. *Jun*: Queen Anne's Captain-General John Churchill forces the surrender of Kaiserswerth on the Rhine. *Sep*: Churchill forces the surrender of Venlo on the River Meuse. *Oct*: Sir George Rooke captures a Spanish treasure fleet at Vigo Bay, although he fails to take Cadiz; Rooke destroys French and Spanish warships. Churchill forces the surrender of Liège. *14 Dec*: Churchill is created Duke of Marlborough. The Forty-Seven Ronin incident in Japan: 47 ronin (unemployed samurai) avenge the death of their master who was ordered to commit suicide last year for fighting at Edo Castle; they kill Kira Yoshinaka. Because Yoshinaka is a kinsman of the Shogun, the 47 ronin are also ordered to commit suicide (in *Feb 1703*).

✎ J. B. Fischer von Erlach: Church of the Holy Trinity, Salzburg

Jakob Prandtauer: Monastery of Melk, Austria

📖 Cotton Mather: *Magnalia Christi Americana*

George Farquhar: *The Inconstant, or The Way to Win Him*

1703 The Grand Alliance proclaims Archduke Charles of Austria King of Spain; the 18-year-old Charles prepares to invade Catalonia. The Duke of Marlborough invades the Spanish Netherlands. Daniel Defoe is sentenced to the pillory and a prison term as punishment for his pamphlet, published last year, *The Shortest Way with Dissenters*. *21 Apr*: Charles XII of Sweden defeats a Russian army at Pultusk and besieges Thorn as the

Great Northern War continues. *1 May*: Peter the Great founds St. Petersburg, making the new city on the Gulf of Finland his new capital and turning Russia towards the west. *3 Sep*: the Ottoman Sultan Mustapha II is deposed and succeeded by his 30-year-old brother Ahmed III. *26 Nov*: in England a great storm destroys the Eddystone Lighthouse and kills thousands of people. *30 Dec*: in Japan, an earthquake and resulting fire destroy the city of Edo, killing 200,000 people.

   Christopher Wren: Church of St. Bride's, Fleet Street (completed)

   Nicholas Rowe: *The Fair Penitent*
   Monzaemon Chikamatsu: *Sonezakishinju* (puppet show)

   Attilo Ariosti: *La più gloriosa fatica d'Ercole*

1704 In Japan, the 44-year-old Kabuki actor Dannjuro Ichikawa is murdered on stage. The weekly *News-Letter*, America's first regular newspaper, begins publication in Boston; it consists of a single sheet covered with news and rumours. *2 Jul*: Charles XII of Sweden secures the election of Stanislas Leszczynski as King of Poland, by using bribery and intimidation. *4 Aug*: English forces under Admiral Rooke take Gibraltar from the Spanish. *13 Aug*: Battle of Blenheim: an English army under Marlborough wins an overwhelming victory over the French-Bavarian-Prussian coalition. The coalition suffers losses of 4,500 dead and 7,500 wounded, while the English lose 670 dead, 1,500 wounded. The 11,000 prisoners taken by Marlborough include the French General Tallard.

   Orangery, Kensington Palace

   Jonathan Swift: *The Battle of the Books*; *A Tale of a Tub*
   Isaac Newton: *Opticks*

   George Frederick Handel: *St. John Passion*

1705 Edmund Halley notices that comets seen in 1531, 1607 and 1682 followed similar tracks; he proposes that they were the same comet and that it will appear again in 1758. Isaac Newton, now 62, is knighted. The English engineer Thomas Newcomen invents an improved steam engine, preparing the way for the Industrial Revolution. *5 May*: the Holy Roman Emperor Leopold I dies, aged 54, after reigning for 47 years and is succeeded by his 26-year-old son Josef I. *24 Sep*: Stanislas is crowned King of Poland, replacing the deposed Augustus II and concluding an alliance with Sweden. *14 Oct*: Charles Archduke of Austria lands in Catalonia; English troops help him to take Barcelona.

   John Vanbrugh and Nicholas Hawksmoor: Blenheim Palace

   John Vanbrugh: *The Confederacy*
     Richard Steele: *The Tender Husband*
     Nicholas Rowe: *Ulysses*
     Prosper Jolyot: *Idoménée*
   Handel: *Almira*

1706   *23 May*: Battle of Ramillies: Marlborough defeats a French army under Villeroi. The cities of Brussels, Antwerp, Ghent and Ostend quickly capitulate to Marlborough's onslaught. British troops raise a French siege of Barcelona, enabling a Portuguese force to install the Austrian Archduke Charles as King in Madrid. *7 Sep*: Prince Eugene of Savoy defeats a French army at Turin; Lombardy submits to Eugene, the French are driven out of Italy and Charles III is proclaimed King of Spain in Milan. *24 Sep*: Frederick Augustus, Elector of Saxony, abdicates the Polish throne, recognizing Stanislas as King of Poland. *Oct*: Philip V of Spain drives Charles III and his supporters out of Madrid. *9 Dec*: Pedro II of Portugal dies, aged 58, and is succeeded by his 17-year-old João V.

   George Farquhar: *The Recruiting Officer*
     John Vanbrugh: *The Mistake*

1707   In Japan, the volcano Fujiyama erupts for the last time (to date). In London, Fortnum and Mason's opens in Piccadilly. *3 Mar*: the Mogul Emperor Aurangzeb dies, aged 88, while on campaign against the Marathas after reigning for 49 years. He has established dictatorial control over the whole of northern and central India, persecuting Sikhs and Hindus; after his death, the Empire will quickly disintegrate. *25 Apr*: Battle of Almanza: a French army under the Duke of Berwick defeats a Portuguese army; Philip V has hired the illegitimate son of ex-King James II of England to lead a mercenary army against the Portuguese. *1 May*: the United Kingdom is created.

🏛 J. B. Fischer von Erlach: Kollegienkirche, Salzburg (completed)

📖 George Farquhar: *The Beaux' Stratagem*
Isaac Watts: *Hymns and Spiritual Songs*
Alain-Rene Lesage: *Crispin, rival de son Maître*
Prosper Jolyot: *Atrée et Tysée*

🎼 Handel: *Rodrigo*; *Nero*
Emanuele d'Astroga: *Stabat Mater*

1708 An alchemist attempting to make gold at Meissen near Dresden in Saxony discovers a way of making white porcelain. The 23-year-old German organist and composer Johann Sebastian Bach becomes Court Organist at Weimar. In 1705, Bach travelled to Lübeck (walking 640km/400 miles) to hear Buxtehude's *Abendmusiken*; Buxtehude (who died, aged 70, two years ago) had a great influence on Bach. In England, the United East India Company is formed by merging two rival companies and quickly becomes the most important European power on the coasts of India. *Jul*: Bruges and Ghent renew their allegiance to France. *11 Jul*: Marlborough defeats the French at the Battle of Oudenarde with help from Prince Eugene of Savoy. *Aug*: Marlborough lays siege to Lille. *Nov*: The tenth Sikh guru Govind Singh is assassinated, apparently on the orders of the new Mogul Emperor Bahadur Shah. *Dec*: Lille capitulates to the Duke of Marlborough's army.

🖼 Antoine Watteau: The Departing Regiment:

📖 Ebenezer Cook: *The Sot Weed Factor*, or *A Voyage to Maryland*
Prosper Jolyot: *Electre*
Joseph Addison: *The Present State of the War*

1709 Kandahar rebels against Persian overlordship as Shah Hussein imposes Shiite fundamentalism on all the Sunnis in his lands; the Ghilzai Chief Mir Vais leads an Afghan revolt. Black Death kills 300,000 people in Prussia. Famine strikes Europe as frost kills crops and hens as far south as the Mediterranean. There are food riots in France. For two months, starting on Twelfth

Night, there is continuous frost in France; the Seine is frozen. British colonies in the West Indies are importing slaves at a rate of 20,000 a year. Almost 7 million African slaves will be taken across the Atlantic to work in the New World during the 18th century. The Industrial Revolution begins in England with the discovery that iron-smelting can be fuelled with coke instead of charcoal; Abraham Darby's breakthrough brings an immediate surge in the demand for coal. *Jan*: the Japanese Shogun Sunayoshi dies, aged 62, and is succeeded by his cousin Ienobu, who releases nearly 9,000 people imprisoned by Sunayoshi for killing animals or eating fish or birds. *8 Jul*: Battle of Poltava: Peter the Great breaks the power of Sweden, forcing Charles XII to take refuge in Anatolia. The Elector of Saxony renews his claim to the Polish crown, deposes Stanislas and assumes the Polish throne which he occupies until *1733. 11 Sep*: Battle of Malplaquet: Marlborough is accused of excessive brutality as 20,000 troops are massacred. *7 Dec*: the painter Meindert Hobbema dies in Amsterdam, aged 71.

 📖 Hermann Boerhaave: *Aphorismi de Cognoscendis et Curandis Morbis*
  Colley Cibber: *The Rival Fools*
  William Dampier: *A New Voyage Round the World*
 🎵 Handel: *Agrippina*
  Emanuele d'Astroga: *Dafni*

1710 Colonel Schuyler of the New York colony takes five Iroquois chiefs to England to show them to Queen Anne and impress them with Britain's power. An English copyright law will be the basis of all future copyright law.

 ✍ Thomas Archer: Birmingham Cathedral
  Christopher Wren: St. Paul's Cathedral (exterior completed); Marlborough House, Westminster
  John Vanbrugh: Castle Howard, Yorkshire (completed)
  Baldassare Longhena: Palazzo Ca'Pesaro, Venice (completed)

 📖 George Berkeley: *Treatise concerning the Principles of Human Knowledge*
  Alain-Rene Lesage: *Tuscaret*

1711 The Black Death kills 300,000 in Austria. Rio de Janeiro is sacked by French troops as Louis XIV fights Britain's Portuguese allies. Afghanistan gains independence after Shah Hussein of Persia sends 25,000 soldiers to suppress the Afghan rising at Kandahar. The Afghans under Mir Vais succeed in beating off the Persian assault against impossible odds; they kill the Persian General Khusrus Khan and fewer than 1,000 Persians escape. *17 Apr*: the Holy Roman Emperor Josef I dies, aged 32, of smallpox and is succeeded by his 26-year-old brother Charles VI. *1 May*: the new Emperor agrees to redress Hungarian grievances; the patriot leader Francis Rakoczi takes refuge in Turkey. *2 Jul*: Peter the Great is forced to sign the Treaty of Pruth when confronted by superior Ottoman forces; he returns Azov to the Turks and Charles XII is allowed to return to Stockholm. *Aug*: British troops attack French Canada aided by 1,500 troops picked up at Boston, but the invasion is halted before it starts by the French, who succeed in sinking 10 ships as they sail into the St. Lawrence. The British give up the idea of invading Canada. *Dec*: Queen Anne of the United Kingdom dismisses the Duke of Marlborough, replacing him with the Duke of Ormonde as Commander-in-Chief of British forces.

    Thomas Archer: Church of St. John, Smith Square, London

    Steele and Addison: *The Spectator* (first issue)
    Alexander Pope: *Essay on Criticism*
    Prosper Jolyot: *Rhadamisthus and Zenobia*
    Handel: *Rinaldo*

1712 French missionary Père d'Entrecolles sends home the first detailed description of the Chinese method of making porcelain. Christopher Hussey, the Nantucket whaling captain, is the first to harpoon a sperm whale from an open boat since Phoenician times; the kill marks the start of a new era in whaling. The Scottish clan Chief Rob Roy is evicted for debt and declared an outlaw; Rob Roy supports himself by raiding the Duke of Montrose's property. Osei Tutu, the founder and King of the Ashanti kingdom in West Africa, is killed in an ambush. The Japanese Shogun Ienobu dies, aged 50, and is succeeded by his three-year-old son Ietsugu. Russian Tsarevich Alexius Petrovich infuriates his father Peter the Great by firing a pistol into his own right hand; Peter has ordered him to do technical drawing and the youth defies him. Bernese forces are victorious at Villmergen in *Jul*, as a second Swiss War between Catholics and Protestants breaks out.

    ✏ J. B. Fischer von Erlach: Trautson Palace, Vienna (completed)

    📕 John Arbuthnot: *The History of John Bull*

1713   Louis XIV is given a coffee bush which is to be the ancestor of all the New World coffee plantations; it is stolen later from the King and taken to Martinique. John Woodward, a London doctor, receives a letter from Emanuel Timoni, a doctor in Constantinople, telling him how to prevent smallpox by inoculation; Timoni describes the method used by a Greek doctor, Giacomo Pylarini, which is the basis of many later inoculation techniques. France turns its fur-trading posts on Hudson Bay over to the Hudson's Bay Company, which now controls the whole region. The Scots-American Andrew Robinson builds the world's first schooner at Gloucester, Massachusetts; other New Englanders soon imitate it and fleets of schooners fish the Grand Banks. *1 Feb*: Ottoman soldiers attack Charles XII in his camp at Bender, Moldavia, taking him prisoner. *25 Feb*: Frederick I, the first King of Prussia, dies, aged 55, and is succeeded by his 24-year-old son Friedrich Wilhelm I. *11 Apr*: Treaty of Utrecht, ending the war of the Spanish Succession. Louis XIV agrees not to unite France and Spain under one crown, recognizes the Protestant succession in Britain, and agrees to fill up Dunkirk Harbour. Gibraltar, Minorca and Newfoundland are ceded to Britain.

    ✏ J. B. Fischer von Erlach: Clam Gallas Palace, Prague (completed)

    📕 Alexander Pope: *Windsor Forest*
        Joseph Addison: *Cato*
    ♬ Handel: *Te Deum*; *Jubilate*

1714   In London, a new Board of Longitude offers a prize of £20,000 to anyone who can devise a means of determining a ship's position to within 30 nautical miles after a six-week voyage. John Woodward publishes the Timoni account of smallpox inoculation. Charles XII, released by the Turks, returns to Stockholm, but the Great Northern War continues. *6 Mar*: Treaty of Rastatt, ending the war between Spain and Austria. *1 Aug*: Queen Anne of Britain dies, aged 48, and is succeeded by Prince George of Hanover, a grandson of James I who speaks no English.

🖎 James Gibbs: Church of St. Mary-le-Strand, London

📖 Bernard Mandeville: *The Fable of the Bees*
 Alexander Pope: *The Rape of the Lock*
 Nicholas Rowe: *The Tragedy of Jane Shore*
🎜 Johann Sebastian Bach: *Ich hatte viel Bekummernis* (cantata)

1715 The Japanese become alarmed at the amount of copper that has been exported by Chinese and Dutch traders and puts limits on future exports. Mir Vais, the Ghilzai Chief of Kandahar, dies and is succeeded by his 18-year-old son Mir Mahmoud; Mahmoud's uncle Abdullah seizes power with the intention of making peace with Persia, assassinates Mahmoud and has himself proclaimed ruler of Kandahar. The French take Mauritius from the Dutch. *1 Sep*: Louis XIV dies, aged 76, at St. Germain-en-Laye after reigning for 72 years. He is succeeded by his five-year-old great-grandson Louis XV with the Duc d'Orléans as Regent. The priest André de Fleury, now 62, is the new King's tutor and will hold great influence over him until his death in *1743*. Louis XIV's death weakens the position of the Jacobite pretender to the British throne, James Edward Stuart; Scottish nobles raise a rebellion on his behalf, but the Lowlands remain loyal to George I. *13 Nov*: Battle of Sheriffmuir: the Jacobites are defeated (the outlaw Rob Roy loots the corpses of both sides). *22 Dec*: The pretender lands near Peterhead to rally support.

📖 Alexander Pope: *The Temple of Fame*
 Nicholas Rowe: *Lady Jane Grey*
 Brook Taylor: *Methodus Incrementorum Directa et Inversa*

Monzaemon Chikamatsu: *Kokusenya Gassen*

🎜 Handel: *Water Music Suite No 1*

1716 The Japanese Shogun Ietsugu dies, aged seven, and is succeeded by Yoshimune, who will allow the Dutch to bring western books into Japan and build irrigation projects to aid agriculture. The Japanese painter Korin Ogata dies, aged 58. The Chinese ban Christian religious teaching. In Scotland, the Duke of Argyll's royalist troops disperse the Jacobite rebels. *5 Feb:* James Stuart flees to France. The Jacobite leaders are executed. *5 Aug:* Prince Eugene of Savoy defeats an Ottoman army at Peterwardein and Charles VI, the Holy Roman Emperor, enters the war against the Ottoman Turks. *26 Aug:* Peter the Great writes to his son Alexius, who wants to become a monk, telling him to return home at once if he wants to remain heir to the throne. Alexius puts himself in the protection of Emperor Charles VI and is sent to the Castle of San Elmo at Naples.

✏ Nicholas Hawksmoor: Church of St. Mary Woolnoth, London

🖎 Antoine Watteau: La Leçon d'amour

🎜 Antonio Vivaldi: *Judithea*

Handel: *Brockes Passion*

1717 The Spanish create the viceroyalty of New Granada with its seat of power at Bogota; this reduces the viceroyalty of Peru to more manageable size. Prussia makes school attendance compulsory. *4 Jan:* the Triple Alliance (Britain, France, Dutch Republic) forces the Old Pretender, James Stuart, to leave France. *5 Jun:* Freemasonry is established in London: the first Grand Lodge is at the Goose and Gridiron Tavern in Covent Garden.

✏ John Gibbs: Church of St. Mary-le-Strand, London (completed)

Schonbrunn Palace, Vienna (completed)

🖎 James Thornhill: Scenes from the Life of St. Paul, Dome of St. Paul's

Antoine Watteau: Embarkation for the Isle of Cythera

📖 Prosper Jolyot: *Electre*

1718 The pirate Edward Teach, known as Blackbeard, is killed in a fight in North Carolina without revealing where he has buried his treasure. Yale University is named after benefactor Elihu Yale. The first English bank notes are issued. New Orleans is founded near the mouth of the Mississippi. *18 Feb*: Peter the Great has the Tsarevich Alexius brought back to Russia and forced to sign a 'confession' implicating his friends, who are then executed. *30 May*: William Penn dies, aged 73. *19 Jun*: The Tsarevich is flogged (25 strokes) at Peter the Great's orders. *24 Jun*: the Tsarevich is given 15 more strokes on being found guilty by the senate of 'imagining' rebellion. *26 Jun*: the Tsarevich dies in the citadel guardhouse at St. Petersburg, aged 28. *Jul*: Philip V of Spain sends troops into Sicily. *21 Jul*: Treaty of Passarowitz, ending the war between Constantinople and Venice. *2 Aug*: the Quadruple Alliance (Holy Roman Emperor, France, Britain: Holland to join next year) is formed to stop Spain upsetting the peace arranged in *1714*. *11 Dec*: Charles XII of Sweden is shot in the head as he looks over a trench parapet close to the fortress of Fredriksten in Norway. He is succeeded by his 30-year-old sister Ulrika, who brings the Great Northern War to an end.

 ☊ Antoine Watteau: Parc Fête
  Godfrey Kneller: The Duke of Norfolk
 📔 Lady Wortley Montagu: *Inoculation Against Smallpox*
  Matthew Prior: *Alma; Solomon* (Prior negotiated the Peace of Utrecht)
  Colley Cibber: *The Non-Juror*
  Voltaire (François Arouet) *Oedipe*

1719 The Principality of Liechtenstein is created by the Holy Roman Emperor Charles VI: Vaduz and Schellenburg are united to make a 155 sq.km/60 square mile state under Count Hans von Liechtenstein, who has bought the territory and its castle. Herat rebels against Persia's imposition of Shiite Islam, declaring independence. A Persian army sent by Shah Hussein to suppress the rising defeats an Uzbek force before engaging Herat's Afghan army. Confusion is caused within the Persian army as Persian artillery hits Persian cavalry; the Afghans exploit the situation, make a decisive charge, destroy a third of the Persian army and capture its artillery.

📖 Daniel Defoe: *Robinson Crusoe*
   Colley Cibber: *Love in a Riddle*
🎵 Handel: *Acis and Galatea*
   Johann Fux: *Gesu Cristo negato da Pietro*

1720 The Belgian composer Jean Faber uses the clarinet for the first time in a serious piece of music. The Japanese Shogun Yoshimune allows western books into Japan, banning only religious books. The last major epidemic of the Black Death in western Europe strikes Marseilles. Ulrika, Queen of Sweden, abdicates in favour of her husband Frederick of Hesse who reigns as Frederick I, but the new constitution removes much of the Swedish monarchy's power. *Jan*: in England the bursting of the 'South Sea Bubble' causes widespread financial loss and a loss of confidence in overseas investment generally. In France a similar speculation, John Law's Mississippi Company, also collapses, ruining its investors. The French playwright Pierre Marivaux is among those financially ruined.

🏛 Colen Campbell: Stourhead, Wiltshire
   John Vanbrugh: Seaton Delaval (begun); Blenheim Palace (completed)
🎨 Giambattista Tiepolo: Martyrdom of St. Bartholomew
📖 Pierre Marivaux: *Arlequin poli par l'amour*
   Monzaemon Chikamatsu: *The Love Suicides at Amijima*
   Alexander Pope: *Iliad* (verse translation); *Haman and Mordecai*
   Daniel Defoe: *Captain Singleton*
🎵 Handel: *Chandos Anthems*; *Music for Haman and Mordecai* (masque)

1721 The Chinese suppress a revolt in Taiwan. The Japanese Shogun Yoshimune bans extravagances, such as sweets and expensive clothes, in an austerity drive. A regular postal service begins between New England and London. During a smallpox epidemic in London, Lady Mary Wortley Montague has her five-year-old daughter inoculated and onlooking physicians are impressed; George I has two of his grandchildren inoculated. The British Chancellor of the Exchequer John Aislabie is imprisoned on fraud charges relating to last year's South Sea Bubble. *Jun*: smallpox reaches Boston by way of the West Indies. Cotton Mather recommends inoculation, but Zabdiel Boylston is the only doctor to take the advice; after successfully inoculating his 13-year-old son he goes on to inoculate over 240 colonists. Six of those inoculated die and Boylston narrowly escapes being lynched. *18 Jul*: the painter Jean Watteau dies of tuberculosis at Nogent-sur-Marne, aged 36. *30 Aug*: Treaty of Nystadt, giving Russia access to the West: Peter the Great obtains Swedish territory that includes Estonia and is proclaimed Emperor of All the Russias.

✏ Orders of Philip V of Spain: Palace of La Granja, above Segovia

📕 Baron de Montesquieu: *Lettres Persanes*

Colley Cibber: *The Refusal, or The Ladies' Philosophy*

Monzaemon Chikamatsu: *The Love Suicides at Sonezaki*

♫ Johann Sebastian Bach: *Brandenburg Concerti*

1722 Jacob Roggeveen, the Dutch explorer, discovers Easter Island. The island is called Rapa Nui by the native Polynesian people, who have cut volcanic rock to create statues up to 11 metres/36 feet tall. The Manchu Emperor Kang Cixi dies in China, aged 68, after reigning for 53 years; he has added Hunan, Gansu and Anhui provinces to the Chinese Empire. In North America, the Iroquois sign an undertaking not to cross the Potomac River or the Blue Ridge without Virginia Governor Alexander Spotswood's permission. Mir Mahmoud of Kandahar conquers Afghanistan and invades Persia, defeating a large Persian army at the Battle of Gulnabad. *12 Oct*: Mir Mahmoud takes Isfahan after a seven-month siege that has starved 80,000 to death. The Shah of Persia, Hussein, abdicates in favour of his son Tahmasp II, who escapes to Mazandaran and tries to organize resistance but without real power; although technically succeeded, Tahmasp had no power, so his position was usurped. Mir Mahmoud makes himself Shah and begins a reign of terror. Peter the Great invades Persia under the pretence of wanting to save the Shahs from Afghan tyranny. He prepares to sweep through the Caucasus and capture the Bosporus and Dardanelles, but the campaign is aborted by an outbreak of ergotism. His horses eat infected rye and his men eat bread made from infected rye: madness and death follow, and the plan has to be abann,donedThe Ottoman Sultan Ahmed III more successfully exploits Persia's weakness, invading Shirwan.

   ✍ Orders of Peter the Great: Palace of Petrodvorets, St. Petersburg

      Matthaus Poppelmann: The Zwinger, Dresden

   📖 Daniel Defoe: *The Adventures and Misadventures of Moll Flanders*

      Pierre de Marivaux: *La Double Inconstance*

      Richard Steele: *The Conscious Lovers*

      Jen Rameau: *Traité de l'harmonie*

      René de Réaumur: *L'Art de Covertier le fer forge en acier* (first technical treatise on steelmaking)

1723 King Agaja of the Dahomey kingdom (Benin) invades the kingdom of Allada. An American coffee industry has its beginnings; French naval officer Gabriel de Cheu breaks into the Jardin Royale at night, steals a seedling and plants it on the island of Martinique. White Kennett, son of the Bishop of Peterborough, writes that the condom can emancipate young English women. In Virginia, Alexander Spotswood resigns his governorship to establish an iron foundry using coal as a fuel. Baku surrenders to the Russian army. Tiflis surrenders to the Ottoman army. Kazbin repels the Afghan invaders, but when Shah Mahmoud arrives he invites the city's noblemen to dinner and has them all murdered; he then gives orders to kill every Persian who has served Shah Hussein and the killing goes on for a fortnight. *25 Feb*: Sir Christopher Wren, the architect, dies aged 90. *5 Apr*: the Austrian architect J. B. Fischer von Erlach dies, aged 66. *10 Oct*: Treaty of Charlottenburg between Britain and Prussia, agreeing royal marriages. *7 Nov*: the painter Kneller dies.

   ✍ J. B. Fischer von Erlach: Kariskirche, Hofburg, Imperial Library in Vienna (work completed by Erlach's brother Joseph Emanuel)

🎶 George Frederick Handel: *Ottone*
Johann Sebastian Bach: *St. John Passion*
Attilo Ariosti: *Coriolano*
Johann Fux: *Costanza e fortezza*

1724 Constantinople and Moscow agree a treaty for the dismemberment of Persia. In South Carolina, black slaves now outnumber white colonists by two to one. The Japanese Ukiyo-ye painter Kiyonobu Torii dies, aged 60.

🏛 Belvedere Palace, Vienna (completed)
📖 Bernard de Fontenelle: *The Origin of Myths*
Colley Cibber: *Caesar in Aegypt*

1725 An Ottoman army takes Tabriz after a siege in which the Turks have lost 20,000 men; Shah Mahmoud has 39 Persian princes executed, the first dies at the Shah's own hands. The surviving Persian nobles elect a nephew of Mir Vais to succeed Mahmoud, who is evidently insane. The new Shah Ashraf kills potential rivals, confiscates their fortunes and is thought to be responsible for ordering the death of Shah Mahmoud. *28 Jan*: Peter the Great Tsar of Russia dies, aged 52, after reigning for 42 years; his widow continues to reign as Catharine I.

🏛 Lord Burleigh and William Kent: Chiswick House, London
The Spanish Steps, Rome
📖 Johann Fux: *Gradus ad Parnassum* (standard textbook on counterpoint)
🎶 George Frederick Handel: *Giulio Cesare*; *Tamerlano*
Johann Sebastian Bach: *Easter Oratorio*
Antonio Vivaldi: *The Four Seasons*

1726 The city of Montevideo is founded at the mouth of the River Plate by Spanish colonists. In France, Bishop André de Fleury is made a Cardinal. *12 Jul*: De Fleury becomes effective Prime Minister of France; he presides over a period of peace, economic growth and religious revivalism.

🏛 James Gibbs: Church of St. Martins in the Fields, London.
🎨 William Hogarth: Illustrations for Samuel Butler's *Hudibras*
📖 Jonathan Swift: *Travels into Several Remote Nations*

of the World by 'English sea-captain Lemuel Gulliver'
('Gulliver's Travels')

🎼 George Frederick Handel: *Alessandro*

1727 Coffee is planted for the first time in Brazil. The border
between China and Russia is fixed by the Kiakhta
Treaty. An Ottoman army advances on Isfahan. Shah
Ashraf of Persia has an army only one-third the size, but
manages by using field guns to kill 12,000 Turks; a treaty
is then concluded acknowledging the Sultan as Caliph
and the Shah himself is confirmed as Shah of Perisia.
Tahmasp II, meanwhile, still holds nominal court at
Farahabad, where the brigand Nadir Kuli joins him.
The German chemist J. H. Schulze takes a step towards
photography, using silver nitrate and chalk under sten-
cils to create a light-produced image. House rats overrun
the city of Astrakhan and then, shortly afterwards, towns
in Germany. *16 May*: Catharine I of Russia dies, aged
44, and is succeeded by her son Peter. *11 Jun*: George I
dies of apoplexy on his way to Hanover, in the room
where he was born at Osnabruck castle; he was 67 and is
succeeded by his 44-year-old son George II.

🏛 Johann von Hildenbrandt: Mirabell Palace, Salzburg (completed)

📖 Stephen Hales: *Vegetable Staticks* (plant physiology)

🎼 George Frederick Handel: *Zadok the Priest; Scipione*

1728 Handel is appointed Co-director of the King's Theatre,
Covent Garden, London. The English astronomer
James Bradley discovers the aberration of light from
stars. John Harrison, an English carpenter, draws a
design for a marine timekeeper that will greatly improve navigation. The Danish explorer Vitus Bering
discovers the Bering Strait separating Asia from North
America.

🎨 Jean Chardin: The Skate; The Rain

📖 Ephraim Chambers: *Cyclopaedia*

Abbé Prevost: *Memoires et aventures d'un homme de
qualité*

Alexander Pope: *The Dunciad*

Pierre de Marivaux: *Le Triomphe de Plutus*

Henry Fielding: *Love in Several Masques*

🎼 John Pepusch and John Gay: *The Beggar's Opera*

George Frederick Handel: *Tolomeo, Re di Egitto; Riccardo Primo*

1729 Diamonds found at Tejuco in Brazil are confirmed in Lisbon, starting a diamond rush to Tejuco, soon to be renamed Diamantina. *Nov:* the 26-year-old John Wesley joins his brother Charles, a 22-year-old student at Oxford. They hold Holy Club meetings each Sunday; these are the beginnings of the Methodist movement. *9 Nov:* Treaty of Seville, ending hostilities between Spain and the Anglo-French alliance; Britain is to retain Gibraltar. *28 Nov:* in Louisiana, Natchez Indians attack and kill over 200 white settlers; the colonists had insisted that the Natchez give up their burial ground.

John Vanbrugh: Seaton Delaval, Northumberland (completed)

Jonathan Swift: *A Modest Proposal*

Johann Sebastian Bach: *St. Matthew Passion*

1730 In England, Lord Townshend finds that he can keep livestock through the winter by feeding them turnips, removing the need to slaughter most of them each autumn and allowing the development of larger cattle. Persian Shah Ashraf is defeated near Shiraz, after which he is murdered by some of his followers; he is succeeded by Tahmasp II, who is little more than a puppet for the brigand Nadir Kuli. *30 Jan:* Tsar Peter II of Russia dies of smallpox, aged 14. *26 Feb:* Peter's cousin Anna enters Moscow and organizes a coup. *8 Mar:* Anna overthrows the Russian Privy Council, summons her lover Ernst Biron and makes him Grand Chamberlain. *17 Sep:* the Ottoman Grand Vizier is strangled when the Janissaries revolt, forcing the Sultan Ahmed III to abdicate, aged 57. *12 Oct:* Frederick IV of Denmark dies, aged 59, at Odense and is succeeded by his 31-year-old son Christian VI. *18 Oct:* the new Ottoman Sultan Mahmud I ascends the throne.

The Serpentine Lake, London

Nicolas Lancret: The Dancer La Camargo
Canaletto (Giovanni Canal): The Symbolic Marriage of Venice to the Adriatic

Pierre de Marivaux: *Le jeu de l'amour et du Hasard*

Henry Fielding: *The Tragedy of Tragedies, or Tom Thumb*

Voltaire: *Brutus*

♫ *Gaudeamus Igitur* (German drinking song first published)

1731 Shah Tahmasp of Persia moves to repel the Ottoman invaders, but is defeated with heavy losses at Arijan and makes a peace treaty that cedes large areas to the Ottoman Empire. Nadir Kuli, now his brother-in-law, denounces the treaty, seizes Tahmasp and imprisons him at Khorasan, setting up his infant son Abbas III on the throne while effectively ruling himself. John Hadley, the English mathematician, invents the reflecting quadrant, which enables latitude to be determined by day or night. In Philadelphia, Benjamin Franklin founds the first circulating library in North America. In Europe, porcelain factories multiply as demand for china cups and plates increases.

⚏ No 10 Downing Street, London

◷ William Hogarth: A Harlot's Progress

⬚ George Lillo: *The London Merchant*

Abbé Prévost: *Histoire du Chevalier des Grieux et de Manon Lescaut*

♫ George Frederick Handel: *Poro*

1732 In London, the average bullock sold at Smithfield cattle market weighs 250 kg/550 lb, compared with 168 kg/370 lb only 20 years ago. Famine strikes Japan; heavy rain and a swarm of grasshoppers destroy crops, causing over 12,000 deaths from starvation. The Swedish botanist Carl von Linné travels through Scandinavia studying plant life. Prussia introduces compulsory military service for males over 18, creating the fourth largest army in Europe (after France, Austria and Russia).

⚏ Edward Shepherd: First Covent Garden Theatre (completed)

Germain Boffrand: Hotel de Soubise, Paris

◷ Jean Chardin: Kitchen Table with Shoulder of Mutton

Niccola Salvi: Fontana di Trevi (sculpture)

⬚ *Philadelphia Zeitung* (first foreign-language newspaper in the British colonies)

Voltaire: *Zaire*
Henry Fielding: *The Debauchees*

George Frederick Handel: *Esther* (first English oratorio)

George Frederick Handel and John Gay: *Acis and Galatea*

1733 The Spanish Plate Fleet, loaded with gold and silver from South America, is wrecked on the Florida Keys. Nadir Kuli's Persian army besieges Baghdad but is itself surrounded at Kirkuk; the army disperses in disorder, retreating to Hamadan. The British colony of Savannah, Georgia, is founded by James Oglethorpe who names this, the last of the 13 British colonies, after George II. The initial colony consists of 120 settlers. In England John Kay the weaver invents the flying shuttle, revolutionizing the textile industry. *1 Feb*: Augustus II of Poland dies, aged 62, precipitating the War of the Polish Succession. Austria and Russia demand the election of Augustus's only legitimate son, the 36-year-old Elector of Saxony, Frederick Augustus; France persuades the Polish nobles to restore Stanislas Leszczynski. Russia sends a large army to invade Poland, forcing Stanislas to flee to Danzig. *10 Oct*: the French declare war on the Holy Roman Empire. The Russians besiege Danzig; the French send an expeditionary force to relieve Danzig and rescue Stanislas.

William Hogarth: Southwark Fair
Stephen Hales: *Haemostaticks* (findings on blood circulation)

Alexander Pope: *Essay on Man*
Jethro Tull: *The New Horse-Hoeing Husbandry*
Voltaire: *La Mort de César*
Pierre de Marivaux: *L'Heureux stratagème*
Johann Sebastian Bach: *Mass in B minor*
Giovanni Pergolesi: *La Serva Padrone*
Jean Rameau: *Hippolyte et Aricie*
Thomas Arne: *Rosamund*

1734 An English sailor suffering from scurvy is marooned on Greenland by his shipmates because the disease is thought to be infectious. He cures himself by eating scurvy grass and is picked up by a passing ship. Schwenkenfelders from Silesia emigrate to North America, landing in Delaware; they introduce the autumn crocus (*Crocus saliva*, which yields spice and the dye saffron) to North America. *2 Jun*: Danzig falls to the Russians after an eight-month siege; Stanislas eludes capture and escapes to Prussia.

✍ Nicholas Hawksmoor: All Souls College, Oxford (completed)

📖 Voltaire: *Lettres anglaises ou philosophiques* (praises the British constitution)
Baron Montesquieu: *Considerations sur les causes de la Grandeur des Romains et leur Décadence*
Henry Fielding: *Don Quixote in England*

1735 English distillers are producing 5.4 million gallons of gin per year – a gallon for every man, woman and child in the country. Auhtorities in the colony of Georgia ban the importing of rum and slaves. John and Charles Wesley embark for Georgia in *Oct*. The War of the Polish Succession ends *5 Oct* with the Treaty of Vienna, legitimizing the Elector of Saxony as Polish King (Frederick Augustus II). The Russians release the last of Peter the Great's Persian acquisitions, joining Nadir Kuli of Persia in an alliance against the Ottoman Turks. Nadir Kuli defeats the Turks at Baghavand and takes Tiflis.

✑ William Hogarth: The Rake's Progress (engravings published)
Nicolas Lancret: The Pleasure Party

📖 Alain Lesage: *Gil Blas*

🎼 Giovanni Pergolesi: *Olimpiade*
George Frederick Handel: *Ariodante*; *Alcina*
Jean Rameau: *Les Indes galantes*

1736 An English surgeon, Claudius Aymand, undertakes the first recorded successful appendecctomy. John Harrison presents his ship's chronometer to the Board of Longitude in London; it is accurate to within one-tenth of a second per day and wins the Board's prize. Pope Clement XII condemns Freemasonry. In China, Qian Long becomes Emperor at the age of 25; during his long reign Chinese control will extend throughout central Asia. Shah Abbas III of Persia dies, aged six, and is succeeded by the Afghan Nadir Kuli as Nadir Shah. Moscow declares war on Constantinople, sending an army into Ottoman lands on the north shore of the Black Sea; the Russians have to retreat to the Ukraine after losing many men. *17 Jan*: the German architect Matthaus Poppelman dies, aged 74.

- William Hogarth: The Good Samaritan
- Leonard Euler: *Mechanica sive motus analytice exposita* (first systematic textbook on mechanics)
- Voltaire: *Les Americains*
- Thomas Arne: *Tom Thumb the Great*
- George Frederick Handel: *Atalanta*
- Giuseppe Bonno: *Trajano*
- Joseph Boismortier: *Les Voyages de l'Amour*

1737 Benjamin Franklin creates the Philadelphia police force, the first city-paid force. In Britain a Licensing Act requires all plays to be submitted to the Lord Chamberlain for censorship. The last Medici Duke of Tuscany, Gastone de' Medici, dies, aged 66, leaving the ducal throne vacant. *Jan*: Vienna declares war on Constantinople to aid Russia in a renewal of the war of the Polish Succession. *11 Oct*: an earthquake kills 300,000 in Calcutta.

- James Gibbs: Radcliffe Camera, Oxford
- Carolus Linnaeus: *Genera Plantarum* (system of taxonomy)
- Pierre Marivaux: *Les Fausses Confidences*
- Henry Fielding: *Tumbledown Dick*
- Jean Rameau: *Castor and Pollux*

1738 The excavation of Herculaneum, the Roman city buried under mud following the eruption of Mount Vesuvius in *AD 79*, begins. John and Charles Wesley, now back in England, form the Methodist Society. *13 Nov*: Treaty of Vienna ratified; Stanislas receives Lorraine in exchange for renouncing the Polish throne.

- Jean Chardin: La Gouvernante
- Louis-Francois Roubiliac: George Frederick Handel (bust)
- Pierre de Maupertuis: *Sur la figure de la terre* (confirms Newton's view that the earth is a spheroid slightly flattened at the poles)

Daniel Bernoulli: *Hydrodynamics* (early version of kinetic theory of gases)

Carolus Linnaeus: *Critica Botanica*

1739 French explorers Pierre and Paul Mallet sight the Rocky Mountains for the first time. Potato crops fail in Ireland. John Wesley begins preaching at Bristol. *20 Mar*: Nadir Shah of Persia defeats the Moghal Emperor's huge army near Karnal and takes Delhi. The collapse of the Moghal Empire creates a major power vaccuum in India; Afghans invade from the north-west, Marathas invade from the west and local feudal lords carve out small independent states, warring with one another. The chaos opens the way for the British to take over the subcontinent. During the sack of Delhi, Nadir Shah seizes the Koh-i-noor diamond. *7 Apr*: the highwayman Dick Turpin is hanged for horse-stealing at York. *18 Sep*: Treaty of Belgrade. Holy Roman Emperor Charles VI deserts Russia and makes peace with the Ottoman Empire. Austria gives up Belgrade; Russia is to retain Azov but undertakes not to keep a Black Sea fleet.

🏛 George Dance the Elder: Mansion House, London

🎨 François Boucher: Le Dejeuner

📖 David Hume: *Treatise on Human Nature*

Carlo Goldoni: *L'uomo di Mondo*

🎼 George Frederick Handel: *Saul; Ode for St. Cecilia's Day*

Jean Rameau: *Les Fêtes d'Herbe*

1740 The Swiss naturalist Abraham Trembley discovers the hydra, a freshwater polyp. The unrestricted sale of gin reaches its peak in England, creating fears that drunkenness will cause the country's social fabric to disintegrate. Admiral Vernon dilutes the navy's rum ration; it becomes known as 'grog', Vernon's nickname. In North America a network of post roads now joins all the Eastern Seaboard colonies; packet boats operate a regular scheduled service linking the main colonial ports. At Sheffield, Benjamin Huntsman rediscovers the crucible method of manufacturing steel, a method in use 2,000 years ago but since lost. *31 May*: Friedrich Wilhelm I of Prussia dies, aged 51, after making his country into a major military power with a standing army of 83,000; he is succeeded by his 28-year-old son Frederick II, who occupies part of Silesia, starting a war with Austria. *5 Oct*: Tsarina Anna of Russia adopts an infant great-nephew as her successor, Ivan VI, naming Count Biron Regent. *17 Oct*: Tsarina Anna dies, aged 47. *20 Oct*: Holy Roman Emperor Charles VI dies, aged 55, and is succeeded by his daughter Maria Theresa as Queen of Hungary and Bohemia, but her right to succeed is contested by Saxony, Bavaria and Spain. The War of the Austrian Succession begins.

 🎨 William Hogarth: Captain Coram
 📖 Samuel Richardson: *Pamela*
  Pierre Marivaux: *L'Epreuve*
 🎼 Thomas Arne: *Rule Britannia*
  Giuseppe Bonno: *The Birth of Jove*

1741 The English Admiral Vernon leads a 100-ship armada against the Spanish citadel of Cartagena, but has to retreat to Jamaica after disease reduces the landing force of 8,000 men to only 3,500 able-bodied men. The colonial Captain Lawrence Washington is decorated for bravery in action at Cartagena; Washington returns to his plantation on the Potomac River and renames it Mount Vernon. Russian explorers set out from Siberia across the Bering Strait with the Danish navigator Vitus Bering; Bering, 61, dies of scurvy during the voyage. The 16-year-old Giovanni Casanova is expelled from the Seminary of St. Cyprian for misbehaviour. Yellow fever at Cadiz kills 10,000 people. *13 Feb*: in the British House of Commons Sir Robert Walpole uses the phrase 'balance of power' to express the British approach to foreign policy. *10 Apr*: Frederick II of Prussia defeats the Austrians at Mollwitz, later going on to capture Brieg, Neisse, Glatz and Olmutz before the British intervene with mediators. *11 Apr*: in Russia, Count Biron is found guilty of treason and sentenced to death, commuted to life banishment to Siberia. The French Ambassador plays on fears of Peter the Great's daughter Elizabeth Petrovna that she may be confined to a convent. He encourages her to stage a coup. *6 Dec*: Elizabeth goes to the barracks of the Preobrazhensky Guards and leads them to the Winter palace, seizes and banishes the

Regent Anna Leopoldovna, deposes the infant Tsar Ivan VI and claims the throne for herself.

🎨 Francois Boucher: Autumn
William Hogarth: The Enraged Musician

📖 Pierre Maupertuis: *Essai de cosmologie* (survival of the fittest) concept: 'These species which we see today are only the smallest part of those which a blind destiny produced'.)
Henry Fielding: *Shamela*

🎵 Christoph Willibald Gluck: *Artaserse*
Thomas Arne: *The Blind Beggar of Bethnal Green*

1742 Anders Celsius devises a centigrade (Celsius) scale of temperature. Benjamin Franklin invents a stove, the 'Pennsylvania fireplace', that heats a room more efficiently using a warm air principle. Coal is discovered in West Virginia. *24 Jan*: Karl Albrecht of Bavaria is elected Holy Roman Emperor Charles VII, but the War of the Austrian Succession continues. Frederick the Great's Prussian troops are struck with dysentery and he is forced to withdraw from the coalition against Austria. *11 Jun*: Treaty of Berlin, ending the Silesian War; Maria Theresa cedes upper and lower Silesia with their coalfields to Prussia. Maria Theresa forms an alliiance with Britain.

📖 Henry Fielding: *The Adventures of Joseph Andrews* (satire on Pamela)
Voltaire: *Le fanatisme, ou Mahomet le prophete*
Edmond Hoyle: *Short Treatise on Whist* (systematization that will lead to contract bridge)

🎵 George Frederick Handel: *Messiah*
Johann Sebastian Bach: *Goldberg Variations*

1743 French entrepreneur Claude Moët founds his Champagne business. The Japanese potter Kenzan dies, aged 81. In Russia there are massacres of Jews. War between Persia and the Ottoman Empire resumes. The Austrians drive the French and Bavarian troops out of Bavaria. An Allied Pragmatic Army (English, Hessian and Hanoverian troops) defeats the French at the Battle of Dettingen on *27 Jun*. Emperor Charles VII has to take refuge at Frankfurt. Nicolas Lancret, the French painter, dies in Paris, aged 53, on *14 Sep*.

📖 Jean d'Alembert: *Traité de dynamique*
Alex Clairaut: *Théorie de la Figure de la Terre*
Henry Fielding: *The History of the Life of the Late
Mr. Jonathan Wild the Great*
Voltaire: *Mérope*

1744 Lord Anson returns from his round-the-world voyage
after losing three-qaurters of his crew to scurvy. In Peru,
the volcano Cotopaxi erupts. Serson, a Scottish engineer,
pioneers the gyroscope stabilizer. Maria Theresa
launches a pogrom intended to drive Jews from Moravia
and Bohemia. *30 May*: the English poet Alexander Pope
dies, aged 56. *Aug*: Frederick II of Prussia opens a
second Silesian War by invading Saxony and Bohemia. *Sep*: The Prussian army takes Prague, then Maria
Theresa's Hapsburg army drives it back into Saxony.
France changes sides, declaring war on Britain and
Austria.

✎ Roger Morris: Inverary Castle, Scotland
Balthasar Neumann: Residenz, Würzburg (completed)

📖 John Newbery: *A Little Pretty Pocket-Book* (one of
the first children's books intended to entertain)

🎵 George Frederick Handel: *Joseph and His Brethren;
Hercules*
Johann Sebastian Bach: *The Well-Tempered Clavier,
Part 2*

1745 The Japanese Shogun Yoshimune abdicates and is
succeeded by Ieshige. The Leyden jar devised independently by Peter van Musschenbroek and Ewald von
Kleist is found to be an electrical capacitator. *20 Jan*:
the Holy Roman Emperor Charles VII dies, aged 47, at
Munich and is succeeded as Elector of Bavaria by his 17-
year-old son Maximilian. *22 Apr*: Treaty of Fussen,
ending the Second Silesian War. Franz Stefan, Maria
Theresa's husband, is elected Holy Roman Emperor
Francis I. *11 May*: Battle of Fontenoy: French forces
defeat the Pragmatic army. *4 Jun*: the Prussian army
defeats the Austrian and Saxon armies at the Battle of
Hohenfriedberg in Silesia. *25 Jul*: Prince Charles Edward Stuart lands in the Hebrides to proclaim his father
James VIII of Scotland, III of England. *2 Sep*: Jacobites

(supporters of the Young Pretender) win the Battle of Prestonpans. *30 Sep*: a Prussian army defeats the Austrians at the Battle of Soor in Bohemia. *4 Dec*: the successful Jacobite army follows Prince Charles Edward into England as far as Derby, then withdraws.

✏ Dominikus Zimmermann: Church of Die Wies, Bavaria

Johann Lucas von Hildebrandt: Schönbrunn Palace, Vienna

🎨 William Hogarth: Marriage à la Mode (series); Self-portrait

Giambattista Tiepolo: Antony and Cleopatra Frescoes, Labia Palace, Venice

📖 Pierre de Maupertuis: *Vénus physique*

Colley Cibber: *Papal Tyranny in the Reign Of King John*

♫ George Frederick Handel: *Belshazzar*

Thomas Arne: *God Save the King*

1746 *17 Jan*: Battle of Falkirk: Jacobite victory over British dragoons. *21 Feb*: Battle of Rocoux: the French under Marshal Saxe free the Netherlands from Austrian rule; French troops occupy Brussels. *16 Apr*: Battle of Culloden; British troops under the Duke of Cumberland rout the Jacobite army, ending Prince Charles Edward's attempt to restore the Stuart dynasty in Britain. *29 Jun*: Prince Charles Edward escapes to Skye disguised as a girl. *9 Jul*: Philip V of Spain dies insane at the age of 62 after reigning for 46 years and is succeeded by his son Ferdinand VI. *6 Apr*: Christian VI of Denmark dies, aged 47, and is succeeded by his 23-year-old son Frederick V. *20 Sep*: Prince Charles Edward escapes to France. *20 Oct*: the Indian city of Madras falls to a French force under Joseph Dupleix.

🎨 Joshua Reynolds: Captain John Hamilton; The Eliot Family

Canaletto: The Vegetable Market at San Giacomo di Rialto

François Boucher: The Milliner

📖 Denis Diderot: *Pensées philosophiques*

1747 Scottish naval surgeon James Lind pioneers the treatment of scurvy. Dahomey is defeated and taken over by the Oyo after 50 years of fighting. The peace that follows is beneficial to the slavers, who can now work uninterrupted by warfare. *10 Jun:* Nadir Shah of Persia is assassinated by one of his own Afghan tribesmen at Fathabad. His death leaves Persia in chaos and Afghanistan an independent state. One of Nadir's generals assumes control of Afghanistan, reigning as Ahmad Shah. *2 Jul:* Battle of Laufeld: the French under Saxe defeat an Anglo Dutch army under the Duke of Cumberland. *16 Sep:* the French overthrow the Republic of the United Provinces; William of Nassau, Prince of Orange, becomes hereditary Stadtholder.

    🏛 Hugh Walpole: Strawberry Hill, Twickenham (England)

       Georg von Knobelsdorff: Sans-Souci Palace, Potsdam

    🎨 William Hogarth: Industry and Idleness

    📖 Thomas Gray: *Ode on a Distant Prospect of Eton College*

       William Collins: *Odes*

    🎵 Johann Sebastian Bach: *Musical Offering*

       George Frederick Handel: *Judas Maccabeus* (tribute to Cumberland's Culloden victory)

1748 In America, colonists cross the Allegheny Divide. *18 Oct:* Treaty of Aix-la-Chapelle, ending the War of the Austrian Succession.

    🎨 Thomas Gainsborough: Mr. and Mrs. Robert Andrews

       William Hogarth: Calais Gate

    📖 Baron de Montesquieu: *De l'esprit des lois*

       John Fothergill: *Account of the Sore Throat Attended with Ulcers* (first detailed description of diphtheria)

       Tobias Smollett: *The Adventures of Roderick Random*

       Samuel Richardson: *Clarissa*

1749 China's population reaches 225 million. The cabinetmaker Thomas Chippendale opens a workshop that will become famous for its graceful furniture. French troops advance into the Ohio valley in America, claiming it for Louis XV.

    📖 George Leclerc, Comte de Buffon: *Histoire naturelle*

Henry St. John: *Letters on the Spirit of Patriotism*:
On the Idea of a Patriot King

Jean-Jacques Rousseau: *Discour sur les Arts et
Sciences*

Henry Fielding: *The History of Tom Jones*

George Frederick Handel: *Royal Fireworks Music*

1750 English doctor Thomas Walker discovers the Cumberland Gap through the Appalachian Mountains. Ojibway (Chippewa) Indians defeat Sioux Indians at the Battle of Kathio, gaining possession of the wild rice lands in northern Minnesota. The Iron Act passed by the British Parliament prohibits the American colonists from manufacturing iron products, while letting them exchange the pig iron for manufactured goods; the act expresses the main principle of the British colonial system, to use the colonies as a source of raw materials for the home industries, and as a market. The Iron Act goes unobserved. Famine strikes France. The population of the world reaches 750 million. *28 Jul*: the composer Johann Sebastian Bach dies, aged 65. *31 Jul*: João V of Portugal dies, aged 61, after reigning for 44 years and is succeeded by his 35-year-old son Jose Manuel. The new King of Portugal appoints the Marques de Pombal as his Chief Minister: Pombal strips the Inquisition of its power.

Westminster Bridge, London

François de Cuvilles: Residenztheater, Munich

John Cleland: *Fanny Hill, or The Memoirs of a
Woman of Pleasure*

Carlo Goldoni: *La botega de caffè*; *Il bugiardo*; *Il
teatro comica*

George Frederick Handel: *Theodora*

Johann Sebastian Bach: *The Art of Fugue*

1751 A young Virginia planter, the 19-year-old George Washington, visits Barbados with his brother Lawrence. Benjamin Franklin discovers the electrical nature of lightning through his famous kite experiment. The Japanese Ukiyo-ye painter Sukenobu Nishikawa dies aged 80. The Japanese Shogun Yoshimune dies, aged 67. *5 Apr*: Frederick I of Hesse-Cassel dies, aged 75, and is succeeded by a distant relation as Adolphus Frederick. *31 Aug*: British troops under Ro-

bert Clive seize Arcot. *22 Oct*: William IV, the Dutch
Stadtholder, dies, aged 40, and is succeeded by his three-
year-old son William (Willem) V. *5 Nov*: in India, Clive
succeeds in driving off a superior French force, for the
first time challenging France's domination of India.

   ✍ Hall of Prayer for Good Harvests, Temple of Heaven, Beijing (restored in timber, but without nails)

   🎨 Giambattista Tiepolo: Frescoes in the Kaisersaal,
Würzburg

     François Boucher: La Toilette de Vénus

     William Hogarth: Gin Lane

   📖 Pierre de Maupertuis: *Système de la Nature*

     Denis Diderot: *Encyclopédie*

     Tobias Smollett: *The Adventures of Peregrine Pickle*

     Henry Fielding: *Amelia*

     Thomas Gray: *Elegy Written in a Country Church-
yard*

1752 George Washington inherits his brother's plantation,
Mount Vernon in Virginia. Benjamin Franklin invents
the lightning conductor. A fire in Moscow destroys
18,000 houses. Philadelphia is the first city in the New
World to have public street lighting: globe lamps are
imported from England. In New York and Boston,
streets are lit by a lamp placed in the window of every
seventh house. Lahore falls to Ahmed Shah of Afghanistan after a four-month siege. The Sudanese Sultan Abu
al-Qasim of Darfur is killed in battle while fighting Funj
forces of the Sultan of Kordofan commanded by General
Abu al-Kaylak. *13 Jun*: Logstown Treaty, in which
Iroquois lands south of the Ohio River are ceded to
the Virginia colony. *3 Sep*: Britain and the British
colonies adopt the Gregorian calendar devised in *1582*.
Sep 14 follows Sep 2 creating confusion, panic and anger:
some believe their lives are shortened by 11 days.

   ✍ George Dance: Mansion House, London (completed)

     Jacques Gabriel: Chateau Choisy (completed); Ecole
Militaire, Paris

   📖 Charlotte Lennox: *The Adventures of Arabella*

     George Berkeley: *On the Prospects of Planting Arts
and Learning in America*

Christopher Smart: *Poems*

John Stanley: *Jephtha*

Michel Blavet: *Le Jaloux Corrigé*

1753 French troops from Canada occupy the Ohio valley, raising two forts. Robert Dinwiddie, Lieutenant Governor of Virginia, sends George Washington with a demand that the French withdraw. *11 Jan*: in England, Sir Hans Sloane dies, aged 92, leaving his library of 50,000 books to the nation; the British government buys his collection of curiosities, creating the foundation for the British Museum and British Library.

Richard Wilson: *Rome from the Villa Madonna*

Tobias Smollett: *Ferdinand Count Fathom*

Christopher Smart: *Hilliad*

James Lind: *Treatise on Scurvy*

Robert Wallace: *On the Numbers of Man*

1754 The French government recalls colonial administrator Joseph Dupleix from India, leaving the British in complete control. Ottoman Sultan Mahmoud I drops dead while dismounting from his horse; he is succeeded by his 55-year-old brother Osman III. English porcelain production is pioneered by William Cookworthy of Plymouth, when he finds deposits of china clay in Cornwall.

17 Apr: French troops rout Virginian frontiersmen who are building a fort and defeat a small British expeditionary force led by George Washington. *19 Jun*: the Albany Convention is a meeting of representatives of the colonies of New England, New York, Maryland and Pennsylvania with chiefs of the Six (Iroquois) Nations, to establish a joint defence plane against the French. *3 Jul*: Washington is defeated again by the French. *10 Jul*: the Albany Convention agrees a proposal by Benjamin Franklin for the union of the 13 British colonies.

Bartolameo Rastrelli: Winter Palace, St. Petersburg (completed)

Nikolaj Eigtoed: Amalienborg Palace, Copenhagen (completed)

Christ Church, Philadelphia (completed)

John Wood, father and son: The Circus, Bath

🐌 William Hogarth: The Election
François Boucher: The Judgment of Paris
📖 Samuel Richardson: *Sir Charles Grandison*

1755 The Venetian playboy Giovanni Casanova, now 30, is imprisoned for spying on his return to Venice after spending 14 years travelling around Europe. *10 Feb*: the French philosopher Montesquieu dies, aged 66. *20 Feb*: General Braddock arrives in Virginia with two regiments of regular soldiers and assumes command as C-in-C of British forces in America. *14 Apr*: Braddock meets colonial governors to plan a four-pronged attack on the French. *7 Jul*: an earthquake in northern Persia kills 40,000 people. *16 Jun*: the French at Fort Beauséjour surrender to British troops. *9 Jul*: the British are defeated on the Monongahela River near Fort Duquesne; nearly 1,000 British colonials are killed or wounded. General Braddock is killed. *8 Sep*: Battle of Lake George: the French are defeated. *1 Nov*: the Lisbon earthquake, originating on the seabed to the west, generates a seismic wave; 30,000 are killed by the earthquake, the fires or the wave that follows.

🏛 Jacques Soufflot: the Panthéon, Paris
🐌 Thomas Gainsborough: Milkmaid and Woodcutter
Jean Greuze: A Father Explaining the Bible to His Children
📖 Samuel Johnson: *A Dictionary of the English Language*
Ephraim Lessing: *Miss Sara Sampson*
Benjamin Franklin: *Observations Concerning the Increase of Mankind* (attacks idea of 'inevitable' poverty)

1756 The Duc de Richelieu invents mayonnaise: he also holds nude dinner parties. The Seven Years' War begins as Prussian troops invade Saxony in response to news that Saxony has formed a coalition with France, Austria, Russia and Sweden against Prussia. The North American War, bringing British and French troops into conflict, becomes an offshoot of the European War. *20 Jun*: the Black Hole of Calcutta incident enrages the British. Surarjak Dowlah, the Nawab of Bengal, imprisons 146 Britons in a small guardroom overnight. *21 Jun*:

when released, only 23 of the Nawab's prisoners are alive.

🖉 Nassau Hall, Princeton
Edmond Wolley and Andrew Hamilton: Pennsylvania State House, Philadelphia

🎨 Thomas Hudson: George Frederick Handel

📖 Edmund Burke: *A Vindication of Natural Society*

1757 London's Royal Library collection is transferred to the British Museum founded four years ago. John Campbell, a British sea Captain, creates the sextant by enlarging the arc of John Hadley's quadrant from 90 to 120 degrees. The Ottoman Sultan Osman III dies, aged 58, and is succeeded by his 40-year-old nephew Mustapha III. *28 Jan*: Ahmed Shah of Afghanistan takes Delhi and the Punjab. *18 Jun*: Battle of Kolin: Fredrick the Great's Prussian army is defeated by a Bohemian army in spite of his shouts of encouragement to his troops: 'You dogs, would you live for ever?' Frederick is forced to withdraw from Bohemia. *23 Jul*: Domenico Scarlatti, composer and son of Alessandro Scarlatti, dies in Madrid, aged 71. *5 Nov*: Battle of Rossbach: the Prussians defeat the French. *5 Dec*: Battle of Leuthen: the Prussians defeat the Austrians. Benjamin Franklin sends advice home from England, suggesting how far American importers and exporters can safely go in breaking British trading laws.

🖉 Jacques Gabriel: Louvre Palace enlargements, Paris

🎨 Thomas Gainsborough: The Artist's Daughter with a Cat
Jean Greuze: The Fowler

📖 James Lind: *On the Most Efficient Means of Preserving the Health of Seamen* (Hygiene as safeguard against typhus)
Edmund Burke: *The Sublime and the Beautiful*

1758 *23 Jun*: Battle of Krefeld: the French are defeated by the Prussian army. *8 Jul*: the French defeat a British force trying to take Fort Ticonderoga. *26 Jul*: the French fortress of Louisburg falls to the British under Generals Amherst and Wolfe. *25 Aug*: Battle of Zorndorff: a victory for the Prussian army over the Russian army that has invaded Prussia. *27 Aug*: in America, the British take Fort Frontenac. *14 Oct*: Battle of Hochkirk: the Austrians defeat the Prussians, but Frederick successfully resists efforts to drive his army out of Saxony and Silesia. *25 Nov*: the British take Fort Duquesne (later Pittsburgh) from the French.

🎨 François Boucher: The Mill at Charenton

📖 François Quesnay: *Tableau Economique*
Emanuel Swedenborg: *De nova Hierosolyma* (The New Jerusalem)
Claude-Adrien Helvétius: *De l'esprit*

🎼 John Smith: *Paradise Lost*
Tommaso Traetta: *Buovo d'Antona* (Bevis of Hampton)

1759 *13 Apr*: a French army defeats Ferdinand of Brunswick at Brunswick. *14 Apr*: The German-British composer George Frederick Handel dies, aged 74. *23 Jul*: Russian forces defeat the Prussians at Kay. *27 Jul*: British troops under Amherst take Fort Ticonderoga. *10 Aug*: Ferdinand VI of Spain dies, aged 45; he has been in a profound depression since his wife Barbara died last year, and is succeeded by his half-brother Carlos III. *12 Aug*: Battle of Kunersdorf: Frederick suffers a major setback when his army is defeated by a combined Austrian and Russian army. *13 Sep*: French Canada falls to the British forces following Wolfe's victory in the Battle of the Plains of Abraham outside Quebec; both the French Commander, the Marquis de Montcalm, and the British, General James Wolfe, are fatally wounded in the battle. Wolfe was only 32.

📐 Nicholas Hawksmoor: Queen's College, Oxford
James Paine and Robert Adam: Kedleston Hall, Derbyshire

🎨 William Hogarth: Sigismonda; The Cockpit

📖 Samuel Johnson: *Rasselas*
Adam Smith: *The Theory of Moral Sentiments*
Voltaire: *Candide*
Carlo Goldoni: *Gl'innamorati* (The Lovers)

🎼 William Boyce: *Heart of Oak* (popular song)

1760 Israel ben Eliezer, the charismatic Polish founder of Nasidism who is also known as the Ba'al Shem Tov, dies, aged 60; he has preached a popular messianic people's movement outside the synagogue. The first roller skates are seen in London, introduced by the Belgian Joseph Merlin; he skates into a party at Carlisle House in Soho Square playing a violin: out of control and unable to stop, Merlin crashes into a large and valuable mirror, smashes his violin and is seriously injured. The Japanese Shogun Ieshige abdicates, aged 49, and is succeeded by the 23-year-old son of Shogun Yoshimune, Ieharu. *23 Jun*: Battle of Landshut: the Austrians defeat and capture a Prussian army. *15 Aug*: Battle of Liegnitz: Frederick the Great's Prussian army defeats the Austrians. *9 Oct*: Russian army takes Berlin and burns it. *12 Oct*: The Russians leave Berlin on hearing that Frederick the Great is rushing back to save the city. *25 Oct*: George II of Britain dies, aged 77, after reigning for 33 years and is succeeded by his grandson George III, who is now 22.

Thomas Gainsborough: Mrs. Philip Thicknesse

Giovanni Morgagni: *On the Seats and Causes of Disease*

Benjamin Franklin: *Some Account of the Success of Inoculation for the Smallpox in England and America*

Laurence Sterne: *The Sermons of Mr. Yorick*; *Tristram Shandy*

James Macpherson: *Fragments of Ancient Poetry Collected in the Highlands of Scotland* (alleged translations, actually hoaxes)

Carlo Goldoni: *I rusteghi* (The Boors)

Franz Joseph Haydn: *Symphonies 2, 3, 4 and 5*

John Stanley: *Zimri*

Thomas Arne: *The Prophetess*

1761 John Harrison's chronometer is taken on a voyage to Jamaica on *HMS Deptford*: the first test is a success. The London doctor John Hill makes the first connection between tobacco and cancer, reporting cases of polyps associated with excessive use of snuff. Slave traders are banned from the Society of Friends by American Quakers, even though many Quakers own slaves. *14 Jan*: Battle of Panipat in India: the Marathas are decisively defeated by Ahmad Shah Abdaii, the Afghan leader. The confusion that follows an Afghan army mutiny favours the transfer of power to the British, who effectively rule India from now until 1947. The French and Spanish invade Portugal; the Portuguese ask the British to help repel the invasion. *15 Aug*: Spain, France and the Bourbon states of Italy form an alliance against Britain. *5 Oct*: William Pitt resigns as British Prime Minister when George III and Parliament refuse to declare war on Spain.

  ⌁ Robert Adam: Osterley Park House, England (rebuilding of Jacobean house in classical style)

  ✇ Louis Françfois Roubiliac: The Nightingale Monument, Westminster Abbey

    Jean Greuze: L'Accordée du Village

  ▯ John Hill: *Cautions Against the Immoderate Use of Snuff*

    Jean Jacques Rousseau: *Julie ou la nouvelle Heloïse*

    Charles Churchill: *The Rosciad*

    Denis Diderot: *Le Père de Famille*

    Carlo Goldoni: *Le Manie della Villeggiatura* (The Rage for Country Life)

  ♯ Thomas Arne: *Judith*

    Micheal Arne: *Edgar and Emmeline*

    Joseph Haydn: *Symphony No 7*

1762 The French reinvent *pâté de foie gras* (known to the ancient Egyptians). In the West Indies, Rear-Admiral George Rodney takes Grenada, St. Lucia, St. Vincent and Martinique. *5 Jan* Tsarina Elizabeth Petrovna dies, aged 52, and is succeeded by her 33-year-old son Peter III. Russia withdraws from the Seven Years' War. Peter III is an admirer of Frederick the Great and returns Pomerania to him. *Jul*: Peter III of Russia is overthrown in a military coup. *18 Jul*: Peter III is put to death and succeeded by his widow Catharine.

  ⌁ Orders of Louis XV: Le Petit Trianon, Versailles

    Robert Adam: Syon House interior, Middlesex

  ✇ George Stubbs: Mares and Foals

    Johann Zoffany: Garrick in 'The Farmer's Return'

    Giambattista Tiepolo: Frescoes for the Royal Palace, Madrid

  ▯ Nils von Rosenstein: *The Diseases of Children and Their Remedies*

Jean Jacques Rousseau: *Le Contrat Social*; *Emile*
Carlo Goldoni: *La baruffe chiozzotte* (The Chioggian Brawls)

🎜 Thomas Arne: *Artaxerxes*
Christoph von Gluck: *Orfeo*

1763 *10 Feb*: Treaty of Paris ends the Seven Years' War. France cedes to Britain territories in Canada and Senegal in Africa. The Mississippi is to be the boundary between British territory and that ceded by France to Spain; Spain cedes Florida to Britain, but regains all British conquests in Cuba. Frederick the Great estimates that the war lost him 853,000 soldiers and that 33,000 civilians have been killed. *5 Oct*: Augustus III of Poland dies, aged 66, at Dresden.

⌂ Church of La Madeleine, Paris (completed)
Touro Synagogue, Newport, Rhode Island

🎨 George Romney: Death of Wolfe
Jean Greuze: The Paralytic Cared for by His Children
Francesco Guardi: The Election of the Doge of Venice

📖 Nevil Maskelyne: *The British Mariner's Guide*
Voltaire: *Treatise on Tolerance*

1764 Frederick the Great moves to improve Prussian food production, inaugurating a rotation system borrowed from the Netherlands and draining marshes. In London, the practice of numbering houses begins. In India, the Muslim soldier Haidar Ali usurps the throne of Mysore. British forces under Sir Hector Munro defeat the Nawab of Oudh at Buxar, giving them control of Bengal, the richest province of India. Britain's Currency Act forbids the colonies from printing their own paper money. *24 May*: James Otis, a Boston lawyer, denounces taxation without representation and urges the colonies to unite in opposing British tax laws. Boston merchants initiate a policy of non-importation from Britain, and the movement towards independence gathers momentum. *12 Sept*: Jean Rameau, composer and friend of Voltaire, dies in Paris, aged 80. *26 Oct*: the English painter William Hogarth dies in London, aged 66.

⌂ Royal Palace, Madrid (completed)

🐚 Jean Houdon: St. Bruno (sculpture)

📖 Pierre Fournier: *Manuel typographie* (first system for measuring and naming sizes of type)

Ts'ao Chan: *The Dream of the Red Chamber*

Oliver Goldsmith: *The Traveller*

Sebastien Chamfort: *La Jeune Indienne*

🎵 Joseph Haydn: *Symphony No 22*

1765 The first true restaurant opens in Paris; a tavern-keeper called Boulanger sells cooked dishes at an all-night place in the Rue Bailleul. French engineer Nicholas Cugnot invents a steam-driven three-wheel gun tractor, pioneering the automobile. James Watt invents a more efficient steam engine than the 1705 Newcomen engine. In Lisbon, the *auto-da-fe* parade, often an excuse for violence against Jews or Christian 'heretics', is abolished. *9 Mar*: judges in Paris declare that Jean Calas, who was tortured and executed cruelly in *1762*, was, after all, innocent of murdering his son Marc-Antoine, who committed suicide in his father's house. The case has been reopened thanks to the intervention of Voltaire, who wrote a series of press articles that proved Calas' innocence. *22 Mar*: the Stamp Act passed by the British Parliament imposes direct taxes on the American colonists. *15 May*: the Quartering Act obliges colonists to provide barracks and supplies for British soldiers. *29 May*: Patrick Henry protests against the Stamp Act in the House of Burgesses. *18 Aug*: Holy Roman Emperor Francis I dies, aged 56, at Innsbruck and is succeeded by his son Josef II.

🏛 Henry Flitcroft and Henry Hoare: Stourhead Landscaped Garden

🐚 Joseph Wright: The Gladiator

Jean Fragonard: The Swing; Bathers

François Boucher: Madame Pompadour

Jean Greuze: Young Girl Weeping Over Her Dead Bird

📖 Horace Walpole: *The Castle of Otranto*

🎵 Thomas Arne: *Love in a Village*

1766 The 10-year-old Wolfgang Amadeus Mozart returns to Salzburg after touring Paris and London with his father as a harpsichord prodigy; he has already started composing. *14 Jan*: Frederick V of Denmark dies, aged 42, and is succeeded by his 16-year-old son Christian VII. *23 Feb*: Stanislas Leszczyncki, ex-King of Poland, dies, aged 89, and Lorraine reverts to France. *18 Mar*: the British Parliament repeals the Stamp Act partly at Franklin's persuasion, but the new Declaratory Act asserts the right of Britain to bind the colonies in all respects.

  🐚 Joseph Wright: The Orrery

    Johann Zoffany: Queen Charlotte and the Two Eldest Princes

  📖 Oliver Goldsmith: *The Vicar of Wakefield*

    Jean Jacques Rousseau: *Confessions*

    David Garrick and George Colman: *The Clandestine Marriage*

  🎵 Samuel Arnold: *Dr. Faustus*

1767 The Burmese invade Thailand and capture its capital Ayutthaya. North Carolina woodsman Daniel Boone goes through the Cumberland Gap, reaching Kentucky in defiance of a decree of King George's; Boone discovers a rich hunting ground contested by several Indian tribes. American whalers venture into the Antarctic for the first time; this is the first attempt at commercial exploitation of the Antarctic region. Jean Jacques Rousseau settles in England.

  🏛 John Wood the Younger: Royal Crescent, Bath

    Robert Adam, Kenwood House, London

  🐚 Joseph Wright: An Experiment on a Bird in an Air Pump

  📖 Joseph Priestley: *The History and Present State of Electricity*

    Laurence Sterne: *The Life and Opinions of Tristram Shandy* (final volume)

    Voltaire: *l'Ingénu*

    Gotthold Lessing: *Minna von Barnhelm; Der Freigeist* (The Freethinker)

    Pierre de Beaumarchais: *Eugénie*

  🎵 Wolfgang Amadeus Mozart: *Apollo et Hyacinthus*

    Christoph von Gluck: *Alceste*

1768 Samuel Hearne, a 23-year-old employee of the Hudson's Bay company, starts walking north-westwards from Hudson Bay; after a year he reaches the Arctic coast with no sign of a north-west passage. In the Himalayas, King Prithwi Naryan Shah unifies Nepal into a single state. *18 Mar*: the writer and cleric Laurence Sterne dies of pleurisy, aged 54. *20 Apr*: the painter Canaletto dies, aged 70, in Venice. *15 May*: France buys Corsica from the Genoese. *25 May*: the English naval officer Lieut. James Cook sails for the Pacific in order to observe a transit of Venus across the face of the sun. *10 Jun*: at Boston, British customs officers seize the sloop *Liberty*. *1 Aug*: angered by the *Liberty* incident, Boston merchants agree not to import from Britain. *22 Sep*: representatives from 26 Massachusetts towns meet and draw up a statement of grievances. *1 Oct*: the British land two infantry regiments at Boston.

  ✐ Jacques Gabriel: Le Petit Trianon, Versailles (completed)

     George Dance the Younger: Newgate Prison, London

     Adam Brothers: The Adelphi, London

  ✍ Joshua Reynolds: Garrick as Kiteley

  📖 Laurence Sterne: *A Sentimental Journey through France and Italy*

     Akinari Ueda: *Tales of the Rainy Moon*

     Oliver Goldsmith: *The Good Natured Man*

  🎼 Joseph Haydn: *Lo speziale* (The Apothecary)

1769 The Great Famine of Bengal kills 10 million people, a third of the population, in the worst natural disaster in human history (in terms of numbers lost). David Garrick inaugurates the first Shakespeare Festival at Stratford-upon-Avon. Richard Arkwright invents a spinning frame. James Cook arrives in Tahiti and sets up the observatory, then he sails west to chart the coasts of New Zealand. Carlos III of Spain authorizes the founding of new missions in California, together with four presidios (armed garrisons) at San Francisco, Santa Barbara, San Diego and Monterey. The Maharajah of Mysore forces the British to agree a treaty of mutual assistance in view of the famine, but the East India Company increases its demands on the reduced population of Bengal, in order to ensure 'a reasonable profit'. The Ottawa Chief Pontiac is murdered at Cahokia on *20 Apr* by another Indian;

there are rumours that he has been killed on British orders. Frederick the Great of Prussia and the Holy Roman Emperor Josef II meet to discuss the partition of Poland.

✐ Thomas Jefferson: Monticello, Virginia (Palladian house)

Old Blackfriars Bridge, London

🖾 Jean Greuze: Offering to Love

📖 William Blackstone: *Commentaries on the Laws of England* ('It is better that ten guilty persons escape than that one innocent suffer.')

Sebastien Chamfort: *Eloge de Molière*

🎵 Wolfgang Mozart: *La finta Semplice*

1770 James Cook explores the east coast of New Holland (later Australia), landing at the site of Sydney and claiming the island for Britain, even though it already has over 250,000 inhabitants. James Hargreaves invents the spinning jenny, automating part of the textile-making process. *19–20 Jan*: Battle of Golden Hill, New York: first open conflict between American colonists and British troops. *5 Mar*: the Boston 'Massacre' leaves three dead. *17 Mar*: the painter Giambattista Tiepolo dies in Madrid, aged 74. *16 May*: the French-Dauphin, 15, marries the 14-year-old Marie Antoinette at Versailles. *30 May*: the French court painter François Boucher dies, aged 66, in Paris. *6 Jul*: Battle of Chesme: a Russian fleet commanded by British officers defeats the Ottoman fleet off the Turkish coast after sailing from the Baltic. *10 Nov*: Voltaire writes, 'If God did not exist, it would be necessary to invent him'.

✐ Robert Adam: Pulteney Bridge, Bath

🖾 John Copley: Paul Revere

Benjamin West: The Death of General Wolfe

George Stubbs: Lion Attacking a Horse

📖 Paul d'Holbach: *Système de la Nature* (denial of any divine plan or purpose in nature)

Johann Wolfgang von Goethe: *Faust, Part 1* drafted, not published

Oliver Goldsmith: *The Deserted Village*

Pierre de Beaumarchais: *Les Deux Amis*

1771 Cossacks conquer the Crimea for Catharine the Great of

Russia; this great Russian success unnerves Frederick
the Great. As he nears the end of his 43-year reign,
Charles Emmanuel III abolishes serfdom in Savoy. *10
Feb:* the Afghans are driven out of Delhi by Marathas
from the Deccan Plateau. *10 Feb:* Adolphus Frederick of
Sweden dies, aged 60, in Stockholm and is succeeded by
his 25-year-old son Gustavus III. *Apr:* the Marathas
reinstate the exiled Moghal Emperor Shah Alam, using
him as a figurehead; this creates anxiety among the
British who have kept Shah Alam imprisoned at Alla-
habad.

 Benjamin West: Penn's Treaty with the Indians
 Joseph Wright: The Alchymist
 Jean Houdon: Diderot

 Louis de Bougainville: *Voyage autour du Monde*
 William Smellie: *Encyclopaedia Britannica*
 Tobias Smollett: *The Expedition of Humphrey Clin-
ker*
 Denis Diderot: *Le Fils Naturel, ou les Epreuves de la
Vertu*
 Carlo Goldoni: *Le Bourru Bienfaisant* (The Bene-
ficent Bear)

1772 Edo, capital of Japan, is destroyed by fire. Joseph Priestley gives rubber its name, finding that it will rub out
pencil marks. Daniel Rutherford distinguishes nitrogen
as a separate gas from carbon dioxide. James Cook sets
sail on a second Pacific expedition, taking Harrison's
chronometer; searching the South Pacific, Cook finds no
large 'southern continent'. The Danish nobility rebel
against the dictator Count Johann von Struense who has
held absolute power for a year; he is deposed, condemned
to death, tortured, beheaded. *5 Aug:* Poland is partitioned, regions going to Russia, Austria and Prussia. *19
Aug:* Gustavus III of Sweden re-establishes absolute
monarchy by taking away the Riksdag's power to legis-
late; he will nevertheless abolish the use of torture,
proclaim religious toleration and the freedom of the
press.

 Giorgio Vasari: Palazzo Grassi, Venice (completed)
 Johann Zoffany: The Members of the Royal Academy

📖 Denis Diderot: *Encyclopédie, Volume 280* (completed)

Gotthold Lessing: *Emilia Galotti*

🎜 Wolfgang Mozart: *Symphony No 21; Divertimento for Strings*

Joseph Haydn: *Symphony No 48*

Thomas Arne: *Squire Badger*

1773 Antigua in Central America is destroyed by an earthquake; the capital of Guatemala is moved to a new site, Guatemala City. The Holy Roman Emperor Josef II expels Jesuits from his Empire and Pope Clement XIV orders the dissolution of the Society of Jesus. In France, Baron de Morveau experiments with chlorine as a disinfectant. In America, Daniel Boone leads a party of pioneers into Kentucky; when Indians attack and Boone's son is killed, the pioneers turn back east of the Appalachians. *12 Jan:* Captain James Cook crosses the Antarctic Circle in his search for a great southern continent; he is the first to travel this far south. *8 May:* Ali Bey dies of wounds received in a skirmish with Ottoman rebels. *10 May:* the British Parliament passes the Tea Act, reducing duty on tea imported into Britain, but retaining higher duty on tea shipped to the American colonies. *16 Dec:* the Boston Tea Party; Lendall Pitts leads a band of colonists disguised as Mohawks to Griffen's Wharf where they board East India Company ships and throw 300 chests of tea into Boston Harbour. At Charlston, tea is left 'unimported' on the docks. *25 May:* Ottoman Sultan Mustapha III dies, aged 57, and is succeeded by his brother Abdul Hamid.

🏛 John Carr, Assize Court, York

🎨 Joshua Reynolds: *The Graces Decorating Hymen*

Jean Greuze: *The Broken Pitcher*

📖 Phyllis Wheatley: *Poems* (Phyllis is a 'Negro, Servant to Mr. John Wheatley of Boston in New England')

Oliver Goldsmith: *She Stoops To Conquer*

Johann von Goethe: *Götz von Berlichingen*

🎜 Samuel Arnold: *The Prodigal Son*

Wolfgang Mozart: *Symphonies 23, 24, 25, 26, 28 and 29*

1774 Connecticut and Rhode Island prohibit the importing of further slaves. Captain Cook charts and names the New Hebrides Islands. *Jan*: news of the Boston Tea Party reaches London. *31 Mar*: the British Parliament passes coercive legislation to bring the American colonies to heel; Boston Harbor is closed until the East India Company is compensated for the lost tea. *10 May*: Louis XV of France dies, aged 64, of smallpox after reigning for 58 years and is succeeded by his 19-year-old grandson Louis XVI. *26 May*: the Virginia House of Burgesses is dissolved by Governor Dunmore. *27 May*: Burgesses meet unofficially in a tavern and call for annual inter-colonial congresses. *16 Jul*: Treaty of Kuchuk-Kaainard-ji, ending the six-year Russo-Turkish War; Russia acquires the north coast of the Black Sea. *5 Sep*: the first Continental Congress assembles at Philadelphia; only Georgia is not represented. *10 Oct*: Battle of Point Pleasant: Shawnee Indians are defeated when they attack frontiersmen on the Ohio River. *14 Oct*: the Continental Congress makes a Declaration of Rights and Grievances, yet Washington writes that no thinking man in North America wants independence. *20 Oct*: the Continental Congress decides to import nothing from Britain and export nothing to Britain after *Dec*, subject to ratification by the individual colonies.

Jacques Louis David: *Artiochus et Stratonice*
Lord Chesterfield: *Letters to His Son* (posthumous)
Johann von Goethe: *Die Leiden des Jungen Werthers* (The Sorrows of Young Werther); *Clavigo*
Sebastien Chamfort: *Eloge de La Fontaine*
Hannah More: *The Inflexible Captive*
Christoph von Gluck: *Iphigenia in Aulis*
Samuel Wesley: *Ruth*
John Smith: *The Redemption*
John Stanley: *The Fall of Egypt*

1775 Cook returns from his second voyage to the Pacific, winning the Royal Society's Copley Medal for conquer-ing scurvy; he has brought 118 men through a three-year voyage 'with the loss of only one man by distemper'. The English actress Sara Siddons makes her stage début, aged 20, at the Drury Lane Theatre. *16 Apr*: Paul

Revere rides to Lexington to warn Samuel Adams and
John Hancock that General Gage intends to arrest them.
19 Apr: Battle of Lexington: in this skirmish, 700 redcoats are met by a small force of colonial minutemen.
Eight minutemen fall and the rest retreat. Battle of
Concord: the British troops are outnumbered 4,000 to
1,800 and 65 British soldiers are killed. Britain hires
25,000 mercenaries from German states and the Royal
Navy opens a siege of Boston. *10 May*: Fort Ticonderoga
is taken by a force of 800 Green Mountain Boys. *12 May*:
Crown Point on Lake Champlain is taken by colonial
forces. The Second Continental Congress meets at
Philadelphia and chooses John Hancock as its President. *17 Jun*: Battle of Bunker Hill: the British win,
but 1,150 redcoats are killed compared with 411 colonists. George Washington is appointed C-in-C of the
Continental Army. *3 Jul*: Washington arrives at Cambridge, Massachusetts to take command. *13 Oct*: the
Continental Congress establishes an American navy –
'two swift sailing vessels'. In England Lord North
reminds the House of Commons that people in England
are each paying 50 times more tax than American
colonists.

✐ John Wood the Younger: Royal Crescent, Bath
(completed)

🕮 Gobelin Factory for Robert Adam: Tapestry Series
'The Love of the Gods'
Joshua Reynolds: Miss Bowles
Jean Chardin: Self-portrait

📖 Samuel Johnson: *Taxation No Tyranny* (against the
colonists)
Edmund Burke: *On Conciliation with the Colonies*
Richard Brinsley Sheridan: *The Rivals*; *St. Patrick's
Day*
Pierre Beaumarchais: *Le Barbier de Seville*
Gotthold Lessing: *Die Juden* (The Jews)

♬ Wolfgang Mozart: *La finta Giardiniera*; *Il Re Pas-
tore*; *Concerto No 5 for Violin and Orchestra*
Thomas Linley: *The Duenna*
Edward Barnes: *Yankee Doodle*

1776 Catharine the Great's favourite, Grigori Potemkin,

builds her a Russian Black Sea fleet. *15 May*: the Virginia Convention instructs its delegate to propose independence for the American colonies. *2 Jul*: the Continental Congress adopts the Virginia Resolution. *4 Jul*: the American Declaration of Independence is signed at Philadelphia. *27 Aug*: Battle of Long Island: General Howe's army of 20,000 regular soldiers defeats an army of 8,000 colonials under General Israel Putnam. *6 Sep*: David Bushnell's *Connecticut Turtle* pioneers the military use of the submarine. A pear-shaped 1-metre/7-foot wooden vessel dives under British ships in New York Harbor with a view to boring holes with an auger and planting explosive charges. The British ships have copper bottoms and the attempt is fruitless. *15 Sep*: General Howe occupies New York City and narrowly misses capturing George Washington. *21 Sep*: the British capture Nathan Hale, a 21-year-old Continental Army captain who has visited Long Island to gather intelligence. He has also started numerous fires in New York to confuse the British. *22 Sep*: Hale is hanged by the British. *28 Oct*: Battle of White Plains: General Howe defeats General Washington. *26 Dec*: Battle of Trenton: a major victory for Washington, who takes over 1,000 prisoners.

Henry Keene: Radcliffe Observatory, Oxford
William Chambers: Somerset House, London

Jean Pigalle: Voltaire
Jean Fragonard: The Washerwoman

Adam Smith: *Inquiry into the Nature and Causes of the Wealth of Nations*
Jeremy Bentham: *A Fragment on the Government*
Edward Gibbon: *The History of the Decline and Fall of the Roman Empire, Volume 1*
Augustus Toplady: *Rock of Ages*
Johann von Goethe: *Stella*
Friedrich von Klinger: *Die Zwillinge* (The Twins); *Sturm und Drang*
Jakob Lenz: *Die Soldaten*
Sebastien Chamfort: *Mustapha et Zeangir*

Wolfgang Mozart: *Serenades Nos 6 and 7*

1777 Spain and Portugal settle differences over their South

American colonies; the capital of Portuguese Brazil is moved from Bahia to Rio de Janeiro. *3 Jan*: Battle of Princeton: Washington's troops defeat three British regiments under Cornwallis. *27 Apr*: Benedict Arnold defeats the British at Ridgefield. *7 Jul*: The American garrison abandons Fort Ticonderoga on hearing that General Burgoyne is on his way: Burgoyne defeats them in retreat. *29 Jul*: the American garrison evacuates Fort Edward, leaving it to the British. *16 Aug*: Battle of Bennington: victory for the Continental troops under Captain Stark. *19 Sep*: First Battle of Saratoga: stalemate, but with heavy British losses. *7 Oct*: Second Battle of Saratoga: General Gates decisively defeats General Burgoyne, who surrenders with his entire force; Burgoyne marches his troops to Boston, embarking for England. *1 Nov*: John Paul Jones sets sail for France with news of Burgoyne's defeat and humiliation. *30 Dec*: Maximilian III Elector of Bavaria dies without a successor.

   🏛 Robert Adam: Culzean Castle, Scotland
       Samuel Wyatt: Doddington, Cheshire
   🎨 Thomas Gainsborough: The Watering Place
   📖 Richard Sheridan: *The School for Scandal*
       Thomas Chatterton: *Poems* supposed to have been written at Bristol, by Thomas Rowley and others, in the fifteenth century
   🎼 Wolfgang Mozart: *Piano Concerto No 9*; *Concerto for Three Pianos*

1778   Joseph Bramah patents the modern valve-and-siphon water closet. Mesmerism is fashionable in Paris. Captain Cook rediscovers the Sandwich Islands (discovered *450*). Philosopher Jean Jacques Rousseau dies. *6 Feb*: the French, excited by Burgoyne's defeat, recognize American independence, signing a treaty with Benjamin Franklin. *4 May*: the Continental Congress ratifies the French treaty, giving it the confidence to reject British peace offers in *Jun*. *28 Jun*: Battle of Monmouth: Washington wins, thanks to drilling at Valley Forge by Friedrich von Steuben during the winter. *4 Jul*: General Lee is courtmartialled for retreating during the Battle of Monmouth and suspended for a year. The War of the

Bavarian Succession opens as Frederick the Great invades Bohemia. *3 Aug*: the Scala Opera House in Milan opens. *9 Nov*: the artist and architect Giovanni Piranese dies, aged 59, in Rome.

🏛 Giuseppe Piermarini: Teatro alla Scala, Milan (completed)

🎨 John Singleton Copley: Brook Watson and the Shark

Joseph Nollekens: Venus Chiding Cupid

📖 Fanny Burney: *Evelina*

Joshua Reynolds: *Seven Discourses delivered in the Royal Academy*

🎼 Wolfgang Mozart: *Les Petits Biens* (ballet); *Symphony No 31*

Dimitri Bortniansky: *Creon*

1779 Samuel Crompton invents a spinning mule, another major advance in the Industrial Revolution. A British force sent by Warren Hastings from Calcutta breaks the coalition between Haidar Ali, Rajah of Mysore, the Marathas and the Nizam. *29 Jan*: the British take Augusta, Georgia. The Spanish ask Britain to cease hostilities and recognize the independence of the North American colonies. The British ask Spain to stop aiding the colonists, going so far as to give Florida, Gibraltar and fishing rights off Newfoundland over to Spain. *21 Jun*: Spain declares war on Britain, besieging Gibraltar. *19 Jul*: Dudley Saltonstall sails from Boston with a fleet of 19 armed American ships, but he is afraid to attack the British fleet, runs his ships ashore and is cashiered for incompetence. *Aug*: John Paul Jones sails round the British isles with five ships. *21 Sep*: Battle of Baton Rouge: the British engage a mixed force of Spanish, French, German, African (freed blacks), Indian and American colonial soldiers – and surrender. *23 Sep*: Jones engages *HMS Serapes* and wins, taking the *Serapes* but losing his own ship. *6 Dec*: the painter Jean Chardin dies, aged 80, in Paris. *14 Feb*: Captain Cook is killed in a skirmish with natives on Hawaii.

🏛 John Carr: Royal Crescent, Buxton, Derbyshire

Abraham Darby III: The Iron Bridge, Coalbrookdale (first iron bridge)

◯ Thomas Gainsborough: Blue Boy
Charles Peale: George Washington at Princeton

▯ Philip Freneau: *The House of Night* (poetry)
Johann von Goethe: *Iphigenia in Tauris*
Richard Sheridan: *The Critic*
William Cowper and John Newton: *Olney Hymns*
(including 'Amazing Grace' and 'Glorious Things
Of Thee Are Spoken')

♫ Christoph von Gluck: *Iphigenia in Tauris*
Wolfgang Mozart: *Symphonies Nos 32* and *33*; *Concerto for Two Pianos*

1780 Holy Roman Emperor Josef II abolishes serfdom in
Hungary and Bohemia. The American Academy of Arts
and Sciences is founded in Boston. The Spanish dancer
Sebastiano Carezo invents the bolero. The 28-year-old
Sebastien Erard builds the first modern pianoforte. *14
Mar*: Mobile falls to the Spanish under de Galvez. *19
May*: a 'dark day' in New England causes those of a
religious turn of mind to think that the world is coming
to an end. *2–8 Jul*: the Gordon Riots in London are a
demonstration against Roman Catholics, whipped up by
Lord George Gordon. *Sep*: a second Mysore War breaks
out in India. Haidar Ali, Muslim ruler of Mysore, forms
an alliance with the Marathas and retaliates when attacked by the British-backed Nawab of Arcot. The
Marathas besiege Madras, where the East India Company has its headquarters, and British troops beat the
Marathas off. *23 Sep*: the British spy Major John André
falls into the hands of the Americans, with papers
showing that Benedict Arnold is plotting to surrender
West Point to the British. Arnold escapes to the British
ship *Vulture*. *2 Oct*: the Americans hang Major André. *7
Oct*: Battle of Kings Mountain: 900 North Carolina
backwoodsmen defeat 900 Loyalist militiamen. *28
Nov*: Maria Theresa of Austria, Hungary and Bohemia
dies, aged 63; her son Josef II now rules alone.

✐ Robert Adam: Osterley Park, Middlesex (completed)

◯ Joshua Reynolds: Mary Robinson as Perdita
John Copley: Death of Chatham

▯ Jeremy Bentham: *Introduction to the Principles of*

Morals and Legislation
George Crabbe: *The Candidate*
🎶 Wolfgang Mozart: *Symphony No 34*
Joseph Haydn: *Symphony No 75*
Luigi Boccherini: *La Clementina*

1781 A Chinese imperial army under Gao Cong puts down a Muslim revolt in Gansu province. Catharine the Great of Russia makes a treaty with Emperor Josef II promising him the eastern half of the Balkans; her aim is to drive the Turks out of Europe and make her grandson, Constantine, ruler of a new Greek empire. *5 Jan:* helped by Benedict Arnold, British troops sack Richmond, Virginia. *17 Jan:* Battle of the Cowpens: victory for Continental infantrymen. *2 Mar:* the United States in Congress assembles. *31 Mar:* William Herschel (German-born English) discovers Uranus, the first new planet to be discovered since prehistory. *1 Jul:* in India, British troops defeat those of Haidar Ali at Porto Novo. *6 Jul:* General Cornwallis defeats General Lafayette at Jamestown Ford, Virginia. *30 Aug:* a French fleet under Comte de Grasse-Tilly arrives in Chesapeake Bay. *5 Sep:* De Grasse-Tilly cripples the British fleet, enabling 16,000 Continental and Allied troops to lay siege to Yorktown on *28 Sep.* *13 Oct:* Emperor Josef II issues an Edict of Tolerance, allowing monasteries to reopen but weakening their links with Rome. *19 Oct:* General Cornwallis surrenders with 7,000 soldiers at Yorktown, ending the American Revolution and War of Independence.

Henry Holland: Berrington Hall, England
Joseph Wright of Derby: Sir Brooke Boothby
Jacques Louis David: Belisarius
Jean Houdin: Voltaire (bust)
Edward Gibbon: *Decline and Fall of the Roman Empire, Volume 6*
Samuel Johnson: *Lives of the English Poets*
Immanuel Kant: *Kritik der Reinen Vernunft* (Critique of Pure Reason)
Philip Freneau: *On the Memorable Victory of Paul Jones*
🎶 Wolfgang Mozart: *Idomeneo, Re di Creta*

Luigi Boccherini: *Stabat Mater*

1782　Spanish forces blockading Gibraltar take Minorca from the British. English prison reformer John Howard visits Newgate Prison and finds people who have been awaiting trial for seven years. In the viceroyalty of Peru, Spanish troops suppress a revolt at Cuzco where Tupac Amaru, a descendant of the Inca kings, has made ineffective attacks; the Spaniards kill him and rout his poorly equipped army. The Maratha War in India ends in the Treaty of Salbai, but the Mysore War continues. Haidar Ali, Rajah of Mysore, dies, aged 60, and is succeeded by his 31-year-old son Tipu Sahib, who continues the war against the British. *6 Apr*: Chao P'ya Chakri founds the Chakri dynasty in Siam, ruling as Rama I and making the city of Bangkok his capital. *12 Apr*: Admiral Rodney defeats a French fleet under de Grasse in the Battle of the Saints between Dominica and Guadeloupe; British control of the Caribbean is re-established. *12 May*: the Painter Richard Wilson dies, aged 67, at Llanberis in Wales. *Jul*: British troops leave Savannah for England. *29 Aug*: the *Royal George* sinks at anchor at Portsmouth while undergoing repairs; 800 men including Admiral Kempenfeld are drowned.

George Dance: Newgate Prison, London (completed)

Samuel McIntire: Pierce Nichols House, Salem

Henry Fuseli: The Nightmare

Francesco Guardi: Fetes for the Grand Duke Paul of Russia

Antonio Canova: Monument to Pope Clement XIV

Thomas Jefferson: *Notes on Virginia*

Joseph Priestley: *A History of the Corruption of Christianity*

Pierre de Laclos: *Les Liaisons Dangereuses*

Johann von Schiller: *Die Rauber*

Wolfgang Mozart: *Die Entfuhrung aus dem Serail; Serenade No 10*

Joseph Haydn: *Orlando Paladillo; Symphony No 77*

1783　In Japan, Mount Asama erupts, devastating crops. In Iceland, an eruption of Mount Skaptar kills one-fifth of the population. Russia annexes the Crimea, which Potemkin has taken from the Turks. *6 Feb*: the siege of Gibraltar ends. *24 Feb*: the British Parliament votes to discontinue the American War. *19 Apr*: the American Congress proclaims victory in the War of Independence, in which some 9,000 American and British lives have been lost. *3 Sep*: Treaty of Paris, recognizing the independence of the 13 colonies, granting full rights to the Newfoundland fisheries, ceding Florida to Spain. *23 Dec*: George Washington resigns as Commander-in-Chief of the Continental Army.

 🖾 Thomas Gainsborough: The Duchess of Hamilton
Jacques Louis David: The Grief of Andromache
 📖 Noah Webster: *Webster's Spelling Book*
 George Crabbe: *The Village*
 Gotthold Lessing: *Nathan der Weise*
 Johann Friedrich von Schiller: *Die Verschworung der Fiesko zu Getza* (Fiesco, or The Conspiracy of Genoa)
 🎼 Wolfgang Mozart: *Symphonies Nos 35* and *36; Piano Concerti Nos 11* and *13; Mass in C minor*

1784 The Japanese famine continues, with 300,000 dying of starvation; abortion and infanticide become common as families despair of finding enough food. In England, Samuel Johnson dies, aged 75. Benjamin Franklin tries in vain to persuade the French to alter their clocks in winter to make the best use of daylight. He also invents bifocal spectacles. The French chemist Antoine Lavoisier pioneers quantitative chemistry. Britain receives its first bales of imported American cotton. *6 Jan*: Treaty of Constantinople, in which the Turks agree to Russia's annexation of the Crimea. *14 Jan*: the U.S. Congress at Annapolis ratifies the Treaty of Paris, bringing the War of Independence to its formal close. *4 Jul*: Emperor Josef II suspends the Hungarian Constitution following revolution in Transylvania.

 🖾 Jacques Louis David: The Oath of the Horatii
 Joshua Reynolds: Mrs. Siddons as The Tragic Muse
 Francisco de Goya: Don Manuel de Zuniga
 📖 Henry Cavendish: *Experiments on Air* (water results from the union of hydrogen and oxygen)

René Haüy *d'une théorie sur la structure des cristaux*

Immanuel Kant: *Notion of a Universal History in a Cosmopolitan Sense*

Johann Friedrich von Schiller: *Kabale und Liebe*

Pierre de Beaumarchais: *La folle journée, ou Le mariage de Figaro*

Wolfgang Mozart: *Piano Concerti Nos 15–19*

Samuel Wesley: *First Symphony*

1785 Warren Hastings, Governor-General of India, resigns amid accusations of autocratic behaviour and returns to England. The U.S. adopts the dollar as its unit of currency using a decimal system devised by Jefferson. Benjamin Franklin returns to America after nine years in Europe. *7 Jan*: the first air crossing of the English Channel is made by François Blanchard (French) and John Jeffries (American-English) using a hot-air balloon. *15 Aug*: Cardinal de Rohan is arrested over the 'diamond necklace affair'; among other scandalous aspects the incident suggests to many that Queen Marie Antoinette has told lies. *Nov 8*: Treaty of Fontainebleau, settling conflicts of interest between Austria and the Netherlands; Austria gives up Maastricht and leaves the mouth of the River Scheldt to the Dutch.

Emerald Buddha Chapel, Bangkok

Baldassare Longhena: Ca' Rezzonico Palazzo, Venice (completed)

Thomas Baldwin: Pulteney Street, Bath

Joshua Reynolds: The Infant Hercules

James Boswell: *The Journal of the Tour to the Hebrides*

William Cowper: *The Task*

Joseph Townsend: *A Dissertation on the Poor Laws*

Wolfgang Mozart: *Le Nozze di Figaro* (The Marriage of Figaro); *Piano Concerto No 22*; *Eine Kleine Nachtmusik*

1786 Mont Blanc is climbed for the first time, by Jacques Balmart and Michel-Gabriel Paccard. In London, Henry Nock invents the breech-loading musket. The Scottish agricultural engineer Andrew Meikle invents the first successful threshing machine, at the age of 67. In Japan, Shogun Ieharu dies, aged 49, and is succeeded by a kinsman, the 13-year-old Ienari. *31 May*: in France, Cardinal de Rohan is acquitted of stealing the necklace. The Comte de La Motte is believed to have it and he has escaped to London; he is given a life sentence in his absence. Both Mme de La Motte and the Queen are suspected of having connived at the Cardinal's downfall. *17 Aug*: Frederick the Great of Prussia dies, aged 72, at Sans-Souci after reigning for 46 years. He is succeeded by his 41-year-old nephew Friedrich Wilhelm II.

  ✐ William Chambers: Somerset House, London (completed)

    Thomas Baldwin and John Palmer: The Pump Room and Colonnade, Bath

  ✑ Joshua Reynolds: The Duchess of Devonshire and Her Daughter

    Johann Zoffany: Colonel Mordaunt's Cock-Match

  📖 William Beckford: *Vathek*

    Robert Burns: *Poems*, chiefly in the Scottish dialect

    William Herschel: *Catalogue of Nebulae*

  🎼 Wolfgang Mozart: *Piano Concerti Nos 23* and *24*; *Symphony No 38*

    Dimitri Bortniansky: *The Falcon*

1787 William Bligh, now 33, sails on *HMS Bounty* to obtain breadfruit from Tahiti for planting in the Caribbean as a food source for colonists. In France, Jacques Charles launches the first hydrogen balloon. In Britain, prisons are becoming overcrowded; it is no longer possible to transport convicts to the American colonies, so they will now be diverted to a new penal colony at Botany Bay, Australia. William Wilberforce begins campaigning for the abolition of slavery in British colonies. George Washington chairs a Constitutional Convention in Philadelphia to draw up a Constitution for the U.S.; Washington resists attempts to make him king. Catharine the Great begins a second war with the Turks in order to gain Georgia. There are rice riots in Japan as the food shortage continues.

  ✑ Jacques Louis David: The Death of Socrates

    Joshua Reynolds: Lady Heathfield

  📖 Thomas Clarkson: *Essay on the Slavery and Commerce of the Human Species*

Royall Tyler: *The Contrast* (first American comedy of any merit)

Johann Friedrich von Schiller: *Don Carlos, Infante von Spanien*

🎜 Wolfgang Mozart: *Don Giovanni*

1788 William Symington, a Scottish engineer, invents the first workable steamboat. The Paris Parlement gives Louis XVI a list of grievances as France plunges into economic chaos; Louis recalls Jacques Necker as Minister of Finance, making him effectively chief minister, and summons the Estates-General to assemble in May next year (first meeting since *1614*). Gustavus III of Sweden invades Finland in an attempt to take it from Russia. *18 Jan*: the first shipload of convicts is landed at Botany Bay; the developing township will be named after the British Home Secretary, Thomas Townsend, Lord Sydney. *Apr*: New York doctors have to go into hiding as a crowd riots in protest against grave robbers who are supplying medics with corpses for study and dissection. *2 Aug*: the painter Gainsborough dies in London, aged 61.

⌁ Karl Langhaus: Brandenburg Gate, Berlin

🎨 Jacques Louis David: Antoine Lavoisier and his Wife; Love of Paris and Helena

Johann Zoffany: Tiger Hunt in the East Indies

📖 *The Times* newspaper (first issue, *1 Jan*)

John Lempriere: *Classical Dictionary*

Mme de Stael: *Lettres sur le Caractère et les Ecrits de J. J. Rousseau*

1789 Johann Friedrich von Schiller becomes Professor of History at Jena. In London, Andrew Pears introduces Pears' soap. *7 Apr*: the Ottoman Sultan Abdul Hamid dies, aged 65, (poisoned) and is succeeded by his 27-year-old nephew Selim III. *28 Apr*: Mutiny on the Bounty; mutineers led by Fletcher Christian cast Captain Bligh and 18 men loyal to him adrift in a 7-metre/22-foot boat, then sail back to Tahiti to collect native women and set up a colony on the uninhabited Pitcairn Island. *30 Apr*: George Washington takes office as first President of the U.S. *12 Jun*: Captain Bligh reaches Timor in the East Indies after navigating across 5,800 km/3,600 miles of open ocean. *17 Jun*: the French Estates-General meets, calling itself the National Assembly. *20 Jun*: the National Assembly meeting is suspended, so the members go to a nearby tennis court where they swear not to disperse until they have given France a constitution; Mirabeau is to head the Assembly. *12 Jul*: members of the third estate (the ordinary people of France) attack the Bastille in Paris. *14 Jul*: the Fall of the Bastille. *5–6 Oct*: riots in Paris; a revolutionary band mainly of women marches on Versailles. General Lafayette rescues the French royal family, moving it to Paris.

  ✎ Robert Adam: Edinburgh University
      Jacques Soufflot: The Panthéon, Paris (completed)
  ✎ Thomas Lawrence: Queen Charlotte
  □ Antoine Lavoisier: *Traité élémentaire de chimie* (first modern chemistry textbook)
      William Blake: *Songs of Innocence*
      Samuel Coleridge: *The Fall of the Bastille* (Coleridge is 16)
  ♭ Wolfgang Mozart: *Gigue in G*
      Franz Beck: *Pandore*
      Karl von Dittersdorf: *Hieronimus Knicker*

1790 In France a committee is founded to settle a uniform system of weights and measures; a metre is 100 centimetres in Paris, 96 in Bordeaux and 102 in Lille. Emperor Josef II dies on *20 Feb*, aged 48, and is succeeded by his 42-year-old brother Leopold II. Louis XVI accepts the constitution drafted by the revolutionaries. Benjamin Franklin dies at Philadelphia, aged 84. Philadelphia becomes the capital of the United States in *Aug*, but Alexander Hamilton has selected a virgin site on the banks of the Potomac as a new national capital site to resolve the rivalries already emerging between north and south.

  ✎ James Wyatt: Castle Combe, Northern Ireland
      Pierre Charles L'Enfant: Federal City of Washington (with Andrew Ellicott and Benjamin Banneker)
  ♭ Henry Raeburn: Sir John and Lady Clark
      William Blake: *Marriage of Heaven and Hell*
      Edmund Burke: *Reflections on the Revolution in France*

William Bligh: *A Narrative of the Mutiny on Board HMS Bounty*

🎵 Wolfgang Mozart: *Piano Concerto No 19*

1791 Captain Bligh sails for Tahiti again to obtain breadfruit, this time on *HMS Providence*. French farmer's wife Marie Harel invents Camembert cheese. The London conductor Peter Solomon invites Haydn to England to conduct his symphonies: Haydn will write six new symphonies this year. The French National Assembly elects Mirabeau President. *2 Apr*: Mirabeau dies, aged 42. *22 Jun*: Louis XVI and his family are recognized by Jean Drouet as they travel east towards the German border, trying to escape. *25 Jun*: Louis XVI and his family are stopped at Varennes and taken back to Paris by National Guardsmen. *5 Dec*: Mozart dies, aged 35, possibly of typhoid. *15 Dec*: the Bill of Rights becomes U.S. law.

✐ James Gandon: Customs House, Dublin
Benedetto Buratti: Campanile, Island of San Giorgio, Venice
Robert Adam: Charlotte Square, Edinburgh

🎨 George Morland: Inside a Stable

📖 James Boswell: *The Life of Samuel Johnson*
Thomas Paine: *The Rights of Man*
Marquis de Sade: *Justine*
Robert Burns: *Tam O'Shanter*
David Everett: *Lines Written for a School Declamation* ('You'd scarce expect one of my age/To speak in public on the stage')

🎵 Wolfgang Mozart: *Die Zauberflöte* (The Magic Flute); *Piano Concerto No 27*; *Ave verum corpus*
Joseph Haydn: *Symphonies Nos 93 and 96*

1792 In Egypt an outbreak of bubonic plague kills 800,000. The 26-year-old Eli Whitney invents the cotton gin, which increases U.S. cotton production and the demand for slave labour. Denmark becomes the first country to give up the slave trade. *23 Feb*: the painter Sir Joshua Reynolds dies in London. *1 Mar*: Holy Roman Emperor Leopold II dies suddenly, aged 44, and is succeeded by his 24-year-old son Francis, the last of the Holy Roman Emperors. *16 Mar*: Gustavus III of Sweden is shot in the back at a midnight masquerade in Stockholm. *29 Mar*: Gustavus III dies, aged 46, and is succeeded by his 13-year-old son Gustavus IV. *20 Apr*: Austria and Prussia form a military alliance against revolutionary France; France declares war on Austria. *11 Jul*: after military setbacks, the French Legislative Assembly announces that the nation is in danger. *10 Aug*: the people of Paris storm the Tuileries Palace, urged on by Georges Danton, after Louis XVI orders the Swiss Guard to fire on them; 600 Guardsmen are massacred and the King is confined in the Temple Prison. The Paris commune takes power under Danton. *19 Aug*: General Lafayette is declared a traitor by the French National Assembly; he escapes to Liège, where he is captured by the Austrians. *20 Aug*: the Prussian army takes Verdun. *21 Sep*: the French National Convention abolishes the monarchy, declaring *22 Sep* the first day of the new French Republic. *19 Nov*: the French National Convention offers help to peoples of all nations who want to overthrow their kings; this is seen as extremely provocative by all the monarchies of Europe.

Joseph Nollekens: Charles James Fox (bust)

Jean Houdon: George Washington (bust)

Mary Wollstonecraft: *Vindication of the Rights of Women*

Robert Burns: *Ye Flowery Banks O'Bonny Doon*

Domenico Cimarosa: *Il Matrimonio Segreto*

Joseph Haydn: *Symphony No 94*

Rouget de Lisle: *La Marseillaise*

Oh! Dear, What Can The Matter Be? (popular song)

1793 Captain Bligh plants breadfruit in Jamaica and St. Vincent. The English navigator George Vancouver discovers Vancouver Island. *1 Jan*: the painter Francisco Guardi dies in Venice, aged 80. *21 Jan*: after a trial before the Convention, Louis XVI is executed in the Place de la Révolution (later Place de la Concorde) in Paris. *1 Feb*: France declares war on Britain, Holland and Spain; those countries join the Holy Roman Empire in an alliance against France. *22 Apr*: President Washington issues a Proclamation of Neutrality in the European war (Hamilton wanted him to support the British, Jefferson wanted him to support the French). *24 Apr*: the radical

Jacobin Jean Paul Marat is brought to trial and acquitted; Marat joins Danton and Robespierre on the Committee of Public Safety in an effort to overthrow the Girondists. *22 Jun*: 31 Girondists are arrested. *13 Jul*: Charlotte Corday stabs Marat to death in his bath. *Oct*: Lyons falls to the French republicans after a siege of two months. A massacre follows. *16 Oct*: Queen Marie Antoinette goes to the guillotine. *31 Oct*: the Girondists arrested in June are guillotined. *23 Dec*: General Westermann routs the Vendée rebel army at Savenay.

    Lansdown Crescent, Bath, England (completed)

    Jacques Louis David: The Death of Marat

    Thomas Banks: Penelope Booth Tomb

    William Godwin: *Enquiry Concerning Political Justice*

    Joel Barlow: *Advice to the Privileged Orders*

    Johann Friedrich von Schiller: *Geschichte des Dreissigjahrigen Krieges*

    William Blake: *Gates of Paradise*

1794   Lutf Ali Khan, Shah of Persia since 1789, is defeated and killed by a brutal usurper, Aga Mohammed, who takes power and founds the Kajar dynasty. In the French colony of Saint Domingue on the island of Hispaniola, Haitian slaves rise in rebellion under the leadership of Pierre Toussaint l'Ouverture; 500,000 blacks and mulattoes have been tyrannized by 40,000 whites. *Mar*: in Paris Robespierre defeats his rivals, sending Danton and others to the guillotine. *8 Jun*: Robespierre names himself High Priest of a new Festival of the Supreme Being as the Reign of Terror reaches its height. *10 Jun*: juries are allowed to convict without hearing any evidence or defence; over 300 people a month are going to the guillotine. Opposition to Robespierre mounts. *26 Jun*: Battle of Fleurus: the French defeat a British fleet in the English Channel. *27 Jul*: a conspiracy of moderates (Thermidoreans) leads to the arrest of Robespierre, Couthon and Saint-Just; they are released by supporters. *28 Jul*: Robespierre and his associates are re-arrested in the Hôtel de Ville; he tries to shoot himself, but is taken, injured, to be guillotined. *20 Aug*: Battle of Fallen Timbers, ending the Indian threat to white settlers in the Kentucky-Ohio region; the Indians have been provoked into attacking the settlers, then hammered by General Wayne's troops.

- John Trumbull: The Declaration of Independence
- Thomas Paine: *The Age of Reason*
- Johann Fichte: Grundlage der gesammten Wissenschaftslehre (Foundation of the Whole Theory of Science)
- William Blake: *Songs of Experience*
- Robert Burns: *Scots Wha Hae*
- Joseph Haydn: *Symphonies Nos 99, 100 and 101*

1795 The British Royal Navy orders that lime juice rations must be carried on all voyages lasting more than five weeks following last year's conclusive testing of James Lind's citrus juice remedy for scurvy. The average weight of cattle being sold at the Smithfield Cattle Market in London is twice what it was in *1710*. The House of Lords acquit Warren Hastings of 'high crimes' allegedly committed while Governor-General of India; during his seven-year trial Hastings, now a ruined man, has been made a scapegoat for all the wrongdoing of the East India Company. The French Convention is threatened by a royalist backlash and calls on the Comte de Barras to defend it. Barras met Napoleon Bonaparte during the siege of Toulon, during which Bonaparte distinguished himself, and gives Bonaparte command of forces defending the Convention. *2 Jan*: the French capture the Dutch fleet as it stands frozen into the River Texel; William V escapes to England as the French establish a Batavian Republic. *5 Mar*: Treaty of Basel, removing Prussia from the French war. *24 Oct*: Stanislas II of Poland abdicates, aged 63, and his country is partitioned for a third time among Austria, Russia and Prussia. The French Convention names Bonaparte Commander of the Armée d'Intérieur as a reward for saving the Tuileries Palace with an artillery bombardment. *26 Oct*: the French National Convention dissolves.

- John Flaxman: Mansfield Monument, Westminster Abbey
- Jacques Louis David: Madame Seriziat and Her Daughter

Francois Gerard: Isabey and His Daughter

Francisco de Goya: The Duchess of Alba

📖 James Hutton: *Theory of the Earth* (modern theory of the earth's great age and doctrine of uniformitarianism)

Marie de Caritat, Marquis de Condorcet: *Tableau Historique des progrés de l'esprit humain* (Condorcet died in *Mar* last year, a victim of the Terror)

Johann von Goethe: *Wilhelm Maisters Lehrjahre*

🎵 Joseph Haydn: *Symphonies Nos 102, 103 and 104*

Ludwig van Beethoven: *Piano Concerto No 2*

1796 The English doctor Edward Jenner develops the technique of vaccination against smallpox. In China, the Manchu Emperor Qian Long abdicates, aged 85, after reigning for 60 years and is succeeded by his 36-year-old son Jia Qing. *Jan*: Charles de Talleyrand arrives in Hamburg after spending over two years in America; he will become French Foreign Minister next year. Ceylon (later Sri Lanka) falls to the British. *Apr*: a French army under Napoleon invades Italy and defeats the Austrians at Millesimo. *10 May*: Babeuf's Conspiracy to overthrow the French Directory fails; the socialist François Babeuf, who wrote the popular song *Mourant de faim, mourant de froid*, is arrested and will be executed next year. *15 May*: Napoleon enters Milan and sets up the Lombard Republic. *10 Nov*: Catharine the Great of Russia dies, aged 67, and is succeeded by her 42-year-old son Paul I. *15 Dec*: a French fleet sets sail from Brest to invade Ireland under the command of General Hoche; a storm disperses the fleet off Kerry and the invasion is called off.

🏛 James Gandon: The Four Courts, Dublin

Rowland Burdon: Sunderland Bridge

James Wyatt: Fonthill Abbey, Wiltshire

🎨 Gilbert Stuart: George Washington

Antoine Gros: The Victor of Arcole

📖 Madame de Staël: *The Influence of the Passions*

Robert Burns: *My Love Is Like A Red Red Rose*; *Auld Lang Syne*

Johann von Goethe: *Egmont*

1797 Cigar-makers in Cuba make little cheap cigars using paper wrappers – cigarettes. The Berlin chemist Martin Klaproth succeeds in reducing uranium oxide from pitchblende. The first copper pennies and pound notes are issued in Britain. Aga Mohammed, the ruler of Persia, is assassinated and succeeded by his nephew Fath Ali Shah. *14–15 Jan*: Battle of Rivoli: Napoleon's first decisive victory over the Austrian army. *2 Feb*: Napoleon takes Mantua after a siege. The Treaty of Tolentino cedes Bologna and Ferrara to France after Napoleon begins a threatening march on Rome. *15 Apr*: the Spithead Mutiny: British sailors demand better conditions, which are granted in *May*. *9 Jul*: the French proclaim a Cisalpine Republic (Milan, Ferrara, Modena, Romagna and Bologna); Genoa is turned into a French-controlled Ligurian Republic. *17 Oct*: Treaty of Campo Formio: Austria is to cede Belgian provinces to France in return for the territory of Venice, Dalmatia and Istria. *16 Nov*: Friedrich Wilhelm II of Prussia dies, aged 53, and is succeeded by Friedrich Wilhelm III, the late King's 27-year-old grandson.

    J. M. W. Turner. Millbank

    Ludwig Tieck: *Der blonde Eckbert*

    Johann von Goethe: *Hermann und Dorothea*

    Frederick Morton: *The State of the Poor*

    Joseph Haydn: *Gott, Erhalte den Kaiser* (becomes Austria's national anthem: words by Lorenz Hoschka); *Emperor Quartet*

    Carlo Cherubini: *Medée* (Medea)

1798 *Feb*: Napoleon occupies Rome, proclaims a Roman Republic and takes the Pope in custody to Valence. *19 May*: after assembling what is clearly an invasion fleet at Boulogne, leading the British to expect an invasion at any moment, Napoleon sails from Toulon with 35,000 servicemen and a staff of scientists. *12 Jun*: Napoleon takes Malta. *21 Jun*: Battle of Vinegar Hill: the British army defeats the Irish rebels, breaking resistance to British rule, for the time being. *1 Jul*: Napoleon lands in Egypt. *2 Jul*: Napoleon takes Alexandria. *21 Jul*: Battle of the Pyramids: the French easily defeat the ill-equipped Mameluke cavalry. *22 Jul*: Napoleon takes Cairo. *1 Aug*: Battle of the Nile: the French fleet is destroyed in Aboukir Bay to the east of Alexandria, cutting Napoleon off. The British fleet is commanded by Nelson.

🎨 Sawrey Gilpin: Horses Frightened by a Thunderstorm

Baron Gerard: Love and Psyche

Francisco de Goya: Caspar de Jovellanos

📖 Dagobert, Baron Cuvier: *Tableau Elementaire de l'Histoire Naturelle des Animaux*

Maria Edgeworth: *Practical Education*

Charles Brockden Brown: *Alcuin, A Dialogue on the Rights of Women*

Samuel Taylor Coleridge and William Wordsworth: *Lyrical Ballads* (including 'Tintern Abbey' and 'Rime of the Ancient Mariner')

Thomas Morton: *Speed the Plough*

Johann Friedrich von Schiller: *Wallenstein's Camp*

Thomas Malthus: *Essay on the Principles of Population* (population increases exponentially while food production increases in arithmetic progression: world food crisis inevitable)

🎼 Ludwig van Beethoven: *Piano Concerto No 1*

Joseph Haydn: *The Creation; Nelson Mass* (not intended as a tribute to the victor of the Nile)

1799 The Prussian naturalist Alexander von Humboldt sails for Spanish America on the *Pizarro*. English chemist Humphry Davy produces laughing gas (nitrous oxide), finds it 'absolutely intoxicating' when inhaled and suggests its use as an anaesthetic in minor surgery. The Rosetta Stone is discovered in Egypt by French army Captain Boucard, who suspects that the three sets of inscriptions in demotic, hieroglyphs and Greek may hold the key to understanding the ancient Egyptian language. *9 Jan*: Britain introduces income tax for the first time. *Feb*: Napoleon invades Syria from Egypt, but is unable to take Acre. Plague breaks out among the French troops, so they retreat to Egypt. *4–7 Jun*: Battle of Zurich: a Russian army defeats a French army. *25 Jul*: Battle of Aboukir: the French under Napoleon and Murat defeat a Turkish-British force. *15 Aug*: Battle of Novi: a French defeat. *24 Aug*: Napoleon sets sail for France. *26 Sep*: the Russian force is driven out of Zurich by the French. *19*

Nov: Napoleon is elevated to First Consul. *14 Dec*: George Washington dies, aged 67, at Mount Vernon. *24 Dec*: the French Directory is ended as a new constitution is approved; Napoleon is installed as Dictator.

✏ James Hoban: United Staes Executive Mansion, Washington (White House)

□ Charles Brockden Brown: *Ormond, or The Secret Witness*

Johann Friedrich von Schiller: *Die Piccolomini* (The Piccolominos); *Wallensteins Tod* (Wallenstein's Death)

Mungo Park: *Travels in the Interior Districts of Africa*

♫ Joseph Haydn: *Theresienmesse*

Ludwig van Beethoven: *Sonate Pathétique*

1800 The world's population reaches 880 million. Sir William Herschel discovers infra-red rays. The techniques of the Industrial Revolution spread to Europe: Lieven Bauwens of Ghent smuggles the spinning jenny into the Low Countries from England. English engineer Richard Trevithick invents a high-pressure steam engine that will later power a road vehicle. Italian physicist Alessandro Volta invents the electric battery. Alexander von Humboldt explores the course of the River Orinoco in South America. In West Africa, Osei Bonshu assumes the throne of the Ashanti kingdom (Ghana) and reigns as Asanthane. The golden throne is alleged by the prophet Okomfo Anokye to have been received 'from heaven' to create and legitimize the holy empire of the Ashanti people. *24 Jan*: Napoleon concludes the Convention of El Arish with the Ottoman Turks, agreeing a French withdrawal from Egypt. *24 Mar*: a French army under Kleber defeats the Turks at Heliopolis. *4 Jun*: Austrian troops starve the Genoese into submission, but then come under attack from Napoleon, who has come through the St. Bernard Pass. *14 Jun*: Battle of Marengo: Napoleon narrowly defeats the Austrians under Baron von Melas. Melas signs a truce, handing over to Napoleon all the Austrian forts west of the River Mincio and south of the River Po. In Cairo, the French General Kleber is assassinated by a Turkish fanatic.

    ✍ Colonel John Taylor: Octagon House, Washington, U.S.

    ✑ Jacques Louis David: Portrait of Madame Récamier
    Thomas Girtin: The White House at Chelsea; Kirkstall Abbey

    ☐ Johann Friedrich von Schiller: *Macbeth*; *Maria Stuart*
    Mason Locke Weems: *The Life and Memorable Actions of George Washington* (includes made-up stories such as chopping down the cherry tree)
    Maria Edgeworth: *Castle Rackrent*

    ♩ Ludwig van Beethoven: *Symphony No 1*; *Piano Concerto in C minor*
    Francois Boieldieu: *The Caliph of Baghdad*
    Luigi Boccherini: *Mass*

1801 The first accurate census shows that China has 295 million people, India 131 million, Russia 33, France 27, Ottoman Empire 21, German states 14, Spain 11, Britain 10, Ireland 5 and the United States 5.3 million. Guangzhou (Canton) is the world's largest city (1.5 million); Nanjing, Hangchow, Kingtechchen and Edo (Tokyo) 1 million each. London is the largest European city with 864,000, while New York is still only 60,000. France adopts the metric system fixed two years ago by the National Convention; most of Europe will quickly follow. *1 Jan*: the United Kingdom of Great Britain and Ireland is created by the Act of Union. *9 Feb*: Treaty of Luneville: Napoleon virtually destroys the Holy Roman Empire. *4 Mar*: Thomas Jefferson becomes third U.S. President. *11 Mar*: Tsar Paul I of Russia is murdered in his bedroom in a palace revolution; insane and dead at 46, Paul is succeeded by his 23-year-old son Alexander I. *14 Mar*: Britain and France end hostilities. *2 Apr*: Battle of Copenhagen: Nelson is responsible for a British victory by ignoring orders from his commander Sir Hyde Parker. *May*: Parker is recalled and Nelson is given command of the British fleet. *Jun*: Nelson is made a Viscount.

    ✍ James Wyatt: Belvoir Castle, Leicestershire
    ✑ Jacques Louis David: Napoléon au Grand Saint-Bernard

J. M. W. Turner: Calais Pier

🍂 Johann Pestalozzi: *Wie Gertrud ihre Kinder lehrt* (How Gertrude Teaches Her Children)
New York Evening Post (first issue *16 Nov*)

Johann Friedrich von Schiller: *Die Jungfrau von Orleans*

🎵 Ludwig van Beethoven: *The Creatures of Prometheus*
Joseph Haydn: *The Seasons*
Francis Boieldieu: *Harp Concerto*

1802 Marie Tussaud opens her wax museum in London; she was commissioned during the Reign of Terror to make death masks of famous victims of the guillotine, and now she puts them on show. Thomas Wedgwood produces the world's first photograph, but because he has no means of fixing the image it quickly fades. William Symington builds the first successful steamship, the *Charlotte Dundas*. *27 Mar*: Treaty of Amiens, a temporary end to European war. *19 May*: Napoleon creates the Légion d'Honneur; he reduces criticism of his policies by keeping courtiers busy with matters of protocol. *2 Aug*: Napoleon is made First Consul for life with the right to name his successor. *9 Nov*: the English artist Thomas Girtin dies, aged 27, in London. *15 Nov*: the English painter George Romney dies, aged 67, at Kendal.

🏛 Arlington House, Washington, U.S.
William Atkinson: Scone Palace, Perthshire

🎨 François Gerard: Madame Recamier
Antonio Canova: Napoleon Bonaparte; The Pugilists

📖 William Wordsworth: *Westminster Bridge*
Nathaniel Bowditch: *The New American Practical Navigator*
Madame de Staël: *Delphine*

🎵 Ludwig van Beethoven: *Moonlight Sonata*
Samuel Wesley: *Fourth Symphony*

1803 Lord Elgin starts shipping portions of the sculpted frieze of the Parthenon home to England. U.S. engineer Robert Fulton is in Paris, developing his submarine *Nautilus*. Cotton is now a more important export for the U.S. than tobacco. The Louisiana Purchase doubles the size of the U.S.; Talleyrand sells the territory to raise funds for

Napoleon's military campaigns. Massachusetts and New York threaten to withdraw from the Union in protest against the Purchase, which Jefferson has agreed without Senate's consent. The Hawaiian chief Kamehameha unifies the eight Sandwich Islands, employing English, Welsh and American Governors. *16 May*: Britain and France re-open war, the French threatening to invade England from Boulogne. *25 Aug*: The Irish rebel leader Robert Emmet is captured by the British. *23 Sep*: Battle of Assaye: British troops under Arthur Wellesley defeat the Marathas in the Second Maratha War.

Henry Raeburn: The McNab

Joseph Lancaster: *Improvement in Education as it Respects the Industrious Classes*

Walter Scott: *Minstrelsy of the Scottish Border*

Johann Friedrich von Schiller: *Die Braut von Messina*

Ludwig von Beethoven: *Symphony No 2*; *Christ on the Mount of Olives*

1804 Nicolas Appert opens the world's first vacuum bottling factory at Massey, France. Richard Trevithick invents a steam railway locomotive that can haul 70 people and 10 tons of iron at 8 kph/5 mph. Frederick Winsor demonstrates gas lighting at the Lyceum Theatre in London. Haiti becomes a black republic when Napoleon's army fails to suppress a slave rebellion; the revolutionaries kill all remaining whites on the island. *20 Mar*: the Duc d'Enghien is shot at Vincennes for plotting to bring back the monarchy to France. *21 Mar*: the Code Napoleon goes into force in France, Belgium, Luxembourg and the Palatinate; it combines Roman law with some of the radical reforms of recent years. *18 May*: Napoleon is proclaimed Emperor by the French Senate; a plebiscite ratifies his elevation. *2 Dec*: Napoleon is crowned in Paris by Pope Pius VII in a ceremony reminiscent of Charlemagne's coronation 1,000 years ago.

Antoine Gros: The Pesthouse at Jaffa

Johann Friedrich von Schiller: *Wilhelm Tell*; *Homage to the Arts*

William Blake: *Jerusalem*; *Milton*

William Wordsworth: *Intimations of Immortality*

1805 French troops gather at Boulogne ready to invade Britain; Vice Admiral de Villeneuve has no confidence in his ships, officers or crews, so he sails south rather than enter the Channel to join the invasion force. Villeneuve is bottled up in Cadiz Harbour by Nelson. British naval officer Francis Beaufort devises the Beaufort Scale for wind velocity. *26 May*: Napoleon crowns himself in Milan Cathedral with the old iron crown of the Lombard kings. Austria, Russia, Sweden and Britain form a Third Coalition against France. *17 Oct*: after he has broken camp at Boulogne and marched across Germany, Napoleon forces a 30,000-strong Austrian army at Ulm to surrender. *21 Oct*: Battle of Trafalgar: the decisive defeat of the French fleet by a British fleet under Nelson ends French aspirations to sea power. Nelson is mortally wounded in the battle. *2 Dec*: Battle of Austerlitz: Napoleon defeats a combined Austrian-Russian army; this dissuades Prussia from joining the Third Coalition. *26 Dec*: Treaty of Pressburg, ending the conflict between France and Austria.

🎨 J. M. W. Turner: Shipwreck
   John Sell Cotman: Greta Bridge
   Francisco de Goya: Doña Isabel de Procal

📖 Walter Scott: *The Lay of the Last Minstrel*
   William Wordsworth: *The Prelude*
   William Hazlitt: *The Principles of Human Actions*

🎵 Ludwig van Beethoven: *Fidelio; Symphony No 3*
   Robert Bochsa: *Trajan*

1806 At Paisley, Scotland, Patrick Clark develops a cotton thread as strong as linen thread. The Lancashire mill owner Robert Owen goes on paying full wages despite a shutdown for lack of raw cotton, winning the confidence and loyalty of his workers. Napoleon installs his brother Joseph on the throne of Naples and his brother Louis on the throne of Holland. *6 May*: the British announce a blockade of the continental coastline from Brest to the River Elbe. *12 Jul*: the Confederation of the Rhine organized by the French ends the Holy Roman Empire; this precipitates war with Prussia. *14 Oct*: the Prussian army is routed at the Battle of Jena. *27 Oct*: Napoleon occupies Berlin. *21 Nov*: Napoleon proclaims a blockade of Britain, denying food and other supplies from mainland Europe.

🏛 Claude Michel: Arc de Triomphe, Paris

🎨 Antoine Gros: The Battle of Aboukir

🎵 Ludwig van Beethoven: *Violin Concerto*

1807 *7 Jan*: the British ban neutral nation ships from trading with France, but the French are self-sufficient in food. *7–8 Feb*: Battle of Eylau: indecisive battle between Prussian and Russian forces. *18 Mar*: British troops occupy Alexandria, but are forced out again by the Turks. *26 May*: the French take Danzig. Former U.S. Vice President Aaron Burr is on trial at Richmond, Virginia, for plotting to set up an independent state comprising Mexico and portions of the Louisiana Territory, but he is acquitted for lack of evidence. *28 May*: the Ottoman Sultan Selim III is deposed by the Janissaries in Constantinople; he is succeeded by the son of Sultan Abdul Hamid. *14 Jun*: Battle of Friedland: the French defeat the Russians. *22 Jun*: the British ship *Leopard* fires on the U.S. frigate *Chesapeake* and takes off four British deserters. *2 Jul*: Jefferson closes U.S. ports to all British warships. *7–9 Jul*: Treaties of Tilsit: Napoleon is to have all German lands between the Rhine and the Elbe and accepts the Russian Tsar's mediation in concluding a peace with Britain. *17 Aug*: the *Clermont*, the first commercially successful steamboat, travels up the Hudson River. *Sep*: the British bombard Copenhagen and seize the Danish fleet, a punishment for joining the Continental System. *29 Nov*: the Portuguese royal family flees to Brazil as the French invade Portugal, which has refused to join Napoleon's Continental System.

🎨 Jacques Louis David: Coronation of Napoleon and Josephine

📖 Thomas Thomson: *System of Chemistry*

Humphry Davy: *On Some Chemical Agencies of electricity*

William Wordsworth: *Poems in Two Volumes*

Charles and Mary Lamb: *Tales From Shakespeare*

🎵 Carl Maria von Weber: *Symphonies Nos 1 and 2*

Ludwig van Beethoven: *Symphony No 4*; *Appassionata Sonata*

1808 The *SS Phoenix* is the first steamboat to be built with an American-built engine; earlier engines have been imported from Britain. *26 Mar:* French troops under Murat occupy Madrid; Carlos IV abdicates in favour of his 23-year-old son Ferdinand, but Napoleon decides to make his own brother Joseph King of Spain, an idea repugnant to the Spanish. *13 May:* Murat threatens the Spanish council after a riot; the council is bullied into asking for Joseph as King. *28 Jul:* Mustafa Bairakdar, the Ottoman Grand Vizier, marches on Constantinople intent on restoring Selim III to the throne, but the Janissaries strangle Selim to prevent this. In retaliation, Bairakdar has the new Sultan Mustapha IV deposed and killed, placing Selim's 23-year-old nephew Mahmud II on the throne instead. *4 Dec:* Napoleon takes Madrid with an army of 150,000 and installs Joseph Bonaparte on the throne.

   ✍ William Porden: The Dome, Royal Pavilion, Brighton
      James Wyatt: Ashridge Park, Hertfordshire
   ✺ Antonio Canova: Pauline Borghese as Venus
      Antoine Gros: The Battle of Eylau
      Francisco Goya: Execution of the Citizens of Madrid
      Jean Ingres: La Grande Baigneuse
      Kaspar David Friedrich: The Cross on the Mountains
   📖 John Dalton: *A New System of Chemical Philosophy*
      Walter Scott: *Marmion*
   ✺ Ludwig van Beethoven: *Symphonies Nos 5 and 6*

1809 Fur trader David Thompson begins to explore and map more than 1 million square miles of Canada between Lake Superior and the Pacific. In India, the Treaty of Amritsar stops the advance of the Sikh confederacy led by Ranjit Singh. *16 Jan:* Battle of Corunna: French forces defeat the British under Sir John Moore, who is killed in the battle; Sir Arthur Wellesley succeeds Moore as commander of British forces in the Peninsula. *13 Mar:* Gustavus IV of Sweden is seized by army officers in the royal apartments and confined in the palace of Gripsholm; a provisional government is proclaimed, led by the Duke of Sudermania. *29 Mar:* Gustavus IV of

Sweden abdicates. *10 May*: the Swedish provisional government announces that Gustavus' family will not succeed to the throne. *21–22 May*: Battle of Aspern: Napoleon's first defeat, by an Austrian army. The French retreat to the island of Lobau in the Danube; they have few supplies and Napoleon rejects his generals' advice to retreat. *5 Jul*: the French annexe the Papal States; Pope Pius VII is taken prisoner. Battle of Wagram: the French win, but at a cost of 20,000 dead. The Austrian army is forced to withdraw after losing 19,000 dead. *27–8 Jul*: Battle of Talavera: the British under Wellesley defeat the Spanish under Joseph Bonaparte; Wellesley is created Duke of Wellington. *4 Aug*: Metternich is made Austrian Minister of State. *8 Oct*: Metternich is made Minister of Foreign Affairs, starting a 40-year career in that post. *14 Oct*: Treaty of Schönbrunn, ending hostilities between France and Austria, which now joins the Continental System.

John Constable: Malvern Hills
Henry Raeburn: Mrs Spiers
Kaspar David Friedrich: Monch am Meer
Jean de Monet: *Zoological Philosophy*
Diedrich Knickerbocker (Washington Irving): *A History of New York*
Johann von Goethe: *The Elective Affinities*

1810 Prussia abolishes serfdom, giving ex-serfs the land they have cultivated for their former masters. *20 Feb*: Austrian patriot Andreas Hofer is shot after leading a rebellion against Bavarian rule. *11 Mar*: Napoleon is married by proxy to the Austrian Archduchess Maria Luisa. *May*: Prince Christian, elected heir to the Swedish throne, dies suddenly; he is replaced as Crown Prince by Napoleon's General Jean Bernadotte. *9 Jul*: France annexes Holland after Louis Bonaparte abdicates. *19 Jul*: Queen Louise of Prussia dies, aged 34. *11 Nov*: the painter Johann Zoffany dies at Kew in Surrey, aged 77.
Column in Place Vendôme to commemorate Napoleon's victory at Austerlitz (modelled on Trajan's Column)

Jacques Louis David: Distribution of the Eagles
François Gerard: The Battle of Austerlitz

Francisco de Goya: *Los Desastres de la Guerra* (engravings)

📖 Madame de Stael: *De l'Allemagne*
Walter Scott: *The Lady of the Lake*

🎵 Ludwig van Beethoven: *Egmont Overture*

1811 The Russian Ambassador to Paris, Prince Alexander Kurakin, introduces the practice of serving meals in courses (*à la Russe*) instead of putting all the food on the table at once. *10 Jan:* a New Orleans slave revolt is suppressed; 66 black workers are killed and their heads displayed on the roadside. *5 Feb:* in England the Prince of Wales, now 49, is to reign as Regent in place of his mad father, George III. *1 May:* Mohammed Ali, the Ottoman Viceroy, invites the Mameluke leaders of Egypt to a banquet at Ciro's citadel, where they are massacred for having plotted against Mohammed Ali. *5 May:* Battle of Fuentes de Onoro: British forces defeat the French. *16 May:* Battle of Albuera: the British are again victorious. *7 Jul:* Venezuela declares itself independent, with Francisco de Miranda in command of the revolutionary forces: Simon Bolivar is one of his lieutenants. *14 Aug:* Paraguay declares its independence. *7 Nov:* Battle of Tippecanoe, ending in defeat for the Shawnee Indians, who have been provoked into battle while their chief Tecumseh is away, and then hammered by General Harrison's troops. *11 Nov:* Cartagena in the viceroyalty of New Granada declares its independence.

✏️ John Nash: Regent's Park, London
Commissioners' Plan: Manhattan Street Plan, New York

📖 Jane Austen: *Sense and Sensibility*
Percy Shelley: *The Necessity of Atheism*

🎵 Carl Maria von Weber: *Abu Hassan*
Ludwig van Beethoven: *Piano Concerto No 5*

1812 François Vidocq forms the French Sûreté. In England, the machine-breaking Luddite riots that started last year spread to Yorkshire, Lancashire, Derbyshire and Leicestershire. *26 Mar:* an earthquake in Venezuela demoralizes de Miranda's revolutionaries. De Miranda is made Dictator in order to control the situation, but he falls into the hands of the Spanish, who send him as a prisoner to

Spain. *Jun*: Napoleon invades Russia with a Grande
Armée of 600,000 soldiers of eight nationalities. *Jul*:
Battle of Ostrowo, seriously weakening Napoleon's
army, which has additional problems with disease. *22
Jul*: Battle of Salamanca: Wellington defeats the French.
Aug: Wellington enters Madrid. *19 Aug*: the British
frigate *Guerriere* is destroyed by the *USS Constitution*.
7 Sep: Battle of Borodino: indecisive battle between the
Grand Army and the Russian army under Field Marshal
Kutusov, who retreats to save his army. Napoleon enters
Moscow to find most of the 300,000 citizen gone. *8–12
Sep*: Moscow is burned down by Russian saboteurs. *19
Oct*: Napoleon begins his retreat from Moscow. *Nov*:
Marshal Kutusov pursues the Grand Army, defeating
armies under Ney and Davout at Smolensk. *Dec*: Napoleon's Grand Army has been reduced (by cold, hunger,
dysentery, typhus and lack of salt) to 100,000 men as the
survivors pass across the River Nieman.

⌂ Mangin: City Hall, New York
✑ Thomas Rowlandson: The Tour of Dr. Syntax
  J. M. W. Turner: Snowstorm: Hannibal Crossing
  the Alps

  Jean Gericault: Mounted Officer of the Imperial
  Guard

📖 Baron Cuvier: *Recherches sur les ossemens fossiles*
  (founding the science of palaeontology)
  Lord Byron: *Childe Harold's Pilgrimage*
🎵 Ludwig van Beethoven: *King Stephen Overture*

1813 The waltz becomes popular in Europe. In the wake of
Napoleon's disastrous Russian campaign, wars of libera-
tion erupt all over Europe. *3 Feb*: Friedrich Wilhelm III
of Prussia appeals for a volunteer corps to liberate
Prussia. *3 Mar*: Swedish treaty with Britain, who will
not oppose a union of Norway and Sweden. *27 Mar*:
Russian and Prussian troops occupy Dresden. *2 May*:
Battle of Lützen: Napoleon defeats an Allied army and
enters Dresden. *20–21 May*: Battles of Bautzen and
Wurschen: Napoleon wins but only with further huge
losses of men. *30 May*: the French take Hamburg. *12
Aug*: Austria declares war on France. *23 Aug*: Battle of
Grossbeeren: a Prussian force under Baron von Bülow

defeats the French and so saves Berlin. *26 Aug*: Battle of Katzbach: another Prussian victory over the French. Battle of Dresden: Napoleon's last major victory in Germany. *6 Sep*: Battle of Dennewitz: the Prussian army under von Bülow is victorious, preventing Marshal Ney from taking Berlin. *14 Sep*: a Mexican Congress at Chilpancingo meets to discuss independence. *5 Oct* Battle of the Thames in Ontario: General Harrison defeats a British army under Proctor; the Shawnee Chief Tecumseh, an ally of the British, is killed in the action. *16–19 Oct*: Battle of Leipzig, ending in defeat for Napoleon, who loses 100,000 men. His Saxon and Württemberg contingents desert him and he begins a retreat. *20 Oct*: the Austrian Emperor Francis I makes Metternich an hereditary Prince. *9 Nov*: in America, General Andrew Jackson defeats Creek Indians at Talledega in a retaliatory attack after the Creeks massacred 500 white settlers in *Aug*. *10 Nov*: Wellington crosses the frontier into France to defeat Marshal Soult. *11 Nov*: Dresden surrenders to Allied forces. *15 Nov*: in Holland, the Dutch expel French officials. *5 Dec*: Lübeck surrenders to the Allies. *26 Dec*: Modlin and Torgau surrender to the Allies. *30 Dec*: Danzig surrenders to the Allies; the allies threaten to invade France itself if Napoleon will not come to terms.

Jane Austen: *Pride and Prejudice*
Johann Wyss: *Der Schweizerische Robinson* (The Swiss Family Robinson)
Percy Shelley: *Queen Mab*
Robert Southey: *The Life of Nelson*

1814 Richard Trevithick's steam locomotive is put to work; George Stephenson's model is used on the Killingworth colliery railway. Most of the Library of Congress is destroyed by fire, allegedly started by British troops; Jefferson offers his library of 6,500 books at cost, which Congress accepts as the nucleus of a new library. The Duke of Sutherland destroys the homes of tenants on his Scottish estates to make way for sheep; he drives up to 10,000 people off his land by *1822*. *1 Feb*: Battle of La Rothière: Napoleon is defeated by von Blücher. *9 Mar*: Battle of Laon: another defeat for Napoleon. *12 Mar*:

Battle of Archis: another defeat for Napoleon. *20 Mar*:
Battle of La Fère-Champenoise: yet another defeat. *30
Mar*: Allied troops storm Montmartre. *31 Mar*: Allied
troops enter Paris. *11 Apr*: Napoleon abdicates and is
given sovereignty of Elba on a substantial income to be
paid by the French. *4 May*: Napoleon lands on Elba. The
French monarchy is restored: the Comte de Provence
becomes Louis XVIII, with Talleyrand as Foreign
Minister. Ferdinand VII is restored to the throne of
Spain. *21 Jun*: the kingdom of the Netherlands is created
by a union of the Austrian Netherlands and Holland. *11
Sep*: a U.S. naval force defeats and captures a British
squadron on Lake Champlain in the Battle of Platts-
burgh; the planned British invasion of the U.S. from
Canada is abandoned.

 🏛 John Soane: Dulwich Picture Gallery, London
 🎨 John Constable: Old Sarum
  Theodore Géricault: The Wounded Cuirassier
  Francisco de Goya: 2 May 1808; General Palafox;
  Ferdinand VII Jean-Auguste Ingres: Odalisque
 📖 Walter Scott: *Waverley*
  Jane Austen: *Mansfield Park*
  William Wordsworth: *The Excursion*
  Matthew Flinders: *A Voyage to Terra Australis*
  René-Charles de Pixerecourt: *Le chien de Montargis*
  (melodrama)

1815 In South Africa, the Zulus begin to expand at the
expense of their neighbours, even though they number
only 1,500. Shaka (Chaka), the 28-year-old son of Chief
Senzangakona, has devised a more effective assegai and a
shield that doubles as a weapon, as well as new military
tactics. The peace in Europe releases Spanish troops for
deployment in South America; 10,000 Europe seasoned
troops land in Venezuela, easily defeat the revolutionary
armies in New Granada and restore royal authority.
Simon Bolivar escapes to Jamaica. *8 Jan*: Battle of
New Orleans, a land victory for the Americans in the
'War of 1812'; the British withdraw after losing 700 men.
1 Mar: Napoleon lands at Cannes with 1,500 men and
begins a march on Paris, gathering thousands to him as
he goes. *20 Mar*: Napoleon reaches Paris and begins a

second reign; Louis XVIII leaves France for Ghent. *5 Apr*: Tambora in the East Indies erupts in the biggest volcanic eruption in modern times; 20,000 are killed. *16 Jun*: Battle of Quatre Bras: the French under Ney win, but not convincingly. *18 Jun*: Battle of Waterloo: a French army of 70,000 faces an Allied (British, German, Dutch) army of the same size under Wellington; the French are decisively defeated, ending Napoleon's career finally. *22 Jun*: Napoleon abdicates, is taken prisoner and exiled to St Helena. *28 Sep*: Joachim Murat, former King of Naples, tries to regain his throne, landing at Pizzo with only 30 men. He is captured. *13 Oct*: Murat is shot by firing squad.

     John Nash: Brighton Pavilion, England
     Adrian Zakharov: Admiralty, St Petersburg
     Charles Bulfinch: University Hall, Harvard University

     John Crome: Boulevard des Italiens
     Thomas Lawrence: Mrs. Wolf
     Francisco de Goya: The Third of May

     Walter Scott: *Guy Mannering*
     Jacob and Wilhelm Grimm: *Kinder- und Hausmarchen* (Fairy Tales)

1816 English dandy Beau Brummell flees to Calais to escape creditors. Friedrich Krupp produces the first steel at Essen, Germany. Chief Senzangakona of the Zulus dies and is succeeded by his son Shaka, who will increase the Zulu army from 400 to 40,000 and rule with tyrannical cruelty. *16 Jan*: Brazil proclaims itself an independent Empire with the Portuguese Prince Regent João as Emperor. *20 Mar*: Queen Maria I of Portugal dies, aged 81; she is succeeded by her son João VI, but he remains in Brazil. *29 Jul*: Argentina (United Provinces of La Plata) declares itself independent of Spain. Cold weather persists through most of the summer in mid-latitudes as a result of the dust veil cretaed by last year's eruption of Tambora; heavy snow falls in north-east U.S. in *Jun* and *Jul* in a year farmers will refer to as 'eighteen-hundred-and-froze-to-death'. *2 Jul*: the French ship *Medusa* is wrecked on a sandbank off the West Africa and the crew and passengers take to the boats; those remaining build a raft. 89 out of the

149 people crowding onto the raft are lost within two days; only 15 survive to reach the Sahara coast, where more die in the sand.

✏ Edward Blore and William Atkinson: Abbotsford, Roxburghshire

🕮 John Crome: Mousehold Heath; Porington Oak

📖 Georg Hegel: *Wissenschaft der Logik*
Jane Austen: *Emma*
Walter Scott: *The Black Dwarf*; *Old Mortality*
Samuel Taylor Coleridge: *Kublai Khan*
John Keats: *On First Looking Chapmand's* Homer
David Ricardo: *Proposals for a Secure Currency*

🎼 Gioacchino Rossini: *Il Barbiere de Siviglia* (Barber of Seville)

1817 Mississippi is admitted to the Union as the 20th state. The Ohio Indians sign a treaty giving their remaining 4 million acres of land to the United States. *12 Feb*: Chile gains its independence from Spain at the Battle of Chacabuco; Bernardo O'Higgins enlists the support of the Argentine commander Jose de San Martin. O'Higgins becomes Supreme-Dictator of Chile. *3 Mar*: The steamboat (sternwheeler) *Washington* leaves Louisville for a round-trip voyage on the Mississippi to New Orleans – the first such voyage.

✏ Orders of Henri Christophe (Henri I): Citadelle La Ferriere, Haiti
John Rennie: Waterloo Bridge, London (opened)

🕮 John Constable: Flatford Mill

📖 David Ricardo: *Principles of Political Economy*
Walter Scott: *Rob Roy*
John Keats: *Poems*
Franz Grillparzer: *Die Ahnfrau* (The Ancestress)

🎼 Gioacchino Rossini: *Le Cenerentola* (Cinderella)

1818 Peter Durant introduces the tin can to America. Johann Siegert invents Angostura bitters at Angostura, Venezuela. Beethoven becomes totally deaf. London surgeon James Blundel performs the first successful human blood transfusion. The Peul Diallo dynasty that has ruled the Niger valley in West Africa for 300 years comes to an end in a takeover by the Muslim usurper Marabout Cheikou Ahmadou. In Venezuela, Simon Bolivar secures the lower Orinoco valley from the Spanish. In India, the Rajput states, Poona and the Holkar of Indore fall into British hands. *5 Feb:* Charles XIII of Sweden dies, aged 69, and is succeeded by the Crown Prince Jean Bernadotte: now 55, he will reign as Charles XIV, founding a new dynasty. *20 Oct:* the U.S.-Canadian border is established as the 49th parallel from the Lake of the Woods to the Rockies, based on David Thompson's survey.

Thomas Lawrence: The Campaign Leaders (18 portraits)

Mary Shelley: *Frankenstein*
Jane Austen: *Northanger Abbey; Persuasion* (posthumous)
Percy Shelley: *Ozymandias*
Walter Scott: *The Heart of Midlothian*
Franz Grillparzer: *Sappho*
Thomas Bowdler: *Family Shakespeare*
Carl Maria von Weber: *Jubel*
Franz Gruber: *Stille Nacht* (Silent Night)

1819 François-Louis Cailler makes the world's first eating chocolate at Vevey in Switzerland. Thomas Stamford Raffles occupies Singapore and makes it a British colony. *22 Feb:* Spain cedes Florida and all its possessions east of the Mississippi to the United States. Alabama joins the Union. *23 Mar:* August von Kotzebue, a reactionary German journalist, is murdered at Mannheim by a student, Karl Sand, who calls Kotzebue an enemy of liberty. Prince Metternich of Austria persuades Friedrich Wilhelm of Prussia to issue the Karlsbad Decrees, establishing an inquisition at Mainz to investigate secret societies and impose strict censorship on publications. *8 May:* Kamehamaha, Chief of Hawaii, dies, aged 82, and is succeeded by his 22-year-old son Kamahameha II, who will welcome missionaries and allow the traditional culture to be undermined. *Aug:* Simon Bolivar liberates New Granada from Spanish rule; the Congress of Angostura proclaims the independence of Great Colombia (New Granada, Quito and Venezuela) and installs Bolivar as President and Military Dictator. *16 Aug:* the Peterloo Massacre in Manchester; British soldiers kill several people engaged in a peaceful demonstration against the Corn Laws.

✐ Thomas Telford: Menai Strait Suspension Bridge
The Prado, Madrid

✐ John Constable: The White Horse
Theodore Gericault: The Raft of the *Medusa*
Thomas Lawrence: Pope Pius VII

📖 Arthur Schopenhauer: *Die Welt als Wille und Vorstellung* (The World as Will and Idea)
Walter Scott: *Ivanhoe*
John Keats: *The Eve of St Agnes; Ode to a Nightingale; On A Grecian Urn; On Melancholy; To Psyche*
Lord Byron: *Mazeppa; Don Juan* (first cantos)

🎼 Franz Schubert: *Stabat Mater*

1820 The Venus de Milo (Aphrodite of Melos) statue is found on the Greek island of Melos by a Greek peasant. The state of Liberia is founded by the Washington Colonization Society for the repatriation of black people to Africa. Edward Bransfield surveys New South Shetland for the Royal Navy, reaching as far south as 64°S. *29 Jan:* George III of England dies, aged 81, and is succeeded by the 57-year-old Prince Regent, George IV. *13 Feb:* the Duc de Berry, France's heir presumptive, is assassinated; his posthumous son, the Comte de Chambord, born *29 Sep*, becomes heir to the French throne. *23 Feb:* the Cato Street Conspiracy comes to light in London; the leaders will be executed for plotting to murder the Cabinet and take over the country. *24 Aug:* a revolt breaks out in Portugal as discontent grows over excessive British influence in the government and the absence of the King, who is still in Brazil.

✐ Royal York Crescent, Bristol (completed)

✐ John Constable: Harwich Lighthouse; Flatford Mill
Bertel Thorvaldsen: The Lion of Lucerne

📖 Percy Shelley: *Prometheus Unbound*
Alphonse de Lamartine: *Meditations Poétiques*
Eugene Scribe: *L'ours et le Pacha* (The Bear and the Pasha)
Frederick Accum: *Adulteration of Foods and Culinary Poisons*

1821 Liberation is in the air after Europe has freed itself of Napoleon. *Feb*: a Greek War of Independence begins. *Mar*: Victor Emmanuel of Piedmont abdicates under pressure and is succeeded by his brother Charles Felix; in the latter's absence the Spanish constitution is proclaimed. *8 Apr*: Battle of Novara: a combined Austrian-Sardinian army defeats the Piedmontese; Savoy regains control over Piedmont. *24 Feb*: Mexico declares its independence from Spain and Agostin becomes provisional Regent of Mexico. *5 May*: Napoleon Bonaparte dies on St Helena, aged 52. *19 Jun*: Battle of Dragasani west of Bucharest: an Ottoman army defeats a Greek nationalist force, but the war will continue for 10 years. *24 Jun*: Simon Bolivar's lieutenant has liberated Quito, while Bolivar himself defeats a royalist army at Carabob in Venezuela. *22 Jul*: José de San Martin declares Peru independent. *30 Aug*: Bolivar is named President of Venezuela. *14 Sep*: El Salvador, Honduras, Costa Rica and Guatemala declare independence from Spain. *Dec*: Panama declares independence from Spain, joining Colombia.

    Jeffry Wyatville: Sidney Sussex College, Cambridge

    William Blake: Illustrations to Jerusalem

    John Constable: The Hay Wain; Hampstead Heath

    Manchester Guardian (first issue)

    Thomas de Quincey: *Confessions of an English Opium Eater*

    Walter Scott: *Kenilworth*

    Michael Faraday: *Principles of the Electric Motor*

    James Fennimore Cooper: *The Spy*

    Franz Grillparzer: *Das goldene Vliess*

    Carl Maria von Weber: *Der Freischütz* (The Free-Shooter); *Konzertstuck for Piano and Orchestra*; *Invitation to the Dance*

    Daniel Auber: *Emma*

1822 Jean Champollion deciphers the Rosetta Stone, making it possible to read ancient Egyptian inscriptions for the first time and giving access to the ancient culture. In West Africa, an Ashanti War breaks out after an Ashanti trader and a Fanti policeman exchange insults. *13 Jan*: a Greek assembly at Epidauros declares independence from the Ottoman Empire. *Apr*: an Ottoman fleet seizes the island of Chios, massacres many of its people. *30 Apr*: at Rotherhithe in England, the world's first iron steamship, the *Aaron Manby*, is launched. *24 May*: Battle of Pichincha near Quito: José de Sucre decisively defeats a Spanish army. *10 Jan*: the *Aaron Manby* goes into cross-Channel service as a cargo ship. *19 Jun*: a Greek flotilla under Admiral Kanaris destroys the Ottoman fleet. *Jul*: the Ottoman army invades Greece, forcing the Greek nationalist government to flee to the islands. *25 Jul*: in Mexico, Agostin de Iturbide is crowned Emperor; he sends troops out to try to bring other Central American states into his Empire. *12 Aug*: in England, Lord Castlereagh commits suicide, aged 53, by slitting his throat with a penknife. *1 Dec*: the Portuguese Regent Dom Pedro proclaims independence for Brazil and is crowned Emperor of Brazil (his father remains João VI of Portugal).

✐ Thomas Rickman: St George's Church, Birmingham

🎨 John Constable: View of the Stour
David Wilkie: Chelsea Pensioners reading the Gazette of the Battle of Waterloo

📖 Chevalier de Lamarck: *Histoire Naturelle des Animaux sans vertebres*
Walter Scott: *The Pirate; Peveril of the Peak*
Frederick Marryat: *Suggestions for the Abolition of Impressment*
Francis Place: *Illustrations and Proofs of the Principles of Population*

🎼 George Kiallmark: *The Old Oaken Bucket*

1823 An electric telegraph offered to the British Admiralty by Francis Ronalds is rejected as 'wholly unnecessary'. Michael Faraday liquifies chlorine, opening the way to its use in water purification and bleaching. Asiatic chloera spreads westwards as far as Astrakhan. The modern petroleum industry begins at Baku on the Caspian Sea: drilling begins. In London, William Wilberforce forms an anti-slavery society. *May*: Chateaubriand, French Foreign Minister, sends troops into Spain to suppress revolution. *6 Jun*: Chateaubriand is dismissed. *1 Jul*: an assembly at Guatemala City declares the sovereignty of the United Provinces of Central America. *31 Aug*: Battle of the Trocadero: French troops defeat Spanish revolutionary forces. *23 Sep*: French troops take Cadiz and the rebels hand over Ferdinand VII, who is restored to the throne. *2 Dec*: the Monroe Doctrine is declared by President Monroe: 'The American continents are not to be considered as subjects for future colonization by any European power'.

Robert Smirke: British Museum, London
Charles Barry: St Peter's Church, Brighton
Thomas Cubitt: Polesden Lacey, Dorking
J. M. W. Turner: The Bay of Baiae
James Fennimore Cooper: *The Pioneers*
Lord Byron: *Don Juan*
Eugene Scribe: *Le Menteur Veridique* (The Truthful Liar)
Walter Scott: *Quentin Durward*
Gioacchino Rossini: *Semiramide*
Henry Bishop: *Home Sweet Home*
Carl Maria von Weber: *Euryanthe*
Franz Schubert: *Rosamunde*

1824 The Rhode Island Red hen is bred at Little Compton, R. I. The hen will become famous for its brown eggs. The Cherokee scholar Sequoya perfects a Cherokee alphabet of 85 letters, which will make the Cherokee the first literate Indian tribe; by *1828* there is a Cherokee language newspaper. *21 Jan*: the Ashanti defeat a Fanti detachment at Essamako; they also capture the British Governor Sir Charles Mcarthy, behead him and use his skull as a royal drinking cup at Kumasi. The Ashanti King Osai Tutu Kwadwo is killed. *26 Jan*: the painter Gericault dies, aged 32, in Paris. *24 Feb*: a Burmese War starts; Lord Amherst, British Governor General of India, declares war when the Burmese capture the island of Shahpuri. *11 May*: Rangoon falls to the British. *14 Jul*: Kamehameha II King of Hawaii and his wife die of measles during a visit to Britain. *24 Aug*: Simon Bolivar and José de Sucre defeat a Spanish force in the Andes. *16 Sep*: Louis XVIII of France dies, aged 68 and is succeeded by his brother Charles X. *Oct*: Greek nationalist forces defeat an Ottoman army at Mitylene. *9 Dec*: Battle of Ayacucho: José de Sucre defeats a Spanish force twice the size of his own army.

🌉 Highgate Falls Bridge, Vermont (first covered bridge in Vermont)
Church of Notre Dame, Montreal

🖼 Caspar David Friedrich: The Polar Sea
Eugene Delacroix: Massacre at Chios

📖 Walter Scott: *Redgauntlet*
Percy Shelley: *Posthumous Poems*

🎵 Ludwig van Beethoven: *Missa Solemnis*; *Symphony No 9*

1825 The Greek War of Independence continues; Ottoman forces under Mustapha Pasha renews the siege of Missolonghi, where Byron died last year (*19 Apr.*). The people of Uruguay rebel against Brazil, encouraged by Argentina which hopes to annexe Uruguay. News of the Hawaiian King's death reaches Hawaii, where Kamahameha III accedes to the throne at the age of 12; he is the dead King's younger brother. *4 Jan*: Ferdinand I King of the Two Sicilies dies, aged 73, and is succeeded by his 47-year-old son Francesco I. *6 Aug*: Bolivia declares itself an independent state at a congress convened by José de Sucre, who will next year become Bolivia's first President. *25 Aug*: Uruguay achieves its independence, but Brazil and Argentina will shortly afterwards go to war over which of them will have Uruguay. *29 Aug*: Portugal formally recognizes the independence of Brazil. *27 Sep*: the Stockton and Darlington railway opens; the 43 km/27-mile railway offers the first passenger rail service in the world. *26 Oct*: the Erie Canal opens, linking the Great Lakes with the Hudson River. *13 Dec*: Tsar Alexander I dies in agony, aged 47, after eating poisonous mushrooms in the Crimea; he is succeeded by his 21-year-old brother Nicholas I. *14 Dec*: the Decembrist rising; young Russian army officers frustrated by the Romanov autocracy challenge its authority. The Tsar injudiciously orders a cavalry charge across icy cobblestones, but the rising is easily suppressed. *29 Dec*: the painter David dies in Brussels, aged 77.

🌉 Thomas Telford: Menai Straits Suspension Bridge

(completed)

Thomas Richman: Ombersley Church, Worcestershire

John Nash: Buckingham Palace (created out of Buckingham House)

Belgrave Square, London

Samuel Palmer: A Valley Thick With Corn

John Constable: The Leaping Horse

Samuel Morse: General Lafayette

Edward Hicks: The Peaceable Kingdom

Thomas Macaulay: *Milton*

William Hazlitt: *The Spirit of the Age, or Contemporary Portraits*

Jacques Thierry: *The Norman Conquest of England*

Franz Grillparzer: *King Ottokar's Rise and Fall*

Charles Wolfe: *The Burial of Sir John Moore*

Emilio Arrieta y Corera: *Ildegonda*

1826 Unter den Linden in Berlin is lit with gas lamps. Munich University is founded. Persian troops invade Russia, but they are halted at the Battle of Ganja by Russian troops under Ivan Paskevich. *24 Feb*: Treaty of Yandabu, ending the Burmese War: Britain acquires Arakan and Assam. *10 Mar*: João VI of Portugal dies, aged 56, and is succeeded by his son Dom Pedro of Brazil as Pedro IV, but Pedro IV refuses to leave Brazil and abdicates in favour of his infant daughter Maria. *5 Apr*: Russia gives Constantinople an ultimatum demanding a return to the status quo along the Danube; Sultan Mahmud II gives in to pressure. *May*: the Ottoman Janissaries revolt when Mahmud orders the formation of a new military corps to replace them; a mob in Constantinople attacks the barracks and kills over 6,000 Janissaries. *4 Jul*: former American Presidents John Adams, 90, and Thomas Jefferson, 83, die on the 50th anniversary of the signing of the Declaration of Independence. *7 Aug*: a British force defeats the Ashanti near Accra (Ghana).

Thomas Telford: Conway Road Suspension Bridge

John Nash: Cumberland Terrace, London (completed)

John Constable: The Cornfield

Eugene Delacroix: Execution of the Doge Marino

Falieri; Greece in the Ruins of Missolonghi

📖 André Ampère: *Electrodynamics*

Walter Scott: *Woodstock*

James Fennimore Cooper: *The Last of the Mohicans*

Alessandro Manzoni: *I Promessi Sposi* (The Betrothed)

Heinrich Heine: *Reisebilder* (Pictures of Travel)

🎜 Carl Maria von Weber: *Oberon* (Weber dies, aged 39, in London)

Franz Schubert: *Marche Militaire*

1827 The English astronomer Frederick William Herschel invents contact lenses. Austrian engineer Joseph Ressel and Scottish engineer Robert Wilson independently invent the screw propeller for ships. U.S. physicist Joseph Henry invents the electromagnet. *26 Jan*: Peru withdraws from Simon Bolivar's Colombia on the grounds that Bolivar is an autocrat. *20 Feb*: Battle of Itzuaingo: the Brazilian force defeat Argentine and Uruguayan troops. *26 Mar*: the composer Beethoven dies, aged 56, in Vienna. *6 Jul*: the Treaty of London between France, Russia and Britain, promising to support the Greek nationalists against the Turks if the Ottoman Sultan will not accept an armistice. *8 Sep*: Egyptian troops are landed at Navarino. *20 Oct*: Battle of Navarino: British, Russian and French squadrons destroy the Egyptian-Turkish fleet.

📐 The Paris Exchange (completed)

🎨 Eugène Delacroix: *Death of Sardanapalus*

James Fenimore Cooper: *The Prairie*

Heinrich Heine: *Buch der Lieder*

Victor Hugo: *Cromwell*

Eugène Scribe: *Le mariage d'argent* (Marriage for Money)

🎜 Felix Mendelssohn: *Overture to A Midsummer Night's Dream*

1828 Radama I King of Madagascar dies and is succeeded by his widow, Ranavaloana I, who remains hostile to Christian missionaries and to the influence of both the French and the British. *22 Feb*: Treaty of Turkmanchai, ending the Russo-Persian War; Russia has the exclusive right to maintain a navy on the Caspian Sea. *16 Apr*: the painter Francisco de Goya dies, aged 82 at Bordeaux. *8 Jun*: after declaring war on the Ottoman Empire (*26 Apr*), Russia sends an army across the Danube. *4 Jul*: Dom Miguel, Regent of Portugal, has himself proclaimed King after a May coup; his niece Maria, a girl of nine, is taken to England for safety as a civil war begins. *15 Jul*: the sculptor Jean Houdon dies, aged 87, in Paris. *27 Aug*: Uruguay declares its independence; mediation by British diplomats establishes the state as a buffer between Brazil and Argentina. *22 Sep*: Shaka, the Zulu King who founded the Zulu nation in southern Africa, is murdered, aged 41, by his brothers Dingane and Mhlangane, who now reign jointly. *19 Nov*: Schubert dies, aged 31.

   Francis Chantrey: Statue of George IV, Trafalgar Square, London

   Walter Scott: *The Fair Maid of Perth*

   Franz Grillparzer: *Ein truer Diener seines Atrin* (A Faithful Servant of His Master)

   Gioacchino Rossini: *Count Ory*

   Franz Schubert: *Fantasy for Piano Four Hands*; *Unfinished Symphony*

1829 Barthelemy Thimmonier invents the first practical sewing machine. George Stephenson's *Rocket* wins the Liverpool and Manchester railway locomotive competition. In Edinburgh, William Burke is hanged for multiple murder to supply doctors with corpses for dissection. Venezuela withdraws from Simon Bolivar's Greater Colombia, becoming an independent republic within the year. *22 Mar*: Greece becomes independent with the signing of the London Protocol. *Apr*: Juan Manuel de Rosas ends the anarchy in Argentina by resorting to military action action against Buenos Aires provincial forces. *15 Sep*: slavery is abolished in Mexico. *8 Dec*: De Rosas makes himself Governor of Buenos Aires.

   Tremont House, Boston (the first modern hotel in the New World)

   Thomas Hamilton: Royal High School, Edinburgh

   John Nash: St James's Park, London

   Decimus Burton: Athenaeum Club, London

   J. M. W. Turner: Ulysses Deriding Polyphemus

Benjamin Haydon: Punch and Judy

Felicia Hemans: *Casablanca* ('The boy stood on the
burning deck/Whence all but he had fled')

Charles Sainte-Beuve: *Joseph Delorme*

Johann von Goethe: *Faust, Part 1*

Franz Berwald: *Leonida*

Gioacchino Rossini: *Guillaume Tell* (William Tell)

Felix Mendelssohn: *St Matthew Passion*; *Symphony
No 1*

1830 World population reaches 1 billion. Cholera spreads
through Russia, killing 900,000 people. *6 Apr*: the
Church of Jesus Christ of Latter-Day Saints is founded
in New York state by Joseph Smith. *13 May*: the
Republic of Ecuador is formed as Gran Colombia dis-
integrates. *24 May*: the first section of the Baltimore and
Ohio Railroad is opened, a 21-km/13-mile stretch from
Baltimore to Ellicott Mills. *4 Jun*: De Sucre is assassinated as he tries to maintain the unity of Gran Colombia;
he is killed, aged 35, near Pasto, Colombia. *5 Jul*: Algiers
surrenders to French forces after a three-week blockade;
France begins a century of colonization of Algeria. *29
Jul*: Charles X of France is deposed and succeeded by the
Duc d'Orléans as Louis Philippe. *4 Oct*: Belgium becomes independent of Dutch control as a provisional
government takes over. *17 Dec*: the 'Great Liberator'
Simon Bolivar dies, aged 47, saying that America is
ungovernable. *20 Dec*: an international conference recognizes the independence of Belgium.

Covent Garden Market, London

Thomas Hamilton: Burns Monument, Edinburgh

Gideon Shrycock: Kentucky State House

Samuel Palmer: Coming from Evening Church

William Etty: The Storm

John Audubon: Birds of America

Joseph Smith: *The Book of Mormon*

Stendhal (Marie Beyle): *Le Rouge et le noir* (Scarlet
and Black)

Alfred Tennyson: *Poems, Chiefly Lyrical* (Tennyson
is 21)

Oliver Wendell Holmes: *Old Ironsides*

Victor Hugo: *Hernani*

William Cobbett: *Rural Rides*

🎼 Vincenzo Bellini: *I Capulleti e i Montecchi* (The Capulets and the Montagues)

Frédéric Chopin: *Piano Concerti Nos 1 and 2*

Hector Berlioz: *Symphonie Fantastique*

Daniel Auber: *Fra Diavolo*

1831 English naturalist Charles Darwin, now 22, sets sail on the *Beagle* on an epoch-making voyage round the world. Scottish explorer James Ross finds the location of the Magnetic North Pole. *Feb*: Italians in northern cities (Modena and Parma) demand independence. *Mar*: insurrections in Italy are put down with assistance from Austrian troops. *9 Mar*: the French Foreign Legion is formed. *26 May*: Battle of Ostrolenka: the Russians defeat Polish troops. *27 May*: Comanche Indians on the Cimarron kill Jedediah Smith. *4 Jun*: Leopold I becomes the first King of the Belgians. *9 Oct*: the Greek President Ioannes Kapodistrias is assassinated, aged 55; his brother Avgoustinos is made provisional President. *17 Oct*: Michael Faraday discovers the principle of the dynamo, successfully generating an electric current. *29–31 Oct*: the Bristol Riots raise fears in Britain that revolution is breaking out; four of the rioters are executed. *18 Nov*: a rising in Bengal against tyrannical Hindu rule is put down and the Muslim leader of the rising, Titu Mir, is killed by government forces.

✎ John Rennie: New London Bridge (completed)

🎨 John Constable Salisbury Cathedral from the Meadows

Eugène Delacroix: Le 28 Juillet 1830

📖 Victor Hugo: *Notre-Dame de Paris*; *Les feuilles d'automne*

Alexander Pushkin: *Boris Godunov*

Franz Grillparzer: *Des Meeres und der Liebe Wellen*

Robert Montgomery Bird: *The Gladiator*

🎼 Vincenzo Bellini: *La Sonnambula*; *Norma*

Giacomo Meyerbeer: *Robert le Diable*

Felix Mendelssohn: *Piano Concerto No 1*

1832 Cholera reaches Scotland, where Thomas Latta injects a saline solution to save the life of a patient and pioneers a new treatment. Greece becomes a monarchy with Otto I, the son of Ludwig I of Bavaria, as King. *22 Mar*: Johann Wolfgang von Goethe dies at Weimar, aged 82. *1 May*: Captain Benjamin de Bournville starts a three-year expedition to explore the Rocky Mountains. *28 Jun*: Metternich insists on the German Confederation's acceptance of the Six Articles, which in effect standardize the behaviour of sovereigns of German states, forbid public meetings and introduce surveillance of suspicious people.

∠ William Wilkins: National Gallery, London
Gota Canal, Sweden

🎨 John Constable Waterloo Bridge from Whitehall Stairs

Eugène Delacroix: A Moorish Couple on Their Terrace

Jean-Auguste Ingres: Louis Bertin

📖 Frances Trollope: *Domestic Manners of the Americans*

George Sand: *Indiana*

Johann von Goethe: *Faust, Part 2*

Sheridan Knowles: *The Hunchback*

🎼 Jean Scheitzhoeffer: *La Sylphide*

Gaetano Donizetti: *L'Elisir d'Amore*

Felix Mendelssohn: *The Hebrides Overture*; *Symphony No 5*

Thomas Hastings: *Rock of Ages*

1833 The German doctor Friedrich Wilde invents the contraceptive diaphragm. The British land on the Falkland Islands and claim them for Britain. Maria II of Portugal is restored to the throne by her father Dom Pedro; he has returned from Brazil and defeated her brother Dom Miguel with help from the French and British. *4 May*: Convention of Kutahya, a truce between Cairo and Constantinople and an agreement that Egypt is to have sovereignty over Syria. *29 Jul*: William Wilberforce dies, aged 73. *23 Aug*: the British Parliament abolishes slavery in the British colonies, thanks to a long campaign by Wilberforce. *29 Sep*: Ferdinand VII of Spain dies, aged 48, and is succeeded by his two year-old daughter Isabella II; Ferdinand's brother Don Carlos claims the throne and civil war threatens. *17 Dec*: the foundling

Kaspar Hauser, believed by some to be Prince of Baden, is stabbed to death at the age of 21 when he goes to meet someone promising information regarding his origins.

- Joseph Hansom: Birmingham Town Hall
- Ando Hiroshige: Fifty-three Stations of Tokaido
- Wilberforce Monument, Westminster Abbey
- Charles Lamb: *Last Essays*
- George Sand: *Lélia*
- Eugène Scribe: *Bertand et Raton*
- John Henry Newman: *Lead, Kindly Light*
- Gaetano Donizetti: *Lucrezia Borgia*
- Felix Mendelssohn: *Die eerst Walpurgisnacht*; *Symphony No 4*
- Alexis Lvov: *God Save the Emperor*

1834 Blind since the age of three, Louis Braille invents a system of raised point writing that will enable the blind to 'read'. The Spanish Inquisition is abolished. Civil war starts in Spain as Don Carlos claims the throne occupied by his niece Isabella II. *6 May*: 4 Sikh troops from the Punjab take Peshawar, led by their ruler Ranjit Singh. *26 May*: the six-year civil war in Portugal ends with defeat for Miguel, who leaves the country. *1 Aug*: 35,000 slaves are freed in South Africa as slavery comes to an end throughout the British Empire. *2 Aug*: South Australia is founded with support from the Duke of Wellington. *16 Oct*: the British Houses of Parliament are destroyed by fire. *23 Dec*: the economist and demographer Thomas Malthus died, aged 68, at Haileybury. *27 Dec*: the essayist and friend of Wordsworth, Charles Lamb, dies.

- Eugène Delacroix: Algerian Women at Home
- Jean Ingres: The Martyrdom of St. Symphorien
- Auguste Préault: Slaughter (bronze)
- Honore de Balzac: *Le Père Goriot*
- Edward George Bulwer-Lytton: *The Last Days of Pompeii*
- Franz Grillparzer: *Der Traum ein Leben* (A Dream is Life)
- Hector Berlioz: *Harold in Italy* Richard Wagner: *Die Feen* (written, not performed)

1835 London doctor James Paget identifies the parasite *Trichina spiralis*, later to be associated with trichinosis, produced by eating raw or undercooked pork. Juan Manuel de Rosas assumes the role of Dictator in Buenos Aires. In South Africa, the Dutch pastoralists begin their Great Trek to the north and east from Cape Province; 10,000 will move to new territories in the Transvaal, depopulating the Cape and bringing them into conflict with the territorial interests of the Zulu nation. In Australia, the city of Melbourne is founded. In Afghanistan, the Khan of Kabul Dost Mohammed takes the title Emir, founding the Barakzai dynasty. *2 Mar*: Francis II, the last Holy Roman Emperor dies; he is succeeded as Emperor of Austria (only) by his four-year-old son Ferdinand I. *5 May*: the first passanger rail service in Mainland Europe opens (Brussels to Mechelen). *26 Jun*: Baron Antoine Gros drowns himself in the River Seine at Meudon, aged 64. *9 Jul*: the passenger rail service between Lyons and St. Etienne opens. *7 Dec*: the first German passenger rail service opens, linking Furth and Nuremberg.

    Charles Barry and Augustus Pugin: Houses of Parliament, London

    Harvey Elmes: Fitzwilliam Museum, Cambridge

    J. M. W. Turner: Burning of the Houses of Lords and Commons

    John Constable: The Valley Farm

    Jean Corot: Homer in the Desert

    Katsushika Hokusai: Hundred Views of Mount Fuji

    Alexis de Tocqueville: *Democracy in America*

    Nicolai Gogol: *Mirgirod*

    Theophile Gautier: *Mademoiselle de Maupin*

    E. G. E. Bulwer-Lytton: *Rienzi*

    Hans Christian Andersen: *Fairy Tales*

    Vincenzo Bellini: *I Puritani*

    Jacques Halevy: *La Juive*

    Gaetano Donizetti: *Lucia di Lammermoor*

    Frederic Chopin: *Grand Polonaise Brillante*

1836 Mount Hekla erupts in Iceland. The Dutch (Boer) settlers in South Africa found Natal, Transvaal and the Orange Free State as the Great Trek continues. In South Australia, the city of Adelaide is founded. The U.S. missionary Marcus Whitman takes Eliza Spalding and his wife Narcissa to the Pacific coast: they are the first white women to cross North America. *6 Mar*: the Alamo at San Antonio falls to a Mexican army commanded by the Mexican President, General Antonio de Santa Anna; the Mexicans kill the entire garrison which includes James Bowie, inventor of the Bowie knife, and Davy Crockett. *21 Apr*: U.S. Colonel Sidney Sherman defeats Santa Anna at the Battle of San Jacinto, taking the Mexican President prisoner. *2 Jul*: the first Canadian railway opens, linking Laprairie and St. Johns.

   ✍ Arc de Triomphe, Paris
      Astor House Hotel, New York
   ✇ Katsushika Hokusai: The Great Wave
      Francois Rude: La Marseillaise (sculpture)
      J. M. W. Turner: Juliet and her Nurse
      Jean Corot: Diana Surprised by Actaeon
   📖 William Miller: *Evidence from the Scripture and History of the Second Coming of Christ, about the Year 1843*
      Thomas Hunt: *The Book of Wealth: in which It Is Proved from the Bible that It Is the Duty of Every Man to Become Rich*
      Ralph Waldo Emerson: *Nature*
      Charles Dickens: *Sketches by 'Boz'*; *Pickwick Papers*
      Frederick Marryat: *Mr. Midshipman Easy*
      Nikolai Gogol: *Revizor* (The Government Inspector)
   ♬ Giacomo Meyerbeer: *Les Huguenots*
      Mikhail Glinka: *A Life for the Tsar*
      Richard Wagner: *Das Liebesverbot*
      Felix Mendelssohn: *St. Paul*

1837 Isaac Pitman devises his shorthand system. Samuel Morse's assistant Alfred Vail devises the 'Morse' code using dots and dashes to represent letters. Friedrich Fröbel opens the first kindergarten at Blankenburg in Thuringia. Smallpox wipes out 15,000 Indians in the Missouri valley. George Grotefend succeeds in deciphering Persian cuneiform inscriptions, opening the way to a deeper understanding of early cultures. Economic depression strikes Britain and the United States.

The Japanese Shogun Ienari abdicates, aged 64, after reigning for 44 years and is succeeded by his son Ieyoshi, who opens Japan's ports to foreign trade. *31 Mar*: the English painter John Constable dies in London, aged 60. *20 Jun*: William IV of Britain dies, aged 71, and is succeeded by his 18-year-old niece Victoria. Salic law forbids succession through the female line in Hanover, so the Hanoverian crown passes to George III's eldest surviving son, the Duke of Cumberland, Ernst August. *Dec*: a French Canadian revolt against British rule begins.

✍ Robert Smirke: British Museum, London
Charles Barry: Reform Club, Pall Mall, London
Euston Station, London (completed)

🎨 Edwin Landseer: The Old Shepherd's Chief Mourner

📖 Simeon Poisson: *Recherches sur la Probabilité des Jugements*
Thomas Carlyle: *The French Revolution*
William Prescott: *History of the Reign of Ferdinand and Isabella*
Charles Dickens: *Pickwick Papers* (completed)
Honoré de Balzac: *Le Curé de Village*
Nathaniel Hawthorne: *Twice-Told Tales*
Eugène-Scribe: *La camaraderie* (The Clique)

🎵 Hector Berlioz: *Requiem*

1838 The French novelist George Sand begins her nine-year liaison with the composer Chopin after her estrangement from the poet Alfred de Musset; she has already shocked polite society by wearing men's clothes and smoking cigars. The first railway in Russia opens, linking St. Petersburg and the Tsar's summer palace, Tsarskoe Selo. The Federation of Central America breaks up as Rafael Carrera leads an Indian rising in Guatemala. The British invade Afghanistan, advancing to Kandahar, Ghazni and Kabul, deposing and imprisoning the Emir Dost Mohammed. *8 May*: in London a People's Charter calls for universal suffrage. *12 Dec*: Chinese officials try to execute an opium dealer at Guangzhou (Canton) and meet resistance from American and British traders, triggering a riot. *16 Dec*: Battle of Blood River in

Natal; the Afrikaners (Boers) defeat a Zulu army, killing over 3,000 Zulus.

🎨 J. M. W. Turner: The Fighting Temeraire
Eugène Delacroix: Medea; Chopin

📖 Casanova: *Memoirs Ecrits par Lui Même* (final volume)
Charles Dickens: *Oliver Twist*
Edgar Allan Poe: *Ligeia*
Karl Immerman: *Munchhausen*
Franz Grillparzer: *Weh dem, der lügt* (Thou Shalt Not Lie)
Victor Hugo: *Ruy Blas*

🎼 Hector Berlioz: *Benvenuto Cellini*
Alicia Spottiswoode: *Annie Laurie*

1839 Scottish blacksmith Kirkpatrick MacMillan invents the first true bicycle. Charles Goodyear accidentally discovers a way to vulcanize rubber, to make it hard. The British-Afghan War continues as the British install the unpopular Shah Shuja in Kabul; resistance to British interference increases. *19 Apr*: the Dutch recognize Belgian independence; Willem I of the Netherlands retains the eastern part of Luxembourg with himself as Grand Duke. *24 Jun*: Battle of Nezib: the Egyptians under Ibrahim Pasha defeat the Ottoman army when the Ottomans invade Syria. *1 Jul*: the Ottoman Sultan Mahmud II is poisoned to death, aged 54, at his summer home in Scutari when his fleet surrenders at Alexandria; he is succeeded by his 16-year-old son Abdul Mejid I. *Nov*: the Opium War begins between China and Britain, after a Chinese official destroys illegal stores of opium in the hands of foreign merchants in Guangzhou. *3 Dec*: Frederick VI of Denmark dies, aged 71, and is succeeded by his 53-year-old nephew Christian VIII.

✏️ Augustus Pugin: St. Chad's Cathedral, Birmingham
Harvey Elmes: St. George's Hall, Liverpool
Richard Upjohn: Kingscote, Bellevue Avenue, Newport, R.I.

🎨 Théodore Chassériau: Suzanne au Bain; Vénus Anadymone
Edwin Landseer: Dignity and Impudence
J. M. W. Turner: The Slave Ship

📖 Stendhal: *La Chartreuse de Parme*
Charles Dickens: *Nicholas Nickleby*
Edgar Allan Poe: *The Fall of the House of Usher*
Henry Wadsworth Longfellow: *Voices of the Night*

🎼 Giuseppe Verdi: *Oberto Conte di San Bonifacio*
Hector Berlioz: *Romeo and Juliet*

1840 Anna Duchess of Bedford introduces afternoon tea, which becomes an enduring British tradition. The wooden steamship *Britannia* makes its first transatlantic voyage for Samuel Cunard and the Royal Mail Steam Packet Company. Rafael Carrera becomes Dictator of Guatemala. *7 Jul*: Friedrich Wilhelm III of Prussia dies, aged 69, and is succeeded by his 44-year-old son Friedrich Wilhelm IV. *5 Jul*: Britain declares war on China; Britain bombards the entrance to Hangchow Harbour and lands troops. *15 Jul*: Treaty of London (Britain, Austria, Prussia, Russia) forms a military alliance against Egypt, which is pressed to give up northern Syria, Mecca, Medina and Crete, and give up the Ottoman fleet. *9 Sep*: British gunboats bombard Beirut and land troops. *10 Oct*: Beirut falls to Napier and the French decide after all not to support Mohammed Ali of Egypt. *20 Oct*: Thiers resigns. *3 Nov*: Acre falls to the British. *27 Nov*: the Convention of Alexandria, drawn up by Napier; Mohammed Ali agrees to return the Ottoman fleet and renounce claims to Syria in return for hereditary rule over Egypt.

🏛 Joseph Paxton: Chatsworth Conservatory (completed)
Prince's Gate, Knightsbridge

🎨 Jean Corot: Flight into Egypt
Eugène Delacroix: Entrance of the Crusaders into Constantinople
Théodore Chassériau: Christ au jardin des Oliviers

📖 Richard Dana: *Two Years Before the Mast*
James Fenimore Cooper: *The Pathfinder*
Mikhail Lermontov: *A Hero of Our Time*; *The Novice*
José Zorilla y Moral: *El Zapatero y el Rey*
Christian Friedrich Hebbel: *Judith*
Eugène Scribe: *Le Verre d'Eau*

    🎵 Gaetano Donizetti: *The Daughter of the Regiment*; *The Favourite*

1841 The first cross-border railway opens, linking Strasbourg and Basel. The Scottish doctor James Baird discovers hypnosis. The Egyptian Viceroy Mohammed Ali agrees to give up Crete. New Zealand becomes a British colony. Carlos Lopez becomes President of Paraguay and begins a despotic rule that will last 20 years. *20 Jan*; the Chinese agree to pay compensation to the British and cede Hong Kong. *13 Jul*; the Straits Convention signed by the five great European powers guarantees Ottoman sovereignty and closes the Bosporus and Dardanelles to all foreign warships. *Nov*: the first emigrant waggon train arrives in Oregon, guided by Thomas Fitzpatrick, after a 3,200 km/2,000 mile trek across hostile Indian territory. *Dec*: the Afghans assassinate the puppet ruler Shah Shuja at Kabul; the British are forced back into the Khyber Pass.

    🏛 Hotel des Anglais, Cairo (later called Shepheard's Hotel)

    Charles Cockerell: Ashmolean and Taylorian Building, Oxford

    Gilbert Scott: Protestant Martyr's Memorial, Oxford

    🎨 Eugène Delacroix: Jewish Wedding in Morocco

    Théodore Chassériau: Pere Lacordaire

    📖 Charles Dickens: *Barnaby Rudge*; *The Old Curiosity Shop*

    James Fenimore Cooper: *The Deerslayer*

    Edgar Allan Poe: *The Murders in the Rue Morgue*

    Robert Browning: *Pippa Passes*

    Mikhail Lermontov *The Demon*

    Dion Boucicault: *London Assurance*

    🎵 Adolphe Adam: *Giselle*

    Robert Schumann: *Symphonies Nos 1 and 4*

    Joseph Haydn (music) & August Hoffman (words: *Deutschland, Deutschland Uber Alles*)

1842 The Florida doctor John Gorrie pioneers air conditioning and refrigeration in an experiment with ammonia. The American doctor Crawford Long performs the first known operation using general anaesthetic, using ether on James Venable to remove a cyst. The British government rejects Charles Babbage's calculating machine; the Prime Minister Robert Peel jokes, 'How about setting the machine to calculate the time at which it will be of use?'. Civil war erupts in Uruguay as the exiled former President Manuel Oribe wins support from de Rosas, the Argentine Dictator. *6 Jan*: British forces under Lord Auckland are massacred in the Khyber Pass: all but 121 of the 16,500 soldiers are killed by Afghans under Akbar Khan. Akbar's father Dost Mohammed regains the throne. *29 Aug*: Treaty of Nanjing, ending the Opium War: China cedes Hong Kong to Britain; Amoy, Guangzhou, Foochow, Ningpo and Shanghai are to be cities where foreign traders will have special privileges.

    ✍ Charles Ellet: Schuylkill River Bridge, Fairmount, near Philadelphia (first wire suspension bridge in U.S.)

    Church of La Madeleine, Paris (completed)

    John Carr and Robert Adam: Harewood House, Leeds

    📖 Nikolai Gogol: *Dead Souls, Part 1*

    Bakin Takizawa: *Nanso Satomi Hakken*

    Edgar Allan Poe: *The Masque of the Red Death*

    Thomas Macaulay: *Lays of Ancient Rome*

    Alfred Tennyson: *The Lady of Shalott*

    🎶 Giuseppe Verdi: *Nabucco*

    Gaetano Donizetti: *Linda di Chamonix*

    Richard Wagner: *Rienzi*

    Mikhail Glinka: *Russlan and Ludmilla*

    Franz Berwald: *Symphonies Nos 1 and 2*

    Felix Mendelssohn: *Symphony No 3*

1843 Maoris kill white settlers in New Zealand in the Massacre of Wairau: a five-year Maori War starts. The British succeed in driving the Boers out of Natal, making it a British colony. The British create a colony in west Africa by separating The Gambia from Senegal. Manuel Oribe lays siege to Montevideo. *17 Feb*: the Muslim Emirs of Sind in India refuse to give up their independence to the East India Company. The British provoke Anglo-Sind conflict so that Sir Charles Napier can attack and defeat the 30,000 Baluch army. *Mar*: Battle of

Hyderabad: Napier destroys the army of the Emirs of Sind, sending to London the one-word dispatch 'Peccavi' (I have sinned). *19 Jul*: the *Great Britain* is launched, the first large, iron-hulled, screw-driven steamship to sail the North Atlantic (designed by Isambard Kingdom Brunel). *Nov*: Hawaii becomes independent (formally recognized by France and Britain).

✍ Edward Bulwer-Lytton: Knebworth House, Hertfordshire
   London Bridge railway station
   Henri Labrouste: Reading Room, Ste Genevieve Library, Paris

🎨 J. M. W. Turner: The Sun of Venice Going to Sea
   Edward Bailey: Statue of Nelson, Trafalgar Square, London

📖 *The Economist* (first issue)
   La Reforme (first issue)
   Soren Kierkegaard: *Euten-Eller* (Either-Or)
   W. H. Prescott: *History of the Conquest of Mexico*
   Charles Dickens *A Christmas Carol*

🎼 Richard Wagner: *Der Fliegende Hollander* (The Flying Dutchman)
   Gaetano Donizetti: *Don Pasquale*
   Felix Mendelssohn: *A Midsummer Night's Dream* (includes 'Wedding March')
   Michael Balfe: *The Bohemian Girl*
   Robert Schumann: *Das Paradies und die Peri*

1844 Santo Domingo gains its independence from Haiti and becomes the Dominican Republic. A band of 15 Texas Rangers under Colonel Hays attacks a band of 300 Comanches, killing half of them using the Colt 'sixshooter' revolver. *8 Mar*: Charles XIV of Sweden (John Bernadotte) dies, aged 81, and is succeeded by his 44-year-old son Oskar I. *24 May*: Samuel Morse transmits the first telegraph message from Washington to Baltimore.

✍ Charles Cockerell: Bank of England, Liverpool
   William Tite: Royal Exchange, London

🎨 Edwin Landseer: Shoeing the Mare
   J. M. W. Turner: Rain, Steam and Speed

📖 Robert Chambers: *Vestiges of the Natural History of Creation*

Margaret Fuller: *Summer on the Lake*
Charles Dickens: *Martin Chuzzlewit*
Alexandre Dumas: *Les Trois Mousquetaires*
Edgar Allan Poe: *The Purloined Letter*
Heinrich Heine: *Deutschland, Ein Wintermarchen*
Giuseppe Verdi: *Ernani*
Friedrich von Flotow: *Alessandro Stradella*
Hector Berlioz: *Roman Carnival Overture*

1845 Potato crops fail throughout Europe; famine kills over 2 million people from Ireland to Russia. The British archaeologist Austen Henry Layard begins excavations at Nimrod in Iraq; his six-year dig will reveal the palaces of the Assyrian kings. English engineer William Armstrong invents hydroelectricity. *May*: Sir John Franklin sets sail on a new expedition to search for a north-west passage; his ships will become icebound and his crew will all die of lead poisoning from the canned provisions they have taken with them. An Anglo-Sikh War starts in India as the British try to conquer the Punjab and Kashmir.

W. H. Playfair: National Gallery, Edinburgh
Prince Albert and Lewis Cubitt: Osborne House, Isle of Wight
George Catlin: North American Indian Portfolio
George Bingham: Fur Traders Descending the Missouri
Scientific American (first issue)
Alexandre Dumas: *Le Comte de Monte Cristo*
Benjamin Disraeli: *Sybil, or The Two Nations*
Robert Browning: *Home Thoughts From Abroad*
Richard Wagner: *Tannhäuser*
Franz Berwald: *Symphonies Nos 3 and 4*
Felix Mendelssohn: *Violin Concerto*
Robert Schumann: *Piano Concerto*

1846 Famine strikes Ireland as the potato crop fails again. The New York printer invents the rotary printing press: it can run off 10,000 sheets per hour. The Smithsonian Institution is founded at Washington by the U.S. Congress, with a large bequest from James Smithson, who died in 1829. *13 Jan*: President Polk starts the Mexican War after he has failed to purchase New Mexico from the Mexican government. *8 May*: Battle of Palo Alto: U.S.

General Zachary Taylor defeats the Mexican force of 6,000 soldiers with 2,000 troops. *9 May*: Battle of Resaca de la Palma: the Mexicans are routed and withdraw across the Rio Grande. *14 Jun*: the Black Bear Revolt starts in California as settlers in the Sacramento valley declare an independent republic (independent of Mexico). *15 Jun*: Oregon Treaty, agreeing the 49th parallel as the boundary between British territory and U.S. in the face of strong insistence within the U.S. on 54°40′ as the frontier. Britain also receives Vancouver Island.

- Charles Barry: The Treasury, Whitehall, London
- Richard Upjohn: Trinity Church, New York
- Edwin Landseer: The Stag at Bay
- John Millais: Pizarro Seizing the Inca of Peru
- Eugène Delacroix: The Abduction of Rebecca
- George Bingham: The Jolly Flatboatmen
- Jules Michelet: *Le Peuple*
- Herman Melville: *Typee*
- Eugène Sue: *Le Juif errant* (The Wandering Jew)
- Edward Lear: *Book of Nonsense*
- Friedrich Hebbel: *Maria Magdalena*
- Robert Schumann: *Symphony No 2*
- Felix Mendelssohn: *Elijah*
- Hector Berlioz: *La Damnation de Faust*
- *Jim Crack Corn* (American popular song)

1847 Over 200,000 emigrants leave Ireland, most going to America. Italian chemist Ascanio Sobrero discovers nitroglycerin. The Russian anarchist Mikhail Bakunin is expelled from Paris for making a speech advocating the overthrow of monarchy in Russia and Poland. *23 Feb*: Battle of Buena Vista: General Taylor's troops rout those of General Santa Anna. *18 Apr*: Battle of Cerro Gordo: Santa Anna is defeated again. *1 Jul*: the first adhesive postage stamps go on sale in the U.S. *10 Jul*: the first Chinese immigrants to New York arrive aboard the junk *Kee Ying* from Guangzhou (Canton); the beginning of Chinatown.

- Charles Barry: Bridgewater House, Green Park, London
- George Bingham: Raftsmen Playing Cards
- Emily Brontë: *Wuthering Heights*

    Charlotte Brontë: *Jane Eyre*
    Frederick Marryat: *Children of the New Forest*
    Herman Melville: *Omoo*
    Giuseppe Verdi: *Macbeth*
    Franz Berwald: *A Rustic Betrothal in Sweden*
    Friedrich von Flotow: *Martha*
    Franz Liszt: *Liebestraum*

1848 Switzerland becomes a federal union with a new constitution. *20 Jan*: Christian VIII of Denmark dies, aged 51, and is succeeded by his 39-year-old son Frederick VI. *24 Jan*: gold is discovered in California by James Marshall; the gold rush brings 6,000 men across to the west. *2 Feb*: Treaty of Guadelupe Hidalgo, ending the Mexican War; Mexico gives all the lands north of the Rio Grande, including California to the United States for 15 million dollars: by this act Mexico loses one-third of its territory. *13 Mar*: revolution in Vienna. *17 Mar*: Milan has its own revolution against Austrian overlordship when it hears the news from Vienna. *28 Mar*: John Jacob Astor, the richest man in America, dies, aged 84 leaving 20 million dollars. *10 Apr*: a Chartist procession in London is called off as troops are mobilized; the British government fears revolution may break out. *17 May*: Emperor Ferdinand of Austria has left Vienna for Innsbruck because of the chaos in the capital. *Aug*: Ferdinand returns to Vienna but a new insurrection forces him to leave again. Serfdom is abolished as a result of student agitation. *2 Dec*: Emperor Ferdinand abdicates and is succeeded by his 18-year-old nephew Franz Josef I.

    Richard Turner and Decimus Burton: Palm House, Kew, London
    High Bridge, New York (an aqueduct to supply Manhattan)

    William Holman Hunt: Love at First Sight; The Eve of St. Agnes
    Théodore Chassériau: Equestrian Portrait of Ala ben Hamid

    John Stuart: *Principles of Political Economy*
    Karl Marx: *Wage, Labour and Capital*
    William Makepeace Thackeray: *Vanity Fair*

Charles Dickens: *Dombey and Son*
Elizabeth Gaskell: *Mary Barton*
Anne Bronte: *The Tenant of Wildfell Hall*
Alexandre Dumas: *La dame aux camélias*
Alfred de Musset: *Infaut Jurer de rien* (You Can't Be
Sure of Anything); *Le Chandelier; Andre del sarto*
Johann Strauss the Elder: *Radetzky March*
Mikhail Glinka: *Kamarinskaya*
Stephen Foster: *Oh! Susanna!*

1849 Canadians seek union with the United States as Canada slides into economic depression. British troops defeat the Sikhs at Gujarat and force a surrender at Rawalpindi; Britain annexes the Punjab. *5 Jan:* Franz Josef's troops arrive to occupy Buda and Pest and suppress the revolution that started there last year. *23 Mar:* Piedmontese forces are defeated by the Austrian army under the 83-year-old General Radetzky; Charles Albert abdicates and is succeeded by his 29-year-old son Victor Emmanuel II. *13 April:* the Hungarian Diet proclaims a republic, electing Lajos Kossuth as President. *30 Apr:* following the declaration of a Roman Republic (*9 Feb*), a large combined French, Spanish, Austrian, Tuscan and Neapolitan army has moved against Garibaldi's nationalist Italian army; Garibaldi inflicts heavy losses but is wounded. *17 Jun:* Russian troops invade Hungary. *Aug:* Garibaldi only just escapes capture; he leaves for the United States. *9 Aug:* Battle of Temesovar: the Russians defeat the Hungarian patriot army decisively and Kossuth has to flee to Turkey two days later. *13 Aug:* the Hungarian nationalists surrender to the Russians who take reprisals, hanging nine generals and shooting four more. *25 Sep:* Johann Strauss the Elder, the Waltz King of Vienna, dies, aged 45, of scarlet fever. *11 Oct:* Strauss's 23-year-old son and namesake takes over his father's orchestra.

The Kremlin, Moscow (completed)
W. Johnston and Thomas Walter: Jayne Building, Philadelphia
William Holman Hunt: Rienzi
Dante Gabriel Rossetti: The Girlhood of Mary Virgin

John Millais: Isabella
Gustave Courbet: After Dinner at Ornans; The Stone Breakers

📖 Henry Thoreau: *A Week on the Concord and Merrimack Rivers*

James Fields: *The Ballad of the Tempest, or The Captain's Daughter*

Friedrich Hebbel: *Herod and Marianne; Genoveva*

🎜 Carl Nikolai: *Die Lustigen Weiber von Windsor* (Merry Wives of Windsor)

Giacomo Meyerbeer: *Le Prophète*

Giuseppe Verdi: *Luisa Miller*

Franze Liszt: *Tasso: lamento e trionfo*

Stephen Foster: *Nelly Was A Lady* (popular song)

Teodoro Cottrau: *Santa Lucia* (popular song)

Richard Storrs Wills: *It Came Upon The Midnight Clear*

1850 The Tai Ping Rebellion starts in China, led by schoolteacher Hong Xiuquan, who thinks he is Christ's brother and calls himself Heavenly Prince. The peasants in the south are stirred up against the government, causing a civil war that will result in the death of up to 30 million people in the next 14 years. The Don Pacifico affair brings Greece and Britain close to war. The 66-year-old Pacifico is an ex-diplomat, a Jew and a British subject: his house in Athens was burned by an anti-Semitic mob last year. The British Foreign Secretary, Palmerston, also 66, orders a naval squadron to blockade the Pireaus until the Greek government compensates Pacifico. *29 Jan*: Senator Henry Clay introduces an 'omnibus bill' in an attempt to reduce the growing friction between northern and southern states in America, *26 Apr*: the Greeks comply with Palmerston's demands. *31 May*: a new French law requires voters to be resident in the same place for at least three years before qualifying for the electoral roll; this is to exclude radical workers who tend to be migratory. *7 Jul*: the Scottish explorer Edward Eyre arrives at Albany in Western Australia after crossing the Nullarbor Plain, the first white man to do so. *9 Jul*: U.S. President Taylor dies of gastroenteritis after gorging iced cherries at a Fourth of July celebration, during which the Washington Monument's cornerstone was laid. *9 Sep*: California joins the Union: the 31st state.

   ✏ Joseph Paxton: Crystal Palace, Hyde Park, London
James Bunning: Billingsgate Market, London

   🎨 Dante Gabriel Rossetti: Ecce Ancilli Domini
Jean Corot: Morning, the Dance of the Nymphs
John Millais: Christ in the House of His Parents
William Holman Hunt: A Converted British Family
Sheltering a Christian Missionary from the Persecution of the Druids
Walter Deverell: Twelfth Night
Charles Collins: The Pedlar; Convent Thoughts

   📖 Charles Dickens: *David Copperfield*
Alfred Tennyson: *In Memoriam*
Nathaniel Hawthorne: *The Scarlet Letter*

   🎼 Richard Wagner: *Lohengrin*
Emilio Arrieta y Corera: *The Conquest of Granada*
Stephen Foster: *De Camptown Races* (popular song)

1851 London is now the world's largest city with 2.4 million people. In Australia, a gold rush follows the discovery of gold near Bathurst in New South Wales by Edward Hargreaves; an inflow of Chinese brings a demand to keep non-white immigrants out. Rama III King of Siam dies and is succeeded by his half-brother Rama IV, who will build roads and canals, stimulate education, reform the government and import an English governess who will later publish her reminiscences. *1 May*: the London Great Exhibition opens: the first world fair. *2 Dec*: in France, the Third Republic ends in a coup engineered by Louis Bonaparte. *19 Dec*: the English painter J. M. W. Turner dies, aged 76, at Chelsea.

   🎨 Emanuel Leutze: Washington Crossing the Delaware
William Holman Hunt: Valentine Rescuing Sylvia from Proteus; The Hireling Shepherd
John Millais: Mariana; Return of the Dove to the Ark; The Woodman's Daughter
Dante Gabriel Rossetti: Hist! said Kate the Queen

   📖 *New York Times* (first issue *18 Sep*)

Herman Melville: *Moby Dick*
Nathaniel Hawthorne: *The House of the Seven Gables*
Heinrich Heine: *Romanzero*
Dion Boucicault: *Dame de Pique; Love in a Maze*
Alfred de Musset: *Les Caprices de Marianne; Bettine*
Eugène Labiche: *Un Chapeau de Paille d'Italie* (An Italian Straw Hat)
♯ Giuseppe Verdi: *Rigoletto*
Mikhail Glinka: *A Night in Madrid*
Robert Schumann: *Symphony No 3*
Franz Liszt: *Hungarian Rhapsody No 2*
Stephen Foster: *Old Folks at Home*

1852 Emigration from Ireland reaches its peak. The New York mechanic Elisha Otis invents the lift, which leads to the development of multi-storey buildings. *3 Feb*: Argentina is forced to relinquish plans to take over Uruguay when de Rosas, the Argentina Dictator, is defeated by insurgents, Brazilians and Uruguayans at the Battle of Caseros; de Rosas flees to Britain. *17 Jul*: Argentina recognizes the independence of Paraguay. *2 Dec*: Louis Napoleon proclaims a second French Empire, reigning as Napoleon III and exiling the Orléans family.

✐ Joseph Paxton: Mentmore, Buckinghamshire
Lewis Cubitt: King's Cross Station, London
Chateau-sur-Mer, Bellevue Avenue, Newport, Rhode Island, U.S.
Baron Haussmann: Bois de Boulogne (designed as a public park)
🎨 Gustave Moreau: Pietà
John Millais: The Huguenot; Ophelia
William Holman Hunt: Our English Coasts; The Awakening Conscience
📖 Peter Roget: *Thesaurus*
Harriet Beecher Stowe: *Uncle Tom's Cabin*
Nathaniel Hawthorne: *The Blithedale Romance*
William Makepeace Thackeray: *History of Henry Esmond*
Alexandre Dumas: *Ange Pitou*
Ivan Turgenev: *A Sportsman's Sketches*
Théophile Gautier: *Émaux et Camées*
Gustav Freytag: *Die Journalisten*

𝄞 Anton Rubinstein: *Dmitri Donskoi; Melody in F*

Robert Schumann: *Manfred Overture; Julius Caesar Overture*

Stephen Foster: *Massa's in de Cold Cold Ground*

1853 The *Great Republic* (built by Donald McKay) is the world's biggest sailing ship, but at 4,500 tons, too big to be commercially successful. Isambard Kingdom Brunel begins work on the *Great Eastern*, an even larger passenger steamer with screws and paddle wheels; this too, is a commercial failure. Transportation to Tasmania comes to an end; 67,000 convicts from Britain have been landed. The Second Burmese War ends; Britain takes over Pegu and Mindon Min becomes King of Burma; he will build Mandalay and make it the capital of Burma. *9 Jan:* Napoleon III marries the Spanish Countess Eugènie at the Tuileries, having failed to get a Hohenzollern or a Vasa. *8 Jun:* U.S. Comodore Perry arrives in Edo Bay with a formal request for a trade treaty. *23 Jul:* the Japanese Shogun Ieoshi dies, aged 61, and is succeeded by his brother Iesada, who agrees to open two ports to foreign trade. *8 Aug:* a Russian fleet arrives at Nagasaki on a trading mission. *7 Sep:* Shanghai falls to rebels as the Tai Ping rebellion continues. *15 Nov:* Maria II of Portugal dies, aged 34, and is succeeded by her 16-year-old son Pedro V

✒ Edward Walters: Free Trade Hall, Manchester

Mount Vernon Hotel, Cape May, New Jersey (world's first hotel with en suite baths)

Mills House, Charleston, South Carolina

🎨 Théodore Chassériau: The Tepidarium

François Rude: Marshal Ney Monument

John Ruskin: Study of Gneiss Rock

John Millais: Kissing Angels design for a Gothic Window

Dante Gabriel Rossetti: Dante Drawing an Angel on the Anniversary of the Death of Beatrice

📖 John Ruskin: *The Stones of Venice*

Charles Dickens: *Bleak House*

Elizabeth Gaskell: *Cranford*

Charlotte Bronte: *Villette*

Nathaniel Hawthorne: *Tanglewood Tales*

Charles Reade: *Gold*

Giuseppe Verdi: *Il Trovatore*

Camille Saint-Saens: *Symphony No 1*

Stephen Foster: *My Old Kentucky Home, Good Night* (popular songs)

1854 A chemistry professor at Yale, Benjamin Silliman, is the first to fractionate petroleum by distillation. *3 Jan*: British and French fleets enter the Black Sea. *6 Feb*: Russia breaks off diplomatic relations with Britain and France. *17 Feb*: the Convention of Bloemfontein is signed: the British agree to withdraw from territory in South Africa to the north of the Orange River, leaving the Orange Free State for Boer settlers. *12 Mar*: Britain and France make an alliance with Constantinople. *20 Mar*: Russian troops cross the Danube in defiance of warnings from Britain and France. *28 Mar*: Britain and France declare war on Russia. *31 Mar*: Treaty of Kanagawa, opening the Japanese ports of Shimoda and Hakodate to U.S. trade. *13 Jul*: Abbas I, Khedive of Egypt, is murdered at the age of 41; he is succeeded by his 32-year-old uncle Said Pasha, *30 Sep*: Battle of the Alma River: after landing on the Crimean Peninsula, Allied (British and French) troops defeat the Russian army. *25 Oct*: Battle of Balaclava: another victory for the Allies overall, even though the battle includes the disastrous cavalry charge (the Charge of the Light Brigade) from which only 200 out of 700 men survive. *5 Nov*: Battle of Inkerman: another victory for the Allies. *30 Nov*: the new Khedive of Egypt grants the concession for a Suez Canal to his friend Ferdinand de Lesseps.

John Ruskin: University Museum, Oxford

James Bogardus: Building for Harper Bros, New York

Louis-Auguste Boileau: Church of St. Eugène, Paris (iron columns)

Jean Millet: The Reaper

Gustave Courbet: Bonjour, Monsieur Courbet

Frederic Church: The Falls of Tacemdama

John Millais: John Ruskin

William Holman Hunt: The Scapegoat

Dante Gabriel Rossetti: Found

Ford Madox Brown: An English Autumn Afternoon
Le Figaro (first issue)
The Age (first issue, Melbourne)
Henry Thoreau: *Walden, or Life in the Woods*
Charles Dickens: *Hard Times*
Timothy Arthur: *Ten Nights in a Barroom and What I Saw There*
Alfred Tennyson: *The Charge of the Light Brigade*
Alexander Ostrovsky: *Poverty is No Crime*; *One Must Not Live as One Likes*
Franz Liszt: *Orpheus*; *Les Preludes*
Hector Berlioz: *L'Enfance du Christ*
Stephen Foster: *Jeanie with the Light Brown Hair* (popular song)

1855 The Ethiopian Chief Ras Kassa deposes Ras Ali, King of Gondar, conquers the neighbouring territories of Shoa, Goijam and Tigre and declares himself 'King of Kings'; he starts a 13-year reign as Emperor Theodore. David Livingstone, now 42, discovers the Victoria Falls on the River Zambezi. In the Crimea, Roger Fenton takes successful photographs of the army encampments, but there is not yet the technology to publish them: engravings made from the photographs nevertheless carry something of the reality of warfare to newspaper readers. Epidemics of typhus and cholera account for more lives than battle wounds in the Crimea. *Feb*: the Japanese Shogun Iesada signs a treaty with Russia. *4 Mar*: Nicholas I of Russia dies, aged 58 and is succeeded by his 36-year-old son Alexander II. *30 Mar*: Treaty of Peshawar: an Anglo-Afghan alliance against Persia, made because the Shah, Nasr Ud-den, plans to take Herat. *16 Aug*: Battle of Chermaia: an Allied victory in the Crimea, helped by a Piedmontese force sent by Count Cavour, the Premier of Savoy. *11 Sep*: the Russian army abandons Sebastopol, blowing up their forts and scuttling their ships to prevent them falling into Allied hands. *Nov*: Japan makes a trading treaty with the Netherlands.

Parker House Hotel, School Street, Boston
Gustave Courbet: Interior of the Studio
Rosa Bonheur: The Horse Fair

John Millais: The Rescue
Ford Madox Brown: The Hayfield; The Last of England

📖 Thomas Bulfinch: *The Age of Fable*
Charles Kingsley: *Westward Ho!*
Elizabeth Gaskell: *North and South*
Anthony Trollope: *The Warden*
Walt Whitman: *Leaves of Grass*

🎼 Giuseppe Verdi: *I Vespri Siciliani* (The Sicilian Vespers)
Franz Liszt: *Piano Concerto No 1*; *Prometheus*
Hector Berlioz: *Te Deum*
Johannes Brahms: *Trio*

1856 Johann Fuhrott discovers the fossil remains of Neanderthal man in the Rhineland; they are recognized at once as the bones of an early form of man thousands of years old. The 18-year-old English chemistry student William Perkins develops Mauve, the world's first synthetic dye. English engineer Henry Bessemer invents the Bessemer converter, which makes low-cost steel. *1 Feb*: the Crimean War ends: Russia yields to an ultimatum from Austria. *18 Feb*: the Hatt-I-Humayun Edict is issued by Abdul Mejid the Ottoman Sultan, guaranteeing Christian subjects normal civil rights, abolishing torture, reforming prisons; following their success in the Crimea, the Allies are able to force these reforms on the Sultan. *30 Mar*: Treaty of Paris, making the Black Sea neutral and asserting the independence of the Ottoman Empire. Cigarettes are introduced to London clubs by veterans of the Crimean War: they discovered them in Russia. Robert Gloag, a Crimean veteran, opens the first British cigarette factory. *12 Jul*: Natal is made a British crown colony.

🏛 Buckingham Palace South Wing (with ballroom)
🎨 Jean Ingres: La Source
Ford Madox Brown: Christ Washing Peter's Feet
John Millais: Autumn Leaves; The Blind Girl
William Holman Hunt: The Light of the World
Arthur Hughes: April Love; The Eve of St. Agnes
John Brett: The Glacier of Rosenlaui
Henry Wallis: The Death of Chatterton

📖 Elizabeth Peabody: *Chronological History of the United States*

Charles Reade: *It's Never Too Late to Mend*

Ivan Turgenev: *Rudin*

🎵 Daniel Auber: *Manon Lescaut*

1857 Giuseppe Garibaldi founds the Italian National Association to work towards the unificatio of Italy: he has been back in Italy for three years after spending five years as a candle-maker in New York. *4 Mar*: Treaty of Paris: Afghanistan's independence is recognized and forced on Persia by the British. *10 May*: the Sepoy Mutiny (Indian Mutiny) begins at Meerut. *15 Jul*: massacre at Cawnpore: the garrison is treacherously murdered after being offered a safe conduct. *17 Jul*: the mutineers are butchered for the Cawnpore Massacre. *11 Sep*: the Mountain Meadows Massacre in Utah. 135 emigrants on the Fancher waggon train are ambushed by 300 Pah-Ute Indians lead by Mormons acting on orders from the Mormon leader Brigham Young; nearly all the emigrants are killed.

🏛 Joseph Paxton: Mentmore Towers, Buckinghamshire

Frederick Olmsted: Central Park, New York

🎨 Frederic Church: Niagara Falls

William Dyce: Titian's First Essay in Colour

John Millais: Sir Isumbras at the Ford

Henry Wallis: The Stonebreaker; A Sculptor's Workshop

📖 Gustave Flaubert: *Madame Bovary*

Charles Dickens: *Little Dorrit*

Anthony Trollope: *Barchester Towers*

Thomas Hughes: *Tom Brown's School Days*

Dion Boucicault: *The Poor of New York*

🎵 Giuseppe Verdi: *Simon Boccanegra*

Franz Liszt: *Piano Concerto; Faust Symphony*

John Henry Hopkins: *We Three Kings of Orient Are*

James Pierpoint: *Jingle Bells* (popular song)

1858 French engineer Ferdinand Carré invents the refrigerator. Tsar Alexander II begins the emancipation of serfs in Russia. The Japanese Shogun Iesada dies, aged 34, and is succeeded by his appointee, the 12-year-old

Iemochi. *14 Jan*: an attempt is made to assassinate Napoleon III; he escapes but 10 others are killed in the bomb explosions. *13 Mar*: in the wake of the assassination attempt, the French execute the Italian revolutionary Felice Orsini. *26–29 Jun*: Treaties of Tientsin, ending the Anglo-Chinese War; China agrees to open more ports to foreign trade. *10 Jul*: Napoleon III has secret meetings with Count Cavour at Plombières, agreeing to join Cavour in a war against Austria. *7 Oct*: Friedrich Wilhelm IV of Prussia is certified insane and unfit to rule; his brother, the 61-year-old Wilhelm, is made Regent. *23 Dec*: Aleksindr Karageorgevic, the Serbian Prince, is deposed, aged 52, and succeeded by Milos Obrenovic, who is 79.

⚓ Chelsea Bridge, London (completed)

Charles Barry: Covent Garden Opera House (rebuilt)

🎨 William Frith: Derby Day

Winslow Homer: Eight Bells

Dante Gabriel Rossetti: Mary Magdalene

John Brett: The Val d'Aosta

William Windus: Too Late

William Dyce: Welsh Landscape with Two Women Knitting

William Morris: Queen Guinevere

📖 Anthony Trollope: *Dr. Thorne*

Oliver Wendell Holmes: *The Deacon's Masterpiece*

Adelaide Procter: *Legends and Lyrics* (incudes 'The Lost Chord')

Dion Boucicault: *Jessie Brown, or The Relief of Lucknow*

Tom Taylor: *Our American Cousin*

🎵 Jacques Offenbach: *Orphée aux Enfers* (Orpheus in the Underworld)

'JK': *The Yellow Rose of Texas* (popular song)

1859 In Australia, Queensland is made into a separate colony with a capital at Brisbane. *1 Jan*: Napoleon III warns the Austrian Ambassador in Paris, in effect leaking his secret alliance with Cavour. *7 Apr*: Austrian troops are mobilized. *23 Apr*: Piedmont defies an Austrian ultimatum to demobilize within three days. *29 Apr*: the Austrian army invades Piedmont. *12 May*: France declares war on Austria, as arranged. *30 May*: the Piedmontese defeat the Austrian army at Palestro. Ferdinand II, King of the Two Sicilies dies, aged 49, and is succeeded by his 13-year-old son Francesco. *24 Jun*: Battle of Solferino: great loss of life on both sides, with no clear outcome. *30 Jun*: Charles Blondel crosses Niagara Falls on a tightrope. *8 Jul*: Oskar I of Sweden dies, aged 60, and is succeeded by his 33-year-old son Charles XV. The Austrian Emperor Franz Josef cannot afford the Piedmont War; faced with revolution in Hungary as well, he meets Napoleon II on *11 Jul* at Villafranca. With Metternich's death at the age of 86, Franz Josef has to negotiate for himself. Hostilities cease, with Napoleon frightened by the nationalism that has been stirred up in Italy. *16 Oct*: John Brown's raid on Harper's Ferry in Virginia; it is to be a signal for a general slave rebellion that will found a new refuge state for blacks. *18 Oct*: Federal troops under Colonel Robert E. Lee overpower Brown at the Federal arsenal. *2 Dec*: John Brown, convicted of treason, is hanged at Charlestown.

🏛 Ferdinand de Lesseps: Suez Canal (work begins *25 Apr*)

Deane and Woodward: Pitt-Rivers Museum, Oxford

Philip Webb and William Morris: The Red House, Bexley Heath

🎨 Edouard Manet: The Absinthe Drinker

Jean Millet: The Angelus

Jean Ingres: The Turkish Bath

James Whistler: At the Piano

Frederic Church: Heart Of the Andes

📖 Charles, Dickens: *A Tale of Two Cities*

George Eliot: *Adam Bede*

Ivan Goncharov: *Oblomov*

Alfred Tennyson: *The Idylls of the King*

Edward Fitzgerald: *The Rubáiyát of Omar Khayyám* (English translation).

Alexander Ostrovsky: *The Thunderstorm*

Dion Boucicault: *The Octaroon, or Life in Louisiana*

🎵 Johannes Brahms: *Serenade for Orchestra*; *Piano*

Concerto No 1
Charles Gounod: *Ave Maria*; *Faust*
Giuseppe Verdi: *Un Ballo in Maschera*
Lowell Mason: *Nearer My God To Thee*
Daniel Decatur Emmet: *Dixie* (popular song)
Sebastian Yradier: *La Paloma* (popular song)

1860 The native population of Hawaii has fallen from 150,000 in *1819* to 35,000 as a result of infectious diseases introduced by Americans and Europeans. Russian pioneers found the port of Vladivostok on the Pacific coast; it is icebound three months in the year. Robert Burke leads the first south-north expedition across Australia, reaching the Gulf of Carpentaria next year. The German adventurer Karl von der Decken explores East Africa with a view to founding a huge German colony there. In America, John D. Rockefeller makes a start in the oil industry at the age of 20. *30 Apr*: Fort Defiance in New Mexico is attacked by a thousand Navajo Indians whose sheep and goats have been shot by the fort's soldiers; the Indians almost succeed in taking the fort. *5 May*: Garibaldi organizes an army of Redshirts at Genoa and sails for Marsala. *11 May*: Garibaldi reaches Marsala. *6 Jun*: Garibaldi takes Palermo. *12 Aug*: Danilo I of Montenegro is assassinated and succeeded by his 19-year-old nephew Nicholas I. The French and British bombard Sinho to force the Chinese to admit diplomats. *22 Aug*: with British help, Garibaldi is able to cross the Straits of Messina into mainland Italy. *7 Sep*: Garibaldi takes Naples and supports the installation of Victor Emmanuel II as King of a united Italy. *Nov*: Abraham Lincoln becomes President of the United States, and disintegration of the Union accelerates. Garibaldi returns to the island of Caprera where he looks after his donkeys Pius IX, Oudinot, Immaculate Conception and Napoleon III.

Edouard Manet: The Guitarist
William Holman Hunt: The Finding of the Saviour in the Temple
Arthur Hughes: The Woodman's Child
William Dyce: Pegwell Bay
John Ruskin: Mer de Glace

📖 George Eliot: *The Mill on the Floss*
Nathaniel Hawthorne: *The Marble Faun*
William Wilkie Collins: *The Woman in White*
Ivan Turgenev: *On the Eve*
Dion Boucicault: *The Colleen Bawn*
🎵 Robert Schumann: *Cello Concerto*
Johannes Brahms: *Serenade No 2*

1861 Richard Gatling invents the Gatling gun: firing hundreds of rounds a minute, it will greatly increase the loss of life in the American Civil War. The Russian anarchist Mikhail Bakunin escapes from Siberia and makes his way via Japan and the U.S. to Europe, where he becomes once again the leading anarchist. Tsar Alexander II completes the emancipation of serfs in Russia. *2 Jan*: Friedrich Wilhelm IV of Prussia dies aged 65, succeeded by his brother and Regent Wilhem I. *17 Jan*: the dancer and former mistress of Ludwig I of Bavaria, Lola Montez, dies, aged 43, in New York. *25 Feb*: the French relieve a blockade of Saigon, defeating a force of 20,000 Annamese; the French extend their control over Cochin (Vietnam). *17 Mar*: a united kingdom of Italy is proclaimed, uniting Parma, Piedmont, Lombardy, Modena, Romagna, Lucca, Tuscany and the Two Sicilies under Victor Emmanuel II. Cavour dies, aged 62, within weeks of the proclamation. *12 Apr*: the American Civil War starts; General Beauregard assumes command of the Confederate Army and bombards Fort Sumter in Charleston Harbour. *25 Jun*: Abdul Mejid the Ottoman Sultan dies, aged 38, of tuberculosis and is succeeded by his 31-year-old brother Abdul Aziz. *Jul*: after calling for volunteers, Lincoln has 30,000 recruits. *2 Oct*: Battle of Ball's Bluff on the Potomac: defeat for the Union. *1 Nov*: Lincoln gives overall command of Federal forces to General McClellan who spends the winter training his 200,000-strong army. *11 Nov*: Pedro V of Portugal dies of cholera, aged 24, and is succeeded by his 23-year-old brother Luiz I. *14 Dec*: Queen Victoria's consort, Prince Albert, dies of typhoid, aged 42.
🏛 Charles Garnier: The Opera, Paris
Edward Godwin: The Guildhall, Northampton
🎨 John La Farge: St. John

Jean Corot: Orphée, Le Repos
Gustave Doré: Illustrations for Dante's *Inferno*
Arthur Hughes: Home from Work
William Windus: The Outlaw
William Dyce: George Herbert at Bemerton
📖 Anthony Trollope: *Framley Parsonage*
George Eliot: *Silas Marner*
Charles Dickens: *Great Expectations*
Friedrich Hebbel: *Siegfrieds Tod*; *Kriemhildes Rache*
🎼 Johannes Brahms: *Quartet for Piano and Strings*
Franz Liszt: *Mephisto Waltz*
William Monk: *Abide With Me* (lyrics by Henry Lyte)

1862 English explorer John Speke discovers the source of the Nile in Lake Victoria. Otto I of Greece is deposed; he takes refuge on a British ship and then returns to Bavaria. *4 Mar*: Confederate forces under Henry Sibley take Santa Fe. *8 Mar*: first naval battle between ironclad ships; the Confederate ironclad *Merrimac* sinks the *Cumberland* and defeated the *Congress* in Hampton Roads. *9 Mar*: the *Merrimac* engages the *Monitor*, with its revolutionary new gun turret, and has to withdraw. *6–7 Apr*: Battle of Shiloh: both sides in the American Civil War claim victory, but both sides suffer great losses. *8 Apr*: British and Spanish troops are withdrawn from Mexico as it becomes clear that Napoleon III intends to set up a Catholic Empire there. *5 May*: Battle of Puebla: Mexicans slaughter well-trained French troops. *31 May*: Federal troops withdraw from the area between the James and York Rivers after sustaining serious losses. *17 Aug*: a Sioux rising in Minnesota under the leadership of Little Crow is suppressed. *30 Aug*: Second Battle of Bull Run: the Confederates under Stonewall Jackson and James Longstreet defeat the Federals under General Pope. *10 Sep*: Carlos Lopez, Dictator of Paraguay, dies, aged 75, and is succeeded as President by his 36-year-old son Francisco Lopez. *17 Sep*: Battle of Antietam: indecisive. The camp followers of General Hooker's Massachusetts become known as 'hookers'. *13 Dec*: General Lee defeats the Federal Army of the Potomac under Burnside at the Battle of Fredericksburg. *26 Dec*:

38 Sioux Indians are hanged at Mankato for their part in the rebellion earlier in the year.

Frederic Church: Cotopaxi
Edouard Manet: La Musique aux Tuileries
Jean Millet: Potato Planters
Honore Daumier: The Third Class Carriage

Victor Hugo: *Les Misérables*
Ivan Turgenev: *Fathers and Sons*
Christina Rossetti: *Boblin Market and Other Poems*
Ellen Price Wood: *East Lynne*

Giuseppe Verdi: *La Forza del Destino*
Hector Berlioz: *Beatrice and Benedict*
Bedrich Smetana: *Wallenstein's Camp*
Robert Schumann: *Scenes from Goethe's* Faust
Johann Strauss: *Motor Waltz*; *Perpetuum Mobile*
General Daniel Butterfield: *Taps* (bugle call)

1863 In China, the Tai Ping rebels lose Soochow to Manchu forces led by Zeng Kuofan and General Charles Gordon, who is now 30. Mohammed Said Khedive of Egypt dies, aged 41, and is succeeded by his 33-year-old cousin Ismail Pasha. The Greek Assembly chooses Prince Alfred to succeed the deposed Greek King, but London rejects the election; the Greeks take a Danish prince as their second choice, the 17-year-old George I. *25 Jan*: Lincoln replaces General Burnside with General Hooker as overall Army commander. *1–4 May*: Confederates defeat Union forces but lose their best general when Stonewall Jackson is wounded. He is shot in the arm by one of his own sentries. *3 May*: Jackson's arm is amputated. *10 May*: Jackson dies of pneumonia. *7 Jun*: French forces occupy Mexico City. *28 Jun*: Lincoln replaces Hooker with Meade. *1–3 Jul*: Battle of Gettysburg: the turning point in the Civil War as the Confederates are routed. The French offer the Mexican throne to the Emperor Franz Josef's brother Archduke Maximilian. *4 Jul*: Vicksburg falls to General Grant. *11 Jul*: Conscription begins for the Union army and draft riots break out in the northern cities, especially New York, where 1,200 people are killed. *19–20 Sep*: Battle of Chickamauga, Georgia: Confederates under General Bragg win, but at a cost of over 2,000 dead and 14,600 wounded. *19 Nov*:

Lincoln dedicates a national cemetery at Gettysburg, making his eloquent Gettysburg Address. *23–25 Nov*: Battle of Chattanooga: the Confederates under Bragg are routed.

London Underground (first underground railway system in the world)

Thomas U. Walter: The Capitol Dome

Frederic Church: Icebergs

Jean Millet: Man with Hoe

Edouard Manet: Le déjeuner sur l'herbe; Olympia

Arthur Hughes: Home from the Sea

Dante Gabriel Rossetti: Beata Beatrix

Edward Hale: *The Man Without a Country*

Jules Verne: *Cinq Semaines en Ballon*

George Eliot: *Romola*

Charles Kingsley: *The Water Babies*

Franz Schubert: *Missa Solemnis*

Max Bruch: *Loreley*

Georges Bizet: *Les Pêcheurs de Perles* (The Pearl Fishers)

Louis Lambert: *When Johny Comes Marching Home* (popular song)

H. S. Thompson: *Clementine* (popular song)

Henry Tucker: *When This Cruel War Is Over* (popular song)

1864   King Kamehameha IV of the Sandwich Islands sells the island of Niihau to Elizabeth Sinclair, a Scot who uses the island to graze sheep and cattle. *10 Mar*: General Ulysses S. Grant is given command of all Union armies. *10 Apr*: Archduke Maximilian accepts the throne of Mexico. *1–3 Jun*: Battle of Cold Springs Harbor: Lee defeats Grant. *12 Jun*: Maximilian arrives in Mexico City: French troops help him drive Juarez over the border into the U.S. *27 Jun*: Battle of Kenesaw Mountain in Georgia: the Confederates defeat Sherman's troops, killing 2,000 while losing only 270 of their own men. *19 Jul*: General Gordon's British army helps Tseng Kuo-fan's army sack Nanjing. Hung Hsiu-chuan poisons himself as over 100,000 are killed and the Tai Ping Rebellion ends (began *1850*). *31 Aug*: Franceso Lopez the Paraguayan Dictator gives Brazil an ultimatum: Brazil may not intervene in Uruguay. *Oct*: Brazil invades Uruguay. *12 Nov*: Lopez seizes a Brazilian arms ship. *30 Nov*: Battle of Franklin: General Hood is defeated with severe casualties (1,750 dead) thanks to the use of the Gatling gun. *1 Oct*: a cyclone destroys much of Calcutta, killing 70,000 people.

🎨 Henri Fantin-Latour: Hommage à Delacroix (who died *13 Aug* last year)
Jean Corot: Souvenir de Mortefontaine
Edouard Manet: The Dead Toreador

📖 Fedor Dostoyevsky: *Letters From the Underground*
Jules Verne: *Voyage au Centre de la Terre* (Journey to the Centre of the Earth)
Jules Goncourt: *Renée Mauperin*
Anthony Trollope: *The Small House at Allington*; *Can You Forgive Her?*
George Marsh: *Man and Nature*

🎵 Jacques Offenbach: *La Belle Hélène*
Stephen Foster: *Beautiful Dreamer* (Foster dies *13 Jan*, aged 37)

1865 William Booth starts a mission in London that will become the Salvation Army. *18 Feb*: Charleston surrenders to a Union fleet. *3 Apr*: Petersburg, Virginia surrenders to the Union army; Grant takes Richmond the same day. *9 Apr*: General Lee surrenders to General Grant at Appomattox Courthouse, bringing the Civil War to an end. The war has cost 618,000 lives. *14 Apr*: Abraham Lincoln is assassinated at Ford's Theatre in Washington by John Wilkes Booth. *26 Apr*: Booth is found and shot. *27 Apr*: the paddle steamer *Sultana* explodes on the Mississippi killing 1,600 people on board. *18 Oct*: the British Prime Minister Lord Palmerston dies, aged 80. *10 Dec*: Leopold I King of the Belgians dies, aged 74, and is succeeded by his 30-year-old son Leopold II.

🏛 Gridley Bryan and Arthur Gilman: City Hall, Boston, U.S.
Gilbert Scott: Grand Midland Hotel, St Pancras Station, London

🎨 Winslow Homer: Prisoners from the Front
George Innes: Peace and Plenty

Gustave Courbet: Girl With Seagulls, Trouville
Ford Madox Brown: Work
📖 John Ruskin: *Sesame and Lilies*
Henry Wheeler Shaw: *Josh Billings: His Sayings*
Lewis Carroll: *Alice's Adventures in Wonderland*
Charles Dickens: *Our Mutual Friend*
Anthony Trollope: *The Belton Estate*
Mark Twain: *The Celebrated Jumping Frog of Calaveras County*
Mary Dodge: *Hans Brinker, or The Silver Skates*
🎵 Giacomo Meyerbeer: *L'Africaine* (Meyerbeer died last year, aged 72)
Richard Wagner: *Tristan und Isolde*
Franz Schubert: *Unfinished Symphony*
Henry Clay Work: *Marching Through Georgia* (popular song)

1866 Bernadette Soubirous of Lourdes enters the convent at Nevers. A Great Tea Race from Foochow to London pits 11 clippers against each other to reduce the spoilage of the tea in their holds; the voyage still takes three months. The cholera epidemic claims many lives – 120,000 in Prussia, 110,000 in Austria, 50,000 in America. *12 Feb*: America demands that French troops leave Mexico. Failing to achieve U.S. recognition, Maximilian sends his wife to get help from Napoleon III or the Pope, but his cause is hopeless. *Jun*: a seven-week war breaks out in Europe, in three theatres connected by telegraphic communication for the first time in the Old World. Bismarck, the 51-year-old Chief Minister of Prussia, precipitates the war, forming an alliance with Italy. *3 Jul*: Battle of Sadowa: Austrian troops are easily defeated by the Prussians under Moltke. *Aug*: the Japanese Shogun Iemochi dies, aged 20, and is succeeded briefly by his kinsman Yoshinobu, the last Tokugawa Shogun.

🎨 Edouard Manet: The Fifer
Gustave Courbet: Sleep
Winslow Homer: The Morning Bell
Albert Bierstadt: A Storm in the Rocky Mountains
📖 Leo Tolstoy: *War and Peace*, first instalment
Fedor Dostoyevsky: *Crime and Punishment*
Victor Hugo: *Les Travailleurs de la Mer* (Toilers of

the Sea)

George Eliot: *Felix Holt the Radical*

Walt Whitman: *O Captain! My Captain!*

Algernon Swinburne: *Poems and Ballads*

Bedřich Smetana: *The Bartered Bride*

Charles Thomas: *Mignon*

Charles M. Barras: *The Black Crook*

Claribel: *Come Back to Erin* (popular song)

1867   *14 Jan*: the painter Jean Auguste Ingres dies aged 86 in Paris. Bismarck organizes a North German Confederation under Prussia's Leadership. *29 Mar*: the British North America Act unites Quebec, Ontario, Nova Scotia and New Brunswick in a Dominion of Canada with its capital at Ottawa. *30 Mar*: Tsar Alexander cedes Alaska to the U.S. for 7-million dollars; even at 2 cents an acre, many Americans think this a pointless acquisition. *15 May*: Maximilian Emperor of Mexico, surrenders to Juarez' forces. *19 Jun*: Maximilian is executed by firing squad. *28 Aug*: Midway Islands in the Pacific are claimed for the U.S. by Captain Reynolds. *9 Nov*: the Japanese Shogun Yoshinobu abdicates as pressure mounts to restore the pre-12th century role of the Emperor and end the feudal military government of the Shoguns. The late Emperor Komei's son Mutsuhito takes power at the age of 15.

James Buchanan Eads: Eads Bridge, St Louis (over the Mississippi)

Lieut-Col H. Scott: Royal Albert Hall, London

Giuseppe Mengoni: Galleria Vittoria Emanuele, Milan (completed)

Edouard Manet: The Execution of Maximilian

Walter Bagehot: *The English Constitution*

Emile Zola: *Thérèse Raquin*

Antony Trollope: *The Last Chronicle of Barset*

Ouida: *Under Two Flags*

Leo Tolstoy: *The Death of Ivan the Terrible*

Charles Gounod: *Romeo et Juliette*

Giuseppe Verdi: *Don Carlos*

Arthur Sullivan & F. C. Burnard: *Cox and Box*

Johann Strauss: *The Blue Danube Waltz*

1868   Christopher Sholes patents a typewriter; he devises the

'QWERTY' layout used on all modern typewriters. In Siam King Rama IV dies, aged 64, and is succeeded by his son Somdeth Chulalongkorn, who is 15. In Madagascar the Hova Queen Rashoherina dies and is succeeded by Queen Ranavalona II. *6 Apr:* the Japanese Shogunate is formally ended as the new Emperor Matsuhito swears an oath to be guided by an assembly. *10 Apr:* the Ethiopian Emperor Theodore is defeated at the Battle of Arogee by an Anglo-Indian army led by Sir Robert Napier. Theodore commits suicide. *13 Apr:* the British reach Magdala, where they free traders, missionaries and others imprisoned by the cruel Theodore. Ethiopia collapses into anarchy as Napier withdraws.

Albert Bierstadt: Among the Sierra Nevada Mountains

Edouard Manet: Zola

Claude Monet: The River

Wilkie Collins: *The Moonstone*

Alexander Ostrovsky: *Diary of a Scoundrel*

Arrigo Boito: *Mefistofele*

Richard Wagner: *Die Meistersinger von Nürnberg*

Jacques Offenbach: *La Perichole*

Peter Tchaikovsky: *Symphony No 1*

Johannes Brahms: *Ein Deutsches Requiem* (A German Requiem)

Anton Bruckner: *Symphony No 1*

Camille Saint-Saëns: *Piano Concerto No 2*

Johann Strauss: *Tales of the Vienna Woods*

John Dykes: *Lead, Kindly Light* (words by Newman)

Lewis H Redner: *O Little Town of Bethlehem*

1869 Mahbub Ali Pasha begins a 42-year reign as Nizam of Hyderabad, a country the size of France in the centre of the Indian Deccan. James Bennett, publisher of the *New York Herald*, commissions correspondent Henry Morton Stanley to go to Africa to 'find' Livingstone, even though Livingstone is not lost or in any difficulty. *Mar:* the Meiji Emperor of Japan accepts the surrendered territories of the four most powerful clans (Choshu, Tosa, Hizen and Satsuma), reappointing the clan Chiefs as Provincial Governors on reduced revenues. *10 Mar:*

the Union Pacific and Central Pacific Railways are joined up in Utah; there is national celebration in America as the travel time separating New York and San Francisco falls from three months to eight days.

Jean-Baptiste Carpeaux: *The Dance*
Leo Tolstoy: *War and Peace*, final instalment
Fedor Dostoyevsky: *The Idiot*
Anthony Trollpoe: *Phineas Finn*
Victor Hugo: *L'homme qui rit*
R. D. Blackmore: *Lorna Doone*
Mark Twain: *Innocents Abroad*
Louisa May Alcott: *Little Women*
Henrik Ibsen: *The League of Youth*
Franz Schubert: *Symphony No 4*
Nikolai Rimsky-Korsakov: *Symphony No 2*
Edvard Grieg: *Piano Concerto*
Anton Bruckner: *Mass*
Richard Wagner: *Das Rheingold*

1870 *1 Mar*: President Lopez of Paraguay is killed. *20 Jun*: Paraguay's six-year war with its neighbours is formally over, leaving 100,000 dead, reducing its population to 28,000 men and 200,000 women; Brazil has lost 165,000 men in the fighting. *25 Jun*: Isabella II of Spain is persuaded in Paris to abdicate; although her 12-year-old son nominally succeeds her, Victor Emmanuel's son the 25-year-old-Duke of Aosta is induced to take the throne as Amadeo I. Wilhelm I of Prussia has persuaded his kinsman Leopold to withdraw his acceptance of the Spanish crown as a result of protests from France contained in the Ems telegram. With Wilhelm's permission, Bismarck publishes enough of the text of the telegram to make it clear that Napoleon has tried to humiliate the Kaiser. *18 Jul*: the Vatican Council votes that the Pope is infallible when speaking on matters of doctrine from his throne. *19 Jul*: France declares war on Prussia, invading the Saar coalfield and gaining a victory at Saarbrücken while three German armies invade France. *1 Sep*: Battle of Sedan: the French army under Marshal MacMahon is crushed. *2 Sep*: Napoleon himself surrenders. *19 Sep*: the Germans begin a siege of Paris and the Second Empire collapses. *12 Dec*: at Triebschen on the shore of Lake Lucerne, Wagner has his newly composed *Siegfried Idyll* performed on his wife's birthday.

    ⚶ Church of Sacré Coeur, Montmartre, Paris

    🖾 Jean Corot: La perle
       Henri Fantin-Latour: Un Atelier a Batignolles
       John Inchbold: Early Spring
       Edward Burne-Jones: The Mill

    📖 William Morris: *The Earthly Paradise*
       Jules Verne: *Vingt mille lieues sous les mers* (Twenty Thousand Leagues Under the Sea)
       Charles Dickens: *Edwin Drood* (unfinished at Dickens' death, *9 Jun*)

    🎜 Léo Delibes: *Coppélia*
       Richard Wagner: *Die Walküre*; *Siegfried Idyll*
       Peter Tchaikovsky: *Romeo and Juliet Overture*
       Camille Saint-Saëns: *Piano Concerto No 3*

1871 The 70-year-old Mormon leader Brigham Young is arrested on polygamy charges at Salt Lake City: he has 27 wives. David Livingstone sees hundreds of African women shot dead by Arab slavers while trying to escape, at Nyangwe; he sends an account to England where efforts are made to force suppression of the slave trade through the Sultan of Zanzibar. *18 Jan*: in the Hall of Mirrors at Versailles a united German Empire is proclaimed (the 'Second Reich'). Wilhelm I of Prussia is to be Emperor and Bismarck Chancellor: the new state is to comprise Saxony, Bavaria, Württemberg and Prussia together with the five Grand Duchies, 13 Duchies and principalities and three free cities of Hamburg, Lubeck and Bremen. *28 Jan*: Paris surrenders to German troops. *1 Mar*: Napoleon III is deposed. The Paris Commune is established. *10 May*: a peace treaty between France and Germany is signed at Frankfurt: France agrees to cede Alsace and part of Lorraine. The Commune falls at the end of *May*, when up to 30,000 Parisians are killed at the barricades.

    ⚶ Basil Champneys: Newnham College, Cambridge

    🖾 James Whistler: Arrangement in Black and Gray
       Thomas Eakins: Max Schmitt in a Single Scull
       George Inness: Woodland Scene

Frederic Church: The Parthenon
Dante Gabriel Rossetti: The Dream of Dante
☐ Fedor Dostoyevsky: *The Possessed*
Alexander Ostrovsky: *The Forest*
🎜 Giuseppe Verdi: *Aida* (intended for the opening of the Suez Canal)
Arthur Sullivan: *Onward Christian Soldiers* (words S. B. Gould)

1872 The Emperor Theodore of Ethiopia is succeeded by the King of Tigre, who rules as Johannes IV, 'King of Kings'. Georg Ebers discovers the oldest known collection of medical writings at Thebes in Egypt, the Ebers Papyrus. *May*: Don Carlos, the Spanish pretender, enters Navarre but his forces are routed at Oroquista: Don Carlos is forced back into the Pyrenees. *18 Sep*: Charles IV of Sweden dies at Malmo, aged 46, and is succeeded by his 43-year-old brother Oscar II. *14 Oct*: the first railway in Japan is opened, a 29-km/18-mile track joining Tokyo (Edo) and Yokohama. *4 Dec*: the brigantine *Mary Celeste* is found drifting with no one aboard; what happened to her crew will never be known.
✐ Henry Hobson Richardson: Trinity Church, Boston
👁 Edgar Degas: Le Foyer de la Danse
Dante Gabriel Rossetti: The Bower Meadow
☐ George Eliot: *Middlemarch*
Thomas Hardy: *Under the Greenwood Tree*
Lewis Carroll: *Through the Looking Glass*
Ambrose Bierce: *The Fiend's Delight*
Franz Grillparzer: *Ein Bruderzwist in Habsburg* (Family Strife in Hapsburg) (Grillparzer dies *21 Jan*, aged 81)
Alphonse Daudet: *L'Arlésienne*
🎜 Camille Saint-Saëns: *La Princesse Jaune*
Max Bruch: *Hermione*
Anton Bruckner: *Mass*
Georges Bizet: *Incidental Music to L'Arlésienne*

1873 Barbed wire exhibited at an Illinois county fair by Henry Rose is taken up by Joseph Glidden and Jacob Haish, who invent a machine to mass-produce barbed wire; this is destined to end the open range in the West. *9 Jan*: the exiled Napoleon III dies in England, aged 64; German

troops begin to evacuate France. *12 Feb*: a Spanish
Republic is proclaimed; Amadeo I abdicates; Foreign
Minister Emilio Cistelar y Ripoli becomes Prime Min-
ister. *1 Apr*: the White Star liner *Atlantic* is wrecked off
Nova Scotia: 502 passengers are drowned. *5 Jun*: the
slave markets in Zanzibar are closed by the Sultan
Barghash Sayyid acting under pressure from Britain.

   🏛 Alfred Waterhouse: Natural History Museum,
South Kensington

   🎨 Thomas Eakins: Oarsmen on the Schuykill
Edouard Manet: Le bon Bock

   📖 Mark Twain and Charles Warner: *The Gilded Age*
Jules Verne: *Le Tour du Monde en Quatre-vingt Jours*
(Around the World in Eighty Days)
Anthony Trollope: *The Eustace Diamonds*

   🎼 Nikolai Rimsky-Korsakov: *Ivan the Terrible*
Camille Saint-Saëns: *Cello Concerto No 1*
Anton Bruckner: *Symphony No 2*
Peter Tchaikovsky: *The Tempest*
Hart Pease Danks: *Silver Threads Among the Gold*
(popular song)
Daniel Kelly: *Home on the Range* (words by Bruce
Higley)

1874 The Fiji Islands are annexed by Britain. *4 Feb*: British
troops led by Sir Garnet Wolseley enter Kumasi, the
Ashanti capital, bringing the second Ashanti War to an
end. *Apr*: Japan invades Taiwan, excusing the action by
pointing to the murder of 54 Japanese sailors who were
shipwrecked there three years ago. *Oct*: China agrees to
pay compensation to Japan and the invasion force is
withdrawn from Taiwan. *1 Dec*: the 17-year-old Alphonso XII of Spain issues a manifesto from Sandhurst in
England, proclaiming himself the sole heir to the Spanish throne and formally beginning his reign.

   🎨 Claude Monet: Impression, Sunrise (the first Im-
pressionist painting)
James Whistler: Nocturne in Black and Gold
Edward Burne-Jones: The Beguiling of Merlin; Pan
and Psyche

   📖 Thomas Hardy: *Far From the Madding Crowd*
Anthony Trollope: *Phineas Redux*

Leopold von Sacher-Masoch: *Die Messalinen Wiens*
Paul Verlaine: *Romances sans paroles*
Adolphe d'Emery: *Les Deux Orphelins*
⚘ Johann Strauss: *Die Fledermaus*
Modest Mussorgsky: *Boris Godunov*
Giuseppe Verdi: *Requiem* (in memory of Manzoni, died *22 May* last year)

1875 The King of Fiji returns home from a visit to Australia taking measles with him: 40,000 of the 150,000 inhabitants of Fiji die in a measles epidemic. Alexander Graham Bell pioneers the telephone. Praxiteles' statue of Hermes (*4th century BC*) is found at Olympia. The Maya-Toltec statue The Great Chac-Mool (made about *1100*) is found at a temple entrance at Chichen-Itza, Central America. *Jan*: the Chinese Emperor Mu Zung dies, aged 19, and is succeeded by his cousin Zaitian as the Guangxu Emperor. *22 Feb*: tension between Beijing and London increases as Augustus Margary, a British official, is killed by bandits close to the Burma-China border. *16 Jul*: a new French constitution provides for a Chamber of Deputies and a Senate, and an elected President. MacMahon is to continue as President until *1879*. *27 Nov*: the Suez Canal comes under British control. Disraeli borrows money (£4 million) from a merchant bank, offering the British Government as security.

✑ Jean Garnier: Paris Opera (completed)
🎨 Claude Monet: Boating at Argenteuil
Thomas Eakins: The Agnew Clinic
📖 Alexander Ostrovsky: *Wolves and Sheep*
Gerard Manley Hopkins: *The Windhover*
Anthony Trollope: *The Way We Live Now*
⚘ Georges Bizet: *Carmen* (Bizet dies aged 36 on *3 June*)
Gilbert and Sullivan: *Trial by Jury*
Ignaz Brull: *Das goldene Kreuz*
Tomas Breton: *Guzman el Bueno*
Camille Saint-Saëns: *Danse Macabre*
Edouard Lalo: *Symphonie Espagnole*
Bedrich Smetana: *The Vltava*
Peter Tchaikovsky: *Piano Concerto No 1*; *Symphony No 3*

1876   The Chiricahua Indian chief Geronimo (real name Goyathlay) leads warriors into Mexico to avenge the killing of his family by Mexicans in *1858*; he begins a 10-year reign of terror. *26 Feb*: Japan recognizes Korea's independence from China. *Apr*: the Royal Titles Act passed by the British Parliament makes Queen Victoria Empress of India. *29 May*: Abdul Aziz the Ottoman Sultan is deposed, aged 46, and is succeeded by his 35-year-old nephew Murad V; Abdul Aziz commits suicide four days later. Murad is himself deposed after three months and replaced by his 33-year-old brother Abdul Hamid II. A Bulgarian insurrection against Turkish rule begins. *25 Jun*: Battle of the Little Big Horn. The Sioux Indians are angry at the slaughter of their buffalo by the advancing white settlers and massacre a 264-strong Seventh Cavalry force under George Custer. *30 Jun*: Serbia declares war on Turkey. *2 Jun*: Montenegro declares war on Turkey. *2 Aug*: Wild Bill Hickok is shot dead at Deadwood, Dakota, aged 39: he is shot from behind while sitting at a poker table in Saloon No 10 by Jack McCall. *1 Sep*: the Serbs are totally defeated at Alexinatz. The Bulgarian insurrection is also suppressed.

◿ Thomas Jackson: Examination Schools, Oxford
Archibald Willard: The Spirit of '76
Winslow Homer: Breezing Up
Alfred Sisley: Flood at Port Marly
Auguste Renoir: Au Moulin de la Galette
Edgar Degas: The Glass of Absinthe; Prima Ballerina

📖 Henry James: *Roderick Hudson*
Anthony Trollope: *The Prime Minister*
Mark Twain: *The Adventures of Tom Sawyer*
Joris Huysmans: *Marthe*
George Eliot: *Daniel Deronda*
Stéphane Mallarmé: *L'Après-midi d'un faune*
Alexander Ostrovsky: *Truth Is Good, but Happiness Is Better*
Henrik Ibsen: *Peer Gynt*
⚏ Amilcare Pochielli: *La Gioconda*
Peter Tchaikovsky: *The Golden Slippers; Marche Slav*

Johannes Brahms: *Symphony No 1*

Thomas P. Westendorf: *I'll Take You Home Again, Kathleen* (popular song)

Henry Clay Work: *Grandfather's Clock* (popular song)

1877   John D. Rockefeller President of Standard Oil of Ohio, signs a contract with the Pennsylvania Railroad strengthening his oil-rail monopoly. *12 Apr*: Britain annexes the South African Republic in breach of the *1852* Sand River Convention recognizing the independence of the Transvaal. *24 Apr*: Russia declares war on Turkey. *21 Jul*: Britain decides to declare war on Russia if Russian troops occupy Constantinople. *Nov*: General Carleton orders Apache Indians in Arizona out of their Chiricahua reservation at Warm Springs, moving them to San Carlos which has summer temperatures rising to 40°C/104°F, no game and no other food supply; any Indian found wandering off the new reservation is to be shot. *31 Dec*: the painter Gustave Courbet dies, aged 58. He was imprisoned for six months in *1871* for destroying the Vendôme Column in Paris, and fled to Switzerland in *1873* after being ordered to pay for the rebuilding of the column.

✏ Charles Shaler Smith: Harrodsburg Bridge, Kentucky (first U.S. cantilever bridge)

Norman Shaw: Old Swan House, Chelsea Embankment, London

🎨 Winslow Homer: The Cotton Pickers

Charles Daubigny: Lever de Lune

Edouard Manet: Nana

Dante Gabriel Rossetti: Astarte Syriaca

Edward Burne-Jones: Perseus Slaying the Sea-Serpent

📖 Leo Tolstoy: *Anna Karenina*

Henry James: *The American*

Sarah Jewett: *Deephaven*

Anna Sewell: *Black Beauty*

🎼 Peter Tchaikovsky: *Swan Lake; Francesca da Rimini*

Camille Saint-Saëns: *Samson et Dalila*

Franz Schubert: *Symphony No 2* (written in *1815*)

Anton Bruckner: *Symphony No 3*

Johannes Brahms: *Symphony No 2*
Jan Blockx: *Jets vergeten*

1878 *9 Jan*: Victor Emmanuel II of Italy dies, aged 57, and is succeeded by his 33-year old son Umberto I. Ottoman forces surrender and ask for an armistice. *23 Jan*: in Russia, a trial of nearly 200 young revolutionaries ends in acquittals, but the police afterwards pick most of the people acquitted and send them to Siberia; systematic terrorism will start next year. *31 Jan*: an armistice between Russia and Turkey is concluded. *15 Feb*: the British fleet arrives at Constantinople. *5 Mar*: Treaty of San Stefano signed outside Constantinople, ends hostilities but angers Britain by reducing Ottoman power, giving Romania, Montenegro and Serbia independence. *Jul*: Berlin Congress: the Ottoman Empire is divided up, leaving few nations satisfied.

   Edward Godwin: White House, Tite Street, Chelsea (for Whistler)

   Albert Bierstadt: Sierra Nevada
   Edgar Degas: Rehearsal on the Stage
   Auguste Renoir: Madame Charpentier and Her Children

   Thomas Hardy: *The Return of the Native*
   Henry James: *The Europeans*
   Henrik Ibsen: *The Pillars of Society*
   Alexander Ostrovsky: *The Girl with No Dowry*

   Peter Tchaikovsky: *Symphony No 4*
   Gilbert and Sullivan: *HMS Pinafore*

1879 The Irish Land League is founded to campaign for independence from Britain. The Zulu nation founded in *1816* by Shaka ends in a blood bath as the British with their breech-loading rifles kill 8,000 Zulu warriors: 1,100 British soldiers lose their lives. *14 Feb*: the War of the Pacific starts as Chilean soldiers occupy Antofagasta and go on to take the whole of the Bolivian coastline. *29 Mar*: the Zulu War ends after the Battle of Rorke's Drift, at which 140 British soldiers hold off 4,000 Zulus; 11 Victoria Crosses will be awarded for this action. *2 Jun*: Louis, the Prince Imperial of France and the prospective Napoleon IV, is killed by a Zulu assegai; the French suspect that he was killed with British connivance. *25 Jun*: Ismail, the Khedive of Egypt, is deposed by the Ottoman Sultan after pressure from the European powers; Ismail is succeeded by his son Tewfik. *3 Sep*: the Afghans rise against the British. The British envoy Sir Louis Cavagnari is murdered. *12 Oct*: the British take Kabul. *19 Oct*: the Afghan Emir Yakub is forced to abdicate; he is succeeded by his cousin Abd-er-Rahman.

🏛 James Renwick: St Patrick's Cathedral, New York (completed)

Frederick Olmsted: Park System, Boston (completed)

Cathedral of St Stephen, Limoges (completed)

🎨 Dante Gabriel Rossetti: The Blessed Damozel

Maray Cassatt: The Cup of Tea

Paul Cézanne: Self-portrait

📖 Henry James: *Daisy Miller*

George Meredith: *The Egoist*

August Strindberg: *The Red Room*

George Washington Cable: *Creole Days*

Henrik Ibsen: *A Doll's House*

Alexander Ostrovsky: *The Heart Is Not Stone*

R. L. Stevenson: *Travels with a Donkey*

🎵 Peter Tchaikovsky: *Eugen Onegin; Variations on a Rococo Theme*

Antonin Dvořák: *Slavonic Dances*

Johannes Brahms: *Violin Concerto*

1880 Thomas Edison patents his incandescent electric light bulb. French Equatorial Africa is established by explorer Pierre Brazza Savorgnani, who founds Brazzaville. *3 Jul*: Morocco is recognized as independent by the European powers and the U.S. *30 Dec*: Paul Kruger proclaims an independent Boer Republic, separate from Britain's Cape Colony, but the revolt is short-lived and the British are able to establish a single South African Rebublic by force, independent but under British suzerainty.

🏛 Cologne Cathedral (completed after 634 years of building)

Charles Clinton: Seventh Regiment Armoury, Fourth Avenue, New York

    Edgar Degas: Petite Danseuse de Quatorze Ans (sculpture)

    Edward Burne-Jones: The Golden Stairs

    Max Liebermann: Old Folks' Home in Amsterdam

    Camille Pissarro: The Outer Boulevards

    Auguste Renoir: Place Clichy

    Paul Cézanne: Château de Medan

    Fedor Dostoyevsky: *The Brothers Karamazov*

    Mark Twain: *A Tramp Abroad*

    Emile Zola: *Nana*

    Guy de Maupassant: *Boule de Suif*

    Jens Jacobsen: *Liels Lyhne*

    Lew Wallace: *Ben Hur*

    Anthony Trollope: *The Duke's Children*

    Steele Mackay: *Hazel Kirke*

    Calixa Lavalle: *Oh Canada*

    Johannes Brahms: *Tragic Overture*

    Luigi Denza: *Funiculi-Funicula* (popular song)

1881   *28 Jan*: Boers in the Transvaal fend off British forces at Laing's Neck. *27 Feb*: the Boers defeat the British at Majuba Hill. *13 Mar*: Tsar Alexander II is assassinated, aged 62, by a band of Nihilists led by Sophia Perovskaya. He is succeeded by his 36-year-old son Alexander III who reacts to the assassination with repressive measures including a persecution of Jews: millions of Jews emigrate from Russia during the next three decades. *5 Apr*: Treaty of Pretoria, giving independence to the South African Republic but under British suzerainty. *2 Jul*: President Garfield of the U.S. is shot by Charles Guiteau at a Washington railway station. *15 Jul*: Sheriff Pat Garrett shoots William Bonney (Billy the Kid) at Fort Sumner in New Mexico; aged 21, Bonney has shot 21 people. *19 Sep*: President Garfield dies.

    Stanford White: Casino, Newport, U.S.

    Augustus Saint-Gaudens: Admiral Farragut (sculpture)

    Auguste Renoir: Boating Party Luncheon

    Max Liebermann: An Asylum for Old Men; Cobbler's Shop

    Claude Monet: Sunshine and Snow

    Edward Burne-Jones: Pelican

📖 Alexander Ostrovsky: *Talents and Admirers*
Johann Spyri: *Heidi*
Henry James: *The Portrait of a Lady*
Anatole France: *Le Crime de Sylvestre Bonard*
Giovanni Verga: *I Malavoglia* (The House by the Medlar Tree)

🎼 Jacques Offenbach: *Les Contes d'Hoffman* (The Tales of Hoffman)
Peter Tchaikovsky: *The Maid of Orleans; Symphony No 2; Violin Concerto*
Gilbert and Sullivan: *Patience*
Camille Saint-Saëns: *Violin Concerto No 3*
Johannes Brahms: *Academic Festival Overture; Piano Concerto No 2*
Franz Schubert: *Symphony No 3*
Anton Bruckner: *Symphony No 4*

1882 *20 May:* the St Gotthard Tunnel opens, the first railway tunnel through the Alps. *11 Jul:* the British fleet under Sir Beauchamp Seymour bombards Alexandria and British troops are landed to defend the Suez Canal from Egyptian nationalist forces. *13 Sep:* Battle of Tel el-Kebir: Sir Garnet Wolseley's troops defeat the Egyptians. *15 Sep:* the British occupy Cairo. *9 Nov:* joint Anglo-French control of Egypt is abolished.

✐ George Street: Law Courts, London (completed)

🎨 John Singer Sargent: Mr. and Mrs. John W. Field
Edouard Manet: Bar at the Folies Bergère

📖 Carlo Collodi: *Pinocchio*
Gabriele d'Annunzio: *Canto novo*
Henrik Ibsen: *Ghosts*
Victorien Sardou: *Fedora*

🎼 Tomas Breton: *Apocalipsia*
Nikolai Rimsky-Korsakov: *The Snow Maiden*
Richard Wagner: *Parsifal*
Bedřich Smetana: *The Devil's Wall; Ma Vlast*
Peter Tchaikovsky: *Serenade for String Orchestra; 1812 Overture*
Claude Debussy: *Le Printemps*

1883 The American engineer Hiram Maxim invents the fully automatic machine gun, which will be adopted by every major army and greatly increase the sum of human suffering; the recoil energy of each bullet fired is used to eject the spent cartridge, insert the next round and fire it. *13 Feb*: the composer Richard Wagner dies in Venice, aged 69. *25 Aug*: the French sign a treaty at Hue, recognizing Tonkin, Cochin China and Annam as French protectorates, but China rejects the treaty and resists French interference in the region. *27 Aug*: Krakatoa in the Sunda Strait erupts with extraordinary ferocity in what is believed to be the most violent volcanic eruption since the Bronze Age eruption of Thera almost 3,500 years ago; 36,000 people lose their lives in the seismic wave generated by the eruption. *3 Sep*: Chinese irregulars, Vietnamese and French troops meet in battle outside Hanoi with great loss of life. *4 Oct*: the Orient Express leaving from the Gare de l'Est in Paris is the first transcontinental train service in Europe. *20 Oct*: Treaty of Ancona, ending the war between Chile, Peru and Bolivia over the Atacama Desert and its nitrate deposits: Chile gains territory from Peru.

　　John Augustus Roebling: Brooklyn Bridge or Great East River Bridge

　　　　Northern Pacific Railway (completed *8 Sep* in Montana)

　　Thomas Eakins: The Swimming Hole

　　Friedrich Nietzsche: *Also Sprach Zarathustra* (Thus Spake Zarathustra)

　　　　Mark Twain: *Life on the Mississippi*

　　　　Robert Louis Stevenson: *Treasure Island*

　　　　Emile Verhaeren: *Les Flamandes* (The Flemish)

　　　　Henrik Ibsen: *An Enemy of the People*

　　　　Imre Madach: *The Tragedy of Man*

　　　　August Strindberg: *Lucky Per's Journey*

　　Léo Delibes: *Lakmé*

　　　　César Franck: *Le Chasseur Maudit* (The Accursed Huntsman)

　　　　Emmanuel Chabrier: *España*

　　　　Johannes Brahms: *Symphony No 3*

　　　　William Tomer: *God Be With You Till We Meet Again* (words, J. Rankin)

1884　*4 Apr*: Treaty of Valparaiso, ending the War of the Pacific between Chile and Peru; the agreement over territory deprives Bolivia of access to the sea and Chile gains the nitrates. *24 Apr*: Bismarck telegraphs Cape Town with the news that Southwest Africa (now Namibia) is henceforth a German colony. *5 Jul*: the German Consul at Tunis proclaims that Togoland is a German protectorate. *26 Oct*: China declares war on France after the French bombard Taiwan as a reprisal for Chinese refusal to acknowledge France's protectorate of Indo-China. *25 Nov*: the English surgeon Rickman Godlee undertakes the first operation to remove a brain tumour.

- Edward Burne-Jones: King Cophetua and the Beggar Maid
  Georges Seurat: Bathers at Asnières
  William Holman Hunt: The Triumph of the Innocents
  Fernand Khnopff: Sphinx
  Augustus Saint-Gaudens: Robert Gould Shaw Memorial (sculpture)
- Leo Tolstoy: *The Death of Ivan Ilyich*
  Joris Huysmans: *Against Nature*
  Mark Twain: *The Adventures of Huckleberry Finn*
- Jules Massenet: *Manon*
  Peter Tchaikovsky: *Mazeppa*
  Zdenek Fibich: *The Bride of Messina*
  Edward MacDowell: *Piano Suite No 2*
  Anton Bruckner: *Symphony No 7*
  Effie Crockett: *Rock-a-bye Baby*

1885 Leopold II King of the Belgians assumes the title Sovereign of the Congo Free State as the Belgian colony is recognized. *26 Jan*: Khartoum falls to the Sudanese Mahdi Mohammed Ahmed; General Gordon and his garrison are massacred just before a British relief force reaches the city. *9 Jun*: Treaty of Tientsin, recognizing France's protectorate of Tonkin in return for France's respect for China's southern frontier. *21 Jun*: the Mahdi dies and is succeeded by the Khalifa Abdullah el Tasshi; his forces gain control of the whole of the Sudan. *24 Nov*: Alphonso XII of Spain dies, aged 27, of tuberculosis; he will be succeeded by his posthumous son Alphonso XIII.

- William LeBaron: Home Insurance Building, Chicago (first skyscraper)

Sagamore Hill, Cove Neck, Long Island (for Theodore Roosevelt)

Vincent van Gogh: The Potato Eaters
William Morris: Woodpecker Tapestry
Augustus Saint-Gaudens: The Puritan
Henrik Ibsen: *The Wild Duck*
Henry Rider Haggard: *King Solomon's Mines*
George Meredith: *Diana of the Crossways*
Emile Zola: *Germinal*
Guy de Maupassant: *Bel Ami*; *Contes et Nouvelles*
Johann Strauss: *The Gypsy Baron*
César Franck: *Fugue for Piano*; *Les Djinns*
Johannes Brahms: *Symphony No 4*

1886 *1 May*: workers in Chicago demonstrate for an eight-hour day and better working conditions; police fire into the demonstration, killing four. *4 May*: the Haymarket Massacre: the Knights of Labor hold a peaceful demonstration in Haymarket Square, Chicago to protest about the May Day killings. A protester throws a bomb that kills seven policemen; the police fire into the crowd, killing three times as many civilians. *24 Jul*: after a third Anglo-Burmese War, China recognizes Burma as a British protectorate. *Sep*: the ground plan of the city of Johannesburg is laid out; it is soon flooded with tens of thousands of people as the South African Gold Rush gets under way.

Daniel Burnham and John Root: Rookery Building, Chicago
Raffles Hotel, Singapore
John Millais: Bubbles
John Singer Sargent: Carnation, Lily, Lily, Rose
Henri Rousseau: Carnaval du Soir
Frederic Auguste Bartholdi: Statue of Liberty (bronze, 46 metres 150 feet high)
Karl Marx: *Das Kapital* (published in English)
Thomas Hardy: *The Mayor of Casterbridge*
Henry James: *The Bostonians*
William Dean Howells: *Indian Summer*
Pierre Loti: *Pêcheur d'Islande*
Robert Louis Stevenson: *The Strange Case of Dr Jekyll and Mr. Hyde*

Marie Corelli: *The Romance of Two Worlds*
Frances Hodgson Burnett: *Little Lord Fauntleroy*
Louisa May Alcott: *Jo's Boys*
Arthur Rimbaud: *Les Illuminations*
🎼 Edward MacDowell: *Ophelia*
Modest Mussorgsky: *Night on the Bare Mountain*
Camille Saint-Saëns: *Symphony No 3*
César Franck: *Symphonic Variations for Piano and Orchestra*
Peter Tchaikovsky: *Manfred Symphony*

1887 Macao off the Chinese coast is ceded to Portugal. In France, the 18-year-old engineering student Léon Bolle invents a calculating machine that automatically multiplies. *11 Jan*: Bismarck warns Europe against war, also advocating that Germany should expand its army. France is agitated by renewed nationalist feeling and wants revenge for defeat in the Franco-Prussian War. *25 Jan*: an Italian-Ethiopian War breaks out, the Ethiopians destroying an Italian army at Dogali. *4 Mar*: the first Daimler car takes to the road. *23 May*: the Canadian Pacific Railway reaches Vancouver; it is the first single-company transcontinental railway in the New World.

✍ Grand Hotel, Mackinac Island, Michigan
Henry Hobson Richardson: Allegheny Courthouse and Jail, Pittsburgh
🖎 Edward Burne-Jones: The Depths of the Sea
Vincent van Gogh: Moulin de la Galette
Thomas Eakins: Walt Whitman
Augustus Saint-Gaudens: Seated Lincoln
📖 Henry James: *The Aspern Papers*
Rudyard Kipling: *Plain Tales from the Hills*
August Strindberg: *The People of Hemso*; *The Father*
Henry Rider Haggard: *She*; *Allan Quartermain*
Arthur Conan Doyle: *A Study in Scarlet*
Henrik Ibsen: *Rosmershom*
Victorien Sardou: *La Tosca*
Georges Feydeau: *Tailleur pour dames*
🎼 Giuseppe Verdi: *Otello*
Emmanuel Chabrier: *Le Roi malgré lui*
Vincent d'Indy: *Suite for Trumpet, Flutes and*

Strings
Johannes Brahms: *Double Concerto*
Nikolai Rimsky-Korsakov: *Capriccio Espagnole*
Modest Mussorgsky: *Pictures at an Exhibition*
Alfred Bruneau: *Kérim*

1888 The first railway in China opens between Tangshan and Tientsin (129 km/80 miles). *9 May*: Wilhelm I of Germany dies in Berlin, aged 90, and is succeeded by his 57-year-old son Friedrich Wilhelm. *13 May*: Brazil's slaves are freed. *15 Jun*: the new Emperor of Germany dies of throat cancer and is succeeded by his 29-year-old son Wilhelm II, who is the last German monarch. *29 Oct*: at Constaninople a Suez Canal Convention is signed, declaring that the canal is to be free and open to all shipping in both peace and war. *30 Oct*: Lobengula the Matabele King accepts a British protectorate and allows Cecil Rhodes exclusive mining rights in Matabeleland and Mashonaland (later Rhodesia/Zimbabwe) *Nov*: the Jack the Ripper murders in the East End of London.

  Louis Sullivan: Auditorium Building, Chicago
Washington Monument
Alfred Mullett: State, War and Navy Department Building, Washington
H. Richardson and L. Elditz: State Capitol Building, New York

  Paul Gauguin: Jacob and the Angel
Georges Seurat: Circus Side Show
Vincent van Gogh: Sunflowers; Night Café
James Ensor: The Entry of Christ into Brussels
Auguste Rodin: Le Penseur (The Thinker)

  Arthur Wing Pinero: *Sweet Lavender*
Oscar Wilde: *The Happy Prince*

  Edouard Lalo: *Le Roi d'Ys* (his first major success at the age of 65)
Gabriel Faure: *Requiem*
Alberto Franchetti: *Asrael*
Peter Tchaikovsky: *Symphony No 5*
Pierre Degeyter: *L'Internationale* (words by Eugene Pettier)

1889 *30 Jan*: Archduke Rudolph of Austria shoots his mistress, the 17-year-old Baroness Marie Vetser, at his hunting lodge at Mayerling near Vienna; he then shoots himself. On his death Franz Ferdinand, now 25, becomes Franz Josef's heir apparent. *11 Feb*: the Japanese Emperor hands his Prime Minister Count Kuroda Japan's first written constitution. *6 Mar*: Milan Obrenovic IV of Serbia abdicates, aged 34, and goes to live in Paris; he is succeeded by his 13-year-old son Alexander I. *12 Mar*: Johannes IV of Ethiopia is killed in the Battle of Metemma as he fights the Mahdists, and is succeeded by Menelek of Shoa, who reigns as 'King of Kings' until *1911*. *2 Oct*: the first Pan-American Conference meets in Washington with the aim of cementing relations among the New World states. *19 Oct*: Luiz I of Portugal dies, aged 51, and is succeeded by his 26-year-old son Carlos I. *15 Nov*: Perdo II of Brazil is deposed by the Brazilian army, which proclaims a republic under General Manoel da Fonseca.

- John Fowler and Benjamin Baker: Forth Bridge, Scotland
  Gustave Eiffel: Eiffel Tower
  Savoy Hotel, London
  Bradford Lee Gilbert: 50 Broadway, New York (13 storeys)
- Winslow Homer: The Gulf Stream
  James Ensor: Portrait of an Old Woman
  Vincent van Gogh: Self-portrait with Bandaged Ear; The Starry Night; Landscape with Cypress Trees
- Maurice Maeterlinck: *Serres chaudes*
  Gabriele d'Annunzio: *Il Piacere* (The Child of Pleasure)
  Henri Bergson: *Time and Free Will*
- Jules Massenet: *Esclarmonde*
  Camille Benoit: *Cleopatra*
  César Franck: *Symphony in D minor*
  Gustav Mahler: *Symphony No 1*
  John Philip Sousa: *Washington Post*

1890 Eugene Dubois discovers fossil remains of Java man, a prehistoric ancestor of modern man who lived in 700,000 BC. *18 Mar*: Kaiser Wilhelm of Germany forces Bismarck's resignation as Chancellor. *11 Jul*: the first-ever elections in Japan, with a limited franchise: only 450,000 vote. *29 Nov*: the first Japanese Diet opens: the representatives elected in *Jul* take their seats for the first time. *15 Dec*: the Sioux Indian chief Sitting Bull is arrested in a skirmish with U.S. troops and then shot dead as braves try to rescue him. *29 Dec*: 'Battle' of Wounded Knee: in truth, a massacre of 300 Indian men, women and children in a South Dakota encampment by the U.S. Seventh Cavalry.

Louis Sullivan: Wainwright Building, St. Louis
Burnham and Root: Monadnock Building, Chicago
Arthur Blomfield: Southwark Cathedral (U.K.)

Claude Monet: Poplars
Paul Cézanne: The Cardplayers
James Ensor: Intrigue
Vincent van Gogh: Portrait of Dr. Gachet; Crows Over the Wheat Fields (his last work; dies *29 Jul* at Auvers, aged 37)
Thomas Hovenden: Breaking Home Ties

James Frazer: *The Golden Bough, Volume 1*
Emily Dickinson: *Poems*
Gerhart Hauptmann: *Das Friedensfest* (The Reconciliation)
Alfred Mahan: *The Influence of Sea Power Upon History*

Peter Tchaikovsky: *The Sleeping Beauty*; *Queen of Spades*
Pietro Mascagni: *Cavalleria Rusticana*
Alexander Borodin: *Prince Igor*
Hector Berlioz: *Les Troyens*
Edward MacDowell: *Lancelot and Elaine*

1891 Work begins at Vladivostok on the eastern end of the Trans-Siberian Railway. In Germany the world's first old age pension scheme goes into operation (as proposed by Bismarck in *1889*): it is based on compulsory contributions from workers and employers and is payable at 70. *20 Jan*: King David Kalalahua of Hawaii dies, aged 54, and is succeeded by his 52-year-old sister Queen Lydia Liliuokalani. The whites who now own 80 per cent of the farmland in Hawaii form a Hawaiian League to oppose the monarchy; an Annexation Club plans to overthrow the Queen. *15 May*: a papal encyclical urges employers to fulfil their moral duty to improve the lot of their workers. *Nov*: the President of Brazil, Fonseca, is ousted; Vice President Floriano Peixoto takes his place.

✐ Stanford White: Newport Casino (U.S.)
Louis Sullivan: Anshe Ma'ariv Synagogue, Chicago
Ames Building, Boston (first skyscraper in Boston: 13 storeys)

🎨 Fernand Khnopff: The Offering
Albert Pinkham Ryder: Toilers of the Sea
Mary Cassatt: The Bath
James Ensor: Maskers Quarrelling Over a Dead Man
Paul Gauguin: Hail Mary

📖 William Morris: *News from Nowhere*
Oscar Wilde: *The Picture of Dorian Gray*; *The Duchess of Padua*
James Barrie: *The Little Minister*
George Gissing: *New Grub Street*
Selma Lagerlof: *The Story of Gosta Berling*
Thomas Hardy: *Tess of the d'Urbervilles*
Henrik Ibsen: *Hedda Gabler*

🎼 Sergei Rachmaninov: *Piano Concerto No 1*
Anton Arensky: *A Dream on the Volga*
Henry J. Sayers: *Ta-ra-ra-boom-der-ay* (popular song)

1892 French troops forcibly depose the King of Dahomey but encounter resistance in native risings. *7 Jan*: Mohammed Tefik Khedive of Egypt dies, aged 39, and is succeeded by his 17-year-old son Abbas II, who will retake the Sudan. *4 Aug*: at Fall River, Massachusetts Lizzie Borden murders her father and stepmother with an axe.

✐ Victor Horta: No 6 rue Paul-Emile Janson, Brussels
George Heins and Christopher La Farge: Cathedral of St. John the Divine, New York (planned to be the world's largest cathedral)
Richard Hunt: Marble House, Newport, Rhode Island

🎨 William Holman Hunt: The Lady of Shalott
Paul Gauguin: The Spirit of the Dead Watching
Henri de Toulouse-Lautrec: At the Moulin Rouge

Aubrey Beardsley: Salome
Augustus Saint-Gaudens: Diana (sculpture)
Mark Twain: *The American Claimant*
Marie Corelli: *The Soul of Lillith*
Rudyard Kipling: *Barrack-Room Ballads*
Oscar Wilde: *Lady Windermere's Fan*
Georges Feydeau: *Monsieur Chasse*
Brandon Thomas: *Charley's Aunt*
Sergei Rachmanininov: *Prelude in C sharp minor*
Anton Bruckner: *Symphony No 8*
Peter Tchaikovsky: *The Nutcracker*
Harry Dacre: *Daisy* (popular song)

1893   *16 Jan*: white settlers on Hawaii succeed in overthrowing
Queen Liliukoalani. Armed marines are landed to protect
U.S. interests and the Queen is forced to abdicate the next
day. *Oct*: Lobengula King of the Matabele leads a revolt
against the British Africa Company of Cecil Rhodes. *23
Oct*: Jameson cuts the Matabele down with machine-gun
fire, suppresses the revolt, drives Lobengula out of his
capital, Bulawayo; the King will die in exile next year.
Fridtjof Nansen explores the Arctic Ocean, reaching
beyond 86°N, the furthest north anyone has so far been.

Frank Lloyd Wright: Winslow House, River Forest,
Illinois
Mormon Temple, Salt Lake City (completed)
Bruce Price: Chateau Frontenac Hotel, Quebec
Claude Monet: Rouen Cathedral
Mary Cassatt: The Boating Party
Edvard Munch: The Scream
Jose Maria de Heredia: *Les Trophées*
Hermann Sudermann: *Heimat*
Henrik Ibsen: *The Master Builder*
Oscar Wilde: *A Woman of No Importance*
Maurice Maeterlinck: *Pelléas et Mélisande*
Arthur Wing Pinero: *The Second Mrs Tanqueray*
Gabriele d'Anunzio: *Il trionfo della morte* (The
Triumph of Death)
Leo Blech: *Aglaja*
Isaac Albeniz: *The Magic Opal*
Giacomo Puccini: *Manon Lescaut*
Giuseppe Verdi: *Falstaff*

Engelbert Humperdinck: *Hansel und Gretel*
Edward MacDowell: *Hamlet and Ophelia*
Peter Tchaikovsky: *Symphony No 6* (he dies of cholera in *Nov*)
Antonin Dvořák: *Symphony No 9* (From the New World)
Mildred Hill: *Happy Birthday To You* (lyrics by Patty Hill)

1894 *20 Mar*: Lajos Kossuth dies in exile in Turin, aged 91. *12 May*: the Congo Treaty between Belgium and Britain gives Britain a lease on a corridor between Lakes Tanganyika and Albert. *22 Jun*: Dahomey in West Africa becomes a French colony. *24 Jun*: the President of France Marie François Carnot dies after being stabbed at Lyons by an Italian anarchist. *4 Jul*: the Republic of Hawaii is proclaimed, with the 50-year-old Judge Sanford Dole as President. *25 Jul*: Japanese forces sink the Kowshing, a British ship carrying Chinese troops to Korea. *27 Jul*: Korea declares war on China. *1 Aug*: China and Japan declare war on each other; the Japanese win easily in the following months.

✍ Reichstag Building, Berlin (completed)
Daniel Burnham: Reliance Building, Chicago (15 storeys)
Horace Jones: Tower Bridge, London
✥ Ferdinand Hodler: The Chosen One
Jan Toorp: Faith Giving Way
Edgar Degas: Femme à sa toilette
📖 Mark Twain: *Pudd'nhead Wilson*
Jose de Heredia: *La Nonne Alfarez*
George du Maurier: *Trilby*
Anthony Hope: *The Prisoner of Zenda*
Rudyard Kipling: *The Jungle Book*
Georges Feydeau: *How to Get Rid of Your Mistress*; *Hotel Paradise*
George Bernard Shaw: *Arms and the Man*
🎼 Anton Arensky: *Raphael*
Anton Bruckner: *Symphony No 5*
Leo Blech: *Cherubina*
Claude Debussy: *Prélude à l'Après-midi d'un Faune*
Jules Massenet: *Thaïs*; *Werther*

1895 The name Rhodesia is given to the territory belonging to the South Africa Company south of the Zambezi, in honour of Cecil Rhodes. The Kiel Canal is opened by the Germans to connect the North Sea and the Baltic without the necessity of passing Copenhagen. The Bavarian physicist Wilhelm Röntgen, now 50, has discovered the X-ray which will revolutionize medical diagnosis in the 20th century. *22 Mar*: the first motion picture theatre in the world opens at 44 rue de Rennes in Paris. *17 Apr*: Treaty of Shimonoseki, ending the Sino-Japanese War which virtually annihilated the Chinese army and navy. *25 Mar*: Vladimir Ulyanov (styles himself Lenin) travels to Geneva, then goes on to Zurich, Berlin and Paris. He later returns to Russia with illegal literature, organizes strikes, prints anti-government literature and Marxist manifestoes. *Dec*: Lenin, now 25, is arrested for illegal political activies. His older brother Alexander was executed in *1887* for similarly plotting against Tsar Alexander II.

   ✐ Holabird and Roche: Marquette Building, Chicago
      Louis Sullivan: Prudential Building, Buffalo, New York
      Stanford White: Washington Arch, Fifth Avenue, New York (completed)
      Richard Morris Hunt: The Breakers, Newport, Rhode Island

   🕭 Winslow Homer: Northeaster
      Auguste Rodin: The Burghers of Calais (Sculpture)

   📖 Joseph Conrad: *Almayer's Folly*
      Thomas Hardy: *Jude the Obscure*
      H. G. Wells: *The Time Machine*
      Hjalmar Soderberg: *Bewilderments*
      Henrik Pontoppidan: *The Promised Land*
      Marie Corelli: *The Sorrows of Satan*
      Oscar Wilde: *An Ideal Husband; The Importance of Being Earnest*

   🎜 Alfred Bruneau: *Requiem*
      Gustav Mahler: *Symphony No 2* (The Resurrection)
      Richard Strauss: *Till Eulenspiegels Lustige Streiche*
      John Palmer: *The Band Played On* (popular song)

1896 French physicist Antoine Becquerel discovers radioactivity in uranium. *1 Jan*: Boers in South Africa defeat Jameson at Krugerdorp. *2 Jan*: Jameson surrenders to the Boers at Doorn Kop; he is turned over to the British for trial in England. *3 Jan*: The German Kaiser sends Kruger a telegram of congratulation which strains Anglo-German relations. *6 Jan*: Cecil Rhodes resigns as Premier of the Cape Colony as a committee of the Cape Assembly finds him guilty of engineering the Jameson Raid. *18 Jan*: British troops take Kumasi and take the Ashanti King prisoner in the Fourth Ashanti War. *1 Mar*: Ethiopian warriors easily defeat Italian soldiers at Adowa, forcing Italy to begin the peace process. *1 May*: Nasr-ed-Din the Shah of Persia is assassinated aged 65, and succeeded by his 43-year-old son Muzaffar-ed-Din. *13 Aug*: the painter Sir John Everett Millais dies in London, aged 67. *26 Aug*: Armenian insurrectionists attack the Ottoman Bank in Constantinople. Ottoman troops retaliate with a three-day massacre of Armenians, killing 3,000. *21 Aug*: Anglo-Egyptian troops begin to reconquer the Sudan under General Kitchener: Dongola is taken. *6 Oct*: Treaty of Addis Ababa, settling the Ethiopian War: Italy agrees to withdraw its plans for an Italian protectorate.

✐ Charles Rennie Mackintosh: Glasgow School of Art

✑ Thomas Eakins: The Cello Player

Henry Tanner: Daniel in the Lions' Den

John Waterhouse: Hylas and the Nymphs

📖 Rémy de Gourmont: *Le Livre des masques*

Henryk Sienkiewicz: *Quo Vadis*

A. E Housman: *A Shropshire Lad*

Georges Feydeau: *Le Dindon* (The Dupe)

Oscar Wilde: *Salomé*

Anton Chekhov: *The Seagull*

Gerhart Hauptmann: *The Sunken Bell*

Henrik Ibsen: *Emperor and Galilean*

Alfred Jarry: *Ubu Roi* (written at the age of 15)

⚜ Isaac Albeniz: *Pepita Jimenez*

Giacomo Puccini: *La Bohème*

Umberto Giordano: *Andrea Chénier*

Hugo Wolf: *Der Corregidor*

Richard Strauss: *Also Sprach Zarathustra*

1897 *6 Feb*: Crete declares that it is part of Greece. *10 Feb*: Athens sends ships and troops. *7 Apr*: a Greek-Ottoman War starts and the Greeks are easily beaten. *9 May*: armistice in the Greek-Ottoman War. *16 Jun*: the U.S. annexes the Hawaiian Islands. *9 Sep*: the Hawaiian Senate ratifies the annexation; sugar planters on the islands have pressed for annexation, but there are some 25,000 Japanese nationals on the islands, too, and Japan registers a formal protest.

    Henry Hardenbergh: Waldorf-Astoria Hotel, New York

       C. H. Townsend: Whitechapel Art Gallery, London

       Anatole de Baudot: Church of St. Jean de Montmartre (concrete)

       August Endell: Elvira Studio, Munich

    Henri Rousseau: The Sleeping Gypsy

       Jean Vuillard: Large Interior

       Camille Pissarro: Boulevard des Italiens

       Auguste Rodin: Balzac Monument (sculpture)

    Bram Stoker: *Dracula*

       Rudyard Kipling: *Captains Courageous*

       H. G. Wells: *The Invisible Man*

       Joseph Conrad: *The Nigger of the Narcissus*

       Rémy de Gourmont: *Les Chevaux de Diomède*

       Raymond Roussel: *La Doublure* (The Understudy)

       André Gide: *Les Nourritures terrèstres* (The Fruits of the Earth)

       Henrik Ibsen: *John Gabriel Borkman*

       George Bernard Shaw: *The Devil's Disciple*

       Edmond Rostand: *Cyrano de Bergerac*

    Vincent d'Indy: *Istar*

       Sergei Rachmaninovs: *Symphony No 1*

       Paul Dukas: *L'Apprenti Sorcier*

       Charles Ives: *Thanksgiving and Forefathers Day for Orchestra and Chorus*

       John Philip Sousa: *The Stars and Stripes Forever*

1898 *18 Jan*: Zola's article 'J'accuse!' is published in *L'Aurore*, an attack on the unfair trial that has led to Captain Dreyfus's imprisonment on Devil's Island in French Guiana. The documents that convicted Dreyfus were forged by two fellow officers: Dreyfus is the victim of an anti-Semitic plot. *15 Feb*: the U.S. battleship *Maine* explodes in Havana Harbour killing 260 sailors. The sinking follows the publication of a letter from the Spanish Ambassador to the U.S. calling President McKinley spineless. *21 Mar*: a U.S. naval court of enquiry reports that the cause of the explosion was external. *28 Mar*: the report is made public. *22 Apr*: the Spanish-American War begins. *1 May*: Battle of Manila Bay; after a long morning's fighting all 10 ships of the Spanish squadron are destroyed. *12 May*: the U.S. North Atlantic Squadron bombards San Juan on Puerto Rico. *1–2 Jul*: Battle of San Juan Hill: a U.S. victory. *3 Jul*: Battle of Santiago Bay: 180 Spaniards are killed, only one American. Captain Philip of the U.S. battleship Texas shouts, 'Don't cheer, boys, the poor devils are dying,' as the Spanish cruiser *Vizcaya* runs aground in flames. *2 Sep*: Battle of Omdurman: Kitchener decisively defeats the forces of the Khalifa of the Sudan; using Maxim machine guns, the British troops are able to kill 11,000 of the Khalifa's dervishes and wound 16,000 more, while sustaining only 48 casualties themselves. *10 Sep*: the Austrian Empress Elizabeth is stabbed to death in Geneva by an Italian anarchist. *19 Sep*: after taking Khartoum, Kitchener goes on to Fashoda, finding it occupied by the French under Marchand. France claims the Nile's left bank, Ethiopia the right. London demands that the French leave the territory at once. *3 Nov*: Paris orders the French force in Fashoda to evacuate it at once.

✐ Antoni Gaudi: Church of Santa Coloma de Cervello, Barcelona

H. P. Berlage: 42 Oude Scheveningsche Weg, The Hague

Charles Voysey: Broadleys, Windermere

Holabir and Roche: Gage Building, South Michigan Avenue, Chicago

✇ George Minne: Kneeling Boy (marble)

▢ Oscar Wilde: *The Ballad of Reading Gaol*

Pierre Louÿs: *La Femme et le Pantin* (The Woman and the Puppet)

Henry James: *The Turn of the Screw*

H. G. Wells: *The War of the Worlds*
Gabriele d'Annunzio: *Sogno d'un mattino di primavera* (The Dream of a Spring Morning)
Arthur Wing Pinero: *Trelawney of the Wells*
Gerhart Hauptmann: *Fuhrmann Henschal* (Drayman Henschel)
Anton Chekhov: *The Seagull* (first effective performance)

♫ Gabriel Fauré: *Pelléas and Mélisande*

1899 In West Africa the Ashanti rise again, for the last time, against the British. Sir Fredric Hodgson provokes the conflict by demanding that the Ashanti surrender their sacred symbol of power, the Golden Stool: Hodgson wants the throne for himself as Governor of the Gold Coast. In response, the Ashanti besiege Hodgson's fort and it is two months before Hodgson and his wife can escape. *19 Sep*: Captain Dreyfus wins a pardon after a retrial forced by public opinion in response to Zola's article. *12 Oct*: in South Africa the Boer War begins as President Kruger of the Boer Republic acts to stop the British acquiring the Transvaal with its gold mines. *13 Oct*: using German weaponry, the Boers lay siege to Mafeking. *15 Oct*: the Boers lay siege to Kimberley. *2 Nov*: the Boers lay siege to Ladysmith.

✐ Post Office, Pennsylvania Avenue, Washington
✑ Edward Burne-Jones: The Mirror of Venus (Burne-Jones died *17 Jun* last year)
Paul Gauguin: Two Tahitian Women
Jean Edouard Vuillard: Paysages et interieurs
Augustus Saint-Gaudens: The Puritan
📖 Frank Norris: *McTeague*
Kate Chopin: *The Awakening*
Rudyard Kipling: *Stalky and Co*
Wladyslaw Reymont: *The Promised Land*
Joaquim Machado de Assis: *Dom Casmurro*
Ernest William Hornung: *The Amateur Cracksman*
Anton Chekhov: *Uncle Vanya*
Ramon Maria del Valle: *Ashes*
Frank Wedekind: *Der Kammersang* (The Tenor)
♫ Jules Massenet: *Cendrillon* (Cinderella)
Jean Sibelius: *Symphony No 1*

Edward Elgar: *Enigma Variations*
Edoardo di Capna: *O Sole Mio*! (popular song)
Scott Joplin: *Maple Leaf Rag*

1900 World population reaches 1.7 billion and there are 16
cities with populations over 1 million. The population of
North America has reached 81 million and is growing
rapidly: it will reach 355 million by 1978. *29 Jan*: Lenin
returns from exile after three years in Siberia with his
wife; he waits in Pskov until his wife is released. *15 Feb*:
French, the British cavalry Commander, relieves Kimberley after a four-month siege. *27 Feb*: General Roberts
forces the Boer leader Piet Conje to surrender near
Paardeberg: Conje has run out of food and ammunition. *28 Feb*: General Buller relieves Ladysmith after a
three-month siege by the Boers. *13 Mar*: General Roberts takes Bloemfontein. *17 Mar*: General Roberts
relieves Mafeking after a siege lasting 215 days: Colonel
Robert Baden-Powell has led the resistance during the
Mafeking siege. *31 May*: the British take Johannesburg.
5 Jun: General Buller takes Pretoria. *20 Jun*: a 'Boxer
Rebellion' begins in China: local Chinese militias murder the German Ambassador to Beijing encouraged by an
anti-foreigner clique at court. The foreign legations are
besieged. *4 Jul*: Generals Roberts and Buller join forces
at Vlakfontein and Britain annexes the Orange Free State
and the Transvaal. Kruger travels to Delagoa Bay and
from there sails to Europe in the hope of enlisting
German support for the Boer cause. *16 Jul*: Lenin and
his wife leave Russia for a five-year exile in Switzerland.
29 Jul: King Umberto of Italy is assassinated, aged 56, by
an anarchist at Monza; he is succeeded by his 30-year-old
son Victor Emmanuel III. *6 Oct*: Kaiser Wilhelm II
refuses President Kruger an audience. *Dec*; Lenin becomes an editor of the newspaper *Iskra* (The Spark)
published in Munich for distribution in Russia.

Antoni Gaudi: Parque Güell, Barcelona
C. H. Townsend: Horniman Museum, London
Pablo Picasso: Le Moulin de la Galette (Picasso is
19)
Paul Cézanne: Still Life with Onions; Mt. Ste-
Victoire

John Singer Sargent: The Wyndham Sisters

Gustav Klimt: Philosophy (Mural for Vienna University)

Sigmund Freud: *Die Traumdeutung* (The Interpretation of Dreams)

Theodore Dreiser: *Sister Carrie*

Booth Trakington: *Monsieur Beaucaire*

Joseph Conrad: *Lord Jim*

H. G. Wells: *Love and Mr. Lewisham*

Gabriele d'Annunzio: *Il fuoco* (The Flame)

Lyman Frank Baum: *The Wizard of Oz*

Helen Bannerman: *Little Black Sambo*

Gerhart Hauptmann: *Schluck und Jau*

Henrik Ibsen: *When We Dead Awaken*

George Bernard Shaw: *You Never Can Tell*

Hermann Sudermann: *St. John's Fire*

Gustave Charpentier: *Louise*

Giacomo Puccini: *Tosca*

Nikolai Rimsky Korsakov: *The Tale of Tsar Saltan*

Enrico Bossi: *Cantico dei cantici*

Edward Elgar: *The Dream of Gerontius*

Harry von Tilzer (Harry Gumm): *A Bird in a Gilded Cage* (popular song)

1901 Persia sells a 60-year concession to explore for oil in Persia to William D'Arcy, a New Zealander; he will sell it to Burmah Oil Co. in 1908. At present over half the world's oil production is from the Baku oilfield in Russia, developed by Ludwig Nobel. *1 Jan*: the Commonwealth of Australia is created by joining all the territories on the island of Australia. *22 Jan*: Queen Victoria of the United Kingdom dies, aged 81, after reigning for 63 years and is succeeded by her 59-year-old son Edward VII. *27 Feb*: the Russian Propaganda Minister is assassinated as a punishment for his repression of student agitators. *2 Sep*: U.S. Vice President Roosevelt says, 'Speak softly and carry a big stick,' laying down a rule for U.S. foreign policy. *6 Sep*: President McKinley is shot by Polish-American anarchist Leon Czolgosz at Buffalo. *7 Sep*: the Peace of Beijing brings the Boxer Rebellion to an end. *14 Sep*: President McKinley dies of gangrene.

Babb, Cook and Willard: Carnegie Mansion, Fifth

Avenue, New York

Horace Trumbauer: The Elms, Newport, Rhode Island

Edvard Munch: Girls on the Bridge

Gustav Klimt: Medicine (mural)

Henri de Toulouse-Lautrec: Femme retroussant Sa Chemise (he dies, aged 36, on *9 Sep*)

Rudyard Kipling: *Kim*

Hjalmar Soderberg: *Martin Birck's Youth*

Thomas Mann: *Buddenbrooks*

Anton Chekhov: *The Three Sisters*

Stanislaw Wyspianski: *The Wedding*

Frank Wedekind: *Der Marquis von Keith* (The Marquess of Keith)

Gerhart Hauptmann: *Der rote Hahn* (The Conflagration)

Richard Strauss: *Feuersnot* (Fire Famine)

Anton Bruckner: *Symphony No 6*

Edward Elgar: *Cockaigne Overture*

Sergei Rachmaninov: *Piano Concerto No 2*

Gustav Mahler: *Symphony No 4*

1902 *20 Jan*: Anglo-Japanese Alliance. Saudi Arabia has its beginnings as the Bedouin warrior Abdul-Aziz ibn Saud the 20-year-old Emir of the Wahabi seizes Riyadh, the fort that serves as the capital of the Nejd; he becomes a focus for the Arab nationalist movement. *15 Apr*: socialist revolutionaries murder the head of the Russian secret police. *16 May*: Alphonso XIII of Spain reaches the age of 16 and begins his reign. *20 May*: Cuba gains its independence from Spain and is established as a republic. *31 May*: the Treaty of Vereeniging brings the Boer War to an end; the Boers agree to accept British sovereignty in South Africa. *4 Jul*: President Roosevelt ends the insurrection in the Philippines.

Daniel Burnham: Fuller ('Flatiron') Building, New York

Aimery Steindl: Hungarian Houses of Parliament, Budapest

Robert Reanor: Old Faithful Inn, Yellowstone National Park

Carrere and Hastings: Whitehall, Palm Beach, Florida

    Claude Monet: Waterloo Bridge
Paul Gauguin: Horseman on the Beach
Gustav Klimt: Beethoven Frieze
Frederick Remington: Comin' Through the Rye (bronze)

Ida Tarbell: *History of the Standard Oil Company* (reveals that John D. Rockefeller controls 90 per cent of U.S. oil-refining capacity and has an annual income of over 40 million dollars)
Arnold Bennett: *Anna of the Five Towns*
André Gide: *The Immoralist*
Alfred Jarry: *Le Surmale* (The Supermale)
Owen Wister: *The Virginian*
P. G. Wodehouse: *The Pothunters* (Wodehouse is 21)
Arthur Conan Doyle: *The Hound of the Baskervilles*
Beatrix Potter: *The Tale of Peter Rabbit*

Claude Debussy: *Pelléas et Mélisande*
Alexander Scriabin: *Symphony No 2*
Jean Sibelius: *Symphony No 2*
Maurice Ravel: *Pavane pour une Infante defunte*
Gustav Mahler: *Symphony No 3*
Hughie Cannon: *Bill Bailey, Won't You Please Come Home* (popular song)

1903 A typhoid epidemic in New York is traced to Mary Mallon, who carries the disease but is not a victim of it; she spreads the disease by taking jobs handling food and refuses to stop. She will be confined from 1915 until her death in 1938. The German doctor Georg Perthes observes that X-rays can inhibit the growth of cancerous cells. William, Walter and Arthur Davidson together with William Harley develop the Harley-Davidson motorcycle. *22 Jan*: the Hay-Herran Treaty is an agreement between Colombia and the U.S. by which a strip across the Isthmus of Panama may be leased to the U.S. for the construction of a Panama Canal. *12 Mar*: Tsar Nicholas II issues a manifesto which includes concessionary reforms; resentment against him nevertheless grows in Russia as famine worsens and (*Oct*) industrial wages fall while food prices rise. *23 May*: the first successful transcontinental car journey begins as a Packard leaves San Francisco for New York (taking 52 days); sales

figures for cars nevertheless remain low owing to the
poor quality of American roads. *10 Jun*: Alexander I of
Serbia is assassinated by Serb conspirators together with
his wife and several courtiers. *15 Jun*: the Serbian
Assembly elects Prince Peter, who is 59, to succeed.
17 Nov: Lenin and his Bolsheviks (extremists) break
away from the Mensheviks (moderates) at the London
Congress of the Social Democratic Party. *17 Dec*: the
Wright brothers achieve a powered flight of 260 metres/
852 feet at a height of 4.5 metres/15 feet above the
ground: only three American newspapers report the
event which takes place at Kitty Hawk, North Carolina.

 Williamsburg Bridge, New York (first big suspen-
 sion bridge with steel towers)
 Antoni Gaudí: Sagrada Familia Church, Barcelona
 John Bentley: Westminster Cathedral, (U.K.)
 (Bentley died last year)
 Pablo Picasso: The Old Guitarist; Sick Child
 Henri Rousseau: Child with Puppet
 Robert Erskine Childers: *The Riddle of the Sands*
 Henry James: *The Ambassadors*
 Samuel Butler: *The Way of All Flesh* (Butler died
 last year, aged 66)
 Jack London: *The Call of the Wild*
 Kate Wiggin: *Rebecca of Sunnybrook Farm*
 W. B. Yeats and Lady Gregory: *The Hour-Glass*
 J. M. Synge: *In the Shadow of the Glen*
 Gerhart Hauptmann: *Rose Bernd*
 Clyde Fitch: *Glad of It*
 Vincent d'Indy: *L'Etranger*
 Eugen d'Albert: *Tiefland* (The Lowland)
 Samuel Coleridge-Taylor: *Hiawatha*
 Béla Bartók: *Kossuth*
 Arnold Schoenberg: *Verklärte Nacht* (Transfigured
 Night)
 Marie Cowan: *Waltzing Matilda* (popular song)

1904 The British passenger liner *Baltic* goes into service; the
largest passenger ship yet built, she is 23,880 tons and
221 metres/726 feet long. *1 Jan*: the wireless radio
distress signal CQD is adopted. *3 Feb*: the composer
Luigi Dallapiccola is born at Pisino, Italy. *8 Feb*: Ad-

miral Togo leads Japanese naval forces in attacking Port Arthur (Lushun) in Manchuria, bottling up a Russian squadron and instigating the first war involving armoured battleships, torpedoes, quick-firing artillery and modern machine guns. *8 Mar*: the first tunnel under the Hudson River is completed. *1 May*: the composer Antonin Dvořvak dies in Prague. The Japanese defeat the Russians at the River Yalu. *30 May*: after occupying Dairen, the Japanese forces lay siege to Port Arthur. *15 Jun*: the New York excursion vessel *General Slocum* is destroyed by fire while taking 1,400 German Americans from Lower East Side to Long Island for a picnic; more than a thousand passengers die in the disaster. *28 Jul*: the Russian Minister of the Interior, the ruthless Vyacheslav Plehve, is assassinated.

✐ Louis Sullivan: Carson Pirie Scott Store, Chicago
　Frank Lloyd Wright: Larkin Building, Buffalo, N.Y.

✐ Claude Monet: Thames
　Emil Nolde: Harvest Day
　Henri Rousseau: The Wedding
　Auguste Rodin: The Hand of God (bronze)
　Augustus Saint-Gaudens: General Sherman Memorial, Central Park
　Mateo Alonzo: Christ of the Andes, Uspallato Pass, Chile/Argentina border (bronze from old cannons)

📖 Luigi Pirandello: *Il fu Mattia Pascal* (The Late Mattia Pascal)
　Hermann Hesse: *Peter Camenzind*
　Joseph Conrad: *Nostromo*
　Frederick William Rolfe: *Hadrian the Seventh*
　W. H. Hudson: *Green Mansions*
　Henrik Pontoppidan: *Lykke Per* (Lucky Peter)
　Anton Chekhov: *The Cherry Orchard*
　J. M. Synge: *Riders to the Sea*
　Gabriele d'Annunzio: *La figlia di Iorio* (The Daughter of Iorio)
　Frank Wedekind: *Die Buchse der Pandora* (Pandora's Box)
　George Bernard Shaw: *Candida*; *John Bull's Other Island*

James Barrie: *Peter Pan*
Leos Janáček: *Jenufa*
Giacomo Puccini: *Madama Butterfly*
Vincent d'Indy: *Symphony No 2*
Maurice Ravel: *String Quartet*
Gustav Mahler: *Symphony No 5*
George M. Cohan: *Give My Regards to Broadway*
(popular song)

1905 The Wright brothers improve their flying machine so
that they can fly in a full circle, a distance of 39 km/24
miles, as they demonstrate at Dayton in Ohio. Commercial rayon production begins in Coventry (U.K.) in
Samuel Courtauld's factory. *2 Jan*: Russian troops at
Port Arthur surrender to the Japanese. *9 Jan*: a Russian
revolution starts with news of the loss of Port Arthur. A
young priest leads a peaceful demonstration to the gates
of the Winter Palace in St. Petersburg; guards machine
gun the demonstrators on the Tsar's orders. *4 Feb*:
revolutionary terrorists murder the Grand Duke Serge
in Moscow. *Mar*: the Japanese defeat the Russians at
Mukden. *27 May*: Battle of Tsushima Straits between
Japan and Korea. The Japanese Admiral Togo fires into
the eight Russian battleships, 12 cruisers and nine
destroyers and manages to destroy or disable all of them
within an hour. *5 Sep*: peace treaty between Russia and
Japan mediated by President Roosevelt. *17 Oct*: after
Russian sailors aboard the cruiser *Potemkin* at Odessa
mutiny (*Jul*), the Tsar feels obliged to agree a constitution, set up a parliament (the Duma) and grant civil
liberties. *Nov*: Lenin returns from exile and addresses
the first workers' Soviet (council) at St. Petersburg, but
the Tsar withdraws his concessions one by one. *9 Dec*: a
revolt led by the Moscow Soviet is suppressed.

Otto Wagner: Post Office Savings Bank, Vienna
Robert Maillart: Tavenasa Bridge (Switzerland)
(first concrete bridge that is entirely modern in
conception)

Pablo Picasso: Young Acrobat on a Ball; The Ab-
sinthe Drinker
Paul Cézanne: Les Grandes Baigneuses
Henri Rousseau: The Hungry Lion

John Singer Sargent: The Marlborough Family

George Santayana: *The Life of Reason, Vol 1*

Soseki Natsume: *Rondon-to* (The Tower of London)

E. M. Forster: *Where Angels Fear To Tread*

H. G. Wells: *Kipps*

Edgar Wallace: *The Four Just Men*

Heinrich Mann: *Professor Unrat*

Richard Strauss: *Salome*

Franz Lehar: *The Merry Widow*

Arnold Schoenberg: *Pelleas and Melisande*

Edward Elgar: *Introduction and Allegro for Strings*

Alexander Scriabin: *Symphony No 3*

Claude Debussy: *La Mer*

1906 In England, Emmeline Pankhurst and her daughters Christabel and Sylvia campaign for women's suffrage. *29 Jan*: Christian IX of Denmark dies, aged 87 and is succeeded by his 62-year-old son Frederick VIII. *10 Feb*: the British battleship *Dreadnought* is launched: with its 10 12-inch guns, it marks a new departure in naval warfare. *18 Apr*: the San Francisco earthquake at 5.13 am: two-thirds of the city is destroyed and 2,500 are killed. *May*: following Britain's lead, Germany decides to launch new, larger battleships, add six cruisers to its fleet and widen the Kiel Canal to allow the warships through. *24 May*: Tsar Nicholas grants universal suffrage in Russia but refuses to grant an amnesty to political prisoners. *12 July*: Captain Dreyfus is restored to rank and awarded the Légion d'Honneur. *21 Jul*: Duma is dissolved in Russia and martial law is declared. *11 Sep*: the Indian Lawyer Mohandas Gandhi, who is now 37, speaks at a meeting in the Empire Theatre, Johannesburg, launching a campaign of peaceful resistance to protest against discrimination in South Africa against Indians.

Vauxhall Bridge, London

Pablo Picasso: **Self-portrait with a Palette; Two Nudes**

Henri Matisse: Le Bonheur de Vivre (his first 'dance' painting)

Maurice Vlaminck: The Red Trees

André Dérain: The Houses of Parliament; Westminster Bridge

Georges Rouault: At the Theatre; Tragedian

Max Beckmann: Young Men by the Sea

📖 Maxim Gorky: *The City of the Yellow Devil*

John Galsworthy: *The Man of Property*

Shimazaki Toson: *Broken Commandment*

Soseki Natsume: *With Grass for Pillow; Little Boy*

Ramon Maria del Valle Inclan: *El marqués de Bradomin*

George Bernard Shaw: *Captain Brassbound's Conversion; Caesar and Cleopatra; The Doctor's Dilemma*

⚓ Gustav Mahler: *Symphony No 6*

Boris Assafiev: *Cinderella*

Ethel Smyth: *The Wreckers*

1907 Muzaffar ud-Din Shah of Persia dies, aged 54, and is succeeded by his 35-year-old son Mohammed Ali. *10 Jun*: the first long distance car rally begins as five motor cars leave Beijing to arrive in Paris in two months' time. A Franco-Japanese Treaty guarantees both Japan and France 'open door' access to China. *14 Jun*: Norway grants suffrage to women. *19 Jul*: Kojong Emperor of Korea abdicates under duress, aged 55, after reigning for 43 years; the Japanese who now occupy his country set up a figurehead ruler. *25 Jul*: Korea becomes a Japanese protectorate. *31 Aug*: an Anglo-Russian entente resolves differences between Russia and Britain over Persia: British pre-eminence in the Persian Gulf is recognized. *Sep*: the maiden voyage of the Cunard Line's *Lusitania*: at 31,500 tons and 241 metres/790 feet long, she is easily the largest liner in existence, burning 1,000 tons of coal a day. *8 Dec*: Oskar II of Sweden dies aged 78, and is succeeded by his 49-year-old son Gustavus V. *15 Dec*: the new Shah of Persia attempts to overthrow his new liberal Chief Minister, but popular risings force him to yield.

✎ Daniel Burnham: Union Station, Washington (modelled on the Baths of Diocletian)

George Bodley and Henry Vaughan: Washington Cathedral

Cass Gilbert: Customs House, New York

Henry Hardenbergh: Plaza Hotel, New York
Antoni Gaudí: Casa Batllo; Casa Mila, Barcelona
Pablo Picasso: Les Demoiselles d'Avignon
Andre Derain: Blackfriars Bridge; The Bathers
Claude Monet: Water Lilies, Giverny
Henri Rousseau: The Snake Charmer
George Bellows: Forty-Two Kids
Joseph Conrad: *The Secret Agent*
Maxim Gorky: *Mother*
E M Forster: *The Longest Journey*
Jack London: *The Iron Heel*
J. M. Synge: *The Playboy of the Western World*
Georges Feydeau: *La puce à l'oreille* (A Flea in Her Ear)
George Bernard Shaw: *The Man of Destiny*
Edward Elgar: *Pomp and Circumstance No 4*
Frederick Delius: *A Village Romeo and Juliet; Brigg Fair*
Jean Sibelius: *Symphony No 3*
Maurice Ravel: *Introduction and Allegro for Harp and Strings*
Oley Speaks: *On the Road to Mandalay* (popular song)

1908 *1 Feb*: Carlos I of Portugal and his son the Crown Prince assassinated in the street in Lisbon; the King is succeeded by his 18-year-old younger son Manoel II, who will end the autocratic rule of his father's Prime Minister Franco. *10 Feb*: Mustapha Kamal of Egypt dies. *23 Jun*: Mohammed Ali Shah of Persia brings off a successful coup with help from the Cossack Brigade: he imposes martial law in Teheran. *23 Aug*: Battle of Marrakesh: Abd-al-Aziz IV the Sultan of Morocco is defeated by his older brother Mulay Hafid, who was proclaimed Sultan at Marrakesh last May. *3 Sep*: Germany formally recognizes Mulay Hafid as the new Sultan, who will rule under the name Abd-al-Hafiz. *5 Oct*: Bulgaria declares independence and Prince Ferdinand takes the title Tsar. *6 Oct*: Austria annexes Herzegovina and Bosnia causing consternation throughout Europe. Berlin supports Vienna; London and Paris support Russia, Turkey and the Balkan nations who object to the move. *7 Oct*: Crete makes the crisis worse by affirming its union with Greece. *2 Dec*: Wilbur Wright wins the Michelin Cup in France by flying 124 km/77 miles in 2½ hours. *28 Dec*: Sicily is shaken by the most severe earthquake known in historic times: 75,000 people are killed in and near the town of Messina.

Louis Sullivan: National Farmers Bank Building, Owatonna, Minn.

Claude Monet: The Grand Canal, Venice
Pierre Bonnard: Nude Against the Light; After Dinner
Gustave Klimt: The Kiss
Marc Chagall: Nu Rouge
Henri Matisse: Harmony in Red

W. H. Davies: *Autobiography of a Super-Tramp*
Anatole France: *L'ile des pingouins* (Penguin Island)
Luigi Pirandello: *The Outcast*
E. M. Forster: *A Room with a View*
Shimazaki Toson: *Haru* (Spring)
Marie Corelli: *Holy Orders*
Kenneth Grahame: *The Wind in the Willows*
Lucy Maud Montgomery: *Anne of Green Gables*
August Strindberg: *The Ghost Sonata*
James Barrie: *What Every Woman Knows*
Leonid Andreyev: *Days of Our Life*

Sergei Rachmaninov: *Symphony No 2*
Maurice Ravel: *Rapsodie Espagnole*
Gustav Mahler: *Symphony No 7*
Alexander Scriabin: *Poem of Ecstasy*
Edward Elgar: *Symphony No 1*:
Frederick Delius: *In a Summer Garden*
Anton Arensky: *Egyptian Nights*
Harry Williams and Jack Judge: *It's a Long Way to Tipperary* (popular song)

1909   *12 Jan*: Constantinople formally accepts the Austrian annexation of Herzogovina and Bosnia. *13 Feb*: Kiamil Pasha, the 76-year-old Ottoman Grand Vizier, is deposed and replaced by Hussein Hilmi Pasha. *13 Apr*: The First Army Corps at Constantinople revolts at the deposition of Kiamil Pasha and forces Hilmi Pasha to resign. *24 Apr*: an army of 'liberation' arrives in Constantinople and after a battle the leaders of the insurrection of April 13 are executed. *16 Jul*: Mohammed Ali Shah the Shah of Persia is deposed by Ali Kuh Khan, the Chief of the Bakhtaiari tribe. The Russian army invades northern Persia, occupying the town of Tabriz ostensibly on the Shah's behalf and they antagonize the Bakhtaiari. Ali Kuh Khan replaces the Shah with his son, the 12-year-old Ahmad. *17 Dec*: Leopold II of the Belgians dies, aged 74, and is succeeded by his 34-year-old nephew Albert I.

✐ Peter Behrens: Turbine Factory, Huttenstrasse, Berlin
Frank Lloyd Wright: Robie House, Chicago
Napoleon LeBrun: Metropolitan Life Insurance Tower, New York (42 storeys: the world's tallest building – until *1913*)
Robert Delaunay: Eiffel Tower

🎨 Henri Matisse: The Dance; The Red Room; Woman in Green
Pierre Bonnard: Standing Nude
Henri Rousseau: The Equatorial Jungle

📖 Gertrude Stein: *Melanctha*
Andre Gide: *La Porte étroite* (Straight is the Gate)
Wladyslaw Reymont: *The Peasants*
Kafu Nagai: *Sumida-gawa* (The River Sumida)
Jamichiro Tanizaki: *The Tattooer*
Rabindranath Tagore: *Gitangali* (Handful of Songs)
John Galsworthy: *Strife*
Gerhart Hauptmann: *Griselda*
August Strindberg: *Earl Birger of Bjalbo*
Israel Zangwill: *The Melting Pot*
Leonid Andreyev: *Anathema*

🎼 Richard Strauss: *Elektra*
Jan Brandts-Buys: *Das Veilchenfest*
Nikolai Rimsky-Korsakov: *Le Coq d'Or*; *Prince Igor*
Sergei Rachmaninov: *The Island of the Dead*; *Piano Concerto No 3*
Gus Edwards: *By the Light of the Silvery Moon* (words E. Madden)

1910 *20 Feb*: Butros Ghali, the Premier of Egypt, is assassinated by a nationalist fanatic; Islamic agitation increases.

10 Mar: the Chinese abolish slavery. *6 May:* Edward VII of the United Kingdom dies aged 68, and is succeeded by his 44-year-old son George V. *31 May:* The Republic of South Africa is established with dominion status but independent of Britain. *4 Oct:* the Portuguese abolish their monarchy (founded in *1143*) in a revolution at Lisbon. Manoel II leaves for England, where he will live until his death in *1932.* The new republic is to be headed by the 67-year-old Teofilo Braga.

    McKim, Mead and White: Pennsylvania Station, New York (modelled on the Baths of Caracalla in Rome and costing 112 million dollars)

    Adolf Loos: Steiner House, Vienna

    Giorgio de Chirico: The Enigma of an Autumn Afternoon

    Fernand Léger: Nudes in the Forest

    Henri Matisse: Blue Nude; The Dance; Music

    Henri Rousseau: Exotic Landscape (Rousseau dies, aged 66, on *22 Sep*)

    Georges Braque: Ambroise Vollard

    Auguste Rodin: The Secret

    Arnold Bennett: *Clayhanger*

    E. M. Forster: *Howards End*

    H. G. Wells: *The History of Mr. Polly*

    Takuboku Ishikawa: *A Handful of Sand*

    J. M. Synge: *Deirdre of the Sorrows*

    Edmond Rostand: *Chantecler*

    George Bernard Shaw: *Misalliance*

    James Barrie: *The Twelve Pound Look*

    Ferenc Molnar: *The Guardsman*

    Igor Stravinsky: *The Firebird*

    Ernest Bloch: *Macbeth*

    Maurice Ravel: *Ma Mère l'Oye* (Mother Goose)

    Ralph Vaughan Williams: *Fantasia on a Theme by Thomas Tallis*

    Gustav Mahler: *Symphony No 8*

1911 The last horse-drawn bus in the London General Omnibus Company is taken out of service; as in cities all over the world, horse-drawn vehicles are giving way to motor vehicles. A revolution begins in China as Sun Yat-sen, the 45-year-old revolutionary leader, returns to China after 16 years of exile in Britain and the U.S. *11 May*: in Mexico the revolutionary Francisco Madero establishes a new capital at Ciudad Juarez. *25 May*: Madero succeeds in overthrowing the Mexican President Porfirio Diaz. *1 Sep*: The Russian Prime Minister Pyotr Stolypin is shot dead in front of the Tsar at the Kiev Opera House. *6 Nov*: Madero makes himself President of Mexico. *14 Dec*: the Norwegian explorer Roald Amundsen, now 39, reaches the South Pole. *29 Dec*: Sun Yat-sen is elected President of the United Provinces of China by a provisional assembly based at Nanjing.

Hans Poelzig: Office Building, Breslau; Chemical Factory, Luban

Frank Lloyd Wright: Taliesin East, Spring Green, Wisconsin

Walter Gropius: Fagus factory, Alfeld (steel framed building)

Marc Chagall: I and the Village

Pablo Picasso: Accordionist

Georges Braque: Man with a Guitar

Auguste Renoir: Gabrielle with a Rose

Henri Matisse: The Red Studio; The Blue Window

Max Beerbohm: *Zuleika Dobson*

Joseph Conrad: *Under Western Eyes*

Thomas Mann: *Death in Venice*

Gaston Leroux: *The Phantom of the Opera*

Edgar Wallace: *Sanders of the River*

Ogai Mori: *The Wild Geese*

Gerhart Hauptmann: *Die Ratten* (The Rats)

Gabriele d'Annunzio: *The Martyrdom of Saint Sebastian*

Frank Wedekind: *Oaha, the Satire of Satire*

Ermanno Wolf-Ferrari: *The Jewels of the Madonna*

Richard Strauss: *Der Rosenkavalier*

Jean Sibelius: *Symphony No 4*

Edward Elgar: *Symphony No 2*

Bela Bartok: *Duke Bluebeard's Castle*

Irving Berlin: *Alexander's Ragtime Band* (popular song)

Harry Lauder (MacLennan): *Roamin' in the Gloamin'* (popular song)

1912 Mount Katmai in Alaska erupts violently burying Kodiak Island 161 km/100 miles away in the Aleutians beneath 1 metre/3 feet of ash. SOS in Morse code is adopted as the universal distress signal. *1 Jan*: China becomes a republic with Sun Yat-sen as President. *15 Apr*: on her maiden voyage, the *Titanic* scrapes past an iceberg during the night and sinks in 2½ hours; over 1,500 of the 2,224 people on board are lost mainly because of the inadequate provision of lifeboats. *14 Jun*: Frederick VIII of Denmark dies aged 69, succeeded by his 41-year-old son Christian X. *30 Jul*: the Japanese Emperor Mutsuhito dies, aged 60, after reigning for 45 years and restoring imperial power in Japan; he is succeeded by his son Taisho. *18 Oct*: Treaty of Lausanne, ending the war between Italy and the Turks. *10 Nov*: the Serbs overrun northern Albania and reach the Adriatic. *3 Dec*: an armistice calms the Balkans temporarily.

    W. S. Richardson: 998 Fifth Avenue (luxury apartment house)

    Pablo Picasso: The Violin
    Juan Gris: Hommage à Picasso
    Fernand Léger: Woman in Blue
    Emil Nolde: The Life of Christ
    Marcel Duchamp: Nude Descending a Staircase

    Romain Rolland: *Jean-Christophe*
    Saki (H. H. Munro): *The Unbearable Bassington*
    Ramon del Valle Inclan: *La Marquess Rosalinda*
    Frank Wedekind: *Tod und Teufel* (Death and Damnation
    Gerhart Hauptmann: *Gabriel Schillings Flucht*
    Ferenc Milnar: *The Wolf*

    Maurice Ravel: *Daphnis et Chloë*
    Claude Debussy: *Images*
    Gustav Mahler: *Symphony No 9*
    Percy Grainger: *Shepherd's Hey*
    Arnold Schoenberg: *Five Pieces for Orchestra*
    Lewis F. Muir: *Waiting for the* Robert E. Lee (words L. W. Gilbert)

1913 *6 Jan*: a peace conference in London breaks down when the Turks refuse to give up Adrianople, the Aegean

Islands and Crete. *23 Jan:* a coup in Constantinopole brings down Kiamil Pasha; he is replaced by Enver Bey representing an extreme nationalist group. *3 Feb:* war breaks out anew in the Balkans (Turkey, Greece, Bulgaria, Serbia). *18 Mar:* George I of Greece is assassinated at Salonica, aged 67, and is succeeded by his 44-year-old son Constantine I. *30 May:* a Treaty of London appears to resolve the Balkan War. *29 Jun:* the Second Balkan War breaks out.

Cass Gilbert: Woolworth Building, New York (60 storeys, the world's tallest habitable structure – until *1931*)

Warren and Wetmore: Grand Central Terminal, New York

Aston Webb: Buckingham Palace Façade (redesigned and heightened)

Oskar Kokoschka: Self-portrait
John Singer Sargent: Henry James
Walter Sickert: L'Ennui
Wilhelm Lehmbruck: Standing Youth (sculpture)
Edvard Eriksen: The Little Mermaid (bronze)

Miguel de Unamuno: *Del sentimiento tragico de la vida* (The Tragic Sense of Life)

Marcel Proust: *Du Côté de chez Swann* (Swann's Way)

Alain Fournier: *Le Grand Meaulnes*
D. H. Lawrence: *Sons and Lovers*
Osip Mandelstam: *Stone*
George Bernard Shaw: *Androcles and the Lion*

Gabriel Fauré: *Penelope*
Erno Dohnanyi: *Aunt Simona*
Igor Stravinsky: *Le Sacré du Printemps* (The Rite of Spring)

Arnold Schoenberg: *Gurre-lieder; Chamber Symphony*

Anton von Webern: *Six Pieces for Orchestra*
Edward Elgar: *Falstaff*
James V. Monaco: *You Made Me Love You* (Popular song)

1914 Gandhi returns to India after 21 years practising law in South Africa; he is now 45. The passenger liner *Bismarck* goes into service in the North Atlantic, the largest of the new generation of liners at 56,600 tons and with a length of 291 metres/954 feet. *15 Jun*: the Cunard Line's *Aquitania* reaches New York on her maiden voyage: she is 47,000 tons and 275 metres/901 feet long. *28 Jun* World War I is sparked off by the assassination in Sarajevo of the Archduke Franz Ferdinand, the 51-year-old heir to the Austrian throne. The Archduke and his wife are travelling in a 1912 Graf und Stift motorcar when they are shot by Gavrilo Princip. *28 Jul*: Austria uses the assassination as an excuse to declare war on Serbia. The war rapidly widens across Europe. *1 Aug*: Germany declares war on Russia. *3 Aug*: Germany declares war on France. On the same day the newly completed Panama Canal opens to traffic. *4 Aug*: German troops invade neutral Belgium and Britain declares war on Germany. *5 Aug*: Montenegro declares war on Austria. *6 Aug*: Serbia declares war on Germany and Austria declares war on Russia. *12 Aug*: Britain and France declare war on Austria. *14 Aug* Battle of the Frontiers (lasting 11 days) costs the lives of 250,000 French soldiers and the very high losses are rigorously censored until the war is over. *23 Aug*: Japan declares war on Germany. *26–30 Aug*: Battle of Tannenberg: a large Russian army invading east Prussia under General Samsonov is decisively defeated by the Germans. *30 Aug*: first German air raid on Paris. *5–12 Sep*: Battle of the Marne: British and French armies halt the German advance. *6–15 Aug*: Battle of the Masurian Lakes: the Russians are again defeated, this time by troops under General von Mackensen. *11 Oct*: the German army takes Ghent as it tries to reach the Channel ports. *14 Oct*: Bruges falls to the Germans. *15 Oct*: Ostend, too, falls, but the Belgians succeed in flooding the Yser district which halts the German push. *30 Oct*: Battle of Ypres (lasting until *24 Nov*): large numbers of soldiers on both sides–German and British-French) are killed without the front line shifting significantly. *1 Nov*: German Vice Admiral Spee surprises a British squadron under Rear Admiral Craddock off the coast of Chile. In the Battle of Coronel, the British are defeated, with the *Monmouth* and *Good Hope* sunk and only the *Gloucester* escaping from the action. *2 Dec*: Battle of Cracow ending today (started *16 Nov*) brings heavy losses to Russians and Austrians. *6 Dec*: Lodz falls to the Germans. *8 Dec*: Battle of the Falkland Islands: victory for a British squadron under Rear Admiral Sturdee, who surprises Graf Spee as he prepares to take the Falklands. Spee goes down with his flagship the *Scharnhorst*: the *Gneisenau*, *Nürnberg* and *Leipzig* are sunk and only the *Dresden* escapes. *15 Dec*: Serbian troops retake Belgrade after driving out the Austrian army. *18 Dec*: Britain proclaims a protectorate over Egypt. *19 Dec*: Abbas Hilmi Khedive of Egypt is deposed and succeeded by Hussein Kamal.

🖉 Bertram Goodhue: St. Thomas Episcopal Church, New York

McKim, Mead and White: Municipal Building, New York

Walter Gropius: Model Factory, Cologne

🎨 Pablo Picasso: Ma Jolie

Giorgio de Chirico: The Enigma of a Day

Paul Klee: The Creator

Oskar Kokoshka: The Bride of the Wind

📖 James Joyce: *The Dubliners*

André Gide: *Les Caves du Vatican* (The Vatican Cellars)

Miguel de Unamuno: *Mist*

Theodore Dreiser: *The Titan*

Junichiro Tanizaki: *A Springtime Case*

Soseki Natsume: *Kokoro*

Edgar Rice Burroughs: *Tarzan of the Apes*

Gerhart Hauptmann: *Der Bogen des Odysseus* (The Bow of Odysseus)

George Bernard Shaw: *Pygmalion*

Paul Claudel: *L'Otage* (The Hostage)

🎵 Tomás Bretón: *Don Gil*

Enrico Bossi: *Joan of Arc*

Riccardo Zandonai: *Francesca da Rimini*

Ralph Vaughan Williams: *London Symphony*; *The Lark Ascending* (written)

Rutland Boughton: *The Immortal Hour*

Jerome Kern: *They Didn't Believe Me* (popular song)

David Davies: *Keep the Home Fires Burning* (popular
song: Davies is 21)
Alonzo Elliott: *There's a Long, Long Trail* (popular
song: Elliott is 23)
F. J. Ricketts: *Colonel Bogey March*

1915 World War I (currently called 'The Great War') intensifies, with huge losses on Eastern and Western Fronts.
18 Feb: Germany begins its U-boat blockade of Britain.
In the Antarctic, Shackleton's *Endurance* becomes stuck
in pack-ice. *19 Feb*: the British begin an attack on the
Dardanelles in an attempt to stop the Germans blocking
supplies to Russia via the Black Sea. *18 Mar*: Admiral de
Robeck (British) withdraws, losing the best opportunity
to take the Dardanelles: the Turks have few supplies. *23
Apr*: the English poet Rupert Brooke dies of blood
poisoning on Skyros on his way to the Dardanelles,
just one of thousands of promising young men to die
in the war. *25 Apr*: British troops land on the Gallipoli
Peninsula but they are pinned down by Turkish artillery.
The Gallipoli campaign has been proposed by First Sea
Lord Sir John Fisher; he now sees his mistake and
resigns, blame for the campaign's failure falling on the
new First Sea Lord, the 41-year-old Winston Churchill.
The Germans use chlorine gas for the first time at the
Second Battle of Ypres. *3 May*: the war is costing Britain
alone £2 million a day. *7 May*: The liner *Lusitania* is
sunk, torpedoed off the south coast of Ireland with a loss
of 1,198 lives. *23 May*: Italy declares war on Austria in
the hope of gaining territory along the Adriatic and in the
Alps; although the Italians launch four offensives during
the war, they lose 250,000 men and gain no territory. *4
Aug*: British nurse Edith Cavell is arrested in Brussels on
suspicion of helping Allied soldiers to escape. *7 Aug*: the
Germans take Warsaw. *12 Oct*: Edith Cavell is shot by
firing squad. *21 Nov*: Shackleton's *Endurance* is crushed
and sunk by pack-ice. *15 Dec*: Sir John French is
replaced as Commander of British forces on the Western Front by Sir Douglas Haig.

Pablo Picasso: Harequin
Marcel Duchamp: The Bride Stripped Bare by
Bachelors

Marc Chagall: Birthday
Ernst Kirchner: Self-portrait
Alexander Archipenko: Woman Combing Hair (sculpture)
Franz Kafka: *Der Verwandlung* (The Metamorphosis)
W. Somerset Maugham: *Of Human Bondage*
D. H. Lawrence: *The Rainbow*
Ivan Bunin: *Gospodin iz San-Francisco* (The Gentleman from San Francisco)
John Buchan: *The Thirty-Nine Steps*
Rafael Sabatani: *The Sea Hawk*
Piero Jahier: *Gino Bianchi*
Louis Anspacher: *The Unchastened Woman*
Leonid Andreyev: *He Who Gets Slapped*
Umberto Giordano: *Madame Sans Gene*
Manuel de Falla: *El Amor Brujo*
Jean Sibelius: *Symphony No 5*
Felix and George Powell: *Pack Up Your Troubles In Your Old Kit Bag* (popular song)

1916 *Jan*: British troops withdraw from Gallipoli. *21 Feb* (until *11 Jul*): Battle of Verdun on the Western Front: huge loss of life on both German and French sides – 350,000 French soldies die. *24 Apr*: Easter Rebellion in Ireland, as patriots try to shed British rule. *31 May–1 Jun*: Battle of Jutland, the great sea battle of the Great War: there are huge losses on both German and British sides with no clear outcome, although the Germans afterwards retreat. *5 Jun*: Lord Kitchener drowns when the *Hampshire* is sunk by a mine off Orkney. *1 Jul* (until *13 Nov*): Battle of the Somme: the largest and bloodiest engagement on the Western Front, in which 420,000 British soldiers are killed in a fruitless attempt to relieve the French. *1 Jul* is the bloodiest day in British history, with over 19,000 men killed and 35,500 wounded; the sound of the artillery can be heard as far away as north London. The Commander-in-Chief Douglas Haig does not visit the front lest the sight of wounded men should affect his judgment. *Aug*: the rebels found guilty of treason in the Easter Rebellion in Ireland are hanged. *21 Nov*: The Austro-Hungarian Emperor Franz Josef dies, aged 86, after reigning for 68 years and is succeeded by his 29-year-old grandson Karl I. *24 Nov*: Sir Hiram Maxim, inventor of the machine gun that has made so much bloodshed possible, dies in London: *31 Dec*: the Russian faith-healer Grigori Efimovich Rasputin is murdered in Petrograd (new name for St. Petersburg) by a group of aristocrats intent on ending the monk's influence on the Isar and Isarina.

   Frank Lloyd Wright: Imperial Hotel, Tokyo
   Vizcaya: The James Deering Mansion, Miami

   Henri Matisse: The Three Sisters
   Giorgio de Chirico: The Disquieting Muse

   Satsume Soseki: *Michigusa* (Grass on the Wayside)
   Rabindranath Tagore: *Gharer baire*
   Henrik Pontoppidan: *De Dodes Rige* (Kingdom of the Dead)
   Giuseppe Ungaretti: *Il Porto Sepolto* (The Buried Harbour)
   Lord Dunsany: *A Night at an Inn*
   Luigi Chiarelli: *La Maschera e il volto* (The Mask and the Face)

   Richard Strauss: *Ariadne auf Naxos*
   Serge Prokofiev: *Scythian Suite*
   Manuel de Falla: *Nights in the Gardens of Spain*
   Haydn Wood: *Roses of Picardy* (popular song: words F. Weatherly)

1917 *17 Jan*: a wireless message from the German Foreign Secretary to the German Ambassador at Washington is intercepted by British intelligence: 'We intend to begin unrestricted submarine warfare. We shall endeavour to keep the U.S. neutral. In the event of this not succeeding, we shall make Mexico a proposal of alliance . . . to recover the lost territory in Texas, New Mexico and Arizona.' *31 Jan*: Berlin formally notifies Washington that unrestricted warfare will begin tomorrow. *3 Feb*: the U.S. break off relations with Germany. *10 Mar*: Russian troops mutiny. *14 Mar*: China breaks off relations with Germany. *15 Mar*: On his way home, Tsar Nicholas II has the train pulled into a siding; he abdicates in favour of his brother Michael. *16 Mar*: Grand Duke Michael abdicates in favour of a provisional

government under Prince George. *Apr*: Lenin and other
Bolshevik leaders arrive in Petrograd. The German High
Command has arranged for them to be sent in a sealed
railway carriage across Germany from Switzerland; it is a
calculated move to destabilize the Russian provisional
government which is known to be sympathetic towards
the Allies. *6 Apr*: the U.S. declares war on Germany. *9
Apr* (until *4 May*): Battle of Arras: the Canadians
succeed in taking Vimy Ridge. *10 May*: since the British
lost 875,000 tons of shipping to enemy U-boat action,
travel by convoy begins. *31 Jul* (until *10 Nov*): Battle of
Passchendaele: 400,000 British soldiers are killed. *15
Oct*: the French dancer Mata Hari (Gertrud Zelle) is
executed for spying for the Germans. *2 Nov*: The Balfour
Declaration says the British Government favours 'the
establishment in Palestine of a national home for the
Jewish people'. *6 Nov*: a Bolshevik revolution begins in
Petrograd with a shot fired, at Lenin's orders, by Alexander Belyshev from the deck of the *Aurora* anchored in
the Neva. Soldiers from the Petrograd garrison and
sailors from Kronstadt seize government offices and
storm the Winter Palace. Alexander Kerensky is forced
to accept Bolshevik support to thwart the efforts of
General Kornilov to make himself Dictator, and the
Bolsheviks secure a majority in the Petrograd Soviet
under the leadership of Leon Trotsky, another extremist who has returned from exile. *7 Nov*: the Kerensky
government falls. Kerensky goes into hiding, later emigrating. A new government under Lenin is formed, with
Trotsky as Commissar for Foreign Affairs and Josef
Stalin as Commissar for National Minorities. *20 Nov*:
Battle of Cambrai: some initial success for the British
army, but the Germans regain the lost ground.

🎨 John Singer Sargent: John D. Rockefeller
   Henri Matisse: Piano Lesson
   Pierre Bonnard: Nude at the Fireplace
   Amadeo Modigliani: Crouching Female Nude
   Wassiliy Kandisnsky: Ladies in Crinoline
   John Stella: Brooklyn Bridge
📖 T. S. Eliot: *Prufrock and Other Observations*
   Denis Thevenin: *Vie des Martyrs*

Norman Douglas: *South Wind*
Frank Swinnerton: *Nocturne*
Abraham Cahan: *The Rise of David Levinsky*
James Barrie: *The Old Lady Shows Her Medals*
Luigi Pirandello: *Cosi e, se vi pare*
Luigi Chiarelli: *La sala di seta*
✤ Erik Satie: *Parade*
Ernest Bloch: *Trois Poemes Juifs*
George M. Cohan: *Over There* (popular song)
Isham Jones: *You're In The Army Now* (popular song)

1918 The worst pandemic to afflict the human race, with the exception of the Black Death, sweeps across Asia, Europe and North America; the so-called Spanish Influenza originates in China and kills 21,640,000 people, over 1 per cent of the world's population. *3 Mar*: Treaty of Brest-Litovsk, ending Russian participation in the First World War; the new Bolshevik régime renounces all claims to Poland, Ukraine, Lithuania, Finland and the Baltic provinces. The Finnish statesman Baron Mannerheim recaptures Helsinki from the Bolsheviks who seized it (in *1919*) and gains Russia's recognition for Finland's status as an independent republic, which he heads. *21 Mar* (until *5 Apr*): a major German offensive on the Western Front gains ground from the British and French. *21 Apr*: Baron von Richthofen, the 26-year-old air ace, is shot down and killed. *9 May*: The French pilot René Fonck (24) shoots down six German fighter planes in 45 seconds. *16 Jul*: the Russian Tsar and his family are shot in the House of Special Purpose at Ekaterinburg; it is just possible that one of the Tsar's daughters, the Grand Duchess Anastasia, escapes. *Aug*: Battle of Amiens: the Germans fall back when the British attack with 450 tanks. *Sep*: General Pershing makes his first major offensive, forcing the exhausted Germans to fall back from positions they have held since *1914*.

26 Sep: René Fock again shoots down six German fighters in 45 seconds; altogether he has shot down 127 enemy planes. *4 Oct*: Ferdinand I of Bulgaria abdicates following the defeat of the Bulgarian army last month in Macedonia; he is succeeded by his 22-

year-old son Boris I. *14 Oct*: the Czechoslovak National Council meeting in Paris organizes a provisional government with Thomas Masaryk as President. *28 Oct*: mutiny breaks out among German sailors at Kiel, spreading rapidly to Hamburg and Bremen. *7 Nov*: insurrection breaks out at Munich. *8 Nov*: the Kaiser abdicates. *11 Nov*: fighting stops on the Western Front, with an armistice signed by Germans and Allies at Compiegne. Karl, the Austro-Hungarian Emperor, is forced to give up participation in the government of Austria. *13 Nov*: Karl renounces active participation in the government of Hungary. *4 Dec*: the Kingdom of the Serbs, Croats and Slovenes is proclaimed under Prince Alexander.

William Orpen: Dead Germans in a Trench
Paul Nash: We Are Making A New World
Paul Klee: Gartenplan
Fernand Léger: Engine Rooms
Juan Gris: Scottish Girl
Oskar Kokoschka: Saxonian Landscape; Friends
Henri Matisse: Odalisques
Robert Delaunay: Portrait of Igor Stravinsky
Vicente Blasco-Ibanez: *The Four Horsemen of the Apocalypse*
Heinrich Mann: *Der Untertan* (Man of Straw)
Lytton Strachey: *Eminent Victorians*
Sacha Guitry: *Deburan*
Vladimir Mayakovsky: *Mystery Buff*
Eugene O'Neill: *The Moon of the Caribees*
Giacomo Puccini: *Il Trittico*
Serge Prokofiev: *Classical Symphony*
Arthur Honegger: *Le Dit des Jeux du Monde* (The Legend of the World at Play)
John Kellette: *I'm Forever Blowing Bubbles* (popular song)
Geoffrey O'Hara: *K-K-K-Katy* (popular song)

1919 *11 Jan*: Romania annexes Transylvania. *18 Jan*: the Peace Conference opens at Versailles; a new German republic is founded with its constituent assembly meeting at Weimar. Thuringia is felt to have humanist traditions, contrasting with the militarist traditions of

Prussia: hence the decision to move the seat of government. Russia is embroiled in civil war between the Bolshevik Red Army and the White Russia Army led by General Denikin with support from the Allies. *3 Feb*: the Red Army captures Kiev. *2 Mar*: in Moscow, the Third International is founded, dedicated to promoting communist doctrine with a view to stimulating worldwide revolution. *7 Apr*: the Allies leave Odessa. *8 Apr*: the Red Army enters the Crimea. *15 May*: Greek troops land at Smyrna with Allied support. *19 May*: the Turkish war hero Mustapha Kemal organizes military resistance to this effort to dismember the Ottoman Empire even further, defending Turkey against the invasion. *28 Jan*: Treaty of Versailles, obliging Germnay to accept sole responsibility for causing the Great War, in which over 8 million people have been killed and 20 million blinded, maimed or otherwise disabled. Germany returns the Alsace-Lorraine conquests of *1871* to France, cedes her colonies to the Allies and has to pay large reparations. *8 Jul*: the new Ottoman Sultan Mohammed VI dismisses Mustapha Kemal. *11 Jul*: the Sultan outlaws Kemal. *5 Aug*: Kemal declares Turkey independent of the Sultan at the Turkish Nationalist Congress. *10 Sep*: Treaty of Saint-Germain, obliging Austria to recognize the independence of Yugoslavia, Poland, Czechoslovakia and Hungary. Austria, too, is to pay large reparations to the Allies. *15 Nov*: the Red Army takes Omsk. *27 Nov*: Treaty of Neuilly, obliging Bulgaria to recognize the independence of Yugoslavia. *17 Dec*: Pierre Auguste Renoir dies, aged 78.

Louis de Soissons: Welwyn Garden City, U.K.
Edwin Lutyens: The Cenotaph, Whitehall, London
Edvard Munch: The Murder
Pablo Picasso: Pierrot
Paul Klee: Dream Birds
Giorgio de Chirico: The Return of the Prodigal Son
Claude Monet: Nympheas
Marc Chagall: Anywhere Out of the World
Constantin Brancusi: Bird in Space (bronze)
John Maynard Keynes: *Economic Consequences of the Peace*

Bertrand Russell: *Introduction to Mathematical Philosophy*

Karl Barth: *Der Romerbrief* (Epistle to the Romans)

André Gide: *La symphonie pastorale*

Shimazaki Toson: *Shinsei* (A New Life)

Marcel Proust: *A l'ombre des jeunes filles en fleurs* (Within a Budding Grove)

W. Somerset Maugham: *The Moon and Sixpence*

P. G. Wodehouse: *My Man Jeeves*

Siegfried Sassoon: *War Poems* (Sassoon threw his Military Cross into the sea)

Karl Kraus: *The Last Days of Mankind*

Paul Claudel: *Tête d'Or*

Ernst Toller: *Die Wandlung* (Transfiguration)

♭ Manuel de Falla: *The Three-Cornered Hat*

Hakon Borresen: *The Royal Guest*

Richard Strauss: *Die Frau Ohne Schatten*

George Gershwin: *Swanee* (popular song)

Walter Donaldson: *How Ya Gonna Keep 'Em Down On The Farm?* (popular song)

1920 The Baltic states (Lithuania, Latvia and Estonia) gain recognition as independent states by Russia after attempts to make them part of the new Union of Soviet Socialist Republics have failed.
7 Feb: the White Russian Admiral Kolchak is executed by the Red Army after he is defetaed at Krasnoyarsk. *28 Mar*: Novorossiysk on the Black Sea is taken by the Red Army. *5 May*: Britain accepts a mandate over Iraq from the Allied Council. *15 May*: the British send more troops into Ireland after attacks by Sinn Fein militants. *21 May*: Venustiano Carranza, President of Mexico, is assassinated. *22 Jun*: Greek forces move against Turkish Nationalist troops with support from Britain. *24 Jun*: the Greeks defeat the Turks at Alashehr. *9 Jul*: the Greeks take Bursa. *25 Jul*: the Greek army takes Adrianople. A great Arab rebellion against the British starts. *27 Jul*: the Red Army takes Pinsk. *10 Aug*: Treaty of Sèvres, obliging the Ottoman Sultan to relinquish claims to territory beyond the borders of Turkey and provide a Kurdish homeland; Syria is to be a French mandate, Palestine and Mesopotamia are to be British mandates,

Rhodes and the Dodecanese are to go to Italy and the other Aegean islands to Greece. *1 Sep*: France proclaims the formation of the state of Lebanon with its capital at Beirut. *12 Oct*: Russia's Polish War ends. *25 Oct*: King Alexander of Greece dies of blood poisoning after being bitten by a monkey. His father, who abdicated in *1917*, resumes the throne, continuing the struggle against Turkey. *1 Nov*: White Russian forces under Baron Wrangel are pushed south into the Crimea. *14 Nov*: Wrangel loses Sevastopol to the Red Army and has to evacuate his White Army to Constantinople, bringing the Russian counter-revolution to an end; the Bolsheviks are now unopposed.

Edwin Lutyens: Britannic House, Finsbury Circus, London

Max Berg: Centenary Hall, Breslau

Fernand Léger: The Tug Boat

Amedeo Modigliani: Reclining Nude (Modigliani dies, aged 35, in Paris)

Juan Gris: Guitar, Book and Newspaper

Max Ernst: Here Everything is Still Floating

Thomas Hart Benton: Portrait of Josie West

F. Scott Fitzgerald: *This Side of Paradise*

Edith Wharton: *The Age of Innocence*

Colette: *Chéri*

D. H. Lawrence: *Women in Love*

Eugene O'Neill: *Beyond the Horizon*; *The Emperor Jones*

Karel Capék: *The Outlaw*

Gerhart Hauptmann: *Der Weisse Heiland* (The White Saviour)

John Galsworthy: *The Skin Game*

George Bernard Shaw: *Heartbreak House*

Darius Milhaud: *Le Boeuf sur le toit* (scenario by Jean Cocteau)

Igor Stravisnky: *Pulcinella* (sets, costumes by Picasso)

Maurice Ravel: *Le Tombeau de Couperin*; *La Valse*

Jerome Kern: *Look For The Silver Lining* (popular song)

1921 *20 Feb*: ex-Cossack soldier Reza Khan Pahlevi, who is now 44, organizes the ejection of all Russian officers from Persia and, without any bloodshed, opens a new régime; Lenin acquiesces and even gives Persia equal right of access to the Caspian Sea. *23 Feb:* a mutiny among Russian sailors at Kronstadt in response to the collapse of the Russian economy. *8 Mar:* Spanish Prime Minister Eduardo Iradier is assassinated by an anarchist. *17 Mar:* the Russian authorites suppress the sailors' mutiny with great force. *23 Jun:* Syria's Faisal I arrives in Basra, Iraq after an Iraqi plebiscite shows 96 per cent approval for his installation as King of Iraq. *21 Jun:* Battle of Anual in Morocco: a Spanish army under General Silvestre is defeated by the Rifs under Abdel-Krim; General Silvestre commits suicide when the Rifs butcher 12,000 of his men. The disaster at Anual precipitates a political crisis in Madrid. U.S. Brigadier General William Mitchell sinks a former German battleship, the 22,800-ton *Ostfriesland,* using air power alone to prove his contention that a strategic air force is more useful than a large navy. The *USS Jupiter,* an 11,000-ton collier, is converted to the first American aircraft carrier: she has a 163-metre/534-foot flight deck and is renamed the *Langley. 16 Aug:* Peter I of Yugoslavia dies, aged 77, and is succeeded by his 33-year-old son Alexander: *4 Nov:* Takashi Hara, Prime Minister of Japan, is assassinated by a fanatic.

- ✍ Simon Rodia: Watts Tower, Los Angeles
  Southwark Bridge, London
- 🎨 George Grosz: Grey Day
  Max Ernst: The Elephant of the Celebes
  Henri Matisse: Odalisque in Red Trousers
  Georges Braque: Still Life With Guitar
  Fernand Léger: Three Women
  Pablo Picasso: Three Musicians
  Piet Mondrian: Composition with Red, Yellow and Blue
  Edvard Munch: The Kiss
- 📖 Ludwig Wittgenstein: *Tractatus Logico-Philosophicus*
  Henrik Willem Van Loon: *The Story of Mankind*
  Aldous Huxley: *Chrome Yellow*

Rafael Sabatini: *Scaramouche*
John Dos Passos: *Three Soldiers*
Agatha Christie: *The Mysterious Affair at Styles*
Luigi Pirandello: *Six Characters in Search of an Author*
Arthur Honegger: *Pastorale d'Eté*; *Le Roi David*
Ralph Vaughan Williams: *Symphony No 3*
Sergei Rachmaninov: *Piano Concerto No 3*
Hakon Børresen: *Kaddara*
Sergei Prokofiev: *The Love of Three Oranges*
Eubie Blake and Noble Sissle: *I'm Just Wild About Harry* (popular song)
Dan Russo: *Toot, Toot, Tootsie* (popular song, words G. Kahn, E. Erdman)

1922 *4 Feb*: the Japanese agree to return Shantung province to China *6 Feb*: the Washington Conference culminates in a naval armaments treaty. For the next 10 years no new ships of more than 10,000 tons with guns bigger than 8-inch calibre are to be built by any of the Allies. *15 Feb*: the Permanent Court of International Justice is opened at The Hague. *16 Apr*: Treaty of Rapallo: Germany recognizes the Soviet Union and adopts normal diplomatic relations with the Lenin government. *15 May*: the Germans cede Upper Silesia to Poland. *Sep*: Constantine I of Greece abdicates under pressure for the second time and is succeeded by his 32-year-old son George II. *28 Oct*: Benito Mussolini leads his black-shirted Fascisti in a 'March on Rome'. *Nov*: Victor Emmanuel III summons Mussolini, who is now 39, to form a Ministry, giving him dictatorial powers to restore order to Italy. *24 Nov*: Erskine Childers, author of the popular spy novel *Riddle of the Sands*, is executed by firing squad for his activities in the newly formed Irish Republican Army. *Nov 25*: Howard Carter opens the inner tomb of Tutankhamun and sees 'wonderful things'.

The Lincoln Memorial, Washington
Jesse Clyde Nichols: Country Club Plaza Shopping Center (the world's first large out-of-town shopping centre)
Paul Klee: Twittering Machine
Daniel Chester French: Statue of Abraham Lincoln

(for memorial)
Joan Miró: The Farm

Oswald Spengler: *Der Untergangdes Abendlandes* (Decline of the West)

James Joyce: *Ulysses* (in Paris)

Hermann Hesse: *Siddhartha*

François Mauriac: *Le baiser au lépreux* (A Kiss for the Leper)

E. E. Cummings: *The Enormous Room*

Barbara Cartland: *Jigsaw* (Cartland is 21)

T. S. Eliot: *The Waste Land*

Osip Mandelstam: *Tristia*

George Bernard Shaw: *Back to Methuselah*

Ernst Toller: *The Machine Wreckers*

Karel and Josef Capék: *The World We Live In* (The Insect Play)

Ralph Vaughan Williams: *Pastoral Symphony*

Arnold Bax: *Symphony No 1*

Arthur Bliss: *A Colour Symphony*

Walter Donaldson: *Carolina in the Morning* (popular song, words G. Kahn)

1923 Lenin establishes the first forced-labour camp in the Solovetsky Islands near Archangel; over the next 30 years the Soviets will build nine cities, 12 railway lines, six industrial centres and three hydroelectric power schemes – all using slave labour. *11 Jan*: French troops occupy the Ruhr coalfield in Germany as the Germans default on coal deliveries promised at Versailles. German inflation soars out of control. *26 May*: Jordan becomes an independent state headed by Emir Abdullah ibn Husein, but remains a British protectorate. *9 Jun*: a coup in Bulgaria removes Prime Minister Stamboliski from office: his policies have antagonized the army. *14 Jun*: Stamboliski is shot 'while trying to escape'. *6 Jul*: the Union of Soviet Socialist Republics set up last year becomes a political reality. *10 Jul*: Mussolini secures his position as Dictator in Italy by dissolving Italy's non-fascist parties. *24 Jul*: Treaty of Lausanne, by which eastern Thrace, Tenedos and Imbros are returned to Turkey, and Greece has the remaining Aegean islands. Britain retains Cyprus, and the Dardanelles are demilitarized; now no provision is made for the Kurds. *23 Aug*: the Allied forces leave Constantinople. *1 Sep*: the Great Kanto earthquake in Japan. The earthquake and ensuing fires destroy Tokyo and Yokohama, killing 100,000, injuring 752,000 and destroying more than 80,000 houses. *12 Sep*: the garrison at Barcelona mutinies. In response, General Primo suspends the constitution and proclaims a directorate of army officers: he has the approval of Alfonso XIII for this coup. *14 Oct*: Ankara is made the capital of the new Turkish state. *29 Oct*: the Turkish Republic is proclaimed with General Mustapha Kemal as President. He has destroyed the political power of the Muslim leaders of the old Ottoman Empire and will develop Turkey into a modern nation, abolishing the veil and insisting that Turks wear Western-style clothes. *8 Nov*: the 34-year-old Adolf Hitler stages a Beer-Hall Putsch in Munich. His Nazi party, founded in 1919 by Anton Drexler, capitalizes on the social unrest in Germany. Hitler's attempt to take over the city government of Munich fails and next year he will be sentenced to five years in prison (serving only nine months).

- Vassily Kandinsky: Circles in the Circle
  Maurice Utrillo: Ivry Town Hall
  Maurice Vlaminck: Village in Northern France
  Raoul Dufy: On the Banks of the Marne
  Marc Chagall: Love Idyll
- Martin Buber: *Ich und du* (I and Thou)
  José Ortega y Gasset: *The Theme of Our Tim*
  Kahlil Gibran: *The Prophet*
  Havelock Ellis: *The Dance of Life*
  Frank Harris: *My Life and Loves*
  Jaroslav Hasek: *The Good Soldier Schweyk* (Haset dies, aged 40)
  Aldous Huxley: *Antic Hay*
  Noel Coward: *The Young Idea*
  Sean O'Casey: *The Shadow of a Gunman*
  George Bernard Shaw: *Saint Joan*
- Howard Hanson: *Symphony No 1*
  Jean Sibelius: *Symphony No 6*
  Roger Sessions: *The Black Maskers*
  William Walton: *Façade* (with Edith Sitwell's poetry)

Darius Milhaud: *La Création du Monde*

Ted Snyder: *Who's Sorry Now?* (popular song, words B. Kalmar, H. Ruby)

Frank Silver: *Yes, We Have No Bananas* (popular song)

1924 Russia returns lands to China that were taken under the Tsars and also returns the Boxer Rebellion indemnities of *1900* for the Chinese to use in education. The Persian Premier Reza Khan Pahlevi establishes government control right through Persia after subduing the Bakhtiari chiefs in the south-west. *21 Jan:* Lenin dies, aged 53, and Petrograd is renamed Leningrad in his honour. A triumvirate takes power in the U.S.S.R. consisting of Josef Stalin, Lev Kamenev and Grigori Zinoviev (real names Dzhugashvili, Rosenfeld, Apfelbaum). *3 Mar:* Mustapha Kemal, Turkey's President, brings the Ottoman dynasty to an end by abolishing the Caliphate and banishing all members of the Osman family. *10 Jun:* Giacomo Matteotti, whose book *The Fascisti Exposed* was published last year, is murdered by the Fascisti. *20 Oct:* Abdul-Aziz ibn Saud, the Wahabi Sultan of Nejd, enters Mecca after forcing the Hashimite King Husein ibn Ali to abdicate in favour of of his son Ali ibn Husein.

✐ Graham, Anderson, Probst and White: Wrigley Building, Chicago Addison Mizner: Villa de Sarmiento, Palm Beach, Florida

✏ Marc Chagall: The Birthday; Ida at the Window
Joan Miró: Catalan landscape
Oskar Kokoschka: Venice
George Bellows: The Dempsey-Firpo Fight

📖 André Breton: *Manifesto of Surrealism*
Thomas Mann: *Der Zauberberg* (The Magic Mountain)
E. M. Forster: *A Passage to India*
Mary Webb: *Precious Bane*
Hermann Melville: *Billy Budd*
Sean O'Casey: *Juno and the Paycock*
Luigi Pirandello: *Ciaseuno a suo modo* (Each in His Own Way)
Noel Coward: *The Vortex*

Ronald Firbank: *Prancing Nigger*

🎼 Ralph Vaughan Williams: *Hugh the Drover* (completed *1914*)

Arnold Schoenberg: *Die glückliche Hand*

Francis Poulenc: *Les Biches*

Georges Auric: *Les Facheux*

George Gershwin: *Rhapsody in Blue*

Jean Sibelius: *Symphony No 7*

Arthur Honegger: *Pacific 231*

Ottorino Respighi: *Pini di Roma* (The Pines of Rome)

Hakon Børresen: *Tycho Brahe's Dream*

Irving Berlin: *What'll I Do* (popular song)

1925 France begins to fortify her border with Germany: the so-called Maginot Line. Norway annexes Spitzbergen. *15 Jan*: U.S. troops land at Shanghai to protect American citizens from violence. *20 Jan*: Japan recognizes the U.S.S.R. and agrees to return the northern part of Sakhalin Island. *Feb*: in Persia, Reza Khan Pahlevi is given dictatorial powers. *28 Feb*: Friedrich Ebert, first President of the new German Reich, dies, aged 53. *12 Mar*: China's leader Sun Yat-sen dies of cancer, aged 57. The U.S. troops leave Shanghai. *30 May*: students demonstrating at Shanghai against 'unfair' treaties are fired on by British troops. *23 Jun*: there are similar demonstrations at Guangzhou. The Chinese boycott British goods and shipping. *Sep*: the Chinese assembly (the Guomindang) appoints General Chiang Kai-shek Commander-in-Chief and he begins the task of bringing the whole of China under central government control. *31 Oct*: the Persian assembly declares the absent Shah deposed. *13 Dec*: Reza Khan is proclaimed Shah.

✐ Eric Mendelsohn: Einstein Tower, Potsdam (completed)

John Howels and Raymond Hood: Tribune Tower, Chicago (completed)

Le Corbusier (Charles Jeanneret): Le Pavillon de l'Esprit, Paris Exposition

✑ Pablo Picasso: Three Dancers

Georges Rouault: The Apprentice

Oliver Hill: Chanctonbury

Marc Chagall: The Drinking Green Pig

Stuart Chase: *The Tragedy of Waste*

Franz Kafka: *Der Prozess* (The Trial)

Boris Pasternak: *Childhood*

François Mauriac: *Le Desert de l'amour* (The Desert of Love)

Ivy Compton-Burnett: *Pastors and Masters*

Virginia Woolf: *Mrs. Dalloway*

Lion Feuchtwanger: *Jud Süss*

F. Scott Fitzgerald: *The Great Gatsby*

Anita Loos: *Gentlemen Prefer Blondes*

Noel Coward: *Hay Fever*

Alban Berg: *Wozzeck*

Maurice Ravel: *L'Enfant et les Sortilèges*

Aaron Copland: *Symphony for Organ and Orchestra*

Conrad Beck: *Symphony No 1*

Joseph Meyer: *If You Knew Susie* (popular song, words B De Sylva)

Jacob Gade: *Jealousy* (popular song)

1926   *8 Jan*: the 43-year-old Abdul-Aziz ibn Saud proclaims himself King of Hejaz and renames the kingdom Saudi Arabia. *2 May*: U.S. troops land in Nicaragua to preserve order and U.S. interests as a revolt against the new President Emiliano Chamorro gets under way. *8 May*: a French fleet shells Damascus in an attempt to suppress the Druse insurrection that started last year. *23 May*: Lebanon is declared a republic. *Oct*: Chiang Kai-shek continues his campaign to unify China, taking the city of Wuchang and establishing it as his power base. In Russia, the Politburo expels Trotsky and Zinoviev as Stalin prepares to establish himself as Dictator of the U.S.S.R., bringing a new era of repression and fear to Russia and its neighbours. *7 Oct*: Mussolini assumes total power in Italy. *25 Dec*: the Japanese Emperor Yoshihito dies, aged 47, and is succeeded by his 25-year-old son Hirohito.

Bertram Goodhue: Central Library, Los Angeles (completed)

Walter Gropius: The Bauhaus, Dessau, Germany

Alfred Edwards and Edwin Lutyens: Grosvenor

House, Park Lane, London

🎼 Marc Chagall: Lover's Bouquet

Edvard Munch: The Red House

Oskar Kokoschka: Terrace in Richmond

René Magritte: The Last Jockey

Henry Moore: Draped Reclining Figure

📖 T. E. Lawrence: *Seven Pillars of Wisdom*

André Gide: *Les Faux Monnayers* (The Counterfeiters)

Ford Madox Ford: *A Man Could Stand Up*

D. H. Lawrence: *The Plumed Serpent*

Franz Kafka: *Das Schloss* (The Castle) (Kafka died in 1924)

Yasunari Kawabata: *The Izu Dancer*

Henri de Montherlant: *Les Bestiaires* (The Bullfighters)

Ernest Hemingway: *The Sun Also Rises*

William Faulkner: *Soldier's Pay*

Graham Greene: *Stamboul Train*

Agatha Christie: *The Murder of Roger Ackroyd*

A. A. Milne: *Winnie-the-Pooh*

🎼 Giacomo Puccini: *Turandot* (Puccini died in *1924*, aged 66)

Béla Bartók: *The Miraculaous Mandarin*

Jean Sibelius: *Symphony No 7*

Dmitri Shostakovitch: *Symphony No 1*

William Walton: *Portsmouth Point Overture*

Arthur Bliss: *Introduction and Allegro*

Harry Woods: *When The Red, Red Robin Comes Bob, Bobbin' Along (popular song)*

1927 *Feb*: Chiang Kai-shek takes Hangchow. *Mar*: Shanghai and Guangzhou fall to Chiang Kai-shek. *24 Mar*: Chiang's troops loot and burn Nanjing. *May*: Chiang negotiates with bankers, who promise up to £5 million if he will break with Moscow; he therefore reverses his political position, establishing a right-wing National Revolutionary Government at Nanjing. *20 May*: Saudi Arabia is recognized as independent by Britain. *21 May*: Charles Lindbergh lands near Paris in his plane, *Spirit of St. Louis*, after completing the first non-stop solo transatlantic flight. *24 May*: London breaks off diplomatic relations with Moscow after reports of widespread Bolshevik espionage and subversion in the British colonies. *9 Jun*: 20 alleged British spies are executed in Moscow in retaliation for the earlier accusation of Russian espionage. *21 Jul*: Ferdinand I of Romania dies, aged 61, and is succeeded by his nephew, the five-year-old Michael I. *14 Oct*: oil is found in large quantities near Kirkuk in northern Iraq. *Nov*: Stalin expels Trotsky from the Central Committee of the Communist party.

Clarence Stein and Henry Wright: Radburn, New Jersey (first modern 'new town' plan)

Mar-a-Lago, Palm Beach, Florida (115-room mansion)

Elizabeth Scott; Shakespeare Memorial Theatre, Stratford-upon-Avon

Georges Braque: Glass and Fruit

Henri Matisse: Figure with Ornamental Background

René Magritte: Man with Newspaper

Max Ernst: The Great Forest

Edward Hopper: Manhattan Bridge

Georgia O'Keeffe: Radiator Building, New York

Joseph Roth: *Die Flucht ohne Ende* (Flight Without End)

Hermann Hesse: *Der Steppenwolf*

Thornton Wilder: *The Bridge of San Luis Rey*

Mazo de la Roche: *Jalna*

T. F. Powys: *Mr. Weston's Good Wine*

B. Traven: *Der Schatz der Sierra Madre* (The Treasure of the Sierra Madre)

Reinhold Glière: *The Red Poppy*

Kurt Weill: *Mahagonny* (libretto by Bertolt Brecht)

Darius Milhaud: *Le Pauvre Matelot*

Georges Auric: *Volpone*

Sergei Rachmaninov: *Piano Concerto No 4*

Edgar Varèse: *Arcana*

Roger Sessions: *Symphony*

Constant Lambert: *The Rio Grande*

Milton Ager: *Ain't She Sweet* (popular song, words by Jack Yellen)

1928 Beijing surrenders to General Chiang Kai-shek, who is elected President of China. The Albanian Republic becomes a kingdom under former Prime Minister Ahme Bey Zogu, who reigns as King Zog. *15 Oct*: the German airship *Graf Zeppelin* arrives at Lakehurst in New Jersey from Friedrichshafen in Germany, covering the 10,600 km/6,600-mile transatlantic voyage in 120 hours.

   ✎ Raymond Hood: National Radiator Building, Gt. Marlborough St. London
      Tyne Bridge, Newcastle

   🎨 Georges Braque: Still Life with Jug
      Marc Chagall: Wedding
      Max Beckmann: Black Lilies
      René Magritte: The Titanic Days
      Georgia O'Keeffe: Nightwave
      Thomas Hart Benton: Crapshooters

   📖 Marcel Proust: *Le Temps retrouvé* (Time Regained: last in series)
      Evelyn Waugh: *Decline and Fall*
      Junichiro Tanizaki: *Tade kuu muhi* (Some Prefer Nettles)
      Shen Yen-ping: *The Eclipse*
      D. H. Lawrence: *Lady Chatterley's Lover*
      Radclyffe Hall: *The Well of Loneliness*
      Virginia Woolf: *Orlando*
      Andre Breton: *Nadja*
      John Galsworthy: *A Modern Comedy*
      Valentin Katayev: *Squaring the Circle*
      Marcel Pagnol: *Topaze*

   ♬ Kurt Weill: *Die Dreigroschenoper* (The Threepenny Opera)
      Georges Auric: *The Birds*
      Herbert Stothard: *I Wanna Be Loved By You* (popular song)
      Irving Berlin: *Puttin' On The Ritz* (popular song)

1929 The Japanese hold their last parliamentary election for 16 years; 20 per cent of the population are now eligible to vote compared with one per cent in 1891. *9 Jan*: at St. Mary's Hospital in London, Alexander Fleming makes the first clinical use of penicillin, using it to treat an assistant's infected sinus. *14 Jan*: Stalin expels Trotsky from the U.S.S.R. *21 May*: Alexander I of Yugoslavia, having proclaimed a dictatorship earlier in the month, dissolves the Croat and other political parties. *7 Jun*: the Lateran Treaties are ratified by the Italian Parliament; the Pope's temporal power is restored and directed onto the 44-hectare/108-acre Vatican City. *25 Jul*: his position now clarified, the Pope is able to leave the Vatican after years of being a virtual prisoner. *3 Oct*: the Kingdom of the Serbs, Croats and Slovenes officially becomes Yugoslavia; the renaming is part of an attempt to disguise the country's deep and historic divisions. *29 Oct*: a record 16.4 million shares trade on New York's Wall Street, causing the Dow Jones Industrial Average to plunge 30.57 points in a single day. A total loss in confidence means that 30 billion dollars disappear from the economy – almost the cost (to America) of the Great War.

Cathedral of St. Vitus, Prague (completed after 580 years of building)

Mies van der Rohe: The Tugendhat House, Brno, Czech

Xanadu, near Havana, Cuba

Giles Gilbert Scott: Battersea Power Station, London

Pablo Picasso: Woman in Armchair

Paul Klee: Fool in a Trance

Marc Chagall: Love Idyll

Piet Mondrian: Composiiton with Yellow and Blue

Robert C. Sherriff: *Journey's End*

Eugene O'Neill: *Dynamo*

Vladimir Mayakovsky: *The Bedbug*

Marcel Pagnol: *Marius*

Sean O'Casey: *The Silver Tassie*

Jean Giraudoux: *Amphitryon '38*

Robert Graves: *Goodbye To All That*

Alberto Moravia: *Gli indifferenti* (Then Time of Indifference)

Jean Cocteau: *Les Enfants Terribles*

Erich Remarque: *Im Westen nichts Neues* (All Quiet on the Western Front)

William Faulkner: *Sartoris*

Ernest Hemingway: *A Farewell to Arms*

🎼 Ralph Vaughan Williams: *Sir John in Love*
Serge Prokofiev: *The Gambler*; *Symphony No 3*
Edward Elgar: *Violin Concerto*
Heitor Villa-Lobos: *Amazonas*
Darius Milhaud: *Viola Concerto*
Anton von Webern: *Symphony for Chamber Orchestra*
Milton Ager and Jack Yellen: *Happy Days Are Here Again!* (popular song)

1930 *28 Jan*: the Spanish dictator Primo de Rivera resigns because of ill health. *16 Mar*: Primo de Rivera dies, aged 59. Students agitate for a Spanish Republic, denouncing the monarchy of Alfonso XIII. *2 Apr*: Zanditu Empress of Ethiopia dies. *24 Mar*: Mussolini argues that the Treaty of Versailles should be reviewed and revised. *30 June*: the last remaining troops of occupation leave the Rhineland five years ahead of the date set by the Treaty of Versailles and, as it turns out, prematurely. *25 Aug*: Augusto Leguia, President of Peru, resigns and flees the country after holding office for 11 years; he has been driven out by a military insurrection led by Colonel Luis Cerro, who will be elected President next year. *5 Sep*: there is a military coup in Argentina. In the German Reichstag elections the Nazi Party wins almost 6½ million votes, compared with the 8 million gained by the Socialists. Adolf Hitler is barred from taking his seat because of his Austrian citizenship. *Oct*: a revolution in Brazil is led by Getulio Vargas, a Provincial Governor. *26 Oct*: Vargas accepts the Presidency of Brazil. *1 Nov*: Vargas dissolves the Brazilian Congress and will rule as Dictator. *2 Nov*: Ras Tafari, who took the name Haile Selassie when he was proclaimed Negus (King) two years ago, is now crowned King of Kings at Addis Ababa. He will reign until *1974* (a rare survival) and be regarded by Jamaican Rastafarians as the living God: he is seen as fulfilling a prophecy of Marcus Garvey, 'Look to Africa, where a black king shall be crowned, for the day of deliverance is near'.

✍ William Van Allan: Chrysler Building, New York (319 metres 1,048 feet high, the tallest brick building in the world – still)

John Howels, Raymond Hood, Andre Fornithran: New York Daily News Building, East 42nd Street, New York

Holabird and Roche: Chicago Board of Trade Building (45 storeys, Chicago's tallest structure for 40 years)

Grant Wood: American Gothic

Edward Hopper: Early Sunday Morning

Diego Rivera: Cortez and his Mercenaries (for Mexico City)

George Grosz: Cold Buffet

Max Beckmann: Self-portrait with saxophone

Piet Mondrian: Composition with Red, Blue and Yellow

Henri Matisse: Tiare (sculpture)

Virginia Woolf: *A Room of One's Own*

Riichi Yokomitsu: *Machine*

Evelyn Waugh: *Vile Bodies*

William Faulkner: *As I Lay Dying*

Dashiell Hammett: *The Maltese Falcon*

Ezra Pound: *The Cantos (III)*

Federico Garcia Lorca: *La Zapatera prodigiosa* (The Shoemaker's Prodigal Wife)

Noel Coward: *Private Lives*

Vladimir Mayakovsky: *Moscow is Burning*; *The Bath House*

Luigi Pirandello: *Questa sera Si recite a soggetto* (Tonight We Improvise)

Dmitri Shostakovitch: *The Nose*

Walter Piston: *Suite for Orchestra*

Arthur Bliss: *Morning Heroes*

Edward Elgar: *Pomp and Circumstance No 5*

George Gershwin: *I Got Rhythm* (popular song, words W. Donaldson and Ira Gershwin)

Hoagy Carmichael: *Georgia On My Mind* (popular song, words S. Gorrell)

1931 The comic strip figures Mickey Mouse (Walt Disney) and Felix the Cat (Otto Mesmer) make their first appearances. *14 Apr*: Alfonso XIII of Spain leaves the country after reigning for 45 years. *30 Apr*: Chinese rebels led by General Chen Jitang break with General

Chiang Kai-shek and take control of Guangzhou. *13 Jul*:
the German Danatbank goes bankrupt, precipitating a
general closure of banks in Germany for almost a month.
3 Aug: the Yangtze River in China bursts a dam during
heavy cyclonic rainfall, flooding 104,000 sq. km 40,000
square miles of farmland and causing widespread famine.
Chiang Kai-shek comes under increasing pressure from
the Communists led by the 37-year-old Mao Tse Tung,
and Chiang is preoccupied with dealing with the Communists and the floods to the extent that he cannot deal
with the threat from the Japanese. *19 Sep*: on a pretext
the Japanese occupy Manchuria: they are angry at
China's boycott of Japanese textiles. *21 Sep*: the Japanese take Kirin. By early *1932* they will control the three
eastern provinces. *11 Dec*: Japan abandons the gold
standard.

✍ Edwin Lutyens: New Delhi, India (with Herbert
　 Baker)
　 Lamb and Harmon: Empire State Building, New
　 York (completed, world's tallest building for over 40
　 years)
　 Joseph Emberton: Royal Corinthia Yacht Club,
　 Burnham-on-Crouch (U.K.)
🎨 Salvador Dali: The Persistence of Memory
　 Paul Bonnard: The Breakfast Room
　 Marc Chagall: The Trick Riders
　 Paul Klee: The Ghost Vanishes
　 Henri Matisse: The Dance
　 Edward Hopper: Route 6, Eastham
　 Jose Clemente Orozco: Zapatistas
　 Constantin Brancusi: Mlle Pognany
　 Paul Landowski: Christ the Redeemer, Rio de
　 Janeiro (concrete)
📖 Antoine de Saint-Exupéry: *Vol de nuit*
　 Tristan Tzara: *L'Homme approximate*
　 Anthony Powell: *Afternoon Men*
　 Virginia Woolf: *The Waves*
　 William Faulkner: *Sanctuary*
　 Henry Miller: *Tropic of Cancer*
　 A. J. Cronin: *Hatter's Castle*
　 Marcel Pagnol: *Fanny*

Ramon de Valle Inclan: *Farce of the Chaste Queen*
Noel Coward: *Cavalcade*
Eugene O'Neill: *Mourning Becomes Electra*
Georges Auric: *Le 14 Juillet*
William Walton: *Belshazzar's Feast*
Paul Hindemith: *Concert Music for Strings and Brass*
Arthur Honegger: *Amphion Suite*
Ferde Grofe: *Grand Canyon Suite*
Ralph Vaughan Williams: *Job*
Noel Coward: *Mad Dogs and Englishmen* (popular song)
Herman Hupfield: *As Time Goes By* (popular song)
Duke Ellington: *Mood Indigo* (popular song, words A. Bigard, I. Mills)

1932   Prospectors strike oil in Bahrain. In India, Mahatma Gandhi begins a 'fast unto death' to press the British authorities into improving their treatment of untouchables; he obtains a pact after six days of fasting. The 36-year-old Sir Oswald Mosley leaves the Labour Party because of its defeatist attitude towards unemployment and founds his own party, the British Union of Fascists: Mosley will be an admirer and supporter of Hitler and Mussolini and demand the expulsion of Jews. The Chinese continue to boycott Japanese goods. *29 Jan*: the Japanese retaliate, landing troops from warships round Shanghai and killing thousands in the first terror bombing of civilians. Aware of the effect on world opinion, the Japanese make it clear that any attempt by the U.S. to interfere with Japan's 'destiny' would precipitate war. *1 Mar*: Charles Lindbergh's infant son is kidnapped and murdered, claiming the world's headlines. *6 May*: Paul Doumer, the French President, is assassinated by a Russian emigré. *15 May*: the Japanese Prime Minister Ki Tauyoshi Inukai is assassinated, effectively bringing Party government in Japan to an end; Inukai is succeeded by the Governor General of Korea, the 73-year-old Makoto Saito. *31 May*: President Hindenburg of Germany invites Franz von Papen to form a government. Papen does so but excludes Nazis. *24 Jun*: absolute government in Siam is ended as radicals capture Rama VII and hold him prisoner until he agrees to reforms and the creation of a senate. *31 Jul*: a general election in Germany makes the Nazi party the biggest in the Reichstag, but still without an overall majority. *13 Aug*: Hitler announces that he will not serve as Vice Chancellor under von Papen. *30 Aug*: another leading Nazi, Herman Goering, is elected President of the Reichstag making von Papen's position untenable. *17 Nov*: von Papen resigns as Prime Minister.

- George Howe and William Lescaze: Savings Fund Society Building, Philadelphia (completed; first International-style skyscraper)

  V. Myers and W. Hart: Broadcasting House, London

  Zuider Zee Barrage (closed *28 May*, creating Lake Yssel & polders)

- Pablo Picasso: Girl Before a Mirror

  Georges Rouault: Christ Mocked by Soldiers

  Maurice Utrillo: Sacré Coeur

  Max Liebermann: Professor Sauerbruch

  Reginald Marsh: The Bowery

  Grant Wood: Daughters of the Revolution

- Ernest Hemingway: *Death in the Afternoon*

  Vladimir Nabokov: *Laughter in the Dark*

  Aldous Huxley: *Brave New World*

  Colette: *La Naissance du jour*

  Georges Duhamel: *Salavin*

  Joseph Roth: *Radetzkymarsch*

  François Mauriac: *Le Noeud de Vipères*

  Hans Fallada: *Kleiner Mann – was nun?* (Little Man, What Now?)

  Wyndham Lewis: *Snooty Baronet*

  Evelyn Waugh: *Black Mischief*

  George Bernard Shaw: *Too True To Be Good*

- Werner Egk: *Columbus*

  Arnold Scoenberg: *Four Orchestral Songs*

  Arnold Bax: *Cello Concerto*

  Frank Bridge: *The Christmas Rose*

  Cole Porter: *Night and Day* (popular song)

  Vernon Duke: *April In Paris* (popular song)

1933   *30 Jan*: Hitler becomes Chancellor as German nationalist feeling swells and economic unrest intensifies. *27 Feb*:

the Reichstag in Berlin is destroyed by fire. The Nazis accuse the Communists of arson and fabricate a case against Dutch Communist Marinus van der Lubbe; he will be found guilty and executed early next year, but there are suspicions that Goering himself may have started the fire. *7 Mar*: Austrian Chancellor Dollfuss proclaims a dictatorship and bans political parades and demonstrations. *20 Mar*: the Nazis open the first concentration camp in Germany at Dachau near Munich. *29 Mar*: Austrian Nazis stage a huge demonstration and riot in deliberate defiance of Dollfuss. Hitler imposes a tourist tax of a thousand marks on any German visiting Austria, wrecking the Austrian tourist industry. *30 Apr*: President Cerro of Peru is assassinated and succeeded by Oscar Benevides. *8 Sep*: King Feial of Iraq dies at Berne in Switzerland and is succeeded by his son Ghazi. *14 Oct*: after Japan announces that it will withdraw from the League of Nations in two years' time, Hitler announces that Germany, too, will withdraw. *8 Nov*: Nadir Shah, King of Afghanistan, is assassinated at Kabul and is succeeded by his son Mohammed Zahir Shah. *16 Nov*: the U.S. establishes diplomatic relations with the U.S.S.R. for the first time since the Russian Revolution.

Hugh Cooper: Dnieper River Dam, Ukraine (HEP scheme)

Giles Gilbert Scott: Cambridge University Library

Diego Rivera: Man at the Crossroads (mural for Radio City Music Hall, New York: destroyed because it includes a portrait of Lenin)

Alberto Giacometti: The Palace at 4 am (sculpture)

Joan Miró: Composition

George Orwell: *Down and Out in Paris and London*

James Joyce: *Ulysses* (in the U.S.)

Andre Malraux: *La Condition Humaine*

Thomas Mann: *Die Geschichten Jaacobs*

Colette: *la Chatte*

Ignazio Silone: *Fontamara*

Franz Werfel: *The Forty Days of Musa Dagh*

Richard Strauss: *Arabella*

Béla Bartók: *Piano Concerto No 2; Hungarian Peasant Songs*

Samuel Barber: *School for Scandal Overture*
Joseph Canteloube: *Vercingetorix*
Al Dubin and Harry Warren: *We're In The Money*
(popular song)
Frank Churchill: *Who's Afraid Of The Big Bad Wolf*
(popular song)

1934   *3 Jan*: France plunges close to civil war as the Russian-born promoter Serge Stavisky, accused of issuing fraudulent bonds, commits suicide at Chamonix amid rumours that many in the French establishment are involved in corruption. *Feb*: in Austria, Dollfuss bans all political parties except his own, the Fatherland Front. In Nicaragua, General Somoza, who commands the National Guard, invites the guerrilla leader General Sandino to a meeting at which Sandino is killed in cold blood. *6–9 Feb*: the Stavisky affair leads to riots in Paris, a general strike follows. The French Republic is saved by the formation of a coalition government made of politicians untouched by any connection with the Stavisky affair. *17 Feb*: Albert King of the Belgians dies in a mountaineering accident, aged 58; he is succeeded by his 32-year-old son Leopold III. *30 Jun*: Hitler orders a purge of the Nazi party; over 70 party members are killed, including Ernst Rohm and Gregor Stresser and their supporters. *13 Jul*: Heinrich Himmler, now 33, is put in charge of German concentration camps. *25 Jul*: the Vienna radio station is seized by Austrian Nazis; the staff are forced to announce that Dollfuss has resigned. The Nazis enter the chancellery and kill Dollfuss. *2 Aug*: Hindenburg President of Germany dies, aged 87, leaving the way clear for Hitler to become head of state. *19 Aug*: a plebiscite of the German people gives Hitler 88 per cent of the votes needed to assume the presidency; he retains the title Führer. *18 Sep*: the U.S.S.R. joins the League of Nations. *9 Oct*: arriving at Marseilles, King Alexander of Yugoslavia is assassinated along with Louis Barthou, the French Foreign Minister. The assassin represents Croat revolutionaries based in Hungary, and the French are tempted to declare war on Hungary, but this is averted by League of Nations intervention. Alexander is succeeded by his 11-year-old son Peter II. In China, Mao

Tse Tung leads his Communist force out of Kiangsi with Nationalist troops in hot pursuit. In the Long March that will last a year and take them 9,600 km/6,000 miles, the Comunists fight a continual rearguard action against the Nationalists; at the end of the Long March Mao will have only 20,000 men left out of his original army of 90,000. *25 Nov*: Mustapha Kemal issues a decree that all Turks must adopt surnames; his own will be Ataturk, Father of the Turks. *1 Dec*: Sergeo Mironovich, Stalin's close associate, is assassinated in Leningrad.

Arthur Brown: Coit Tower, San Francisco (completed)

Edward Burra: The Serpent's Egg
William Coldstream: The Studio
Henry Moore: Two Forms

Robert Graves: *I, Claudius*
Mikhail Sholokhov: *And Quietly Flows the Don*
Lao She: *Rickshaw Boy*
George Orwell: *Burmese Days*
Henri de Montherlant: *Les Celibataires*
F. Scott Fitzgerald: *Tender is the Night*
Aldo Palezzeschi: *Sorelle Materassi* (The Materassi Sisters)
Evelyn Waugh: *A Handful of Dust*
Agatha Christie: *Murder on the Orient Express*
Tsao Yu: *Thunderstorm*
Federico Garcia Lorca: *Yerma*
Ronald Mackenzie: *The Maitlands*

Dmitri Shostakovitch: *Lady Macbeth of Mtensk*
Howard Hanson: *Merry Mount*
Ernest Bloch: *Sacred Music*
Roy Harris: *Symphony – 1933*
Béla Bartók: *The Enchanted Deer*
Sergei Rachmaninov: *Rhapsody on a Theme of Paganini*
Ralph Vaughan Williams: *Symphony No 4*
Arnold Bax: *Symphony No 6*
James Hanley: *Zing! Went the Strings of My Heart* (popular song)
Richard Rodgers: *Blue Moon* (popular song, words Lorenz Hart)

1935 Seismologist Charles Richter devises the Richter scale for measuring earthquakes; on it each increase of a whole number means a ten-fold increase in magnitude. Hitler denounces the Versailles Treaty clauses concerning German disarmament and creates the Luftwaffe to give Germany air superiority. Persia is henceforth to be caled Iran by the Shah's order. *13 Jan*: the League of Nations plebiscite carried out in the Saar region shows that the people of the area would overwhelmingly prefer to be reunited with Germany. *1 Mar*: the League of Nations returns the Saar, with its coalfield, to Germany. *2 Mar*: King Rama VII of Siam abdicates and is succeeded by his 10-year-old nephew Rama VIII. *3 Jun*: the new French Line passenger liner, the *Normandie*, arrives in New York Harbour after her maiden voyage, crossing the Atlantic in four days 11 hours; the 79,000-ton liner is 34 metres/1,029 feet long. *12 Jun*: the three-year war between Paraguay and Bolivia over the disputed Chaco region ends. *2 Sep*: a hurricane destroys the Florida East Coast Railroad line between Key West and Florida City and kills 400 people. *3 Oct*: Italian troops invade Ethiopia. *8 Nov*: Italian troops take the Ethiopian provincial capital Makale. *18 Nov*: the League of Nations imposes economic sanctions on Italy in retaliation for the Ethiopian invasion. *14 Dec*: Thomas Masaryk, first President of Czechoslovakia, resigns, at the age of 85, and is succeeded by Eduard Beneš. *18 Dec*: President Gomez of Venezuel dies, aged 78; during his 26-year dictatorship he has seen his country become a major oil producer.

   Ralph Modjeski: Huey P. Long Bridge, Metairie Louisiana (the longest railway bridge in the world – 7 km/4.35 miles long)

   William Perry: Williamsburg, Virginia (reconstructed to its original colonial state at a cost of 95 million dollars, the bill footed by John D. Rockefeller)

   Cass Gilbert: U.S. Supreme Court Building (Gilbert died *1934*, aged 75)

   League of Nations Building, Geneva

   Pablo Picasso: Minotauromachy

   Wyndham Lewis: Edith Sitwell

Paul Nash: Equivalents for Megaliths
Ben Nicholson: White Relief
📖 Shimasaki Toson: *Before the Dawn*
Osamu Dazai: *Gyakko*
Alberto Moravia: *Le ambizoni sbagliate* (Wheel of Fortune)
Sinclair Lewis: *It Can't Happen Here*
George Orwell: *A Clergyman's Daughter*
A. J. Cronin: *The Stars Look Down*
Christopher Isherwood: *Mr. Norris Changes Trains*
John Steinbeck: *Tortilla Flat*
T. S. Eliot: *Murder in the Cathedral*
Jean Giraudoux: *La Guerre de Troie n'aura pas lieu* (Tiger at the Gates)
🎼 Boris Assafiev: *Lost Illusion*
William Walton: *Symphony No 1*
Michael Tippett: *String Quartet No 1*
Cole Porter: *Just One of Those Things*; *Begin the Beguine* (popular songs)
George Gershwin: *Summertime* (words by I. Gershwin)
Jimmy McHugh and Dorothy Fields: *I'm in the Mood for Love* (popular songs)

1936 Stalin liquidates his enemies in the Soviet Union in a great purge that lasts two years and costs up to 10 million lives. The *Queen Mary* goes into service on the North Atlantic run. *20 Jan*: George V dies in London, aged 70, and is succeeded by his 41-year-son Edward VIII. *26 Feb*: in an army mutiny at Tokyo, young officers assassinate the former Premier Saito and Finance Minister Takahashi in a futile attempt to set up a military dictatorship. *7 Mar*: Hitler takes advantage of the crisis over Italy's invasion of Ethiopia to reoccupy the Rhineland. *28 Apr*: King Ahmed Fuad of Egypt dies, aged 68, and is succeeded by his 16-year-old son Farouk. *5 May*: Italian troops take Addis Ababa. *9 May*: Mussolini proclaims the annexation of Ethiopia by Italy: with Eritrea and Italian Somaliland it will be named Italian East Africa. *2 Jun*: a coup in Nicaragua is led by General Somoza, who deposes President Sacasa and will make himself President next year. *30 Jun*: the Ethiopian Emperor Haile

Selassie appeals to the League of Nations in person, 'to
claim the justice that is due to my people,' adding, 'It is
us today: it will be you tomorrow'. *7 Jul*: in Japan, 17 of
the army officers involved in the attempted coup in *Feb*
are sentenced to death. *18 Jul*: the Spanish Civil War
begins as army officers in Spanish Morocco start an
insurrection against the Madrid government, rallying
behind Generals Emilio Mola and Francisco Franco:
the revolt spreads to garrisons at Cadiz, Saragossa,
Burgos and Seville. *20 Jul*: Mola and Franco form a
junta at Burgos. *6 Nov*: the junta's troops lay siege to
Madrid using equipment from Germany and Italy. *10
Dec*: in England, Edward VIII abdicates in favour of his
brother George VI.

    Edward Maufe: Guidford Cathedral (U.K.)
    Erno Goldfinger: Hill Pasture, Essex (U.K.)

    René Magritte: The Black Flag
    Max Ernst: La Ville Entière
    Jose Orozco: Victims
    Meret Oppenheim: Fur-lined Teacup (sculpture)
    Henry Moore: Two Forms

    John Dos Passos: *The Forty-Second Parallel*
    William Faulkner: *Absalom! Absalom!*
    John Steinbeck: *In Dubious Battle*
    Aldous Huxley: *Eyeless in Gaza*
    Vladimir Nabokov: *The Gift*
    Isaac Bashevis Singer: *The Brothers Ashkenazi*
    Margaret Mitchell: *Gone With The Wind*
    Wan Chia-pao: *Sunrise*
    Terence Rattigan: *French Without Tears*

    Samuel Barber: *String Quartet*
    John Ireland: *A London Overture*
    Benjamin Britten: *Our Hunting Fathers*
    Sergei Prokofiev: *Peter and the Wolf*
    Cole Porter: *I've Got You Under My Skin* (popular
    song)

1937 The Spanish Civil War continues, in spite of General
Mola's death in a plane crash. *23 Jan*: the Moscow show
trials begin as Stalin makes examples of disloyal and
prominent party members. *8 Feb*: Franco takes Malaga.
26 Apr: the unarmed Basque town of Guernica is

destroyed by German bombers, which drop explosives
and incendiaries for three hours, while Heinkel fighter
planes strafe the surrounding fields, killing civilians
trying to escape. *12 Jun*: in Moscow, Marshal Tukha-
chevski and seven Generals are shot for treason. *2 Jul*:
the aviatrix Amelia Earhart disappears on a flight from
New Guinea to Howland Island. *16 Jul*: the Buchenwald
concentration camp is opened near Weimar: in the next
eight years 56,500 will die in its gas chambers. *11 Aug*:
General Bake Sidqi, Dictator of Iraq, is assassinated by a
Kurd. *11 Oct*: in the Spanish Civil War, Gijon falls to
Franco. *Oct 28*: the Spanish government moves from
Valencia to Barcelona.

◢ Joseph Strauss: Golden Gate Bridge, San Francisco
John Burnet: Senate House, London University
Frank Lloyd Wright: Falling Water, Bear Run,
Pennsylvania

🎨 Georges Rouault: The Old King
Paul Klee: Revolution of the Viaducts
Pablo Picasso: Guernica
Joan Miró: Still Life with Old Shoe
René Magritte: Not to Be Reproduced

📖 John Steinbeck: *Of Mice and Men*
Ernest Hemingway: *To Have and Have Not*
Yasunari Kawabata: *The Snow Country*
Georges Bernanos: *Nouvelle Histoire de la Mouchette*
Andre Breton: *L'amour fou* (Mad Love)
A. J. Cronin: *The Citadel*
J. R. R. Tolkien: *The Hobbit*
Christopher Isherwood and W. H. Auden: *The
Ascent of F6*
Jean Anouilh: *Le voyageur sans baggage*

🎵 Alban Berg: *Lulu*
Grazyna Bacewicz: *Violin Concerto No 1*
Reinhold Glière: *Leyli and Mejnun*
Ernest Bloch: *La Voix dans le desert* (Voice in the
Wilderness)
Benjamin Britten: *Variations on a Theme by Frank
Bridge*
Robert Schumann: *Violin Concerto* (written in *1853*)
Dmitri Shostakovitch: *Symphony No 5*

William Walton: *Crown Imperial*
Frederick Delius: *Florida Suite* (written *1887*; Delius died in *1934*)
Richard Rodgers: *My Funny Valentine* (popular song, words by L. Hart)
George Gershwin: *Let's Call The Whole Thing Off* (popular song, words by I. Gershwin; Gershwin dies of brain tumour *11 Jun*, aged 38)

1938 *4 Jan*: London announces that any partition of Palestine to create a Jewish homeland must be postponed, which provokes terrorist attacks during the ensuing months. *4 Feb*: John Baird gives the first demonstration of colour television at the Dominion Theatre, London. *23 Feb*: oil is discovered in Kuwait. *6 Mar*: Japanese troops advancing along the Hangchow Railway through Shansi province reach the Yellow River. *14 Mar*: Hitler annexes Austria to 'protect' 10 million Germans living outside the Reich's frontiers. *10 Apr*: an Austrian plebiscite shows that nearly 100 per cent of Austrian voters want union with Germany. *29 Sep*: Britain and France appease Hitler at Munich by allowing him to take the Sudetenland, in effect part of Czechoslovakia. Arab extremists seize Bethlehem and part of Jerusalem. *10 Oct*: British troops retake Bethlehem. *18 Oct*: the British retake Jerusalem. *21 Oct*: the Japanese take Guangzhou. *25 Oct*: the Japanese take Hankow. *7 Nov*: Herschel Grynzpan, a 17-year-old Polish Jew, assassinates Edouard vom Rath, a German official at the Paris embassy. *9 Nov*: the Nazis use the assassination as an excuse for a pogrom, the worst in German history; in the *Kristalnacht* riots Jewish shop windows are smashed, synagogues are looted and up to 30,000 Jews are carried off to concentration camps. *10 Nov*: Kemal Ataturk President of Turkey dies aged 57; the 54-year-old Ismet Inonu is elected to succeed him. *18 Dec*: the German chemist Otto Hahn succeeds in splitting the uranium atom, releasing energy.

✍ Walter Gropius: Gropius House, Lincoln, Massachusetts (completed)
Frank Lloyd Wright: Taliesin West, Paradise Valley, Arizo (completed)
Bartlett Dam, Arizona (completed)

- Henry Moore: Recumbent Figures
  Georges Rouault: Italian Women
  Thomas Hart Benton: Cradling Wheat
  Paul Klee: Park near Lucerne
- George Orwell: *Homage to Catalonia*
  Jean-Paul Sartre: *La Nausée*
  Elizabeth Bowen: *The Death of the Heart*
  Nordahl Grieg: *Men ung ma verden ennu vaere* (But the World Must Be Young)
  Graham Greene Greene: *Brighton Rock*
  Evelyn Waugh: *Scoop*
  Isak Dinesen: *Out of Africa*
  Daniel Fagunwa: *ogboju ode iinn igbo irummale* (The Forest of a Thousand Demons)
  C. S. Lewis: *Out of the Silent Planet*
  Jean Anouilh: *Le bal des voleurs* (Thieves' Carnival)
- Paul Hindemith: *Mathis der Maler*
  Henry Barraud: *La Farce de Maitre Pathelin*
  Howard Hanson: *Symphony No 3*
  Ralph Vaughan Williams: *Serenade to Music*
  Arnold Bax: *Violin Concerto*
  Frank Churchill: *Heigh-Ho* (popular song, words L. Mose)
  Hoagy Carmichael: *Two Sleepy People* (popular song, words F. Loesser)
  Ralph Rainger: *Thanks for the Memory* (popular song, words L. Robin)

1939 *28 Mar*: the Spanish Civil War ends as Madrid falls to Franco's troops. Spain will remain neutral in the European war, having lost 410,000 men in fighting or by execution and a further 200,000 by starvation and disease. *4 Apr*: King Ghazi of Iraq is killed in a car accident and is succeeded by his three-year-old son Faisal II. The British Consul is killed by rioters who suspect that the British have arranged the car accident. *1 Sep*: German troops and aircraft invade Poland. *3 Sep*: Britain and France declare war on Germany. *17 Sep*: Soviet troops invade Poland from the east. Charles Lindbergh makes a speech on U.S. radio arguing that Stalin is as much to be feared as Hitler. *21 Sep*: Armand Calinescu, Premier of Romania, is murdered by members of the pro-fascist

Iron Guard. *27 Sep*: Warsaw falls to the Germans. *28 Sep*: Poland is partitioned between the U.S.S.R. and Germany. *1 Oct*: Churchill says in a radio broadcast, 'I cannot forecast to you the action of Russia.' *13 Dec*: Battle of the River Plate in the South Atlantic. The British cruiser *Exeter* is badly damaged by the German pocket battleship *Graf Spee*, which is then driven into Montevideo Harbour by the *Ajax* and *Achilles*. *18 Dec*: The *Graf Spee* is scuttled in Montevideo Harbour.

Frank Lloyd Wright: Johnson Wax Research Tower, Racine, Wisconsin

Walter Gropius and Maxwell Fry: Impington Village College (U.K.)

Paul Klee: Ubermut

René Magritte: Objective Stimulation

Thomas Hart Benton: Weighing Cotton; Threshing Wheat

James Joyce: *Finnegans Wake*

Joyce Cary: *Mister Johnson*

Ernst Junger: *On the Marble Cliffs*

Cora Sandel: *Alberte*

John Steinbeck: *The Grapes of Wrath*

Thomas Wolfe: *The Web and the Rock*

Antoine de Saint Exupéry: *Wind, Sand and Stars*

Christopher Isherwood: *Goodbye to Berlin*

Rumer Godden: *Black Narcissus*

Sholem Asch: *The Nazarene*

Henri de Montherlant: *Les Jeunes Filles*

Henry Miller: *Tropic of Capricorn*

Raymond Chandler: *The Big Sleep*

Anatoly Bogatirev: *In the Thick Woods of Polesye*

Elliott Carter: *Pocahontas*

Luigi Dallapiccola: *Volo di notte*

Michael Tippett: *Concerto for Double String Orchestra*

Charles Ives: *Sonata No 1 for Piano and Orchestra*

Roy Harris: *Symphony No 3*

Béla Bartók: *Violin Concerto No 2*

Dmitri Shostakovitch: *Symphony No 6*

Arthur Honegger: *Joan of Arc at the Stake*

Ross Parker and Hugh Clark: *There'll Always Be An*

England (popular song)
Hugh Charles: *We'll Meet Again* (popular song)
Harold Arlen: *Somewhere Over The Rainbow* (popular song, words E. Harburg)

1940   *Mar*: the Katyn Forest Massacre. The Red Army imprisons 4,143 Polish officers near Smolensk, ties them up and shoots them, burying them in a mass grave. *Apr*: German troops seize Norway and Denmark. *7 May*: British Prime Minister Neville Chamberlain resigns. *10 May*: a British National Government is formed under Churchill's leadership. *13 May*: the Dutch Queen and her court arrive in Britain as German troops, armoured divisions and aircraft pour into Belgium and the Netherlands. *14 May*: Rotterdam is virtually destroyed by air raids. *21 May*: Amiens and Arras fall to the Germans. *28 May*: Belgium surrenders. *29 May*: evacuation of French and British troops from Dunkirk begins. *4 Jun*: Dunkirk is evacuated after five days of frantic activity: 340,000 French and British soldiers are successfully ferried across to Britain before they can be captured by the advancing German army. *10 Jun*: Italy declares war on France. *14 Jun*: German troops enter Paris; the French make a desperate appeal to the U.S. for help. *15 Jun*: the U.S. declines to help. *16 Jun*: French Premier Reynaud resigns and is replaced by Marshal Pétain, who is 83. *17 Jun*: Pétain asks Germany for an armistice. France is occupied by the Germans for the remainder of the war. *27 Jun*: Soviet troops invade Romania. *3 Jul*: the British navy sinks French warships at Oran in North Africa. *5 Jul*: the French Vichy government breaks off diplomatic relations with Britain. General de Gaulle forms a Free French government in exile in Britain. *15 Aug*: the Battle of Britain reaches its height, with British Spitfires fighting off German Stukas; today 180 German planes are shot down. *21 Aug*: Stalin settles an old score in Mexico. His agent Ramon Mercader succeeds in gaining Trotsky's trust and friendship, then murders him with an ice-pick. *15 Sep*: Hitler prepares an all-out air attack on Britain in readiness for an invasion by sea. *27 Sep*: the Axis is created, an alliance joining the economic and political destinies of

Italy, Germany and Japan for 10 years. *2 Oct*: U-boats
sink the *Empress of Britain*, carrying children to Canada
for safety. *15 Dec*: the Italians in North Africa are driven
back across the Libyan border by British troops under
General Wavell.

Eric Ravilious: Submarines in Dry Dock
Wassily Kandinsky: Sky Blue
Max Beckmann: Circus Caravan
Ruffino Tamayo: The Red Mask
Georgia O'Keeffe: Stump in Red Hills
Paul Klee: Death and Fire (Klee dies 29 Jun, aged
60)

Dino Buzatti: *Il deserta de Tartari* (The Tartar
Steppe)
Tarjei Vesaas: *Kimen* (The Seed)
Ernest Hemingway: *For Whom the Bell Tolls*
Graham Greene: *The Power and the Glory*
Cesar Vallejo: *España, aparta de me este caliz* (Spain,
Take Thou This Cup From Me)
T. S. Eliot: *East Coker*
Benjamin Britten: *Sinfonia da Requiem; Les Illumi-
nations*
Boris Assafiev: *A Feast in Time of Plague*
Renzo Bossi: *Rosa Rossa*
Paul Hindemith: *Violin Concerto*
Heitor Villa-Lobos: *Fantasia de Movementos Mixtos;
Izaht*
Arnold Schoenberg: *Violin Concerto*
Leigh Harline: *When You Wish Upon A Star*
(popular song, words N. Washington)

1941 *27 Mar*: revolution breaks out in Yugoslavia. *6 Apr*:
German troops invade Greece and Yugoslavia; the
Croats support the Germans and the hundreds of
thousands of Serbs who are killed die mostly at the
hands of Croat irregulars. *10 May*: Hitler's deputy
Rudolf Hess flies alone to Scotland on a mission that
has never been understood; the British imprison him.
10 May: the German battleship *Bismarck* leaves port
(Gdynia) for the Atlantic. *24 May*: *Bismarck* sinks the
British battleship *Hood*: only three out of the crew of
1,421 survive. *24 May*: the *Bismarck* is sunk by a British

squadron: 1,200 of her crew die. *31 May*: British troops arrive in Iraq to forestall an Axis takeover. *Jun*: British troops move into Syria and Lebanon, again to prevent the Germans from taking over. *22 Jun*: in a major escalation of the war, the German army invades Soviet Russia, advancing rapidly mainly because Stalin's purges have left the Russia military high command very depleted. The Germans are able to reach Leningrad easily and lay siege to the city. *Aug*: Soviet and British troops invade Iran. *16 Sep*: the Shah of Iran abdicates in favour of his 21-year-old son, Mohammed Reza Phlevi, who is pro-Allies. *29 Sep*: at Babi Yar outside Kiev the Nazi invasion force slaughters up to 96,000 Ukrainians: the magnitude of this massacre is made possible by the efficiency of Sir Hiram Maxim's machine gun. *Dec*: the British help the Ethiopians to drive the Italians out of Ethiopia and regain their independence. *7 Dec*: Japanese fighter planes led by Mitsuo Fuchida raid Pearl Harbor, the U.S. base in Hawaii sinking five battleships at anchor and killing 2,344 men. *8 Dec*: the U.S. declares war on Japan after the Pearl Harbor attack, which was an undeclared act of war. *9 Dec*: the Japanese sink two British warships, *Repulse* and *Prince of Wales*, off the coast of Malaya. *11 Dec*: Germany declares war on the U.S.

Giles Gilbert Scott: New Bodleian Library, Oxford

Edward Hopper: Nighthawks

John Borglum: Mount Rushmore National Monument (sculpture)

Jackson Pollock: Bird

Francis Picabia: Women with Bulldog

Fernand Leger: Divers Against Yellow Background

Paul Nash: Totes Meer

Alberto Moravia: *La mascherato* (The Fancy Dress Party) (Mussolini personally censors the novel)

Arthur Koestler: *Darkness at Noon; Scum of the Earth*

Francois Mauriac: *La Pharisienne* (A Woman of the Pharisees)

Sadig Hidayat: *The Blind Owl*

Joyce Cary: *Herself Surprised*

F. Scott Fitzgerald: *The Last Tycoon* (Fitzgerald died last *Dec* aged 44)

A. J. Cronin: *The Keys of the Kingdom*

Joseph Kesselring: *Arsenic and Old Lace*

Bertolt Brecht: *Mother Courage*

Benjamin Britten: *Paul Bunyan* (composed, not performed)

Michael Tippett: *A Child of Our Time* (completed, not performed)

Sergei Rachmaninov: *Symphonic Dances*

Paul Hindemith: *Cello Concerto*

Samuel Barber: *Violin Concerto*

Paul Creston: *Symphony No 1*

Aaron Copland: *Piano Sonata*

Virgil Thomson: *Symphony No 2*

Norbert Schultze: *Lili Marlene* (popular song, words written by Hans Leip, a German soldier in the First World War)

Nat Burton and Walter Kent: *The White Cliffs of Dover* (popular song).

1942 The Chinese get U.S. help in resisting Japanese aggression. General Stilwell starts work on a supply road over the Himalayas, the 770-km/478-mile Burma-India Ledo Road, so that supplies can be sent in from the Indian subcontinent. *2 Jan*: the Japanese take Manila. *10 Jan*: the Japanese invade the Dutch East Indies, then experience defeat at the Battle of Macassar Strait. *15 Jan*: an Inter-American Conference at Rio de Janeiro seeks to co-ordinate the defence of the New World against aggression. *15 Feb*: Singapore falls to the Japanese. *9 Apr*: on the Bataan Peninsula in the Philippines, 36,000 U.S. troops are forced to surrender to General Yamashita, who succeeds in killing most of them on forced marches to internment camps. *18 Apr*: bombers from the U.S. aircraft carrier *Hornet* raid Tokyo. *May*: the Battle of the Coral Sea: the Japanese are defeated but sink the carrier *Lexington*. *2 May*: the Japanese take Mandalay, completing their conquest of Burma. *31 May*: Czech patriots assassinate the Reich Protector of Czechoslovakia Reinhard Heydrich. *6 Jun*: the Germans exact terrible revenge for Heydrich's murder, choosing a village at random – Lidice – executing every male and destroying the buildings. Battle of Midway: U.S. planes based on aircraft carriers stop rather than defeat the Japanese. *21 Jun*: Tobruk in North Africa falls to German forces under Rommel, who takes 25,000 British soldiers prisoner and then moves quickly across towards Alexandria. He is checked by British troops under General Montgomery at El Alamein (*2 Oct*). *16 Jul*: the Germans round up 30,000 Parisian Jews and bus them to concentration camps: only 30 survive the war. *22 Aug*: Battle of Stalingrad begins. Hitler has directed his campaign in this direction in order to take control of the Baku oilfield. The huge battle drags on for five months: in it 750,000 Russian soldiers and 400,000 German soldiers will die. *27 Nov*: the French scuttle their warships at Toulon rather than see them fall into German hands. *24 Dec*: at Peenemunde Wernher von Braun perfects the first flying bomb.

    Giles Gilbert Scott: Waterloo Bridge, London

    Georges Braque: Patience

    Jackson Pollock: Male and Female

    Pierre Bonnard: L'Oiseau Bleu

    Albert Camus: *L'Etranger* (The Stranger)

    Antoine de Saint-Exupéry: *Pilote de la guerre* (Flight to Arras)

    Camilo Jose Cela: *La familia di Pascal Duarte* (The family of Pascal Duarte)

    Evelyn Waugh: *Put Out More Flags*

    John Steinbeck: *The Moon Is Down*

    Mary McCarthy: *The Company She Keeps*

    William Faulkner: *Go Down, Moses*

    Thornton Wilder: *The Skin of Our Teeth*

    John Cage: *Imaginary Landscape No 3*

    Dmitri Shostakovitch: *Symphony No 7* (Leningrad)

    Aaron Copland: *Lincoln Portrait*; *Rodeo*

    Heitor Villa-Lobos: *Bachianos Brasileiras No 9*

    Benjamin Britten: *A Ceremony of Carols*

    Michael Tippett: *String Quartet No 2*

    Ferenc Farkas: *The Magic Cupboard*

    Aram Khatchaturian: *Gayaneh*

1943   *23 Jan*: the British Eighth Army takes Tripoli in North

Africa; Axis forces fall back with the British pursuing. *27 Jan*: Casablanca Conference (Roosevelt, Giraud, de Gaulle, Churchill) culminates in the appointment of General Eisenhower as Commander of unified forces in North Africa. *Feb*: the new Mexican volcano Paricutin starts empting. *8 Feb*: Allied forces take Guadalcanal in the Solomons. *Mar*: Battle of the Bismarck Sea: the U.S. sink 21 Japanese transports taking troops to New Guinea. *15 Mar*: after losing Kharkov to the Russians, the Germans recapture the city. The Germans have lost 500,000 during winter fighting on the eastern front. *18 Apr*: Battle of the Warsaw Ghetto begins as 500,000 Jews bottled up in the ghetto defend themselves heroically for six weeks against attacks by German tanks and artillery. The losses are about 5,000 on each side, but the survivors are deported to death camps. *7 May*: the British take Tunis and Bizerte falls to the Americans, bringing Axis resistance in North Africa to an end. *5 Jul*: Battle of Kursk begins: after a week of heavy fighting the Soviet Fifth Army wins: 70,000 German troops are lost. *9 Jul*: U.S. airborne invasion of Sicily by U.S. and British paratroopers. *19 Jul*: U.S. bombing raid on Rome. *25 Jul*: Mussolini resigns under pressure and Marshal Badoglio takes over at the age of 72. *5 Aug*: Allied forces seize the Japanese air base at Munda in the Solomon Islands. *17 Aug*: Allied troops take Messina in Sicily, cross into southern Italy; the Badoglio régime signs an armistice with Allies at Algiers. *23 Aug*: Russian troops retake the city of Kharkov. *8 Sep*: although Italy surrenders unconditionally, German forces in Italy continue fighting. *25 Sep*: Soviet troops retake Smolensk. *4 Oct*: Heinrich Himmler outlines in a speech to his Gruppenführer his plan for 'the extermination of the Jews': it will be a 'never-to-be-written page of glory.' *6 Nov*: Soviet forces retake the city of Kiev as they advance westwards. *24 Dec*: the Pas de Calais is attacked by Allied planes.

✎ The Pentagon, Arlington, Virginia (world's largest office block)

Jefferson Memorial, Washington (completed)

෴ Max Beckmann: Odysseus and Calypso

Piet Mondrian: *Broadway Boogie-Woogie*
Jackson Pollock: *The She-Wolf*
Willem de Kooning: *Queen of Hearts*
Grandma Moses: *The Thanksgiving*

Jean Paul Sartre: *L'Être et le Néant* (Being and Nothingness)
Jose Lins do Rego: *Fogo Morto* (Dead Fires)
Ayn Rand: *The Fountainhead*
Robert Musil: *Der Mann ohne Eigenschaften* (The Man Without Qualities)
Arthur Koestler: *Arrival and Departure*
C. S. Lewis: *Perelandra*
Sholem Asch: *The Apostle*
Antoine de Saint-Exupéry: *Le Petit Prince* (The Little Prince)
Bertolt Brecht: *Der gute Mensch von Sezuan* (The Good Woman of Setzuan); *Galileo*
Noel Coward: *Present Laughter*; *This Happy Breed*
Terence Rattigan: *While the Sun Shines*

Marc Blitzstein: *Freedom Morning*
Dmitri Shostakovitch: *Symphony No 8*
Howard Hanson: *Symphony No 4*
Ralph Vaughan Williams: *Symphony No 5*
Benjamin Britten: *Serenade for Tenor, Horn and Strings*
Richard Rodgers: *Oh, What A Beautiful Morning* (popular song, from the musical *Oklahoma*, words by Oscar Hammerstein)

1944　*22 Jan*: Allied troops fight their way ashore on Anzio beach 40km/25 miles from Rome. The RAF bombs Berlin. *6 Feb*: Allied forces in the Pacific capture Kwajalein Island. *15 Feb*: Allied bombers destroy the abbey at Monte Cassino in Italy. *15 Jun*: American bombers attack Kyushu. *19 Jun*: Battle of the Philippine Sea: the Americans lose only 27 planes, the Japanese 402. *3 Jul*: the city of Minsk falls to the Russians, who capture 100,000 German soldiers. *9 Jul*: U.S. troops succeed in taking Saipan in the Marianas; U.S. bombers can reach Tokyo from here, so the conquest of this island marks a major turning-point in the war. *17 Jul*: Iceland gains its independence from Denmark. *18 Jul*: the Tokyo government falls. *20 Jul*: Hitler survives an attempts by his generals to assassinate him; he is injured by the bomb, but not seriously. *4 Aug*: the Amsterdam Jew Otto Frank and his family are betrayed to the Gestapo after two years in hiding; they are sent to the Auschwitz death camp. *11 Aug*: Allied forces cross the River Loire. *15 Aug*: U.S. troops land in southern France and move north along the Rhone valley. *19 Aug*: General Patton's Third Army reaches the River Seine. *23 Aug*: French troops retake Marseilles. *25 Aug*: Paris is retaken and General de Gaulle returns. *30 Aug*: the Soviet army enters Bucharest. *4 Sep*: the Allies take Antwerp. *5 Sep*: the U.S.S.R. declares war on Bulgaria. The Allies take Brussels. *16 Sep*: Soviet troops enter Sofia. *17 Sep*: British paratroopers are dropped at Eindhoven and Arnhem but they are unable to outflank the German army and sustain heavy losses. *13 Oct*: British and Greek forces retake Athens from the Germans. *20 Oct*: Soviet and Yugoslav partisan troops take Belgrade. *21 Oct*: Allied troops retake Aachen. *12 Nov*: the Allies sink the German battleship *Tirpitz* in Norway. *24 Nov*: the Allies take Strasbourg. *16 Dec*: Battle of the Bulge: the Germans launch an offensive in the Ardennes causing serious losses to the U.S. army. *27 Dec*: Soviet troops surround Budapest.

Francis Bacon: Three Studies for Figures at the Base of a Crucifixion
Pablo Picasso: Death's Head
Romare Bearden: Factory Workers
Frido Kahlo: The Broken Column
Max Ernst: The King Playing with the Queen

W. Somerset Maugham: *The Razor's Edge*
Charles Jackson: *The Lost Weekend*
Par Lagerkvist: *Dvargen* (The Dwarf)
Robert Graves: *The Golden Fleece*
Isak Dinesen: *Winter tales*
Jean Anouilh: *Antigone*
Jean-Paul Sartre: *Huis Clos* (No Exit)
Philip Yordan: *Anna Lucasta*
Terence Rattigan: *O Mistress Mine*

Arnold Schoenberg: *Ode to Napoleon*; *Theme and Variations*

Leonard Bernstein: *Jeremiah*
Samuel Barber: *Symphony No 2*
Walter Piston: *Symphony No 2; Fugue for a Victory Tune*
Béla Bartók: *Concerto for Orchestra*
William Walton: *Music for Henry V*
Aaron Copland: *Appalachian Sprin*
Michael Tippett: *Symphony No 1* (composed)
Robert Allan and Doris Fisher: *You Always Hurt The One You Love* (popular song)
Fred Heatherton: *I've Got A Lovely Bunch Of Coconuts* (popular song)

1945   *9 Jan*: major U.S. invasion of the Philippines under General MacArthur. *26 Jan*: Soviet troops liberate the Polish death camp Auschwitz, but find only 3,000 prisoners; the SS have deported the rest to camps inside Germany. Over a million people have died at Auschwitz. *3 Feb*: a thousand U.S. bombers raid Berlin in an effort to produce a surrender. *4 Feb*: General MacArthur enters Manila. *13 Feb*: British bombers raid Dresden, killing 135,000 civilians. *9 Mar*: U.S. bombers raid Tokyo, killing more than 124,000 civilians. *10 Mar*: U.S. troops invade Mindanao in the Philippines. *22 Mar*: the League of Arab States is founded to co-ordinate the thrust towards complete independence. *11 Apr*: General Patton liberates Buchenwald concentration camp. *12 Apr*: U.S. President Roosevelt dies, aged 63. *21 Apr*: the U.S. Seventh Army takes Nuremberg. *24 Apr*: Dachau concentration camp is liberated. *25 Apr*: Soviet and U.S. armies meet on the River Elbe just south of Berlin and celebrate far into the night. Himmler begins negotiations for a surrender. *28 Apr*: Mussolini and 12 of his associates are executed at Lake Como; Hitler is unnerved by the news of Mussolini's death. *29 Apr*: German troops in Italy surrender unconditionally. *30 Apr*: Hitler commits suicide, aged 56, in his bunker in Berlin. Goebbels kills his family and then commits suicide. *7 May*: Germany surrenders unconditionally, bringing the European war to an end. *10 Jul*: the U.S. wages full-scale air war against the islands of Kyushu and Honshu, beginning today. *30*

Jul: the Japanese torpedo the U.S. warship *Indianapolis* in the Indian Ocean after she has delivered atom bomb components to the Marianas; the ship sinks in 12 minutes and only 316 of her crew of 1,996 survive. *2 Aug*: Potsdam Conference ends (Truman, Stalin, Churchill), determining that Germany is to be disarmed and demilitarized, its leaders to be tried for war crimes. *6 Aug*: the atom bomb dropped on Hiroshima kills 100,000 Japanese civilians outright; another 100,000 die in ensuing months form burns and radiation sickness. *8 Aug*: the U.S.S.R. declares war on Japan. *9 Aug*: the U.S. drops an atom bomb on a civilian population at Nagasaki, killing 75,000 people outright. *10 Aug*: Japan asks for peace. *14 Aug*: President Truman formally declares the Second World War over. 55 million people have died. Europe has 10 million displaced persons. *15 Aug*: in France Marshal Pétain is sentenced to death for treason (collaborating with the Germans), but his sentence is commuted to life imprisonment: he is 89 and will live until *Jul 1951*.

🎨 Philip Guston: If This Be Not I
   Arshile Gorky: The Diary of a Seducer
   Max Ernst: The Temptation of St. Anthony
   Stuart Davis: For Internal Use Only
   Diego Rivera: Greta Tenochtitlan
   Alexander Calder: Red Pyramid (mobile)
   Henry Moore: Family Group (sculpture)
📖 George Orwell: *Animal Farm*
   Jean-Paul Sartre: *L'âge de raison* (The Age of Reason)
   Carlo Levi: *Christ Stopped at Eboli*
   Stig Dagerman: *The Serpent*
   Cora Sandel: *Krane's Café*
   John Steinbeck: *Cannery Row*
   C. S. Lewis: *That Hideous Strength*
   Evelyn Waugh: *Brideshead Revisited*
   Federico Garcia Lorca: *La Casa de Bernada Alba* (Lorca died in *1936*)
   Tennessee Williams: *The Glass Menagerie*
   Jean Giraudoux: *La Folle de Chaillot* (The Madwoman of Chaillot)

Arthur Laurents: *Home of the Brave*
Benjamin Britten: *Peter Grimes*
Edmund Rubbra: *Canterbury Mass*
Bjarne Brustad: *Atlantis*
Serge Prokofiev: *Symphony No 5*
Dmitri Shostakovitch: *Symphony No 9*
Arnold Schoenberg: *Prelude for Orchestra and Mixed Choir*
Grazyna Bacewicz: *Symphony No 1*
Richard Rodgers: *You'll Never Walk Alone* (popular song, words O. Hammerstein II)

1946 *3 Jan*: William Joyce ('Lord Haw Haw') is hanged by the British for broadcasts made during the war; Joyce claimed to be American but held a British passport, making the charge of treason legally allowable. *7 Jan*: an Austrian Republic is formed. *10 Jan*: the United Nations General Assembly begins its first session in London. *17 Jan*: the U.N. Security Council holds its first meeting. *3 Jan*: Yugoslavia adopts a Soviet-style constitution. *1 Apr*: an earthquake on the seabed in the Aleutian trench generates a seismic wave that destroys Scotch Cap Lighthouse (14 metres/45 feet above sea level) on Unimak Island and reaches Hawaii five hours later. *25 Apr*: Moscow agrees to draw its troops out of Iran. *17 May*: Ion Antonescu, the wartime leader of Romania, is sentenced to death. *1 Jun*: after Ho Chi Minh tries to drive the French out of Indo-China, they proclaim an autonomous Republic of Cochin China. *2 Jun*: an Italian referendum narrowly rejects the monarchy. *3 Jun*: ex-King Umberto II leaves Italy to join his family in Lisbon: Italy becomes a republic. *27 Jun*: Italy loses the Dodecanese Islands to Greece. *15 Sep*: Bulgaria also gets rid of its monarchy and declares itself a People's Republic. *28 Sep*: George II returns to Greece in response to a referendum showing that the majority of Greeks want a return to the monarchy. *30 Sep*: the Nuremberg Trials reach their climax as 12 leading Nazis are sentenced to death, including Ribbentrop and Goering; Rudolf Hess and Walter Funk are sentenced to life imprisonment; Franz von Papen is acquitted. *10 Oct*: the Chinese Guomindang re-elects

Chiang Kai-shek as President, but Mao Tse Tung has a million Communists in uniform and 2 million guerrillas and broadcasts a radio message ordering all-out war against the Nationalists. *21 Nov*: Bulgarian Communist Georgi Dimitrov returns from the USSR to become premier of Bulgaria.

James Stirling: History Faculty Building, Cambridge (U.K.)

Jackson Pollock: Eyes in the Heart

Fernand Léger: Composition with Branch

Pablo Picasso: Faun Playing the Pipe; Françoise with Yellow Necklace

Jean Genet: *Miracle de la rose*

Eudora Welty: *Delta Wedding*

Miguel Asturias: *The President*

Nikos Kazantzakis: *Zorba the Greek*

Benjamin Spock: *The Common Sense Book of Baby and Child Care*

Edouardo de Filippo: *Questi Fantasmi*! (Those Ghosts!)

Christopher Fry: *A Phoenix Too Frequent*

Terence Rattigan: *The Winslow Boy*

Friedrich Wolf: *Beaumarchais, or the Birth of Figaro*

Max Frisch: *The Chinese Wall*

Jean-Paul Sartre: *La putain respectueuse* (The Respectful Prostitute)

Lillian Hellman: *Another Part of the Forest*

Simone de Beauvoir: *Tous Les Hommes sont Mortels*

Benjamin Britten: *The Rape of Lucretia*

Gian-Carlo Menotti: *The Medium*

Alan Bush: *The Press Gang*

Igor Stravinsky: *Symphony in Three Movements; Ebony Concerto*

Richard Strauss: *Metamorphosen*; *Oboe Concerto*

Béla Bartók: *Piano Concerto No 3* (Bartok died, aged 63, last *Sep*)

Darius Milhaud: *Clarinet Concerto; The Bells; Piano Concerto No 3*

Samuel Barber: *Cello Concerto*

Charles Ives: *Symphony No 3*

Paul Hindemith: *For Those We Love*

Arthur Honegger: *Symphony No 3*
Aaron Copland: *Symphony No 3*
Aram Khatchaturian: *Cello Concerto*
Michael Tippett: *String Quartet No 3*
Irving Berlin: *Anything You Can Do* (popular song)

1947 Mount Hekla in Iceland erupts causing widespread destruction. A Bedouin boy discovers the first of the Dead Sea Scrolls, a text of the Book of Isaiah written in the first century BC. U.S. scientist Willard Libby discovers that all organic material contains carbon-14 atoms which decay at a fixed and measurable rate, making it possible to date prehistoric archaeological material for the first time. *7 Feb*: both Arabs and Jews reject the British proposal to divide Palestine into Arab and Jewish zones, so Britain refers the matter to the United Nations. *1 Apr*: George II of Greece dies, aged 56, after his second reign and is succeeded by his 45-year-old brother Paul I. *20 Apr*: Christian X of Denmark dies, aged 76, and is succeeded by his 48-year-old son Frederick IX. *15 Aug*: India becomes an independent state; the 58-year-old Jawaharlal Nehru becomes Hindu India's first Prime Minister. *29 Nov*: the UN decides on partition for Palestine, with Jerusalem to be under UN trusteeship; the Jews approve, the Arabs reject the plan. *17 Dec*: the Arab League declares it will forcibly resist partition of Palestine. *30 Dec*: dispute over the control of Kashmir is referred to the UN after many have died in riots following partition.

Tishman Brothers: 445 Park Avenue, New York (start of building boom)
Carson and Lundin: Esso Building, Rockefeller Center, New York
Giles Gilbert Scott: Bankside Power Station, London
Frederick Gibbard: Harlow New Town (U.K.)
Henri Matisse: Young English Girl
Jean Dubuffet: Portrait of Henri Michaux
Pablo Picasso: Ulysses with his Sirens
Oskar Kokoschka: Das Matterhorn
Jackson Pollock: Full Fathom Five
Saul Bellow: *The Victim*

Osamu Dazai: *The Setting Sun*
Yasunari Kawabata: *Thousand Cranes*
Jose Lins do Rego: *Euridice*
Jean Genet: *Querelle de Brest*
Malcolm Lowry: *Under the Volcano*
Alberto Moravia: *The Woman of Rome*
Hans Nossack: *Nekyia*
Albert Camus: *La Peste*
Arthur Miller: *All My Sons*
Carlo Terron: *Il diamante del profeta* (The Prophet's Diamond)
Robinson Jeffers: *Medea*
Jean Anouilh: *L'invitation au château* (Ring Around the Moon)
Tennessee Williams: *A Streetcar Named Desire*
Benjamin Britten: *Albert Herring*
Francis Poulenc: *Les Mamelles de Tiresias*
Roger Sessions: *The Trial of Lucullus; Symphony No 2*
Gian Carlo Menotti: *The Telephone*
Arthur Honegger: *Symphony No 4*
Paul Hindemith: *Symphonia Serena; Piano Concerto*
George Antheil: *Violin Concerto*
Morton Gould: *Symphony No 3*
Darius Milhaud: *Suite for Harmonica and Orchestra; Symphony No 3*
Serge Prokofiev: *Symphony No 6*
Henry Barraud: *Les Mystères des Saints Innocents*
Elliott Carter: *The Minotaur*

1948 *4 Jan*: Burma becomes independent. *30 Jan*: Gandhi is assassinated at the age of 78 by a Hindu extremist. *25 Feb*: a Communist coup in Czechoslovakia. *14 May*: the state of Israel is proclaimed. *24 Jul*: Soviet forces occupying East Germany set up a blockade to cut off Berlin from West Germany. *25 Jul*: an airlift begins, continuing until *Sep* next year: British and U.S. planes fly supplies into Berlin. *4 Sep*: Queen Wilhelmina of the Netherlands abdicates, aged 68, in favour of her daughter, the 39-year-old Juliana. *13 Sep*: Nehru sends Indian troops into the state of Hyderabad; the Nizam refuses to join India and has appealed to the United Nations, but gives way in the end. The Nizam keeps his title, palaces and private property, but Hyderabad is subsumed into India. *23 Dec*: Hedeki Tojo, Japan's wartime Prime Minister, and six others convicted of war crimes are hanged.

Giorgio Morandi: Natura Morta
Willem de Kooning: Woman
Robert Motherwell: Elegy to the Spanish Republic
Graham Sutherland: The Crucifixion

Halldor Laxness: *Atom stooin* (The Atom Station)
Yukio Mishima: *Confessions of a Mask*
Carl Sandburg: *Remembrance Rock*
Norman Mailer: *The Naked and the Dead*
Irwin Shaw: *The Young Lions*
William Faulkner: *Intruder in the Dust*
Patrick White: *The Aunt's Story*
Alan Paton: *Cry the Beloved Country*
Graham Greene: *The Heart of the Matter*
Nathalie Sarraute: *Portrait d'un inconnu* (Portrait of an Unknown Man)
Bertolt Brecht: *The Antigone of Sophocles*; *The Caucasian Chalk Circle*
Christopher Fry: *The Lady's Not for Burning*
Jean Anouilh: *Ardele* (The Cry of the Peacock)
Terence Rattigan: *The Browning Version*; *Harlequinade*

Heitor Villa-Lobos: *Magdalena*; *Mandu-Carara*
Igor Stravinsky: *Orpheus*; *Mass*
Arnold Schoenberg: *A Survivor of Warsaw*
Benjamin Britten: *Saint Nicolas*
Samuel Barber: *Knoxville – Summer of 1915*
David Diamond: *Symphony No 4*
Ralph Vaughan Williams: *Symphony No 6*
Darius Milhaud: *Symphony No 4*
Roger Sessions: *Symphony No 2*
Francis Poulence: *Sinfonietta*
Frank Loesser: *On A Slow Boat To China* (popular song)

1949 *21 Jan*: Chiang Kai-shek resigns as President of China as his Nationalist armies are defeated by Mao's Communist armies. *4 Apr*: the North Atlantic Treaty Organization (NATO) is created with pledges of mutual assistance against aggression. *18 Apr*: the Republic of Eire is proclaimed in Dublin. *5 May*: in London the Council of Europe statute is signed, setting up a Consultative Assembly with headquarters at Strasbourg. *11 May*: Siam is renamed Thailand. *17 May*: the British recognize Eire's independence, but reaffirm Northern Ireland's position within the United Kingdom. *23 May*: the German Federal Republic (West Germany) is established, with its seat of government at Bonn; West Berlin remains the nominal capital. *2 Jun*: Transjordan becomes the Hashemite Kingdom of Jordan. *30 Sep*: the Berlin airlift comes to an end; the Russians officially lifted their blockade of Berlin on *12 May*. *1 Oct*: the People's Republic of China is proclaimed in Beijing as Mao Tse Tung turns China into a Communist state: he is to be its Chairman (and virtual emperor). *7 Oct*: the German Democratic Republic (East Germany) is founded, under Soviet control. *16 Dec*: in Indonesia, Achmed Sukarno is elected President. *27 Dec*: the Dutch give Indonesia its independence; the new country's capital is to be Jakarta (formerly Batavia).

Jackson Pollock: Number 2
Pablo Picasso: The Kitchen
Graham Sutherland: Portrait of Somerset Maugham
Simone de Beauvoir: *Le Deuxième Sexe*
Alberto Moravia: *Conjugal Love*
Cesare Pavese: *La Casa in Collina* (The House on the Hill)
Jean-Paul Sartre: *La Mort dans l'âme* (Iron in the Soul)
Anais Nin: *The House of Incest*
Naguib Mahfouz: *The Beginning and the End*
Par Lagerkvist: *Barabas*
Graham Greene: *The Third Man*
George Orwell: *Nineteen Eighty-Four* (Orwell will die next *Jan*, aged 46)
Arthur Miller: *Death of a Salesman*
Friedrich Durrenmatt: *Romulus the Great*
Albert Camus: *Les Justes*
Reinhold Glière: *Ghulsara*
Benjamin Britten: *Spring Symphony*

Ernest Bloch: *Concerto Symphonique*

Paul Hindemith: *Concerto for Organ, Brass and Woodwind*

Ralph Vaughan Williams: *The Pilgrim's Progress*

Richard Rodgers: *Some Enchanted Evening*; *Happy Talk* (popular songs, words by Oscar Hammerstein)

Johnny Marks: *Rudolph the Red-Nosed Reindeer* (popular song)

1950 *29 Jan*: race riots in Johannesburg as blacks begin to protest about the apartheid laws that came into operation last year. *14 Feb*: a treaty of friendship and mutual support is signed by China and the U.S.S.R. *1 Mar*: the German-born physicist Klaus Fuchs is found guilty of giving British information about atomic energy to the Soviet Union, yet Fuchs was employed by the British knowing that he was a Communist. *8 Mar*: Marshal Voroshilov announces that the Soviet Union now has the atom bomb. *25 Jun*: Communist forces from North Korea invade the Republic of South Korea, starting a Korean War. *27 Jun*: the UN Secretary-General Trygve Lie asks UN members to help South Korea. U.S. President Truman orders air and sea forces to defend South Korea. *28 Jun*: Seoul falls to North Korean troops. *9 Jul*: General MacArthur takes command of a UN force in Korea. *22 Jul*: Leopold III of the Belgians returns to Belgium after six years in exile. *23 Jul*: there are leftist demonstrations against Leopold in Brussels. *1 Aug*: Leopold abdicates in favour of his 19-year-old son Baudouin. *26 Sep*: UN forces retake Seoul, but fail to defeat the North Korean army. *21 Oct*: a Chinese army invades Tibet. *29 Oct*: Gustavus V of Sweden dies, aged 91, and is succeeded by his 66-year-old son Gustavus VI. *1 Nov*: President Truman escapes an assassination attempt by two Puerto Ricans. *26 Nov*: Chinese and North Korean troops attack UN forces in freezing conditions in Korea, inflicting heavy losses; the Americans retreat in disorder leaving 15,000 marines trapped.

⚏ Le Corbusier: Notre-Dame-du-Haut, Ronchamp (France)

Wallace Harrison: United Nations Secretariat

Building, New York

Henri Matisse: *Zulma*

Barnett Newman: *Tundra*

Jackson Pollock: *Lavender Mist*

Willem de Kooning: *Excavation*

Fernand Léger: *The Constructors*

Franz Kline: *Chief*

Alberto Giacometti: *Seven Figures and a Head*

Pablo Picasso: *The Goat*

Immanuel Velikovsky: *Worlds in Collision*

Simon Vestdijk: *Anton Wachter*

Cesare Pavese: *La luna e il falo* (The Moon and the Bonfire)

Juan Carlos Onetti: *La vida breve* (The Short Life)

Ernest Hemingway: *Across the River and into the Trees*

Barbara Pym: *Some Tame Gazelle*

Doris Lessing: *The Grass is Singing*

T. S. Eliot: *The Cocktail Party*

Eugene Ionesco: *La Cantatrice chauve* (The Bald Primadonna)

Jean Anouilh: *La répétition* (The Rehearsal)

Norman dello Joio: *The Triumph of St. Joan*

Darius Milhaud: *Bolivar; Piano Concerto No 4*

Gian Carlo Menotti: *The Consul*

Francis Poulenc: *Piano Concerto*

Serge Prokofiev: *On Guard for Peace*

Benjamin Britten: *Variations and Fugue on a Theme by Purcell*

Virgil Thomson: *Cello Concerto*

David Diamond: *Timon of Athens*

Stephen Weiss and Bernie Baum: *Music! Music! Music!* (popular song)

Lew Quadling: *Sam's Song* (popular song, words J. Elliott)

1951 *4 Jan*: Communist forces again take Seoul. *14 Mar*: UN troops take Seoul back from the Communists, to find that 80 per cent of the city is destroyed. *29 Mar*: General MacArthur offers to discuss a truce, but Beijing refuses. *30 Mar*: Ethel and Julius Rosenberg and Morton Sobell are found guilty in New York of selling atomic secrets to the Soviets. *5 Apr*: the Rosenbergs are sentenced to death. *11 Apr*: General MacArthur is dismissed after publicly recommending air attacks on Chinese cities. Truman appoints General Ridgway in his place. *2 May*: the new Nationalist Front government in Iran nationalizes the oil industry, in breach of a *1933* concession treaty with Britain. *3 May*: Japan regains its independence after six years of military occupation. *8 May*: the first thermonuclear reaction is tested at the Pacific atoll of Eniwetok. *26 May*: Britain appeals to the International Court of Justice over Iran's nationalization of the Iranian oil industry. *Jun*: British diplomats Burgess and Maclean flee to Moscow amid suspicion that they are Soviet agents. *5 Jul*: the International Court of Justice rules against Iran. President Truman calls for a compromise. *20 Jul*: King Abdullah of Jordan is assassinated in Jerusalem and is succeeded by Emir Talal, who next year will be declared unfit to rule. *Sep*: UN forces in Korea now number 500,000 and new peace talks begin. *27 Sep*: Iranian troops occupy the Abadan oilfields. *4 Oct*: Anglo-Iranian Oil removes its personnel from Abadan for safety. *1 Nov*: the U.S. explodes an atomic device over the Nevada desert. *10 Dec*: Iran agrees to resubmit its case to the Court of Justice.

  Harrison and Abramovitz: Alcoa Building; U.S. Steel Building, both in Pittsburgh
Robert Matthew and Leslie Martin: Royal Festival Hall, London

  Jean Dubuffet: Natural History
Edward Hopper: First Row Orchestra
Jackson Pollock: Black and White Painting
Pablo Picasso: Massacre in Korea

  Truman Capote: *The Grass Harp*
Anthony Powell: *A Question of Upbringing*
Graham Greene: *The End of the Affair*
William Styron: *Lie Down in Darkness*
Herman Wouk: *The Caine Mutiny*
James Jones: *From Here to Eternity*
J. D. Salinger: *The Catcher in the Rye*
Alberto Moravia: *Il Conformiste* (The Conformist)
Heinrich Böll: *Wo warst du, Adam?* (Adam, Where

Art Thou?)
Albert Camus: *L'Homme Revolte* (The Rebel)
Tennessee Williams: *The Rose Tattoo*
Max Frisch: *Count Oderland*
Eugene Ionesco: *La leçon* (The Lesson)
Lillian Hellman: *The Autumn Garden*
Christopher Fry: *A Sleep of Prisoners*
Peter Ustinov: *The Love of Four Colonels*
Alan Bush: *Wat Tyler*
Gian Carlo Menotti: *Amahl and the Night Visitors*
Benjamin Britten: *Billy Budd*
Igor Stravinsky: *The Rake's Progress*
Béla Bartók: *The Miraculous Mandarin*
Francis Poulenc: *Stabat Mater*
Walter Piston: *Symphony No 4*
Arthur Honegger: *Symphony No 5; Suite Archaique*
Charles Ives: *Symphony No 2* (written about *1900*)

1952   Michael Ventris deciphers the Minoan-Mycenean script known as Linear B, finding it to be an early form of Greek. His discovery will make it possible to learn more about the beginnings of civilization in Europe. *6 Feb*: George VI of Britain dies, aged 56, of lung cancer (he was a heavy smoker) and is succeeded by his 25-year-old daughter Elizabeth II. *10 Mar*: there is a military coup in Cuba: President Socarras is overthrown and replaced by General Zaldivar (dictator *1933–40*). *Apr*: General Eisenhower steps down form his post as Supreme Allied Commander; Truman appoints General Ridgway to replace him and General Clark to replace Ridgway in the Far East. The Republican Party nominates Eisenhower as its presidential candidate. *26 Jul*: King Farouk of Egypt abdicates three days after a coup by General Naguib. *11 Aug*: King Talal of Jordan is deposed and replaced by his 16-year-old son Hussein, who will ascend the Jordanian throne next year and remain there for over 40 years in spite of at least 10 assassination attempts and other attempts to depose him. *10 Sep*: General Naguib of Egypt forms a government. *20 Oct*: Kikuyu tribal leader Jomo Kenyatta organizes the Mau Mau (black terrorists) to drive out the white settlers in Kenya. The British send out troops to try to suppress the Mau Mau. *7 Nov*:

Israel's first President Chaim Weizmann dies, aged 77. *8 Dec*: The Israeli Knesset replaces Weizmann with Itzhak Ben-Zvi.

Gordon Bunshaft: Lever House, Park Avenue, New York (completed)

Owen Williams: BOAC Hangars at Heathrow Airport, UK

Helen Frankenthaler: Mountains and Sea

Lucien Freud: Francis Bacon

John Minton: The Death of Nelson

Barnett Newman: Adam

Willem de Kooning: Woman and Bicycle

Ad Reinhardt: Red Painting

Ernest Hemingway: *The Old Man and the Sea*

William Styron: *The Long March*

Bernard Malamud: *The Natural*

John Steinbeck: *East of Eden*

Jules Romains: *Les hommes de bonne volonté* (Men of Good Will)

Barbara Pym: *Excellent Women*

Carlo Terron: *Non ce pace per L'antico Fauno* (No Peace for the Ancient Faun)

Frederick Knott: *Dial 'M' for Murder*

Friedrich Dürrenmatt: *Die Ehe des Herrn Mississippi* (The Marriage of Mr. Mississippi)

Terence Pattigan: *The Deep Blue Sea*

Jean Anouilh: *La valse des toréadors* (The Waltz of the Toreadors)

Paul Hindemith: *Die Harmonie der Welt*

Serge Prokofiev: *Symphonic Concertante* (Prokofiev will die 5 Mar next year)

John Cage: *Water Music*; *4'33"*

Darius Milhaud: *West Point Suite*

Roy Harris: *Symphony No 7*

Gian Carlo Menotti: *Violin Concerto*

Dmitri Tiomkin: *Do Not Forsake Me* (Popular song, words N. Washington)

1953 A huge uranium deposit is found in Ontario, Canada; this will make Canada a supplier of world significance of the fuel for nuclear energy. *5 Mar*: Josef Stalin dies aged 73, and he is succeeded as Chairman of the Council of

Ministers by Georgi Malenkov. *31 Mar*: the Swedish diplomat Dag Hammarskjold is elected Secretary-General of the United Nations. *8 Apr*: Jomo Kenyatta and five other Kikuyu are found guilty of organizing the terrorist campaign to drive white settlers out of Kenya. With their conviction a 10-year campaign for Kenyan independence begins. *May*: U.S. planes bomb dams in North Korea, flooding rice fields and spoiling crops. *29 May*: Hillary and Tensing reach the summit of Mount Everest at 11.30 am: they are the first people to climb the highest mountain in the world. *19 Jun*: Ethel and Julius Rosenberg are executed in the U.S. for espionage. *10 Jul*: the Soviet Minister of Internal Affairs Lavrenti Beria is dismissed. *27 Jul*: an armistice is signed at Panmunjom in Korea, ending the three-year war that has wrecked the whole region; North Korean and Chinese casualties amount to 1½ million and about 2 million Korean civilians have been killed. *12 Aug*: the U.S.S.R tests a hydrogen bomb and raises physicist Andrei Sakharov to full membership of the Soviet Academy of Sciences. *9 Nov*: King Saud of Saudi Arabia dies, aged 73; he founded the country which is named after him. He is succeeded by his son Saud ibn Abdel Aziz. *23 Dec*: the dismissed Soviet Minister of Internal Affairs, Beria, is shot as a traitor.

Francis Bacon: Pope Innocent X
Larry Rivers: Washington Crossing the Delaware
Jackson Pollock: Blue Poles
Henry Moore: King and Queen (sculpture)
Ian Fleming: *Casino Royale*
Ray Bradbury: *Fahrenheit 451*
Nathalie Sarraute: *Martereau*
Saul Bellow: *The Adventures of Augie March*
Alain Robbe-Grillet: *Les Gommes* (The Erasers)
Heinrich Böll: *Acquainted with the Night*
Samuel Beckett: *Waiting for Godot*
Terence Rattigan: *The Sleeping Prince*
John Patrick: *The Teahouse of the August Moon*
Dylan Thomas: *Under Milk Wood*
Jean Anouilh: *Medée* (Medea)
Tennessee Williams: *Camino Real*

Arthur Miller: *The Crucible*

Marc Blitzstein: *The Harpies* (composed in *1931*)

Benjamin Britten: *Gloriana*

Grazyna Bacewicz: *Symphony No 4*

Dmitri Shostakovitch: *Symphony No 10*

Michael Tippett: *Fantasia Concertante on a Theme of Corelli*

Masao Oki: *Atomic Bomb*

Darius Milhaud: *Symphony No 5*

William Walton: *Te Deum; Orb and Sceptre*

Arthur Honegger: *Une Cantata de Nöel*

Alexander Borodin: *Stranger in Paradise* (popular song, words added by Robert Wright and George Forest)

1954 *21 Jan*: the *Nautilus*, launched today in Connecticut, is the world's first nuclear-powered submarine. *1 Mar*: the U.S. Atomic Energy Commission explodes the first American hydrogen bomb at Bikini Atoll in the South Pacific. *2 Mar*: President Lopez of Paraguay dies, aged 54, at Asunciòn; General Alfredo Stroessner is elected President in his place and he will head a military dictatorship that will give refuge to Nazi war criminals. *17 Apr*: in Egypt, General Naguib is replaced as Premier by Colonel Gamal Nasser, who is now 36. *22 Apr*: in America, Senator McCarthy conducts hearings beginning today as Chairman of the 'Permanent Investigations Subcommittee', charging that a Communist spy ring is operating at Fort Monmouth. McCarthy's colleagues become increasingly alarmed at his methods. *27 Jun*: the world's first nuclear power station goes into operation at Obninsk near Moscow. *21 Jul*: the Geneva Conference ends, having decided on the 17th parallel as the frontier between North and South Vietnam. Ho Chi Minh becomes President of the Democratic Republic of North Vietnam. *24 Aug*: President Vargas of Brazil resigns under pressure and commits suicide. He is succeeded by Vice President Filho. *19 Oct*: Egypt's Colonel Nasser signs a treaty with Britain providing for British withdrawal from the Suez Canal Zone within two years. *31 Oct*: a revolt against French rule breaks out in Algeria, organized by the Front de Liberation. *2 Dec*:

the U.S. Senate votes to censure Senator McCarthy for misconduct. *29 Dec*: Laos gains full independence from France.

- Morris Lapidus: Fontainebleau Hotel, Miami Beach, Florida

  Basil Spence: Coventry Cathedral (U.K.)

- Graham Sutherland: Portrait of Sir Winston Churchill (later destroyed by Lady Churchill)

  Francis Bacon: Figure with Meat

  Jean Dubuffet: Les Vagabonds

  Stuart Davis: Colonial Cubism

  Robert Rauschenberg: Charlene; Collection

  Jackson Pollock: White Light

  Felix de Weldon: Iwo Jima Memorial (bronze figures)

  Joseph Cornell: The Caliph of Baghdad (sculpture)

- Iris Murdoch: *Under the Net*

  Doris Lessing: *A Proper Marriage*

  Françoise Sagan: *Bonjour Tristesse*

  Simone de Beauvoir: *The Mandarins*

  William Golding: *Lord of the Flies*

  Cyprian Ekwenski: *People of the City*

  Yasunari Kawabata: *The Sound of the Mountain*

  Heinrich Böll: *Haus ohne Hüter* (The Unguarded House)

  Thomas Mann: *Felix Krull*

  Ilya Erenburg: *The Thaw* (first reference to the iniquities of the Stalin regime)

  Terence Rattigan: *Separate Tables*

- Lennox Berkeley: *Nelson*

  Gian Carlo Menotti: *The Saint of Bleeker Street*

  William Walton: *Troilus and Cressida*

  Benjamin Britten: *The Turn of the Screw*

  Arnold Schoenberg: *Moses and Aaron*; *De Profundis*

  Samuel Barber: *Prayers of Kierkegaard*

  Luciano Berio: *Nones*

  Dominick Argento: *Sicilian Limes*

  Charles Ives: *Washington's Birthday* (Ives dies, aged 79, in New York)

  Darius Milhaud: *Piano Concerto No 4*

  Heitor Villa-Lobos: *Odisseia de una raca* (Odyssey of

a Race)

Roger Sessions: *String Quartet No 2*

Igor Stravinsky: *In Memoriam Dylan Thomas* (Thomas died *9 Nov* 1953)

Jule Styne: *Three Coins in the Fountain* (popular song words S. Cahn)

Charles Calhoun: *Shake, Rattle and Roll* (popular song)

1955　*15 Jan*: U.S.S.R. recognizes the independence of West Germany. *8 Feb*: Soviet premier Malenkov resigns, succeeded by Marshal Bulganin, who affirms the ties between U.S.S.R. and China and appoints Marshal Zhukov Minister of Defence. *5 Apr*: the 81-year-old Winston Churchill resigns as British Prime Minister and is succeeded by Foreign Secretary Anthony Eden. *19 Sep*: a military coup in Argentina overthrows the dictator Juan Perón, who goes into exile, first to Paraguay, then Nicaragua. He lost popularity after the death of his charismatic wife Eva in *1952*. *5 Nov*: the painter Maurice Utrillo dies, aged 71, at Dax.

Jasper Johns: Target with Four Faces

Robert Rauschenberg: Rebus; Bed

Jackson Pollock: Scent

Larry Rivers: Double Portrait of Birdie

Giorgio de Chirico: Italian Square

Pablo Picasso: The Women of Algiers

J. R. R. Tolkien: *Lord of the Rings*

Graham Greene: *The Quiet American*

Anthony Powell: *The Acceptance World*

William Golding: *The Inheritors*

Alain Robbe-Grillet: *The Voyeur*

Vladimir Nabokov: *Lolita*

Tennessee Williams: *Cat on a Hot Tin Roof*

Arthur Miller: *A View from the Bridge*

Frances Goodrich and Albert Hackett: *The Diary of Anne Frank*

Malcolm Arnold: *Rinaldo and Armida*

Michael Tippett: *Piano Concerto*

Ralph Vaughan Williams: *Symphony No 8*

Walter Piston: *Symphony No 6*

Howard Hanson: *Symphony No 5*

William Haley: *Rock Around The Clock* (popular song)

Sammy Fain: *Love Is A Many-Splendoured Thing* (popular song words P. Webster)

1956 *1 Jan*: Sudan becomes an independent republic, joining the Arab League. *1 Mar*: Morocco becomes an independent kingdom. *20 Mar*: Tunisia gains its independence. *21 May*: the U.S. Atomic Energy Commission tries out its first airborne hydrogen bomb as it begins a series of bomb tests in the Pacific. *4 Jun*: Egypt announces that it will not be renewing the Suez Canal Company's concession when it runs out in *1968*. *13 Jun*: the last British troops leave the Suez Canal base in Egypt. *26 Jun*: President Nasser of Egypt orders the seizure of the Suez Canal, outlawing the Suez Canal Company. *2 Aug*: British and French families are airlifted out of the Canal Zone this week. *18 Sep*: Britain gives the Gold Coast its independence. *23 Sep*: Britain and France put their grievances over the Suez Canal before the UN Security Council. *23 Oct*: students in Budapest demand a return to democratic government, the return of Imre Nagy to the partnership, the withdrawal of Soviet troops and the release of Cardinal Mindszenty who has been held in solitary confinement since *1948*. *24 Oct*: Imre Nagy is reinstated as Hungarian Premier to appease the demonstrators. *25 Oct*: withdrawal of Soviet troops from Polan begins. *29 Oct*: Israeli troops invade the Sinai Peninsula. *31 Oct*: British and French planes bomb Egyptian airfields. Washington sends aid to Israel; Jordan bans British planes from using its bases in any action directed against Egypt. Soviet troops are withdrawn from Budapest and Cardinal Mindszenty is released from prison. *2 Nov*: Gaza falls to British troops. The Hungarian Premier Imre Nagy goes on the radio to denounce the Warsaw Pact of *1954*. *4 Nov*: 16 Soviet divisions move into Hungary with 2,000 tanks to suppress the Hungarian rebellion. Nagy is replaced by Janos Kadar. Cardinal Mindszenty takes refuge in the U.S. Embassy at Budapest, where he occupies a floor for the next 15 years. The UN General Assembly condemns Russian interference in Hungary. *5 Nov*: British paratroopers land at Port Said in Egypt to recover control of the Suez Canal. In answer to protests from around the world, Britain says she will evacuate her troops only when a UN force arrives. *15 Nov*: the UN force arrives. *22 Nov*: Imre Nagy is seized by Russian troops as he leaves the Yugoslav embassy in Budapest. Five days earlier, at a Kremlin reception, Khrushchev said 'History is on our side. We will bury you!' to Western diplomats. *29 Nov*: Eisenhower offers asylum to Hugarian patriots, but makes no attempt to intervene. *22 Dec*: the last British and French troops leave Port Said. *27 Dec*: the UN fleet begins the task of clearing the scuttled ships which the Egyptians used to block the canal and make it unusable.

✍ Orders of Dean Walter Hussey: The Arundel Screen, Chichester Cathedral (medieval, reinstated)

🎨 Richard Hamilton: Just what is it that makes today's homes so different, so appealing? (photo-collage)
Piero Manzoni: Pins
Willem de Kooning: Easter Monday

📖 Angus Wilson: *Anglo-Saxon Attitudes*
Compton Mackenzie: *Thin Ice*
Rose Macaulay: *The Towers of Trebizond*
Françoise Sagan: *Un Certain Sourire* (A Certain Smile)
Albert Camus: *La Chute* (The Fall)
Mary Renault: *The Last Of the Wine*
William Golding: *Pincher Martin*
Par Lagerkvist: *Sybil*
Yevgeny Yevtushenko: *Zima Junction*
Friedrich Dürrenmatt: *Der Besuch der alten Dame* (The Visit)
Enid Bagnold: *The Chalk Garden*
John Osborne: *Look Back in Anger*
Brendan Behan: *The Quare Fellow*
Eugene O'Neill: *A Long Day's Journey into Night* (O'Neill died in 1953)

🎵 Arnold Schoenberg: *Modern Psalm*
William Walton: *Johannesburg Festival Overture*
Charles Ives: *Robert Browning Overture*
Edmund Rubbra: *Piano Concerto*

Lennox Berkeley: *A Dinner Engagement*
Elvis Presley and Vera Walson: *Love Me Tender*
(popular song)
Elvis Presley, Mae Axton, Tommy Durden: *Heartbreak Hotel* (popular song)

1957 Mao Tse Tung organizes the Great Leap Forward in
China; over 500 million peasants are reorganized into
'people's communes' with few individual rights and no
private ownership of property. *9 Jan*: broken by his
failure to handle the Suez Crisis, the British Prime
Minister Anthony Eden resigns; he is replaced by
Harold Macmillan, who is now 62. *23 Jan*: Ku Klux
Klansmen force a 25-year-old truck driver, Willie Edwards, to jump to his death from a bridge into the
Alabama River; they accuse him of making remarks to
a white woman – a mild offence of which he is, in any
case, entirely innocent. *2 Feb*: Israel rejects a UN call to
withdraw from Egypt's Gaza Strip. *1 Mar*: Israel withdraws from the Gaza Strip on the assumption that the
UN will administer it. *25 Jul*: the Bey of Tunis is
deposed and Tunisia becomes a republic under President Bourguiba. *11 Aug*: the Sherifian Empire of Morocco becomes the Kingdom of Morocco: the Sultan
changes his title to King Mohammed V. *21 Sep*: Haakon
VII of Norway dies, aged 85, and is succeeded by his 54-
year-old son Olaf V. *4 Oct*: the U.S.S.R. launches the
world's first man-made satellite, *Sputnik I*. *26 Oct*: in the
U.S.S.R. Marshal Zhukov is dismissed. Molotov is
exiled to Siberia for conspiring against Khrushchev.
Nov: *Sputnik II* is sent into orbit with a dog inside.

Morris Lapidus: Americana Hotel, Bal Harbour,
Florida
Jodrell Bank Radio Telescope U.K.

Robert Rauschenberg: Painting with Red Letter 'S'
Clyfford Still: 1975D No 1
Alberto Giacometti: Annette
Diego Rivera: Sandias (Riveria dies, aged 70, *25 Nov*
at Mexico City)
Victor Vasarely: Betelgeuse
Ad reinhardt: Black on Black

Jack Kerouac: *On the Road*

Mordecai Richler: *A Choice of Enemies*
Bernard Malamud: *The Assistant*
Carlo Gadda: *That Awful Mess on Via Merulana*
Nevil Shute: *On the Beach*
Alain Robbe-Grillet: *La Jalousie* (Jealousy)
Vladimir Nabokov: *Pnin*
Boris Pasternak: *Doktor Zhivago*
Eugene O'Neill: *A Moon for the Misbegotten*
John Osborne: *The Entertainer*
Samuel Beckett: *Endgame*
Tennessee Williams: *Orpheus Descending*
Igor Stravinsky: *Agon*
Benjamin Britten: *The Prince of the Pagodas*
Morton Gould: *Declaration*; *Jekyll and Hyde Variations*
William Walton: *Cello Concerto*
Michael Tippett: *Symphony No 2*
Charles Ives: *Symphony No 2* (composed around 1900)
David Diamond: *Symphony No 6*
Heitor Villa-Lobos: *Symphony No 10*
Walter Piston: *Symphony No 4*
Arthur Honegger: *Symphony No 5*
Dmitri Shostakovitch: *Piano Concerto No 2*; *Symphony No 11*
Francis Poulenc: *Stabat Mater*
Pierre Boulez: *Polyphonie X*
Roger Sessions: *Symphony No 3*
Peter Tchaikovsky: *Symphony No 7* (performing version A. Bogatirev)
Jerry Leiber and Mike Stoller: *Jailhouse Rock* (popular song)

1958 U.S. scientists begin measuring ozone levels in the atmosphere, suspecting that nuclear weapons testing and high-altitude flying by jet aircraft may be damaging the ozone. During the next 13 years ozone levels increase, possibly owing to recovery as atom bomb tests cease. The U.S. submarine *Nautilus* crosses the North Pole beneath the sea-ice. *14 Feb*: Iraq and Jordan join in an Arab Federation under King Feisal of Iraq, following the formation earlier in the month of a United Arab Republic by the union of Egypt and Sudan under Nasser. *31 May*: General de Gaulle becomes France's Premier as the Algerian revolt threatens to cause civil war within France. *17 Jun*: French troops withdraw from Tunisia with the exception of Bizerte. *14 Jul*: King Feisal of Iraq, his son and Premier are assassinated in a coup by General Kassem, who proclaims a republic. Hussein of Jordan becomes head of the Arab Federation. *15 Jul*: U.S. troops land near Beirut to protect U.S. lives and property during rioting. *1 Aug*: King Hussein of Jordan dissolves the Arab Federation. *28 Sep*: a French referendum approves the formation of a Fifth Republic. Nikita Krushchev engineers the removal of Bulganin, his principal rival: Bulganin is dismissed from the Communist Party Presidium. *25 Oct*: U.S. troops withdraw from the Lebanon. *Nov*: General de Gaulle emerges from the French elections as President for a seven-year term beginning next *Jan*. *4 Nov*: Britain, U.S.S.R. and the U.S. agree to stop nuclear weapons testing because of fears about radiation levels in the atmosphere.

Pier Luigi Nervi: Palazzetto dello Sport, Rome (completed)

Pier Luigi Nervi: Pirelli Building, Milan (completed)

Oskar Niemeyer: Presidential Palace, Brasilia (completed)

Stevenage Town Centre

Jacob Epstein: St. Michael and the Devil

Mark Rothko: Four Darks on Red

Pablo Picasso: Peace

Jasper Johns: Three Flags

Cyril Parkinson: Parkinson's Law

Chinua Achebe: *Things Fall Apart*

Mario Llosa: *La ciudad y los perros* (The City and the Dogs)

Yasar Kemal: *Ince Memed* (Memed, My Hawk)

Cora Sandel: Leech

Alan Sillitoe: *Saturday Night, and Sunday Morning*

Doris Lessing: *A Ripple from the Storm*

Evelyn Waugh: *The Ordeal of Gilbert Pinfold*

Leon Uris: *Exodus*

Eugene Ionesco: *Tueur sans gages* (The Killer)
Harold Pinter: *The Birthday Party*
Peter Shaffer: *Five Finger Exercise*
Brendan Behan: *The Hostage*
Samuel Beckett: *Krapp's Last Tape*
Bertolt Brecht: *The Resistible Rise of Arturo Ui*
Samuel Barber: *Vanessa*
Benjamin Britten: *Noye's Fludde; Nocturne*
Dmitri Shostakovitch: *Piano Concerto No 2*
William Walton: *Partita for Orchestra*
Sem Dresden: *François Villon*
Duke Ellington, Bill Strayhorn, Johnny Mercer:
Satin Doll (popular song)
Dominico Modugno: *Volare* (popular song)
Carl Sigman, R. Rascel, S. Giovanni, J. Fishman:
Arrivederci Roma (popular song)

1959 *1 Jan*: the Cuban dictator Batista resigns and flees to
Miami as Fidel Castro, the rebel leader, captures San-
tiago. *3 Jan*: Castro enters Havana and assumes office as
Head of State. *2 Feb*: the 22-year-old singer Buddy Holly
dies in a plane crash in a snowstorm in Iowa. *15 Apr*:
Fidel Castro makes an unofficial visit to Washington. *17
Apr*: Castro emphasizes that his revolution in Cuba is
humanistic rather than Communist. *27 Apr*: Mao Tse
Tung resigns as China's Head of State in favour of Liu
Shao-chi: Mao remains Chairman of the Chinese Communist Party. *3 Jun*: Singapore becomes independent,
with Lee Kuan Yew as Prime Minister of a republic. *5
Jul*: President Sukarno of Indonesia dissolves the constituent assembly as he moves steadily towards a more
authoritarian regime.

Mies van der Rohe and Philip Johnson: Seagram
Building, New York
Frank Lloyd Wright: Guggenheim Museum, New
York (Wright dies *9 Apr*, aged 89)
Franz Kline: Zinc Yellow
Kenneth Noland: Virginia Site
Frank Stella: Jill
Jasper Johns: Numbers in Color
Philip Roth: *Goodbye, Columbus*
Saul Bellow: *Henderson the Rain King*

William Burroughs: *The Naked Lunch*
Mordecai Richler: *The Apprenticeship of Duddy Kravitz*
William Faulkner: *The Mansion*
Muriel Spark: *Memento Mori*
Heinrich Böll: *Billiards at Half-Past Nine*
Nathalie Sarraute: *The Planetarium*
Françoise Sagan: *Aimez-vous Brahms?*
Alan Sillitoe: *The Loneliness of the Long Distance Runner*
Shelagh Delaney: *A Taste of Honey*
Deryck Cooke: *The Language of Music*
William Golding: *Free Fall*
Richard Arnell: *The Petrified Princess*
Luciano Berio: *Allez-Hop*
Paul Hindemith: *Pittsburgh Symphony*
Benjamin Britten: *Missa Brevis*
Tadeusz Baird: *Expressions*
Neil Sedaka and Howard Greenfield: *Breaking Up is Hard To Do* (popular song)

1960 Many European colonies in Africa gain their independence: Togo, Cameroun, Malagasy Republic, Independent Congo Republic, Somalia, Ghana, Dahomey, Upper Volta, Ivory Coast, Chad, Central African Republic, Gabon, Mali, Niger, Senegal, Nigeria, Mauritania. *13 Feb:* France tests its first atom bomb over the Sahara in an attempt to prove its status as a world power. Castro signs an agreement with the Soviet Minister Mikoyan: the U.S.S.R. will buy Cuban sugar and provide Cuba with credit. *21 Mar:* the Sharpeville Massacre. 20,000 black people besiege a Johannesburg police station to protest against the law requiring all blacks to carry identification papers; the police open fire, causing 72 deaths. *26 Mar:* the pass law is suspended in South Africa. *1 May:* Soviet missiles bring down an American U-2 spy plane at Sverdlovsk; the pilot Gary Powers is captured by the Russians. Washington has no alternative but to admit that the U.S. has carried out high-altitude reconnaissance over the Soviet Union; Khrushchev calls off his Paris summit meeting with Eisenhower, scoring a major propaganda victory. *22*

May: an earthquake near Concepciòn in Chile causes tsunamis that create havoc in many towns along the coast of Chile; waves travelling at over 640 kph/400 mph reach Hawaii and Japan. *23 Jun*: Castro threatens to seize American-owned property on Cuba to counter American economic aggression. *12 Jul*: Khrushchev says the Monroe Doctrine of *1823* has died a natural death, defending Soviet influence in the Caribbean. *14 Jul*: Washington confirms that the U.S. still adheres to the Monroe Doctrine. *12 Oct*: Inajiro Asanuma, leader of the Japanese Socialist Party, is assassinated on a public stage by a right-wing extremist; Asanuma supported the U.S. Japanese mutual defence treaty.

Lucio Costa (Plan) and Oscar Niemeyer (buildings): Brasilia
Basil Spence: University of Sussex (U.K.)
René Magritte: The Postcard
Andy Warhol: Campbell's Soup Can
Jasper Johns: Painted Bronze
Joseph Beuys: Bathtub (sculpture)
Albert Giacometti: walking Man (sculpture)
David Storey: *This Sporting Life*
Anthony Powell: *Casanova's Chinese Restaurant*
Andrei Sinyavsky: *The Trial Begins*
William Styron: *Set This House on Fire*
John Updike: *Rabbit, Run*
John Barth: *The Sotweed Factor*
Tennessee Williams: *Period of Adjustment*
Robert Bolt: *A Man For All Seasons*
Jean Genet: *Le balcon* (The Balcony)
Harold Pinter: *The Dumb Waiter*
Lillian Hellman: *Toys in the Attic*
Benjamin Britten: *A Midsummer Night's Dream*
Pablo Casals: *El Pesebrio* (The Manger)
Don Banks: *Horn Concerto*
Alun Hoddinott: *Piano Concerto No 2*
Roger Sessions: *Symphony No 4*
Charles Ives: *Lincoln, The Great Commoner* (composed in *1912*)
John Cage: *Music for Amplified Toy Pianos*
William Schuman: *Symphony No 7*

Walter Piston: *Violin Concerto No 2*
William Walton: *Symphony No 2*
Ferde Grofe: *San Francisco Suite*
Darius Milhaud: *Symphony No 9*
Paul Hindemith: *Sinfonietta*
Hank Ballard: *The Twist* (popular song – and popular dance)
Manos Hadjidakis: *Never On Sunday* (popular song)
Lee Pockriss and Paul Vance: *Itsy Bitsy Teenie Weenie Yellow Polka Dot Bikini* (popular song)

1961 The *France* launched by the Compagnie Générale Transatlantique is the longest and the last of the great transatlantic liners: she is 315 metres/1,035 feet long. Tanganyika and Sierra Leone gain independence. *3 Jan*: the U.S. severs diplomatic relations with Cuba. *17 Jan*: Patrice Lumumba, Congolese ex-Premier, is killed under mysterious circumstances; Moscow charges UN Secretary General Hammarskjold with complicity. *15 Jan*: the Cuban Foreign Minister claims at the UN that the U.S. is preparing to invade Cuba. *17 Jan*: the Bay of Pigs; the U.S. bungles its invasion of Cuba and Castro's troops are able to repel the invaders as well as gaining a huge propaganda victory. *18 Jan*: Khrushchev demands that the Cuban invasion stop; Kennedy replies that the U.S. will not permit military intervention from outside. *30 May*: Rafael Trujillo, the 70-year-old Dictator of Dominica, is assassinated. *31 May*: South Africa withdraws from the British Commonwealth. *3–4 Jun*: Kennedy and Khrushchev meet in Vienna, ostensibly to agree the neutrality of Laos but disarmament, nuclear test bans and the German question are also on the agenda. *13 Aug*: the East Germans close the border between East and West Berlin. *15–17 Aug*: the Berlin Wall is built, a masonry barrier making it almost impossible to cross from East to West Berlin. The garrison of West Berlin is reinforced. *18 Sep*: UN Secretary General Dag Hammarskjöld is killed, aged, 56, when his plane crashes in the Congo. *23 Oct*: Zhou En-lai, Chinese Premier, walks out of a party congress in Moscow, initiating a break in relations between China and the U.S.S.R. *30 Oct*: a Soviet hydrogen bomb is eploded in Novaya Zemlya. *3 Nov*: Burmese diplomat U Thant is elected UN Secretary-General.

    Skidmore, Owings and Merrill: Chase Manhattan Bank, New York

    Century City, Los Angeles

    Eero Saarinen: U.S. Embassy, London

    Morris Louis: Delta Nu

    Frank Stella: New Madrid

    Pablo Picasso: Still Life with Lamp Light

    Joan Miró: Blue II

    David Hockney: We Two Boys Forever Clinging

    Graham Sutherland: Noli me tangere

    Günter Grass: *Katze und Maus* (Cat and Mouse)

    Joseph Heller: *Catch-22*

    Patrick White: *Riders in the Chariot*

    Muriel Spark: *The Prime of Miss Jean Brodie*

    Bernard Malamud: *A New Life*

    Juan Carlos Onetti: *El astillero* (The Shipyard)

    Angus Wilson: *The Old Men at the Zoo*

    Tennessee Williams: *The Night of the Iguana*

    Max Frisch: *Andorra*

    John Osborne: *Luther*

    Edward Albee: *The American Dream*

    William Mathias: *Piano Concerto No 2*

    Dmitri Shostakovitch: *Symphony No 12*

    Walter Piston: *Symphony No 7*

    Francis Poulenc: *Gloria*

    Henry Mancini: *Moon River* (popular song, words J. Mercer)

1962 More European colonies gain their independence: Burundi, Jamaica, Trinidad and Tobago, Western Samoa, Uganda. *22 May*: the South Vietnamese army launches Operation Sunrise to eliminate the Vietcong guerrillas using U.S. money, arms and field observers. *21 May*: Adolf Eichmann is hanged by the Israelis for war crimes against Jewish people during the Second World War. *3 Jul*: France proclaims Algeria independent after an Algerian referendum has shown an overwhelming wish for independence. *Sep*: Mohammed Ben Bella becomes Algeria's first President.

    Basil Spence: Coventry cathedral (complete) (U.K.)

Frederick Gibberd: Roman Catholic Cathedral of Christ the King, Liverpool (begun, replacing Lutyens' *1929* design)

Kenneth Noland: *Cantabile*

Bridget Riley: *Movements with Squares*

Robert Rauschenberg: *Ace*

Roy Lichtenstein: *Blam!*

Andy Warhol: *Green Coca-Cola Bottles; 100 Cans*

Francis Bacon: *Three Studies for a Crucifixion*

Graham Sutherland: *Christ in Glory* (tapestry)

Vladimir Nabokov: *Pale Fire*

Giorgio Bassani: *The Garden of the Finzi Continis*

James Baldwin: *Another Country*

Anthony Burgess: *A Clockwork Orange*

Philip Roth: *Letting Go*

Anthony Powell: *The Kindly Ones*

William Faulkner: *The Reivers* (Faulkner dies 6 *Jul*, aged 64)

Ken Kersey: *One Flew Over the Cuckoo's Nest*

Alexander Solzhenitsyn: *One Day in the Life of Ivan Denisovich*

Edward Albee: *Who's Afraid of Virginia Woolf?*

Arnold Wesker: *Chips with Everything*

Ann Jellicoe: *The Knack*

Friedrich Dürrenmatt: *Die Physiker* (The Physicist)

Dmitri Shostakovitch: *Katerina Ismailova; Symphony No 13*

Michael Tippett: *King Priam*

Benjamin Britten: *War Requiem*

Roy Harris: *Symphony No 8*

David Diamond: *Symphony No 7*

Darius Milhaud: *Symphony No 12*

William Schuman: *Symphony No 8*

Sten Broman: *Symphony No 1*

Pierre Boulez: *Pli selon pli*

Beach Boys: *Surfin' Safari* (popular song)

1963   *1 Jan*: Martin Luther King makes a speech at the Lincoln Memorial in Washington: 'I have a dream that one day sons of former slaves and the sons of former slaveowners will be able to sit down together at the table of brotherhood'. *10 Apr*: the nuclear-powered submarine *USS*

Thresher sinks in the North Atlantic killing all 129 men on board; it is the world's worst submarine disaster. *16 Jun*: David Ben Gurion, Israel's Premier, resigns aged 76, and is succeeded by Levi Eshkol. *26 Jun*: during a four-day visit to West Germany, President Kennedy makes a speech in West Berlin designed to make the people of the beleaguered city feel supported: 'Ich bin ein Berliner'. *18 Oct*: the British Prime Minister Harold Macmillan resigns believing, on his doctor's advice, that he is terminally ill with cancer. He is not. *1 Nov*: a coup organized by General Duong Van Minh overturns the South Vietnamese government of Ngo Dinh Diem. *22 Nov*: President John F. Kennedy is assassinated in Dallas by Lee Oswald. *24 Nov*: nightclub owner Jack Ruby murders Lee Oswald while Oswald is in custody at the Dallas city jail. *12 Dec*: Kenya gains its independence, with Jomo Kenyatta as President.

⌂ Pietro Belluschi and Walter Gropius: Pan Am Building, New York

   Ronald Ward: Millbank Tower, London

✇ Roy Lichtenstein: Whaam!; Hopeless; Girl at Piano

   Francis Bacon: Man and Child

   Andy Warhol: Jackie

   David Hockney: Second Marriage; Picture Emphasizing Stillness

   Bridget Riley: Fall; Fission

   Josef Albers: Homage to the Square 'Curious'

📖 Julio Cortazar: *Hopscotch*

   Heinrich Böll: *The Clown*

   Günter Grass: *Hundejahre* (Dog Years)

   Kingsley Amis: *One Fat Englishman*

   Yukio Mishima: *The Sailor Who Fell From Grace With The Sea*

   John Fowles: *The Collector*

   John Updike: *The Centaur*

   John Le Carré: *The Spy Who Came in from the Cold*

   Andrei Sinyavsky: *The Icicle*

   Sylvia Plath: *The Bell Jar* (Plath commits suicide *11 Feb*, aged 31)

♫ Richard Rodney Bennett: *The Mines of Sulphur*

   Paul Hindemith: *The Long Christmas Dinner*

Benjamin Britten: *Cantata Misericordium*
Howard Hanson: *Song of Human Rights*
Michael Tippett: *Concerto for Orchestra*
John Lennon and Paul McCartney: *I Want To Hold Your Hand* (popular song)

1964 More European colonies gain their independence: Malta, Malawi, Zambia, Tanzania. *Jan*: the Boston Strangler makes his final attack. *1 Apr*: President Goulart of Brazil is overthrown in a military coup: President Johnson of the U.S. prepares to move in to stop a socialist takeover in Brazil. *27 May*: Prime Minister Nehru of India dies suddenly, aged 74, and is succeeded by Lal Shastri. *11 Jun*: after fighting has broken out in Cyprus between Greeks and Turks, the Greek government in Athens refuses to open talks with Ankara. *9 Aug*: the UN orders a cease-fire in Cyprus. *17 Aug*: Greece withdraws her military support from NATO. *27 Sep*: the Warren Commission Report is published; it claims that Lee Oswald alone was responsible for the assassination of President Kennedy and that there was no conspiracy; the report only serves to fuel conspiracy theories about the murder. *2 Nov*: King Saud of Saudi Arabia is deposed and replaced by his brother Faisal.

Prudential Tower, Boston (completed)
Washington Cathedral Tower
Bertrand Goldberg: Marina City, Chicago
Denys Lasdun: Royal College of Physicians, Regent's Park, London
Richard Sheppard: Churchill College, Cambridge
Andy Warhol: Shot Orange Marilyn
Hans Hofmann: Rising Moon
Frank Stella: Fez
René Magritte: The Sin of Man; The Man in the Bowler Hat
Robert Rauschenberg: Retroactive II
Jean Arp: Classic Figure (sculpture)
Roger Sessions: *Montezuma*; *Symphony No 5*
Benjamin Britten: *Curlew River*
Luigi Dallapiccola: *Parole di San Paolo*
John Lennon and Paul McCartney: *She Loves You*; *A Hard Day's Night* (popular songs)

Brian Wilson: *I Get Around* (popular song)

Antonio Jobim: *The Girl From Ipanema* (popular song, words V. de Moraes)

1965 The Maldives and The Gambia gain their independence. *7 Feb*: U.S. bombers begin bombing targets in North Vietnam. *Mar*: the Romanian Premier Gheorghiu-Dej dies and is succeeded by Nicolae Ceausescu, who is now 47 and will rule despotically until *1989*. *8 Mar*: U.S. marines are landed at Da Nang, in the first deployment of ground troops in Vietnam. *28 Jul*: as many as 125,000 Americans are now in Vietnam. President Johnson announces a doubling of draft calls. *Sep*: in Indonesia the army crushes a Communist revolt. *Oct*: Ian Smith, Prime Minister of Rhodesia travels to London to demand immediate independence for Rhodesia. Harold Wilson, the British Prime Minister, refuses unless better representation of black Rhodesians is envisaged with a view to eventual majority rule. *8 Oct*: in Indonesia a general massacre of Communists leaves 400,000 dead. *11 Oct*: Rhodesia declares independence unilaterally; London calls the declaration illegal and announces economic sanctions against Rhodesia. *12 Oct*: the UN calls on all nations to refuse aid to the illegal regime in Rhodesia. *25 Oct*: in the Congo Republic, General Mobutu deposes President Kasavubu and makes himself President in a bloodless coup.

✉ Zeeland Bridge, Netherlands (longest bridge in Europe)

Eero Saarinen: Gateway Arch, St. Louis; CBS Building, New York

Gunther Franke: TV Tower, Alexanderplatz, Berlin

Mies van der Rohe: Neue Nationalgalerie, Berlin

Hugh Casson: Elephant House, London Zoo

Post Office Tower, London (completed)

🎨 Pablo Picasso: Self-portrait

Ed Ruscha: Every Building on the Sunset Strip

📖 Jerzy Kosinski: *The Painted Bird*

Alain Robbe-Grillet: *La maison de rendezvous* (The House of Assignation)

Ian Fleming: *Thunderball*

Joe Orton: *Loot*

> Neil Simon: *The Odd Couple*
> James Baldwin: *The Amen Corner*
> Harold Pinter: *The Homecoming*
> Leonard Bernstein: *Chichester Psalms*
> Michael Tippett: *The Vision of St. Augustine*
> William Walton: *The Twelve*
> John Taverner: *Cain and Abel*
> Charles Ives: *From the Steeples and Mountains* (composed in *1901*)

1966 Lesotho and Guyana gain their independence. *11 Jan*: Lal Shastri Prime Minister of India dies, aged 61, and is succeeded by Mrs. Indira Gandhi, the 48-year-old daughter of Jawaharlal Nehru. Alberto Giacometti the artist and sculptor dies, aged 64, at Chur in Switzerland. *17 Feb*: the artist Hans Hofmann dies, aged 85, in New York. *22 Feb*: Milton Obote Prime Minister of Uganda assumes full powers. *24 Feb*: in Ghana, President Nkrumah is deposed while away on a visit to Beijing. *11 Mar*: President de Gaulle announces that France will take her troops out of NATO and that NATO must remove its bases and headquarters from France within the year. *17 Jun*: the artist Jean Arp dies, aged 78, at Basel. *1 Jul*: President Mobutu of the Democratic Rebulic of Congo, having taken legislative power away from Parliament earlier in the year renames the main towns; Stanleyville is now Kisingani, Elizabethville Lubumbashi and Leopoldville Kinshasa. *6 Sep*: South African Prime Minister Henrik Verwoerd is assassinated, ironically, by a poor white. *13 Nov*: Israeli tanks and planes attack Sammu, a Jordanian village, in retaliation for PLO raids. *Dec*: Ian Smith, President of Rhodesia, meets Harold Wilson the British Prime Minister for talks on a warship and makes tentative agreements that Rhodesia will have majority rule within 15 years. *5 Dec*: Smith's government in Salisbury rejects the agreement. *6 Dec*: Wilson appeals for UN sanctions against Smith and the UN readily agrees: only Portugal and South Africa refuse to participate in sanctions.

> Seifert and Partners: Centrepoint, London
> Jacques Brownson: Civic Center, Chicago (completed)

John Portman: Hyatt Regency Hotel, Atlanta (completed)

Wallace K. Harrison: Metropolitan Opera House, New York (completed)

Marc Chagall: Le triomphe de la musique

Bridget Riley: Drift 2

Roy Lichtenstein: Yellow and Red Brushstrokes

Bruce Nauman: Sculpture Platform (sculpture)

Cesar Baldaccini: The Thumb

Mao Tse Tung: *Sayings of Chairman Mao*

Konrad Lorenz: *On Aggression*

Truman Capote: *In Cold Blood*

Paul Scott: *The Jewel in the Crown*

John Fowles: *The Magus*

Anthony Powell: *The Soldier's Art*

Mario Vargas Llosa: *The Green House*

Jose Lezama Lima: *Paradise*

Shusaka Endo: *Silence*

Mary Renault: *The Mask of Apollo*

James Goldman: *The Lion in Winter*

Peter Shaffer: *Black Comedy*

Samuel Barber: *Antony and Cleopatra* (opening the new Metropolitan Opera House)

Havergal Brian: *Symphony No 1* (written in *1919*)

John Taverner: *The Whale*

Harrison Birtwistle: *Punch and Judy*

Gordon Crosse: *Changes*

Benjamin Britten: *The Burning Fiery Furnace*

Tadeusz Baird: *Tomorrow*

Gunter Bialas: *Hero und Leander*

Dmitri Shostakovitch: *Cello Concerto No 2*

Roger Sessions: *Symphony No 6*

John Kander: *Money, Money* (popular song, words Fred Ebb)

John Lennon and Paul McCartney: *Eleanor Rigby* (popular song)

Brian Wilson: *Good Vibrations* (popular song)

1967 *Feb*: Martin Luther King speaks out against U.S. involvement in Vietnam; popular feeling increasingly runs against the war as more young men are shipped to Vietnam and casualties mount. *15 Apr*: anti-war demonstrations in San Francisco and New York gain massive support. *21 Apr*: a right-wing coup in Greece puts the colonels in power for seven years, led by George Papadopoulos and General Styliano Patakos. Left-wing leaders, including George Papandreou, are arrested. *5 Jun*: the Six-Day Arab-Israeli War starts. *7 Jun*: the Israelis take the Arab part of Jerusalem. *10 Jun*: Moscow severs diplomatic relations with Israel. *17 Jun*: the Chinese explode their first hydrogen bomb, increasing tension between Moscow and Beijing. *4 Jul*: the UN asks Israel to withdraw from Arab Jerusalem. *15 Jul*: Tel Aviv refuses to comply with the UN request, also retaining its hold on the strategic Golan Heights. *25 Jul*: during a state visit to Canada General de Gaulle encourages French-speaking Quebec to break away; he is rebuked for this breach of etiquette by the Canadian Prime Minister and returns to France. *9 Oct*: the revolutionary and terrorist Che Guevara is shot, aged 39, by Bolivian soldiers. *21 Oct*: in the U.S., anti-war demonstrators march on the Pentagon. *3 Dec*: in South Africa, Christian Barnard carries out the world's first heart transplant: the patient lives for only 18 more days, but it is a breakthrough in heart surgery.

Vincent Ponte: Bonaventure Complex, Montreal
Moshe Safde: Habitat, Montreal
John Hancock Center, Chicago (337 metres/1,107 feet, second in height only to the Empire State Building in New York)
Arup Associates: The Snape Maltings (U.K.)
Jean Dubuffet: Borne au logos VII (sculpture)
Barnett Newman: Broken Obelisk (sculpture)
Louise Bourgeois: Homage to Bernini (sculpture)
Bruce Nauman: Henry Moore Bound to Fail (sculpture)
Chaim Potok: *The Chosen*
William Styron: *The Confessions of Nat Tuner*
Gabriel Marquez: *Cien años de soledad* (100 Years of Solitude)
Ngugi wa Thiong'o: *A Grain of Wheat*
Claude Simon: *Histoire*
Günter Grass: *Ausgefragt*

Angus Wilson: *No Laughing Matter*
William Golding: *The Pyramid*
Peter Nichols: *A Day in the Death of Joe Egg*
Tom Stoppard: *Rosencrantz and Guildenstern are Dead*
Rolf Hochhuth: *Soldaten*
Brendan Behan: *Borstal Boy*
♫ William Walton: *The Bear*
Alexander Goehr: *String Quartet No 2*
Peter Maxwell Davies: *Antichrist*

1968 The richest deposits of oil in North America are discovered on the North Slope of Alaska; work begins on
designing a pipeline to take the oil across Alaska's tundra
wilderness to the ice-free port of Valdez (rebuilt since the
1964 earthquake). More European colonies are given
their independence: Nauru, Mauritius, Swaziland and
Equatorial Guinea. The political geography of Africa has
been transformed: within six years only South Africa,
South-West Africa (Namibia) and Rhodesia will remain
under white control. *30 Jan*: the Communists begin a
great Tet offensive: Vietcong and North Vietnamese
troops attack 30 towns in South Vietnam, including
Saigon and Hue. *16 Mar*: the My Lai Massacre: hundreds of innocent civilians in a Vietnamese village are
machine-gunned to death by young U.S. soldiers. *4 Apr*:
Martin Luther King is shot dead on the balcony of a
motel where he is staying. *8 Jun*: King's alleged assassin,
James Earl Ray, is arrested by British police at Heathrow
Airport and sent back to the U.S.: next year Ray will be
found guilty and sentenced but doubts remain about
whether he really acted alone. *27 Aug*: Czech leaders
summoned to the Kremlin return home to announce the
cancellation of various reforms; the Kremlin has become
very anxious about the liberalization of the past few
months.

✐ Henry Cobb: John Hancock Building, Copley
Square, Boston
G.L.C. Architects: Queen Elizabeth Hall and Pur-
cell, Room, London
🌀 Richard Hamilton: The Beatles
Bridget Riley: Late Morning

Frank Stella: Untitled

Michelangelo Pistoletto: Orchestra of Rags (sculpture)

Eva Hesse: Accession III (sculpture)

📖 Muriel Spark: *The Public Image*

Gore Vidal: *Myra Breckenridge*

John Updike: *Couples*

Kurt Vonnegut: *Welcome to the Monkey House*

Alexander Solzhenitsyn: *First Circle*; *Cancer Ward*

Anthony Burgess: *Enderby*

Paul Scott: *The Day of the Scorpions*

Peter Luke: Hadrian VII

🎼 Peter Maxwell Davies: *Taverner*

Humphrey Searle: *Hamlet*

Pierre Boulez: *Livre*

Franz Berwald: *The Queen of Golconda* (composed 1864)

Howard Hanson: *Symphony No 6*

Roger Sessions: *Symphony No 8*

Benjamin Britten: *The Prodigal Son*

Alun Hoddinott: *Symphony No 3*

Havergal Brian: *Symphony No 32* (composed)

Mick Jagger and Keith Richard: *Jumpin' Jack Flash* (popular song)

Michel Legrand: *The Windmills of Your Mind* (popular song, words A. Bergman)

1969 *8 Jun:* U.S. President Richard Nixon meets President Thieu of South Vietnam and announces the beginning of U.S. troop withdrawal. *18 Jul:* Senator Edward Kennedy drives off Dike Bridge into Poucha Pond on Chappaquiddick Island; although he manages to escape from the sinking car, his companion Mary Jo Kopechne does not. Unaccountably, Kennedy does not report Miss Kopechne's death to the police for 10 hours; questions are raised concerning the Senator's judgment at a critical moment in his political career. *21 Jul:* people walk on the moon for the first time: Neil Armstrong and Buzz Aldrin step out of the *Apollo 11* module and walk about on the moon's dusty surface; many Americans believe it has been staged in a studio as a diversion from the Vietnam War.

    ✎ Derek Walker, Richard Llewellyn-Davies and Milton Keynes Development Corporation Architects: Milton Keynes, (U.K.) (new city)

    ✎ Mark Rothko: Orange Yellow Orange
Willem de Kooning: Montauk
Gilbert Proesch and George Passmore: Underneath the Arches
Richard Serra: One-Ton Prop (sculpture)
Louise Bourgeois: Cumul I (sculpture)

    📕 Vladimir Nabokov: *Ada*
Mikhail Bulgakov: *The Monster and Margarita* (Bulgakov died, aged 48, in *1940*)
Alberto Moravia: *La vita e gioco*
Nathalie Sarraute: *Entre la vie et le mort* (Between Life and Death)
Mario Puzo: *The Godfather*
Kurt Vonnegut: *Slaughterhouse Five*
Philip Roth: *Portnoy's Complaint*
Yukio Mishima: *Spring Snow*
Joe Orton: *What the Butler Saw*

    𝄞 Harrison Birtwistle: *Down By The Greenwood Side*
Peter Maxwell Davies: *Eight Songs for a Mad King*
Dmitri Shostakovitch: *Symphony No 14*
Burt Bacharach: *Raindrops Keep Falling On My Head* (popular song)

1970 Tonga and Fiji are given their independence. *Jan*: Israeli jets raid the suburbs of Cairo. *12 Jan*: the civil war in Nigeria ends as General Effiong, the Biafran chief of staff, surrenders; 2 million people, mostly civilians, have died during the war. *16 Jan*: Colonel Muammar Gadaffi, who is now 27, assumes power in Libya. *25 Feb*: the artist Mark Rothko commits suicide in New York, aged 66. *29 May*: the artist Eva Hesse dies of a brain tumour at the age of 34. *24 Jul*: President Nasser of Egypt accepts a peace formula put forward by the U.S. *26 Jul*: Jordan accepts the peace formula. *27 Jul*: the Portuguese Dictator Antonio Salazar dies, aged 81 and is replaced as Premier by Marcello Caetano. *31 Jul*: Israel accepts the peace formula. *2 Aug*: while diplomats of many countries work to make peace, the Arabs and Israelis begin fighting again. *9 Aug*: Israeli jet fighters attack what they believe are guerrilla bases in southern Lebanon. *15 Sep*: a civil war breaks out in Jordan, ending *26 Sep*. King Hussein narrowly escapes yet another assassination attempt. *28 Sep*: President Nasser of Egypt dies, aged 52. *14 Oct*: Nasser's associate Anwar Sadat, who is now 51, is elected President of Egypt. *3 Nov*: the 62-year-old Salvador Allende takes office as President of Chile. He will nationalize much of the Chilean economy, recognize the Castro administration in Cuba, and be regarded as a danger by the U.S. *9 Nov*: Charles de Gaulle (born *1890*) dies, aged 79. *25 Nov*: the Japanese novelist Yukio Mishima harangues a thousand troops on the disgrace of losing the war in *1945* and tries to persuade them to join his private army and launch a military coup. When he realizes his efforts are futile Mishima commits suicide in a ceremonial act of *seppuku*.

Denys Lasdun: University of East Anglia U.K.

Romare Bearden: Patchwork Quilt

Alice Neel: Andy Warhol

Robert Smithson: Spiral Jetty (sculpture)

Eva Hesse: Untitled (sculpture)

Robertson Davies: *Fifth Business*

Nadine Gordimer: *A Guest of Honour*

Saul Bellow: *Mr. Sammler's Planet*

Ernest Hemingway: *Islands in the Stream*

Yukio Mishima: *Runaway Horses*

Anthony Shaffer: *Sleuth*

Paul Zindel: *The Effect of Gamma Rays on Man-in-the-Moon Marigolds*

Alan Ayckbourn: *How the Other Half Loves*

Luciano Berio: *Laborintus II*

Tadeusz Baird: *Goethe Letters*

Michael Tippett: *The Knot Garden*

Richard Rodney Bennett: *Victory*

David Bedford: *The Garden of Love*

Nicholas Maw: *The Rising of the Moon*

Simon and Garfunkel: *Bridge Over Troubled Water* (popular song)

Elton John: *Your Song* (popular song)

John Lennon and Paul McCartney: *Let It Be* (popular song)

1971   *25 Jan*: President Obote of Uganda is ousted while away on a conference. The coup is engineered by 44-year-old General Idi Amin, who seizes power and begins a brutal and capricious reign of terror. *10 Feb*: an earthquake measuring 6.6 on the Richter scale shakes Los Angeles, killing 51 people. *13 Feb*: South Vietnamese troops aided by U.S. troops invade Laos to take out North Vietnamese supply depots but they are driven out with heavy casualties. *31 Mar*: Lt. William Calley is convicted by a military tribunal of killing civilians at My Lai. *6 Apr*: President Nixon frees Calley pending further enquiries. *22 Apr*: 'Papa Doc', President Duvalier of Haiti, dies and is succeeded by his 19-year-old son Jean-Claude as 'President for life'. *May*: the East German Communist Party leader Walter Ulbricht retires, aged 78, and is succeeded by Erich Honecker. *13 Sep*: Lin Pao, the 65-year-old Chinese Defence Minister who has led a futile coup against Mao Tse Tung, dies in a plane crash in Mongolia as he tries to escape from China. *27 Oct*: President Mobutu changes the name of the Democratic Republic of Congo to Zaire; he also renames the River Congo the River Zaire.

    Aswan High Dam, Egypt (completed)
       Standard Oil of Indiana Building, Chicago (completed, 337 metres 1,107 ft high)
    Willem de Kooning: Amityville
       David Hockney: Mr. and Mrs. Clark and Percy
    Anthony Powell: *Books Do Furnish a Room*
       Kingsley Amis: *Girl, 20*
       V. S. Naipaul: *In a Free State*
       Dee Brown: *Bury My Heart at Wounded Knee*
       John Updike: *Rabbit Redux*
       E. M. Forster: *Maurice*
       Es'kia Mphahlele: *The Wanderers*
       Heinrich Böll: *Group Portrait with Lady*
       Yukio Mishima: *The Decay of the Angel; The Temple at Dawn*
       Herman Wouk: *Winds of War*
       Simon Gray: *Butley*
       David Storey: *The Changing Room*
    Benjamin Britten: *Owen Wingrave*

Egon Wellesz: *Symphony No 9*
John McCabe: *Symphony No 2*
Andrew Lloyd Webber: *Jesus Christ Superstar* (musical, words Tim Rice)
Stephen Schwartz: *Godspell*

1972 *5 Jan:* President Nixon authorizes a 5½ billion dollar space shuttle programme for the U.S. *14 Jan:* Frederick IX of Denmark dies, aged 72, and is succeeded by his 31-year-old daughter Margrethe II. *20 Feb:* U.S. President Nixon arrives in Beijing to meet Chairman Mao and Premier Zhou En-lai, bringing the period of U.S. hostility towards China that began in *1949* to an end. *3 Mar:* Beijing's UN representative claims Hong Kong for China. Zhou En-lai assures the North Vietnamese that no secret deals were made with Nixon regarding the future of Indo-China. *10 Apr:* an earthquake in Iran kills 5,000. *16 Apr:* U.S. bombers attack Hanoi, the first raid on a North Vietnamese city by the U.S. since *1968.* *19 Apr:* heated debate in the U.S. Senate about the resumption of bombing. *22 May:* Ceylon becomes the republic of Sri Lanka. Nixon arrives in Moscow for talks with Party Secretary Brezhnev. *17 Jun:* the Watergate affair begins as five men are arrested while burgling the Democratic party's national headquarters in the Watergate complex in Washington. *31 Jul:* Paul Spaak dies, aged 73; he was one of the founders of the European Community which this year has expanded to become, with 257 million people, the world's most powerful trading bloc. *1 Aug: Washington Post* reporters publish a link they have found between the break-in at the Watergate building and the Committee for the Re-Election of the President (CREEP). *22 Dec:* an earthquake in Nicaragua badly damages the city of Managua, killing thousands.

✍ Minoru Yamasaki: World Trade Center, New York (411-metre/1,350-foot high twin towers, 110 storeys: it is the world's tallest building)
William Pereira: Transamerica Corp. Building, San Francisco

✆ Andy Warhol: Mao
Vito Acconci: Seedbed (sculpture)

Duncan Grant: The Sharaku Scarf
MIT Scientists: *The Limits to Growth*
Frederick Forsyth: *The Day of the Jackal*
Richard Adams: *Watership Down*
Margaret Drabble: *The Needle's Eye*
Robertson Davies: *Manticore*
Alexander Solzhenitsyn: *August 1914*
Tom Stoppard: *Jumpers*
Tennessee Williams: *Small Craft Warnings*
Aaron Copland: *Three Latin American Sketches*
Michael Tippett: *Symphony No 3*
Dominick Argento: *A Ring of Time*
Alexander Goehr: *Piano Concerto*
Andrew Lloyd Webber: *Joseph and the Amazing Technicolor Dreamcoat* (musical, words Tim Rice)

1973 An energy crisis grips the developed countries of the world. *Jan*: hostilities begin in the Near East as Israeli fighters shoot down 13 Syrian MIG-21 jets. Fighting erupts along the Suez Canal, where Egyptians cross at five places to threaten Israel and the Syrians attack at two points in the Golan Heights. *28 Jan*: a cease-fire in Vietnam ends the ground fighting as far as U.S. troops are concerned. *1 Apr*: after five men have been found guilty of the break-in at Watergate, President Nixon announces 'major developments in the case'; White House aides Haldeman and Erlichman resign under pressure, while legal aide John Dean is pressed to implicate others in testimony before an investigating committee set up by the Senate. *8 Apr*: Pablo Picasso dies, aged 91, at Mongins in France. *25 May*: the Peronist Hector Campora is elected President of Argentina. *20 Jun*: the former Dictator Juan Peron returns to Argentina after 17 years in exile: he is now 77. *29 Jun*: Nixon tells Congress, 'While we (the U.S.) have only six per cent of the world's population, we consume one-third of the world's energy output. The supply of energy is not keeping pace with demand.' This marks the dawning of an awareness among politicians that the world's resources are finite and need more careful husbanding. *11 Sep*: in Chile, General Augusto Pinochet overthrows the Marxist Allende government in a violent coup. In an account that stretches credibility, Pinochet claims that President Allende machine-gunned himself to death during the takeover. Pinochet begins a repressive anti-communist rule. *15 Sep*: Gustavus VI of Sweden dies aged 90, and is succeeded by his 23-year-old son Carl Gustavus XVI. *6 Oct*: the Yom Kippur War begins in the Near East, the fiercest Arab-Israeli war of the four since *1948*. *12 Oct*: Israeli forces press north to within 29 km/18 miles of Damascus. *15 Oct*: Moscow announces that it will give every assistance to the Arabs to help them regain territory lost to Israel in *1967*. *17 Oct*: tank battles begin in Sinai between Egypt and Israel. *20 Oct*: Soviet Premier Kosygin meets President Sadat of Egypt in Cairo for talks; U.S. Secretary of State Kissinger meets Brezhnev in Moscow. The U.S. and U.S.S.R. make a joint call for a cease-fire. The Watergate prosecutor Cox is dismissed after insisting that Nixon hand over tapes of conversations with aides relevant to the Watergate break-in. Attorney-General Richardson resigns in protest. Nixon appoints Leon Jaworski to succeed Cox and hands over the tapes, but they turn out to have gaps. *24 Oct*: Israel and Egypt agree to a cease-fire in the Yom Kippur war. Israel has suffered 4,100 casualties in the war, Syria 7,300 and Egypt 7,500.

✈ New London Bridge (U.K)
Skidmore, Owings and Merrill: Sears Tower, Chicago (completed; 110 storeys, 443 metres/1,455 feet high, the world's tallest building)

✎ Robert Smithson: Amarillo Ramp (Smithson dies *20 Jul* in a plane crash)

📖 Gore Vidal: *Burr*
Iris Murdoch: *The Black Prince*
Anthony Powell: *Temporary Kings*
Thomas Pynchon: *Gravity's Rainbow*
Italo Calvino: *The Castle of Crossed Destinies*
Octavio Paz: *The Bow and the Lyre*
Peter Shaffer: *Equus*
Alan Ayckbourn: *Absurd Person Singular*
David Storey: *Cromwell*

♫ Alun Hoddinott: *Symphony No 5*
Benjamin Britten: *Death in Venice*

Cornelius Cardew: *The Old and the New*
Harrison Birtwistle: *Grimethorpe Aria*
Elton John: *Goodbye Yellow Brick Road; Don't Shoot Me I'm Only The Piano Player* (popular songs)
Irwin Levine and L. Russell Brown: *Tie A Yellow Ribbon Round The Old Oak Tree* (popular song)

1974 Hundreds of thousands die in the famine in Bangladesh. In the developing countries economic recession deepens as the effects of the major rise in crude oil prices set by OPEC are felt. *28 Jan*: General Grivas, the Cypriot leader, dies, aged 75. *3 Mar*: a DC-10 crashes outside Paris killing 346. *2 Apr*: President Pompidal of France dies, aged 62. He is succeeded (*19 May*) by Valery Giscard d'Estaing. *18 Mar*: it is announced in Delhi that India has successfully carried out an atom bomb test. The Canadian government protests and suspends aid to India's atomic energy programme. *20 Jul*: Turkish forces invade Cyprus with the intention of restoring Makarios, who has been overthrown by Greek Cypriot troops earlier in the month. Greece mobilizes its army; Moscow puts its troops on alert; the UN calls for a halt to hostilities; heavy fighting continues. *23 Jul*: the military junta in Athens resigns and former premier Caramanlis comes out of exile to head a new civilian government. *9 Aug*: U.S. President Nixon resigns in disgrace one week after The House Judiciary Committee voted to impeach him on charges of obstructing the course of justice, failing to uphold the law and refusing to produce material subpoenaed by the committee. Gerald Ford is sworn is President. *19 Aug*: the U.S. Ambassador to Nicosia, Rodger Davies, is shot dead during a Greek Cypriot demonstration outside his Embassy. *11 Nov*: in Pakistan, a car carrying Ahmad Kasuri is ambushed and Kasuri's father is killed; Kasuri is a vehement critic of President Zulfikar Ali Bhutto and it transpires that the perpetrators of the ambush are members of Bhutto's security force. *26 Nov*: Kakuei Tanaka is forced to resign as Prime Minister of Japan as financial scandals come to light. *7 Dec*: President Makarios returns to Nicosia to find that Turkish forces now occupy almost half of Cyprus. *25 Dec*: the town of Darwin, Australia, is destroyed by a cyclone. *28 Dec*: an earthquake in the mountains in northern Pakistan kills over 5,000 people.

Seifert and Partners: Grand Metropolitan Hotel, Knightsbridge (U.K.)

Minato Ohashi Bridge, Kyoto (completed; world's 3rd longest cantilever bridge)

Charles de Gaulle Airport, Paris (opens)

Don Eddy: New Shoes for H.

Jasper Johns: Corpse and Mirror

Louise Bourgeois: The Destruction of the Father (sculpture)

Joseph Beuys: Coyote (sculpture)

Chris Burden: Trans-Fixed (sculpture)

Jacob Bronowski: *The Ascent of Man*

Bob Woodward and Carl Bernstein: *All the President's Men*

Alexander Solzhenitsyn: *The Gulag Archipelago*

Graham Greene: *The Honorary Consul*

Anthony Burgess: *Napoleon Symphony*

Robert Pirsig: *Zen and the Art of Motorcycle Maintenance*

Vladimir Nabokov: *Look at the Harlequins*

Robert Lowell: *The Dolphin*

Anne Sexton: *The Death Notebooks* (Sexton commits suicide *4 Oct* aged 45)

Tom Stoppard: *Travesties*

Gordon Crosse: *The Story of Vasco*

Iain Hamilton: *The Catiline Conspiracy*

Günter Bialas: *Der Gestiefelte Kater*

1975 More former European colonies achieve independence: Cape Verde Islands, Mozambique, Angola, Surinam and Papua New Guinea; Dahomey changes its name to Benin. *19 Feb*: the Italian composer Luigi Dallapiccola dies in Florence, aged 71. *21 Feb*: former White House aides Mitchell, Haldeman, Erlichman and Mardian are given prison sentences for their part in covering up White House involvement in the Watergate break-in. *6 Mar*: there are huge demonstrations in New Delhi against Indira Gandhi's government. *25 Mar*: King Faisal of Saudi Arabia is assassinated, aged 69, by his 27-year-old nephew Prince Faisal Musad Abdel Aziza;

arrested for selling drugs in the U.S., the Prince will now be beheaded for murder. The new King is the late King's brother Khalid, who will continue Faisal's moderate OPEC policies. *21 Apr*: President Thieu of South Vietnam resigns as North Vietnamese troops close in on Saigon; he leaves the country. *30 Apr*: General Duong van Minh surrenders Saigon as U.S. helicopters try to airlift as many Americans and Vietnamese out as possible. This brings the Vietnam War to an end; it has cost the lives of 56,000 Americans and 1.3 million Vietnamese. *5 Apr*: Chiang Kai-shek President of the Nationalist Republic of China (Taiwan) dies, aged 87, his son Chiang Chingkuo takes over the role of Premier. *11 Jun*: a high court in India rules that Indira Gandhi used unfair practices to gain election in *1971*, that her election was invalid as a result and that she must resign. Mrs. Gandhi refuses to resign. *30 Jun*: Indira Gandhi suppresses dissent and imposes press censorship. *20 Nov*: in Spain, Generalissimo Franco dies, aged 82, after ruling Spain as Dictator for 36 years. Prince Juan Carlos, now 39, is to become King in a return to constitutional monarchy.

✏ Denys Lasdun: The National Theatre, London (completed)

🎨 David Hockney: Sets for *The Rake's Progress* at Glyndebourne
Philip Guston: Blue Light; The Magnet
Roy Lichtenstein: Cubist Still Life with Lemons
Willem de Kooning: Whose Name Was Writ in Water

📖 Malcolm Bradbury: *The History Man*
Patrick White: *The Cockatoo*
Mario Vargas Llosa: *Conversation in the Cathedral*
Gabriel Marquez: *Autumn of the Patriarch*
Paul Scott: *A Division of Spoils* (completing the Raj Quartet)
Anthony Powell: *Hearing Secret Harmonies*
Saul Bellow: *Humboldt's Gift*
Bernard Slade: *Same Time, Next Year*
Edward Albee: *Seascape*
Harold Pinter: *No Man's Land*

Simon Gray: *Otherwise Engaged*
Pierre Boulez: *Rituel in memoriam Bruno Maderna*
Bruce Springsteen: *Born To Run* (popular song)

1976 *8 Jan*: The Chinese Premier Zhou En-lai dies, aged 77, and is succeeded by Hua Guofeng. *3 Mar*: Mozambique closes its border with Rhodesia: now independent of Portuguese control, the people of Mozambique can join in imposing economic and political sanctions on the illegal regime in Rhodesia. *24 Mar*: there is a bloodless coup in Argentina: the new military junta arrests Isabel Martinez de Peron and declares martial law. *2 Apr*: Prince Sihanouk of Cambodia resigns; the Khmer Rouge leader Pol Pot becomes Prime Minister. *14 Apr*: Spain withdraws troops from Spanish Sahara allowing Morocco to annexe most of the phosphate-rich country. *9 May*: the terrorist Ulrike Meinhof hangs herself in her prison cell in Stuttgart at the age of 42. *17 Jun*: the Ambassador to Lebanon, Francis Meloy, is assassinated in Beirut; Washington advises all U.S. citizens to leave Lebanon. *4 Jul*: Palestinian terrorists have hi-jacked an Air France plane and forced the pilot to fly it to Uganda. Airborne Israeli commandoes storm the plane at Entebbe Airport and successfully free 104 hostages. *26 Jul*: the former Japanese Prime Minister Kakuei Tanaka is arrested on charges of taking a huge bribe from Lockheed. *28 Jul*: Tangshan earthquake kills 655,000 in China in the worst earthquake disaster in recorded history. *21 Sep*: the former Chilean ambassador to the U.S. Orlando Letelier is killed in a car bomb explosion in Washington; he was an outspoken critic of President Pinochet. *10 Sep*: Chairman Mao Tse Tung dies, aged 82. The 'Gang of Four', including Mao's widow Jiang Qing, is arrested and imprisoned in Oct for subverting the party and the economy. *24 Sep*: Ian Smith agrees to accept a scheme for majority rule in Rhodesia by *1978*. *26 Oct*: the South African government gives the province of Transkei nominal independence; the UN calls it a sham: by declaring the 1.3 million Xhosa people citizens of the Transkei it effectively deprives them of South African citizenship. *4 Dec*: the English composer Benjamin Britten dies, aged 63.

    ✐ World Trade Center, Los Angeles
John Portman: Bonaventure Hotel, Los Angeles (completed)
James Rouse: Quincy Market, Boston (restoration of historic city)
Milton Keynes Development Corporation: Cofferidge Close, Stony Stratford, Milton Keynes U.K.
National Exhibition Centre, Birmingham

🎨 Andy Warhol: Skull
Elizabeth Murray: Beginner
Alfred Leslie: Our Family in 1976
David Hockney: Gregory with Gym Socks
Carl André: Bricks (sculpture)
Lucien Freud: Portrait of Frank Auerbach
Christo: Running Fence (sculpture)
Claes Oldenburg: Batcolumn

📖 Michael Harrington: *The Twilight of Capitalism*
Alex Haley: *Roots*
Alice Walker: *Meridian*
Manuel Puig: *Spider Woman*
Patrick Grainville: *Lesa Flamboyants*
Margaret Atwood: *Lady oracle*
Marge Piercy: *Woman on the Edge of Time*
Ira Levin: *The Boys from Brazil*
Daphne du Maurier: *The Winding Stair*
Tom Stoppard: *New-Found Land*
Neil Simon: *California Suite*
Preston Jones: *A Texas Trilogy*

🎵 Harrison Birtwistle: *For O for O, the Hobby Horse is Forgot*
Peter Maxwell Davies: *Symphony No 1*
Gordon Crosse: *Symphony No 2*
Andrew Lloyd Webber: *Don't Cry For Me, Argentina* (musical, popular song)
Philip Glass: *Einstein on the Beach*

1977 *Feb*: General Benti, the 55-year-old President of Ethiopia and 10 other people are killed in a gun battle at a council meeting at Addis Ababa; Colonel Mariam is appointed Head of State. *27 Mar*: at Santa Cruz de Tenerife in the Canary Islands a Boeing 747 collides on take-off with another 747 still on the ground: 582

people die in the two planes. *7 Apr*: in West Germany, terrorists murder the Attorney General who is in charge of the Baader-Meinhof gang prosecutions. *30 Apr*: Andreas Baader and two accomplices are convicted for murder and further outrages follow. *2 Jul*: in China, the 73-year-old leader Deng Xiaoping is restored to power. *3 Jul*: the Prime Minister of Pakistan Zulfikar Ali Bhutto loses power. *3 Sept*: Bhutto is arrested on charges of conspiring to murder Ahmad Kasuri in *1974*. *2 Dec*: a South African magistrate finds that the security police were blameless in the death in police custody of Steve Biko. *4 Dec*: the Central African Republic is renamed Central African Empire as President Jean-Bedel Bokassa has himself crowned Emperor in an extravagant ceremony costing around 10 million pounds.

Hugh Stubbins: Federal Reserve Bank, Boston (completed)

Hugh Stubbins: Citicorp Center, New York (completed)

Skidmore, Owings and Merrill: Olympic Tower, New York (completed)

Colin St. John Wilson: New British Library, London

David Hockney: My Parents; Looking at Pictures on a Screen

Robert Moskowitz: The Swimmer

Balthus: Nude in Profile

Chuck Close: Self-portrait

John Kenneth Galbraith: *The Age of Uncertainty*

James S. Fixx: *The Complete Book of Running* (popularizes jogging)

P. G. Wodehouse: *Sunset at Blandings*

Anne Tyler: *Earthly Possessions*

John Le Carré: *The Honourable Schoolboy*

J. R. R. Tolkien: *The Silmarillion*

Thomas Keneally: *A Season in Purgatory*

John Fowles: *Daniel Martin*

Margaret Drabble: *The Ice Age*

Philip Roth: *The Professor of Desire*

Günter Grass: *Der Butt* (The Flounder)

James Merrill: *Divine Comedies*

Bernard Pomerance: *The Elephant Man*
David Mamet: *A Life in the Theatre*
Per Olov Enquist: *The Night of the Tribades*
Sten Broman: *Symphony No 10*
Milton Babbitt: *A Solo Requiem*
Michael Tippett: *Symphony No 4*; *The Ice Break*
Frederick Delius: *The Magic Fountain*
Iain Hamilton: *Tamburlaine*

1978 Former European colonies Tuvalu, Dominica and the Solomon Islands gain their independence. *7 Jan*: on the 15th anniversary of the Shah's land reform and women's emancipation decrees there are religious riots in the holy city of Qom in Iran. *15 Mar*: Red Brigade terrorists in Italy abduct and later murder Aldo Moro, the 61-year-old former Prime Minister of Italy. *27 Apr*: pro-Soviet socialists in Afghanistan overthrow President Daud, replacing him with Mur Muhammad Taraki, who concludes a long-term military treaty with Moscow. *9 May*: Aldo Moro's bullet-riddled body is found in a car boot in Rome. *9 Jun*: the Shah of Iran arrests the Chief of the Savak secret police on charges of torturing prisoners. *24 Jun*: the President of North Yemen is killed by a bomb as he receives the credentials of a new Ambassador from South Yemen. *6 Aug*: Pope Paul VI dies, aged 80; he is succeeded by John Paul I. *20 Aug*: a packed cinema in Abadan, Iran, burns down killing 377 people; the Shah's enemies say Savak agents started the fire, while the Shah's supporters say Islamic Marxists did it. *22 Aug*: President Jomo Kenyatta of Kenya dies, aged 86, and is succeeded by Daniel Mori. In Nicaragua, left-wing guerrillas seize the National Palace in Managua and hold hundreds of people hostage in an attempt to depose Somoza. The Sandinista rebels take their name from the guerrilla leader General Sandino. *16 Sep*: President Chaudry of Pakistan comes to the end of his term of office; General Mohammed Zia ul-Haq declares himself the new President. *17 Sep*: the Camp David Accord: after a fortnight of discussion mediated by U.S. President Carter, Prime Minister Begin of Israel and President Sadat of Egypt come to an agreement on a 'framework for peace'. *28 Sep*: Pope John Paul I dies after only 34 days as Pope. *16 Oct*: the Polish cardinal Karol Wojtyla becomes the first non-Italian pope since *1523*, John Paul II. *6 Nov*: the Iranian cabinet resigns and it is replaced by a military government. *29 Dec*: the Shah of Iran asks Shahpur Bakhtiar to form a new civilian government.

🎨 Elizabeth Murray: Children Meeting
Andy Warhol: Self-portrait
Marc Chagall: Arts to the Glory of God, Chichester Cathedral
David Hockney: Le Plongeur; Sets for The Magic Flute
Edward Bawden: Walled Garden

📖 Ian McEwen: *The Cement Garden*
John Cheever: *Falconer*
John Updike: *The Coup*
John Irving: *The World According to Garp*
David Malouf: *An Imaginary Life*
Iris Murdoch: *The Sea, The Sea*
Herman Wouk: *War and Remembrance*
David Hare: *Plenty*
Tom Stoppard: *Night and Day*
Harold Pinter: *Betrayal*

🎼 Dominick Argento: *Miss Havisham's Fire*
John Adams: *Shaker Loops*
Michael Berkeley: *The Wild Winds*

1979 Kiribati (Gilbert Islands) gains its independence. *16 Jan*: the Shah of Iran appoints Prime Minister Bakhtiar to head a Regency and leaves for Egypt after 37 years in power. *30 Jan*: Whites in Rhodesia vote to ratify the new constitution which extends the franchise to the black community; the country is renamed Zimbabwe Rhodesia. *1 Feb*: the Shiite Muslim leader Ayatollah Khomeini, now 78, flies into Teheran from Paris after 15 years in exile. *11 Feb*: after rioting, Bakhtiar resigns; the chaos in Iran worsens during the year as thousands are killed in executions and riots. *14 Feb*: Afghan Muslim extremists abduct the U.S. Ambassador to Kabul, Adolph Dubs; local police try to rescue him and Dubs is killed during the ensuing gunfight. *17 Feb*: Iran's new government announces that oil exports from Iran will resume on 5

Mar, but at a price 30 per cent higher than that agreed by OPEC. *3 Apr*: China warns the U.S.S.R. that it will not seek to renew the *1950* treaty of friendship when it expires in *1980*. *4 Apr*: the former Prime Minister of Pakistan Zulfikar Ali Bhutto is hanged in Rawalpindi Prison for conspiracy to murder. There are protests throughout Pakistan against the execution. *10 Apr*: President Idi Amin is forced into exile as Ugandan exiles and Tanzanian soldiers occupy Kampala, Uganda's capital. Amin's eight years in power have left Uganda over £100 million in debt. *27 Jun*: a reverse discrimination suit in the U.S. courts ends with a startling verdict. Brian Weber sued his union and employer over a training progarmme that gave preference to blacks. The Supreme Court's decision in United Steel Workers v. Weber condones 'affirmative action programmes'. *17 Jul*: the Nicaraguan Dictator Somoza resigns after a civil war and takes refuge in Miami. *20 Jul*: Sandinista rebels enter Managua and set up a five man junta. *27 Aug*: IRA terrorists detonate a bomb planted on Lord Mountbatten's fishing boat; it explodes, killing Lord Mountbatten and others. *20 Sep*: Emperor Bokassa is overthrown. Even though accused of taking part in a massacre of children, Bokassa is given refuge in the Ivory Coast. Former President Dacko returns to power, restoring the Central African Republic. *15 Oct*: President Romero of El Salvador is deposed in a military coup after several weeks of violence. *22 Oct*: ill with cancer, the Shah of Iran is allowed into the U.S. at Henry Kissinger's insistence, but against the advice of the U.S. Ambassador in Teheran. *4 Nov*: Iranian extremists seize the U.S. embassy in Teheran, taking 66 hostages and demanding that the U.S. extradite the Shah. *15 Nov*: the English art historian Sir Anthony Blunt is exposed as a one-time Soviet spy; he is stripped of his knighthood. *16 Dec*: the Shah leaves the U.S. for Panama. *24 Dec*: Soviet troops invade Afghanistan, apparently invited by the new President, Amin. *27 Dec*: a 'revolutionary tribunal' in Kabul convicts President Amin of treason and orders him to be executed. He is replaced by a figurehead President, Babrak Karmal.

    Helmut Jahn: Xerox Centre, Chicago (completed)
I. M. Pei and Partners: John F. Kennedy Library, Boston (completed)
David Hockney: Divine
Miton Resnick: Elephant
Claes Oldenburg: Crusoe Umbrella (mural)
Vito Acconci: The People Machine
Telford Taylor: *Munich: the Price of Peace*
Ezra Vogel: *Japan as Number One*
Margaret Atwood: *Life Before Man*
Nadine Gordimer: *Burger's Daughter*
Muriel Spark: *Territorial Rights*
William Styron: *Sophie's Choice*
V. S. Naipaul: *A bend in the River*
Es'kia Mphahlele: *Chirundu*
William Golding: *Darkness Visible*
Penelope Fitzgerald: *Offshore*
Peter Shaffer: *Amadeus*
Malcolm Arnold: *Beckus the Dandipratt*
Michael Tippett: *Triple Concerto for Violin, Viola and Cello*
Alexander Goehr: *Babylon the Great is Fallen*

1980 In the U.S., smoking has dropped 28 per cent among male adults, 13 among women, 20 per cent among boys: the habit has increased 50 per cent among girls. *6 Jan*: Indira Gandhi regains power in India in an election victory managed by her 33-year-old son Sanjay. *24 Mar*: in El Salvador, the human rights activist Archbishop Oscar Romero is assassinated by a sniper while he is saying mass. *18 Apr*: Zimbabwe (formerly Rhodesia) gains its independence and a new government takes power under black Marxist Robert Mugabe. *30 Apr*: Queen Juliana of the Netherlands abdicates, aged 71, in favour of her 42-year-old daugher Beatrix. *4 May*: President Tito of Yugoslavia dies, aged 87; his death leaves a power vacuum raising fears that the country may quickly disintegrate into many small warring states again. *18 May*: The Mount St. Helens volcano erupts, sending enormous quantities of ash sideways, rather than upwards, as the north slope of the mountain unexpectedly collapses. *23 Jun*: Indira Gandhi's 33-year-old son

Sanjay, who was expected to follow her in the 'dynastic' succession, is killed in a plane crash while he is performing illegal aerial acrobatics. *26 Jan*: the Shah of Iran dies of cancer after being invited to Cairo for surgery by President Sadat. *14 Aug*: Polish shipyard workers at Gdansk go on strike in protest at rising food prices. The strike spreads, with workers demanding the legal right to strike and to form unions without Communist party control. The strikes are orchestrated by electrician Lech Walesa, who is now 37. *17 Sep*: Anastasio Somosa, the 54-year-old former Nicaraguan Dictator, is machine gunned to death in Asuncion, Paraguay while being driven in his Mercedes. *8 Dec*: the singer John Lennon is murdered outside his New York apartment; his death leads to renewed calls for laws controlling the ownership of guns.

 Philip Johnson and John Burgee: Crystal Cathedral, Garden Grove, California.

 Ralph Erskine: Byker Development, Newcastle-upon-Tyne, (U.K.)

 Gruzen and Partners: Grand Hyatt Hotel, New York (completed)

 Anselm Keifer: To the Unknown Painter

 Howard Brenton: *The Romans in Britain*

 Carl Sagan: *Cosmos*

 Umberto Eco: *The Name of the Rose*

 Anthony Burgess: *Earthly Powers*

 William Golding: *Rites of Passage*

 Shirley Hazzard: *The Transit of Venus*

 Mark Medoff: *Children of a Lesser God*

 Ronald Harwood: *The Dresser*

 Willy Russell: *Educating Rita*

 Isabel Colegate: *The Shooting Party*

 Angus Wilson: *Setting the World on Fire*

 J. L. Carr: *A Month in the Country*

 William Mathias: *The Servants*

 Harrison Birtwistle: *On the Sheer Threshold of the Night*

 George Benjamin: *Ringed by the Flat Horizon*

 Philip Glass: *Satyagraka*

1981 World population reaches 4.5 billion with about 960 million in China alone. Acquired Immune Deficiency Sydrome (AIDS) is positively identified in California and New York, where the disease at first perplexed doctors; AIDS will quickly spread wolrdwide and draw comparisons with the Black Death of the 14th century. Belize, Antigua and Barbuda gain their independence. *20 Jan*: Iran releases all the U.S. hostages, who have been held captive for more than a year. *13 May*: Pope John Paul II is wounded in an assassination attempt in St. Peter's Square in Rome. *7 Jun*: Israel sends jets into Iraq to destroy the Osirak nuclear reactor, determined to stop her neighbours from developing nuclear weapons. President Bani-Sadr of Iran is dismissed; he leaves Iran for France. *Jun 28*: a bomb attack in Teheran kills Ayatollah Beheshti, the Chief Justice and Head of the Islamic Republican Party, and four major government ministers. *30 Aug*: another bomb attack in Teheran kills the President, Ali Rajai, the Prime Minister, Hojatolislam Bahonar, and Colonel Dagsgerdi. *Sep*: President Sadat of Egypt takes a firmer line with dissidents, having as many as 1,600 arrested in a single night. *11 Sep*: in Teheran, a grenade kills one of Khomeini's aides, Ayatollah Madani. *6 Oct*: President Anwar Sadat of Egypt is assassinated by extremists while he is watching a military parade in Cairo. He is succeeded as President by Hosni Mubarak who affirms his commitment to the peace treaty with Israel that Sadat arranged. *31 Dec*: in a coup in Ghana, Jerry Rawlings seizes power (for the second time), accusing President Limann of ruinous economic policies.

✍ Maya Ying Lin: Vietnam War Memorial, Washington (Lin is 21)

I. M. Pei: City Hall, Dallas (completed)

The Barbican Centre, London (completed)

Humber Bridge, U.K. (world's longest suspension bridge, 1,410 metres 4,626 feet long)

✑ Romare Bearden: Artist with Painting and Model

Alice Neel: Self-portrait (Neel is 81; the portrait is nude)

Robert Moskowitz: Red Mill

Robert Ryman: Paramount

Richard Serra: Tilted Arc (sculpture)

📖 Martin Cruz Smith: *Gorky Park*
John Updike: *Rabbit is Rich*
Salman Rushdie: *Midnight's Children*
Paul Theroux: *The Mosquito Coast*
Nadine Gordimer: *July's People*
Simon Gray: *Quartermaine's Terms*
Harvey Fierstein: *Torch Song Trilogy*
🎼 Peter Maxwell Davies: *Symphony No 2*
Simon Bainbridge: *Landscape and Woods*
Pierre Boulez: *Répons*

1982 *27 Feb*: Wayne Williams, a 23-year-old Black, is found guilty of at least two of the Atlanta child murders. *2 Apr*: the Falkland War begins: Argentine forces invade and capture the Falkland Islands. *5 Apr*: a British fleet sails for the Falklands. *21 Apr*: Israel strikes PLO strongholds in Lebanon in retaliation for PLO guerrilla activities within Israel. *25 Apr*: British troops recapture South Georgia. Israeli troops complete their withdrawal from Sinai as agreed in the Camp David Accord. *2 May*: the Argentine cruiser *General Belgrano* is torpedoed and sunk even though outside the Exclusion Zone demarcated by the British. *9 May*: Israeli jets raid PLO bases south of Beirut; the PLO retaliate with artillery fire across the border into Israel. *14 Jun*: Argentine forces surrender as the British recapture Port Stanley. Fighting ceases in the Falklands. King Khalid of Saudi Arabia dies, aged 68, and is succeeded by his 60-year-old brother Fahd. *17 Jan*: General Galtieri, the Argentine leader, is deposed. *27 Jul*: Israeli jets attack civilian areas in West Beirut, killing 120. *14 Sep*: President Bashir Gemayel of Lebanon is killed in a bomb explosion at his party headquarters in Beirut. He is succeeded by his brother Amin Gemayel, who is 40. *16 Sep*: Israeli troops move into West Beirut too late to prevent a massacre of Palestinians by 'Christian' Falangists. The level of bloodshed brings calls for Prime Minister Begin's resignation. *10 Nov*: Brezhnev dies, aged 75: he is succeeded as Soviet Party Secretary by Yuri Andropov.

✏ I. M. Pei: Texas Commerce Tower, Houston (completed)
I. M. Pei: Fragrant Hills Hotel, Beijing (completed)

The Thames Barrier, London
🐾 Joseph Beuys: Monuments to the Stag
Elizabeth Murray: Keyhole
📖 Saul Bellow: *The Dean's December*
Mario Vargas Llosa: *Aunt Julia and the Scriptwriter*
Gabriel Garcia Marquez: *Chronicle of a Death Foretold*
Yevgeny Yevtushenko: *Berry Patches*
William Golding: *A Moving Target*
Heinrich Böll: *The Safety Net*
Graham Greene: *Monsignor Quixote*
William Boyd: *An Ice-Cream War*
Timothy Mo: *Sour Sweet*
Bruce Chatwin: *On the Black Hill*
Michael Frayn: *Noises Off*
Athol Fugard: *Master Harold . . . and the Boys*
Tom Stoppard: *The Real Thing*
Anthony Shaffer: *Whodunnit*
🎼 Philip Glass: *The Photographer*
David Bedford: *Sun Paints Rainbows on the Vast Waves*
Robin hollaway: *Serenata Notturna*
George Benjamin: *At First Light*
Luciano Berio: *La Vera Storia*
Jack Nitzsche and Buffy Sainte-Marie: *Up Where We Belong* (popular song)

1983   *8 Mar*: U.S. President Reagan calls the U.S.S.R. 'an evil empire.' *23 Mar*: Reagan outlines his plan for a Strategic Defence Initiative to defend the U.S. and its allies with flocks of satellites that will intercept incoming missiles. The projected cost is astronomical and the U.S.S.R. sees this as a move to carry the arms race into outer space. *21 Aug*: former Philippine Senator Benigno Aquino is shot dead by an assassin on arrival at Manila airport as he returns to his country. He has been warned that agents of President Marcos or his wife Imelda would kill him, but he decided it was time to organize opposition to Marcos within the Philippines. The assassin is instantly shot dead in what looks like a well-organized conspiracy. *1 Sep*: a Boeing 747 carrying 269 passengers and crew from New York inadvertently strays across Soviet air space off

Sakhalin Island. A Soviet fighter fires an air-to-air missile bringing the plane down in the sea: there are no survivors. The Soviet authorities insist the violation was not a mistake but a deliberate attempt to spy on military installations; Washington reveals that U.S. spy planes have recently been in the area. *15 Sep*: the ailing Israeli Prime Minister Menachem Begin resigns and is succeeded by Yitzhak Shamir, who is now 67. *12 Oct*: a coup in Grenada leaves Prime Minister Maurice Bishop and his cabinet dead as Deputy Prime Minister Bernard Coard takes over. *25 Oct*: U.S. marines land, ordered in by President Reagan; Queen Elizabeth II of the United Kingdom is angered by the intervention of the U.S. in a Commonwealth country's internal affairs. *Dec*: Argentina returns to a civilian government after eight disastrous years of military rule that have led the country into an expensive and abortive war with Britain. *25 Dec*: the artist Joan Miró dies, aged 90, at Palma, Majorca.

Edward Barnes: IBM Building, New York (completed)
Terry Farrell: TV-am Studios, London
Frank Gehry: The Norton House, Venice, California (completed)
Philip Johnson: American Telephone and Telegraph Building, N. Y.

Brice Marden: Elements IV
Jasper Johns: racing Thoughts

Kingsley Amis: *Stanley and the Women*
Philip Roth: *The Anatomy Lesson*
J. M. Coetzee: *The Life and Times of Michael K.*
Peter Ackroyd: *The Last Testament of Oscar Wilde*
Iris Murdoch: *The Philosopher's Pupil*
Malcolm Bradbury: *Rates of Exchange*
William Trevor: *Fools of Fortune*

Peter Maxwell Davies: *Into the Labyrinth*
Harrison Birtwistle: *The Mask of Orpheus*
John Butler: *Towards Aquarius*
John Adams: *Bridge of Dreams*
Michael Jackson: *Beat It* (popular song)
Sting (Gordon Sumner): *Every Breath You Take* (popular song)

1984   *9 Feb*: the Soviet leader Yuri Andropov dies, aged 69;
he is succeeded by Konstantin Chernenko, who is 72.
5–6 Jun: Sikh extremists have occupied the Golden
Temple at Amritsar. Indira Gandhi, India's Prime
Minister, orders troops to storm the temple and as
many as 1,200 Sikhs are killed in the fighting. The
Sikhs have pressed for an independent Sikh state but
Mrs. Gandhi is determined not to let India fragment. *20
Jul*: James Fixx, who has encouraged and popularized
jogging, dies of a heart attack while jogging at Hardwick,
Vermont; he was 52. *3 Aug*: Upper Volta changes its
name to Burkina Faso. *19 Oct*: the pro-Solidarity priest
Jerzy Popieluszko is abducted and murdered by Polish
security police. Public indignation is so great when his
body is found in a reservoir that the policemen have to be
brought to trial; they will be convicted in *Feb* next year.
19 Dec: an agreement is signed in Beijing by Margaret
Thatcher for Britain and Zhao Ziyang for China providing for the transfer of Hong Kong to Chinese control in
1997.

Andy Warhol: Polestar
Vito Acconci: Bad Dream House No 1
Jean Dubuffet: Monument with Standing Beast
Mario Vargas Llosa: *The War of the End of the World*
Gore Vidal: *Lincoln*
Saul Bellow: *Him with His Foot in his Mouth and
Other Stories*
Alan Sillitoe: *Down from the Hill*
Milan Kundera: *The Unbearable Lightness of Being*
Marguerite Duras: *L'Amant*
Anita Brookner: *Hotel du Lac*
Angela Carter: *Nights at the Circus*
William Golding: *The Paper Men*
J. G. Ballard: *Empire of the Sun*
Michael Frayn: *Benefactors*
Beth Henley: *The Miss Firecracker Contest*
Philip Glass: *Akhnaten*
Iain Hamilton: *Lancelot*
Luciano Berio: *Un Re in Scolto*
Peter Dickinson: *Mass of the Apocalypse*
David Deltradici: *Child Alice*

Peter Maxwell Davies: *The No. 11 Bus*
Michael Tippett: *The Mask of Time*
Andrew Lloyd Webber: *Requiem; Starlight Express*
(musical, words R. Stilgoe)

1985   *8 Jan*: Moscow and Washington agree to negotiate
towards limiting and reducing nuclear weapons arsenals
and preventing an arms race in space. *Mar*: British
scientists report the annual development of a huge hole
in the ozone layer over Antarctica, stimulating concern
that industrialization, too, may need to be strategically
limited. *1 Mar*: Uruguay returns to civilian rule under
President Sanguinetti after 12 years of military dictatorship, under which inflation has risen to 66 per cent and
foreign debts amount to £3 billion. U.S. President
Reagan compares the Nicaraguan contras to 'our Founding Fathers'. *11 Mar*: Chernenko dies aged 73 and is
replaced as General Secretary of the Soviet Communist
Party by Mikhail Gorbachev, who is now 54. *15 Mar*:
Brazil returns to civilian rule under President Jose
Sarney after 21 years of military dictatorship. *28 Mar*:
Marc Chagall dies, aged 97. *11 Apr*: Enver Hoxa Dictator of Albania dies aged 78, after 41 years in power, and
is succeeded as Head of the Albanian Communist Party
by Ramiz Alia. *May*: President Reagan visits West
Germany to commemorate the 40th anniversary of the
liberation of the Buchenwald concentration camp but
makes the diplomatic gaffe of visiting the Bitburg Cemetery where officers of the Waffen SS are buried; many
find his visit offensive. *1 Jun*: a TWA airliner is hijacked
between Athens and Rome and diverted to Beirut, where
the passengers are held hostage for 17 days. *23 Jun*: an
Air India Boeing 747 crashes into the North Atlantic
west of Ireland, killing all 329 on board. *18 Jul*: U.S.
Congress votes to stop Reagan supplying arms to the
contras. *21 Jul*: film actor Rock Hudson collapses at the
Paris Ritz. *27 Jul*: President Obote of Uganda leaves the
country following a military coup; he is replaced by
General Tito Okello. *Aug 12*: a Japan Air Lines Boeing
747 on a domestic flight crashes into a mountain, killing
520 in the worst single-plane air accident ever. *17 Aug*: in
the Iran-Iraq War, Iraqi jet fighters carrying French

Exocet missiles bomb Kharg Island, the main Iranian oil terminal. *27 Aug*: President Buhari of Nigeria is overthrown in a coup and replaced by Major General Babangida. *19 Sep*: an earthquake near Mexico City measures 7.8 on the Richter Scale and kills over 5,000. *2 Oct*: film actor Rock Hudson dies, aged 59, of AIDS, heightening American awareness of the impact and seriousness of the disease. *7 Oct*: hijackers seize the cruise ship *Achille Lauro* in the Mediterranean, killing an American passenger in cold blood. *14 Nov*: a volcano erupts in Colombia causing mudflows and floods that kill 25,000 people. *21 Nov*: Gorbachev and Reagan meet to discuss arms control. *23 Nov*: an Egyptian airliner is hijacked between Athens and Cairo and forced to land in Malta; the hijackers kill two people and 58 more are killed during the Egyptian commandoes' inept storming of the plane. *27 Dec*: terrorists attack Vienna and Rome airports, killing 20 people.

Andy Warhol: Van Heusen
Richard Diebenkorn: Ocean Park No. 139
Dorothea Rockbourne: Interior Perspective
Joseph Beuys: Capri-Batterie
Garrison Keillor: *Lake Woebegone Days*
Robertson Davies: *What's Bred in the Bone*
Philip Roth: *Zuckerman Bound*
Iris Murdoch: *The Good Apprentice*
Peter Ackroyd: *Hawksmoor*
Anthony Burgess: *The Kingdom of the Wicked*
John Fowles: *A Maggot*
Herb Gardner: *I'm Not Rappaport*
Keri Hulme: *The Bone People*
Oliver Knussen: *Higglety, Pigglety, Pop!*
Peter Maxwell Davies: *Symphony No 3*
Leonard Bernstein: *Jubilee Games*
Paul McCartney: *We All Stand Together* (popular song)
Eric Clapton and Michael Kamen: *Edge of Darkness* (popular song)

1986 World oil prices collapse. The U.S. national debt exceeds 2 trillion dollars, double what it was in 1981. The U.S. trade deficit worsens; a world recession is on the way. *29*

Jan: a coup in Kampala topples the government: Yoweri Museveni is declared President but fighting continues in northern Uganda. The unmanned spacecraft *Voyager 2* (launched *1977*) flies past Neptune, sending back pictures of previously undiscovered rings and moons. The U.S. programme has a major setback with the explosion one minute after take-off of the shuttle *Challenger*: all seven of its crew are killed instantly. *6 Feb*: President Jean-Claude Duvalier of Haiti resigns, aged 34, and takes sanctuary in France. The régime in Haiti continues much as before. *11 Feb*: in the U.S.S.R. political prisoners, including Anatoly Scharansky and Yuri Orlov, are released and allowed to leave the country. This is one stage in Gorbachev's liberalization programme. *28 Feb*: Olof Palme, the 59-year-old Prime Minister of Sweden, is assassinated on his way home from the cinema with his wife. Who the assassin was may never be known. *6 Mar*: in South Africa police fire on a demonstration, killing 30. *15 Apr*: using Britain as a base, U.S. fighter planes make an 11-minute attack on Gadaffi's headquarters in Tripoli. Reagan ordered the attack as a reprisal for Libyan or Libyan-organized terrorist actions against U.S. citizens in Europe. 15 civilians are killed in the controversial attack: Colonel Gaddafi escapes unharmed. In Lebanon three hostages are killed in retaliation for the U.S. action. *26 Apr*: the nuclear power station at Chernobyl near Kiev in the Ukraine explodes releasing clouds of radioactive fall-out, contaminating much of northern Europe. 30 fire-fighters and plant workers die during the first few weeks after the accident; future cancer deaths resulting from exposure to the radioactive fall-out may range between 7,000 and 40,000. Confidence in nuclear energy and its reliability as a power source is severely shaken throughout Europe. *26 Aug*: in Cameroon, a volcanic eruption beneath a lake releases large volumes of toxic gas, killing 1,500 people in the villages round the lake. *28 Oct*: King Fahd of Saudi Arabia dismisses Sheik Yamani from the Oil Ministry post he has held for 24 years; the King is dissatisfied with the modest prices Sheik Yamani has set for Saudi oil. *Dec*: Gorbachev telephones Andrei Sakharov in Gorky to tell him his exile is over; he may return to Moscow.

Jacob K. Javits Convention Center, New York (completed)

Richard Rodgers: Lloyd's, Leadenhall Street, London

Roy Lichtenstein: Mural with Blue Brushstroke

Louise Bourgeois: Nature Study (bronze)

Donald Judd: Untitled '88 (sculpture)

Kingsley Amis: *The Old Devils*

Mario Vargas Llosa: *The Real Life of Alejandro Mayta*

Margaret Atwood: *The Handmaid's Tale*

John Updike: *Roger's Version*

Alan Ayckbourn: *A Woman in Mind*

Hugh Whitemore: *Breaking the Code*

Harrison Birtwistle: *Yan Tan Tethera*

Robin Holloway: *Inquietus*

Oliver Knussen: *Hell's Angels*

Elliott Carter: *Fanfare*

Peter Maxwell Davies: *Winterfold*

Andrew Lloyd webber: *Phantom of the Opera* (musical, words C. Hart)

1987 Zulu chief Mangosuthu Buthelezi launches a war against the African National Congress in South Africa, dividing the black cause. Chief Buthelezi founded Inkatha, a mainly Zulu organization, in *1975*. General Ben Ali, Prime Minister of Tunisia, declares President Bourguiba unfit to rule and removes him from office at the age of 84. *6 Mar*: the *Herald of Free Enterprise*, a roll-on, roll-off cross-Channel ferry, leaves Zeebrugge Harbour with its bow doors still open. The ship takes on water, capsizes in shallow water and causes the deaths of 192. *11 Jun*: Margaret Thatcher is returned for a third term as British Prime Minister. *25 Jun*: Gorbachev announces plans for a new direction in U.S.S.R. economic policy. He believes central planning is inhibiting economic develpment and that more decisions should be made (and responsibilities taken) at local level. *Jul*: Oliver North testifies before a U.S. congressional committee that his secret activities had support from senior officials in the administration. Admiral Poindexter confirms that he authorized use of profits from arms sales to Iran to support the contra rebels. *4 Jul*: a French court finds Klaus Barbie guilty of war crimes, sentencing him to life imprisonment. Now 73, Barbie was Gestapo chief in Lyons, *1941–45*. *29 Jul*: a treaty between India and Sri Lanka is signed with the aim of ending ethnic violence in Sri Lanka. *9 Nov*: a bomb explosion in Colombo kills 32. *10 Nov*: although he has become popular by sacking corrupt officials, Moscow Communist Chief Boris Yeltsin is himself dismissed after complaining that Gorbachev's reforms (*perestroika*) are taking too long. *18 Nov*: Yeltsin's dismissal is unpopular, so he is given a new senior post. *7 Dec*: Gorbachev arrives in Washington for talks on arms limitation. *10 Dec*: Reagan and Gornachev sign the first treaty to reduce the size of nuclear weapons arsenals; there is to be mutual weapons inspection. *20 Dec*: a Filipino passenger ferry collides with a tanker: at least 1,500 are drowned.

Brice Marden: *Diptych*
Elizabeth Murray: *The Hunger Artist*
Willam de Kooning: *Untitled*
Robert Ryman: *Constant*

Gore Vidal: *Empire*
Tom Wolfe: *The Bonfire of the Vanities*
Tahar Ben Jelloun: *La Nuit Sacrée* (The Sacred Night)
Toni Morrison: *Beloved*
Penelope Lively: *Moon Tiger*
Philip Roth: *The Counterlife*
Allan Bloom: *The Closing of the American Mind*
William Golding: *Close Quarters*
Peter Ackroyd: *Chatterton*
Alfred Uhry: *Driving Miss Daisy*
Peter Shaffer: *Lettice and Lovage*
Peter Wright: *Spycatcher*

Harrison Birtwistle: *Endless Parade*
Michael Jackson: *Bad* (popular song)
Fleetwood Mac: *Tango in the Night* (popular song)

1988 *13 Jan*: President Chiang Ching-kuo of Taiwan dies, aged 77, and is succeeded by Lee Teng-hui. *5 Feb*: General Noriega, the Panamanian Head of State, is indicted in Miami on charges of drug trafficking. *16 Mar*: Iraqi troops use poison gas against Kurds in the town of Halabja, killing over 4,000. German companies have built gas-manufacturing facilities for the Iraqi army. *14 Apr*: the U.S.S.R. agrees to pull its troops out of Afghanistan. President Nicolae Ceausescu of Romania plans to demolish 8,000 villages in a compulsory urbanization programme. *18 Apr*: after a two-day battle Iraqi troops recover the town of Fao; over 53,000 Iraqis and maybe as many as 120,000 Iranians have been killed in the struggle for the town. *May*: General Zia ul-Haq, the 64-year-old President of Pakistan, dismisses Prime Minister Junejo and dissolves the National Assembly with the criticism that progress towards the establishment of Islamic law has been too slow. *29 May*: Reagan visits Moscow but antagonizes Gorbachev with demands for increased civil liberty in the U.S.S.R. *23 Jun*: U.S. climatologist James Hansen warns the Senate Committee on Energy and Natural Resources that increased carbon dioxide levels in the atmosphere (and the addition of other 'greenhouse' gases) is leading to global warming and this constitutes a threat to the human race. *1 Jul*: delegates at a Moscow Communist Party conference endorse Gorbachev's radical proposals to transfer some power from the party to elected legislatures and inaugurate a presidency. *3 Jul*: the US warship *Vincennes* in the Persian Gulf mistakes an Iran Air A300 Airbus for an attacking bomber and shoots it down; the mistake costs 290 civilian lives. *31 Jul*: King Hussein of Jordan cedes the West Bank to the PLO; he questions the usefulness of American peace initiatives in the region. *8 Aug*: Iran accepts an Iraqi truce plan that will lead to an end to the eight years of conflict that has cost 105,000 Iraqi lives and a million Iranian lives. *18 Aug*: President Zia is killed when his plane explodes mid-air. *Dec*: Benazir Bhutto, the 35-year-old daughter of Ali Bhutto, who was hanged at Zia's orders in *1979*, is elected Prime Minister. *7 Dec*: in an address at the UN in New York Gorbachev promises to reduce Soviet armament and troop levels on the western frontiers

of the Warsaw Bloc. Armenia experiences an earthquake measuring 6.9 on the Richter Scale; it kills over
25,000 people. *21 Dec:* a terrorist bomb destroys a
Pan-Am 747 in mid-air over the town of Lockerbie
in Scotland, all 259 on board and 11 on the ground are
killed. *22 Dec:* Chico Mendes, a Brazilian rubber tapper
who has rallied local people to try to stop the clearance
of the rainforest by ranchers, is shot dead at his home.

📖 Benjamin Friedman: *Day of Reckoning: The Consequences of American Economic Policy Under Reagan
and After*

Salman Rushdie: *The Satanic Verses*

Bharati Mukherjee: *The Middleman and Other Stories*

Umberto Eco: *Foucault's Pendulum*

Gabriel Garcia Marquez: *Love in the Time of Cholera*

Elmore Leonard: *Freaky Deaky*

Stephen Hawking: *A Brief History of Time*

Graham Greene: *The Captain and the Enemy*

Alan Bennett: *Talking Heads*

Peter Carey: *Oscar and Lucinda*

David Mamet: *Speed-the-Plow*

🎼 Keith Richard: *Talk Is Cheap* (popular song)

1989 The year of *perestroika*. *7 Jan:* the Japanese Emperor
Hirohito dies, aged 87, after reigning for 62 years and is
succeeded by his 55-year-old son Akihito. *2–3 Feb:* a
coup in Paraguay leads to the overthrow of dictator
Alfredo Stroessner, who is now 76. He is replaced by
General Rodriguez. *Mar:* Soviet voters have an opportunity to elect members of the Presidium of the Supreme
Soviet, the newly constituted parliament; Boris Yeltsin
wins a landslide victory. *24 Mar:* the oil tanker *Exxon
Valdez* runs aground on Bligh Reef releasing 240,000
barrels of Alaskan crude oil into Prince William Sound, a
sanctuary for whales, porpoises, otters, fish and sea-
birds; it is environmentally the worst U.S. tanker spill
so far. The *Exxon Valdez* Captain is sacked for drinking.
7 May: an election in Panama defeats General Noriega
but he ignores the election result and remains in power. *4
Jun:* Ayatollah Khomeini dies, aged about 86; he is
replaced as President of Iran by Hashemi Rafsanjani.

18 Aug: 40 years of strict Communist rule end in Poland after party candidates have been defeated in the *Jun* elections. A new cabinet is formed headed by Tadeuz Mazowiecki with support from Lech Walesa and Cardinal Glemp. *23 Aug:* Latvians, Lithuanians and Estonians join hands to form a human chain that crosses their three republics as they demand independence from the U.S.S.R. *Sep:* after P. W. Botha's resignation as President of South Africa, F. W. de Klerk becomes President; he is conspicuously more liberal than any previous South African leader, pledging to make the government more representative. Yeltsin visits America and says that there will be insurrection in the U.S.S.R. if Gorbachev does not make progress faster. *17 Oct:* an earthquake in San Francisco measures 7.1 on the Richter scale. It is the most destructive earthquake experienced in North America since *1906*, killing about 90 people, most crushed in their cars when the upper level of the Nimitz Highway collapses; it causes about 6 billion dollars' worth of damage to property. President Erich Honecker is forced to resign in East Germany, but he is replaced by his protegé, the equally hard-line Egon Krenz. *23 Oct:* Hungary proclaims itself a democratic republic, adopting a new constitution and renaming the Communist Party the Socialist Party. Soviet Foreign Minister Eduard Shevardnadze publicly admits that the Soviet invasion of Afghanistan was illegal. *9 Nov:* the East German government allows citizens to leave the country without visas. Hundreds of thousands of joyful East Germans visit the West. Demolition of the Berlin Wall begins. In China, Deng Xiaoping retires from politics at the age of 85. *17 Nov:* in Czechoslovakia, Prague police beat student demonstrators. Large-scale demonstrations follow in Wenceslas Square demanding the resignation of Milos Jakes, General Secretary of the Communist Party. *24 Nov:* Jakes is replaced but the Czech people are still not satisfied, demanding new rights. *10 Dec:* President Husak of Czechoslovakia resigns and a new cabinet with a Communist minority is installed. *16 Dec:* in Romania the Securitate (secret police) shoot thousands of protestors. *19 Dec:* the Czech parliament votes to move to a Western-style democracy. *21 Dec*: more Romanian demonstrators are shot by the Securitate, but soldiers go over to the side of the demonstrators as Ceausescu and his régime lose support. *22 Dec*: the Brandenburg Gate in Berlin is opened as East and West Berlin are reunited. After battles between the Securitate and the Romanian army, Nicolae Ceausescu and his wife Elena are captured. *24 Dec*: following the U.S. invasion of Panama (*20 Dec*), General Noriega has eluded capture, but he turns himself in to Vatican representatives in Panama City and remains in political asylum for 10 days; after that he will surrender to the U.S. for trial in Miami. *25 Dec*: Ceausescu and his wife Elena are executed by firing squad. Ion Iliescu heads a provisional government. *29 Dec*: the Czech parliament elects playwright and dissident Vaclav Havel as President, with Dubcek as Chairman of parliament.

🖋 Baikal-Amur Mainline (new trans-Siberian railway, 322 km/200 miles north of the old one: it has 3,000 bridges and four major tunnels)

Kevin Roche: Morgan Building, New York (completed)

I. M. Pei: Bank of China Building, Hong Kong (tallest in Hong Kong)

Marriott Hotel, Warsaw

Pierre Fakhoury: Basilica of Our Lady of Peace, Yamoussoukro, Ivory Coast (tallest church in the world, 160 metres/525 feet high dome)

📖 Simon Schama: *Citizens: A Chronicle of the French Revolution*

William Golding: *Fire Down Below*

Elmore Leonard: *Killshot*

Allan Gurganus: *Oldest Living Confederate Widow Tells All*

Bharati Mukherjee: *Jasmine*

Kazuo Ishiguro: *The Remains of the Day*

Iris Murdoch: *Message to the Planet*

Ronald Harwood: *Another Time*

William Nicholson: *Shadowlands*

Athol Fugard: *My Children, My Africa*

🎵 Michael Tippett: *New Year*

Mark-Anthony Tunage: *Greek*
Alain Boubil: *Miss Saigon* (musical, words Richard
Maltby)

1990   *11 Feb*: the 71-year-old Nelson Mandela is released from
prison near Cape Town; President de Klerk asks him to
help negotiate a political settlement between Whites and
Blacks. *11 Mar*: the Lithuanians decide to secede from
the U.S.S.R. Gorbachev deplores the decision and sends
Soviet tanks into Vilius. *18 Mar*: East Germans hold
their first free elections since *1932*. *Apr*: Gorbachev cuts
off oil supplies to Lithuania in an effort to persuade the
Lithuanians to change their minds. *21–24 Jun*: earthquakes in northern Iran cause 50,000 deaths and leave
500,000 without homes. *2 Jul*: pilgrims visiting Mecca
block a pedestrian tunnel, the ventilating system fails and
1,426 are suffoctaed or trampled to death. *2 Aug*: Iraqi
forces invade Kuwait after Kuwait refuses to comply
with impossible demands from President Saddam of
Iraq: that Kuwait pay compensation for drilling oil on
territory allegedly belonging to Iraq and cede disputed
land to Iraq. Teheran, Beijing, London, Moscow and
Tokyo denounce Saddam's action; the UN Security
Council votes for economic sanctions against Iraq. *7
Aug*: U.S. President Bush sends forces to Saudi Arabia. *8 Aug*: Iraq annexes Kuwait. *10 Aug*: 12 Arab
countries vote to oppose Iraq with military force. *18
Aug*: Saddam holds 10,000 foreigners hostage. *29 Aug*:
Saddam releases the women and children. *25 Sep*:
Gorbachev is given virtually free rein to decontrol the
economy of the U.S.S.R. but he moves cautiously and
prices rise sharply. *3 Oct*: the reunification of Germany
after 43 years of division. the joining of East and West
Germany has been approved in Ottawa (*Feb*) by Foreign
Ministers of Britain, France, the U.S. and the U.S.S.R.
17 Nov: Gorbachev asks for special powers as the Soviet
economy collapses and is granted them in spite of fears
that he may abuse them. *29 Nov*: UN Security Council
votes to authorize member nations to use military force
to eject Iraqi forces from Kuwait if they are still there
after *15 Jan 1991*. *20 Dec*: Eduard Shevardnadze resigns
as Soviet Foreign Minister warning the Congress of the

People's Deputies against 'reactionaries': his warning is
unheeded. Lech Walesa becomes President of Poland
after a second ballot.

    Philip Frohman: National Cathedral, Washington
(completed)

    Kenzo Tange: City Hall, Tokyo (completed)

    Fernando Botero: Venus, Broadgate, London

    Shintaro Ishihara: *The Japan That Can Say No*

    Nadine Gordimer: *My Son's Story*

    Thomas Pynchon: *Vineland*

    Mordecai Richler: *Solomon Gursky Was Here*

    A. S. Byatt: *Possession*

    Harold Pinter: *The Dwarfs*

    Derek Walcott: *Omeros*

    David Hare: *Racing Demon*

    Robin Holloway: *Clarissa*

    Rodney Castleden: *The Songs of Mary Magdalene*

1991 17 *Jan*: Olaf V of Norway dies, aged 87, and is succeeded
by his 53-year-old son Harald V. U.S. British and Allied
missiles and planes attack targets in Kuwait and Iraq
beginning early in the morning. *18 Jan*: Iraqi missiles hit
Haifa and Tel Aviv. Israel shows great restraint in not
retaliating; the Israelis fear damaging the coalition of
allies. *22 Jan*: Iraqis set fire to two Kuwaiti oil refineries
and oil wells near the Saudi border; by the end of the war
732 of Kuwait's oil wells are on fire. *24 Jan*: Iraqis release
Kuwaiti crude oil into the Gulf, creating a vast slick that
takes a heavy toll on wildlife. *26 Jan*: President Mohammed Siad Barre flees from Mogadishu, the capital of
Somalia, as United Somali Congress rebels overthrow
his regime. The rebel leader Ali Mahdi Mohammed,
becomes interim President. *24 Feb*: Operation Desert
Storm begins (and ends in four days). U.S. General
Schwarzkopf plans and commands the successful expulsion of Iraq from Kuwait, driving Iraqi forces well back
inside Iraq. 270,000 American, French and British
troops are involved. 100,000 Iraqis die in the conflict:
over 100,000 Iraqi soldiers surrender, but at the end of
the operation Saddam remains in power. *3 Mar*: Los
Angeles policemen brutally beat an unarmed black
motorist, Rodney King; fortunately for Mr. King, the

incident is recorded on videotape. *30 Apr*: a cyclone
strikes Bangladesh, flooding farmland, destroying crops
and killing 138,000 people. *21 May*: former Prime
Minister of India, 46-year-old Rajiv Gandhi, is assassinated with a bomb as he campaigns for re-election. *Jun*:
Mount Pinatubo on Luzon in the Philippines erupts with
great violence; it is one of the biggest volcanic eruptions
of the century, ejecting enormous quantities of ash and
19 million tonnes of sulphur dioxide (forming droplets of
sulphuric acid in the atmosphere). *20 Jun*: the German
Bundestag votes to move the seat of government from
Bonn to Berlin in spite of the cost. *25 Jun*: the long-
feared disintegration of Yugoslavia begins as Croatia and
Slovenia declare their independence from the rest of
Yugoslavia. Battles between Serbs and Croats erupt.
19–23 Aug: an attempted coup by Communist hardliners (Shevardnadze's 'reactionaries') fails largely
thanks to the heroic efforts of Boris Yeltsin who manages to enlist the support of a handful of tank commanders; the coup leaders flee. President Gorbachev returns
to Moscow from his brief imprisonment in his summer
home in the Crimea. *24 Aug*: Yeltsin suspends the
Communist Party, bringing 74 years of continuous rule
by the party to an end. *5 Sep*: Gorbachev persuades the
all-Soviet Congress to give up its power: its real control
over the constituent republics has in any case evaporated
and both economy and polity are on the verge of collapse.
6 Sep: Gorbachev recognizes the independence of the
three Baltic republics. *5 Nov*: the Czech-born British
publisher Robert Maxwell (real name Ludvik Hoch) falls
to his death from his yacht in the North Atlantic.

- The Dartford Bridge, Thames Estuary (U.K.)
  Norman Foster: Sackler Galleries, Royal Academy,
  London
- Louise Bourgeois: Cleavage (marble)
  Vito Acconci: Adjustable Well Bras (sculpture)
- Nicholas Lemann: *The Promised Land: The Great
  Black Migration and How it Changed America*
  Susan Hill: *Air and Angels*
  Milan Kundera: *Immortality*
  Anne Tyler: *St. Maybe*

Neil Simon: *Lost in Yonkers*
Marc Camoletti: *Don't Dress for Dinner*
Margaret Forster: *The Battle for Christabel*
Julian Barnes: *Talking it Over*
George Lloyd: *Symphony No 12*
Michael Tippett: *Byzantium*
Harrison Birtwistle: *Gawain*
Mark-Antony Turnage: *Momentum*
Guns n' Roses: *Use Your Illusions* (popular song)

1992　*1 Jan*: Butros Butros Ghali, a 69-year-old Egyptian diplomat becomes the 6th Secretary General of the United Nations. *7 Jan*: Zviad Gamsakhurdia, the former Head of State in Georgia, is accused of having been a dictator; he flees to Armenia. *9 Jan*: a woman in Zurich claims that the 5,000-year-old Iceman recently found in the Alps is her father. Bosnian Serbs declare their own republic under the leadership of Radovan Karazic, bringing fears that the civil war will spread right to the heart of the disintegrating Yugoslav federation. *13 Jan*: Aileen Wuornos, a 35-year-old prostitute, goes on trial in Florida for the murder of seven men. *17 Jan*: IBM announces an annual loss of 564 million dollars – its biggest loss ever. *3 Feb*: the discovery is announced of the lost ancient city of Ubar (around *2,000 BC*) in the Arabian Desert on the border of Yemen and Oman; satellite images have helped to identify ancient caravan routes converging on the site. *12 Feb*: Bill Clinton comes clean about avoiding the Vietnam War draft; contemporary correspondence proves that he was strongly opposed to the war. *15 Feb*: U.S. composer William Schuman dies, aged 81. *21 Feb*: Jeanne Calment, France's oldest citizen, celebrates her 117th birthday today in Arles, where she knew van Gogh. *22 Feb*: the Pope visits Goree Island near Dakar, Senegal and describes 'the forgotten holocaust': an estimated 15 million Africans captured from as far south as Angola passed through Goree Island on their way to slavery in the New World. *21 Mar*: the population of the world reaches 5.4 billion of which 1.2 billion are Chinese. The American Census Office projects that world population may be over 8 billion by 2020. *8 Apr*: the Palestinian leader Yasir

Arafat's plane crashes in the Sahara but he is not seriously injured. German scientists confirm that human remains found in Brazil in *1985* are those of Josef Mengele, the infamous doctor at Auschwitz who was responsible for the deaths of tens of thousands. *12 Apr*: Euro Disney opens in France. *21 Apr*: Vladimir Romanov, the pretender to the Russian throne, dies aged 74. *22 Apr*: an earthquake in California registers 6.1 on the Richter Scale. *26 Apr*: as feared, the earthquake aftershock is stronger than the initial shock – 6.5. *28 Apr*: the French composer Olivier Messiaen dies, aged 83. The English painter Francis Bacon dies in Madrid, aged 82. *30 Apr*: there are serious riots in Los Angeles following the acquittal of the policemen who beat up black motorist Rodney King; the riots cause 600 million dollars' worth of damage. *23 May*: Judge Giovanni Falcone, the leading anti-Mafia investigator, is assassinated with a massive bomb which makes a crater 38 metres/126 feet deep. *11 Jun*: the last survivor of the *Titanic* sinking, Marjorie Robb, dies in Boston, aged 103. *16 Jun*: Cory Aquino is defeated in the Philippine election by General Fidel Ramos. *24 Jun*: cigarette companies expect a flood of legal claims in the U.S. after the successful claim brought by Rose Cipollone's family after her death from lung cancer following 42 years of smoking. 400,000 deaths a year in the U.S. alone are believed to be smoking-related. *28 Jun*: two earthquakes strike uninhabited desert areas in southern California, both registering above 7 on the Richter Scale. *29 Jun*: the 73-year-old president of Algeria, Mohammed Boudiaf, is assassinated while making a speech at a political rally. *Jul*: Sarajevo is under siege. *10 Jul*: General Noriega of Panama is sentenced in Miami to 40 years in prison for offences relating to drug trafficking. *17 Jul*: President Vaclav Havel of Czechoslovakia resigns after a proclamation of Slovak sovereignty: he can see that the country will split in two. *3 Aug*: Washington confirms reports of torture and illegal killings in Serb-run prison camps in Bosnia. *12 Aug*: U.S. composer John Cage dies, aged 79. *1 Sep*: Alexander Dubcek, aged 70, is badly injured in a car crash. *14 Sep*: Northern India and Pakistan are devastated by river

floods and landslides following three days of torrential
rain: over 2,000 die. *28 Sep*: photographs taken by
astronomers confirm that there is a 10th planet in the
solar system, 6,000 million km/3,700 million miles from
the sun. *4 Oct*: a Boeing 747 crashes into a residential
suburb of Amsterdam shortly after taking off; about 150
are killed, fewer than at first feared. *12 Oct*: an earthquake registering 5.9 on the Richter scale strikes Cairo,
killing 340 people; there is concern about what might
happen if such an earthquake struck close to the Aswan
Dam. *14 Oct*: Moscow hands secret KGB documents to
Lech Walesa revealing that it was Stalin and his Politburo who ordered the killing of Polish officers in *1940*
(the Katyn Forest Massacre); for years the Russians
maintained the Germans committed the war crime. *31
Oct*: the Vatican absolves Galileo of heresy, in effect
admitting that the earth is round. *7 Nov*: Alexander
Dubcek dies of his injuries. *11 Nov*: Israel sends tanks
into Lebanon following two nights of rocket attacks by
Hezbollah, the pro-Iranian guerrilla organization. *17
Nov*: cave paintings discovered at Cosquer in southern
France are found to date to *25,100 BC* which puts them
among the earliest known works of art. *18 Nov*: Benazir
Bhutto is put under house arrest after police stop a
political demonstration. *25 Nov*: it is announced in
Prague that Czechoslovakia will cease to exist on *1
Jan, 1993*, becoming the Czech and Slovak Republics.
3 Dec: the Greek tanker *Aegean Sea* runs aground at
Corunna, Spain, spilling 550,000 barrels of oil to make a
19-km/12-mile slick which then catches fire. *7 Dec*:
Hindu militants at Ayodhya in Northern India destroy
the 16th-century Babri Masjid mosque with their bare
hands; over 800 are killed in the ensuing riot. *12 Dec*: an
earthquake registering 6.8 on the Richter Scale in Indonesia kills 1,500 people. *20 Dec*: the Folies Bergère, the
Paris music-hall which opened in *1869*, closes down.

  ✍ Canary Wharf Tower, London
    Euro Disney, Marne-La-Vallée
    Expo 91, Seville
    Norman Foster: Library, Cranfield Institute of
    Technology

    ✉ John Keene: The Gulf War
    Statue of Sir Arthur 'Bomber' Harris, The Strand,
    London
    📖 Michael Ondaatje: *The English Patient*
    Barry Unsworth: *Sacred Hunger*
    Peter Hoeg: *Miss Smilla's Feeling For Snow*
    🏛 Philip Glass: *The Voyage*

1993   *5 Jan*: The oil tanker *Braer* runs aground in the Shetland
Islands after losing power in a storm; she loses all her
cargo of crude oil and there are fears that the Shetland
coast will be ruined for years to come, but the energy of
the storm waves quickly disperses the oil. *15 Jan*: the
Sicilian Mafia boss Salvatore Riina is arrested after
eluding capture for 22 years. *19 Jan*: IBM announces
an annual loss of £3.3 billion in 1991, the worst ever. *26
Jan*: Bill Clinton is sworn in as President of the U.S. *17
Feb*: the UN suspends relief operations in Bosnia. An
overloaded ferry sinks off the coast of Haiti (a disaster
waiting to happen): over 1,200 die. *19 Feb*: British Prime
Minister John Major rejects the idea of pardons for First
World War servicemen executed for cowardice or desertion on the grounds that it would be 'rewriting history'.
12 Mar: car bombs in Bombay kill 200. *14 Mar*: severe
storms along the east coast of the U.S. kill 66 people. *24
Mar*: President de Klerk admits that South Africa had
nuclear weapons. *10 Apr*: Chris Hani, the black South
African Communist leader who might have 'succeeded'
Nelson Mandela as the black voice of South Africa, is
assassinated. *17 Apr*: two Los Angeles policemen are
convicted of beating up Rodney King. *19 Apr*: the Waco
Siege in Texas ends in a fire that kills 97 people including
David Koresh, the charismatic cult leader. *24 Apr*: the
City of London is badly damaged by an IRA bomb;
initial estimates put the damage at £1 billion. *30 Apr*: the
tennis player Monica Sales is stabbed by a dissatisfied
spectator during a match in Hamburg. *1 May*: President
Ranasinghe Premadasa of Sri Lanka is assassinated by a
suicide bomber. *5 May*: Asil Nadir, the Chairman of
Polly Peck, jumps bail and flees to Cyprus. *13 Jun*:
Pakistani UN troops in Somalia fire into a crowd killing
20 people. *2 Jul*: 40 people die in an arson attack on a

hotel in Turkey by Islamic fundamentalists who are protesting against Salman Rushdie's book *Satanic Verses*, which they see as blasphemous. *6 Jul*: 40 unpublished poems by T. S. Eliot are discovered. *13 Jul*: an earthquake in Japan kills at least 80. *23 Aug*: U.S. police raid the singer Michael Jackson's homes after allegations of child abuse have been made by a 13-year-old boy. *9 Sep*: Israel and the PLO agree to recognize each other's legitimacy and right to exist in a major step forward in the Middle East peace process. *13 Sep*: Yitzhak Rabin and Yasir Arafat sign a peace accord at the White House. *21 Sep*: President Boris Yeltsin dissolves the Russian parliament and announces that he is taking control. *22 Sep*: a train plunges into a swamp in Alabama; at least 40 die. *30 Sep*: an earthquake strikes the central Deccan Plateau killing more than 10,000 people as it shakes down their lightly built houses on top of them. *3 Oct*: President Yeltsin declares a state of emergency in Russia after the worst outbreak of political violence since the Russian Revolution in *1917*. *4 Oct*: Communist hardliners in Moscow surrender after a short but violent siege. *15 Oct*: President F. W. de Klerk and Nelson Mandela are awarded the Nobel Peace Prize. *1 Nov*: in Britain the trial begins of two boys accused of the murder of James Bulger, a 2-year-old, in Liverpool. *24 Nov*: two 11-year-old boys, Robert Thompson and Jon Venables, are convicted of abducting and murdering James Bulger; there is widespread horror in Britain at the crime, mixed with disbelief that the normal, harmless-looking boys could have committed it. *25 Nov*: the English author and composer Anthony Burgess dies, aged 76. *3 Dec*: the Princess of Wales announces that she will be withdrawing from public life next year. *9 Dec*: three British prisoners are released by the Iraqis after the British ex-Prime Minister Sir Edward Heath meets and makes a direct appeal to President Saddam of Iraq. *12 Dec*: the first free elections are held in Russia. *14 Dec*: the result of the Russian election is a move to the right; about 50 per cent vote for conservative-nationalist groups, with Vladimir Zhirinovsky (Liberal Democratic Party leader) emerging as overall leader. Yeltsin remains

President, Viktor Chernomyrdin Prime Minister, but the Baltic States fear that the extreme right-wing Zhirinovsky could become President soon and take revenge on them for precipitating the collapse of the Soviet Union. *15 Dec*: the Downing Street Declaration: John Major and Albert Reynolds, Prime Ministers of the United Kingdom and the Irish Republic, agree an arrangement within which a united Ireland might be created. It is hoped that the terrorist violence that has killed 3,111 people in Britain and Ireland in the last 25 years will end. In Geneva the World Trade Organization is founded, replacing GATT (General Agreement on Tariffs and Trade) set up in *1947*.

   Daniel Libeskind: Jewish Museum, Berlin

   Eldred Evans and David Shalev: Tate Gallery, St. Ives (U.K.)

   Nicholas Grimshaw: Waterloo International Terminal, London

   Rachel Whiteread: House (Grove Road, London)

   Terry Frost: Banner for the Opening of the Tate

   Robert Greenhay: Sheep in the Orchard

   Jimmie Durham: We Have Made Progress (sculpture)

   Judy Boyt: Rebellion (bronze)

   David Bellos: *Georges Perec: A Life in Words*

   Bharati Mukherjee: *The Holder of the World*

   Rodney Castleden: *The Making of Stonehenge*

   Vladimir Zhirinovsky: *The Last Thrust to the South*

   Peter Ackroyd: *The House of Dr. Dee*

   Tom Stoppard: *Arcadia*

   Harold Pinter: *Moonlight*

   Richard Holmes: *Mr. Johnson and Mr. Savage*

   Roberto Calasso: *The Marriage of Cadmus and Harmony*

   Roddy Doyle: *Paddy Clarke Ha Ha Ha*

   August Wilson: *The Piano Lesson*

   Arthur Miller: *The Last Yankee*

   Davis Mamet: *Oleanna*

   Tony Kushner: *Perestroika*

   George Lloyd: *Symphonic Mass*

   Hans Werner Henze: *Requiem*

Rodney Castleden: *There is no Rose*
Michael Finnissey: *Thérèse Raquin*
Michael Berkeley: *Baa Baa Black Sheep*

APPENDICES

APPENDIX I: THE SEVEN WONDERS OF THE WORLD

The seeds of this ancient idea may be found in the *Histories* of Herodotus (about 485–425 BC), in which he described the city of Babylon and the Pyramids as towering achievements of past civilizations. There was an implication that the Minoans and Mycenaeans had left nothing that was by then (i.e. 450 BC) visibly impressive, and Herodotus was evidently deeply impressed by *size*. The two latest monuments on the 'standard' list of the Seven Wonders were the Colossus and the Pharos, and the 30-year period between the building of the Pharos and the destruction of the Colossus is the most likely time for the compilation of the list. It was, in fact, then that Callimachus of Cyrene (305–240 BC), a senior librarian at Alexandria, wrote *A Collection of Wonders in Lands Throughout the World*. This work has not survived, but its existence would certainly have favoured the compilation of rival lists, improved lists and short-lists. The first list of seven occurs in a short poem by Antipater, a Greek poet from Sidon, written about a century after Callimachus' death.

'I have gazed on the walls of impregnable Babylon, along which chariots may race, and on the Zeus by the banks of Alpheus. I have seen the Hanging Gardens and the Colossus of Helios, the great man-made mountains of the lofty pyramids, and the gigantic tomb of Mausolus. But when I saw the sacred house of Artemis that towers to the clouds, the others faded into shadows, for the sun himself has never looked upon its equal outside Olympus.'

Different lists of the Seven Wonders were compiled thereafter. Diodorus Siculus, in describing the great obelisk of Queen Semiramis at Babylon, said that it should be numbered among the seven most notable works of his day, yet it is the list of Antipater of Sidon that has survived. The idea of Seven Wonders gained in popularity during the Roman Empire. In AD 80, the poet Martial considered the Colosseum in Rome the equal of the Seven Wonders; he also proposed the Horned Altar on Delos. Other lists looked back to the palace of King Cyrus at

Ecbatana, Egyptian Thebes and the Roman Capitol with its great temple dedicated to Jupiter, Juno and Minerva. The later lists are less convincing, because the authors had clearly not seen all the sites they listed. Gregory, Bishop of Tours (AD 536–594), included Solomon's Temple at Jerusalem and Noah's Ark. Bede (AD 673–735) included a statue of Bellerophon, the stadium at a city called Heraclea and an unidentifiable bath house. It is worth remembering that the earlier lists were of *theamata*, not *thaumata* – sights to be seen, rather than wonders.

What follows is the standard list, the one referred to in Antipater of Sidon.

The Pyramids of Egypt

The oldest and the only surviving 'wonder'. About 80 pyramids are still standing, but it is the three at Cairo – the Pyramids of Gizeh – that are usually meant. They are arranged in a straight line from south-west to north-east, the Pyramids of Mycerinus, Chephren and Cheops. The largest is the Great Pyramid of Cheops (Khufu). It is 147 metres/482 feet high, 229 metres/751 feet square, and almost complete; it only lacks its apex (the top 10 metres/33 feet) and marble casing. King Khufu's architect and clerk of works was his cousin, the Vizier Hemon, whose statue is in the Pelizaeus Museum at Hildersheim in Germany.

The Hanging Gardens of Babylon

Terraced and artificially irrigated gardens adjoining the palace of Nebuchadnezzar II in the city of Babylon, they were built in about 575 BC at Nebuchadnezzar's orders, allegedly to make his wife, a princess from the mountains, feel more at home. The Hanging Gardens have not survived in any recognizable form and even their location is uncertain. Some believe, (because Herodotus did not mention the gardens as such) that they adorned the flanks of the ziggurat, but the difficulty of irrigating terraces that high above the river would seem to rule out such a location. Others believe the Hanging Gardens were created on walled terraces outside the city between the Ishtar Gate and the River Euphrates, 300 metres/980 feet away to the north-west. Diodorus Siculus wrote that 'the galleries rose little by little above one another . . . the uppermost gallery was 50 cubits high, level with the circuit wall of the battlements of the city'. The walls were 6.7 metres/22 feet thick, their roofs made with

5 metre/16-foot beams covered with layers of reeds, bitumen, baked brick, lead, then soil deep enough for the roots of trees.' Remains of walls fitting Diodorus' description have survived outside the northern city walls, beside the River Euphrates, where watering would have been easy.

Temple of Artemis (Diana) at Ephesus

This was first built at King Croesus' orders by the Knossian architects Chersiphon and his son Metagenes. It was destroyed by Herostratus in 356 BC and rebuilt. The second temple, of gleaming white Parian marble, stood in a huge and imposing precinct on a raised platform 131 by 79 metres/430 by 259 feet. The large temple had 127 graceful fluted Ionic columns 20 metres/66 feet high. There were no figures, only dentils, on the high frieze. The pediment was punctured by three large openings, the central one furnished with large doors; these were for 'appearances' specially staged epiphanies of 'gods' and 'goddesses' during religious ceremonies. The second temple was destroyed by the Goths in AD 262: only debris remains.

The Statue of Zeus at Olympia (Elis)

The colossal seated statue of Zeus was made by Pheidias in 435 BC. A wooden framework was built in the temple to the exact size and shape of the finished figure. Plates of ivory were carved to represent the flesh areas and nailed onto the wooden armature; sheets of gold and silver were moulded to represent drapery and hair and similarly pinned into position, so that the finished figure appeared to be solid. Contemporary coins show what the statue of Zeus looked like – a seated, draped figure on a high-backed throne, holding a staff-like sceptre with a bird on top in his left hand, and a winged Victory figure in his right hand. The temple of Zeus was huge, but the statue seems – and seemed to some contemporaries – too large for it. At 13 metres/43 feet high, its gigantic form soaring into the rafters, it must have been overpowering. In AD 391 the statue was transported to a palace in Constantinople; there, it was destroyed in a fire in 462. It seems that no copy of it was ever made.

The Mausoleum at Halicarnassus (Bodrum)

This funerary monument was raised by Queen Artemisia and King Mausolus of Caria as a memorial to themselves; he died in

353 BC, but work almost certainly began on it during his lifetime. It consisted of a substantial pillared temple about 30 metres/98 feet square perched on a very high tiered plinth, making the entire monument 43 metres/141 feet high. Numerous pieces of sculpture survive, including statues believed to represent Artemisia and Mausolus.

The Colossus of Rhodes

This gigantic bronze statue of Helios the sun god stood about 36 metres/118 feet high – three times taller than any other known classical statue – and dominated the harbour at Rhodes. Its exact site is unknown: it may have stood on the waterfront or up the slope in Rhodes town. The statue was made by Chares of Lindos, who completed it in 280 BC. It was felled by an earthquake in 244 BC, breaking off at the knees. Even the fallen figure was a great tourist attraction until AD 654, when the bronze fragments were taken by Arabs to Asia Minor, sold to a Jew and then transported east; they were last seen travelling towards Syria on the backs of 900 camels.

The Pharos of Alexandria

A lighthouse built in about 290 BC and of unknown height; it was certainly not 560 metres/1,837 feet high, as Epiphanes said, but probably around 100–125 metres/328–410 feet. The light was produced by a huge fire maintained in the base, which was reflected out to sea by mirrors fixed in the top of the tower. Similar, but smaller lighthouses were built at Ostia and Ravenna, also in three stages. There were windows in the sides, presumably to light an interior staircase. The best description comes from an Arab traveller who saw it and took measurement in 166. He describes a square ground plan for the first stage, 8.5 metres/28 feet square, with no stairway but a ramp gradually ascending round a cylindrical core. The first stage was 57.7 metres/1189 feet high, with a 1.8-metre/6-feet high parapet. The second stage, built on top with an octagonal cross section, was 27 metres/89 feet high. The third stage was cylindrical and 7 metres/23 feet high. On top of that was a 'mosque' 5.5 metres/18 feet high with four 'doors' and a dome. The building was partly ruined by the year 1326 and had deteriorrated so badly by 1349 that it was unsafe to enter. The Pharos fell down in an earthquake in 1375 and its site is now covered by the Kait Bey Fort.

APPENDIX II: RULERS OF ANCIENT EGYPT

Proto-historic or Early Dynastic Period

1st Dynasty	3,200–2,980 BC	Men/Menes/Nar-Mer/Narmerza
		Ahai
2nd Dynasty	2,980–2,780 BC	Djer
		Den-Semti
		Udimu
		Peribsen

The Old Kingdom

3rd Dynasty	2,780–2,680 BC	Zoser
		Sekhemkhet
		Khaba
4th Dynasty	2,680–2,565 BC	Snefru
		Khufu (Greek: Cheops)
		Khafre (Greek: Chephren)
		Menkaure (Greek: Mycerinus)
		Dedefre
		Nebka
		Shepseskaf
5th Dynasty	2,565–2,420 BC	Weserkaf/Userkaf
		Sahure
		Neferirkare
		Neferefre
		Niuserre
		Isesi
		Unas
6th Dynasty	2,420–2,258 BC	Teti
		Pepi I
		Merenre
		Pepi II (reigned for 94 years)

First Intermediate Period

7th–10th Dynasties	2,258–2,040 BC	Khety I
		Khety II
		Ibi
		Merikare
		Mentuhotep I

The Middle Kingdom

11th Dynasty	2,040–1,991 BC	Mentuhotep II
		Mentuhotep III
12th Dynasty	1,991–1,786 BC	Amenemhet I
		Senusret I/Sesostris I
		Amenemhet II
		Senusret II/Sesostris II
		Senusret III/Sesostris III
		Amenemhet III
		Amenemhet IV
		Queen Sebekneferura

Second Intermediate Period (Hyksos Period)

13th–16th Dynasties	1,786–1,600 BC	(most rulers names are lost from this period)
		Khendjer
		Salitis
		Khyan
		Apopi I
17th Dynasty	1,600–1,570 BC	Sekenenre II
		Kamose

The New Kingdom

18th Dynasty	1,570–1,342 BC	Ahmose I (Greek: Amasis I)
		Amenhotep I/Amenophis I
		Thutmose I
		Thutmose II
		Queen Hatshepsut
		Thutmose III
		Amenhotep II/Amenophis II
		Thutmose IV
		Amenhotep III/Amenophis III
		Amenhotep IV/Amenophis IV/ Ikhnaten
		Tutankhamun
		Horemheb
19th Dynasty	1,342–1197 BC	Ramesses I
		Seti I
		Ramesses II
		Seti II
		Merenptah

20th Dynasty	1197–1085 BC	Setnakht
		Ramesses III
		Ramesses IV
		Ramesses V
		Ramesses VI
		Ramesses VII
		Ramesses VIII
		Ramesses IX
		Ramesses X
		Ramesses XI

Third Intermediate Period

21st Dynasty	1085–950 BC	Smendes/Nesubanebdet
		Herihor
22nd Dynasty	950–730 BC	Sheshonk I/Shishak I
		Osorkon I
23rd Dynasty	817–730 BC	Pedibast
24th Dynasty	730–715 BC	Tefnakht
		Bakenrenef/Bocchoris

The Late Kingdom

25th Dynasty	715–656 BC	Shabaka
		Taharka
26th Dynasty	663–525 BC	Psamtek I/Psammetichus (reigned for 54 years)
		Necho
		Psamtek II (594–588)
		Apries/Hophra (588–568)
		Ahmose II (Greek: Amasis II) (568–526)
		Psamtek III (526–525)
27th Dynasty	525–404 BC	Cambyses (525–522)
		Darius I (522–486)
		Xerxes (486–465)
28th Dynasty	404–398 BC	Amyrtaeus
29th Dynasty	398–378 BC	Nefeuret I
		Achoris
		Nefeuret II
30th Dynasty	378–341 BC	Nectanebo
		Tachos/Teos
		Nectharheb
31st Dynasty	341–332 BC	Darius III

Alexandrian Conquest (332–323 BC)
Alexander the Great

Ptolemaic Period (323–30 BC)

323–285	Ptolemy I Soter (Governor 323–305, then King)
285–246	Ptolemy II Philadelphus
246–221	Ptolemy III Ceranus
221–204	Ptolemy IV Philopater
204–181	Ptolemy V Epiphanes
181–146	Ptolemy VI Philomentor
146–116	Ptolemy VII Euergetes II or Physkon (Bloated)
116–108, 88–80	Ptolemy VIII Soter II or Lathyros
108–89	Ptolemy IX Alexander I
80	Ptolemy XI (killed for killing his stepmother)
80–51	Ptolemy XI Philopater Philadelphus
51–47	Ptolemy XII Philopater
47–44	Ptolemy XIII Philopater
44–30	Queen Cleopatra Philopater and Ptolemy XIV ('Caesarion')

Roman Period (30 BC – AD 395)
Direct rule by Roman Emperors under equestrian prefects, beginning with
Cornelius Gallus and then Aelius Gallus, under Augustus' direct control.

APPENDIX III: RULERS OF BABYLON

First Dynasty of Babylon		Kassite Dynasty	
Sumu-abum	1894–1881 BC	Gandash	?
Sumulael	1881–1845 BC	—	
Sabium	1845–1831 BC	Agum II	c. 1570 BC
Apil-Sin	1831–1813 BC	Burna-Buriash I	c. 1510 BC
Sin-muballit	1813–1793 BC	Kashtiliashu III	c. 1490 BC
Hammurabi	1993–1750 BC	—	
Samsu-iluna		Agum III	c. 1465 BC
Abi-eshuh	1712–1684 BC	Kara-indash	c. 1415 BC
Ammi-ditana	1684–1647 BC	Kadashman-Harbe I	?
Ammi-saduqa	1647–1626 BC	Kurigalzu I	c. 1390 BC
Samsu-ditana	1626–1595 BC	Kadashman-Enlil I	c. 1370 BC

Burna-Buriash II	c. 1350 BC
Kara-hardash	?
Nazi-Bugash	?
Kurigalzu II	1345–1324 BC
Nazi-Maruttash	1324–1298 BC
Kadashman-Turgu	1298–1280 BC
Kadashman-Enlil II	1280–1265 BC
Kudur-Enlil	1265–1256 BC
Shagarakti-Shuriash	1256–1243 BC
Kashtiliashu IV	1243–1235 BC
interregnum	1235–1228 BC
Enlil-nadin-shumi	1228–1225 BC
Kadashman-Harbe II	
Adad-shuma-iddina	1225–1219 BC
Adad-shuma-usur	1219–1189 BC
Meli-Shipak	1189–1174 BC
Marduk-apla-iddina I	1174–1161 BC
Zababa-shuma-iddina	1161–1160 BC
Enlil-nadin-ahi	1160–1157 BC

Second Dynasty of Isin

Marduk-kabit-ahheshu	
	1157–1141 BC
Itti-Marduk-balatu	1141–1133 BC
Ninurta-nadin-shumi	1133–1127 BC
Nebuchadnezzar I	1127–1105 BC
Enlil-nadin-apli	1105–1101 BC
Marduk-nadin-ahhe	1101–1083 BC
Marduk-shapil-zeri	1083–1070 BC
Adad-apla-iddina	1070–1048 BC
Marduk-ahhe-eriba	1048–1047 BC
Marduk-zer-x	1047–1035 BC
Nabu-shumu-libur	1035–1027 BC

Second Dynasty of the Sealand

Simbar-Shipak	1027–1009 BC
Ea-mukin-zeri	1009 BC
Kashshu-nadin-ahi	1008–1006 BC

Dynasty of Bazi

Eulmash-shakin-shumi	1006–989 BC
Ninurta-kudurri-usur I	989–986 BC

Shirikti-Shuqamuna	986 BC

Elamite Dynasty

Mar-biti-apla-usur	985–980 BC
Nabu-mukin-apli	980–944 BC
Ninurta-kudurri-usur II	944 BC
Mar-biti-ahhe-iddina	943 BC
—	
Shamash-mudammiq	c. 905 BC
Nabu-shuma-ukin I	c. 895 BC
Nabu-apla-iddina	c. 870 BC
Marduk-zakir-shuma I	c. 840 BC
Marduk-balassu-iqbi	c. 815 BC
Baba-aha-iddina	c. 812 BC
(5 unknown kings)	?
Ninurta-apla-x	?
Marduk-bel-zeri	?
Marduk-apla-usur	?
Eriba-Marduk	?–760 BC
Nabu-shuma-ishkun	760–748 BC
Nabonassar	748–734 BC
Nabu-nadin-zeri	734–732 BC
Nabu-shuma-ukin II	732 BC

'Ninth Dynasty'

Nabu-mukin-zeri	732–729 BC
Tiglath-Pileser III	729–727 BC
Shalmaneser V	727–722 BC
Merodach-Baladan II	722–710 BC
Sargon II	710–705 BC
Sennacherib	705–703 BC
Marduk-zakir-shumi II	703 BC
Merodach-Baladan II	703 BC
Bel-ibni	702–700 BC
Assur-nadin-shumi	694–693 BC
Nergal-ushezib	693 BC
Mushezib-Marduk	693–689 BC
Sennacherib	689–681 BC
Esarhaddon	681–669 BC
Shamash-shuma-ukin	669–648 BC
Kandalanu	648–627 BC
Assyrian interregnum	627–626 BC

Chaldean Dynasty

Nabopolassar	626–605 BC
Nebuchadnezzar II	605–562 BC
Evil-Merodach	562–560 BC
Neriglissar	560–556 BC
Labashi-Marduk	556 BC
Nabonidus	556–539 BC

Achaemenid Rulers

Cyrus II	538–530 BC
Cambyses II	530–522 BC
Bardiya	522 BC
Nebuchadnezzar III	522 BC
Nebuchadnezzar IV	522 BC
Darius I	522–486 BC
Xerxes I	486–465 BC
Bel-shimanni	465 BC
Shamash-eriba	464 BC
Artaxerxes I	464–424 BC
Darius II	424–405 BC
Artaxerxes II	405–359 BC
Artaxerxes III	359–338 BC
Arses	338–336 BC
Darius III	336–331 BC

Macedonian Rulers

Alexander the Great (III)	
	330–323 BC
Philip Arrhidaeus	323–316 BC
Alexander IV	316–307 BC

Seleucid Dynasty

Seleucus I Nicator	311–281 BC
Antiochus I Soter	281–261 BC
Antiochus II Theos	261–246 BC
Seleucus II Callinicus	246–225 BC
Seleucus III Soter	225–223 BC
Antiochus III	223–187 BC
Seleucus IV Philopater	187–175 BC
Antiochus IV Epiphanes	
	175–164 BC
Antiochus V Eupator	164–162 BC
Demetrius I Soter	162–150 BC
Alexander Balas	150–145 BC
Demetrius II Nicator	145–139 BC
Antiochus VI Epiphanes	
	145–142 BC
Antiochus VII Sidetes	139–129 BC
Demetrius II Nicator	129–125 BC

APPENDIX IV: RULERS OF ANCIENT ROME

Kings of Rome

Romulus	753–716 BC
Numa Pompilius	716–673 BC
Tullus Hostilius	673–640 BC
Ancus Martius	640–616 BC
Tarquinius Priscus	616–579 BC
Servius Tullius	579–534 BC
Tarquinius Superbus	534–509 BC

The Republic of Rome

Dictatorship of Sulla	82–78 BC
First Triumvirate	60–53 BC
(Julius Caesar, Pompey and Crassus)	
Dictatorship of Pompey	52–47 BC
Dictatorship of Julius Caesar	45–44
Second Triumvirate	43–27
(Octavian, Mark Anthony and	
Marcus Lepidus)	

Emperors of the Roman Empire

Augustus (previously Octavian)	
	27 BC–AD 14
Tiberius I	AD 14–37
Caligula (Gaius Caesar)	37–41
Claudius I	41–54
Nero	54–68

Galba	68–69
Otho	69
Vitellius	69
Vespasian	69–79
Titus	79–81
Domitian	96–98
Nerva	96–98
Trajan	98–117
Hadrian	117–138
Antoninus Pius	138–161
Marcus Aurelius	161–180
Lucius Verus (jointly)	161–169
Commodus	180–192
Pertinax	193
Didius Julianus	193
Septimus Severus	193–211
Caracalla	211–217
Geta (jointly)	211–212
Macrinus	217–218
Elagabulus (Heliogabalus)	218–222
Alexander Severus	222–235
Maximinius I (the Thracian)	235–238
Gordian I	238
Gordian II	238
Balbinus and Pupienus Maximus	238
Gordian III	238–244
Philip (the Arab)	244–249
Decius	249–251
Gallus and Hostilianus (Volusianus)	251–253
Aemilianus	253
Valerian and Gallienus	253–260
Gallienus	260–268
Claudius II (Gothicus)	268–270
Quintillus	270
Aurelianus	270–275
Tacitus	275–276
Florianus	276
Probus	276–282

Carus	282–283
Carinus and Numerianus	283–284
Diocletian (divides empire)	284–305
Maximian (jointly)	286–305
Constantius I	305–306
Severus	306–307
Licinius (jointly)	307–323
Constantine I (reunites empire)	308–337
Constantine II (jointly)	337–340
Constans (jointly)	337–350
Constantius II (jointly)	337–361
Magnentius (jointly)	350–353
Julian (the Apostate)	361–363
Jovianus	363–364
Valentinian I (rules West)	364–375
Valens (rules East)	364–378
Gratian (rules West)	375–383
Magnus Maximus (usurper in West)	383–388
Valentinian II (rules West)	375–392
Eugenius (usurper in West)	392–394
Theodosius I (the Great) (rules East, then unites East and West)	378–395

Emperors of the Eastern Roman Empire

Arcadius	395–408
Theodosius II	408–450
Marcian	450–457
Leo I	457–474
Leo II	474
Zeno	474–491
Anastasius	491–518

Emperors of the Western Roman Empire

Honorius	395–423
Maximus	410–411
Constantius III	421

John	423–425	Anthemius	467–472
Valentinian III	425–455	Olybrius	472
Petronius Maximus	455	Glycerius	473
Avitus	455–456	Julius Nepos	473–480
Majorian	457–461	Romulus Augustus	475–476
Severus III	461–465		

APPENDIX V: POPES

St. Peter (Established Church in Rome)	42	St. Marcellinus	296
St. Linus	67	St. Marceilus I	308
St. Anacletus (Cletus)	76	St. Eusebius	309
St. Clement I	88	St. Melchiades	311
St. Evaristus	97	St. Sylvester I	314
St. Alexander I	105	St. Marcus	336
St. Sixtus I	115	St. Julius I	337
St. Telesphorus	125	Liberius	352
St. Hyginus	136	Felix II (A.P.)	355
St. Pius I	140	St. Damasus I	366
St. Anicetus	155	Ursinus (A.P.)	366
St. Soter	166	St. Siricius	384
St. Eleutherius	175	St. Anastasius I	399
St. Victor 1	189	St. Innocent I	401
St. Zephyrinus	199	St. Zosimus	417
St. Callistus I	217	St. Boniface I	418
St. Hippolytus (A.P.)	217	Eulalius (A.P.)	418
St. Urban I	222	St. Celestine I	422
St. Pontian	230	St. Sixtus III	432
St. Anterus	235	St. Leo I	440
St. Fabian	236	St. Hilary	461
St. Cornelius	251	St. Simplicius	468
Novatian (A.P.)	251	St. Felix III (II)	483
St. Lucius I	253	St. Gelasius I	492
St. Stephen I	254	Anastasius II	496
St. Sixtus II	257	St. Symmachus	498
St. Dionysius	259	Lawrence (A.P.)	498–505
St. Felix I	269	St. Hormisdas	514
St. Eutychian	275	St. John I, the Martyr	523
St. Caius	283	St. Felix IV (III)	526
		Boniface II	530

Dioscorus (A.P.)	530
John II	532
St. Agapitus I	535
St. Silverius, the Martyr	536
Vigilus	538
Pelagius I	555
John III	561
Benedict I	575
Pelagius II	579
St. Gregory I	590
Sabinian	604
Boniface III	607
St. Boniface IV	608
St. Deusdedit (Adeodatus)	615
Boniface V	619
Honorius I	625
Severinus	640
John IV	640
Theodore I	642
St. Martin I, the Martyr	649
St. Eugene I	655
St. Vitalian	657
Adeodatus II	672
Donus	676
St. Agatho	678
St. Leo II	682
St. Benedict II	684
John V	685
Conon	686
Theodore (A.P.)	686
Paschal (A.P.)	687
St. Sergius I	687
John VI	701
John VII	705
Sisinius	708
Constantine	708
St. Gregory II	715
St. Gregory III	731
St. Zachary	741
Stephen II (dropped from offical list 1961)	752
Stephen III (II)	752
St. Paul I	757
Constantine II (A.P.)	767
Philip (A.P.)	768
Stephen IV (III)	768
Adrian I	772
St. Leo III	795
Stephen V (IV)	816
St. Paschal I	817
Eugene II	824
Valentine	827
Gregory IV	827
John (A.P.)	844
Sergius II	844
St. Leo IV	847
Benedict III	855
Anastasius (A.P.)	855
St. Nicholas I	858
Adrian II	867
John VIII	872
Marinus I	882
St. Adrian III	884
Stephen VI (V)	885
Formosus	891
Boniface VI	896
Stephen VII (VI)	896
Romanus	897
Theodore II	897
John IX	898
Benedict IV	900
Leo V	903
Christopher (A.P.)	903
Sergius III	904
Anastasius III	911
Landus	913
John X	914
Leo VI	928
Stephen VIII (VII)	928
John XI	931
Leo VII	936
Stephen IX (VIII)	939

Marinus II	942	Sylvester IV (A.P.)	1105
Agapitus II	946	Gelasius II	1118
John XII	955	Gregory VIII (A.P.)	1118
Leo VIII	963	Callistus II	1119
Benedict V	964	Honorius II	1124
John XIII	965	Celestine II (A.P.)	1124
Benedict VI	973	Innocent II	1130
Boniface VII (A.P.)	974	Anacletus II (A.P.)	1130
Benedict VII	974	Victor IV (A.P.)	1138
John XIV	983	Celestine II	1143
John XV	985	Lucius II	1144
Gregory V	996	Blessed Eugene III	1145
John XVII (A.P.)	997	Anastasius IV	1153
Sylvester II	999	Adrian IV	1154
John XVII	1003	Alexander III	1159
John XVIII	1004	Victor IV (A.P.)	1159
Sergius IV	1009	Paschal III (A.P.)	1164
Benedict VIII	1012	Callistus III (A.P.)	1168
Gregory (A.P.)	1012	Innocent III (A.P.)	1179
John XIX	1024	Lucius III	1181
Benedict IX	1032	Urban III	1185
Sylvester III	1045	Clement III	1187
Benedict IX	1045	Gregory VIII	1187
Gregory VI	1045	Celestine III	1191
Clement II	1046	Innocent III	1198
Benedict IX	1047	Honorius III	1216
Damasus II	1048	Gregory IX	1227
St. Leo IX	1049	Celestine IV	1241
Victor II	1055	Innocent IV	1243
Stephen IX (X)	1057	Alexander IV	1254
Benedict X (A.P.)	1058	Urban IV	1261
Nicholas II	1059	Clement IV	1265
Alexander II	1061	Blessed Gregory X	1271
Honorius II (A.P.)	1061	Blessed Innocent V	1276
St. Gregory VII	1073	Adrian V	1276
Clement III (A.P.)	1080	John XXI	1276
Blessed Victor III	1087	Nicholas III	1277
Blessed Urban II	1088	Martin IV	1281
Paschal II	1099	Honorius IV	1285
Theodoric (A.P.)	1100	Nicholas IV	1288
Albert (A.P.)	1102	St. Celestine V	1294

Boniface VIII	1294	Gregory XIII	1572
Blessed Benedict XI	1303	Sixtus V	1585
Clement V	1305	Urban VII	1590
John XXII	1316	Gregory XIV	1590
Nicholas V (A.P.)	1328	Innocent IX	1591
Benedict XII	1334	Clement VIII	1592
Clement VI	1342	Leo XI	1605
Innocent VI	1352	Paul V	1605
Blessed Urban V	1362	Gregory XV	1621
Gregory XI	1370	Urban VIII	1623
Urban VI	1378	Innocent X	1644
Clement VII (A.P.)	1378	Alexander VII	1655
Boniface IX	1389	Clement IX	1667
Benedict XIII (A.P.)	1394	Clement X	1670
Innocent VII	1394	Blessed Innocent XI	1676
Gregory XII	1406	Alexander VIII	1689
Alexander V (A.P.)	1409	Innocent XII	1691
John XXIII	1410	Clement XI	1700
Martin V	1417	Innocent XIII	1721
Eugene IV	1431	Benedict XIII	1724
Felix V (A.P.)	1439	Clement XII	1730
Nicholas V	1447	Benedict XIV	1740
Callistus III	1455	Clement XIII	1758
Pius II	1458	Clement XIV	1769
Paul II	1464	Pius VI	1775
Sixtus IV	1471	Pius VII	1800
Innocent VIII	1484	Leo XII	1823
Alexander VI	1492	Pius VIII	1829
Pius III	1503	Gregory XVI	1831
Julius II	1503	Pius IX	1846
Leo X	1513	Leo XIII	1878
Adrian VI	1522	St. Pius X	1903
Clement VII	1523	Benedict XV	1914
Paul III	1534	Pius XI	1922
Julius III	1550	Pius XII	1939
Marcellus II	1555	John XXIII	1958
Paul IV	1555	Paul VI	1963
Pius IV	1559	John Paul I	1978
St. Pius V	1566	John Paul II	1978

APPENDIX VI: RULERS OF ENGLAND

Saxons

Egbert	827–839
Ethelwulf	839–858
Ethelbald	858–860
Ethelbert	860–865
Ethelred I	865–871
Alfred the Great	871–899
Edward the Elder	899–924
Athelstan	924–939
Edmund	939–946
Edred	946–955
Edwy	955–959
Edgar	959–975
Edward the Martyr	975–978
Ethelred II, the Unready	978–1016
Edmund Ironside	1016

Danes

Canute	1016–1035
Harold I Harefoot	1035–1040
Harthacanute	1040–1042

Saxons

Edward the Confessor	1042–1066
Harold II	1066

House of Normandy

William I, the Conqueror	1066–1087
William II	1087–1100

Henry I	1100–1135
Stephen	1135–1154

House of Plantagenet

Henry II	1154–1189
Richard I, the Lionheart	1189–1199
John	1199–1216
Henry III	1216–1272
Edward I	1272–1307
Edward II	1307–1327
Edward III	1327–1377
Richard II	1377–1399

House of Lancaster

Henry IV	1399–1413
Henry V	1413–1422
Henry VI	1422–1461

House of York

Edward IV	1461–1483
Edward V	1483
Richard III	1483–1485

House of Tudor

Henry VII	1485–1509
Henry VIII	1509–1547
Edward VI	1547–1553
Mary I	1553–1558
Elizabeth I	1558–1603

APPENDIX VII: RULERS OF SCOTLAND

Malcolm II	1005–1034	Donald Bane (restored)	1094–1097
Duncan I	1034–1040	Edgar	1097–1107
Macbeth	1040–1057	Alexander I	1107–1124
Malcolm III (Cranmore)	1057–1093	David I	1124–1153
Donald Bane	1093–1094	Malcolm IV	1153–1165
Duncan II	1094	William the Lion	1165–1214

Alexander II	1214–1249	**House of Stewart**	
Alexander III	1249–1286	Robert II	1371–1390
Margaret of Norway	1286–1290	Robert III	1390–1406
		James I	1406–1437
(Interregnum	1290–1292)	James II	1437–1460
		James III	1460–1488
John Balliol	1292–1296	James IV	1488–1513
		James V	1513–1542
(Interregnum	1296–1306)	Mary, Queen of Scots	1542–1567
		James VI (I of Great Britain)	
Robert I, the Bruce	1306–1329		1567–1625
David II	1329–1371		

APPENDIX VIII: RULERS OF ENGLAND AND SCOTLAND

House of Stuart		**House of Stuart**	
James I	1603–1625	Charles II	1660–1685
Charles I	1625–1649	James II	1685–1688
		Mary II (jointly)	1689–1694
Commonwealth	**1649–1653**	William III (jointly)	1689–1702
Protectorate	**1653–1660**	Anne	1702–1714
Oliver Cromwell	1649–1658		
Richard Cromwell	1658–1659		

APPENDIX IX: RULERS OF THE UNITED KINGDOM

House of Hanover		**House of Saxe-Coburg**	
George I	1714–1727	Edward VII	1901–1910
George II	1727–1760		
George III	1760–1820	**House of Windsor**	
George IV	1820–1830	George V	1910–1936
William IV	1830–1837	Edward VIII	1936
Victoria	1837–1901	George VI	1936–1952
		Elizabeth II	1952–

APPENDIX X: PRIME MINISTERS OF THE UNITED KINGDOM

	In office	Party
Sir Robert Walpole	1721–1742	Whig
Earl of Wilmington	1742–1743	Whig
Henry Pelham	1743–1754	Whig
Duke of Newcastle	1754–1756	Whig
Duke of Devonshire	1756–1757	Whig
Duke of Newcastle	1757–1762	Whig
Earl of Bute	1762–1763	Tory
George Grenville	1763–1765	Whig
Marquess of Rockingham	1765–1766	Whig
William Pitt the Elder (Earl of Chatham)	1766–1768	Whig
Duke of Grafton	1767–1770	Whig
Lord North	1770–1782	Tory
Marquess of Rockingham	1782	Whig
Earl of Shelburne	1782–1783	Whig
Duke of Portland	1783	Coalition
William Pitt the Younger	1783–1801	Tory
Henry Addington	1801–1804	Tory
William Pitt the Younger	1804–1806	Tory
Lord Grenville	1806–1807	Whig
Duke of Portland	1807–1809	Tory
Spencer Perceval	1809–1812	Tory
Earl of Liverpool	1812–1827	Tory
George Canning	1827	Tory
Viscount Goderich	1827–1828	Tory
Duke of Wellington	1828–1830	Tory
Earl Grey	1830–1834	Whig
Viscount Melbourne	1834	Whig
Sir Robert Peel	1834–1835	Tory
Viscount Melbourne	1835–1841	Whig
Sir Robert Peel	1841–1846	Tory
Lord John Russell	1846–1852	Whig
Earl of Derby	1852	Tory
Earl of Aberdeen	1852–1855	Peelite
Viscount Palmerston	1855–1858	Liberal
Earl of Derby	1858–1859	Conservative
Viscount Palmerston	1859–1865	Liberal
Earl Russell	1865–1866	Liberal

Earl of Derby	1866–1868	Conservative
Benjamin Disraeli	1868	Conservative
William Gladstone	1868–1874	Liberal
Benjamin Disraeli	1874–1880	Conservative
William Gladstone	1880–1885	Liberal
Marquess of Salisbury	1885–1886	Conservative
William Gladstone	1886	Liberal
Marquess of Salisbury	1886–1892	Conservative
William Gladstone	1892–1894	Liberal
Earl of Rosebery	1894–1895	Liberal
Marquess of Salisbury	1895–1902	Conservative
Arthur Balfour	1902–1905	Conservative
Sir Henry Campbell-Bannerman	1905–1908	Liberal
Herbert Asquith	1908–1915	Liberal
Herbert Asquith	1915–1916	Coalition
David Lloyd-George	1916–1922	Coalition
Andrew Bonar Law	1922–1923	Conservative
Stanley Baldwin	1923–1924	Conservative
James Ramsay MacDonald	1924	Labour
Stanley Baldwin	1924–1929	Conservative
James Ramsay MacDonald	1929–1931	Labour
James Ramsay MacDonald	1931–1935	National Coalition
Stanley Baldwin	1935–1937	National Coalition
Neville Chamberlain	1937–1940	National Coalition
Winston Churchill	1940–1945	Coalition
Winston Churchill	1945	Conservative
Clement Attlee	1945–1951	Labour
Sir Winston Churchill	1951–1955	Conservative
Sir Anthony Eden	1955–1957	Conservative
Harold Macmillan	1957–1963	Conservative
Sir Alec Douglas-Home	1963–1964	Conservative
Harold Wilson	1964–1970	Labour
Edward Heath	1970–1974	Conservative
Harold Wilson	1974–1976	Labour
James Callaghan	1976–1979	Labour
Margaret Thatcher	1979–1990	Conservative
John Major	1990–	Conservative

APPENDIX XI: HOLY ROMAN EMPERORS
Dates given are period of reign.

Charlemagne	800–814
Louis I (the Pious)	814–840
Lothair I	840–855

Saxon dynasty

Otto I, the Great	936–973
Otto II	973–983
Otto III	983–1002
Henry II	1002–1024

Franconian dynasty

Conrad II	1024–1039
Henry III	1039–1056
Henry IV	1056–1106
Henry V	1106–1125
Lothair III, Duke of Saxony	1125–1137

Hohenstaufen dynasty

Conrad III	1138–1152
Frederick I, Barbarossa	1152–1190
Henry VI	1190–1197
Philip of Swabia	1197–1208
Otto IV of Brunswick	1198–1212
Frederick II	1212–1250
Conrad IV	1250–1254

Interregnum

Electors gain power	1254–1273

Transition period

Rudolf I of Habsburg	1273–1292
Adolf of Nassau	1292–1298
Albert I, King of Germany	1298–1308

Henry VII of Luxembourg	1308–1314
Louis IV of Bavaria (co-regent)	1314–1347
Frederick of Austria (co-regent)	1314–1322
Charles IV, of Luxembourg	1347–1378
Wenceslas of Luxembourg	1378–1400
Rupert, Duke of Palatine	1400–1410
Sigismund of Luxembourg	1410–1434

Habsburg dynasty

Albert II	1437–1439
Frederick III	1440–1493
Maximilian I	1493–1519
Charles V, King of Spain	1519–1556
Ferdinand I	1556–1564
Maximilian II	1564–1576
Rudolf II	1576–1612
Matthias	1612–1619
Ferdinand II	1619–1637
Ferdinand III	1637–1657
Leopold I	1658–1705
Joseph I	1705–1711
Charles VI	1711–1740
War of Austrian Succession	1740–1748
Charles VII of Bavaria	1742–1745
Francis I of Lorriane	1745–1765
Joseph II	1765–1790
Leopold II	1790–1792
Francis II	1792–1806

APPENDIX XII: HABSBURG EMPERORS OF AUSTRIA

Francis II	1804–1835	Francis Joseph	1848–1916
Ferdinand	1835–1848	Charles	1916–1918

APPENDIX XIII: HOHENZOLLERN EMPERORS OF GERMANY

William I (of Prussia)	1871–1888	William II	1888–1918
Frederick III	1888		

APPENDIX XIV: RULERS OF GERMANY

Weimar Republic

Friedrich Ebert	1919–1925
Paul von Hindenburg	1925–1934

Third Reich

Adolf Hitler	1934–1945

Post World War II

Germany under Allied control

1945–1949

APPENDIX XV: CHANCELLORS OF THE FEDERAL REPUBLIC OF GERMANY (WEST GERMANY)

Konrad Adenauer	1949–1963	Willy Brandt	1969–1974
Dr. Ludwig Erhard	1963–1966	Helmut Schmidt	1974–1982
Kurt Georg Kiesinger	1966–1969	Helmut Kohl	1982–1990

APPENDIX XVI: CHAIRMEN OF THE DEMOCRATIC REPUBLIC OF GERMANY (EAST GERMANY)

Walter Ulbricht	1949–1971	Egon Krenz	1989–1990
Erich Honecker	1971–1989		

APPENDIX XVII: CHANCELLORS OF UNITED GERMANY

Helmut Kohl   1990

APPENDIX XVIII: RULERS OF FRANCE

The Carolingians

Charles I, the Bald	843–877
Louis II	877–879
Louis III	879–882
Charles II	885–888
Eudes	888–898
Charles III	898–922
Robert	922–923
Rudolph	923–936
Louis IV	936–954
Lothair	954–986
Louis V	986–987

The Capets

Hugh Capet	987–996
Robert II, the Pious	996–1031
Henry I	1031–1060
Philip I	1060–1108
Louis VI	1108–1137
Louis VII	1137–1180
Philip II	1180–1233
Louis VIII	1223–1226
Louis IX	1226–1270
Philip III	1270–1285
Philip IV	1285–1314
Louis X	1314–1316
Philip V	1316–1322
Charles IV	1322–1328

House of Valois

Philip VI	1328–1350
John II	1350–1364
Charles V	1364–1380
Charles VI	1380–1422
Charles VII	1422–1461
Louis XI	1461–1483
Charles VIII	1483–1498
Louis XII	1498–1515
Francis I	1515–1547
Henry II	1547–1559
Francis II	1559–1560
Charles IX	1560–1574
Henry III	1574–1589

House of Bourbon

Henry IV, of Navarre	1589–1610
Louis XIII	1610–1643
Louis XIV	1643–1715
Louis XV	1715–1774
Louis XVI	1774–1793

The First Republic and First Empire

Napoleon Bonaparte (First Consul)	1799–1804
Napoleon I (Emperor)	1804–1814

Restoration of monarchy

Louis XVIII	1814–1824
Charles X	1824–1830
Louis-Philippe	1830–1848

Second Republic

Louis Napoleon Bonaparte (President)	1848–1852
Napoleon III (Emperor)	1852–1870

Third Republic

Louis Adolphe Thiers	1871–1873
Marshal Patrice de MacMahon	1873–1879
Paul Grévy	1879–1887
Marie Carnot	1887–1894
Jean Casimir-Périer	1894–1895
François Faure	1895–1899
Émile Loubet	1899–1906
Armand C. Fallières	1906–1913
Raymond Poincaré	1913–1920
Paul Deschanel	1920
Alexandre Millerand	1920–1924
Gaston Doumergue	1924–1931
Albert Lebrun	1932–1940

Vichy government (under Germans)
1940–1944
Provisional government 1944–1946

Fourth Republic
Vincent Auriol 1947–1954
René Coty 1954–1959

Fifth Republic
Charles de Gaulle 1959–1969
Georges Pompidou 1969–1974
Valéry Giscard d'Estaing 1974–1981
François Mitterrand 1981

APPENDIX XIX: RULERS OF SPAIN

Habsbury dynasty
Charles I (V of Germany) 1516–1556
Philip II 1556–1598
Philip III 1598–1621
Philip IV 1621–1665
Charles II 1665–1700

Bourbon dynasty
Philip V 1700–1724
Louis I 1724
Philip V (restored) 1724–1746
Ferdinand VI 1746–1759
Charles II 1759–1788
Charles IV 1788–1808
Joseph Bonaparte 1808–1814
Ferdinand II 1814–1833
Isabella II 1833–1868

Other monarchs
Amadeus of Savoy 1870–1873

First republic 1873–1874
Restoration of Monarchy
Alfonso XII 1874–1885
Primo de Rivero (dictator)
1923–1930
Alfonso XIII 1886–1931
Second Republic
Niceto Alcalá Zamora 1931–1936
Manuel Azaña 1936–1939
General Francisco Franco
1939–1975

Restoration of Monarchy
Juan Carlos 1975

Prime Ministers
Admiral Luis Blanco 1973
Carlos Navarro 1973–1976
Adolfo Suárez 1976–1982
Felipe González 1982

APPENDIX XX: PERIODS OF JAPAN

Yamato	*c.* 300–592	
Asaka	592–710	Empress Suiko (592–628)
		Emperor Temmu (673–686)
Nara	710–794	Emperor Kammu (781–806)
Heian	794–1185	Japan ruled from Heian (now called Kyoto)
Fujiwara	858–1160	Fujiwara clan rules
Taira	1159–1185	Taira clan take control

Kamakura	1185–1333	Minamoto Yoritomo defeats Taira clan; in 1192 he becomes Shogun
Namboku	1334–1392	End of Shogun rule in 1333; Emperor Godaigo rules alone 1333–1339; imperial line splits into northern and southern courts
Ashikaga	1338–1573	Ashikaga Takauji becomes Shogun in 1338
Muromachi	1392–1573	Two rival courts are unified
Sengoku	1467–1600	Emperor Gonara (1527–1557)
Momoyama	1573–1603	Oda Nobunaga, a Daimyo (baron), deposes the Shogun and becomes dictator to 1582
Edo	1603–1867	Ieyasu Tokugawa becomes Shogun in 1603; Tokugawa Shoguns rule until 1867
Meiji	1868–1912	Emperor Mutsuhito (Meiji) is restored; he ends the shogunate and modernizes Japan
Taisho	1912–1926	Emperor Yoshihito
Showa	1926–1989	Emperor Hirohito
Heisei	1989–	Emperor Akihoto

APPENDIX XXI: TSARS OF RUSSIA

Ivan III, the Great	1462–1505	Peter I	1689–1725
Basil III	1505–1533	Catherine I	1725–1727
Ivan IV, the Terrible	1533–1584	Peter II	1727–1730
Fyodor I	1584–1598	Anna	1730–1740
Boris Godunov	1598–1605	Ivan VI	1740–1741
Fyodor II	1605	Elizabeth	1741–1762
Demetrius	1605–1606	Peter III	1762
Basil (IV) Shuiski	1606–1610	Catherine II, the Great	1762–1796
(Interregnum	1610–1613)	Paul I	1796–1801
Michael Romanov	1613–1645	Alexander I	1801–1825
Alexis	1645–1676	Nicholas I	1825–1855
Fyodor III	1676–1682	Alexander II	1855–1881
Ivan V & Peter I, the Great		Alexander III	1881–1894
	1682–1689	Nicholas II	1894–1917

APPENDIX XXII: RULERS OF THE U.S.S.R.

Vladimir Lenin	1917–1922	Yuro Andropov	1982–1984
Joseph Stalin	1922–1953	Konstantin Chernenko	1984–1985
Nikita Khrushchev	1953–1964	Mikkhail Gorbachev	1985–1992
Leonid Brezhnev	1964–1982		

APPENDIX XXIII: PRESIDENTS OF RUSSIA

Boris Yeltsin	1992–

APPENDIX XXIV: PRESIDENTS OF THE UNITED STATES OF AMERICA

George Washington	1789–1797	None
John Adams	1797–1801	Federalist
Thomas Jefferson	1801–1809	Democratic-Republican
James Madison	1809–1817	Democratic-Republican
James Monroe	1817–1825	Democratic-Republican
John Quincy Adams	1825–1829	Democratic-Republican
Andrew Jackson	1829–1837	Democratic
Martin Van Buren	1837–1841	Democratic
William H. Harrison	1841	Whig
John Tyler	1841–1845	Whig
James K. Polk	1845–1849	Democratic
Zachary Taylor	1849–1850	Whig
Millard Fillmore	1850–1853	Whig
Franklin Pierce	1853–1857	Democratic
James Buchanan	1857–1861	Democratic
Abraham Lincoln	1861–1865	Republican
Andrew Johnson	1865–1869	National Union
Ulysses S. Grant	1869–1877	Republican
Rutherford Hayes	1877–1881	Republican
James Garfield	1881	Republican
Chester Arthur	1881–1885	Republican
Grover Cleveland	1885–1889	Democratic
Benjamin Harrison	1889–1893	Republican
Grover Cleveland	1893–1897	Democratic
William McKinley	1897–1901	Republican
Theodore Roosevelt	1901–1909	Republican
William Taft	1909–1913	Republican
Woodrow Wilson	1913–1921	Democratic
Warren Harding	1921–1923	Republican
Calvin Coolidge	1923–1929	Republican
Herbert Hoover	1929–1933	Republican
Franklin D. Roosevelt	1933–1945	Democratic
Harry S. Truman	1945–1953	Democratic

Dwight D. Eisenhower	1953–1961	Republican
John F. Kennedy	1961–1963	Democratic
Lyndon Johnson	1963–1969	Democratic
Richard Nixon	1969–1974	Republican
Gerald Ford	1974–1977	Republican
Jimmy Carter	1977–1981	Democratic
Ronald Reagan	1981–1989	Republican
George Bush	1989–1993	Republican
Bill Clinton	1993–	Democratic

APPENDIX XXV: PRIME MINISTERS OF CANADA

Sir John MacDonald	1867–1873	William King	1926–1930
Alexander MacKenzie	1873–1878	Richard Bennett	1930–1935
Sir John MacDonald	1878–1891	William King	1935–1948
Sir John Abbott	1891–1892	Louis St. Laurent	1948–1957
Sir John Thompson	1892–1894	John Diefenbaker	1957–1963
Sir Mackenzie Bowell	1894–1896	Lester Pearson	1963–1968
Sir Charles Tupper	1896	Pierre Trudeau	1968–1979
Sir Wilfrid Laurier	1896–1911	Charles (Joe) Clark	1979–1980
Sir Robert Borden	1911–1920	Pierre Trudeau	1980–1984
Arthur Meighen	1920–1921	John Turner	1984
William King	1921–1926	Brian Mulroney	1984–
Arthur Meighen	1926		

APPENDIX XXVI: PRIME MINISTERS OF AUSTRALIA
Australia was established as a Commonwealth in 1901.

Sir Edmund Barton	1901–1903	Stanley Bruce	1923–1929
Alfred Deakin	1903–1904	James Scullin	1929–1932
John Watson	1904	Joseph Lyons	1932–1939
Sir George Reid	1904–1905	Sir Earle Page	1939
Alfred Deakin	1905–1908	Sir Robert Menzies	1939–1941
Andrew Fisher	1908–1909	Sir Arthur Fadden	1941
Alfred Deakin	1909–1910	John Curtin	1941–1945
Andrew Fisher	1910–1913	Francis Forde	1945
Sir Joseph Cook	1913–1914	Joseph Chifley	1945–1949
Andrew Fisher	1914–1915	Sir Robert Menzies	1949–1966
William Hughes	1915–1923	Harold Holt	1966–1967

Sir John McEwen	1967–1968	John Fraser	1975–1983
John Gorton	1968–1971	Robert Hawke	1983–1991
William McMahon	1971–1972	Paul Keating	1991–
Edward Gough Whitlam	1972–1975		

APPENDIX XXVII: PRIME MINISTERS OF NEW ZEALAND

Sir Joseph Ward	1906–1912	Sir Walter Nash	1957–1960
Thomas MacKenzie	1912–1915	Keith Holyoake	1960–1972
William Massey	1915–1925	Sir John Marshall	1972
Sir Francis Bell	1925	Norman Kirk	1972–1974
Joseph Coates	1925–1928	Hugh Watt	1974
Sir Joseph Ward	1928–1930	Wallace (Bill) Rowling	1974–1975
George Forbes	1930–1935	Robert Muldoon	1975–1984
Michael Savage	1935–1940	David Lange	1984–1989
Peter Fraser	1940–1949	Geoffrey Palmer	1989–1990
Sir Sidney Holland	1949–1957	Michael Moore	1990
Keith Holyoake	1957	James Bolger	1990–

APPENDIX XXVIII: PRESIDENTS OF THE REPUBLIC OF ITALY

Alcide de Gasperi (acting head of state)	1946	Giuseppe Saragat	1964–1971
Enrico de Nicola (provisional President)	1946–1948	Giovanni Leone	1971–1978
		Amintore Fanfani	1978
Luigi Einaudi	1948–1955	Alessandro Pertini	1978–1985
Giovanni Gronchi	1955–1962	Francesco Cossiga	1985–1992
Antonio Segni	1962–1964	Oscar Luigi Scalfaro	1992–

APPENDIX XXIX: PRESIDENTS OF INDIA

Dr. Rajendra Prasad	1949–1962	Fakhruddin Ahmed	1974–1977
Dr. Sarvapalli Radhakrishnan	1962–1967	Basappa Jatti	1977
		Neelam Reddy	1977–1982
Dr. Zahir Hussain	1967–1969	Giani Zail Singh	1982–1987
Varahgiri Giri	1969–1974	Ramaswamy Venkataraman	1987–

APPENDIX XXX: MAJOR WARS

Date	Name of war	Warring parties
c. 1250 BC	Trojan wars	Mycenaeans *v.* Trojans
431–404 BC	Peloponnesian War	Athens *v.* Sparta
264–241 BC	First Punic War	Rome *v.* Carthage
218–101 BC	Second Punic War	
149–146 BC	Third Punic War	
1096–1099	First Crusade	Saracens *v.* Christians over Palestine
1147–1149	Second Crusade	
1189–1192	Third Crusade	
1202–1204	Fourth Crusade	
1337–1453	Hundred Years War	England *v.* France
1455–1485	Wars of the Roses	House of York *v.* House of Lancaster
1562–1598	French Wars of Religion	Huguenots *v.* Catholics
1642–1648	English Civil War	Cavaliers *v.* Roundheads
1618–1648	Thirty Years War	Catholic League (Germany, Austria, Spain) *v.* Denmark, Sweden, France
1689–1697	War of League of Augsburg	France *v.* the League, England and the Netherlands
1700	Great Northern War	Sweden *v.* Russia, Denmark, Poland, Holland
1701–1713	War of Spanish Succession	Spain, France and Bavaria *v.* England, Holland, Austrian Empire and Portugal
1730–1738	War of Polish Succession	Russia, Poland *v.* France
1740–1748	War of Austrian Succession	Austria, Britain *v.* Prussia, Bavaria, France, Spain
1756–1763	Seven Years War	Britain and Prussia *v.* France, Austria and Russia
1775–1783	American War of Independence	American colonies *v.* Britain
1793–1815	Napoleonic wars	France *v.* Britain, Austria, Sweden, Russia and Prussia
1821–1829	Greek War of Independence	Greece *v.* Ottoman Turkey
1846–1848	Mexican-American War	Mexico *v.* U.S.
1854–1856	Crimean War	Russia *v.* Britain, France and Turkey
1859	War for Italian Independence	France, Piedmont-Sardinia *v.* Austria

1861–1865	U.S. Civil War	Confederates v. Unionists
1866	Austro-Prussian War	Prussia v. Austria
1870	Franco-Prussian War	France v. Prussia
1894–1895	Chinese-Japanese War	China v. Japan
1899–1902	Boer War	Britain v. Boers (Dutch) in South Africa
1904–1905	Russo-Japanese War	Russia v. Japan
1914–1918	World War I	Germany and Austria-Hungary v. France, Russia, Britain and other nations
1918–1921	Russian Civil War	Bolsheviks v. White Russians
1936–1939	Spanish Civil War	Nationalists (Franco) v. Republicans
1939–1945	World War II	Britain, France, U.S.S.R., U.S. and other nations v. Germany, Italy and Japan
1967	Six Days' War	Israel v. Arab states
1950–1953	Korean War	N. Korea v. S. Korea
1964–1973	Vietnam War	N. Vietnam v. S. Vietnam and U.S.
1982	Falklands War	United Kingdom v. Argentina
1991	Gulf War	U.S., U.K. & France v. Iraq
1991–	Yugoslav Civil War	

APPENDIX XXXI: INVENTIONS

BC

6,400	Wheel (Sumerians)
6,000	Pottery (Jericho)
4,000	Brick (Egypt, Assyria)
500	Abacus (China)
45	Julian Calendar of 365¼ days, year beginning 1 Jan (Sosigenes of Alexandria)
30	Sundial (China)

AD

105	Paper (Tsai Lun)
444	Wheelbarrow (China)
850	Astrolabe (Arabs)
863	Cyrillic alphabet (Cyril and Methodius)

905	Book printing from woodblocks (Printers of Chengdu, China)
975	Modern arthmetical notation introduced (Arabs)
1000	Use of the zero in Mathematics (Sridhara)
1026	Do-re-mi in music (Guido d'Arezzo)
1036	Modern musical notation (Guido d'Arezzo)
1041	Movable printing type (Pi Sheng)
1086	Magnetic compass (Shen Kua)

1120	Measurement of latitude and longitude in degrees (Welcher of Malvern)
1259	Firearms (China)
1278	Glass mirror
1298	Spinning wheel
1300	Brandy (Arnaldus de Villa Nova)
1454	Movable metal type for printing (Printers at Mainz)
1520	Rifle (August Kotter)
1532	Frangipani pastry (Count Cesare Frangipani)
1582	Gregorian (modern) calendar (Aloysius Lilius)
1585	Decimals (Simon Stevin)
1589	Knitting machine (William Lee)
1593	Thermometer (Galileo)
1608	Telescope (Hans Lippershey)
1614	Logarithms (John Napier)
1642	Calculating machine (Blaise Pascal)
1643	Mercury barometer (Evangelista Torricelli)
1650	Air pump (Otto von Guericke)
1656	Pendulum clock (Christian Huygens)
1675	Pressure cooker (Denis Papin)
1677	Microscope (Anthony van Leeuwenhoek)
1698	Steam pump (Thomas Savery)
1709	Alcohol thermometer (Gabriel Fahrenheit)
1712	Steam engine (Thomas Newcomen)
1713	Smallpox inoculation (Giacomo Pylarini)

1731	Quadrant (John Hadley)
1733	Flying Shuttle (John Kay)
1735	Chronometer (John Harrison)
1742	Celsius temperature scale (Anders Celsius)
1752	Lightning conductor (Benjamin Franklin)
1756	Mayonnaise (Duc de Richelieu)
1757	Sextant (John Campbell)
1760	Roller skates (Joseph Merlin)
1765	Condensing steam engine (James Watt)
1767	Carbonated water (Joseph Priestley)
1780	Modern pianoforte (Sebastian Evrard)
1783	Parachute (Louis Lenormand)
	Hot air balloon (Joseph and Jacques Montgolfier)
1784	Bifocal spectacles (Benjamin Franklin)
1785	Power loom (Edmund Cartwright)
1786	Breech-loading musket (Henry Nock)
	Threshing machine (Andrew Meikle)
1788	Steamboat (William Symington)
1790	Sewing machine (Thomas Saint)
1793	Cotton gin (Eli Whitney)
1794	Semaphore long-distance signalling system (Claude Chappe)
1796	Vaccination against smallpox (Edward Jenner)
	Lithography (Alys Senefelder)

1800	Electric battery (Alessandro Volta)
	Lathe (Henry Maudsley)
1804	Steam locomotive (Richard Trevithick)
1815	Miners' safety lamp (Humphry Davy)
1816	Metronome (Johann Malzel)
	Bicycle (Karl von Sauerbronn)
1817	Kaleidoscope (David Brewster)
1822	Camera (Joseph Niepce)
1823	Digital calculating machine (Charles Babbage)
1826	Photography (Joseph Niepce)
1827	Phosphorus matches (John Walker)
1833	Diaphragm contraceptive (Friedrich Wilde)
1834	Reaping machine (Cyrus McCormick)
1836	Revolver (Samuel Colt)
1837	Telegraph (Samuel Morse)
1837	Morse code (Andrew Vail)
1839	Electric telegraph (Charles Wheatstone and William Cooke)
	Vulcanized rubber (Charles Goodyear)
1849	Safety pin (Walter Hunt)
1851	High-speed photography (Fox-Talbot)
1853	Passenger lift (Elisha Otis)
1855	Celluloid (Alexander Parkes)
	Steel converter (Henry Bessemer)
	Bunsen burner (Robert Bunsen)
1858	Refrigerator (Ferdinand Carre)
1858	Washing machine (Hamilton Smith)
1861	Linoleum (Frederick Walton)
1862	Rapid-fire gun (Richard Gatling)
1876	Telephone (Alexander Graham Bell)
1887	Motor car engine (Gottlieb Daimler & Karl Benz, independently)
1888	Celluloid film and movie camera (William Friese-Greene)
	Pneumatic tyre (John Dunlop)
1892	Zip fastener (Whitcomb Judson)
1895	Wireless (Guglielmo Marconi)
	Safety razor (King Gillette)
1897	Diesel engine (Rudolf Diesel)
1898	Submarine (John Holland)
1899	Tape recorder (Valdemar Poulsen)
1901	Vacuum cleaner (Cecil Booth)
1903	Aeroplane (Orville and Wilbur Wright)
1908	Bakelite (Leo Baekeland)
	Cellophane (Jacques Brandenberger)
1911	Combine harvester (Benjamin Holt)
1912	Mouldable PVC (I. Ostromislensky)
1913	Geiger counter (Hans Geiger)
1914	Tank (Ernest Swinton)
1919	Non-rusting stainless steel (Elwood Haynes)
1925	Television (John Logie Baird)
	Frozen food process (Clarence Birdseye)

1926	Liquid-fuel rocket (Robert Goddard)
1928	Electric shaver (Jacob Schick)
1930	Jet engine (Frank Whittle)
1935	Nylon (Wallace Carothers) Radar (Robert Watson-Watt)
1938	Teflon (Roy Plunkett)
1939	Electron microscope (Vladimir Zworykin)
1946	Electronic computer (J. P. Eckert and J. W. Mauchly)
1948	Transistor (J. Bardeen, W. Brattain, W. Shockley)
1948	Long-playing record (Peter Goldmark)
1955	Artificial diamonds Hovercraft (Christopher Cockerell) Contraceptive pill (Gregory Pincus)
1960	Radiocarbon dating (Willard Libby) Laser (Theodore Maiman)
1965	Holography (D. Gabor)
1990	Hydrofluorocarbon Klea 134a, substitute for CFCs (ICI chemists)

APPENDIX XXXII: DISCOVERY AND EXPLORATION

Date	Place	Achievement	Discoverer
BC			
600	Africa	circumnavigated anticlockwise	Egyptians
325	British Isles	known as 'Britannic Islands'	Mediterranean navigators
AD			
450	Hawaii	discovered after 3,000 km/ 2,000 mile voyage	Hawaii-Loa, Polynesian
860	Iceland	landed	Vikings
982	Greenland	landed	Eric the Red
986	Labrador	sighted	Bjarni Herjolfsson
995	Labrador	landed, overwintered	Leif Ericsson
1003–6	Labrador	explored	Thorfinn Karlsfeni
1194	Spitzbergen	disc.	Norsemen
1272	China	reached from the West	Marco Polo
1432	Azores	disc.	Gonzalo Cabral
1433	C. Bojador	disc., rounded	Gil Eannes
1444	R. Senegal	disc.	Nino Tristram
1445	Cape Verde	disc., rounded	Dinis Diaz
1455	C. Verde Is.	disc.	Alvise da Cadamosto
1472	Fernando Po Is.	disc.	Fernando Po
1472	Equator	crossed	Lopo Goncalves

1483	Mouth of R. Zaire	disc.	Diogo Cao
1488	Cape of Good Hope	rounded	Bartholomew Diaz
1492	West Indies	disc.	Christopher Columbus
1494	Jamaica	disc.	Christopher Columbus
1497	Natal	disc.	Vasco da Gama
1497	Newfoundland	rediscovered	John Cabot
1498	Cape route to India	disc.	Vasco da Gama
1498	Trinidad and Orinoco mouth	disc.	Christopher Columbus
1498	SE N. America	disc.	Duarte Pareira
1499	Venezuela	explored	Alonso de Ojeda
1500	S. Labrador & E. Greenland	explored	Gaspard Corte
1500	Brazil	disc. and explored	Pedro Cabral
1503	Panama	disc.	Christopher Columbus
1505	Sri Lanka	disc.	Portuguese navigators
1506	Tristan da Cunha	disc.	Tristan da Cunha
1508	Hudson Bay	disc.	John Cabot
1513	Pacific Ocean	sighted	Vasco de Balboa
1515	Bermuda	explored	Juan de Bermudez
1516	River Plate	disc.	Juan de Solis
1519–21	World	circumnavigated	Ferdinand Magellan
1520	Tierra del Fuego	disc.	Ferdinand Magellan
1521	Mexico	explored	Hernando Cortes
1524	New York	disc.	Verrazano
1530–8	Peru	explored	Francisco Pizarro
1534–6	St. Lawrence River	Explored	Jacques Cartier
1540	R. Colorado	disc.	Hernando de Alarcon
1541	R. Mississippi	disc.	Hernando de Soto
1541	R. Amazon	disc. & descended	Francisco de Orellana
1549	Japan	visited	Francis Xavier
1550	Australia	sighted	Dutch navigators
1576	Baffin Is.	disc.	Martin Frobisher
1596	Spitzbergen	rediscovered	Willem Barents
1603–9	Canada, interior	explored	Samuel de Champlain
1610	Hudson Bay	explored	Henry Hudson
1616	Cape Horn	disc.	Willem Schouten
1642	Australia	visited	Abel Tasman
1642	New Zealand	sighted	Abel Tasman
1722	Easter Is.	disc.	Jacob Roggeveen
1728	Alaska	disc.	Vitus Bering

1769	New Zealand	landed	James Cook
1773	Antarctic Circle	crossed	James Cook
1789	R. Mackenzie	disc.	Alexander Mackenzie
1795	R. Niger	explored	Mungo Park
1820	Antarctica	sighted	Nathaniel Palmer
1819–21	Antarctica	circumnavigated	Fabian von Bellingshausen
1828	Australia, interior	explored	Charles Sturt
1838–42	Antarctica, interior	explored	Charles Wilkes
1851	R. Zambezi	disc.	David Livingstone
1852–5	Sudan	explored	Heinrich Barth
1855	Victoria Falls	disc.	David Livingstone
1858	L. Tanganyika	disc.	Richard Burton and John Speke
1860–1	Australia	crossed	Robert Burke and William Wills
1877	R. Zaire	explored	Henry Stanley
1888	Greenland	explored	Fridtjof Nansen
1900	Arctic Ocean	explored	Duke of the Abruzzi
1909	North Pole	reached	Robert Peary
1911	South Pole	reached	Roald Amundsen
1957–8	Antarctica	crossed	Vivian Fuchs
1961	Earth	orbited	Yuri Gagarin
1969	Moon	landed	Neil Armstrong

APPENDIX XXXIII: WINNERS OF THE NOBEL PRIZE FOR LITERATURE

1901	René Sully-Prudhomme	1839–1907 (France)
1902	Theodor Mommsen	1817–1903 (Germany)
1903	Björnstjerne Björnson	1832–1910 (Norway)
1904	Frédéric Mistral	1830–1914 (France)
	José Echegaray	1832–1916 (Spain)
1905	Henryk Sienkiewicz	1846–1916 (Poland)
1906	Giosuè Carducci	1835–1907 (Italy)
1907	Rudyard Kipling	1865–1936 (U.K.)
1908	Rudolf Eucken	1846–1926 (Germany)
1909	Selma Lagerlöf	1858–1940 (Sweden)
1910	Paul von Heyse	1830–1914 (Germany)
1911	Maurice Maeterlinck	1862–1949 (Belgium)

1912	Gerhart Hauptmann	1862–1946 (Germany)
1913	Rabindranath Tagore	1861–1941 (India)
1914	—	
1915	Romain Rolland	1866–1944 (France)
1916	Verner von Heidenstam	1859–1940 (Sweden)
1917	Karl Gjellerup	1857–1919 (Denmark)
	Henrik Pontoppidan	1857–1943 (Denmark)
1918	—	
1919	Carl Spitteler	1845–1924 (Switzerland)
1920	Knut Hamsun	1859–1952 (Norway)
1921	Anatole France	1844–1924 (France)
1922	Jacinto Benavente y Martinez	1866–1954 (Spain)
1923	William Butler Yeats	1865–1939 (Ireland)
1924	Wladyslaw Reymont	1868–1925 (Poland)
1925	George Bernard Shaw	1856–1950 (Ireland)
1926	Grazia Deledda	1875–1936 (Italy)
1927	Henri Bergson	1859–1941 (France)
1928	Sigrid Undset	1882–1949 (Norway)
1929	Thomas Mann	1875–1955 (Germany)
1930	Sinclair Lewis	1885–1951 (U.S.)
1931	Erik Axel Karlfeldt	1864–1931 (Sweden)
1932	John Galsworthy	1867–1933 (U.K.)
1933	Ivan Bunin	1870–1953 (U.S.S.R.)
1934	Luigi Pirandello	1867–1936
1935	—	
1936	Eugene O'Neill	1888–1953 (U.S.)
1937	Roger Martin du Gard	1881–1958 (France)
1938	Pearl Buck	1892–1973 (U.S.)
1939	Frans Emil Sillanpää	1888–1964 (Finland)
1940–43	—	
1944	Johannes V. Jensen	1873–1950 (Denmark)
1945	Gabriela Mistral	1889–1957 (Chile)
1946	Hermann Hesse	1877–1962 (Switzerland)
1947	André Gide	1869–1951 (France)
1948	T. S. Eliot	1888–1965 (U.K.)
1949	William Faulkner	1897–1962 (U.S.)
1950	Bertrand Russell	1872–1970 (U.K.)
1951	Pär Lagerkvist	1891–1974 (Sweden)
1952	François Mauriac	1885–1970 (France)
1953	Winston Churchill	1874–1965 (U.K.)
1954	Ernest Hemingway	1898–1961 (U.S.)

1955	Haldór K. Laxness	1902– (Iceland)
1956	Juan Ramón Jiménez	1881–1958 (Spain)
1957	Albert Camus	1913–1960 (France)
1958	Boris Pasternak (declined)	1890–1960 (U.S.S.R.)
1959	Salvatore Quasimodo	1901–1968 (Italy)
1960	Alexis Léger	1887–1975 (France)
1961	Ivo Andric	1892–1975 (Yugoslavia)
1962	John Steinbeck	1902–1968 (U.S.)
1963	Giorgos Seferis	1900–1971 (Greece)
1964	Jean-Paul Sartre (declined)	1905–1980 (France)
1965	Mikhail Sholokhov	1905–1984 (U.S.S.R.)
1966	s. y. Agnon	1888–1970 (Poland)
	Nelly Sachs	1891–1970 (Sweden)
1967	Miguel Asturias	1891–1970 (Guatemala)
1968	Yasunari Kawabata	1899–1972 (Japan)
1969	Samuel Beckett	1906–1989 (Ireland)
1970	Alexander Solzhenitsyn	1918– (U.S.S.R.)
1971	Pablo Neruda	1904–1973 (Chile)
1972	Heinrich Böll	1917–1985 (Germany)
1973	Patrick White	1912–1990 (Australia)
1974	Harry Martinson	1904–1978 (Sweden)
	Eyvind Hohnson	1900–1976 (Sweden)
1975	Eugenio Montale	1896–1981 (Italy)
1976	Saul Bellow	1915– (U.S.)
1977	Vicente Aleixandre	1898–1984 (Spain)
1978	Isaac Bashevis Singer	1904–1991 (U.S.)
1979	Odysseus Elytis	1911– (Greece)
1980	Czeslaw Milosz	1911– (Poland)
1981	Elias Canetti	1905– (Bulgaria)
1982	Gabriel Márquez	1928– (Colombia)
1983	William Golding	1911– (U.K.)
1984	Jaroslav Seifert	1901–1986 (Czechoslavakia)
1985	Claude Simon	1913– (France)
1986	Wole Soyinka	1934– (Nigeria)
1987	Joseph Brodsky	1940– (U.S.S.R.)
1988	Naquib Mahfouz	1911– (Egypt)
1989	Camilo José Cela	1916– (Spain)
1990	Octavio Paz	1914– (Mexico)
1991	Nadine Gordimer	1923– (S. Africa)
1992	Derek Walcott	1930– (Trinidad)
1993	Toni Morrison	1931– (U.S.)